Creative Teaching in
Early Childhood Education

Creative Teaching in Early Childhood Education

A SOURCEBOOK FOR CANADIAN EDUCATORS AND LIBRARIANS

SECOND EDITION

Donald K. McKay
The School of Early Childhood Education
Ryerson Polytechnical Institute

Wendy E. Mitchell
St. Lawrence College

Bonnie Mack Flemming

Darlene Softley Hamilton

JoAnne Deal Hicks

HBJ

HARCOURT BRACE JOVANOVICH CANADA INC.

Toronto Montreal Orlando Fort Worth San Diego Philadelphia London
Sydney Tokyo

Canadian Cataloguing in Publication Data

McKay, Donald K., 1947–
    Creative teaching in early childhood education:
a sourcebook for Canadian educators and librarians

2nd Canadian ed.
Includes bibliographical references and index.
ISBN 0-7747-3221-0

1. Education, Preschool — 1965–   . 2. Education,
Preschool — Activity programs.   3. Teaching — Aids
and devices.   4. Creative activities and seat work.
I. Mitchell, Wendy E. II. Title.

LB1140.2.M33 1993   372.21   C92-094446-9

Acquisitions Editor: Heather McWhinney
Developmental Editor: Dianne Horton
Editorial Assistants: Lisa Stamp and Charlene Sue Low Chee
Director of Publishing Services: Jean Lancee
Editorial Manager: Marcel Chiera
Editorial Co-ordinator: Semareh Al-Hillal
Production Manager: Sue-Ann Becker
Production Co-ordinator: Denise Wake
Copy Editor: Claudia Kutchukian
Cover and Part-Opener Design: Dave Peters
Interior Design: Jack Steiner Graphic Design
Typesetting and Assembly: Bookman Typesetting Co.
Printing and Binding: Webcom Limited

Cover Art: Handprints provided by Robert Stephen Hnatejko, Jennifer Elyse Case, and Brian Michael Case.

∞ This book was printed in Canada on acid-free paper.

1 2 3 4 5   97 96 95 94 93

*To all educators of young children.
Your respect for and dedication to children
encourages the joy and sense of wonder of
childhood.*

Preface

Young children develop individually, progressing through developmental stages at different rates and at different times. Their backgrounds, interests, needs, and abilities are similarly varied. As a result, exemplary programming for young children demands that educators be flexible, creative, and resourceful.

The second edition of *Creative Teaching in Early Childhood Education* is designed to enrich the resource base of Canadian educators and librarians. It includes up-to-date, extensive, and readily available resources featuring Canadian content, and recognizes the comprehensive and excellent resources produced in Canada for use by and with young children.

The text is organized according to broad topics that are meaningful to children and their world. The book also emphasizes a cognitive developmental approach to the education and care of young children. Part 1, Basic Resources, sets up the developmental strands that continue throughout the text and provides basic organizational and curriculum strategies. Parts 2 to 8 are divided into topic-based chapters that respond to the interests and issues that concern young children.

Each chapter of the text features an introduction to its broad topic or theme, followed by suggestions for introducing the topic and for setting up active learning centres. Resources for planning group activities are provided. Each chapter concludes with lists of related materials and resources.

The appendix lists possible sources for commercially available materials, while the indices provide flexible access to the material in the text.

The second edition of *Creative Teaching in Early Childhood Education* has been prepared in response to the suggestions of users of the first edition. Specific changes include:

☐ Suggestions for adapting curriculum for children with special needs. The positive trend toward integration of children with special needs into their community child care and education programs makes it necessary for all teachers to consider how their programs may be modified for such children. Examples of activity modifications are flagged throughout the text using the following symbol: ■.

☐ New activities with a greater emphasis on active learning. Detailed instructions for some activities provide particular guidance for the beginning early childhood educator.

☐ A focus on education that reflects the diversity of children's families.

☐ Relevant new photographs that provide visual support for the written material in the text. Their captions often provide suggestions for observation and classroom practice.

☐ Updated and revised book and film lists.

☐ Revised music resources. The Basic Resources for Music Centres has been revised to reflect current thinking about music for young children. New songs have been inserted in most chapters, and the song lists have been revised to be consistent throughout.

☐ Indexing and clearer cross-referencing. Books, songs, verses, and films are indexed by title and author. Art activities are indexed by the art medium used, dramatic activities by topic, and suggested activities by developmental domain.

The input of users of the first edition has been most helpful in the preparation of this edition. Educators using this second edition can contribute to further editions by sending their comments and suggestions to the publisher on the reply card provided at the back of the book. These suggestions are invaluable and assist us in keeping this as a useful project in the important field of early childhood education.

Note to Educators

Creative Teaching in Early Childhood Education has been prepared to meet the needs of the many educators working in child care centres, nursery schools, kindergartens, and parent–child programs across the country. In addition to providing many specific activities and resources, it is designed to demonstrate current approaches to the education of young children. The curriculum strategies in this book allow maximum flexibility in planning, so that your programming will meet the developmental needs of all children with whom you work. This book is intended as a reference that you can consult as you plan activities for children.

Note to Librarians

Creative Teaching in Early Childhood Education is a useful resource for the many librarians across the country who run varied and excellent programs for young children. In addition to providing many specific activities and resources, this book demonstrates current approaches to working with young children. We hope that you will be able to benefit from our models in developing your own programs and in meeting the developmental needs of all the children with whom you work. The book may also be useful as you select titles for your collections.

Acknowledgements

This second edition of *Creative Teaching in Early Childhood Education* is still inspired by the original American edition prepared by Bonnie Mack Flemming, Darlene Softley Hamilton, and JoAnne Deal Hicks. Our debt to these authors continues for their original concept and their insights into the day-to-day needs of early childhood educators. The many people who contributed to the original edition are acknowledged in that book.

The support of the team at HBJ-Holt has made working on this edition of the text a pleasure. Heather McWhinney inspired the first Canadian edition and has continued as a mentor for this edition. Dianne Horton injected the project with life and vitality and an amazing insight into the issues that are critical to this venture. Semareh Al-Hillal has put in long creative hours to produce an accurate and attractive text. Popular films and fiction frequently portray battles between editors and authors. My experience completely negates this portrayal. Thanks also to Dave Peters and freelancer Jack Steiner, who created a design that gives the book a fresh and vibrant new look.

On behalf of HBJ-Holt, I wish to thank Mary Clare Courtland, Carol Saliba, Debbie Sheppard-Chisholm, Judy Wainwright, Carolyn Warberg, and Marilynn Yeates for their thoughtful and helpful reviews of the first edition of this book.

The co-operation and support of my colleagues at Ryerson is greatly appreciated. Special thanks to Kenise Murphy Kilbride, June Pollard, and Gary Woodill. Monique Richard is particularly supportive of the ongoing revision of this text.

Finally, special acknowledgement is due to Margaret McKay, John McKay, the Denis family, and Jim Laughlin for believing in my ability and always being here when I need them.

Donald McKay

I would like to acknowledge with gratitude my mentor, Marilynn Yeates. I would also like to say a special thank you to Peter, David, and Kendra, for being patient when Mom couldn't play with you.

Wendy Mitchell

PART 7 Transportation

PART 8 My World

How to Use This Book

The order of the parts of this guide does not imply any prearranged teaching sequence. A logical grouping of subjects under headings such as Family Celebrations, Seasons, Animals, and Transportation has been made for easier reference.

Basic Understandings

Concepts children can grasp from the subject are written as statements. Choose the simplest statements for the children with the least experience and the statements with more detailed information for the children with previous experience. Some statements contain more than one concept and may be simplified as needed.

Additional Facts the Teacher Should Know

1. Carefully research information about the subject.
2. Precautions about the subject or activities.
3. Care and maintenance of materials, equipment, plants, or animals.

Introducing This Subject to Children

A conversation, story, picture, special event, shared items, visitor, or trip may be the stepping-stone to the subject. Your choice will depend on:

1. Your children's previous experiences.
2. Your children's most recent interests.
3. The season, the weather, staff skills, and community resources.

Vocabulary

1. Create a basic list of new words to be discovered while exploring the subject.
2. Add familiar words within your group's previous experiences.

Learning Centres

Discovery Centre

First-hand experiences to help the children grasp the basic concepts include:

1. Physics and chemistry experiments, including cooking.
2. Exploring nature — plants, animals, and the five senses.
3. Exploring our world — sun, water, air, soil, and rocks.
4. Books and magazines with pictures that show discovery concepts.

Dramatic Play Centres

Suggestions are included here for encouraging children to play out learning experiences in the sections on home-living centre, block-building centre, and other dramatic play centres (see Dramatic Play Centres in Part 1). Select ideas considering your own equipment, space, budget, community resources, and the creative interest and ability of your staff.

Art Centre

It is assumed that basic art media are offered on a daily basis in your art centre (see Art Centre in Part 1). Variations of the basic media and special activities related to each subject are included in this section. Bullets serve as a guide to the selection of experiences for your group:

- Youngest and least skilled.
- •• More skilled.
- ••• For the most experienced child.

Experiences are grouped as follows:

1. Creative art experiences, which include painting, crayoning, moulding and sculpting, cutting and pasting, collage, printing and mixed media.
2. Other experiences in the art centre using art media include creating objects or materials to be used for games, as dramatic play props, as gifts, or for teaching skills.

Learning and Language Materials Centre

Included here are manipulative, language, and cognitive materials related to learning new concepts and to making judgements about colours, shapes, numbers, spatial relationships, and classifications. These materials are divided into two sections:

1. *Commercially made games and materials.* Listed are types of manipulative and cognitive materials that are available commercially and the criteria for choosing them. As suppliers vary so widely across the country, it was decided to include criteria for choice and examples that meet the criteria, rather than listing specific equipment and manufacturers. Most of these items are included in educational catalogues and many are sold in good independent toy stores.
2. *Teacher-made games and materials.* Suggestions are included for teacher-made cognitive materials. Variations of learning games are described in Learning Games in Part 1.

Well-chosen toys stimulate problem-solving skills and fine motor development.

Book Centre

Books here are to be explored by children individually or read to one or two children by a teacher or an aide (see Book Centre in Part 1). Listed alphabetically by author, the books are coded by text length, type of illustration, concept level, and the age and experience of children. Bullets serve as a guide to the selection of experiences for your group:

- Assumes no previous exposure; brief text and simple illustrations.
- •• Assumes some previous exposure; longer text and simple illustrations.
- ••• Assumes much previous exposure; longer text and more detailed illustrations.
- •••• More informative text and excellent illustrations (often photographs); read or read–tell; use primarily in the discovery centre or as a basis for a language or cognitive experience.

 # Planning for Group Time

The following suggestions may be used when children are gathered in small groups of three to seven, or larger groups when everyone is involved. Your group size will vary with the interest and maturity of the children, the number of children enrolled, and the size of your staff.

Music

1. Original songs are listed by title and page number.
2. Parodies are included to supplement your music library program.
3. Copyrighted songs from Core Library music books (see Teacher Resources in Part 1) are listed by title and page number for easy reference.
4. Rhythms and singing games are listed in the same manner as songs.
5. Records and cassettes are listed by artist, title, and recording company.

Fingerplays and Poems

1. Original or traditional fingerplays and poems are written out, with actions.
2. Copyrighted material from Core Library books (see Teacher Resources in Part 1) is listed by title and page number for easy reference.

Stories

(To read, read–tell, or tell to a group.)
This section gives suggestions on how one or two books from the Book Centre list may be used for storytelling. For suggestions on storytelling, see Book Centre in Part 1.

Games

Games in this section can be played successfully with children in a small or large group during group time. Some of these games may have been listed under Teacher-Made Games and Materials (for an explanation, see Learning Games in Part 1). *Flannelboard ideas* will be noted in the appropriate sections depending on their use: to illustrate a song, to illustrate a story, fingerplay, poems, or games, or when used with an individual child. For instructions on how to make and use flannelboards, see the section Flannelboards in Part 1.

Routine Times

Suggestions are made for capitalizing on teachable moments during routine times. Appropriate activities for learning concepts related to a subject are listed to use during snack time, meal time, toileting, resting, dressing, transitions, or in transit (busing or walking).

Large Muscle Activities

These suggestions will primarily be used outdoors. When the weather is unsuitable, use a basement, gym, or other large space indoors. Circle games, direction games, and problem-solving games described in Learning Games in Part 1 are included as appropriate.

Extended Experiences

Suggestions are noted for utilizing trips, visitors, films, and other special experiences to extend children's knowledge of a subject (see Extended Experiences in Part 1).

Teacher Resources

Pictures and Displays

Suggestions are given for creating your own bulletin boards or displays and for re-arranging the room to best use the materials suggested.

Books and Periodicals

These are primarily teacher references, but some of the resources may be materials for older children that the teacher or librarian could adapt for use with young children. See the discussion on developmentally appropriate material for a Book Centre on p. 36.

Films and Videos

This section lists materials that can be used to support your program.

Community Resources and Organizations

This section lists people, places, groups, associations, and things in your community that may assist you in planning your program.

Government Agencies

This section lists various government agencies that supply materials that will assist you in planning your program.

Part 1 Basic Resources

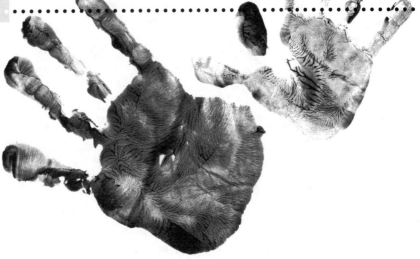

1 *Basic Resources*

Basic Resources

Principles of Good Curriculum Planning

Designing a suitable and interesting curriculum is one of the exciting challenges that faces teachers of young children. The challenge can be met by using the following principles:

1. Good curriculum plans are based on a knowledge and understanding of the development of young children.
2. Outstanding curriculum plans also recognize the individual needs of each child.
3. Curriculum plans should respond to the interests of the children with whom you are working.
4. Curriculum plans should recognize the diversity among children and their families and be sensitive to family traditions and beliefs.
5. Curriculum plans should incorporate the community and current events.
6. Curriculum strategies reflect the strengths and special skills of each member of the staff.
7. Make the most of the physical setting and location of your school or centre.
8. Children should be involved in the curriculum planning process.

The following checklist will assist you in implementing curriculum plans based on the planning principles. It will also help you to evaluate your curriculum strategies.

1. Knowledge and understanding of children's development:
   a. Ensure that your curriculum covers all domains of children's development (i.e., cognitive, fine and gross motor, language, and social-emotional skills).
   b. Develop and use activities that require a variety of skills.
   c. Design activities so that children at different developmental levels will experience different developmental challenges.
2. Recognition of children's individual needs:
   a. Present a balance of activities: structured/unstructured; informative/creative; active/quiet; indoor/outdoor; observing/participating; and individual/group.
   b. Plan activities that can be adapted to meet specific needs of individual children.

   c. Offer opportunities to discover, explore, be challenged, and solve problems through direct experiences.
3. Respond to the interests of the children:
   a. Offer diverse choices in activities.
   b. Listen and observe to learn the children's evaluation of activities.
4. Design a curriculum that recognizes diversity among children and their families:
   a. Talk to parents about their family customs. Attempt to incorporate some of these into your program.
   b. Celebrate differences among children, but focus on commonalities, too. Encourage children to take pride in their individuality.
   c. Involve parents in your curriculum planning.
   d. Recognize diversity on a daily basis, as well as through major celebrations. For example, when you plan cooking activities, include favourite recipes from all the cultures in your group.
5. Incorporate the community and current events in your plans:
   a. Involve resource people from the community in your program.
   b. Ask parents to notify you about upcoming events in their communities so that you can develop activities to include these events.
   c. Pay attention to the local news for items that might interest the children.
6. Reflect the strengths and special skills of each member of the staff:
   a. Identify particular curriculum interests among your staff.
   b. Plan together, so that ideas can be shared among the whole staff.
7. Encourage staff members to continue their professional development and growth through:
   a. Using the Core Library in this text.
   b. Attending workshops.
   c. Joining professional organizations, such as the Canadian Association for Young Children and the Council for Exceptional Children.
   d. Visiting other centres and schools.
8. Make the most of the physical setting and location of your school or centre:
   a. Set up your centre or class so that there is easy movement from one area to another.
   b. Place quiet activities with other quiet activities and noisy activities with other noisy activities.
9. Involve children in your curriculum planning:
   a. Ask them what they would like to do.
   b. Respond to their immediate interests.
   c. Be prepared to be spontaneous and flexible so that you can change your plans when children become interested in a particular activity or subject.

Many child-care and preschool programs are successfully integrating children with special needs. Their aim is to provide *all* children with a typical experience in their home community while meeting all of their educational and care needs. Throughout this text, there are examples of activities that are modified to assist children with a variety of special needs. They will be marked with a ■. Further information on designing programs for children with special needs can be found in Penny Deiner's book *Resources for Teaching Young Children with Special Needs* (1983), listed in the Core Library.

Short- and Long-Range Planning with Staff

Base all of your planning on the developmental needs of the children in your centre. It is critical that the strengths and needs of the children be the main criteria for deciding whether an aspect of the program is appropriate. Your child or human development text is a major support for program planning. A number of resources that describe programs based on developmental needs are listed in the Core Library (pp. 68–75); as are a few human development texts.

1. Block out a general program by the year/month/week/day:
   a. Choose subject guides as aids, considering the need for repetition and the particular interests, needs, and experience of your group.
   b. Study your overall plan to determine the equipment and materials most necessary for carrying out your projected plans.
   c. Familiarize yourself with this Basic Resources section for ways your staff can augment your budget and extend the educational opportunities offered.
   d. Expand your resources by purchasing some of the recommended Core Library books.
   e. Make a plan for starting or supplementing your art, music, science, fingerplay, and other idea files. Encourage input by all members of the staff and the parents.
   f. At appointed intervals evaluate your daily plans, noting recommendations for the future. Modify and adapt the plans for use again with another group at another time.
   g. Organize the teacher storage space and periodically reorganize it. Repair and replace or duplicate items that are most needed and used.
2. Make a detailed program plan for the week:
   a. Consider every learning centre in the classroom and each time segment of the day.
   b. Make special plans for individual children; be selective in the choice of materials and ideas you will present by considering each child's needs, abilities, and interests.
   c. Build on previous experience of the children. Cross-references in this book will help you plan related experiences.
   d. Gather the materials needed.
   e. Try out recipes, patterns, ideas, or experiments in advance, especially when they involve foods, arts, and science.
   f. Be flexible — be ready to change plans, expand, or substitute when the children are ready.
   g. Anticipate the need for alternative plans. Consider changes of weather, shortages of staff, personal crises, and limitations on space caused by multiple uses of a facility.
   h. Define and assign specific responsibilities to staff members. Outline ways in which volunteers may be enlisted to assist staff. Encourage substitutes (volunteers and parents) to attend staff planning meetings for better continuity.
   i. Each staff member should be encouraged to accept a learning centre, a routine time, or a program activity for which she or he is totally responsible.
3. Make your plans unique:
   a. Be selective — choose only those basic understandings and curriculum ideas that meet the needs of your children as reflected by their ability, previous experience, opportunity, ethnic culture, geographic environment, and economic situation.
   b. Choose ideas for development that best fit your teaching philosophy, style, and skills, and about which you can be most enthusiastic.
   c. Adapt to the potential and the limits of your type of program, length of school day, physical environment, and community resources.

   NOTE: This resource book is not all-inclusive; you should continue to add your own ideas. It is unlikely, and inappropriate, that you will use all the materials and activities suggested under any one subject with any one child or group.

Children often learn by watching other children. The child on the left is completely involved in the activity of his friend, even though he seems to be only watching.

 # Learning Centres

Learning centres are areas in a school or a classroom that define a special focus or that afford a specific opportunity not otherwise possible. Centres planned for young children often include a discovery centre; dramatic play centres, including a home-living centre, a block-building centre, and others; an art centre; a learning and language materials centre; a book centre; a music centre; and a centre for large muscle activities. Space for sleeping, resting, and eating, apart from the above or in a multiple use of the above, may also be provided as needed.

These centres allow children to make choices, to move freely and independently, and to develop their skills. Centres also provide opportunities for a large number of children to learn individually or in smaller groups so that the teacher can take advantage of the children's interests and desires. In a more structured grouping, these activities might not be possible.

Invite children into the mainstream of learning in the least coercive way. The shy child may choose to enter a quiet corner and pursue learning in his or her own way, while a child who seeks and needs companionship can join a co-operative play group. A child with a keen interest and ability in art or science may wish to begin the day in an area where he or she feels more confident, comfortable, and eager.

Learning centres invite children to come and see, come and do, and come and learn. A wise staff invites, guides, and encourages children to explore all the centres and, ultimately, learn in several. The staff should offer enough opportunities to learn concepts so that, whether a child selects one centre or another, the end result will be the learning necessary for that particular child's growth. By helping each child find that there are alternative ways of learning the same thing, you will help a child discover the best way for him or her to learn.

Room arrangements, materials and equipment, staff, and concepts to be learned will all influence the organization of a good learning environment for young children. By setting up a series of centres within this environment, you can provide opportunities:

1. For children to make choices.
2. For children to discover and learn through direct experience.
3. For children to gain self-confidence and competence as a result of learning skills.
4. For children to enlarge their vocabularies and to develop communication skills through the creative use of language, materials, and equipment.
5. For imaginative dramatic play through role playing.
6. For children to learn to think and to solve problems by using a variety of materials.
7. For children to develop physical and motor skills — co-ordination and manipulation — as they use the equipment.
8. For children to develop socially as they learn to relate to others.
9. For children to share and to be responsible to others as members of a group.
10. For children to use and care for materials and equipment.
11. For children to complete tasks and to plan group projects.
12. For children to discover and expand their learning of specific information relating to a subject.

Some considerations in planning for centres

1. Space (floor, table, display, and storage).
2. Light, ventilation, and heat.
3. Exits, entrances, and traffic patterns.
4. The number of children and their interests, abilities, and needs.
5. Availability of enough sturdy, safe, multipurpose equipment and materials.
6. Size of budget for additions to basic equipment, supplemented with homemade and donated or recycled materials.
7. Number of staff (permanent and volunteer).
8. Length of school day, program services offered, and size and form of the building.
9. Availability of extended classroom space such as a gym, a park, or an outdoor yard.

Remember, providing a rich environment is not enough. Adults must be facilitators, participants, and supervisors interacting with the children, other staff members, and the environment (see the section Notes for Guiding Behaviour for specific suggestions).

Arrange centres in such a manner as to allow easy supervision by staff from strategic spots without limiting the children's use of materials. There are times when a teacher may need to supervise several centres alone, such as the beginning or the end of each day. At these times, some centres may need to be closed or "off limits." If so, make the alternatives challenging, interesting, and exciting.

Discovery Centre

Guidelines for Teaching Science in the Discovery Centre

1. Encourage each child to observe keenly:
   a. What do you see?
   b. What is it like?
2. Invite each child to think by posing such questions as:
   a. Why do you suppose?
   b. What do you think?

Even lenses with very low magnification reveal textures and details imperceptible to the naked eye.

    c. What might happen if?
    d. How can we find out?
3. Help each child to look for explanations.
4. Encourage each child to grow and know. Invite and listen to questions and predictions. Help the child to discover misconceptions.
5. Give each child a variety of experiences. Provide a well-balanced program using:
    a. Living things — plants, animals — to illustrate growth and life.
    b. Matter and energy — heat, wind, electricity, sound, motors, fire, magnetism, cooking.
    c. The earth and its elements — rocks, soil, sand, metals, water, air.
    d. Regions beyond the earth — sun, moon, stars, outer space.
6. Give each child an opportunity to discover. Provide the equipment and materials that will make experimentation and discovery possible (see the lists below).
7. Repeat experiences; relate them to whatever else the child is doing and learning; provide opportunities for progressive learning.
8. Use a variety of media — real specimens, models, filmstrips, pictures, books, resource persons, and trips — that allow for direct observation and experimentation.
9. Develop in each child a respect for all living things.
10. Teach safety in the use of equipment.

> **NOTE:** You don't need elaborate equipment. Observe nature in water, shadows, sky, and earth. You can do many things with only a magnifying glass, a measuring cup, and a ruler.

Discovery centre equipment

A quiet centre should be planned where discoveries and explorations of materials can be made by individuals and small groups of children. A closet or ample cupboard space to store equipment is needed. The centre should be furnished with shelves, a variety of containers, small tables, nooks, and a few comfortable chairs or cushions. Items that will be referred to in this book include:

Metric and imperial measuring devices
mass/weight — balance pans; bathroom, kitchen, and spring scales
area/length — measuring tapes, rulers, metre sticks
fluid/volume — measuring cups and spoons
temperature — thermometers

Specimens

rocks, minerals, fossils, gems	seashells	coconut shells
halite (salt in original form)	sponges	corn, wheat, other seeds
wool (raw, carded, spun, dyed)	driftwood	bird nests, eggs
cotton ball, thread, cloth	feathers	flowers, growing plants
silkworms (preserved), cocoons	animals	
leaves (pressed in wax paper)	insects (preserved)	

Discovery aids

magnifying glasses (tripod and hand)	colour paddles	binoculars
magnets (horsehoe and bar)	globe	telescope
simple machines or tools (pulleys	tuning fork	flashlight
with rope and chains, wheels,	mirrors	microscope
wedges, screws, levers, springs)	prisms	stethoscope
animal cages (with exercise wheel	ant farm	telephone
or chambers and tunnels to allow	compass	terrarium
small animals to exercise)	cheesecloth	vivarium
vases, pots, bowls	rubber tubing	aquarium
electric clock	switch box	

This discovery centre is set up with labelled activities that children can complete on their own. Displaying a familiar book in the centre may remind children of some of the ideas presented in the book.

Science opportunities are everywhere — what can children discover?

☐ **Under or beside a rock or a log?**

slugs	insects	damp soil
snails	worms	mushrooms, moulds
toads	lizards	moss
turtles	snakes	small animals

☐ **On a sidewalk?**

footprints	grass or weeds in cracks	sections to count
wet leaves/leaf prints	ice, snow, puddle of water	a game marked with chalk
ants	crevices	worms after rain

☐ **On, in, or under a tree or a bush?**

nuts	crevices	small animals
fruits	holes	mushrooms, moulds
birds	knots	protection from rain
insects	branches	for people and animals
flowers	twigs	designs and shapes made
pine-cones	sap	by shadows and
bark	nests	formation of branches

☐ **In or near a pond or a lake?**

cattails	minnows	crayfish
water lilies	insects	mud
swans	leaves, seeds	rocks, stones, sand
ducks	algae	place for birds and animals
snakes	twigs	to find water for
skunks	grass, moss	drinking and bathing
reflections	frogs, tadpoles	
fish	turtles	

☐ **At the beach?**

sand	driftwood	crabs
seagulls	seaweed	clams
water	insects	stones
seashells	fish	

☐ **In a pile of soil?**

insects	worms	different colours of soil
seeds	rocks, pebbles	gravel, sand

☐ **In a garden or on a lawn?**

turtles	birds	grasses
dandelion and other seeds	rabbits	feathers
anthills	bird feeder, birdbath	worms
four-leaf clovers	kitchen garden	insects
weeds	flowers	slugs
squirrels		

☐ **In the centre, school, or library?**

conservation	weight	texture
how foods are made	how colours are made	how light works
gravity	how sound is produced	

Storage

A key to taking advantage of a spontaneous interest in science is *accessibility* of resources. Science trays allow for stacking and compact storage. Fruit shipping cartons with rope handles are easily transported. Cover the top half of a carton with a large plastic bag to make it airtight; the bottom half can be used as another tray. Label the side for quick identification of contents. Other suitable storage boxes for smaller items include see-through unbreakable plastic boxes and shoe boxes, available from most department stores. These are sometimes colour-coded, which may help you with storing by categories.

Items for tray storage

Shapes — circle, square, triangle, star, ellipse, oval or egg shape, rectangle, octagon, hexagon.

Leather and fur — sheepskin, suede, cowhide, etc; good sources are gloves, purses, shoes, and scraps from leather shops.

Colour — include prisms, coloured glasses, colour paddles and paint, carpet and upholstery samples in primary and secondary colours (see Colour in My World, Chapter 27).

Wood — include crosscuts of a tree and a limb, wood shavings, shingles, sawdust, plywood, samples of various colours and grains of wood, bark, toys, and other items made of wood.

Tree, flower, fruit, and vegetable seeds — place in closed, clear, unbreakable containers (pill bottles or 35 mm film canisters).

This is a teacher-made puzzle box that all children enjoy. To open each lock requires slightly different motor skills.

■ This is an excellent activity for all children, but particularly supports children in their motor development.

Nest and broken bird eggshells — have donor help you label the type of bird and location of the nest; include a picture of the bird.

Plumbing equipment — include faucets, elbows, T's, adapters, long and short lengths of pipe; check with plumbing companies for supplies.

Lock box or treasure box — padlock, chain lock, cupboard latch.

> **NOTE:** See also the specimens listed on p. 17 for many more items that can be stored in trays.

Dramatic Play Centres

Home-living centre

1. Set up the centre in an accessible, contained area. Locating it adjacent to the block-building centre or special dramatic play centres will allow interaction and co-operative play.
2. Try to simulate a real home. Set the scene by posting pictures and putting out accessories to develop interest and related play.
3. Keep the centre orderly — clothes clean and mended and equipment repaired. Orderliness invites constructive use.
4. Equipment should be sturdy enough for group use and easy for a child to use alone.
5. Post rules and suggestions for guiding or modifying behaviour, such as:
   a. Mops stay on the floor; brooms are for sweeping.
   b. It is easier to walk when the floors are clear.
   c. Food should stay on the table, in the cupboards, or in the pans on the stove.
   d. Dolls, doll clothes, and dishes should be kept off the floor (except for picnics).
   e. All members of the family should help to keep the house clean and neat.
6. If the family is too large, invite some of the children to participate in another activity, or encourage them to build another house, sharing the furniture.
7. Help a child to join the group by asking if the family could use a grandmother or an uncle.
8. Avoid or monitor the use of shared accessories that might pose a health hazard, for example, combs, wigs, pacifiers, teething rings, or plastic cutlery.
9. Remove or add special items to renew interest in the centre and to encourage an expanded use of basic equipment.
10. Encourage the children to reflect a nonsexist viewpoint toward dramatic play roles chosen by themselves or others.

Block-building centre

> **NOTE:** Low-pile carpeting reduces the noise level.

1. Allow enough space away from classroom traffic.
2. Arrange blocks according to shape and size so they are accessible on the shelves.
3. Provide sufficient accessory toys to expand and develop broader use of the blocks as interest demands. Remove items that are not needed.
4. Wooden blocks require extra supervision for safety.
5. Chalked boundaries on the floor will prove helpful in ensuring property rights.
6. Label buildings for children to develop their interest in language.
7. To prevent hoarding, limit the number of blocks accumulated by one child before construction begins.

Blocks of a variety of shapes and sizes are of great interest to young children. They help children to learn about balance, shape, size, and mass and develop their co-ordination.

The children are using blocks to experiment with balance and position. The block-building centre has a clear working space and an accessible storage area. This encourages the children to take responsibility for their activities.

■ Building with blocks encourages both fine and gross motor development.

8. Pick up or help pile stray blocks that may otherwise bother the work or movement of children. Keep the area clean and orderly and all equipment in good repair.

9. Expand interests with the use of books, excursions, pictures, and other aids.

10. Post rules and suggestions for guiding or modifying behaviour, such as:
    a. We build with blocks.
    b. We need an open path to the block shelves.
    c. Put blocks that are alike together when picking them up. Remember that teachers and others can help in the clean-up task.
    d. Build no higher than your chin. (This rule keeps a child visible and gives him or her a measurement for safety.)

11. Encourage children to build with blocks before using accessories. It will encourage more constructive and creative uses of both.

   NOTE: An exception might be a new, shy, or insecure child who may wish to hold an accessory while observing or before joining play.

Collect dramatic play props

☐ **Letter carrier/post office worker**
hat (see p. 473)
stamps
mailbag
mailbox
letters
packages
play money
rubber stamps
cash drawer

☐ **Railway worker (engineer, brakeman, conductor, porter, dispatcher)**
lunch box
overalls
ticket punch
coloured tickets
lantern (without glass)
hat (see p. 26)
watch
pillows
luggage
trays
bandana

☐ **Ranch hand**
hat
chaps
rope
bolero
stickhorse
bandana

☐ **Grocery clerk**
apron
vendor's hat (see p. 27)
baskets
play money
cash register
food cartons, boxes
pad and pencil
shopping bags
shelves
plastic or papier-
mâché fruits and
vegetables

☐ **Pilot/flight attendant**
cap
airplane
instrument panel
(see p. 472)
serving trays
travel folders
packing-box
cockpit
plank from gym
equipment
wing

☐ **Baker**
hat (see p. 27)
pans
apron
rolling pin
wooden spoons
plastic bowls
cookie cutters

☐ **People who fish**
net
cardboard oars
poles with string, spools
paper, cardboard,
or plastic fish
box for boat
styrofoam packing
worms

☐ **Circus performers/
workers**
tickets
crepe paper to
decorate wheels
black hat for
ringmaster
crazy hats, costumes,
and ruffled collars
for clowns
cardboard cartons cut
to resemble cages
with bars
stands for animals to
perform on
white hats for popcorn
vendors (see p. 27)

☐ **Painter**
cap
paintbrushes
paint roller
paint tray
bucket and water
ladder

☐ **Sanitary engineer**
cloth or paper sacks
garbage cans
wagons
Soveralls
gloves

☐ **Firefighter**
rubber hose (short
lengths)
wagon
ladder
rubber or cardboard
hatchet
hat (see p. 473)

☐ **Service station
attendant**
oil can
cap
flashlight
rubber hose (short
lengths)
rope (short lengths)
sponge and bucket
rubber or soft plastic
tools
cash register
credit cards
play money

☐ **Police officer**
hat
badge
tickets
licence
traffic signs
handcuffs
keys to jail
pencil and pad

☐ **Doctor, nurse, nursing
attendant**
nurse's cap
tape, cotton
pad and pencil
two telephones
kit or bag
thermometer container
sunglasses (without
lenses)
unbreakable supplies
(pill bottles)
bandages (strips of
sheeting)
stethoscope
baby scale
tape measure or
height chart

Adapt dramatic play props
....

☐ **Save accessories**
   length of hose (protect nozzle or
      remove; a bicycle handle grip
      makes a good nozzle)
   empty oil cans
   empty food containers
   paper punch or empty stapler
   buckets and brushes
   pads and pencils
   rubber stamp with handle

☐ **Make your own**
   temporary props or paper or cardboard: hat
      bands, money, signs
   fishing poles, smokestacks, and oars can be
      made of empty upholstery rollers
   enlist aid of volunteers to sew simple cloth
      hats such as bakers' hats, engineers' caps,
      scarves, stoles, shortened skirts with elastic
      waistbands, white bib aprons using elastic
      instead of ties

☐ **Build equipment**
   mount laundry, fat, or flour
      barrels for tunnel or airplane
      (add wings)
   use empty boxes and cartons
   use discarded tires for swings,
      climbers, or tunnels
   mount a steering wheel for a
      multiple-use vehicle

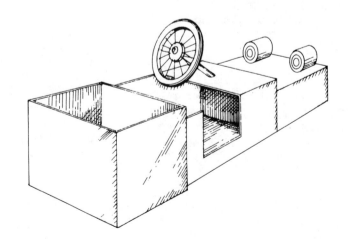

☐ **Alter shirts**
  cut off sleeves
  reverse collars
  adjust neck buttons and sew on a large
    button
  helper shirts that are often available: letter
    carrier; work shirt; white or pastel shirts for
    doctors, orderlies, nursing attendants; lab
    coats; nurses' uniforms
  grocery or ice cream aprons can be made
    with elastic neck straps and an elastic
    waist in back

☐ **Collect real hats**
  discontinued or damaged letter carrier's cap
  paint cap (free at a paint dealer)
  sailor's hat
  nurse's cap
  construction hard hat
  old felt or straw hat
  bright-coloured woman's hat, turban, scarf
  service station attendant's cap
  chef, firefighter, or police officer's hat

Patterns for dramatic play props

NOTE: Seam allowance measurements included for all patterns.

☐ **Mail bag**
  Cuff open edge of large paper sack
  with a strip of cardboard, folding top
  edge of sack twice over cardboard
  for durability. Staple ends of strap on
  inside of sack as shown in diagram.

  NOTE: Strap must be attached to
  opposite side.

☐ **Train engineer's cap**

Take overlapping tucks at points A-AB-B, C-CD-C,
E-EF-F, and so on, and then gather remaining shape
into headband. Attach bill at one of the short sides
and line with upholstery material or plastic for
sturdiness.

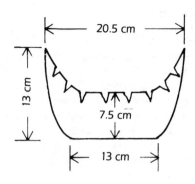

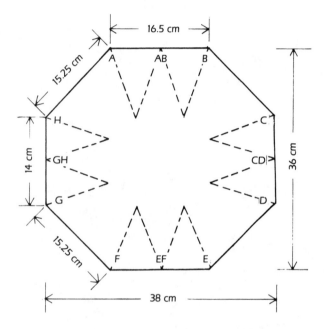

Cut two 5 cm x 58 cm bands
with 2 cm slashes on inside edge
of bill (finished bill 5.5 cm deep)

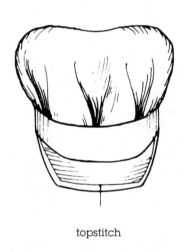

topstitch

☐ **Grocer's apron**

Use 28 cm elastic for neck and 18 cm
elastic for waist. Bottom hem is
indicated by dotted lines. Attach
elastic at neck and waist. Allow for
other hems when cutting;
measurements are finished size.

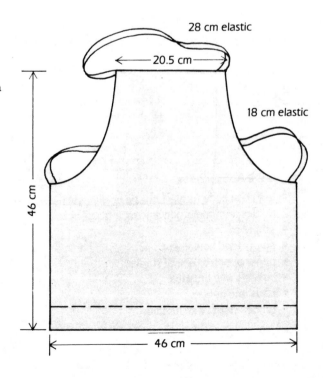

☐ **Baker's hat**

Gather a circle 53 cm in diameter into a double band about 46 cm long and 2.5 cm wide. When circle is completely gathered into headband, insert a 5 cm long piece of wide elastic as shown. Allow for adjustment to various head sizes.

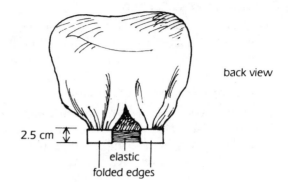

back view

2.5 cm

elastic
folded edges

☐ **Food vendor's hat**

Sew two part A pieces together around curve between points *bacd*, leaving straight edges at *bd* open. Sew two more part A pieces in same manner, and turn inside out to form lining for first crown. Cut two part B pieces, and open both pieces out flat. Sew pieces together (one on top of the other), bind curved edges with bias tape, and leave straight edges open. Insert straight open edges of brim into open ends of both crown and lining at *bd* (headband). Top stitch, and tuck in raw edges.

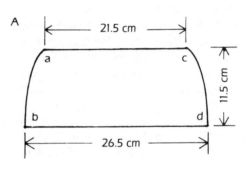

A

21.5 cm

a   c

11.5 cm

b   d

26.5 cm

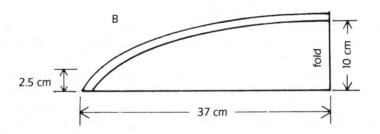

B

2.5 cm

fold

10 cm

37 cm

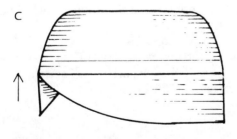

C

D

Cardboard and Cartons

The common box or carton can offer an endless number of possibilities for temporary equipment. Students in one early childhood education program pooled their ideas and listed 100 uses for cartons in an E.C.E. centre. Here are a few of those ideas.

Home-living centre

1. *Stove:* Make from a sturdy rectangular box about 60 to 80 cm high. Paint circles for burners. Attach wooden beads or knobs on the front of the carton for heat selector dials. Secure them with plastic-coated wire and a disc of plastic on *both* sides of the cardboard to prevent tearing. Cut a three-sided opening for a door and use masking tape to reinforce the fold instead of a hinge. Insert an inverted box inside for an oven floor. To make a latch, hook a yarn loop on a button that has been secured with plastic discs on both sides of the cardboard.
2. *Doll's bed:* Make from a shallow box of appropriate size. Turn the top flaps to the inside of the box and secure by stapling, sewing, or taping them down. Use a pillow for a mattress and cover it with sheets or a blanket.
3. *Tote box:* Make as for bed except add rope loops for handles. Paint box for greater durability and attractiveness.
4. *Partition or room divider:* Use three sides of a large desk, stereo, or cupboard carton to make a three-way play screen. Cut an opening for a door or window in one section. Can be painted or wallpapered.
5. *Mailbox:* Paint a rectangular cardboard box red, cut a slot for depositing the mail, and label with "Canada Post." Add a list of pick-up times beneath the mail slot.
6. *Shelves and a cupboard:* Set cartons inside other cartons.
7. *Desk or dressing table:* Invert a rectangular carton, open end down. Cut out a square for a kneehole space. Fold and tape the square into the box to reinforce the desk. This can also be used as a fireplace.
8. *Television:* Cut a hole in the side of a carton to form the television screen.
9. *Table:* Turn a carton upside down. Reinforce two opposite sides with an extra thickness of cardboard, and cut off the other two opposite sides and top flaps.

Block-building centre

1. *Road segments:* Make cardboard highway sections to use with proportional blocks and cars. Use proportional double longs, Y and X shapes, and arches and curves as guides, and make your cardboard road segments double size for two-lane traffic. Draw a median strip on each. Let children lay out these cardboard roadways and save the blocks for buildings along the highway.
2. *Tabletop play board:* Use a mattress, stereo, or pool-table carton cut in two. Hinge in the centre with masking tape so that it can be stored. Paint the surface green except where you wish to leave roadways or cement areas. Paint an irregularly shaped lake in the centre of one section (see Learning Centres, Chapter 7, for illustration). VARIATION: Make a cloverleaf roadway or a subdivision street pattern. Leave grass space for constructing houses or public buildings.
3. *Vehicles:* Use rectangular cartons for trains, cars, boats, and wagons. Glue fabric to the bottom of each box so it will pull smoothly and not scratch the floor. Attach rope pulls or use rope to link cartons together.
4. *Zoo cage:* See the instructions in Learning Centres, Chapter 19.
5. *Hollow blocks:* Reinforce boxes on the inside by inserting two slotted pieces of strong corrugated cardboard that have been formed into an X-shaped partition. Tape the box lids shut and paint. These blocks will be sturdy enough for long use.

The teacher is commenting on the structures the children are building with their blocks. Judicious comments from the teacher can extend any learning experience.

Art Centre

An art centre is best placed in an area with a washable floor, near a sink. It should have ample storage space and be away from traffic. No one but the child can create the picture or idea that is in his or her mind; the creations will reflect each child's *experience*. Art experiences can release emotions to allow for creativity; a child often expresses feelings as well as ideas through art. The process is more important than the product. When working with children in the art centre:

1. Introduce a variety of media.
2. Be prepared.
3. Provide choices.
4. Offer support.
5. It is better to ask, "Would you tell me about it?" than, "What is it?"
6. Let children explore.
7. Provide space for drying finished products.
8. Supervise.
9. Compare creations only against a child's previous efforts.
10. Offer large sheets of paper, long-handled brushes, thick chalk, and pencils.

The art activity is extended as a language activity by having the children dictate a story to the teacher to write down. In writing down the story, the teacher correlates sound and symbol and also shows that the child's story is valued and that language is purposeful.

Favourite Recipes for Art Materials

NON-HARDENING NO-COOK PLAY DOUGH

500 mL/2 cups self-rising flour
25 mL/2 T powdered alum
25 mL/2 T salt
25 mL/2 T cooking oil
250 mL/1 cup, plus 25 mL/2 T boiling water

Mix and knead.

COOKED PLAY DOUGH

250 mL/1 cup flour
125 mL/$\frac{1}{2}$ cup salt
250 mL/1 cup water
15 mL/1 T vegetable oil
10 mL/2 tsp cream of tartar

Heat until ingredients form ball, then add food colouring.

······························

SALLY WYSONG'S PLAY DOUGH

This play dough is similar to the commercial type and more durable. Store in a plastic bag or closed container when not in use.

250 mL/1 cup flour
250 mL/1 cup water
15 mL/1 T oil
15 mL/1 T powdered alum
125 mL/½ cup salt
25 mL/2 T vanilla
food colouring

Mix all dry ingredients. Add oil and water. Cook over medium heat, stirring constantly until the mixture reaches the consistency of mashed potatoes. Remove from heat and add vanilla. Divide into balls and work in food colouring by kneading.

······························

POTTER'S CLAY

125 mL/½ cup flour
125 mL/½ cup cornstarch
250 mL/1 cup salt dissolved in 925 mL/3¾ cups of boiling water

Blend flour and cornstarch with enough water to make paste. Boil water and salt. Add to cornstarch mixture and cook until clear. Cool overnight, then add 1.5 L to 2 L (6 to 8 cups) of flour and knead until you have the right consistency.

NOTE: Keep a salt shaker full of flour handy for the children to keep their clay from sticking.

······························

IRIDESCENT SOAP BUBBLES

250 mL/1 cup water
25 mL/2 T liquid dish detergent
15 mL/1 T glycerine
2 ml/½ tsp sugar

Mix all ingredients.

······························

SUGAR FLOUR PASTE

250 mL/1 cup flour
250 mL/1 cup sugar
0.95 L/1 qt warm water
15 mL/1 T powdered alum

Mix dry ingredients together. Slowly stir in 250 mL/1 cup of water. Bring remainder of water to boil and add the mixture to it, stirring constantly. Continue to cook and stir (1/2 hour in a double boiler) until fairly clear. Remove from heat. Makes almost 1 L. Paste keeps a long time. Keep moist by adding small piece of wet sponge to top of small jar of paste.

BOOKBINDER'S PASTE

5 mL/1 tsp flour
10 mL/2 tsp cornstarch
1 mL/¼ tsp powdered alum
75 mL/⅓ cup water

Mix dry ingredients. Add water slowly, stirring out lumps. Cook mixture in a double boiler over low heat, stirring constantly. Remove from heat when paste begins to thicken; it will thicken more as it cools. Keep covered. Thin with water when necessary.

FINGERPAINT

150 mL/⅔ cup dry laundry starch
250 mL/1 cup cold water
750 mL/3 cups boiling water
250 mL/1 cup soap flakes

Dissolve starch in cold water. Stir until smooth and add boiling water. On a stove, bring to a boil and then simmer on low heat until thickened. This should take approximately one minute. Remove from heat and stir in the rest of the ingredients. Use on coated paper, newsprint, or wrapping paper.

SALT PAINT

75 mL/⅓ cup salt
1 mL/¼ tsp food colouring

Spread in pan to dry before putting in salt shakers. Shake onto surface brushed with glue.

SAND PAINT

125 mL/½ cup sand (washed, dried, and sifted)
15 mL/1 T powdered paint

Mix ingredients and shake onto surface brushed with watered glue.

NOTE: Empty plastic vitamin or soap bubble bottles make excellent containers.

SOAP PAINT

375 mL/1½ cups soap flakes
250 mL/1 cup hot or warm water

Mix ingredients and whip with an eggbeater until stiff.

Creative Art Tips

1. A candy box or cheese box with holes cut in its lid to hold small cans or jars makes an excellent paint holder that resists tipping.

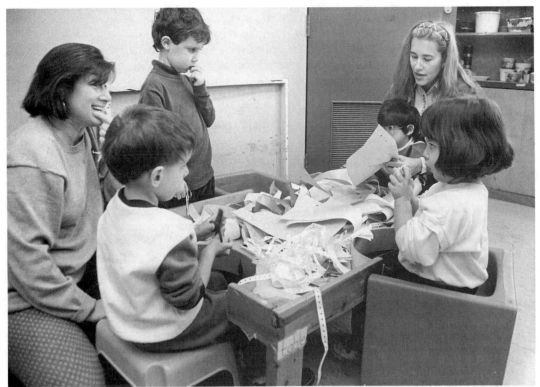

Using scraps for art activities allows the children to use their imagination and to explore a variety of forms and shapes. Children also solve problems by experimenting with visual effects and ways of fastening scraps together.

2. Foam rubber with holes makes an excellent chalk holder.
3. Pieces of sponge may be obtained from upholstery shops and cut into geometric shapes for sponge printing.
4. Baskets and margarine tubs make good crayon holders.
5. Buy white glue by the litre and pour it into small detergent or squeeze bottles.

   ▼ CAUTION: Clear spout after each use and insert round toothpick for a stopper.

6. Old toothbrushes can be used for spatter painting.
7. Old toothbrushes with a hole in one end may be cut off to about 8 cm in length and filed to make blunt needles for weaving yarn through mesh vegetable bags. Thread bright yarn through the hole in the toothbrush and tie a button at the other end of the yarn to prevent the end from sliding through the mesh.
8. When children are cutting paper, tape a paper bag to the edge of the table for scraps.
9. A printing shop is an excellent source for small scraps of coloured paper and cardboard.
10. Mark a storage box for art supplies on the end or top with a picture to identify its contents, or use clear plastic boxes.
11. Place a piece of wet sponge inside the lid of a jar of paste to keep the paste moist between uses.
12. Ask department store clerks to save paper inserts from lingerie and blouses.

Creative Art Media

1. *Brayers:* These can be made of wooden or plastic spools and a piece of coat hanger that has been cut and bent in half. Insert one of the prongs in each end of a spool to make

a handle. For a smooth brayer, cover the spool with a piece of foam or upholstery fabric. Use brayer without covering to make stripes.

2. *Cardboard overlays:* Have children glue layers of geometrically shaped cardboard scraps on a surface. Children may choose to paint on top of the overlay. A print can be taken from the painted surface using a monoprint technique (see number 11 below).

3. *Sewing cards:* Styrofoam meat and pastry trays make good forms for sewing with yarn. Punch holes with a nail or an ice pick randomly in the tray. Use a threaded bobby pin for a needle by taping the prongs shut with cellophane tape. With supervision, older children can use blunt tapestry needles. Bright-coloured rug yarn works well.

4. *Weaving cards:* Different shapes of notched cardboard can be wrapped with one colour yarn and then woven with another colour. The best weaving needle for young children is made by dipping the end of the yarn in glue or melted wax. Let dry before using. A cellophane-taped end also works well.

5. *Crayon sandpaper prints:* Have children draw pictures with crayons on sandpaper. Place a plain piece of white paper over the picture and press with a warm iron. The result is a stippled painting on the paper and a vivid blurred print on the sandpaper. Use discarded sandpaper belts from a free source.

6. *Colour cones:* Melt small pieces of crayons in pans set in hot water. (Scrape the surfaces of light colours before melting them to keep the pure colours, and melt crayons in sequence — light to dark — so you can use the same pans.) When slightly cool, pour into paper cones. Children love the result. Colour cones can be gripped point up by the wider end, or they can be rubbed on the side for a fast sweep of colour. VARIATIONS:
    a. *Colour cups:* Pour 3 cm or more of the melted crayon was into muffin tins. These use less wax than the colour cones. To remove, dip muffin tin quickly in and out of a pan of hot water.
    b. *Colour caps:* Spoon melted crayon wax into pop-bottle caps. Leave the hardened wax in the caps and use for counting, collage material, or colour games.
    c. *Crayon chubbies:* Pour melted crayon wax into large, wide, or tall plastic pill bottles. When hardened, dip or roll in very hot water to remove.

7. *Imagination paper:* Glue a scrap of coloured paper to a larger piece of paper. Prepare as many sheets of paper as necessary for each child to have one. Let children choose the piece that makes them think of a beginning for a picture. Using crayons and their imagination, children can complete their pictures by adding to the scrap. VARIATION: Instead of a scrap of paper, use a felt-tip marker to make wavy, straight, zigzag, or dotted lines on a sheet of paper.

8. *Wire sculptures:* Cast-off plastic-coated telephone or electric wires are excellent materials for wire sculptures. Offer different lengths, colours, and thicknesses.

9. *Clay boards/monoprint surfaces:* Cut formica or linoleum scraps into squares or rectangles to use as bases for clay, play dough, or fingerpaint. You could also use individual linoleum tiles.

10. *Monoprinting:* Children fingerpaint directly on a surface and then place a piece of newsprint on the painting. As the paper is lifted off, a reverse print is revealed.

11. *Displaying children's work:* Provide a space for each child. Let each child choose a picture for the display. Avoid displaying a dozen of one kind of picture together.

Learning and Language Materials Centre

This centre needs good lighting, easy access to shelves, and groups of tables arranged for individual or group use. Sometimes placing a table against a dividing wall allows a child more room for activity without having to disturb or compete with another child across the table for space. Other times, centre materials can be shared more easily when children's chairs are placed around the end of a table or by using a round table.

Computer software is available for young children. Choose software with clear graphics that a child can operate alone. Try to choose programs with open-ended activities that foster creativity and problem solving rather than skill and drill activities. If your staff has no experience with this software, ask a knowledgeable parent to help you with purchasing and setting up programs.

In some centres, you may choose to hinge narrow tables to a wall; these can then be lowered and braced for extended table space when needed, and used for displaying pictures when raised. These hinged tables also free up floor space when raised.

When this centre is adjacent to the book centre, children can easily move from one to the other for language development activities that may be offered in either area.

Language arts in this centre and the book centre should include opportunities for:

1. *Listening:* Help the children discover that thoughts can be expressed aloud.
2. *Thinking:* Give opportunities for problem solving.
3. *Speaking:* Encourage the children to speak in all centres in the program. Invite them to talk about what they are doing, will do, and can do in sharing times; to name objects; to talk into a telephone. Accept what the children have to say as important. Listen to their expressed thoughts and ideas. Use fingerplays and learning games to build vocabulary and to help children learn nouns, verbs, adjectives, adverbs, and prepositions.
4. *Writing:* Help children discover that words and thoughts can be written down by labelling objects in the centre; using signs, song charts with words, and words lettered on bulletin boards with pictures; or lettering children's thoughts about their pictures.
5. *Reading:* Read to children. Show them that words and pictures are symbols for thoughts. Relate words to pictures or objects to help children realize the need for, and excitement of, reading signs, books, and other matter in their world. Let them see their thoughts when you have written them down to encourage them to want to write for themselves.

Puppets provide opportunities for role play and storytelling. Children can act out their own stories or retell familiar ones. Puppets also encourage motor development and social interaction.

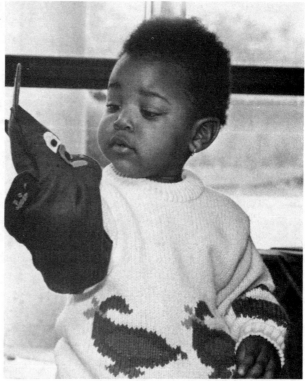

Book Centre

Select books for young children with care. The following are some guidelines for choosing books:

1. The story and illustrations should be captivating and imaginative. Select books with one to three characters in a story for the youngest children.
2. Attractive pictures with vivid colours and interesting detail appeal to children.
3. The plot should not be too complex.
4. Look for use of repetitive catch phrases, humour, surprise, action, rhyme, direct conversation, and a reasonable, satisfying conclusion.
5. Books should be sturdily bound and easy for children to handle.

Consider putting books in all areas of your classroom so that invitations to read are everywhere. You may also wish to focus on and celebrate reading in a special part of your room: the book centre.

Setting up a book centre

This centre requires good lighting, some privacy, and quiet. It should be located away from more active work and play. By placing this centre next to the science area, the books will be within easy reach for reference, and any aquarium, terrarium, or plants will give a homey touch to this comfortable spot for looking at or reading books. When next to the home-living centre, this area may become an extended study or library.

Change the books frequently. Have a special display for the books that relate to your current theme and also leave out a selection of the children's favourites, including any that you have made together. When you are going to change the books, invite the children to help you choose which ones to take out of storage. When going to the public library, take the children along to help you select books. It is useful and enjoyable to talk to the children about their particular choices. Take advantage of public library reading programs.

Provide books and other reading materials for children of all ages. Placed throughout the room in learning centres as well as in a special book centre, such materials invite reading at any time of the day. This infant selected a book with a baby on the cover. She sat down with it, looked at the pictures, and turned the pages as any fluent reader would.

Some equipment that will make the book centre more enjoyable includes:

1. A round table with chairs, and space in the centre for a few selected books.
2. Two or three child-size rocking chairs.
3. A few small beanbag chairs or a large one to share.
4. A stack of upholstery fabric or carpet squares or cushions for sit-upons.
5. An overstuffed couch or chair (plastic or washable fabric is best) with legs removed so it is low enough to get on and off easily.
6. A small area rug with pad (so it will not slip if the area is not carpeted).
7. Mobiles that are more visible from a beanbag or rocking-chair position.
8. A bulletin board with pictures that relate to special books on display.
9. Murals or framed pictures.
10. A flannelboard with figures for acting out stories.
11. Taped background music or tape-recorder with musical or story tapes.
12. Headsets for listening to pre-recorded stories; tape-recorders for recording tapes of children's stories; VCRs for screening recorded stories.
13. Puppets and a puppet theatre or TV box for dramatic play and story presentations.

Some Do's and Don'ts for Storytelling

When you select a story

1. *Don't* read aloud any story without scanning and evaluating it first.
2. Adapt a story for your group. Shorten, expand, or change wording for the age level, the time allowance, and the occasion. Emphasize the incidents that appeal to children (sound, humour, action). Remember that for very young children three minutes is a long time. *Don't* memorize word by word and recite the story. Leave out unimportant details. The storytelling will not be as much fun if you concentrate on a recitation. Quote only words that cannot be improved.

The children prepared this mural after listening to Maurice Sendak's *Where the Wild Things Are*. In addition to extending the story, the children learned about co-operation and teamwork.

3. Evaluate and edit a story. If a phrase, paragraph, or picture needs to be omitted because of insensitivity to an ethnic group, to people with special needs, or to people's economic status, paper-clip the page or write in the change. *Don't* discard a book because of one offensive illustration or paragraph — modify the picture or the text.

As you prepare the story

1. Know the story. If you need prompts, clip and mark key pages where you want to read a section or be reminded of a sequence of subjects. Be sure you understand the story as a whole and the relationship of every character to the main plot so that you can better set the scene. Tell the story slowly; pause for emphasis; speed up for excitement or urgency; vary the volume of your voice to suggest emotion or change of character. Speak distinctly. *Don't* tack on facts you have forgotten after the sequence is past. *Don't* forget the punch line. *Don't* read too rapidly or mumble.

2. Rehearse the story before you tell it so you will be able to make eye contact with the children. Practise telling it aloud in front of a mirror. Tape-record your reading for a revealing self-criticism. *Don't* ad lib unless you are an experienced and very talented storyteller. Your off-the-cuff rendition may be unsuccessful and may ruin a story for the children.

3. Locate any props you will use. Make sure they relate well to the story. Manipulation of puppets or flannelboard materials should not distract you or your listeners from the story. *Don't* take too long a pause locating the next prop.

Before you begin the story

After practising the story so that you are thoroughly familiar with it, get comfortable. Make certain the children can see and hear and are not crowded. Consider the personalities and individual needs of the children. Sit where they will be least distracted by the surroundings. Be flexible; regroup children if necessary. *Don't* allow children to sit too close to one another. *Don't* let yourself be driven by a time schedule.

When you tell the story

Make the characters come alive. Use direct conversation. Involve yourself by empathizing with the main characters. Use gestures and facial expressions, vary your voice, and pace your delivery for emphasis. Maintain eye contact with children. *Don't* tell the story using vague characters in an obscure setting. *Don't* make your delivery monotonous by using the same pattern of inflection regardless of the story line.

During and after the story

Listen for children's responses and comments. Let them think, ponder, and show pleasure or displeasure. Allow the story to state its message or entertain the children. Allow them to identify with the story from their own experience. Answer children's questions but *don't* editorialize, moralize, or interpret.

Extended Experiences with Books

After the children have heard a story one or more times and are familiar with it, you might try the following:

1. Use a flannelboard.
2. Use background music.
3. Use puppets.
4. Use props and pictures.
5. Use a tape-recorder for individual listening.
6. Let children dramatize the story.
7. Talk about the story.
8. Tell part of the story and let the children make up a new ending for it.

When and How to Use Poetry

1. Get into the habit of sharing poetry with children every day.
2. Instead of reading a story at group time, substitute a poem.
3. Use poetry to supplement another activity in the classroom.
4. Use poetry to encourage active participation (fingerplays and action rhymes).
5. Read poems with background mood music.
6. Use poetry as a chant with a large muscle activity.
7. Record a child's chant or verse recited while playing.
8. Share a child's poem with the whole group.
9. Make a file of poems printed on cards. Illustrate one side of the card to show the children as you read the poem printed on the back of the card.
10. Hang illustrated poems on the walls in the various centres for easy reference while teaching.

 # Planning for Group Time

A part of every well-planned program for young children includes directed learning experiences in a group. These experiences are possible when children are gathered into small or large groups for a specific activity with one teacher. Several types of groups might include:

1. A small group, with three to five children focussing on a special need or interest and interacting with an adult. This type of grouping may occur spontaneously in an existing learning centre or elsewhere during the day.
2. A larger group when all the children or a group of six or more are gathered for a longer period of directed learning with a lead teacher (other teachers may assist). Experiences in this larger group often include the use of music, fingerplays, stories, games, poetry, and rhythms.
3. An outdoor group (or indoor in inclement weather), with more structure, for large muscle activities such as circle games, exercises, or practising a motor skill.
4. A routine time group, when all the children may be eating, resting, or moving indoors or outdoors at one time.
5. A group formed for a trip or excursion, when there is a need for children to be in a more controlled grouping.

   NOTE: See special suggestions under the Planning for Group Time sections in each chapter of this guide.

Music Centre

Provide a centre for the exploration and creative use of music and musical instruments.

1. Let children listen to tapes (vocal and instrumental) for music appreciation and to increase their vocabulary.
2. Make rhythm band instruments available to encourage awareness and sensitivity to sound.
3. Encourage self-expression through music. Record children's original songs on tape and play them back.
4. Encourage children to sing songs for their own enjoyment.
5. Plan opportunities for rhythmic movement. It will encourage dramatic expression and develop motor control.
6. Invite musicians to come and play for the children.

Music in the Child's World

Music is a part of every child's environment, whether it be in the form of the song of a bird, a whistler on the street, or music played on instruments. By inviting children to explore instruments, to listen to nature, and to participate in singing, we offer them the opportunity and experience to express their feelings or ideas naturally through music. Listen for the children's creative interpretations and encourage their spontaneous responses when they are exploring sound. Tape segments of original songs or chants with or without their instrumental accompaniment. If one of the teachers can play back on a piano or other instrument an original composition by a child, the other children will be encouraged in their musical expression and will be delighted at the recognition of their creative effort.

Listed below are several sounds or emotions that may be suggested by the use of instruments as you plan music with your children:

1. *Triangle:* Raindrops, night sounds, birds, flowers, sunset, water, waterfalls, tiptoeing, dawn, snow, splashing, falling leaves, quiet, tears.
2. *Drum:* Thunder, Native dances, marching bands, heavy footsteps, anger, hammering.
3. *Tambourine and maracas:* Dancing, the word *suddenly*, fluttering, eerie Halloween sounds.

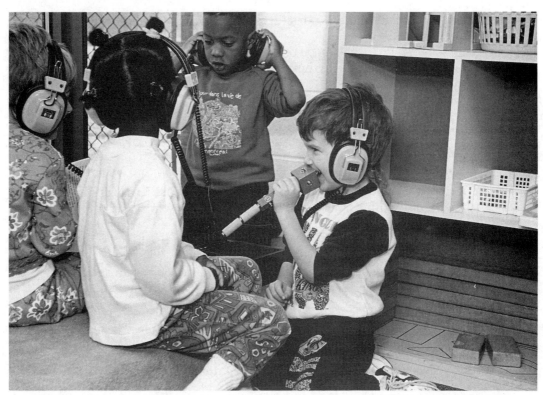

Children enjoy listening to and singing along with taped music. This child has added dramatic play by building a microphone from blocks. Other children have joined in and are enjoying his performance.

4. *Bell:* Fire alarms, school or church bells, clock alarms, buoys, fire trucks.
5. *Cymbals:* Garbage can lids, pan lids when cooking.
6. *Finger cymbals:* Seeds, dawn, very small flowers, first raindrops.
7. *Sand block:* Feet shuffling, rustling sounds, shredding, sanding, wood in the wood-shop, squirrels in the leaves, trash rattling.
8. *Rhythm sticks, claves, tone blocks, or wood blocks:* Clocks ticking, hoofbeats, running, pecking, raindrops, footsteps, hammering, ascending or descending stairs.

When choosing instruments for young children, it is important to consider the following:

1. How sturdy is the instrument? Will it last for a long time?
2. Do the notes played by the children sound in tune? Many instruments made for children as toys are not in tune.
3. Does the instrument encourage children to create musical sounds or does it encourage noise?

(You will find more information about music in the child's world in the book *Move, Sing, Listen, Play* by Donna Wood.)

The choice of songs for children is very important, because children's voices and language abilities are still developing. The song lists in each chapter of this guide do not have bullets to indicate the developmental level for which individual songs are appropriate. The choice of songs is determined by many factors, but the children's experience with music is a critical one. As a result, a given song could be equally suitable for a group of four-year-olds or a group of two-year-olds. When choosing songs, carefully consider the amount and type of musical experience the children have had and the following criteria:

1. Is the song within the children's range? It should be approximately one octave starting at the B below middle C.
2. Is the key appropriate for the mood of the song? A minor key is good for a sad song.
3. Can the children manage the rhythmic pattern? A simple, repetitive rhythmic pattern is best for young children.
4. Do the words match the music? If the song is about birds flying high in the sky or low to their nest, does the music go high and low with the words?
   (For more detail, refer to Donna Wood's book *Move, Sing, Listen, Play*.)

Teaching Songs to Children

1. Before introducing a new song, you may wish to use it first as background music or as a segment for rhythms or an accompaniment for a rhythm band if it has a strong rhythmic beat.
2. Since children learn by repetition, sing a new song to them first. They will soon master a short segment (one verse or just the refrain).
3. Invite children to join you, if they wish, as you sing the song again and again.
4. Use prompts such as pictures, flannelboard figures, or hand actions to help the children remember the words.

   NOTE: If you have an overhead projector, you might show selected pictures or illustrations as the children sing.

5. Play a simple accompaniment with a guitar, an autoharp, or a recorder. If you play the piano, use a few basic chord variations or a one-hand accompaniment since the melody should be recognizable. Elaborate accompaniment is not recommended.
6. Make sure all the teachers on your staff are familiar with the new song.

   NOTE: To aid volunteers or substitutes, post the words of the song on a wall above the lead teacher's head.

7. Sing the new song often until the children know it.
8. Teach one song at a time.
9. Give the children opportunities to sing songs at other times during the day. Encourage them to sing at play by taping their original songs or by echoing their chants when they sing.

Music Accessories

1. *Dance costumes:* Ask dancing schools to post a request for discarded dance costumes or tutus to use for dressup. Remove crotches and hem costumes to allow children to pull them on over their clothes.

   NOTE: Commercial tutu bands are ideal because they fit all young children without alterations.

2. *Drapery sheer skirts:* (See the diagram on p. 43.) Ask a drapery shop to save colourful cutoff lengths of sheer curtains. It usually takes two scraps of a width of sheer material to make a full skirt. Alternate colour with white or a complementary shade. Make a casing at the top to allow for gathering with elastic. Discarded pantyhose make an excellent source of soft, sturdy elastic and is the right circumference for a young child. Use the selvage edges of the fabric as the bottom hem. French-seam or serge the side seams so the material will not fray.
3. *Scarf lengths:* Gather drapery sheer scraps roughly 15 cm wide and 60 cm long. Hem the ends and sides. Attach a yarn ball or a loop of discarded pantyhose elastic to one end. The ball can be held in the hand but does not need a tight grip so children's muscles are relaxed. The wristlet of soft elastic allows free movement of the wrist,

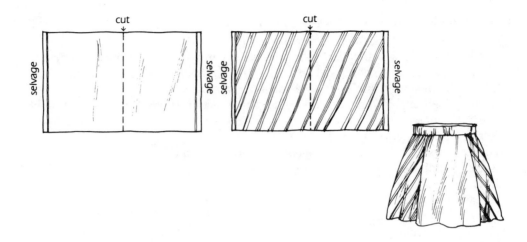

fingers, and hand. When the wristlet is attached to shoulder straps or belts, the scarf can simulate wings or a tail.

4. *Ankle bells:* Make a 15 to 20 cm circle of elastic from discarded pantyhose. Tie two or three jingle bells together loosely with a piece of plastic-coated wire. Sew the wire on the wristlet or ankle band. The wire keeps the metal bells from cutting the thread that attaches them to the elastic. Tennis wristbands with bells sewn on also work well.

5. *Tambourines:* Encircle the outside of an embroidery hoop with plastic-covered wire threaded through four large jingle bells. Cover the wire with yarn, using a 10 m ball of yarn. Beginning between bells, make a tassel where the yarn ends meet.

6. *Flags:* Make a casing on one side of a chiffon scarf large enough and tight enough to slide over a length of thick dowel or broomstick (18 cm to 20 cm). The scarf can then be removed easily for laundering.

7. *Jingle paddles:* Lace large jingle bells with pipecleaners. Push the ends of the pipe-cleaners through drilled holes in a discarded wooden paddle. Lightweight paddles are usually available in variety stores with a small rubber ball attached with an elastic.

8. *Music and rhythms:* Use a taped sequence of appropriate music, marking the beginnings of different music segments on the tape. This works well when you cannot play the piano or afford a large collection of tapes, and leaves you free to watch the children. A tape also allows a segment to be a predetermined, reasonable length.

9. *Gymnastic ribbons:* Ribbons similar to those used by gymnasts can be made by cutting 2 m wide pieces of felt into 5 cm by 2 m strips. Children can use their imagination to move with these in time to music.

Fingerplays and Action Songs

Originally these rhyme games were written to use only the fingers and hands to act out the words. They were used primarily by parents to help teach their youngest children body parts, numbers, and shapes. Some of them date back nearly 2000 years.

In the nineteenth century, Friedrich Froebel, who developed the kindergarten in Germany, adapted adult games and songs for children for educational purposes. He used them to integrate meanings and the emotional satisfaction of sensing relationships among parts.

Today, the best fingerplays and action songs use the whole body (large and small muscles) for total participation.

Value of fingerplays and action songs

1. Increase manual dexterity and muscular control.
2. Develop an understanding of rhythms of speech and music, and life's activities.
3. Encourage an understanding of concepts of size, shape, place, and direction.
4. Build vocabulary and aid in language development.
5. Allow for self-expression, encouraging a child's own response in the use of body and speech for interpreting concepts.
6. Help teach numbers, especially one to ten.
7. Provide relaxation (a legitimate opportunity to move and wiggle).
8. Assist the child in learning to follow directions.
9. Teach order and sequence.
10. Increase attention span.
11. Develop listening skills.
12. Give an opportunity to have fun.

Suggestions for teaching fingerplays and action songs

1. Demonstrate appropriate actions as you say or sing the words to the group.
2. Repeat the fingerplay, encouraging the children to imitate only the actions.
3. Repeat the fingerplay, allowing those who wish to participate to use both actions and words.
4. Keep actions slow enough so that children do not have trouble keeping up.
5. Repeat the fingerplay until children become familiar with it.
6. Introduce variations or a new approach to an old favourite.
7. Be enthusiastic; use songs that you enjoy.
8. Repeat old favourites (children enjoy repetition).
9. Occasionally, send parents the words and music to fingerplays currently being used so that they can try them at home.
10. You may wish to make a fingerplay card file for yourself to use as a prompt during group time, although it is better to memorize the fingerplays.
11. When learning a new fingerplay or song, letter a large sign to post on an adjacent wall at eye level for the staff and volunteers.

▼ CAUTION: Select one or two fingerplays for each subject, making certain they teach *best* the concept to be learned. As with books, poems, and songs, watch for the difficulty of vocabulary, the length of verse, the concept to be learned, and the maturity level of your group. Use the simplest fingerplays with the youngest or the least mature group; increase the complexity as the group shows readiness.

Flannelboards

A flannelboard is a felt- or flannel-surfaced board (sometimes cardboard) used as a visual teaching aid. It supports materials that have a textured back that will adhere to the board's surface.

Value of a flannelboard

1. It provides a focus of attention.
2. It helps to sustain interest by providing an element of surprise or continuing suspense as materials are added to the board.
3. It can be inexpensively made from a variety of available materials.
4. It can be a versatile and flexible medium if made in various sizes and forms.

5. A flannelboard allows teachers to expand understanding through both visual and verbal means.
6. Its use (as far as what can be done on the surface) is limited only by the creativity and resourcefulness of the teacher.
7. Flannelboard cutouts can prompt children as to the sequence of a game, story, song, fingerplay, or poem.
8. It can encourage children to participate verbally, thus building their language skills.

Using a flannelboard

1. Select a game, story, song, fingerplay, poem, or concept to be introduced.
2. Decide on subjects or pictures that best highlight sequences of events or steps in learning.
3. Gather or prepare cutout materials.
4. Arrange cutouts in sequence, or number them on the back.
5. Rehearse before presenting to the group.
6. Consider visibility for all who are to view the presentation.
7. Eliminate cutouts that seem contrived.

   NOTE: Manipulating cutouts should not distract you or your listeners or detract from the presentation.

8. Evaluate after use of the flannelboard to improve your next presentation.
9. Let children participate or let them use flannelboard materials on their own.
10. Store the flannelboard where it will be readily available for spontaneous use.

Types of flannelboards and their construction

Easel flannelboard

You can make changeable sections, using the same base for a flannelboard or for a painting easel. Staple, glue, or tape felt or heavy flannel to pieces of masonite or heavy cardboard. Enamel or spray paint the pieces to make a painting easel that is washable. A carton is used for the base. Cover its edges with masking tape before painting it. Slash diagonal notches in the carton's sides at the angle desired for the easel. An inverted carton wedged inside the box will brace the easel and provide shelf space to store extra boxes of cutouts. Use spring clothespins to hold paper on the painting easel.

Pocket apron flannelboard

The pocket on this design is handy for holding cutouts. This flannelboard leaves your arms free to place cutouts on the board. To make a 5 cm pocket, allow 10 cm of material to fold back. Make the board your trunk length (chin to lap) when seated. Staple, glue, or tape felt or heavy flannel to heavy cardboard. Use braided yarn for a soft strap.

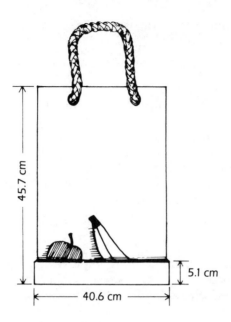

Triangle tent/tabletop flannelboard

This design can be constructed from masonite to be freestanding or can be cut out of the bottom of a square cardboard carton. Slit one side and overlap the flaps as shown to form a triangle. Staple, glue, or tape felt or heavy flannel to one or all sides. The measurements will vary with the box used.

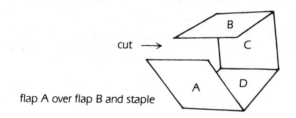

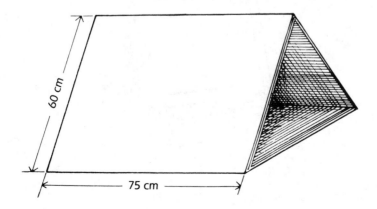

Freestanding flannelboard

A triangular flannelboard can be braced so that it will not tip over. Lace the edges together with plastic or leather strips threaded through holes drilled in flannel-covered masonite. This flannelboard can be placed upright on a floor or on one side on a tabletop. It can be used by three children at a time.

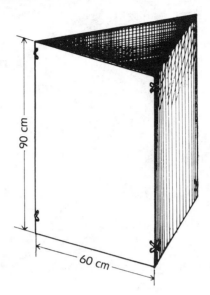

Flannelboard tips

1. Magnetize your flannelboard by inserting a piece of wire screen between the backing and flannel or by making one side metal. Cookie sheets make good magnetic boards.
2. Flannel, felt, sandpaper, flocked paper, and pellon can all be used as cutouts or as backings for cutouts.
3. Colouring books of food and animals are excellent sources of outlines for cutouts.

Learning Games

Value of Games

Games offer an excellent vehicle for learning while having fun. With games a child can:

1. Increase vocabulary by learning to identify objects, pictures, and materials.
2. Develop the senses of sight and hearing.
3. Learn to discriminate and classify.
4. Learn to follow directions and take turns.
5. Discover cause and effect.
6. Gain experience and social skills with other children and adults.

Uses of Games

Games without props can be used at any time and are especially useful in assisting the transition from one activity to another:

1. While children are assembling for a story group, a singing time, or a snack time.
2. While children are waiting for something to be prepared.

The teacher is leading the children in a game that teaches them how to follow directions. Through imitation of the teacher *and other children*, they develop their ability to follow directions, and learn gross motor control.

■ A physiotherapist is a part of the team. She is working with all the children in this group to encourage gross motor development and does not isolate children with special needs from the other children.

3. While children are slowly dispersing to go home and are leaving at different times.
4. While children wait for others to finish lunch, to finish their nap, to go outside, or to go to another room.
5. While children are riding to and from the school or centre.
6. While children are removing or putting on outdoor clothes.
7. When the teacher is diverting silly or unacceptable conversation or behaviour.
8. When preparing for a specific activity, such as introducing a new idea in art or science or continuing a story.
9. During group time, as a tool to teach a concept.

     NOTE: Games with props can be planned for the whole group, with a small group, or with an individual child during a free-choice time. These games extend the opportunities for learning because of the sensory properties of the props used.

Suggestions for Teaching Games

1. Young children learn best in a small group, because it eliminates long waiting periods and offers more person-to-person opportunities.
2. Remember that young children's attention spans for any concentrated effort last about one minute more than their age. By varying the pace and activity you may, however,

keep children in an organized group for longer periods, such as for group time, stories, songs, and games.

3. In the games, introduce only one or two concepts at a time.
4. Keep games simple, making sure instructions are clear. Try to demonstrate as much as possible.
5. Ensure each child's opportunity to participate and succeed.
6. Watch for restlessness, stop when interest wanes.
7. Rather than insist that every child participate in a game, appeal through a special interest or past experience to encourage each to want to play.

> **NOTE:** Some young children may appear never to enjoy a group game but will learn a song or game by observing and will frequently repeat it at home. Sometimes unwillingness to follow rules is an indication that the game has gone on too long or is too structured. Perhaps those who wish to continue could do so and the others could be given an alternative activity.

8. Relays and competitive games are not recommended. Children should be encouraged to compete only against their own past performances. They need many opportunities to succeed and to feel good about themselves, and failures can defeat this purpose. Avoid games that require waiting or inactivity.

Identification Games

> ▼ **CAUTION:** When introducing the materials to be used, always identify an object as being real or just a picture, model, or toy.

Name it

Place three or more objects in a row and identify each object. Have children name them from left to right. Rearrange or scramble them and let children name the objects in their new order.

> **NOTE:** Excellent for developing vocabulary and observation skills or for developing interest in a particular theme.

I see something, what do you see?

This game and its variations are excellent to play while on a walk, a sightseeing excursion, or a ride in a car. The leader simply states what he or she sees and asks the children to respond with what they see. VARIATION: Use other senses.

Look and see

Select three or more familiar objects. Ask the children to close and cover their eyes. Hide one of the objects behind your back or under a cover. Then say to the children, "Look and see." Let the children guess which object is missing by noting what remains. As their skill develops, add or remove more than one object at a time. When a child guesses successfully, let that child hide the next object. Flannelboard cutouts may also be used.

> ▼ **CAUTION:** Make sure every child gets an opportunity to hide an object. Suggest that a child who is eligible for a second turn choose a child who has not had a turn to be next.

Sniff and smell

Place a very small amount of several seasonings or spices that have a distinctive odour familiar to the children in small, unbreakable containers. Film canisters with holes punched in their lids are excellent. A pantyhose scrap glued over the opening will also prevent spills but still allow sniffing. Teach children to smell unknown substances by fanning above the container with one hand and smelling the scent that wafts toward them (rather than directly inhaling). Include items such as cinnamon, onion salt, coffee, cocoa, talcum, and dry mustard. VARIATION: Make a double set of the sniff and smell cans. Children can match cans with the same contents by their odour. You may wish to code the bottoms of the containers for your convenience. Tape over the lid holes to preserve the odours while they are stored.

▼   CAUTION: Breakable plastic bottles should be used only under careful supervision, which limits their use. Plastic is extremely dangerous when broken, especially if a piece is swallowed.
Be aware of allergies in your group.

Reach and feel

Set out a series of objects with different textures and shapes, and identify them (children may assist). Discuss how the objects are alike and how they are different. Let the children touch, feel, and hold the objects before you begin the game. Then place the objects inside a cloth or paper bag. Let the children reach inside the bag and identify one of the objects by feeling it inside the bag before removing it to verify their guess. If objects are different enough, the children can be encouraged to guess by feeling a single object through the bag. Keep the bag securely closed. VARIATION: Let the children guess by feeling through a hole or holes of a "feel it box." Leave the opposite side of the box open for the children in the group to watch as one child guesses. Children can clap if the child guesses correctly or shake their heads or call out "Guess again!" if the child's guess is wrong.

Listen and hear

Identify objects and drop or manipulate them to produce their characteristic sounds. Have the children close and cover their eyes. You may choose to produce the sound from behind a screen. Let the children recall the sound heard and identify it. VARIATION: Tape-record and play back familiar sounds for children to guess.

▼   CAUTION: Children resist blindfolds and they are not sanitary. Alternatives are closing eyes and covering them with hands, using a screen, having children turn their heads, or using a sleepmask (available in drug stores and travel shops) with a fresh tissue covering for each child.

Chew, lick, and taste

Distribute toothpicks or coffee stir sticks and small paper cups containing samples of foods. Avoid children dipping into the main source. Identify the foods as the children taste them. Talk about differences in flavours and textures.

▼   CAUTION: Be aware of allergies or restricted foods in your group.

Can you remember?

Show a group of children a tray of objects related to a special interest. Help identify the objects by name. Remove the tray or cover it, and ask the children to recall what was on the tray. Display five items at first, increasing the number as the children become more skilful.

Language Games

Guess who? or Who am I?

Begin by saying, "I see somebody who is wearing a red ribbon. Guess who it is?" Eventually include each child. Continue to add clues if children cannot identify the person from the first clue. When they make a mistake say, "Guess again," and restate the statement as a fact: "Mary is wearing a blue ribbon and she has blonde hair, doesn't she?" (Re-establish facts in order to unlearn mistakes.) VARIATION: Describe a community helper, a storybook character, or an animal.

Guess what? or What am I? or What can I do?

Begin by describing something in the form of a question: "What is sometimes soft, always round, and bounces when you drop it?" Answer: a ball. Descriptions can also include sounds and uses.

What did you hear?

Encourage the children to duplicate (or describe) the sounds of animals in the nature centre, the sounds of eating, or the sounds of well-known vehicles. Let them try to duplicate a clapping rhythm or imitate a rhythm beaten on a rhythm stick or a drum.

Listening

Choose one child to be the listener. The child should be seated on the floor or on a chair in front of the group with his or her face turned away from the group. Point to another child in the group who will be the mystery voice. She or he can say, "Hi" or any other greeting. The first child guesses who the mystery voice is. If the child cannot guess correctly, the mystery voice says something else. You may wish to use two telephones while playing the game.

Who's missing?

Select a child to be "it." Ask the child to close and cover his or her eyes. Select another child in the group to hide in a designated place. When that child is safely hidden, ask the child who is "it" to look and guess who is missing. You may give hints or rename all the children who are present that day.

Let's tell a story

Show children a picture and ask one of them to make up a story by telling what *is* happening, what *did* happen, or what *will* happen.

News time

Encourage each child to prepare something to tell or show the group. Encourage more telling and less showing, as traditional "show and tell" often ends up as a time for showing off how many expensive toys a child has rather than as a time for encouraging language development. Be ready to ask questions that will assist the children to talk, as some children become shy in front of a group.

Problem-Solving Games

How many?

Ask any question that demands problem solving. Choose questions that allow for a variety of possible answers. For example: "How many ways can you think of to get to school?"

How can I? or How can you?

Ask a child to solve a simple problem: "How could I (you) turn on the tape-recorder if it were on a high table and I (you) were too short to reach it?" "How can you get from one side of the room to the other without walking?"

Which?

This is similar to the previous game. Often your first question, "Which?" is followed by the second question, "Why?" Select questions about things that involve a judgement or opinion.

NOTE: See also *Sorting and grouping by association.* After the child has told you "which," ask "Why?" "Which one do you wear on your feet?" "Which one do you use to brush your teeth?" "Which animal would make a good pet?"

Why? or If?

Preface questions with the word "why" or "if." For example: "Why do cows live in the country? Let's think, what is it that cows eat? Is there much grass in the city?" "What do you think would happen if you put blue paint on top of yellow paint?" "If it snows, what clothes will we need for playground time?"

Sequence or Which comes first?

Present pictures depicting before and after an event to see if children can identify the sequence. Then move on to a story sequence or series of three or four pictures. Ask children to reorder the pictures and give reason for their decisions. Some pictures might be reversible: clean/dirty, chicken/egg.

Classification Games

Match-them

This is a matching game similar to the commercial games Perception Plaques and Match-Ems. Show and identify several sets of identical picture cards, squares, objects, or flannelboard figures. Scramble the items, and then let the children find matching pairs. You may hold the item to be matched or the children may be given half of a pair and then take turns finding the match. If children make mistakes, call their attention to the differences. Praise their success. VARIATION: Place draw cards facedown on the table.

Alike, different, and the same

Show children several identical items. Then introduce something different but similar, such as an item that is smaller, larger, a different colour, or belongs to a different group. Begin with obvious differences and progress to more subtle differences as the children are ready. You may use real objects, pictures, or models.

Sorting and grouping by association

Encourage children to sort and group real objects, pictures, or models into trays, boxes, or circles of yarn. Sort by content (e.g., furniture into various rooms), by rhyme (e.g., a goat, coat, boat, note), by type (e.g., hat–clothes, apple–fruit), or by use (e.g., saddle with horse, cup with saucer). Begin with simple, obvious groupings, such as all red or all dogs, and then progress to finer differentiations such as farm animals, pets, and zoo animals.

Lotto

There are many commercial lotto games available. You may make your own lotto cards using cards and large gummed seals or paper cutouts. Any game that is played with cards divided into four, six, or nine squares with corresponding cards that are drawn to complete the squares is a lotto-like game. The first child to cover all the spaces or a row on his or her card completes the game.

NOTE: For very young children, continue the game until all the children's cards are complete. Those who finish first may help the other children find the missing cards.

Ring it

Cut 6 cm to 8 cm diameter circles from the centres of plastic lids. Wrap the remaining plastic rings with bright-coloured yarn. Encourage children to use these rings to circle matching colours in any picture or on a game. This game is self-correcting.

Direction Games

Follow the leader

Select a child to be the leader. Children all follow the leader and do as he or she does. This is an excellent game for a rainy day. Make suggestions if a child cannot think what to do. VARIATION: Set up a maze so children can crawl under a table, step over some blocks; and walk around a pole. You may make the maze more complex by having the children follow the actions of the leader (changing arm, head, and leg positions) as they go.

Directions

Fill a small, shallow carton with a number of items familiar to the children. Select a child or call for a volunteer. Give a direction to move an object to a certain place. Clap if the child succeeds. If not, assist the child with, "What was it you were going to put where?"

Together, together

This game is similar to "follow the leader" but can be played sitting down. The teacher says, "Together, together, let's all (do something) together." This game may be used to direct a group to another activity.

Sally says/Sam says

This game is similar to "together, together." Instead of using a simple instruction to do something, you preface it with, "Sally says do_____." When the leader omits the statement, "Sally says," the children are instructed to stay as they were. With older children, another type of limitation might be to say, "All those wearing white may go to the table."

NOTE: The name used does not matter. Children enjoy alliteration.

Counting Games

How many objects?

Set out a number of familiar objects: one to five for the younger children, one to ten for older children. Then ask: "How many _____ are there?" Select by kind, colour, or any other grouping.

Circle Games

Save these games for the most mature group or modify them without a formal circle formation. Play traditional action songs, such as:
"Farmer in the Dell"
"Round and Round in the Village"
"Hokey Pokey"
"This Is the Way"
"Sally Go Round the Sun"
"Did You Ever See a Lassie (Laddie)?"
"Looby Loo"
"Mulbery Bush"

"Pop! Goes the Weasel"
"Skip to My Lou"/"Fly Little Bluebird"

Fly little bluebird

(tune: "Skip to My Lou")

Fly little bluebird, through my window	Hop little bluebird, in my garden
Fly little bluebird, through my window	Hop little bluebird, in my garden
Fly little bluebird, through my window	Hop little bluebird, in my garden
Um diddle um dum dey.	Um diddle um dum dey.

Children form a circle holding hands with arms raised in verse 1 to make windows. One child is selected to be the bluebird. After this child finishes hopping in the garden (inside the circle), the teacher selects a successor.

Friend, friend from over the way

The children choose a friend who will come to visit to begin the game. Then they say together:

Friend, friend from over the way,
Please come over now and play *(child knocks on the table or door)*

Children say:

Come in **John** from over the way, (use child's name)
What would you like to play today?

The child chooses what he or she would like to play. Everyone pantomimes the action.

Musical stars or Skip squat

Set on the floor enough paper stars for all the children. Play a short interlude of music and have the children skip around the room as it plays. Explain to the children that when the music stops they are to stand on a star. Have one less star than there are children to add excitement and an element of chance. VARIATIONS: Use puddles, brown rocks or snowflakes instead of stars.

▼   CAUTION: Never eliminate more than one star during the entire game. Make no emphasis on the last one down and assist each child to land safely on a star sometimes. Then no one is left out of the game; instead, the child left without a star rejoins the group as soon as the music begins.

Sally go round the sun

Sally go round the sun,
Sally go round the moon,
Sally go round the chimney pots,
On a Sunday afternoon. Whoops!

(You will find the music for "Sally Go Round the Sun" in Chapter 25.)

Children make a circle with hands joined and slide to the left as they sing. They drop each other's hands and with hands raised over heads, jump into the air and clap when they sing "Whoops!"

Hot potato

Make a "hot potato" by tying up a small towel, clean cloth, or nylon stocking into a soft, light ball. The children sit in a circle with their feet spread out and touching the feet of the child on either side. As the ball is tossed to them, they quickly toss it to someone else. Since cloth does not bounce and is soft, this is safer than a regular ball or beanbag.

Singing games help children develop a sense of music through movement. Through repetitive language and predictable melodies and rhythms, they also build familiarity with language and allow children to enjoy the playfulness of language.

Beanbag toss

Select a target such as a wastebasket, carton, or inner tube. (A clown face can be painted on a cardboard box with a hole for a mouth or nose.) The children toss or throw a beanbag into the target. Encourage success by offering toss (underhand thrust) or throw (forceful thrust) opportunities side by side.

Singing Games Using Action Songs

There are many action songs that invite children to respond to music. A child may even choose to sing along as he or she moves to the music. These songs will be suggested in each chapter of this guide under the sections Large Muscle Activities or Rhythms and Singing Games.

Accompaniment Tapes

Some singing games and songs that describe a series of responses are available on tapes and can be used as accompaniments if you are not a singer or do not have anyone to play the piano, guitar, or autoharp.

Routine Times
••••••••••••••••••••••••

Parts of the program that vary little from day to day are considered routine times and become a framework for the daily program. They give the children the security that comes with knowing what will happen next. Most often, arrival, health inspection, snack time, toileting, meal time, nap time, group movement, and dismissal are considered the routine times of the school day.

If not planned for as an integral part of the total program these times may become boring and humdrum. A matter-of-fact acceptance of routine by the staff will assist children to accept the routine for their basic physical comforts and needs. There is no need for bribes, cajoling, threats, punishment, or excessive praise.

Accidents involving elimination should be handled in a matter-of-fact way.

Remember that the children's ability to accept and function within the school routines will vary considerably.

1. Some children are members of a group for the first time (an only child).
2. School routines are often quite different from home routines.
3. The school or centre may have different values, rules, and limits from those of the child's home.
4. Some children are more flexible and willing to imitate, while others are more independent and may need time and assistance to adjust.
5. Physical needs and skills will also vary with each child's age, sex, past experience, and development.

Everyone assists in cleaning up. The teacher models cleaning up and gently directs the children. Labelling the shelves with words and pictures can help the children put their toys where they belong.

The children sit comfortably to hear the teacher tell a story. The poster on the window helps the children to preview the story and its presentation.

Flexibility is a valuable trait for children in today's world. The extreme conformist has as much trouble as the rebel. Help the children become more flexible with regard to routines by:

1. Giving them a few minutes' notice before making a necessary change in the program.
2. Encouraging everyone to help so that they can all be ready sooner to participate in the next experience.
3. Giving reasons for routine tasks required.
4. Assisting children to recognize the benefits of group experience as well as individual achievement.

When planning for routine times, refer to the suggestions noted in each chapter of this guide, and take advantage of opportunities for learning and variations that will make these times more pleasant. See also the earlier sections Fingerplays and Action Songs and Uses of Games. Plan for a happy balance between activity and rest, with opportunities for refreshments and toileting at necessary intervals.

Large Muscle Activities

Opportunities for the development of motor skills through large muscle activities should be a part of every daily program for very young children. Plans should include both indoor and outdoor experiences, with specific plans for your group and for individual children in the group. Children attending an all-day program will have a greater need for these activities as they have less chance to do them at home. Days of inclement weather, especially rainy days, will increase the need to implement opportunities for these experiences indoors.

Outdoor Large Muscle Activities Centre

Consider Your Playground an Extension of Your Classroom

1. Provide adequate space for the size and age of your group. Enclose your playground with a hedge, a fence, or walls; include a gate with a lock to provide safety from street traffic and easier supervision of the children. When there are no local licensing standards, define boundaries by using ropes, sidewalks, or other natural boundaries.
2. If your outdoor space is limited, consider scheduling playground use at different intervals during the day with fewer children in the yard at one time.
3. Augment your playground and allow for alternative space by using nearby parks, gymnasiums, or other play space.
4. Use space wisely by planning and evaluating the potential of every nook and corner and by purchasing and making multipurpose equipment. Make certain that no less than one-third of the playground space is free of permanent equipment.
5. Build a storage unit for extra equipment and seasonal items. If the unit is built with a flat roof and a sturdy guardrail and deck on the upper level, it can be used as a play area. Add ladders, stairs, or ramp from one level to another.

Playing with sand is fun and it stimulates experimentation. Providing a wide variety of inexpensive plastic containers helps children create varied structures. Yogurt, ice cream, and other plastic food containers can take on a second life as sandbox toys.

6. Plan for your playground's accessibility to the classroom, toilet, and cloakrooms. Use large doors and a ramp for easier mobility.
7. Consider the climate and the need for protection from harsh weather. Build sheltering walls and windbreaks, plan for drainage, and landscaping with trees and bushes to provide shade and prevent soil erosion. Plan to utilize the playground all year.
8. Arrange for open areas, equipped areas, and secluded areas with space for individuals and for groups.
9. When weather permits, move some of your learning centres to the playground.

Designing Your Playground

1. Digging space: Use a sandbox or an enclosed sandpile to provide an area for mud play, construction, and digging. Remember, sand needs to be covered when not in use so that it is not used as a litter box by animals.
2. *Shade:* Plant a variety of trees, shrubs, and vines of different sizes, colours, and growing cycles. Consider the use of canopies, covered patios, or terraces, as well as temporary shelters such as tents, hung blankets, or beach umbrellas.
3. *Pathways:* Construct a wide, curved pathway that circles around or returns to a larger paved area, allowing for group play and preventing traffic jams. When possible, include a slope and hill for variation. Hard surfaces can be asphalt or concrete. When paving surfaces, consider drainage to avoid standing water. Spread cedar chips near play equipment to allow drainage and to cushion children's falls.
4. *Active play areas:* Include low-branched trees, a large cement tunnel under a mound of dirt, tree trunks or logs relocated in a bed of sand or wood chips, cubbies to crawl into, bushes, and self-pumping swings. Climbing equipment can be made from telephone poles or logs cut into various lengths and set vertically in cement to form a series of stumps of various heights. Consider the need for social interaction and co-operative play.
5. *Quiet play areas:* Allow for areas of grass and have cushions, a blanket, a shallow pool, or a single swing away from other equipment. Consider the need for solitary play space.
6. *Discovery areas:* Provide places to explore and discover, including animal cages, bird feeders, birdhouses, birdbaths, a garden, and bushes and plants for insects and small animals. Include an automatic weather gauge, a weather vane, a thermometer, flowers and trees, and areas where children can enjoy snow, leaves, seeds, and water.
7. *Surfaces and terrain:* Plan a variety of surfaces and levels.

Plan for a Variety of Play Equipment

1. Budget for the repair, replacement, and maintenance of existing equipment as well as for the addition of new equipment each year.
2. Contact members of the community for the possible acquisition of an old boat to be used for dramatic play. Be alert to hinges or openings in which a child's hand, head, or foot might be caught. Paint the boat with a wood or metal preservative to avoid weathering or rusting.
3. Build your own multiple-use equipment, such as a playhouse/storage shed with stairs, a railing around the roof, or a cubby underneath.
4. Recycle discarded items into valuable, durable play equipment.
5. Include play equipment that offers simple and complex challenges and meets the needs and abilities of your group. Add accessories to make this equipment more versatile.
6. If you have a square playground which is one of the more difficult to use, put a sandpile, one major piece of equipment for multiple use, or a large surface area for dramatic play in the centre. The outside corners can be smaller play areas.

Riding toys encourage social interaction, teach children about the movement of vehicles, promote fitness, and help develop co-ordination.

Obstacle course

Plan an obstacle course in the shape of a broken circle, square, rectangle, octagon, or U-shape that allows the children to begin again once they have completed one cycle. This encourages a continual flow of participants, incurs less traffic confusion, and discourages haphazard sampling by children who may not wish to attempt a more difficult task. Vary skill opportunities by changing the obstacle course as group or individual needs are identified. Provide for a broad variety of motor experiences that will allow children to balance, climb, slide, jump, tumble, push, pull, and swing.

Tires

1. Tractor tires can enclose sandpiles if they are placed on a sand-based, tiled, or bricked area that will allow drainage. Cover the sandpile when not in use.
2. Tires can be used as jumping circles.
3. Slit tires in two along worn tread lines to make canals for sailing toy boats.
4. Stand large tires upright and bury them in the ground up to the centre to form an archway or tunnel.
5. Three tires of varying size can be hung on three cables beside each other with space between each to create an interesting swing.
6. Seven or more tires can be bolted together to make a flat bed. Hang this from cables from four poles to make a conversation swing.
7. Twelve tires can be bolted together in rows of three and attached to two posts to make a climbing wall. Remember to drill drain holes in the tires so that rainwater will not accumulate in them.

Telephone cable spools

1. Paint telephone cable spools and use them as tables near the sandpile or a shady tree.

2. Smaller spools can be used for platforms if children wish to perform like clowns or animals. Make sure the spools are securely anchored to the ground.

Laundry or fat barrels

1. Cut out both ends of a barrel and mount it on a platform to make a tunnel. Add a cleated ramp for an obstacle course.
2. Cut out the top end and a large hole in one side of a barrel and use it for ball-tossing games. The hole in the side allows children to retrieve the ball without help. It also can suggest the more difficult feat of throwing a ball or beanbag into the side hole.
3. Leave both ends of a barrel in and cut a door in one side to form a cozy nook.
4. Cut a cockpit hole in one side of a barrel. If you wish, add wings and a propeller.
5. Windows may be cut in the side of a barrel for a puppet theatre, window counter, or small playhouse.

Cartons or packing crates

While not very durable, cartons provide a variety of play experiences if children are allowed to explore freely.

Duffel bag or one trouser leg

Both of these can be stuffed with a pillow or foam rubber and used as punching bags. Attach a spring or a canvas strap to the bag and hang it from a hook.

Tree trunks, logs, stumps, and railroad ties

1. A solid tree trunk with many sturdy branches, stripped of bark and treated for weathering, makes an interesting climber.
2. A log makes another interesting climber when laid on its side in sand or dirt.

The playground can provide a safe environment for many activities, from climbing and jumping to observing and measuring.

3. Tree stumps or crosscuts of a telephone pole embedded in sand or cement can be used for sitting or climbing on.
4. Screw a plywood circle to a stump to make a low table.
5. Railroad ties used as boundaries also make steps or balance boards.

Concrete sewer pipe

1. Use this as a tunnel or attach it to other equipment.
2. Use a pipe as a base for creating both a tunnel and a small hill. To maintain the hillside, turf or seed the dirt piled on the pipe.

Enclosure walls, fences, and stair rails

1. Paint murals or learning aids on walls.
2. Suspend easels on fences for outdoor artists. When you dismiss the children from the playground, use clothespins to clip take-home pictures to the fence.
3. Hang planters (can be large oil cans) on a stair rail to discourage sliding or climbing on it and to provide an opportunity to discover and explore while moving between indoors and outdoors.
4. If you have a good view, plan your enclosures to allow the children to take full advantage of their surroundings.

Tips for Supervising the Playground

1. Face the children you are supervising. Position yourself near equipment where accidents could occur.
2. Do not have more children on the playground than can be safely supervised.
3. Remind children to bend their knees when jumping.
4. Allow creative use of equipment but with consideration for children's safety and for care of equipment.
5. Encourage children to grasp bars with a monkey grip (thumb under, fingers over) when climbing or swinging.
6. Limit turns on popular equipment by using a timer or counting the number of turns. Encourage one-way traffic on obstacle courses to avoid collisions.

Indoor Large Muscle Activities Centre

To individualize your program for motor development, you will need to provide for large muscle activity space indoors as well as outdoors. The indoor space will also be needed when inclement weather keeps the children inside. Rainy days do not have to be dreaded by either the children or the teacher if alternative plans have been made. Some suggestions for creating an indoor large muscle activity centre follow.

Designing Your Play Area

1. Use centre areas of the classroom for large muscle activities. Provide additional opportunities by equipping a large muscle activity centre with one or more of the following:
    a. Tumbling mat.
    b. Punching bag.
    c. Climbing gym or ladder box.
    d. Rocking horse or boat.
2. Use converted classroom space. Move furniture out of the way or close off an area such as the block-building centre and use that floor space to set up portable large muscle play equipment. Select a seldom-used doorway for hanging climbing ropes, a rope ladder, or a swing. Other portable equipment might include:

Plan indoor large muscle activities for cold and rainy days. This climber was designed and built by the teachers and parent volunteers. It provides children with a wide variety of motor activities and encourages dramatic play.

    a. Balance beam or walking board.
    b. Ladders, sawhorses, or planks.
    c. Swing, climbing rope, rope ladder, or bar (doorway equipment).
    d. Laundry or fat barrel (see p. 61).
    e. Tunnel.
    f. Indoor–outdoor climber (e.g., Quadro climber).

3. Take advantage of other indoor space when the weather does not permit children to go outdoors. This might include a wide hallway, a gymnasium, or an adjacent room.

   ▼ **CAUTION: Consider the need for clear traffic routes in halls and emergency exits when using these spaces. A narrow passageway or single exit should not be blocked with a swing, bar, or other equipment.**

4. Plan for large muscle games and group exercises. See the games described earlier and in each chapter of this guide for specific suggestions.
5. Provide for an expanded use of music and rhythm activities. Use accompaniment tapes, and see the earlier music section for specific suggestions.
6. Plan skill games with equipment, such as:
    a. Horseshoes.
    b. Balls (nylon, sponge, rubber).
    c. Skill-toss games.
    d. Wadded balls for indoor snowball fights (crumple tissue or newspaper for balls).
    e. Feathers, blown to keep in midair.
    f. Bubbles or balloons (blow and catch them).
    g. Bleach bottle scoops for catching balls.
    h. The equipment listed in numbers 1 and 2.

Teachers, parents, and children have created a waterfall and beach in a corner of their classroom as part of a summer theme. As the children enjoy this entertaining area, they learn about water and gravity, and they learn words such as *up, down, pour,* and *flow.*

Extended Experiences
· ·

Trips and Excursions

To go or not to go? That is the question

1. Weigh whether the trip is the best way to introduce children to this discovery and learning experience.
2. Is each child secure enough with the group and with the centre to leave on a trip?
3. Is this trip best taken at this age?
4. Exactly what can the children learn, see, and do on this trip?
5. Will your group be welcomed? Will young children be accepted?
6. When did you take your last trip? Remember, once a week is too often.

Have you made reservations?

1. Make contacts. Call ahead regarding a visit.
2. Set a time and date, and make reservations.
3. Don't forget to confirm the reservation the day before you go.
4. Make suggestions to the person conducting the tour as to what the children will be interested in, what they might understand, and what their attention span is.

This child discovered a new motor skill as she followed her older friend through the tunnel.

Are you and the children prepared?

1. Scout the area before you go. Are you knowledgeable about the destination? Have you defined what is to be explored?
2. Enlist extra help: parents, volunteers, and drivers.
3. Plan for special means of transportation.
4. Plan with staff. Define individual teaching responsibilities, and discuss concerns, such as crossing a busy street.
5. Accidents may happen. Take a survival kit for assurance.
6. Take along snacks and drinks, and make provisions for toileting.
7. Watch the clock. Children have built-in timers for their needs, such as resting, eating, and toileting.
8. If the destination is far away, you may want to stop en route for a rest or snack break.
9. A walk in the rain might be fun, but what about a downpour?
10. You can always cancel, but have an excellent alternative plan ready.
11. Alert parents to needs, such as special clothing, funds for tickets, a bag lunch, boots, mittens, and swimsuits. Get written permission slips and inform parents of specific plans (the destination, date, and time).

Keep a travel log

1. Take photos, make a tape-recording (e.g., sounds of a zoo), or take notes for the next trip.
2. Learn from your mistakes and build on what was positive.
3. Note signs of learning; sometimes they are not immediately evident.

Are you a good tour leader?

1. Prepare the children by introducing the idea and letting them help plan the trip.
2. When plans are definite, share them with the children, but not too far ahead of the date.

3. Brief your travellers on the rules.
4. Use travel time for learning as well as helping the children to pass the time.

Follow up with follow-through

1. Be prepared for an energetic response when you get back to your centre by:
   a. Having appropriate dramatic play props and costumes ready for use.
   b. Having related books available in the book centre before and after the trip.
   c. Collecting poems, games, and songs that might be used when interest is shown.
   d. Planning art activities around the focus of the trip.
2. Provide for instant replay. Listen en route for children's initial responses.
3. Allow chances for children to verbalize their experiences during group time and in small groups.
4. Treasures and souvenirs may be shared in "show and tell."

Evaluate the trip

1. Give children time to react and respond to the experience. Then evaluate the trip with your staff.
2. Would you do it again? What would you do differently?

Planning for Visitors

Select the visitor

1. Choose someone who likes and is interested in young children.
2. Invite educational officers from community organizations or people who have very young children of their own. When invited on their day off, working parents can be more flexible about time.
3. Select members of both sexes and of different cultural groups.
4. Choose someone most knowledgeable about or skilled in the resource you need. Remember grandparents, students, and retired citizens.

Interview the visitor

1. Interview the visitor by telephone or in person. Set a specific date and time that best suits both of you.
2. Visit the person at his or her place of work if appropriate. The visitor may then suggest other items or subjects you may want to include in the visit.

Brief the visitor

1. List questions the children might ask.
2. Suggest items to wear or share (within children's experience).
3. Caution the visitor about safety with regard to tools or other items to be shared.
4. Describe the setting the visitor will be in.
5. Offer a few tips on ways to deal with behaviour that may occur.

Plan for the visit

1. Set the scene. Give children opportunities to discover related information from other activities before the visitor arrives.
2. Plan some follow-through experiences for the children after the visit.
3. Encourage children to help prepare an invitation and later a thank-you note for the visitor.

Using Films and Filmstrips

1. Preview a film or filmstrip. Double-check that extension cords and extra projector bulbs are handy.
2. Select a film much as you would a book — for content, pictures, length, age level, appropriateness, interest, and authenticity.
3. Reserve the film or filmstrip, projector, and screen.
4. Edit the film or, if a filmstrip, the storyline to meet your needs. Make a note of sections you wish to roll past.
5. Select a room that can be darkened. Leave a small light on for children who may be frightened of the dark.
6. Mark the floor for placement of the screen and projector after you have focussed the picture. Choose a clear wall for projection if no screen is available.
7. Have a table for the projector handy so it can be placed on the marked space.
8. If the children are seated on the floor, project the film so they can all see but not so high that they must sit with their necks in an uncomfortable position.
9. While viewing the film, listen and watch for children's responses (verbal, facial, and body language). When you can, encourage children to answer their own questions by following a question with another question. If they cannot, answer the questions yourself or help children to discover the answers. You may wish to rerun the filmstrip.

Planning a Party for Parents and Friends

1. Make sure every child can have one parent, family member, or friend attend the party.
2. If you plan to let visitors observe children in a group-time experience, select activities that children enjoy: play games, sing songs, and tell or read a story just as you usually do. Make certain there is no focus on any one child! Keep things simple and unrehearsed, and follow the usual routine if possible.
3. Seat visitors behind the children or along the side of the room so children will be less aware that they are being observed. Ideally, let visitors and children sit together and both participate.
4. There should be no pressure on performance.
5. The group should be only those children who are normally in the room together.
6. Hold the party during regular school hours.
7. Plan the party for a time of year when the days are not likely to be filled with events, when the weather is usually good, and when most parents and children can attend (in the fall, children beginning school may be coming down with the usual childhood communicable diseases — measles, chickenpox, and mumps). You may wish to invite visitors for only one small group of your whole class at a time. Invite these different groups of visitors over a series of successive days.

 # Teacher Resources

Pictures, Displays, and Special Room Arrangements

1. Create your own resources. Start or add to a picture file. Have parents, staff, and volunteers help collect pictures. Besides clipping magazines, watch for good picture sources in your community. Seasonal or topical posters in grocery stores, drugstores, department stores, travel agencies, or the post office may be available for the asking.

2. Talk to store managers about discarded cardboard shelf displays. These have many uses with little change except a coat of paint.
3. Make your own cardboard display boards or scrapbooks. Pegboard is another sturdy surface for displays.
4. Screw a section of plasterboard to the wooden frame of a blackboard. This will instantly transform the blackboard into a bulletin board.
5. Make a kiosk for displaying science or art items by stacking cartons. Use flat surfaces to display pictures and niches to display treasures for examination or exploration.

Mounting Pictures

1. Whenever possible, mount teaching pictures to a uniform size for easier filing.
2. File smaller pictures in see-through envelopes.
3. Label pictures on the back or place them in alphabetical folders.
4. If you mount pictures in colour, dramatize the most important subject or object by repeating its colour in the border. Always leave a wider margin at the bottom of a mat than along the other three sides, which may have equal margins. Occasionally, use an abstract or odd shape behind a picture to mount it more attractively. Use pinking shears or tear the edges of a picture for other variations.
5. Try to get a complete figure of an animal, a person, or an object in the picture. If mounted and displayed with other pictures, choose appropriate sizes (relative to one another) so children will not be confused by the misproportions.

Displaying or Posting Teaching Pictures

1. Use thumbtacks at the edges, *not* through a picture. If you use tape, remove it before you return the picture to the file.
2. Save some duplicate pictures for expanded use. Look for sequence pictures.
3. Use walls, hallways, and stairwells as display spaces for children's art. Change displays often. Invite a local artist to paint a mural or child-scaled wall design.
4. Don't forget the ceiling of the resting area. Hang mobiles or pictures to suggest relaxation or pleasant memories, such as nature scenes, children holding pets, or parents hugging children.
5. Hang bulletin boards near an entrance for parents' notices and messages, in the group-time area for focus of theme, for interest development, or for reference, or inside an entrance door for children to discover as they arrive.
6. Dress up a bulletin board with twisted crepe paper strips and abstract shapes of paper in complementary colours (if you doubt your own judgement, look at fabrics or paintings for shades or tints that are used together). Cut out coloured or black letters for bold messages. Use coloured yarn or string to circle related pictures.

   NOTE: Suggestions are made in each chapter for specific uses of pictures in games, language development, and other activities.

Core Library

The following titles can be obtained through bookstores or from the publishers. Titles that are no longer in print can be found at the public library.

General Books about Child Development

Cohen, Dorothy H., and Virginia Stern with Nancy Balaban. *Observing and Recording the Behavior of Young Children.* New York: Teachers College Press, 1983.

Elkind, David. *The Hurried Child*. Reading, MA: Addison-Wesley, 1981.

Evans, Richard. *Piaget: The Man and His Ideas*. New York: Dutton, 1973.

Ginsberg, H., and S. Opper. *Piaget's Theory of Intellectual Development*. Englewood Cliffs, NJ: Prentice-Hall, 1979.

Harris, Judith Rich, and Robert M. Liebert. *The Child* (3rd ed.). Englewood Cliffs, NJ: Prentice-Hall, 1991.

Irwin, D.M., and M.M. Bushnell. *Observational Strategies for Child Study*. New York: Holt, Rinehart and Winston, 1980.

Kagan, Jerome. *The Nature of the Child*. New York: Basic Books, 1984.

Katz, Lilian G. *Current Topics in Early Childhood Education*. 7 volumes. Norwood, NJ: Ablex, 1981–1987.

Morrison, George S. *The World of Child Development: Conception to Adolescence*. Albany, NY: Delmar, 1990.

Piaget, Jean. *The Child's Conception of Number*. New York: Norton, 1965.

———. *The Child's Conception of the World*. Totowa, NJ: Littlefield, 1975.

———. *The Grasp of Consciousness*. Cambridge, MA: Harvard University Press, 1976.

Snow, Charles W. *Infant Development*. Englewood Cliffs, NJ: Prentice-Hall, 1990.

Turner, J.S., and D.B. Helms. *Lifespan Development*. New York: Holt, Rinehart and Winston, 1983.

General Curriculum Resources

Baratta-Lorton, Mary. *Workjobs*. Don Mills, ON: Addison-Wesley, 1972.

Charlesworth, Rosalind, and Karen K. Lind. *Math and Science for Young Children*. Albany, NY: Delmar, 1990.

Coombs, Ernie, and Shelley Tanaka. *Mr. Dressup's Book of Things to Make and Do*. Toronto: CBC Enterprises, 1985.

Croft, Doreen J., and Robert D. Hess. *An Activities Handbook for Teachers of Young Children* (4th ed.). Boston: Houghton Mifflin, 1985.

Daniels, Betty Ternice. *The Prairie Kid's Cookbook*. Cochin, SK: Prairetopian Enterprises, 1983.

Debelak, M., et al. *Creating Innovative Classroom Materials for Teaching Young Children*. San Diego: Harcourt Brace Jovanovich, 1981.

Deiner, Penny L. *Resources for Teaching Young Children with Special Needs*. Toronto: Harcourt Brace Jovanovich, 1983.

Indenbaum, Valerie, and Marcia Shapiro. *The Everything Book*. Livonia, MI: Partner Press, 1985.

MacDonald, Kate. *Anne of Green Gables Cookbook*. Don Mills, ON: Oxford University Press, 1985.

Martin, Elaine. *Baby Games: The Joyful Guide to Child's Play from Birth to Three Years*. Philadelphia: Running Press, 1988.

Martin, Toy. *The Pre-School Craft Book*. Poole, UK: Blandford Press, 1981.

Maxim, George W. *The Sourcebook: Activities for Infants and Young Children* (2nd ed.). Columbus, OH: Merrill, 1990.

Owl's Summer Fun. Toronto: Greey de Pencier, 1982.

Owl's Winter Fun. Toronto: Greey de Pencier, 1980.

Penrose, Gordon. *Dr. Zed's Dazzling Book of Science Activities*. Toronto: Greey de Pencier, 1987.

———. *Dr. Zed's Science Surprises*. Toronto: Greey de Pencier, 1989.

———. *Magic Mud and Other Great Experiments*. Toronto: Greey de Pencier, 1987.

Rockwell, R.E., et al. *Hug a Tree and Other Things to Do Outdoors with Children*. Mt. Rainier, MD: Gryphon, 1983.

Walker, Lois. *More Wonderful Puppcorn Puppets.* Toronto: Puppcorn Productions, 1986.
Walker, Lois, and Hub Walker. *Crafts for Kids: The Puppcorn Way.* Toronto: Deneau, 1982.

Children's Literature
Butler, D. *Babies Need Books.* Markham, ON: Penguin, 1980.
Caseearli, A. *Good Books to Grow On.* New York: Warner, 1985.
Charlton, J., ed. *Children's Choices of Canadian Books.* Ottawa: Citizen's Committee on Children, 1978–1985.
Children's Literature in Canada: A Guide to Authors and Illustrators. Toronto: Harcourt Brace Jovanovich, 1988.
Ciancids, P.J. *Picture Books for Children* (2nd ed.). Chicago: American Library Association, 1981.
Growing with Books: Children's Literature in the Formative Years and Beyond. Toronto: Ontario Ministry of Education, 1988.
Landsberg, Michele. *Michele Landsberg's Guide to Children's Books.* Markham, ON: Penguin 1985.
Norton, Donna E. *Through the Eyes of a Child: An Introduction to Children's Literature.* Columbus, OH: Merrill, 1983.
Russell, William. *Classics to Read Aloud to Your Children.* New York: Crown, 1984.
Saltman, J. *Modern Canadian Children's Books.* Toronto: Oxford University Press, 1987.
Stott, Jon C. *Children's Literature from A to Z.* New York: McGraw-Hill, 1984.
Sutherland, Zena, and May Hill Arbuthnot. *Children and Books* (8th ed.). New York: HarperCollins, 1991.
Trelease, Jim. *The New Read-Aloud Handbook.* New York: Penguin, 1989.

Alphabet Books
Good programs for young children encourage and enhance the development of language and communication. All of the activities in this text encourage the appropriate use of language, but they do not deal directly with children's interest in letters and words. Letters and words should be themes that run through your program at all times.

- Blades, Ann. *By the Sea: An Alphabet Book.* Toronto: Kids Can Press, 1986.
- Cleaver, Elizabeth. *ABC.* Toronto: Oxford University Press, 1982.
- ••• Feelings, Muriel. *Jambo Means Hello: Swahili Alphabet Book.* New York: Dial Press, 1974.
- •• Harrison, Ted. *A Northern Alphabet.* Montreal: Tundra, 1982.
- • Hoban, Tana. *A, B, See.* New York: Greenwillow, 1982.
- ••• Isadora, Rachel. *City Seen from A to Z.* New York: Greenwillow, 1983.
- •• Johnson, Odette, and Bruce H. Johnson. *Apples, Alligators and Also Alphabets.* Toronto: Oxford University Press, 1990.
- ••• Lessac, Frane. *Caribbean Alphabet.* London, UK: Macmillan, 1989.
- ••• Martin Jr., Bill. *Chicka Chicka Boom Boom.* New York: Simon & Schuster, 1989.
- ••• Mastin, Colleayn. *Canadian Wild Animals A–Z.* Kelowna, BC: Sandhill, 1986.
- •• Moak, Allan. *A Big City ABC.* Montreal: Tundra, 1984.
- •• Morgan, Nichola. *The Great B.C. Alphabet Book.* Markham, ON: Fitzhenry & Whiteside, 1985.
- ••• Musgrove, Margaret. *Ashanti to Zulu.* New York: Dial, 1976.
- • Paré, Roger. *The Annick ABC Activity Set.* Willowdale, ON: Annick Press, 1985.
- ••• Poulin, Stéphane. *Ah! belle cité!/A Beautiful City ABC.* Montreal: Tundra, 1985.
- ••• Shelby, Anne. *Potluck.* New York: Orchard, 1991.

Films and Videos

NOTE: Check with your distributor about public performance rights.

Alligators All Around. Weston Woods.
Alphabet. National Film Board.
Korean Alphabet. National Film Board.

Language Games, Fingerplays, and Poetry

Bennett, Jill, ed. *People Poems.* Toronto: Oxford University Press, 1990.
———. *A Cup of Starshine.* Vancouver: Walker, 1991.
Booth, David, ed. *'Til All the Stars Have Fallen: Canadian Poems for Children.* Toronto: Kids Can Press, 1989.
Brown, Marc. *Finger Rhymes.* New York: Dutton, 1980.
———. *Hand Rhymes.* New York: Dutton, 1985.
Champlin, Connie, and Nancy Renfro. *Storytelling with Puppets.* Chicago: American Library Association, 1985.
Cole, Joanna. *A New Treasury of Children's Poetry.* New York: Doubleday, 1984.
Doray, Maya. *J Is for Jump!* Belmont, CA: Pitman Learning, 1982.
Downie, Mary Alice. *The New Wind Has Wings.* Toronto: Oxford University Press, 1984.
Fowke, Edith. *Sally Go Round the Sun.* Toronto: McClelland & Stewart, 1969.
Glazer, Tom. *Eye Winker, Tom Tinker, Chin Chopper.* Garden City, NY: Doubleday, 1973.
Grayson, Marion. *Let's Do Fingerplays.* Bridgeport, CT: Luce, 1962.
Heidbreder, Robert, and Karen Patkau. *Don't Eat Spiders.* Toronto: Oxford University Press, 1985.
King, Karen, and Ian Beck. *Oranges and Lemons.* Toronto: Oxford University Press, 1985.
Lee, Dennis. *Alligator Pie.* Toronto: Macmillan, 1974.
———. *Jelly Belly.* Toronto: Macmillan, 1984.
———. *Lizzy's Lion.* Don Mills, ON: Stoddart, 1984.
Prelutsky, Jack, ed. *The Random House Book of Poetry for Children.* New York: Random House, 1983.
Prelutsky, Jack, and Marc Brown. *Read-aloud Rhymes for the Very Young.* New York: Knopf, 1986.
Silverstein, Shel. *A Light in the Attic.* New York: Harper & Row, 1981.
———. *Where the Sidewalk Ends.* New York: Harper & Row, 1974.
Simmie, Lois. *An Armadillo Is Not a Pillow.* Saskatoon: Western Producer Prairie, 1986.
———. *Auntie's Knitting a Baby.* Saskatoon: Western Producer Prairie, 1984.
Sneyd, Lola. *The Asphalt Octopus: A Child's World in Poetry.* Toronto: Simon & Pierre, 1982.
———. *The Concrete Giraffe.* Toronto: Simon & Pierre, 1984.
Stacey, Ann. *The Enchanted Bear and Other Poems.* Winnipeg: Prairie Publishing, 1986.
Stangl, Jean. *Paper Stories.* Belmont, CA: David S. Lake, 1984.
Weimer, Tonja E. *Fingerplays and Action Chants* (vol. 1: "Animals"; vol. 2: "Family and Friends"). Text and cassette. Pittsburgh: Pearce Evetts, 1986.
Williams, Sarah. *Round and Round the Garden.* Toronto: Oxford University Press, 1983.
Wynne-Jones, Tim. *Mischief City.* Vancouver: Douglas & McIntyre, 1986.

Art Books

Bartlett, Nancy Lewis. *Children's Art and Crafts.* Sydney, Aust.: Australian Women's Weekly Home Library Division, 1989.

Cherry, Clare. *Creative Art for the Developing Child.* Belmont, CA: Fearon Teacher Aids, 1990.

Irvine, Joan. *How to Make Pop-Ups.* Toronto: Kids Can Press, 1987.

Jenkins, Peggy Davison. *Art for the Fun of It: A Guide for Teaching Young Children.* New York: Prentice-Hall, 1980.

Reid, Barbara. *Playing with Plasticine.* Toronto: Kids Can Press, 1988.

Schirrmacher, Robert. *Art and Creative Development for Young Children.* Albany, NY: Delmar, 1988.

Music Books

Biene, Susanna. *Sing Through the Seasons; Ninety-Nine Songs for Children.* Ulster Park, NY: Plough, 1972.

Birkenshaw, Lois. *Music for Fun, Music for Learning* (3rd ed.). Toronto: Holt, Rinehart and Winston, 1982.

Birkenshaw, Lois, and David Walden. *The Goat with the Bright Red Socks.* Toronto: Toronto Board of Education, 1978.

Burton, Leon, and William Hughes. *MusicPlay.* Don Mills, ON: Addison-Wesley, 1979.

Cass-Beggs, Barbara. *Your Child Needs Music.* Oakville, ON: Frederick Harris, 1986.

———. ed. *Canadian Folk Songs for the Young.* Vancouver: Groundwood/Douglas & McIntyre, 1991.

Fowke, Edith. *Sally Go Round the Sun.* Toronto: McClelland & Stewart, 1969.

Glazer, Tom. *Do Your Ears Hang Low?* New York: Doubleday, 1980.

———. *Eye Winker, Tom Tinker, Chin Chopper: Fifty Musical Fingerplays.* New York: Doubleday, 1973.

Gordon, Shelley. *Songs to Sing and Sing Again.* Toronto: S. Gordon, 25 Belsize Dr. Toronto, ON M4S 1L3, 1984.

Haines, J.E., and L.L. Gerber. *Leading Young Children to Music.* Toronto: Merrill, 1984.

Hart, Jane, ed. *Singing Bee! A Collection of Favorite Children's Songs.* New York: Lothrop, Lee & Shepard, 1982.

Magadini, Peter. *Music We Can See and Hear.* Oakville, ON: Frederick Harris, 1982.

Murray, Helen. *Stepping Along in Music Land.* Books I and II. London, ON: Middlesex Printing, 1983.

Nelson, Esther. *Musical Games for Children of All Ages.* New York: Sterling, 1976.

Raffi. *The Baby Beluga Book.* Toronto: McClelland & Stewart, 1986.

Sharon, Lois, and Bram. *Elephant Jam.* Toronto, McGraw-Hill Ryerson, 1980.

Warren, Jean. *Piggyback Songs for Infants and Toddlers.* Everett, WA: Warren, 1985.

———. *More Piggyback Songs.* Everett, WA: Warren, 1984.

———. *Piggyback Songs.* Everett, WA: Warren, 1983.

Warner, L., and P. Berry. *Tunes for Tots.* Carthage, IL: Good Apple, 1982.

Winn, Marie, ed. *What Shall We Do and Alee Galloo! Playsongs and Singing Games for Young Children.* New York: Harper & Row, 1970.

Wood, Donna. *Move, Sing, Listen, Play.* Toronto: Gordon V. Thompson, 1982.

Guides for Taking Trips

Clarke, Sheila, Marilyn Linton, and Jeanne Scargall. *Toronto Is for Kids.* Toronto: Greey de Pencier, 1976.

MacKay, Claire. *The Toronto Story.* Toronto: Annick Press, 1990.

Murray, Kristen, and Allan Shute. *Kidmonton.* Edmonton, AB: Tree Frog Press, 1978.

Small, Cecile. *Saskatchewan: 2 Kids and a Camera.* Saskatoon: Turner Warwick, 1982.

Stein, Sherry, and Howard Shapiro. *Kidding Around Montreal.* Don Mills, ON: Collier Macmillan, 1976.

Wood, Daniel, and Betty Campbell. *Kids! Kids! Kids! and Vancouver.* Vancouver: Fforbez Enterprises, 1978.

———. *Kids! Kids! Kids! and Vancouver Island.* Vancouver: Fforbez Enterprises, 1977.

Special Canadian Resources

Anderson, Karen, and Gary Woodill. *Community Resources for Canadian Families.* Orillia, ON: Ptarmigan, 1985.

Burnaby, B. *Language in Education Among Canadian Native Peoples.* Toronto: OISE Press, 1982.

Linton, Marilyn. *The Maple Syrup Book.* Toronto: Kids Can Press, 1983.

Luke, Carmen. *Television and Your Child: A Guide for Concerned Parents.* Toronto: Kagan and Woo, 1988.

Marsh, James, ed. *The Canadian Encyclopedia.* Edmonton: Hurtig, 1985.

McKay, Kenneth B. *Puppetry in Canada: An Art to Enchantment.* Ontario Puppetry Association, 1987.

Smallwood, J. *The Encyclopedia of Newfoundland and Labrador.* St. John's: Newfoundland Book Publishers, 1981.

Woodill, Gary, and Karen Anderson. *Canadian Resources for Children with Special Needs.* Orillia, ON: Ptarmigan, 1985.

Multicultural Resource Books

Cass-Beggs, Barbara. *A Musical Calendar of Festivals: Folk Songs of Feast-Days and Holidays from Around the World.* London, ON: Ward Lock, 1983.

Cech, Maureen. *GlobalChild.* Ottawa: Cech, 1990.

Chud, Gyda, and Ruth Fahlman. *Early Childhood Education for a Multicultural Society.* Vancouver: Pacific Education Press, 1985.

Derman-Sparks, Louise, and the A.B.C. Task Force. *Anti-Bias Curriculum Tools for Empowering Young Children.* Washington, DC: NAEYC, 1989.

Fralick, Paul. *Make It Multicultural: Musical Activities for Early Childhood Education.* Hamilton, ON: Mohawk College, 1989.

Graeme, Jocelyn, and Ruth Fahlman. *Hand in Hand: Multicultural Experiences for Young Children.* Don Mills, ON: Addison-Wesley, 1990.

Kehoe, John W. *A Handbook for Enhancing the Multicultural Climate of the School.* Vancouver: University of British Columbia, 1984.

Kilbride, Kenise Murphy. *Multicultural Early Childhood Education: A Discovery Approach for Teachers.* Toronto: Ontario Ministry of Community and Social Services, 1990.

Lee, Enid. *Letters to Marcia: A Teacher's Guide to Anti-Racist Education.* Toronto: Cross Cultural Communication Centre, 1989.

McLeod, Keith A., ed. *Multicultural Early Childhood Education.* Toronto: University of Toronto, 1984.

Mock, K. *Multicultural Preschool Education: A Resource Manual for Supervisors and Volunteers.* Toronto: Ontario Ministry of Citizenship and Culture, 1985.

Neugebauer, Bonnie, ed. Alike and Different: Exploring Our Humanity with Young Children. Redmond, WA: Exchange Press, 1987.

One Child, Two Cultures. Winnipeg: Manitoba Employment Services and Economic Survey, 1987.

Parry, Caroline. *Let's Celebrate! Canada's Special Days.* Toronto: Kids Can Press, 1987.

Secretary of State. *Publications List.* Ottawa: Multiculturalism Directorate, Government of Canada, 1980.

Saracho, Olivia N., and Bernard Spodek, eds. Understanding the Multicultural Experience in Early Childhood Education. Washington, DC: NAEYC, 1983.

Sawyer, Don, and Howard Green. *The NESA Activities Handbook for Native and Multicultural Classrooms.* Vancouver: The Tillacum Library, 1984.

The Children's Book Centre

A very special Canadian resource is the Children's Book Centre, a national, nonprofit organization that was established in 1976 to promote the reading and writing of Canadian children's books. This organization serves parents, teachers, librarians, booksellers, publishers, students, writers, illustrators — in fact, anyone who cares about children and the books they read. Regardless of where you live, the Children's Book Centre can provide you with information about Canadian children's books. Further, it offers:

☐ A reference library that is open to the public.

☐ A quarterly newsletter to keep you up to date on the latest books, personalities, developments, and great ideas for introducing books to children.

☐ Print and audio-visual materials on authors, illustrators, book production, and publishing.

☐ Workshops on writing for children.

☐ Staff presentations on all aspects of Canadian children's literature.

☐ An annual national Children's Book Festival to salute Canadian books, which includes author and illustrator presentations, special kits, and celebrations from coast to coast.

The Centre has its national office in Toronto and regional officers across the country. At time of writing, these were:

National Office:
The Canadian Children's Book Centre
35 Spadina Road
Toronto, ON
M5R 2S9
(416)975-0010

Alberta:
Marg Stephen
Wordworks
10523 – 100 Ave.
Edmonton, AB
T5J 0A8
(403)424-7764

Saskatchewan:
Lynda Newson
3142 Eastview
Saskatoon, SK
S7J 3J4
(306)477-1308

Manitoba:
Cheryl Archer
130 Oakview Ave.
Winnipeg, MB
R2K 0R8
(204)667-7032

Atlantic:
Norene Smiley
3552 Windsor St.
Halifax, NS
B3K 5G8
(902)453-0365

Additional resources for children's books are:

BC Association of Learning Materials and Educational Representatives
c/o Ren Speer, 1–2336 South Grandview Highway
P.O. Box 66019, Station F
Vancouver, BC
V5N 5L4
(604)872-3042

Canadian Society of Children's Authors, Illustrators and Performers
P.O. Box 280, Station L
Toronto, ON
M6E 4Z2
(416)651-3759

Notes for Guiding Behaviour
••

Suggestions for Guiding Behaviour

1. Know everything you can about each child.
2. Decide what you want each child to learn.
3. Plan the children's environment.
4. Establish positive, friendly relationships with each child.
5. Encourage each child in his or her growth and development of a good self-image.

Ways to Build Trust

1. Like the child. Take her or him seriously. Assure the child that you like and care about her or him.
2. Talk to the child at her or his level. Bend down, put your arm around the child's shoulder, hold hands gently, or kneel down beside the child. Eye contact is very important.
3. Be positive, not harsh; gentle, not weak; pleasant, calm, firm, sincere, and matter-of-fact. Be consistent and dependable about your expectations and guidance.
4. Speak softly, slowly, and patiently, and be friendly but firm.
5. Make a suggestion rather than give a command. Save commands for emergencies.
6. Listen to the child's explanation of how he or she feels. Accept his or her right to feelings.
7. Encourage the child to share success, give praise, show understanding, and learn through discovery and failure.
8. Set an example, expect co-operation, and make co-operation possible.
9. Offer choice only when it is legitimate. Offer compromises or alternatives if needed.

Remember, if I Know Each Child, I Can

1. Protect each child's rights.
2. Divert.
3. Allow a child the opportunity to resolve his or her own problems.
4. Offer a compromise to children in a dispute when I do not know which child is correct.
5. Show a child how.
6. Ask a child a question.
7. Overlook certain behaviour (always considering safety).
8. Be flexible.
9. Make allowances for age/phase behaviour.
10. Give a child a chance to rebel (within reason).
11. Stop certain behaviour (when safety is a factor).
12. Offer duplicate materials or equipment rather than expect a child to share arbitrarily.

I Can Prevent Difficulties By

1. Preparing for a variety of activities, using materials and equipment in good repair that offer opportunities for every child to succeed.
2. Defining areas, arranging rooms attractively, and rotating activities and materials to invite challenge.
3. Planning for total supervision for each space, with defined roles for all teachers (remembering to consider each one's abilities and special interests).
4. Giving guidance and support when needed, and allowing discovery, exploration, and creativity.

If I Plan I Can

1. Allow time to complete tasks.
2. Substitute when alternatives are needed.
3. Arrange equipment, space, and program to avoid accidents, overstimulation, or cross-traffic.
4. Set reasonable limits for safety.
5. Effect smooth transitions for individuals (and group) by allowing for individual differences and experiences.
6. Use the proximity of an adult to help modify behaviour.

Part 2 Self-Concept

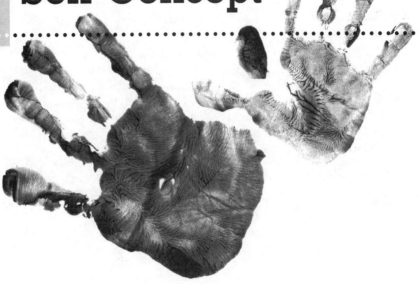

PART

2 Self-Concept

1 I'm Me, I'm Special

Basic Understandings
(concepts children can grasp from this subject)

- [ ] I'm me, I'm special. *There is no one else just like me.*
- [ ] I have a special name given to me when I was born. It is on my birth certificate.
- [ ] I may also have a secret name that only my family knows.
- [ ] No one has a voice just like mine; no one has fingerprints just like mine.
- [ ] I am like others in some ways; I am different from others in some ways.
- [ ] I can do some things easily; I can do some things well.
- [ ] Some things are hard to do; some things I cannot do well yet.
- [ ] I can do many things now that I could not do when I was a baby.
- [ ] As I get older, I will be able to do more things than I can do now.
- [ ] I do not have to be good at everything; I can make mistakes.
- [ ] I have feelings; at different times I may be glad, sad, angry, tired, or have other feelings.
- [ ] I can learn some good ways to show my feelings.
- [ ] No one can know what I think or how I feel unless I tell them or show them.
- [ ] If I know I am special, I know others are special too.
- [ ] Others need to know that I think they are special. Sometimes I need to know them better to know how special they are and in what ways they are special.
- [ ] When I share my own ideas or do things in my own way I am being creative.
- [ ] My thoughts and ideas are important. Other people have good ideas, too.
- [ ] I am likable and lovable. I can learn to like and love others.
- [ ] I have a right to share the materials, the equipment, and the attention of the teacher and to be safe and protected in school.
- [ ] Some children have special needs: braces, glasses, hearing aids, a wheelchair, speech therapy.
- [ ] Each year I have a special day called my birthday. (See Chapter 29, Mathematics in My Everyday World, for experiences related to birthday celebrations.)

Some things about me are very special

- [ ] My family is very special.
- [ ] My friends are very special. I may not have the same friends as another child.

- ☐ I have special thoughts. I can dream, wonder, wish, and enjoy just by looking at things or watching others.
- ☐ Sometimes I keep my thoughts to myself and sometimes I tell others my thoughts.
- ☐ I have special places, special toys, special treasures, and special pets that are mine.
- ☐ I can have special quiet times just for me; I don't always have to be busy with activities.
- ☐ I have a wonderful body. It has many parts: eyes, ears, nose, mouth, feet, hands, hair, skin, fingers, toes.
- ☐ I can do many things with my body — I can see, touch, taste, smell, hear, talk, move, think, and learn.

I am a member of a family and a community

- ☐ I am someone's son/daughter (grandson/granddaughter).
- ☐ I may also be someone's brother/sister/cousin/nephew/niece.
- ☐ I can be a part of a group (my family, my class, my neighbourhood).
- ☐ Someday I may choose to become a wife/husband and a mother/father.
- ☐ Someday I may become an aunt/uncle, grandmother/grandfather, or cousin to someone.
- ☐ A friend is someone who likes me just as I am.
- ☐ A neighbour is someone who lives close to where I live.
- ☐ I need to help my family and group by caring for and sharing the things we own, helping in plans, sharing my ideas, and doing what I am asked to do or need to do.
- ☐ I live in Canada. I may have been born in another country. I may have relatives in another country.

My family is special

- ☐ My family is made up of _____ , _____ , and _____ .
- ☐ Adults in my family can be helpful because they know many things that I do not know.
- ☐ My family has certain beliefs and special ways of living and doing things. (See Chapter 7, Living in Families, and Chapter 8, Families at Work.)
- ☐ My family celebrates days that are important to us: birthdays, Mother's Day, Father's Day, Valentine's Day, anniversaries, and graduations. (See Part 4, Family Celebrations and Part 5, Seasons.)
- ☐ My family and I have different customs, beliefs, and celebrations from other families. (See Parts 4 and 5.)
- ☐ My family and I may speak a different language from others near us.
- ☐ Adoption is one way a child can become a member of a family.
- ☐ I may be a part of two families. (Many children share time between two homes.)
- ☐ I love the people in my family.

I live in a special place

- ☐ I live with my family:
- ☐ in a home _____ (what kind?).
- ☐ in a city _____ (name).
- ☐ in a _____ (village, town, municipality, or country).
- ☐ in a _____ (province or territory).
- ☐ in the world (on the planet Earth).

I can change by growing

- ☐ I can get bigger (taller and heavier) until I am a grown-up.
- ☐ I need food, exercise, and rest to help me grow.
- ☐ Each year I have a birthday and become one year older.

I can change by learning

- ☐ When I think, remember, and decide, things can be better.
- ☐ I can learn about my body and make it work for me and for others.
- ☐ I can learn to do many things. If I try over and over again I should be able to learn to do something very well.
- ☐ I can learn by doing and discovering when I use my mind to think, eyes to see, ears to listen, fingers to feel, tongue to taste, and nose to smell.
- ☐ I can learn to do things for myself.
- ☐ I can help to keep myself clean and healthy.
- ☐ I can be thoughtful of others in what I do and what I say.
- ☐ I can learn to follow directions and rules.
- ☐ I can learn to take care of and help other people.
- ☐ I can learn to take care of other things in my world: plants, animals, parks, streams, sidewalks, and so on.
- ☐ I can learn how to use things the right way and how to care for them properly.

I can change by pretending

- ☐ I can play that I am someone else.
- ☐ I may wear a costume to make myself look like someone else.
- ☐ I may wear a wig to change the colour of my hair and to change its style.

I can change by dressing differently

- ☐ I can get a haircut or change the way I wear my hair so that I look different.
- ☐ I can wear various kinds of clothes and look different.
- ☐ I may look different when I get cleaned up and when I get dirty.
- ☐ I may wear glasses if I need them.
- ☐ I may wear a cast if I break an arm or leg, but ... I am still me!

I can change by getting sick/well

- ☐ If I skin or bruise myself, I look different until the injury heals.
- ☐ If I break a bone, I may look different until it mends.
- ☐ When I get a fever or feel sick, I do not look the same as when I am well.
- ☐ When I am tired I look different from when I am rested; sometimes I become cross and unhappy.
- ☐ Doctors, nurses, my family, and my teachers help me to keep healthy and help me to grow.

I can change by acting differently

- ☐ I can learn better ways to show my feelings: talk when I am angry, tell someone when I need help.
- ☐ I can let others know how I feel. I can listen to others and find out how they feel and what they think.
- ☐ I can work and play by myself; I can work and play with others.
- ☐ I can feel good about myself when I do my share of work at home and at school.
- ☐ Sometimes I help my friends and share things. Because we are different, we sometimes argue, disagree, or even fight.
- ☐ I can learn good manners; I can learn to be polite.
- ☐ I can show others I like or love them.
- ☐ Sometimes I am not proud of what I have done. I feel happier if I am allowed to help make things better by fixing what I have spoiled, cleaning up if I have made a mess, or being more thoughtful or friendly the next time.
- ☐ People like me better if I am friendly. I am still me, I like myself, and I am proud to be me.
- ☐ I can make some things better by:

1. Learning to do things as well as I can, and helping when I can.
2. Understanding that others have problems too.
3. Preventing accidents that may cause problems or make people unhappy.
4. Asking for help from adults to learn what I can do and to become the person I would like to become.

Some things I cannot change

☐ I cannot change my height or skin colour.

☐ I may not like some things about myself that I cannot change, but these things are a part of me that I will learn to accept.

☐ I cannot change my family or where I live.

☐ I cannot solve problems that make my parents or guardians drink, take drugs, argue, or fight.

☐ I cannot provide food, clothes, or a place to sleep for myself.

☐ I cannot keep my parents or guardians from getting a divorce, going to jail, or leaving me; but I can tell someone else who could help me if my parents hurt me or leave me alone.

☐ Some things I cannot change until I am older because they are the problems or responsibilities of grown-ups.

☐ Sometimes I am not proud of what I have done. I can try to be more thoughtful or friendly the next time.

Additional Facts the Teacher Should Know

1. A good self-image is often considered a prerequisite to learning or a beginning toward achieving whatever one is capable of becoming. Each child is unique and deserves to be accepted at whatever level of development he or she has attained physically, mentally, socially, and emotionally. Many early childhood classes include children whose first language is neither English nor French and whose cultural heritage may be different from the majority of children in the class or the majority of teachers in the centre. Also, many integrated classes include children who have special physical, cognitive, cultural, or emotional needs.

   a. Teachers should familiarize themselves with each child and the child's family or living group. Background information gathered from a pre-enrolment interview, completed information forms, and a home visit prior to the opening of school should provide a good beginning to understanding. The staff should operate on the basis that the parents or guardians are the primary educators of the child and that they will all have to work together throughout the year for the benefit of the child.

   b. Traditional family structures have changed. Accept the cultures and lifestyles of all children and help them feel good about themselves, their families, and their lifestyles. Help children to share their knowledge, skills, and culture with one another on a level that all children can comprehend. (See Part 3, Families, and Part 4, Family Celebrations.)

   c. Assess all children individually to determine their present skills and knowledge, and devise a plan for supplementing their education regardless of any special needs. Individual records are important, but do not stereotype or pigeonhole a child because a previous teacher recorded a lack of success. A year of maturation or a change in staff can make a great deal of difference. Remember to teach to a child's needs and to build on strengths and interests.

Do not assume that a child with special needs has a poor self-concept. Many such children have been nurtured and respected by their families so that they have a good self-concept.

d. A child in your classroom with special needs should be more a matter for celebration than concern. Such children enrich the lives of others in the class.

e. Parents or guardians must become partners in the education of their children if real progress is to be made. The staff should try to make the parents or guardians feel welcome in the classroom. Share the plans you have for a particular child and keep the parents or guardians informed as to the child's progress throughout the year by using conferences and written reports.

f. A rich and varied environment will help develop the ability to function independently in the world. The children should be encouraged to do what they can for themselves, but they should be helped with tasks that are too difficult before frustration sets in. Provide materials and directed learning experiences that are appropriate to the age and ability of each child in order to capitalize on their abilities, minimize frustration, and structure success.

g. At times you may wish to group children with similar needs together, such as at story time, in some cognitive learning sessions, and during some art experiences. At other times you should group children so that those with fewer skills or knowledge are able to learn from those with more skills and knowledge.

h. Positive rather than negative guidance builds a positive self-image. The staff should be constantly alert for praiseworthy actions by the children in order to reinforce them with their warm approval. Artificial or unwarranted praise should not be given, as children can detect insincerity. Staff members should accept each child's feelings as important, then they can help each child work through negative feelings.

Teachers should respect the dignity of each child. If corrective action is needed, it should be done quietly, firmly, and without shaming a child in front of peers. By your manner, the child will discover that you are still friends and that it is the behaviour of which you disapprove, not the child. Young children easily confuse discipline with personal rejection.

i. Children should be encouraged to share their ideas and to respect those of others. Self-concept should be an ongoing theme throughout the daily program, not merely an aid toward getting acquainted.

j. It is now the law in most provinces that you must report child abuse you are aware of. It is critical that any suspected abuse be reported to the appropriate community authorities as quickly as possible. Remember that your first responsibility is to the child. In instances of abuse, the teacher is of utmost importance in giving the child security and emotional support. Many colleges, universities, government departments, and community agencies offer short courses on reporting and preventing child abuse.

k. Stress professionalism at all times. You will be in possession of privileged information about children and their families. Never discuss this information with others who are not professionally involved. If you wish to share a positive or humorous incident, do so without using names. Be sure to share these incidents with the child's family, too.

l. Avoid gender stereotyping.
   ☐ Teach children nonsexist language by example. For example, use proper but comfortable nonsexist English: instead of firemen, say firefighters. Use he and she only when referring to particular people, otherwise use a specific noun or the third-person plural.
   ☐ Avoid dividing children into groups by gender. Group children using a variety of factors, such as by colour of shoes, simple counting games, etc.

   ☐   Don't judge children's sex-role attitudes, as they may be expressing a strongly held view from their own families. Instead, offer them alternative opinions.

2. Cultural awareness is important to each child's self-image. Canada provides a home to immigrants and a haven for refugees. Although the English and French cultures dominate our educational traditions, there is now a need to incorporate other cultural heritages into our curricula. A number of organizations provide teaching resources to assist you with planning heritage programs.

     Unfortunately, space does not permit us to discuss each cultural group that resides in Canada. In our research, we soon discovered that we could not generalize about any cultural group. Within each group are people who are seeking to preserve and practise their individual beliefs, with differing emphasis on traditions. Further modification occurs as each succeeding generation adapts cultural traditions to suit itself and the ever-changing times. All these factors make it difficult to describe a single set of values or a uniform method of celebrating a special event.

     In view of this, we wish to share some guidelines for becoming more sensitive to and aware of cultural diversity.

   a. Recognize and accept that each child and each family has a cultural heritage and unique way of life. The individual family's mode of living has been shaped not only by its culture, but by its religious beliefs, education, economic circumstances, geographic location, experiences, and interpersonal relationships. Recognize that families are simply different and not "deficient" or "superior," for example.

   b. If you have children from other cultures in your class, educate yourself to a knowledgeable level about each culture, as needed, so that you can help every child develop his or her potential to the fullest. Staff meetings and on-the-job training should be planned to increase cultural understanding and improve teaching skills. Capitalize on opportunities to meet and make friends with people from another culture. Ask questions, read (see Books and Periodicals at the end of this chapter), and discuss. Avoid isolating yourself from life and the world as it is concerned with only your small segment of it.

   c. Staff attitudes toward children with special needs or cultural differences will influence the attitudes of other children. Examine your attitudes, personal views, and behaviour toward others as honestly as you can. Remind yourself to look at questions from a parent's or child's point of view. How might they feel? Why?

   d. Call everyone by their preferred name. Never give a child a nickname or attempt to simplify his or her name. Similarly, adults in the class should be called by their preferred name and title. Children can easily understand diversity in names and titles.

   e. When children wear special clothes for religious or other reasons, respect this right and teach other children to respect it as well.

   f. Keep in mind that children will have the various mores and customs of their families or cultural community. For example, some children may feel severely admonished or disciplined when embarrassed or shamed in front of others. They may wish to stand aside and observe until they feel comfortable enough to join an activity. Similarly, some children have been taught to show respect for adults by holding back and waiting for adults to speak first. They may also lower their eyes when they are speaking to an adult. Do not assume that any of these behaviours are signs of disrespect or negative feelings.

   g. Many black Canadians have emigrated from Caribbean countries. Do not assume that curriculum materials prepared for black Americans will be relevant for children from the Caribbean, as the traditions are quite different. Parents and local cultural associations can help you assess the suitability of materials.

h. When non-English-speaking children are enroled, a competent, trained staff member who is able to communicate with these children should be available on a full-time basis. This person may speak a pure form of the language but must be willing to accept a family's dialect as an authentic form of communication. A child's first language should be respected and used, as necessary, while a second language is being learned. Neither language is right or wrong; each is unique. If the first language escapes a negative label, the child will learn to use both languages in their appropriate place and will become truly bilingual.

i. Each culture has many individuals who have made outstanding contributions to Canada, and each culture has traditional foods, dances, songs, games, art, ceremonial dress, and celebrations that can be appreciated by most young children. We have included some of these in the sections on Family Celebrations and Seasons (Parts 4 and 5, respectively). We realize this is only a beginning, and that there are many local celebrations and customs that can, and should, be included in your program. Enlist the help of parents and local resource people as you plan your program. Every family has skills, hobbies, household articles, toys, picture books, instruments, and art objects that can be shared in some meaningful way with encouragement from an imaginative and understanding staff.

j. When children from diverse cultures are sharing with their classmates, avoid embarrassing them or making them feel uncomfortable. Do not expect very young children to teach others, but allow them to share when they are ready to do so. They are anxious to be part of the group and not to be isolated. They cannot be expected to know all the history of their ancestry any more than any other child of their age. Ask yourself, "What could I share about my heritage when I was a child?"

k. Be alert to prejudice being shown by children or their parents in car pools, on playgrounds, or at parent meetings. Give assistance and be supportive whenever possible. Focus on ways to deal with misunderstanding or ignorance. Whenever you can, disprove stereotypes or misconceptions and help others to do the same.
   - ☐ Note contributions of Canadians from every ethnic group.
   - ☐ Focus on the need for equal opportunities for education and career training.

l. Try not to make misrepresentations of a culture by careless use of a phrase, story, song, or joke. Guard against subtle ridicule of a group by using an inaccurate imitation of its language, dress, customs, gestures, or mannerisms. In a quote, always use actual words and correct pronunciation.

m. Being informed will help you to take advantage of learning opportunities. If an illustration in a book or picture is inaccurate or patronizing, you will be able to discuss why. Offer a book or picture that portrays the same subject more accurately or positively.

n. Many multicultural materials are available. Some are very good and will be helpful; others are reactionary or inaccurate. Be selective — good multicultural materials should meet these criteria:
   - ☐ Accurate content.
   - ☐ If portraying the present, accurate in their representations of current attitudes and customs.
   - ☐ If portraying the past, historically accurate.
   - ☐ Cultural relevance and significance to the child.
   - ☐ Easily understood and related to the curriculum.

No one can instantly sensitize you. We hope that you will be challenged to make your teaching of young children truly a "small world" of living and learning that will have meaning for all the families you work with.

Introducing This Subject to Children

1. Introduce children and teachers to one another when they enter school. Encourage children to call one another by their first name.
2. Names of children should be placed near coat hooks or in cubbies, with a special picture to help children identify their things. (Names should be lettered clearly on artwork in the upper left-hand corner to teach left-to-right orientation.)
3. A child may bring a special possession from home to share with the group.
4. Daily health inspection provides an opportunity for learning about body parts and general health care.
5. Ask parents to write their child's name on a couple of old shirts with a waterproof marker or have names put on at a T-shirt shop. The children can wear these shirts until the teachers learn their names. Name tags can also be made of colourful fabric and pinned to the children's clothes. Be sure that the names are printed in both upper- and lower-case letters; for example, Julie not JULIE. Use permanent markers or fabric crayons to print the names on the fabric.
6. Take pictures of the children and post them with their names on each. The children will enjoy seeing their pictures, and visitors and student teachers in the class will have a quick reference to help them call a child by name.
7. Tape-record the children's voices, songs, or conversations. Play back the tapes, and have the children guess who is speaking or singing. Have a simple tape-recorder with earphones available in a quiet area so that children may tape and listen to their own voices.
8. Have full-length and hand mirrors available for children to help them develop a sense of body image.
9. Ask the children for their ideas when planning activities or when solving problems. Only do this when you will be able to follow up and use the children's ideas.
10. Encourage the children to talk about their family activities.
11. Play a game or sing a song that includes everyone's name.

Children can learn about their bodies through activities such as making a hand and foot collage.

Vocabulary

learn	hers	region	haircut
easy	ours	county	care for
hard	you	province	doctor
play	yours	territory	dentist
work	theirs	apartment	nurse
help	them	home	hairdresser
share	avenue	friend	barber
like/love	street	cavity	examination
feelings	country	sick	neighbourhood
I	city	well	names of family members
me	house	healthy	names of classmates
mine	farm	checkup	names of ethnic groups
myself	village	shots	colours of skin, hair, eyes
we	field	wash	names of body parts
us	port	clean	names for body actions
they	town	brush	names for celebrations
his	municipality	dirty	

Learning Centres

Discovery Centre

1. Introduce a full-length mirror or small hand mirrors to explore individual characteristics, such as eyes, skin, clothing, and hair.
2. Use a magnifying glass to explore skin, fingers, and hair.
3. Weigh and measure children at the beginning of and regularly during the year to be aware of individual growth changes. Compare growth against a child's own previous record, not someone else's.
4. Make hand or footprints. Compare and note differences. Notice that no two are alike — only one person can make a certain print. Comment on the use of footprints for identifying newborn infants.
5. For older children who live within a kilometre of the school or in a small town, post a map of the district or draw a simplified version. Put a map pin on the street where each child lives. Around the map, put pictures of the children or their houses with the addresses printed underneath. Run yarn from each map pin to its corresponding picture. Add pictures of the school and other places the children visit throughout the year. Talk about who lives closest or farthest from the school, the fire hall, the grocery store, and so on.
6. Prepare a display of various materials used for identification: ID cards from a university, a company, or the armed forces; birth certificates; ID bracelets; name labels in clothing; name tags; library cards; licence plates; a driver's licence; credit cards; an office name plate; monograms; personalized clothing, jewellery, and pencils. Choose items that are most appropriate for your group. Allow children to examine these and to help identify the ones they know. Discuss the use of the various items.
7. Purchase a simple camera and teach the children how to take pictures of one another (individually and in groups). Have the children assemble a storyboard using the

pictures. They can make up a story using themselves as characters. Extend the activity by allowing the children to take photos of things that they have made in the block-building art centres.

■ This is an excellent activity for helping children develop a better self-concept, and it may be especially useful for children who need positive behavioural models.

Dramatic Play Centres

Home-living centre

1. Offer a wide variety of men's and women's dressup clothes and a full-length mirror. Invite interested children to select a suitable style or colour. This will help children with their awareness of self, will encourage them to enact home experiences, and will help them to understand various roles of family members. (See Home-Living Centre in Chapter 7, Living in Families.)
2. Providing boy and girl dolls, dolls of different ethnic groups with authentic features, brother and sister dolls, and drink-wet dolls gives children many concept possibilities about the self.

▼ CAUTION: Avoid commercial dolls where only skin colour is changed.

Block-building centre

1. Label with a sign any buildings made by the children, such as "Pete's Garage."
2. Encourage children to take photographs of their block constructions. Label and display the photographs on an adjacent wall, and then send them home with the children. Alternatively, the children might develop a collaborative scrapbook for the year, and include any photographs they have taken.

Other dramatic play centres

1. Set up a variety of dramatic play centres that represent sites in your community. These could include a doctor's office, a dairy, a grocery store, a feed store, a marine supply store, a fire hall, etc. A shoe store could include shoeboxes, old shoes, a ruler for measuring feet, money, and a cash register. Encourage all children to experiment with various roles in the centres. For instance, encourage both girls and boys to be firefighters, doctors, nurses, store clerks, captains of fishing boats, hairstylists, etc.

▼ CAUTION: Use only plastic or washable hats and wigs for sanitary reasons.

2. A variety of puppets representing people of both genders and various ages and races will offer children the opportunity to act out their feelings about themselves and others. Animal puppets can be fun, but they are not appropriate when used in place of people puppets. Encourage children to use animal puppets as animals, not as people.
3. Make and send seasonal cards. This activity can be part of a trip to the post office, and gives the children a sense of being a part of their community. It also shows them a way to be kind to other people.

Art Centre

••• 1. Children can paint or draw pictures of themselves, family, and friends (accept a child's picture as is; do not prod for more finished work that may be developmentally beyond the child).
••• 2. In the late part of the year or with older children, have the children lie on the floor on large sheets of paper and trace around them. They can paint the figures to correspond with the clothing they are wearing. Cut out the figures after they are painted and

display them on classroom walls. Have different skin-tone paints mixed for children, or allow them to mix colours they need.

- 3. A fingerpaint activity can end with each child making a handprint on a separate piece of paper. This helps use up excess fingerpaint before children go to wash and also gives them a concept of their own hand size. Children can also make fingerprints on paper and will notice that each person's is different. You can use stamp pad ink for this instead of fingerpaint. VARIATION: Make footprints.
- 4. Handprints made of play dough or plaster of Paris can be given to parents as gifts.
- 5. Clay people can be made by older children. Natural clay soil in some areas is excellent and can be baked in a kiln if desired. Pulling features out of a ball of clay is more successful for baking; these features are less likely to break off than those put on as appendages.
- 6. A class mural can be made by putting a role of newsprint on the floor and having each child add to the group effort by choosing the medium he or she prefers; for example, paints, crayons, chalk, or charcoal. If some children choose to work with dough or clay, their creations can be displayed in a kiosk or on a low shelf below the mural.
- 7. Imagination paper: Offer a variety of paper scraps in all shapes, sizes, and colours. Circles, ovals, triangles, and long narrow strips make interesting pictures. (See Art Centre in Part 1 for a detailed description.)
- 8. Finish the picture: Paste small, irregular shapes of coloured paper to sheets of paper. Let the children choose a sheet that suggests an idea to them. You could also draw curved or wavy lines, dots, and squares on sheets of paper.
- 9. For special occasions, have the children plan how the class will be decorated. Use a group time for planning and then provide the children with the materials they need in the art centre. Use another group time to complete the decorating.

Children can learn about their own bodies by painting or colouring their own silhouettes.

■ A child with a negative self-concept may find this a challenging activity, but teacher support can bring enjoyment and help the child accept him- or herself. Similarly, mirrors placed at child level throughout the classroom will build familiarity with appearance.

••• 10. Papier-mâché puppets: Make family puppets. When dry, paint with skin-tone paints. Paper and fabric scraps can be used for clothes.

••• 11. Paper bag puppets: Paint paper bags with skin tones. Add facial features using paint, crayons, yarn, or trims.

> **NOTE:** Throughout the year, display each child's creative efforts frequently. Let each child select what he or she would like to display. Group a variety of media together, focusing on individuality and avoiding unfair comparisons and competition. Change displays frequently. Use hallways, stairwells, bulletin boards, and classroom walls for flat work and kiosks or low shelves for three-dimensional pieces.

Learning and Language Materials Centre

Commercially made games and materials

1. *Puzzles:* Those that show children and adults of a wide variety of races and cultures. Be sure to have puzzles with knobs for younger children.
2. *Construction and manipulative toys:* Dolls, animals, and dressing boards that help children develop skills in buttoning, lacing, zipping, etc. Be sure the toys can be placed so that the children are practising the skill in the same position as they would be if they were dressing themselves.
3. *Dolls and puppets:* Choose dolls and puppets that reflect a variety of races and cultures.
4. *Flannelboards:* There are a large number of flannelboard kits that aid the development of body and cultural awareness.

Teacher-made games and materials

> **NOTE:** For detailed descriptions, see Learning Games in Part 1.

1. *Name it:* Use photographs of the children.
2. *Name it, Look and see,* or *Reach and feel:* Play using:
   a. A nail file, comb, toothbrush, and hand mirror.
   b. Things we wear on our hands, such as rings, gloves, and mittens.
   c. Headwear such as a scarf, hat, helmet, bathing cap, or beret.
   d. Footgear such as boots, rubbers, slippers, sandals, and shoes.
   e. Brushes that help us keep clean such as nailbrushes, toothbrushes, bath brushes, hairbrushes, shoe brushes, and clothes brushes.
   f. Dolls or pictures to represent family members.
   g. A stethoscope, dentist's mirror, thermometer, and eye chart.
3. *Match-them:* Use pairs of socks, mittens, or shoes.
4. *Alike, different, and the same:* Use the items in number 3.
5. *Sorting and grouping by association:* Use things we wear on our head, feet, and hands.
6. *Which?*
   a. Show a pair of shoes for a man, woman, child, and baby. Ask, "Which pair is worn by a man? A woman? A child? A baby? Which is heaviest? Lightest? Biggest? Smallest? Has the highest heel? Is brown?" and so on.
   b. Use pictures of hands doing things, such as handshaking, waving goodbye, clapping, holding something, and washing.
   c. Use pictures of children doing things, such as getting a haircut, putting on shoes, brushing teeth, getting a checkup, running, swimming, climbing, or swinging.
7. *Guess who?* "I'm thinking of someone who is wearing ... (describe child)."
8. *Listening:* See Identification Games in Part 1.

9. *Who's missing?* See Identification Games in Part 1.
10. *How can I? How can you?* See Problem-Solving Games in Part 1.
11. *Find your name:* Prepare a name card with each child's first name (you may add last names later in the year). Let children find their cards.
12. *Can you remember?* See Identification Games in Part 1.
13. *Let's tell a story:* See Language Games in Part 1.
14. *Faces:* Make flannel faces with interchangeable eyes, noses, and mouths that depict various feelings and skin tones. Use natural skin tones, not pink or white.
15. Paper dolls mounted on flannel can represent family members to use with identification games or storytelling. Provide a variety of paper clothes so the children can dress the dolls as they wish. Pattern books are a good source of multicultural figures.
16. Make your own self-help frames or learning vests. Include zippers, buttons, laces, snaps, and hooks. You might also include some pockets.

Book Centre

- Aliki. *A Weed Is a Flower.* Englewood Cliffs, NJ: Prentice-Hall, 1965. (Read–Tell)
- ••• Anglund, Joan. *A Friend Is Someone Who Likes You.* New York: Harcourt Brace Jovanovich, 1966.
- •••• ———. *What Colour Is Love?* New York: Harcourt Brace Jovanovich, 1958.
- ••• Bingham, Mindy, and Penelope Colville Paine. *My Way Sally.* Santa Barbara, CA: Advocacy Press, 1988.
- •• Bourgeois, Paulette. *Big Sarah's Little Boots.* Toronto: Kids Can Press, 1987.
- •• ———. *Hurry Up, Franklin.* Toronto: Kids Can Press, 1989.
- • Brenner, Barbara. *Bodies.* New York: Dutton, 1973.
- • ———. *Faces.* New York: Dutton, 1970.
- •• Brott, Ardyth. *Jeremy's Decision.* Toronto: Oxford University Press, 1990.
- •• Brown, Ruth. *I Don't Like It!* New York: Dutton, 1990.
- ••• Carle, Eric. *Do You Want to Be My Friend?* New York: Harper & Row, 1986.
- •• Carlson, Nancy. *I Like Me.* New York: Penguin, 1990.
- ••• Caseley, Judith. *Harry and Willy and Carrothead.* New York: Greenwillow Press, 1991.
- ••• Chislett, Gail. *Pardon Me Mom.* Willowdale, ON: Annick Press, 1986.
- ••• ———. *The Rude Visitors.* Willowdale, ON: Annick Press, 1984.
- ••• Damrell, Liz. *With the Wind.* New York: Orchard, 1991.
- •• de Paola, Tomie. *The Art Lesson.* New York: Putnam, 1989.
- •• ———. *Andy (That's My Name).* Englewood Cliffs, NJ: Prentice-Hall, 1973.
- •• Dickson, Barry. *Afraid of the Dark.* Toronto: James Lorimer, 1986.
- ••• Downie, Mary Alice. *Jennie Greenteeth.* Toronto: Kids Can Press, 1984.
- ••• Dumas, Jacqueline. *And I'm Never Coming Back.* Willowdale, ON: Annick Press, 1986.
- •• Etherington, Frank. *When I Grow Up Bigger than Five.* Willowdale, ON: Annick Press, 1986.
- • Ets, Marie H. *Just Me.* New York: Viking Press, 1965.
- ••• Fernandes, Eugenie. *A Difficult Day.* Toronto: Kids Can Press, 1986.
- ••• Fujikawa, Gyo. *See What I Can Be!* New York: Putnam, 1990.
- ••• Gill, Gail. *There's an Alligator Under My Bed.* Toronto: Three Trees Press, 1984.
- ••• Gilman, Phoebe. *Jilian Jiggs.* Richmond Hill, ON: Scholastic, 1985.
- ••• Goennel, Heidi. *When I Grow Up....* Boston: Little, Brown, 1987.
- ••• Green, Carrolle. *The Too Busy Day.* Willowdale, ON: Annick Press, 1985.
- ••• Havill, Juanita. *Jamaica's Friend.* Toronto: Scholastic, 1987.
- ••• Heide, Florence Parry. *The Day of Ahmed's Secret.* New York: Lothrop, Lee, & Shepard, 1990.

••• Jensen, Virginia. *Sara and the Door.* Don Mills, ON: Addison-Wesley, 1977.

••• Keats, Ezra Jack. *Peter's Chair.* New York: Harper & Row, 1967.

••• ———. *Jeannie's Hat.* New York: Harper & Row, 1966.

••• ———. *Whistle for Willie.* New York: Viking Press, 1964.

••• Kellogg, Steven. *Much Bigger than Martin.* New York: Dial Press, 1973.

••• Klein, Norma. *Girls Can Be Anything.* New York: Dutton, 1973.

••• Lasker, Joe. *He's My Brother.* Chicago: Albert Whitman, 1974.

•••• Leaf, Munro. *Who Cares? I Do.* Philadelphia: Lippincott, 1971.

••• Levine, Ellen. *I Hate English.* Toronto: Scholastic, 1990.

• Lineham, Patricia. *See What I Can Do!* New York: Putnam, 1990.

•••• MacEwen, Gwendolyn. *The Chocolate Moose.* Toronto: New Canada, 1981. (Read–Tell)

•• Mazer, Anne. *Watch Me.* New York: David McKay, 1990.

•• Munsch, Robert. *Thomas's Snowsuit.* Willowdale, ON: Annick Press, 1985.

••• Newman, Marjorie. *School Concert.* Markham, ON: Penguin, 1986.

• O'Brien, Anne Sibley. *Don't Say No.* Markham, ON: Fitzhenry & Whiteside, 1986.

• ———. *I Don't Want To Go.* Markham, ON: Fitzhenry & Whiteside, 1986.

• ———. *It Hurts.* Markham, ON: Fitzhenry & Whiteside, 1986.

• ———. *It's Hard To Wait.* Markham, ON: Fitzhenry & Whiteside, 1986.

••• Plantos, Ted. *Heather Hits Her First Home Run.* Windsor, ON: Black Moss, 1986.

• Polivy, Betsy Bober, and Jan Gelbard, *My Dressing Book.* New York: Putnam, 1989.

••• Rice, Melanie, and Chris Rice. *All About Me.* New York: Doubleday, 1987.

•• Rockwell, Anne. *When We Grow Up.* New York: Dutton, 1981.

•• Roe, Eileen. *All I Am.* New York: Macmillan, 1990.

••• Sheehan, Patty. *Kylie's Song.* Santa Barbara, CA: Advocacy Press, 1988.

••• Stein, Sarah B. *Making Babies.* New York: Walker, 1974.

• Stinson, Kathy. *The Bare Naked Book.* Willowdale, ON: Annick Press, 1986.

• ———. *Big or Little.* Willowdale, ON: Annick Press, 1983.

•••• Strauss, Joyce. *How Does It Feel...?* New York: Human Sciences Press, 1979.

••• Surat, Michele Maria. *Angel Child, Dragon Child.* Toronto: Scholastic, 1989.

•••• Viorst, Judith. *Alexander and the Terrible Horrible No Good Very Bad Day.* New York: Atheneum, 1972.

••• Williams, Vera. *Something Special for Me.* New York: Greenwillow Press, 1983.

•• Wolde, Gunilla. *Thomas Is Different.* Toronto: Hodder and Stoughton, 1989.

Planning for Group Time

NOTE: All music, fingerplays, poems, stories, and games listed here may be used at other times during the session as appropriate.

Music

Songs

Please see "Hello Everybody" at the end of this chapter.

From *The Baby Beluga Book*, Raffi
"To Everyone in All the World," p. 21
"Over in the Meadow," p. 28

From *The Goat with the Bright Red Socks*, Birkenshaw and Walden

"This Is Me," p. 2
"These Are My Eyes, Eyes, Eyes," p. 3
"I Feel Glad," p. 7
"I Can Count," p. 8
"Theleftrightfrontbackupanddown Dance," p. 13
"Rig a Jig Jig," pp. 14–15
"What Makes a House a Home?" p. 21

From *Sally Go Round the Sun*, Fowke
"If You're Happy," p. 44
"Head and Shoulders," p.46
"It Doesn't Really Matter," p.46
"Foot and Finger Plays," pp. 100–106 (good for body image)

From *Songs to Sing And Sing Again*, Gordon
(See index for songs in languages other than English.)
"Here Is What I Can Do," p. 36
"One Finger, One Thumb," p. 44

From *What Shall We Do and Alee Galloo!*, Winn
"Come On and Join in the Game," p. 4
"This Is What I Can Do," p. 10
"Who's That Knocking at My Door?" p. 84

Rhythms and Singing Games

1. Body exercise songs: Touch body parts as you sing. With the older children, you may add other verses using other parts of the body.

....
HEADS AND SHOULDERS

(tune: "Oats, Peas, Beans")

Heads and shoulders, knees and toes
Heads and shoulders, knees and toes
Heads and shoulders, knees and toes
Let's point to them together.

....
MY HEAD, MY SHOULDERS

(tune: "Mulberry Bush")

My head, my shoulders, my knees, my toes
My head, my shoulders, my knees, my toes
My head, my shoulders, my knees, my toes
Then we stand together.

....
GOOD GROOMING

(tune: "Mulberry Bush")

This is the way we wash our face ...
This is the way we put on our clothes ...
This is the way we brush our teeth ...

2. Rhythms in names: When children have had some rhythm experience, beat out a rhythm and chant their names to it. For example, 1-2-3 for Mei-lin Cheung, and 1-2-3-4

for Mi-chael Saun-ders. Later in the year, beat out a rhythm and have children guess the names in the class that fit the pattern.

3. The twist: Encourage children to respond to rhythmic music in their own way. When space is limited, provide each child with a piece of 30.5 cm by 30.5 cm carpet. Place these squares on a smooth floor, nap side down. Each child may move, twist, and sway in any way as long as his or her feet remain on the square. Children become quite skilful as they twist on the carpet. Use music with a fast beat.

From *Finger Play and Action Rhymes*, Jacobs
"Good Morning," p. 7
"A Big Boy," p. 41

From *Finger Rhymes*, Brown
"My Book," p. 5
"Five Little Babies," p. 6

From *Fingers, Feet, and Fun*, Evans
"Five Little Fingers," p. 24
"One, Two, Three, Four, Five," p. 30
"Peter Hammers," p. 40
"There Was a Little Girl," p. 42
"Growing," p. 46
"My Mirror," p. 82
"Hide and Seek," p. 83
"Me," p. 85

From *The New Wind Has Wings*, Downie
"Laughter," p. 10
"O Earth, Turn," p. 19

> **NOTE:** Any rhythm activity tape you have that features large muscle activities could be used, as well as any songs that feature self-concept.

Records and Cassettes

Sandy Tobias Oppenheim. *If Snowflakes Fell in Flavours.* (Berandol Records)
"Let's Play the Statue Game"
"I Am Sick"
"I Feel Grouchy"
"My Wish Song"

Sharon, Lois, and Bram. *Smorgasbord.* (Elephant Records)
"Peanut Butter"
" 'A' You're Adorable"

Fingerplays and Poems

TEN LITTLE FINGERS

I have ten little fingers *(hold up both hands)*
And they all belong to ME *(point to self)*
I can make them do things
Would you like to see? *(point to child)*
I can shut them up tight *(make fist)*
I can open them up wide *(open fingers)*
I can clap them together and make them hide *(clap, then hide)*
I can jump them up high, I can jump them down low *(over head and down)*
And fold them together and hold them just so. *(fold in lap)*

....

THIS LITTLE HAND

This little hand is a good little hand *(hold up one hand)*
This little hand is his brother. *(hold up other hand)*
Together, they wash and they wash and they wash *(washing hands)*
One hand washes the other.

....

WHERE ARE YOUR _____ ?

Where are your eyes? Show me your eyes — baby's eyes can see.
Where are your eyes? Show me your eyes — shut them quietly.
Where is your nose? Show me your nose — baby's nose can blow.
Where is your nose? Show me your nose — wiggle it just so.
Where is your mouth? Show me your mouth — it can open wide.
Where is your mouth? Show me your mouth — how many teeth inside?

Stories

(To read, read–tell, or tell. See Book Centre earlier in this chapter for a complete list.)
There is a wealth of stories relating to self-concept. Choose stories that are relevant to
the current interests and concerns of the children.

A book such as Chislett's *The Rude Visitors* is a good choice if the children are
concerned with manners and being considerate of other people.

Anglund's *A Friend Is Someone Who Likes You* is an excellent story to read when
children are going through a stage of having a new "best friend" every day.

Games

(See Learning Games in Part 1 and Teacher-Made Games and Materials earlier in this
chapter for directions.)

1. *Guess who?*
2. *Who's missing?*
3. *Listening.*
4. *Look and see.*
5. *Traffic police:* Have the children stand in their own spaces, facing in the same
   direction. Choose one child to be the police officer; provide a whistle and a hat. The
   officer gives directions, such as "Walk very slowly" or "Hop on one foot." The group
   must stop moving when the officer blows the whistle. Allow every officer three
   directions, and then choose a new officer. In a small group, the game ends when
   everyone has had an opportunity to be the officer.

   NOTE: You may need to model giving directions for very young children when the
   game is first played. Be sure to wipe the whistle with a non-toxic disinfectant
   before you give it to the next officer.

Routine Times

1. All routines: Explain to new children the reasons for inspection, resting, eating,
   washing hands, and brushing teeth. Throughout the year, continue to teach the value
   of these routines.
2. Greeting children: Always try to welcome each child individually upon arrival. Special
   attention should be given to those who have been absent.

3. Inspection: Talk about keeping clean and healthy, and help children to learn their body parts. Watch for healing of bruises and scrapes.
4. Children can take turns telling one another's names at snack time or meal time.
5. Children may find their place identified by a name card or place card. You might use these for snack time, meal time, or any activity time.
6. Throughout the year, serve foods at snack time or meal times that are enjoyed by various cultural groups.
7. Washing hands: Talk about the importance of washing hands after toileting and before eating.
8. When toileting, use correct biological terms for body parts and bodily functions; for example: genitals, penis, anus, rectum, navel, eliminate, bowel movement, and feces.

Large Muscle Activities

1. Note special progress and praise accomplishments in any skill, game, or exercise, such as using the balance beam, walking boards, slide, or swing, or running, hopping, climbing, crawling, and skipping.
2. Encourage the children to try new feats. Compare their progress only against their *own* former efforts.
3. Use gym mats for somersaults and other tumbling exercises.
4. Playing in the snow offers children the opportunity to learn more about their bodies. Activities such as making snow angels, houses, and people use large muscles and improve co-ordination. Building snow people also encourages co-operation.

Extended Experiences

NOTE: See Planning for Visitors in Part 1.

1. Invite a police officer to show the children fingerprinting.

   ▼ CAUTION: Be sure you have facilities planned so that the children can wash their fingers after being fingerprinted. You should contact the police officer ahead of time to discuss what you think your children will be able to understand.

2. Invite a doctor or dentist, through the local public health nurse, to perform any required checkups in the school if adequate space can be provided for the examinations.
3. Invite a dental hygienist to talk to the children about taking care of their teeth and to demonstrate the correct method of brushing.
4. Invite a nurse to talk to the children about good health habits and to assist you in weighing and measuring the children. Record each child's height and mass on a measuring chart. Post the chart, or save it until late spring or summer and measure the children again. Compare the results. You might also consider asking a nurse to demonstrate blood-pressure monitoring equipment.
5. Invite a physical education teacher or dance instructor to teach the children exercises or simple dance movements.
6. Arrange to visit children's parents at work to give children a sense of their community and an understanding of the diversity in their families.
7. Select suitable filmstrips.
8. Create a quiet space that may be used by one or two children. The space should be scaled for children's use only. Tell the children that teachers will come into the space only with their permission, unless children are having a problem (e.g., two children are arguing). Be sensitive to children who may need some time in a quiet space, and suggest that they use it.

■ This can be especially useful for children who have difficulty attending to tasks. The space should never be used as a consequence of problem behaviour — it should be a space that children enjoy.

9. A quiet space could be used by an individual child when:
   a. Listening to tapes.
   b. Looking at books.
   c. Exploring cognitive or manipulative materials.
   d. Thinking or resting.

This space can be created:
   a. On a raised platform — add carpet or pillows.
   b. In a closet — take off the door, and provide a light and a pillow or a beanbag chair.
   c. In a barrel with the top and one side cut away — add a round pillow.
   d. In a quiet corner by partitioning it off with shelves or a screen — add a carpet, overstuffed chairs with their legs removed, or beanbag chairs.
   e. By arranging 1.5 m to 1.75 m high bookshelves to enclose a corner of the room — drape a light blanket or piece of cloth over the shelves to suggest a roof.

 # Teacher Resources

Pictures and Displays

☐ Photographs of the children can be taken with a camera and displayed with their names underneath.

☐ Children's artwork should be displayed throughout the year with everyone having their work selected frequently.

☐ Display pictures of children illustrating many skills, such as dressing, brushing teeth, climbing a tree, riding a tricycle, and so on.

☐ Display pictures that include children and adults from a variety of cultures. Do not use commercial products that have children dressed in ceremonial costumes as these only reinforce stereotypes. National magazines are good sources of pictures.

☐ Try also to display photographs of individuals who are physically disabled engaged in a variety of everyday activities.

Books and Periodicals

Ames, L.B., et al. *Don't Push Your Preschooler.* New York: Harper & Row, 1980.

———. *Your Two Year Old: Terrible or Tender.* New York: Dell, 1980.

———. *Your Three Year Old: Friend or Enemy.* New York: Dell, 1980.

———. *Your Four Year Old: Wild or Wonderful.* New York: Dell, 1980.

Anderson, Eugene. *Self-Esteem for Tots to Teens.* Deephaven, MN: Meadowbrook, 1984.

Berne, Patricia. *Building Self-Esteem in Children.* New York: Continuum, 1981.

Caplan, Theresa, and Frank Caplan. *The Early Childhood Years: The 2 to 6 Year Old.* Toronto: Bantam, 1983.

Cole, Joanna. *The Magic School Bus Inside the Human Body.* Richmond Hill, ON: Scholastic, 1989.

Greenspan, Stanley, and Nancy Thorndike Greenspan. *First Feelings.* New York: Penguin, 1985.

Harrison, Barbara G. *Unlearning the Lie: Sexism in Schools.* New York: Liveright, 1973.

Hart, Carole, et al. *Free to Be ... You and Me* (conceived by Marlo Thomas). New York: McGraw-Hill, 1974, 1987.

Lorin, M.J. *The Parents' Book of Physical Fitness for Children.* New York: Atheneum, 1978.

Oppenheim, Joanne. *Kids and Play.* New York: Ballantine, 1978.

Patrick, Denise. *Look Inside Your Body.* New York: Putnam, 1989.

Popper, Adrienne. *Parents' Book for the Toddler Years.* New York: Ballantine, 1986.

Prudden, Suzy. *Exercise Program for Young Children.* New York: Workman, 1983.

Films and Videos

NOTE: Check with your distributor about public performance rights.

Body Talking. National Film Board, 1983.

The Circus Baby. Weston Woods.

I Like Me. Weston Woods (sound filmstrip).

I'll Find a Way. National Film Board, 1977.

Noises in the Night. Stephen Bosustow Productions (released in Canada by BFA Educational Media), 1969.

Smile a Day. Nelvana (released in Canada by Marvin Melnyk Associates), 1973.

Step by Step. Hubley Studios Productions (released in Canada by International Tele-Film), 1978.

Tikki Tikki Tembo. Weston Woods.

The Toymaker. Manitoba Education and Training Instructional Resources Library, 1964.

The Ugly Duckling. Weston Woods.

Community Resources and Organizations

☐ Parents of children in your classroom, friends from diverse cultures, or foreign students at a nearby college.

☐ Pediatrician and nurse.

☐ Dentist and dental hygienist.

☐ Speech and hearing clinic.

☐ Mental health clinic.

☐ Department of Public Health.

☐ Child development department of school of childhood education at a local college or university.

☐ Community cultural organizations.

☐ The Canadian Mental Health Association.

☐ Provincial and territorial mental health associations.

Government Agencies

☐ The federal Department of Multiculturalism and Citizenship is an invaluable resource.

☐ Provincial and territorial cultural and multicultural ministries.

☐ Provincial, territorial, and federal ministries concerned with health, welfare, and social services.

Hello Everybody

Lucile Panabaker (adapted)

1. Hel - lo eve-ry bo-dy and how do you do? How do you do? How do you do? Hel-

lo eve-ry bo-dy and how do you do?   How are you to-day?   (Shake)

2. Shake hands everybody and how do you do? How do you do? How do you do?
   Shake hands everybody and how do you do? How are you today?
3. Walk around everybody. . .
4. Stand on one foot everybody. . .
5. Wave your arms everybody. . .

Have the children add other verses.

2 Sight

Basic Understandings
(concepts children can grasp from this subject)

- [ ] We see with our eyes.
- [ ] We learn things by using our eyes.
- [ ] We need light to help us to see; if is completely dark, we cannot see.
- [ ] Some animals, such as cats, can see in the dark.
- [ ] We need to take good care of our eyes so that we can see.
- [ ] Some people need glasses to help them to see.
- [ ] Some people cannot see at all; they are blind (see other chapters on senses).
- [ ] Our eyes take pictures somewhat like a camera does.
- [ ] Our eyes help tell us the colours of things.
- [ ] Our eyes help tell us the sizes of things.
- [ ] Our eyes help tell us the shapes of things.
- [ ] Things that are far away look smaller than when we are close to them.
- [ ] The coloured part of the eye is called the iris.
- [ ] The black centre of the eye, called the pupil, is really an opening to let in light so that we can see.
- [ ] If the sun is too bright, our eyes may not keep out enough light. We can protect our eyes when we are out in bright sun by wearing a peaked cap or a sun visor.

   NOTE: Some doctors suggest that sunglasses, especially the cheap ones made for children, weaken children's eyes and should be discouraged.

- [ ] Eyebrows and eyelashes help protect our eyes from dust particles.
- [ ] If something gets in one of our eyes, our eyes shed tears to help wash it out.

Additional Facts the Teacher Should Know

1. The optic nerve relays the image viewed by the retina to the brain. Nerve fibres from the retina run through the optic nerve. It is the nerve cells in the retina that make sight possible.

2. The *iris* is the coloured part of the eye. The *pupil* is an opening in the iris. The *lens* of the eye is located behind the pupil. The *retina* is the inner layer of the eyeball. Light enters the eye via the pupil and passes through the colourless liquid contained in the eyeball cavity. The muscles of the eye focus the lens.

3. Some people are near-sighted; some are far-sighted. A concave lens in glasses corrects near-sightedness; a convex lens corrects far-sightedness.

4. Some children have visual difficulties, such as seeing reverse images, colour blindness, near-sightedness, far-sightedness, and strabismus (crossed-eyes). Squinting, holding objects or books close to the eyes, bumping into objects, tripping, or persistently erring in colour identification may indicate vision problems. Ask parents to refer such children to an eye doctor for further examination and testing.

   NOTE: This is an excellent area for introducing children to basic eye care and safety. See Teacher Resources in this chapter for sources of information on this subject, or consult your centre's nurse. Other chapters related to this subject are Chapter 25, Day and Night, and Chapter 27, Colour in My World.

Introducing This Subject to Children

1. Place eyeglasses, binoculars, a microscope, magnifying glasses, a kaleidoscope, and slide viewers or View Masters on a table. Talk about why some people need or use these.

2. Ask children to put their hands over their eyes, and then ask, "Can you see?"

3. If children are willing, put a sleepmask over their eyes, and ask, "How could you walk around if you couldn't see? What do you think would happen?"

   ▼ CAUTION: Wrap the mask with fresh tissue for each child.

4. If you have a doll with broken eyes, show it to the children and say, "If a doll gets an eye pushed out, we can fix the eye. But children cannot get new eyes, so they need to take very good care of the ones they have."

5. All activities in this chapter are well-suited for use with children who have hearing impairments. To ensure that all children understand the directions, demonstrate all activities.

Vocabulary

glasses	eyelash(es)	vision	frames
spectacles	look	blind	nosepiece
contact lenses	see	iris	magnifying glass
eye(s)	sight	pupil	microscope
eyebrow(s)	sighted	lens	telescope
sunglasses	sun visor	tear	
monocle	binoculars		

Learning Centres
• •

Discovery Centre

1. Go for an observation walk. This can be a general or a specific walk, such as "Look for bugs," or "Look for leaves." Take some binoculars, a magnifying glass, and a sack for the treasures you may find.
2. Have children look at objects through a magnifying glass. Provide a supply of interesting specimens, such as rocks, shells, or insects. Decide which are shiny and which are dull.
3. Use a magnifying glass to look at a telephone book. Invite the children to choose or bring in objects that they wish to observe under the magnifying glass.
4. Use a visual theme for a treasure hunt in which children look for objects in the room with particular visual attributes; for example, all red objects, all round objects, etc.
5. Use cooking activities to demonstrate differences in appearance *before* and *after.* You might try:

gelatine	pancakes	scrambled eggs	bacon
gingerbread	pudding	waffles	cupcakes

    Making popcorn involves all five senses. You can *see* it pop if you have a popper with a glass or plastic lid; you can *hear* it popping; you can *smell* it; you can *taste* it; and you can *feel* the shapes of the kernels. Sing "Catch the Popcorn if You Can" (words and music in Chapter 3).

    ▼ CAUTION: Be sure you have all the required utensils and ingredients available before you start.

6. Have a table for the children to display their special finds of the week. Ask the children to bring objects with special visual attributes.
7. Look at an object that is far away. Talk about how small it looks. Walk closer to it and see how much bigger it looks.
8. When you see an airplane in the sky, talk about how small it looks and how big it really is when you are close to it. Compare pictures of far away and close airplanes.
9. Hang an eye chart for children. Talk about the reasons why some people need glasses. Recall the magnifying-glass exploration.
10. If staff, parents, or children wear glasses or contact lenses, ask them to show the group what they look like and how they fit.
11. Make a peep box with a small light in it. Let children look in when it is dark and when the light is on.
12. Talk about some objects that are round, big, or a particular colour. For example, "Look at this ball. What colour is it? What shape is it? What size is it? How do you know it was blue, round, and big? Did you hear it? Did you taste it? Did you feel it? No, you saw it with your eyes."
13. Display different things that help us to see when it is dark, such as a lamp, a candle, a lantern, a flashlight, or a kerosene lamp.
14. Observe or "make" a rainbow — for directions, see Chapter 27, Colour in My World.
15. Make a display of things people read, such as books, magazines, Braille books, newspapers, pamphlets, posters, or instructions on a computer screen.

    NOTE: Choose illustrated items if possible.

16. Display items we need to read or see to help us; for example, thermometers, clocks, television, filmstrips, cookbooks, traffic signs, street and house numbers, maps, timetables, tour brochures, telephone books, picture dictionaries.
17. Take pictures of the children and have the film developed at a one-hour photo shop, if possible, to demonstrate how photos are developed. Use a Polaroid camera if you have access to one. Allow older children to take their own pictures. Remember to keep track of which child shot which picture.
18. Have a special colour day when everyone is asked to wear a specific colour and all the activities revolve around that colour. For example, on green day, green, blue, and yellow paints would be provided and green vegetables would be served at lunch along with green pasta, etc. [Source: Indenbaum, Valerie, and Marcia Shapiro. *The Everything Book.* Livonia, MI: Partner Press, 1985.]
19. Rent a video camera and recorder, or ask a parent who has this equipment to record and show a special event in the centre.

Dramatic Play Centres

Home-living centre

1. Have a flashlight available to look for things in dark places.
2. Have a discarded or toy camera available to take pretend pictures of the dolls.
3. Set out sunglass frames with the lenses removed.
4. Provide unbreakable hand and wall mirrors.
5. Place a magnifying glass and a telephone book by a toy telephone.

Familiar play equipment encourages dramatic play and expression of emotion. This quiet child became quite expressive while playing in the home-living centre.

Block-building centre

1. Set out road signs and traffic signals for use with road building.
2. Display pictures of traffic at night. Talk about the use of headlights at night and during the day (if you are in a province or territory that has a daytime headlight law.)
3. When you are talking to children about their constructions, say to them, "Tell me how your construction looks."

Other dramatic play centres

1. Eye doctor: Set out an eye chart, a lab coat, a flashlight, a mirror, and eyeglass frames with the lenses removed.
2. Set up a shop to sell eyeglasses and sunglasses. Remove lenses from frames.
3. Make a movie (see Art Centre) and let children pretend to run a movie theatre or drive-in theatre.
4. Play library after a visit to a library. Collect books, set out reading tables, and put up bookshelves. Provide the librarian with a desk or a counter, a stamp and stamp pad, cards, and a telephone. Paste card pockets in the books.

Art Centre

- 1. Easel painting: Let the children mix colours or add black and white to make shades and tints.
- 2. Stained glass: Paint with tempera on clear cellophane and hang paintings in a window to let light shine through them.
- 3. Paint with tempera on aluminum foil or foam trays.
- •• 4. Drip painting: Use two parts salt and one part flour to three parts water. Add powdered tempera for desired colour. Drip from a brush onto paper.
- •• 5. Spatter painting: Place small items found on the observation walk on a piece of paper and spatter paint over them. Children might use small stones, leaves, flowers, twigs, pine cones, seeds, or feathers.
- ••• 6. Mural painting: Put large sheets of paper on a wall or the floor and let the children paint or colour what they saw on the observation walk.
- •• 7. Make a collage using different shapes and colours of paper, yarn, ribbon, or items found on the observation walk.
- ••• 8. Encourage older children to make a "movie" about a pet. Together, write a story and glue a series on a long strip of shelf paper. Thread the movie through slots in a carton "movie screen."

   NOTE: See Chapter 27, Colour in My World, for many other suggestions. When possible, take easels, play dough, and a carpentry workbench outdoors. If weather does not permit working outdoors, place easels near the discovery centre, where live pets and plants can serve as inspiration to young artists.

Learning and Language Materials Centre

Commercially made games and materials

1. *Puzzles:* Colourful and visually stimulating puzzles. Be sure to have some puzzles with knobs for younger children.
2. *Construction and manipulative toys:* coloured pegboards. Pegboards with illuminated pegs. Inexpensive binoculars. Plastic magnifying glasses of different sizes. Magnifying glasses on stands, available in most science stores. Microscopes.
3. *Outdoor toys:* Prisms for observing the colours in sunlight (suitable for older children).

   NOTE: Be sure to remind the children not to look directly at the sun.

The children try to identify objects that are hidden under the cloth by looking at the shapes. The teacher uses open-ended questions as clues. The theme is "fun at the beach": the fish on the bulletin board, made by the children, and the shells relate to the theme.

Teacher-made games and materials

NOTE: For detailed descriptions, see Learning Games in Part 1.

1. *Look and see:* Use several objects of different colours or shapes.
2. *I see something, what do you see?*
3. *Who's missing?*
4. *Guess who?*
5. *Match-them.*
6. *Sorting and grouping by association:* Sort by size, shape, and colour.
7. *Alike, different, and the same.*
8. *Wallpaper dominoes:* Dominoes can be made using blocks of wood and wallpaper scraps. Cut a board that is 5 cm wide and 2.5 cm thick into pieces 10 cm long. Glue 5 cm by 5 cm pieces of wallpaper to the blocks to make a set of dominoes. [Source: Adapted from Debelak, M., et al. *Creating Innovative Classroom Materials for Teaching Young Children.* San Diego: Harcourt Brace Jovanovich, 1981.]
■ Try to choose wallpapers with textures that a visually impaired child can feel. Textures dominoes may also be used in games with all children covering their eyes. If you can obtain sleepmasks from airlines, they make excellent blindfolds.

Book Centre

••• Aliki. *My Five Senses.* New York: Crowell, 1962.
   • Asch, Frank. *I Can Blink.* Toronto: Kids Can Press, 1985.
   • Astrop, Caroline, and John Astrop. *Chatterbooks: Senses: See.* St. John's: Breakwater, 1991.
••• Brown, Margaret Wise. *Walk with Your Eyes.* Danbury, CT: Watts, 1979.
  •• Domanska, Janina. *What Do You See?* New York: Macmillan, 1974.

•• Emberly, Ed. *Green Says Go.* New York: Little, Brown, 1968.

••• Fiday, Beverly. *Eyes, Ears, Nose & Mouth.* Cincinnati: Standard, 1986.

• Fisher, Leonard Everett. *Look Around! A Book about Shapes.* Markham, ON: Penguin, 1986.

• Hoban, Tana. *Look! Look! Look!* New York: Greenwillow Press, 1988.

• ———. *Look Again.* New York: Macmillan, 1971.

• ———. *Take Another Look.* New York: Greenwillow Press, 1981.

•• Jonas, Ann. *Round Trip.* New York: Greenwillow Press, 1983.

••• Keats, Ezra Jack. *Goggles.* New York: Macmillan, 1969.

•• Lionni, Leo. *Little Blue and Little Yellow.* New York: Pantheon, 1969.

••• Littler, Angela. *What Can You See?* Englewood Cliffs, NJ: Messner, 1988.

• Livermore, Elaine. *Find the Cat.* Boston: Houghton Mifflin, 1973.

• Lundell, Margo. *What Does Baby See?* New York: Putnam, 1990.

•• MacLachlan, Patricia. *Through Grandpa's Eyes.* New York: Harper & Row, 1980.

•• Newth, Philip. *Roly Goes Exploring.* New York: Collins, 1981.

•• Parramon, J.M., and J.J. Puig. *Sight.* New York: Barron, 1985.

• Patrick, Denise, and Lewis Patrick. *What Does Baby See?* New York: Western, 1990.

•• Pluckrose, Henry. *Seeing.* Danbury, CT: Watts, 1986.

•• Polland, Barbara Kay. *The Sensible Book: A Celebration of Your Five Senses.* Millbrae, CA: Celestial Arts, 1974.

•• Price, Matthew. *Do You See What I See?* Toronto: Kids Can Press, 1985.

•• Raskin, Ellen. *Spectacles.* New York: Macmillan, 1972.

•• Reuter, Margaret. *My Mother Is Blind.* Chicago: Children's Press, 1974.

•••• Rice, Melanie, and Chris Rice. *All About Me.* New York: Doubleday, 1987.

• Stinson, Kathy. *Red Is Best.* Toronto: Annick Press, 1982.

•• Wolfe, Ashley. *Only the Cat Saw.* New York: Dodd Mead, 1985.

 # Planning for Group Time

NOTE: All music, fingerplays, poems, stories, and games listed here may be used at other times during the session as appropriate.

Music

Songs

Please see "Let's Take a Walk" at the end of this chapter.

From *Do Your Ears Hang Low?*, Glazer
"Lavender's Blue," p. 60
"Long-Legged Sailor," p. 72

From *Eye Winker, Tom Tinker, Chin Chopper*, Glazer
"Jenny Jenkins," p. 42
"The Little White Duck," p. 46

From *Elephant Jam*, Sharon, Lois, and Bram
"Jenny Jenkins," p. 122

From *The Goat with the Bright Red Socks*, Birkenshaw and Walden
"These Are My Eyes, Eyes, Eyes," p. 3

From *More Piggyback Songs for Infants and Toddlers*, Warren
"When I Look into the Sky," p. 22
"Oh Rainbow, Oh Rainbow," p. 28
"Mr. Oil," p. 92

From *Sally Go Round the Sun*, Fowke
"Monkey See and Monkey Do," p. 17

From *Stepping Along in Music Land*, Murray
"My Five Senses," p. 1
"Coloured Sticks," p. 33
"Little Green Man," p. 42
"Colour Song," p. 44
"Make a Rainbow," p. 46

From *What Shall We Do and Alee Galloo!*, Winn
"Two Little Blackbirds," p. 39

Records and Cassettes

Bob Homme. *The Giant Concert of Concerts Presents the Friendly Giant.* (A & M Records)
"Ribbon Concert"

Bob Schneider. *When you Dream a Dream.* (Capital Records)
"In the Morning"
"Over the Rainbow"

Fingerplays and Poems

From *Don't Eat Spiders*, Heidbreder
"Sun, Sun," p. 9

From *Finger Rhymes*, Brown
"Grandma's Spectacles," p. 6
"Where Is Thumbkin?" p. 10
"Whoops! Johnny," p. 21

From *A New Treasury of Children's Poetry*, Cole
"Little Black Bug," p. 23

From *The New Wind Has Wings*, Downie
"Windshield Wipers," p. 78
"Indian Summer," p. 100

From *Read Aloud Rhymes for the Very Young*, Prelutsky and Brown
"Hide and Seek Shadow," p. 25
"Look," p. 25
"Poor Shadow," p. 25
"Yellow Butter," p. 67

From *Round and Round the Garden*, Williams
"Clap Your Hands," p. 45
"Ten Little Fingers," p. 18

From *Where the Sidewalk Ends*, Silverstein
"Colours," p. 24

....

I HAVE SO MANY PARTS TO ME

I have two hands to clap with *(clap)*
One nose with which to smell *(sniff)*
I have one head to think with *(tap head)*
Two lungs that work quite well. *(take a deep breath)*
I have two eyes that let me see *(point to eyes)*
I have two legs that walk *(walk in place)*
I have two ears that help me hear *(cup hands to ears)*
A mouth with which to talk. *(point to mouth)*

....

BEAR HUNT

(Leader gives a line — others repeat. Pat thighs in rhythm.)

Would you like to go on a bear hunt?
Okay — all right — come on — let's go!
Open the gate — close the gate. *(clap hands)*

Coming to a bridge — can't go over it — can't go under it
Let's cross it. *(thump chest with closed fists)*

Coming to a river — can't go over it — can't go under it
Let's swim it. *(pretend to do crawl stroke)*

Coming to a tree — can't go over it — can't go under it
Let's climb it! *(pretend to climb tree and look around)*
No bears! *(pretend to climb down)*

Coming to a wheat field — can't go over it — can't go under it
Let's go through it! *(rub palms together to make swishing noise)*

Oh! Oh! I see a cave — it's dark in here — *(cover eyes)*
I see two eyes — I feel something furry — *(reach out hand)*
It's a bear! Let's go home! *(running motion with feet)*
(repeat above actions in reverse using fast motions)
Slam the gate. *(clap hands)*
We made it!

....

GRANDMOTHER'S GLASSES

These are grandmother's glasses *(make glasses over eyes)*
This is grandmother's cap *(peak hands on head)*
This is the way she folds her hands *(fold hands)*
And puts them in her lap. *(place in lap)*

These are grandfather's glasses *(make glasses over eyes)*
This is grandmother's hat *(flat hand on head)*
This is the way he folds his arms *(cross arms on chest)*
And stands there just like that. *(look straight ahead)*

....

LOOK LOOK

Look up, look down
Look all around
Look here, look there
Look everywhere.

··································

LITTLE BOY BLUE

Little Boy Blue, come blow your horn,
The sheep's in the meadow, the cow's in the corn,
Where's the little boy that looks after the sheep?
He's under the haystack, fast asleep.

Stories

(To read, read–tell, or tell. See Book Centre earlier in this chapter for a complete list.) When choosing stories for reading or telling in this section, choose ones with vivid visual images and visually stimulating pictures. Stinson's *Red Is Best* and Brown's *Walk with Your Eyes* are good examples of books that meet these criteria.

Games

(See Learning Games in Part 1 and Teacher-Made Games and Materials earlier in the chapter for directions.)

1. *Can you remember?*
2. *Look and see.*
3. *I see something, what do you see?*
4. *Who's missing?*
5. *Sorting and grouping by association.*
6. *Sequence.*
7. *Guess who?*
8. *Match-them.*
9. *Alike, different, and the same.*
10. *Easter egg hunt:* Hide plastic or paper eggs or familiar objects for the children to find.
11. *Pin the tail on the donkey:* Older children might enjoy this game.

   ▼ **CAUTION: Use "hold-it" or double-sided tape on paper "donkey tails" instead of pins, or magnets with a magnetic flannelboard.**

Routine Times

1. At snack or meal times, emphasize the use of sight to identify foods. For example: Teacher: "What are we having for a snack?" Child: "Carrots." Teacher: "How do you know they are carrots?" Child: "They look like carrots." Teacher: "What colour (or shape or size) are they?" Child: "Orange and long ..." Teacher: "That's right, our eyes help us tell us what they are."
2. When walking or busing, talk about how our eyes help us to drive or walk safely. Discuss traffic lights, road signs, and median lines. Ask, "Could you drive if you were blind? What would you need to help you walk if you were blind?"
3. When walking or busing children on a sunny day, talk about the use of sunglasses and the sun visor while driving. On a rainy day or late afternoon in the winter, discuss how the use of headlights, streetlights, and windshield wipers helps us to see.
4. At rest time, talk about the eyelids and how we close them to keep the light out and give our eyes a rest.

Large Muscle Activities

1. Take a "magic circle walk." (See Extended Experiences in Chapter 13.)
2. Throw a large ball into a wastepaper basket.
3. Toss beanbags into a box.
4. Try to kick a ball to a fence or to another designated spot.
5. Bowling: Make an alley with large hollow blocks. Use empty dish detergent bottles for pins. Plastic bowling sets are available commercially.
6. Woodworking: Emphasize how we use our eyes when measuring, sawing, and hammering. Buy safety glasses to use at woodworking tables.
7. Try to hit a ball with a bat or small plank (for older children). Plastic bats and whiffle or cloth balls are safest.

   NOTE: This activity requires adult supervision at all times.

8. Johnny can you jump the brook? Put two lengths of rope parallel to each other on the floor about 15 cm apart, and let each child "jump the brook." Increase the distance between the ropes after each child has had a turn.
9. Have the children imitate animals walking (with pictures as cues) to encourage them to translate visual ideas into actions.
10. Bring a bright light into a large room with a white wall and turn off all the other lights. Have the children stand facing the wall with their backs to the light. Then ask them to stand or dance in different ways to see their shadows.
11. Use a 75-watt spotlight (available in most hardware stores) and a screen to create hand shadow people and animals.

Extended Experiences

1. Take a sightseeing trip or walk to see what you can see.
2. Visit an optometrist or have one visit the group.
3. Take slides or movies of the children, or rent commercial films, slides, or filmstrips.

   ▼ CAUTION: Leave a light on in the room or leave the door ajar, in case any children are afraid of the dark.

4. If you have access to a video camera, take a video of the children. Turn off the microphone and ask the children to mime actions for the film (it would be useful to set a theme for the mimes). When you show the video, have the children guess what their friends are imitating.
5. Visit the children's section of your library.
6. Have a blind person with a seeing-eye dog visit your centre.

   ▼ CAUTION: This activity is perhaps best for older children, as the children cannot touch the dog while he is visiting because he is specially trained to see for and guard his owner.

7. Invite a lapidary or rock hound to bring a black light and some fluorescent rocks and minerals to be viewed in a dark room.
8. After a heavy snowstorm, go outside and look for all the colours you can find in the snow.

■ If you have a visually impaired child in your group, invite one of the child's friends (not an adult) to be the child's guide on this walk. Ask the guide to help the child feel the snow and to tell the child about the colours in the snow. Do not worry about the visually impaired child's concept of colour; through the perceptions of the seeing child, the non-seeing child will begin to understand colours associated with objects, although not the concept of colour itself. Variations on this "buddy system" can be used in most visual activities.

9. Go on a colour treasure hunt. On a walk, have the children hunt for all the things they can collect that are a particular colour. When you return from the walk, display the "treasures" and talk about how all of the objects are one colour, even though they are many different shades of that colour.

Teacher Resources

Pictures and Displays

☐ Display pictures of eyes, or people looking at things.
☐ Display pictures of a blind person with a seeing-eye dog.
☐ Display an eye chart on a wall.
☐ Display things we use with our eyes: mirror, magnifying glass, telescope, microscope, kaleidoscope, or slide viewer.

Books and Periodicals

Canadian Association of Optometrists publishes many picture books and pamphlets. Often these are available from your local optometrist.

Caplan, Theresa, and Frank Caplan. *The Early Childhood Years: The 2 to 6 Year Old.* Toronto: Bantam, 1983.
Cole, Joanna. *The Magic Bus Inside the Human Body.* Richmond Hill, ON: Scholastic, 1989.
Liepman, L. *Your Child's Sensory World.* New York: Dial Press, 1973.
Martin, Paul D. *Messengers to the Brain: Our Fantastic Five Senses.* Washington, DC: National Geographic Society, 1984.
Patrick, Denise. *Look Inside Your Body.* New York: Putnam, 1989.
Rivlin, Robert. *Deciphering the Senses: The Expanding World of Human Perception.* New York: Simon & Schuster, 1984.
Smith, Kathie B., and Victoria E. Crenson. *Rand McNally Question Books: The Senses.* New York: Macmillan, 1986.
Sully, Nina. *Looking at the Senses.* Batsford, UK: David and Charles, 1982.
Suzuki, David. *Looking at Senses.* Don Mills, ON: Stoddart, 1986.

Films and Videos

NOTE: Check with your distributer about public performance rights.

Body Talking. National Film Board, 1983.
My Friends Call Me Tony. National Film Board, 1975.
Sound of Sunshine, Sound of Rain. Hallinan Plus Productions (released in Canada by Marlin Motion Pictures), 1984.
Whazzat? Manitoba Education and Training Instructional Resources Library, 1975.

Community Resources and Organizations

☐ Optometrist.
☐ Nurse — school nurse may lend you an eye chart.
☐ Local office of the Canadian National Institute for the Blind.
☐ Children's librarian at local library.
☐ Check with local rock and mineral club for a lapidary or rock hound.
☐ Parent with a video camera or Polaroid camera.
☐ Photographer.

Let's Take a Walk

Donna Wood

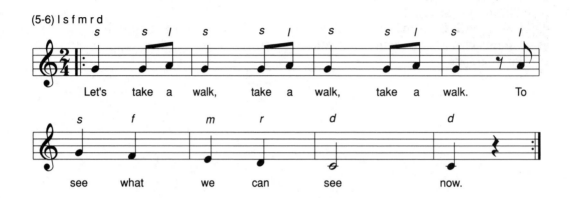

Formation: When the children can step with the beat and are ready to move as a group, they are ready to try this game. The children stand along a wall, holding hands.

Game 1: Hold the first child's hand and ask all to watch and follow "so we can sing and walk in a long line." Turn your face and body a little, so you can see where to go. Keep holding hands and "see what we can see."

Game 2: After singing "see what we can see now," everyone stands still and the leader calls out "I can see _____ [e.g., a red shoe]. Can you?" The other children answer "yes" when they can see the object. After everyone has said yes, the leader moves to the back of the line, and a new leader takes over.

3 Sound

Basic Understandings
(concepts children can grasp from this subject)

- [ ] We hear with our ears.
- [ ] We listen to many sounds.
- [ ] We learn many things by listening.
- [ ] Sounds are made by things that vibrate.
- [ ] Sounds are air vibrations that go into the ear.
- [ ] The outside of the ear acts as a funnel to catch vibrations that go into the ear.
- [ ] Some animals hear better than we do; for example, dogs.
- [ ] Some animals hear sounds different from those that we can hear.
- [ ] Some people cannot hear at all; they are deaf. Some are hard of hearing (cannot hear well).
- [ ] Most people who are deaf "hear" by *feeling* sound vibrations (waves).
- [ ] We can recognize some things by the sounds they make — dogs, birds, motors.
- [ ] Some sounds help to warn us of danger — sirens, horns, whistles, bees, rattlesnakes, growling animals, cracks of lightning, thunder.
- [ ] Some sounds help us — alarm clock bells, chimes, voices, telephone bells, doorbells.
- [ ] We can make sounds as well as hear them.
- [ ] Some sounds we like; some sounds we do not like.
- [ ] Some sounds are loud, soft, high, low, pleasant, or harsh.
- [ ] We need to take good care of our ears.

    ▼ CAUTION: When presenting this concept, avoid giving children ideas by telling them, "Don't stick thing in your ears." Instead say, "We must keep our ears clean by washing them. We must not hurt our ears or the ears of other people."

- [ ] Some people who cannot hear "talk" by using sign language; they move their hands in a special way. Sometimes they can read other peoples' lips and can know what they are saying.

Additional Facts the Teacher Should Know

1. People have nerves in the inner ear to relay sound vibrations to the brain. The outer ear acts as a funnel to channel vibrations to the eardrum, which separates the outer ear from the middle ear. Behind the eardrum are three small bones that carry sound to the inner ear, where the balance and hearing organs are found. Each of these organs has a nerve that connects it with the brain.

2. The eustachian tube connects the middle ear with the throat and ordinarily allows a balance of air pressure on both sides of the eardrum.

3. Some people are born deaf. Some become deaf because of injury or nerve damage; others become deaf because of repeated infections that result in scar tissue on the eardrum that interrupts the flow of sound vibrations. When a cold settles in the inner ear (often due to blowing the nose too hard), medicine may be needed to stop the infection. Sometimes it becomes necessary for the doctor to lance the eardrum (puncture a small hole) to relieve the pressure of the infection and allow for drainage so that the eardrum will not burst. While the eardrum heals rapidly, a star-shaped scar may form after the pressure is broken if the eardrum is not lanced. As scar tissue forms with repeated infections a person may become more hard of hearing. Surgery can improve hearing if the cause of deafness is not nerve damage. Alert parents or a doctor if a child develops an earache at school.

4. Some children may be hearing impaired. If a child repeatedly loses interest during story time or does not respond readily to questions, he or she may have a hearing loss. Consult the parents and recommend that the child go to a doctor for examination and testing. Many public health departments will come to a centre to screen children for hearing problems.

Introducing This Subject to Children

1. Play tapes of recorded sounds to see if the children can identify them.

2. Have a variety of sound-producing objects for the children to identify without seeing or touching them; for example, drop objects or make sounds behind a screen.

3. Use a piano or other musical instrument to illustrate the concepts "high," "low," "soft," and "loud." If you use a stringed instrument, demonstrate the vibrations. This can also be done with an open, empty box encircled with several rubber bands.

4. A visitor might play a musical instrument for the children, or a child might bring in a music box to share.

5. Discuss sound when you hear a siren or thunder.

6. Obtain a telephone teaching unit from the telephone company for the children to use, or bring in a homemade telephone for the home-living centre.

   NOTE: Real phones that ring and have a dial tone or a busy signal (but are not connected to a phone line) can often be borrowed at no charge from a telephone company. Children will be able to hear one another through the receiver.

Vocabulary

ear(s)	talk	tone	pleasant
hear	hum	high	harsh
deaf	sing	low	tape-recorder
sound	whistle	loud	telephone
buzz	whisper	soft	stereo
listen	shout	noise	speaker
vibration	ring	silence	microphone

Learning Centres

Discovery Centre

1. Pop popcorn: Listen for the sounds of crackling hot oil and popping kernels.
2. Record children talking or singing on a tape-recorder, and play the tape back.
3. Play previously taped segments of:
   a. Sounds around the house — mixer, vacuum cleaner, doorbell, door shutting, toilet flushing, water running, dryer, washing machine.
   b. Sounds of nature — bird chirping, cricket chirping, dog barking, rain, wind blowing through trees, crunch of leaves.
   c. Street sounds — police whistle, cars, bus, siren, brakes, clatter of garbage can lids.
4. Provide rhythm band instruments for exploring different sounds.
5. Tune bottles or glasses of water to various pitches. Play a tune and let the children experiment (supervise for safety).
6. Make a double set of sound tubes from unbreakable plastic pill bottles or metal or plastic 35 mm film canisters. Fill with various ingredients in varying amounts, such as flour, rice, beans, pebbles, salt, a peachstone, and so on, and then glue the lids on. After shaking the tubes and listening to them, the children can match those that sound alike or arrange them from loudest to softest.
7. Go on a sound scavenger hunt in the playground or on a walk. Ask the children to listen for and identify as many different sounds as possible. Record the sounds using a portable tape-recorder. At group time, play back the tape and ask children to identify the different sounds. The sounds they identify can also be classified in a number of different ways — soft sounds and loud sounds, sounds they like and sounds they dislike, for example.

■ Most children enjoy sitting in one place and listening for sounds. This activity is very effective for physically disabled children when all the children sit in a group and hunt with their ears. Older children enjoy sitting with their eyes closed, hunting for sounds.

8. Set out step bells, tone blocks, and a xylophone for children to try out.
9. Use a tuning fork to help explain vibrations.
10. Examine, operate, and make musical instruments.
11. Examine a typewriter, a see-through music box, or an alarm clock.
12. Examine a stethoscope, and let the children listen to one another's heartbeat.
13. Invite the children to explore a sound tray filled with objects that can be used to make sounds. Include:

bell	coconut shell	tone block and mallet	seashell
feather	gong	eggbeater	castanet
whisk broom	triangle	crisp paper	cotton ball
comb	alarm clock	tissue	

   Prompt the children to compare and classify the different sounds they can make with the objects in the sound tray.
14. Encourage children to compare the sound of items being dropped, struck, or handled; for example, wood against wood, metal against metal, metal against wood, paper being torn and crumpled.

Dramatic Play Centres

Home-living centre

1. Put an alarm clock that ticks loudly in this centre.
2. Encourage the use of the telephone. Make paper cup telephones; put one in this centre and another in the block-building centre or in other dramatic play centres, such as a store or an office. Make sure there is more than one telephone available to encourage co-operative interaction.
3. Invite children to listen for kitchen sounds, such as a wooden or metal spoon stirring different kinds of foods in pans or bowls made of metal, glass, plastic, and so on.
4. Add sound-making tools, such as a toy eggbeater, a small hand sweeper, and a broom. Note the sounds when these are used.

Block-building centres

1. Set out toy fire engines. Encourage the children to build a fire station — either a small one (made with wooden blocks) or one large enough for them to play in (made with hollow blocks). Allow the children to imitate sirens.
2. Set out toy airplanes and encourage the making of runways for takeoffs and landings. Children can imitate the airplane motors.

   NOTE: Other vehicles that are often associated with sounds include ambulances and police cars.

3. Set out other motor and machine accessories.

Other dramatic play centres

1. Make a train from cardboard, wooden boxes, or a row of small chairs. An occasional conductor's call, "All aboard," and piano background sounds for a train whistle or engine will add to the dramatic play. Authentic train whistles are available at a reasonable price from *VIA* Rail.
2. Doctor's office: Set out stethoscopes to give opportunities to listen to heartbeats.
3. Carpenter's shop: Encourage the use of woodworking tools, and invite the children to listen to or describe the sounds their saws, hammers, or sandpaper blocks make.

Art Centre

••• 1. After returning from a sound scavenger hunt, encourage children to make pictures of the sounds they heard during the hunt.
  • 2. Make shakers or rattles from gourds or boxes filled with seeds, rice, or sand. These can be painted. Trial-size plastic lotion bottles can be decorated with contact paper or pictures.
  • 3. Make drums from yogurt or ice cream containers:
     a. Colour or paint each container.
     b. Wind yarn around the outside or cover with wallpaper.
     c. Make a beater by piercing a rubber ball with a sharpened dowel.
 •• 4. Make tambourines: Use bells and paper plates or foil pie plates. Let children paint or crayon the paper plates or glue paper or fabric scraps on the metal plates.
  • 5. Make sand blocks: Glue sandpaper to wooden blocks. You might want to paint the blocks first.

- 6. Make jingle paddles and let children paint them (see Music Accessories in Part 1).
- 7. Decorate cardboard tubes (from paper towels and toilet paper) to use as sound tubes. In group time, have the children sing or hum through the tubes and explore the different sounds they can make with them.
- 8. While children are at the art centre, suggest that they listen to all the sounds they are making while they are working.

Learning and Language Materials Centre

Commercially made games and materials

1. *Construction and manipulative toys:* Include a variety of musical instruments or toys. Be sure that the instruments are durable and that they play notes that are in tune. Best choices are xylophones, drums, maracas, bells, and triangles. Toy pianos are not appropriate; play telephones are.
2. *Outdoor toys:* Metal wind chimes can add a touch of sound to an outdoor playground.
3. *Miscellaneous:* Sturdy cassette tape-recorders for the children to use.

Teacher-made games and materials

NOTE: For detailed descriptions, see Learning Games in Part 1.

These children are listening to and reading a familiar story.

■ A listening centre can be useful for identifying possible hearing impairment in a child. Watch for a child who consistently seems to need a higher playback volume than other children.

1. *Listen and hear.*
2. *Listening:* You may wish to try whispering.
3. *Guess who?* or *Who am I?* Imitate an animal.
4. *Guess what?* or *What am I?* Imitate a tool or machine sound.
5. *Match them:* Match sound tubes (see Discovery Centre earlier in this chapter).
6. *What did you hear?* Recall sounds:
   a. Of a zoo.
   b. Of a kitchen.
   c. Of a street.

Book Centre

••• Arthur, Catherine. *My Sister's Silent World.* Chicago: Children's Press, 1979.

• Asch, Frank. *I Can Roar.* Toronto: Kids Can Press, 1985.

• Astrop, Caroline and John. *Chatterbooks: Senses: Hear.* St. John's: Breakwater, 1991.

••• Bennett, Jill, ed. *Noisy Poems.* Toronto: Oxford University Press, 1987.

•• Berry, Joy W. *Teach Me about Listening.* Danbury: Grolier, 1986.

•• Bloom, Freddy. *The Boy Who Couldn't Hear.* London: The Bodley Head, 1977.

••• Brown, Margaret Wise. *The Little Brass Band.* New York: Harper & Row, 1955.

•• ———— . *The Quiet Noisy Book.* New York: Harper & Row, 1950.

• Bruna, Dick. *I Can Make Music.* New York: Methuen, 1984.

•• Curry, Peter. *I Can Hear.* Los Angeles: Price Stern, 1984.

••• Fiday, Beverly. *Eyes, Ears, Nose & Mouth.* Cincinnati: Standard, 1986.

•• Flack, Marjorie. *Ask Mr. Bear.* New York: Macmillan, 1971.

• Forrester, Patricia. *The Magnificent Moo.* New York: Macmillan, 1983.

• Hearn, Emily. *Woosh! I Hear a Sound.* Willowdale, ON: Annick Press, 1983.

• Hutchins, Pat. *The Good Night Owl.* New York: Macmillan, 1972.

••• Isadora, Rachel. *Ben's Trumpet.* New York, Macmillan, 1979.

•• Keats, Ezra Jack. *Whistle for Willie.* New York: Viking Press, 1964.

• Kline, Suzy. *Shhhh!* Niles, IL: Whitman, 1984.

••• Kuskin, Karla. *The Philharmonic Gets Dressed.* Markham, ON: Fitzhenry & Whiteside, 1986.

•• Lemieux, Michèle. *What's That Noise?* Toronto: Kids Can Press, 1989.

••• Littler, Angela. *What Can You Hear?* Englewood Cliffs, NJ: Messner, 1988.

•• nichol, bp. *Once: A Lullaby.* Windsor, ON: Black Moss, 1983.

•• Parramon, J.M. and J.J. Puig. *Sound.* New York: Barron, 1986.

•• Patrick, Denise. *Look Inside Your Body.* New York: Putnam, 1989.

• Patrick, Denise, and Lewis Patrick. *What Does Baby Hear?* New York: Western, 1990.

•• Perkins, A.L. *The Ear Book.* New York: Random House, 1968.

••• Peterson, Jean. *I Have a Sister, My Sister Is Deaf.* New York: Harper & Row, 1977.

•• Polland, Barbara Kay. *The Sensible Book: A Celebration of Your Five Senses.* Millbrae, CA: Celestial Arts, 1974.

•••• Rice, Melanie, and Chris Rice. *All About Me.* New York: Doubleday, 1987.

• Scarry, Richard. *Splish Splash Sounds.* New York: Western, 1986.

• Shine, Deborah. *The Pudgy Noisy Book.* New York: Putnam, 1988.

•• Showers, Paul. *How You Talk.* New York: Crowell, 1967.

•• ———— . *The Listening Walk.* New York: Crowell, 1961.

••• Spier, Peter. *Gobble, Growl, Grunt.* Garden City, NY: Doubleday, 1971.

•• Stecher, Miriam, and Alice Randall. *Max the Music Maker.* New York: Lothrop, 1980.

••• Stevenson, James. *Clams Can't Sing.* New York: Greenwillow Press, 1980.

•• Wells, Rosemary. *Noisy Nora.* New York: Dial Press, 1973.

•••• Wolf, Bernard. *Anna's Silent World.* New York: Lippincott, 1977.

• Ziefert, Harriet. *Little Bunny's Noisy Friends.* New York: Puffin, 1990.

• ——— . *Baby Ben's Bow-Wow Book.* New York: Random House, 1984.
•• Zion, Gene. *Harry and the Lady Next Door.* New York: Harper & Row, 1960.

Planning for Group Time

> **NOTE:** All music, fingerplays, poems, stories, and games listed here may be used at other times during the session as appropriate.

Most group-time activities make use of sounds through listening, singing, and talking. Choose activities that emphasize sounds and having fun with sounds.

Music

Songs

Catch the Popcorn if You Can

by Jean Warren

(tune: "This Old Man")

C
Watch me pop in the pan.
F   G7
Try to catch me if you can,
       C   F   C
While I hop and pop and jump to and fro.
G7   C G7 C
Try to catch me as I go.

(As a second verse, have the children sing just the word "pop" as they hop around the room. This song can also be sung while you are making popcorn.)

From *More Piggyback Songs for Infants and Toddlers*, Warren
"I Hear the Animals," p. 73
"Farm Sounds," p. 80
"Can You Clap?" p. 84
"Old Volcano," p. 90

From *Sally Go Round the Sun*, Fowke
"Oranges and Lemons," p. 31
"Do Your Ears Hang Low?" p. 139

From *Stepping Along in Music Land*, Murray
"Five Senses," p. 1 (Book I)
"Strike Up the Band," p. 8 (Book I)
"Ten Little Notes," p. 58 (Book I)
"Mr. Clock," p. 1 (Book II)

Rhythms and Singing Games

1. All tapes and songs are appropriate for listening to sound. Use your favourites and point out high and low sounds, loud and soft sounds, fast and slow tempos, rhythms, and moods (e.g., happy, sad, dreamy, excited). Use a piano, xylophone, autoharp, and tone bells to demonstrate sounds, tempo, and moods.
2. Rhythm band: Use all instruments that are available and any good marching tune (e.g., "Little Brass Band").
3. Using rhythm band instruments separately:
   a. Bells: "Sleigh Ride" or "Jingle Bells."
   b. Drums: Any good marching music or authentic Native Canadian music.
   c. Sand blocks: "I've Been Working on the Railroad."
4. Listening and moving to interpret music: Have the children move to the following pieces of classical music, listening for the suggested mood:
   ☐ "Brahm's Lullaby," Strauss.
   ☐ Any waltz by Strauss.
   ☐ Any march by Sousa.
   ☐ "Pomp and Circumstance March," Elgar.
   ☐ "Papageno's Aria," Mozart.
   ☐ "Ein Fogelfanger Bin Ich, Ja," Mozart.
5. Echo games: Sing a short melody, make sounds, or play tapes of sounds, and invite the children to imitate, identify, or describe the sounds.
6. Rhyming words: Older children enjoy stringing together rhyming words to make collaborative nonsense rhymes. Start with words that have many possible matches, such as cat, mat, rat ... Extend the activity by having the children chant their own nonsense rhymes to a beat.
7. Matching pitch: Sing a child's name high or low, and ask the child to sing it back in the same way. Do not correct a child's singing; instead, label the way he or she sang (for example, "You sang your name on a high note"). Then sing the name in the same pitch as the child.

Records and Cassettes

Bob Homme. *The Giant Concert of Concerts Presents the Friendly Giant.* (A & M records)
"Band Concert"
"Buzzy Concert"
Raffi. *The Corner Grocery Store.* (Troubadour Records)
Bob Schneider. *When You Dream a Dream.* (Capitol Records)
"Band of Songs"
"Grandpa's Song"
Sharon, Lois, and Bram. *Smorgasbord.* (Elephant Records)

Fingerplays and Poems

From *Hand Rhymes*, Brown
"Here Is the Beehive," p. 14
"Quack, Quack, Quack," p. 22

From *Let's Do Fingerplays*, Grayson
"Clap Your Hands," p. 10
"Thing That Go" (series), pp. 21–28
"Hickory Dickory Dock," p. 31
"Kitty, Kitty," p. 42
"Raindrops," p. 47

"The Finger Band," p. 86
"Noise Makers" (series), pp. 86–90
"I Am a Fine Musician," p. 87
"Hammering," p. 88
"Shake, Shake, Knock, Knock," p. 88
"Balloons," p. 89
"Pound Goes the Hammer," p. 89

From *Mischief City*, Wynne-Jones
"Talking," p. 6
"They Are Having a Party Downstairs," p. 19
"The Vacuum Monster," p. 27

From *Read Aloud Rhymes for the Very Young*, Prelutsky and Brown
"Whistling," p. 6
"Chook, Chook," p. 42
"Quack, Quack," p. 43
"A Little Talk," p. 43
"Ears Hear," p. 84

From *Round and Round the Garden*, Williams
"Clap Clap Hands," p. 10
"Knock at the Door," p. 30
"I Hear Thunder," p. 37

Stories

Choose stories for reading aloud that have lots of interesting sounds and rhythms in the words, such as Scarry's *Splish Splash Sounds* or Hearn's *Woosh! I Hear a Sound*.

Games

(See Learning Games in Part 1 and Teacher-Made Games and Materials earlier in this chapter for directions.)

1. *Guess Who?* and *Guess What?* Imitate animal sounds and tool sounds.
2. *Listening:* Use play telephones; guess who's on the other phone.
3. *Listen and hear:* Have some objects that make noise behind a screen, such as an alarm clock, a bell, a rattle, an eggbeater, or crumpled paper.
4. *Sally says/Sam says:* Crow like a rooster, bark like a dog.
5. *What did you hear?* A language-development game for discovering sounds; ask children what sounds they could hear if they were in the county, at the seashore, in the city, or in a park.

Routine Times

1. At meal or snack times, serve crunchy foods like carrot sticks, celery sticks, crisp crackers, or dry cereal.
2. At meal or snack times, talk about chewing quietly with the mouth closed and not slurping beverages and soups.
3. At pickup time, suggest moving as quietly as possible without talking, and occasionally walking on tiptoe.
4. At rest time, listen for sounds when sitting or laying on blankets outside or with windows open, when weather permits.

5. At rest time, use one of the suggested records or cassettes (see p. 126) or play a quiet lullaby.
6. When walking or busing, listen for sounds — birds, sirens, hammers.
7. When playing outside, make note of sounds — a squeaky trike, a chirping cricket, an approaching helicopter, the thud of a falling block, and so on.

Large Muscle Activities

1. Take a listening walk outdoors and listen for sounds made by animals, insects, people, machines, bells, and sirens.
2. Organize a marching band.

Extended Experiences

1. Invite a parent or a musician to bring a musical instrument and play it for the children.
2. Visit a school during band, orchestra, or choir rehearsal. Arrange with the teacher in advance to select two or three short pieces that the children would enjoy. Perhaps the band or choir could practice and play one or two pieces that the children know best (if music is provided to them in advance). A ten-minute program is sufficient. Also ask that some of the instruments be played separately and identified for the children.
3. Borrow a telephone company teaching unit and talk about how to answer the telephone, how to dial the telephone, and how to lay the receiver down carefully. Younger children should be taught not to play with the telephone, and older children should be encouraged to learn their own telephone number.

 # Teacher Resources

Pictures and Displays

☐ Display pictures of cars and of things that make sounds, such as animals, clocks, machines, and bells. Ask children to imitate the different sounds.
☐ Display a few musical instruments.
☐ Tune drinking glasses to various pitches by filling them with varying amounts of water.

Books and Periodicals

(See the list of music books in the Core Library in Part 1.)

Caplan, Theresa, and Frank Caplan. *The Early Childhood Years: The 2 to 6 Year Old.* Toronto: Bantam, 1983.

Cole, Joanna. *The Magic Bus Inside the Human Body.* Richmond Hill, ON: Scholastic, 1989.

Liepmann, L. *Your Child's Sensory World.* New York: Dial Press, 1973.

Martin, Paul D. *Messengers to the Brain: Our Fantastic Five Senses.* Washington, DC: National Geographic Society, 1984.

Rivlin, Robert. *Deciphering the Senses: The Expanding World of Human Perception.* New York: Simon & Schuster, 1984.

Smith, Kathie B., and Victoria E. Crenson. *The Rand McNally Question Books: The Senses.* New York: Macmillan, 1986.

Films and Videos

NOTE: Check with your distributor about public performance rights.

Band Concert. Walt Disney (released in Canada by Magic Lantern Films), 1935.
Body Talking. National Film Board, 1983.
Harry and the Lady Next Door. Barr Films (released in Canada by Visual Education Centre), 1989.
The Mole and the Music. Kratky Films, Prague (released in Canada by International Tele-Film), 1974.
Noises in the Night. Stephen Bosustow Productions (released in Canada by BFA Educational Media), 1969.
A Sense of Sound. National Film Board, 1986.
The Sound Collector. National Film Board, 1982.
Sylvester. Screenscope (released in Canada by International Tele-Film), 1973.
Sylvester: the Mouse with the Musical Ear. Golden Book Films (released in Canada by Omega), 1972.
Why Mosquitoes Buzz in People's Ears. Kratky Films, Prague (released in Canada by Weston Woods), 1984.

Community Resources and Organizations

- ☐ Local telephone company — borrow a teaching unit.
- ☐ Local school band, orchestra, or choir director.
- ☐ Church organist.
- ☐ Hearing-aid companies (often give free ear charts and pamphlets).
- ☐ Canadian Hearing Society.
- ☐ Canadian Association of the Deaf
- ☐ Canadian Amateur Musicians Association.

4 Taste

Basic Understandings
(concepts children can grasp from this subject)

☐ We taste through parts of our tongues called taste buds.
☐ Each food has a particular taste.
☐ Some foods taste sweet, sour, salty, or bitter. Some foods combine these tastes.
☐ We may add flavouring to a food when preparing it to make it taste better.
☐ The flavour of a food or a drink is a combination of the way it tastes and the way it smells.
☐ We like the taste of some foods; we dislike the taste of other foods.
☐ Sometimes we have to get used to a new taste by trying it several times. We may learn to like the taste.
☐ Every family has different favourite foods.

Additional Facts the Teacher Should Know

1. For the senses of smell and taste, people need the olfactory nerves in the nose and the taste buds on the tongue. People have difficulty with taste discrimination when their olfactory nerves or their taste buds are not properly developed. The senses of smell and taste are based on a sensitivity to chemicals. Different nerve endings are sensitive to particular chemical stimuli; for example, salts, sugars, or acids. Some children are born without a sense of taste or a sense of smell, either of which will affect their ability to discriminate flavours.

2. Most young children do not have a keen sense of taste and therefore do not require as much seasoning in their food. The way the food is displayed and the size of the serving can affect children's attitudes toward eating and trying new foods. Try to serve foods from the four food groups in an attractive manner. Keep the portions small. With new foods, expect only one bite. If foods are served family-style, children gain independence in serving themselves and can more easily express their food taste needs. Sometimes the texture of a food affects a child's attitude toward it.

3. Encourage children to learn to like different foods by inviting parents to come and help make simple recipes that are favourite family foods. Consult your public health department about laws regulating the preparation of foods in your centre. Encourage the children to keep preparation surfaces sanitary, to keep hands clean while cooking,

and to handle equipment safely. For recipe books, see Teacher Resources at the end of this chapter. (For related information and activities, see Chapters 5, 6, and 27.)

4. All activities in this chapter are well-suited for use with children who have special needs. Having tea parties and sharing foods generally encourages children to socialize with one another.

5. Food is a critical part of the identity of many families. In some cases, food is one of the few links a family can maintain with its cultural roots. In large cities, it is possible to find the ingredients for foods from around the world. This becomes more difficult in smaller cities and towns. As educators, we can enhance the educational experience of all children by being aware of the food preferences of all their families. Food can be a basis for program planning throughout the year, as we encourage children to explore new tastes.

▼ **CAUTION: Many children have special diets for health or religious reasons. Be sure you are aware of any dietary restrictions before planning any of the activities in this section.**

Introducing This Subject to Children

1. Prepare a favourite food that has a distinctive flavour and odour.
2. Introduce a story about food, such as *Bread and Jam for Frances* by Russell Hoban.
3. Have a tasting party.
4. Have a parent visit the school and bring or prepare a typical food from his or her culture.

Vocabulary

taste	salty	bad	seasoning
taste bud	bitter	tart	salt
tongue	spicy	cold	pepper
sweet	hot	pleasant	cinnamon
bland	flavour	unpleasant	sugar
sour	good	delicious	

Learning Centres
· ·

Discovery Centre

1. Make a milk shake. Add chocolate, strawberry, vanilla, or banana flavouring.
2. Make a pitcher of lemonade or unsweetened fruit drink. Have the children taste it before and after adding sugar.
3. Make popcorn. Have the children taste it with and without salt.
4. Mix cinnamon and sugar. Sprinkle the mixture onto enriched white toast or raisin toast.
5. Provide a shaker full of sugar and a shaker full of salt. Let the children shake a little of each onto their clean hands and taste them. Talk about how the tastes are different.
6. Melt bitter chocolate. Have the children taste it before and after adding sugar.

7. Bake pumpkin cupcakes. Let children taste some of the ingredients and the final product.
8. Mix a muffin batter. Add blueberries to some of the batter, chopped dates or nuts to some, peanut butter to some, and mashed banana to some. Compare the flavours before and after baking.
9. Compare the flavours of cooked and uncooked foods and the flavours of fresh and canned foods.
10. Have a tasting party: Set out bite-size portions of a variety of foods that have distinctive flavours — salty, sweet, sour, bitter, spicy, and bland. Let children match cheese shapes with corresponding cracker shapes. To stimulate discussion, consider colour, texture, and odour when providing foods for the children to taste; for example, orange carrot coins, green pickle slices, yellow cubes of cheese, red radish roses, candy orange slices, shavings of bitter chocolate. Serve grapefruit juice, pink lemonade, and chocolate mild to drink.

▼ CAUTION: Before serving foods to children, be aware of any food allergies and special diets in your group.

This cheerful poster was made by the teacher to show children the connection between print and their daily routine. It outlines the responsibilities of parent volunteers in the centre, and the daily snack menu can be posted with it.

Dramatic Play Centres

Home-living centre

1. Encourage the preparation of pretend foods in this centre.
2. Collect empty food boxes and cans (make sure all sharp edges are covered with layers of tape) to put on the shelves.
3. Hang pictures of people preparing and eating foods. Include pictures of workers who serve, sell, grow, deliver, cook, prepare, or handle food or food products.
4. Allow the use of weak tea or a fruit drink with pretend meals.
5. Provide utensils and ingredients to make no-cook foods; for example, thin slices of cheese cut with a cookie cutter, dates rolled in sugar, instant puddings, no-bake cookies, or candy.

Other dramatic play centres

1. Set up a bakery at snack time and let the children "buy" their snacks. Provide a variety of cookies, rolls, or muffins. Provide hats and aprons for the bakers and servers, and "money" for the customers. A cash register will also be needed.
2. Set up an ice-cream stand for snack time. Provide a choice of ice creams or sherbets to be scooped into cones or dishes. Offer a choice of fruits to put on top.
3. For snack or meal time, set up a cafeteria that offers a variety of raw vegetables, crackers, dry cereals, fruits, sandwiches, and drinks. TV trays, a cash register, and play money will be needed.
4. Make banana freeze for a snack. Peel ripe bananas and freeze them for 24 hours. With the children watching, place the frozen bananas in a blender or food processor and process until the bananas are smooth and fluffy (the texture should be the same as soft ice cream). The bananas will change texture and the blender will make different sounds during blending. Children find it fun to watch and then eat the results.

Art Centre

NOTE: Many teachers are using foods (such a dried pasta and instant pudding) for art activities. In a time when there are food banks in most major cities, these activities are inappropriate, as they give children the message that food is cheap and disposable. The following activities do not use foods in recognizable form, except for cooking and eating activities.

- 1. Save coloured water from boiling brown onion skins (yellow) and red onion skins (purple) for the children to use as watercolour paints.
- 2. Prepare some coloured salt (pickling or table salt) by mixing it with dry or liquid tempera. When dry, let children paint pictures with thinned glue and sprinkle on the desired colours to make textured paintings.
- 3. Make a book of food pictures cut from magazines. Write captions with what children say about their choices of pictures as they cut and paste them.

  NOTE: For younger children, you might provide precut or preselected pictures from which to choose.

- 4. Save seeds and eggshells from food preparation at the beginning of the week to be dried out. Use as collage materials later in the week for an extended experience.
- 5. Offer a variety of art media in the colours of foods tasted or cooked during the day, so children will have the colours they need to tell about their experiences through art.
- 6. Provide gummed geometric shapes for children to make a "lick and stick" picture. Discuss the taste of the glue with the children.

Learning and Language Materials Centre

Commercially made games and materials

1. *Puzzles:* Puzzles that show a variety of foods or people preparing foods.
2. *Small toys for imaginative play:* Plastic foods and cooking utensils. Try to find foods that look realistic and are non-toxic. Sturdy toy stoves and refrigerators — do not buy any electric toys, as they require very close supervision and discourage independent play.
3. *Outdoor toys:* Child-size gardening equipment for planting a small garden in the playground. Choose equipment that is strong enough to be useful and small enough for small hands.
4. *Flannelboards:* A number of flannelboard kits on food and nutrition are available.

Teacher-made games and materials

NOTE: For detailed descriptions, see Learning Games in Part 1.

1. *Name it:* Have a tray of fresh fruits and vegetables available. Identify the foods by name and have the children taste and smell them. Ask the children to close and cover their eyes, and have them identify a fruit or vegetable by taste alone. This game is best played at snack time.
2. *Look and see:* Make flannelboard cutouts of foods that have different tastes. Ask children which is missing — salty, spicy, sweet, or sour foods?
3. *Chew, lick, and taste:* Select appropriate foods to illustrate different tastes.
4. *Sorting and grouping by association:* Categories could be salty, sweet, spicy, or sour. Use labelled boxes, a flannelboard, or a cardboard game board divided into sections with pictures of foods — for example, a carton of salt, a piece of candy, a peanut, a pickle — glued in each section.
5. *Guess what?* Describe a food, making sure to include its taste. For instance, say, "It is yellow, smaller than an orange, and tastes sour. What is it?"

Book Centre

NOTE: Select one of the foods mentioned in a book for the children to taste before, during, or after the story.

••• Aliki. *A Medieval Feast.* Toronto: Fitzhenry & Whiteside, 1983.
•• ——— . *My Five Senses.* New York: Crowell, 1962.
••• Allington, Richard L., and Kathleen Krull. *Tasting.* Milwaukee, WI: Raintree, 1980.
•• Andrews, Jan. *Fresh Fish and Chips.* Toronto, Women's Press, 1973.
••• Armitage, Rhonda. *The Lighthouse Keeper's Lunch.* New York: Deutsch, 1979.
• Astrop, Caroline, and John Astrop. *Chatterbooks: Senses: Taste.* St. John's: Breakwater, 1991.
••• Berry, Joy W. *Teach Me about Tasting.* Danbury, CT: Grolier, 1986.
••• Buchanan, Joan. *Nothing Else but Yams for Supper!* Windsor, ON: Black Moss, 1988.
••• Burningham, John. *Avocado Baby.* New York: Crowell, 1982.
•• Curry, Peter. *I Can Smell, I Can Taste.* Surrey, UK: World's Work, 1982.
• de Paola, Tomie. *Pancakes for Breakfast.* New York: Harcourt Brace Jovanovich, 1978.
••• ——— . *The Popcorn Book.* New York: Holiday, 1978.
• Gelbard, Jane. *My Eating Book.* New York: Putnam, 1989.
• Greenaway, Kate. *A — Apple Pie.* New York: Warne, 1987.
••• Hoban, Russell. *Bread and Jam for Frances.* New York: Harper & Row, 1964.
••• Lottridge, Celia. *One Watermelon Seed.* Toronto: Oxford University Press, 1986.
•••• MacEwen, Gwendolyn. *The Chocolate Moose.* Toronto: New Canada, 1981. (Read–Tell)
• Mayer, Mercer. *Frog Goes to Dinner.* New York: Dial Press, 1974.

••• McCloskey, R. *Blueberries for Sal.* New York: Viking Press, 1948.

•• Morris, Ann. *Bread, Bread, Bread.* New York: Lothrop, Lee & Shepard, 1989.

••• Orbach, Ruth. *Apple Pigs.* New York: Philomel, 1981.

• Oxenbury, Helen. *Eating Out.* New York: Dial Press, 1983.

•• Parramon, J.M., and J.J. Puig. *Taste.* New York: Barron, 1985.

•••• Pasternak, Carol, and Alan Sutterfield. *Stone Soup.* Toronto: Women's Press, 1975.
    (Read–Tell)

•• Patrick, Denise. *Look Inside Your Body.* New York: Putnam, 1989.

••• Polland, Barbara Kay. *The Sensible Book: A Celebration of Your Five Senses.* Millbrae, CA:
    Celestial Arts, 1973.

• Poulet, Virginia. *Blue Bug's Vegetable Garden.* Chicago: Children's Press, 1973.

•• Rayner, Mary. *Mrs. Pig's Bulk Buy.* New York: Macmillan, 1981.

••• Rice, Eve. *Benny Bakes a Cake.* New York: Greenwillow Press, 1981.

•••• Rice, Melanie, and Chris Rice. *All About Me.* New York: Doubleday, 1987.

••• Robart, Rose. *The Cake that Mack Ate.* Toronto: Kids Can Press, 1986.

••• Spohn, Kate. *Ruth's Bake Shop.* New York: Orchard, 1990.

• Tetherington, Jeanne. *Pumpkin, Pumpkin.* New York: Greenwillow Press, 1986.

• Vincent, Gabriel. *Breakfast Time, Ernest and Celestine.* New York: Greenwillow Press,
    1985.

••• Wallace, Ian, and Angela Wood. *The Sandwich.* Toronto: Kids Can Press, 1985.

•• Watson, Clyde. *Tom Fox and the Apple Pie.* New York: Crowell, 1972.

•••• Wheeler, Bernelda. *I Can't Have the Bannock, but the Beaver Has a Dam.* Winnipeg:
    Pemmican, 1985. (Read–Tell)

•• Ziefert, Harriet. *What Do I Taste: The Five Senses.* New York: Bantam, 1988.

 # Planning for Group Time
• •

NOTE: All music, fingerplays, poems, stories, and games listed here may also be used
at other times during the session as appropriate.

Music

NOTE: Combine the singing of these songs with a sample taste of the foods to which
they refer, or sing the appropriate song as the activity is being carried out, such
as making gingerbread or butter.

Songs

From *Do Your Ears Hang Low?*, Glazer
    "The Donut Song," p. 24

From *The Goat with the Bright Red Socks*, Birkenshaw and Walden
"Those Rumbling, Tumbling Down in the Stomach Junk Food Blues," p. 34
"The Good Food Song," p. 35

From *Sally Go Round the Sun*, Fowke
"Oats and Beans and Barley Grow," p. 14
"My Aunt Jane," p. 122
"Found a Peanut," p. 138

From *Stepping Along in Music Land*, Murray
"Gingerbread Boy," p. 19 (Book I)
"Table Manners," p. 26 (Book I)
"Making Butter," p. 8 (Book II)
"Making Bread," p. 9 (Book II)
"Be a Honey Bee," p. 17 (Book II)

From *What Shall We Do and Alee Galloo!*, Winn
"Pease Porridge Hot," p. 58

Records and Cassettes

Sandy Tobias Oppenheim. *If Snowflakes Fell in Flavours.* (Berandol Records)
Raffi. *The Corner Grocery Store.* (Troubadour Records)
Sharon, Lois, and Bram. *Smorgasbord.* (Elephant Records)

Fingerplays and Poems

NOTE: Most of the following are about food: finding, serving, or eating it.

....

THE ICE CREAM CONE

by Lois Birkenshaw

I'm an ice cream cone,
I was bought today,
But I've been left in the sun
And I'm melting away.

I'm running over the sides,
I'm dripping down, down, down.
Lick me quick!
Before I'm all ... gone.

Have the children imitate the melting ice cream, running slowly over the edges of the cone and finally ending up as a puddle on the floor.

From *Don't Eat Spiders*, Heidbreder
"Nutty Chat," p. 19
"Don't Eat Spiders," p. 23
"Sticky Maple Syrup," p. 29 (also in Chapter 6 in this book)
"The Apple and the Worm," p. 38

From *Mischief City*, Wynne-Jones
"Don't Drink the Bathwater," p. 18
"Invasion from the Planet Pizza," p. 32

From *A New Treasury of Children's Poetry*, Cole
"The Cupboard" p. 38
"Mix a Pancake," p. 39
"Soft Boiled Egg," p. 89
"I Eat My Peas with Honey," p. 104

From *The New Wind Has Winds*, Downie
"Eating Fish," p. 18

From *Read Aloud Rhymes for the Very Young*, Prelutsky and Brown
"The Picnic," p. 31
"The Toaster," p. 35
"Crunch and Lick," p 67
"Yellow Butter," p. 67
"The Meal," p. 68
"Two Sad," p. 68
"Table Manners," p. 69
"Toothsome," p. 69
"Tickles, Tickles," p. 79

From *Round and Round the Garden*, Williams
"Five Fat Sausages," p. 8
"Five Fat Peas," p. 29
"Pat-a-Cake," p. 38
"Here Are the Lady's Knives and Forks," p. 43
"I'm a Little Teapot," p. 44

From *Where the Sidewalk Ends*, Silverstein
"I Must Remember," p. 14
"Pancake?" p. 34
"Boa Constrictor," p. 45
"Peanut Butter Sandwich," p. 84
"Spaghetti," p. 100
"Me Stew," p. 122

....
LUNCH

by Darlene Hamilton

Crunch, munch
There's food for our lunch!
Today we have berries, or you may have cherries,
There's salad with peas, a sandwich with cheese.
Or — a slice of browned roast on your own buttered toast.
Crunch, munch, eat your lunch!

....
TASTES

by Darlene Hamilton

Syrup and honey are sweet.
Pickles and lemons are sour.
Peanuts and crackers a treat
For a snack most any hour!

Stories

(To read, read–tell, or tell. See Book Centre earlier in this chapter for a complete list.) Stories for the taste theme can be greatly varied. Wallace and Wood's *The Sandwich* deals with problems concerning food and culture. Parramon and Puig's *Taste* introduces some scientific concepts about taste.

Games

(See Learning Games in Part 1 and Teacher-Made Games and Materials earlier in this chapter for directions.)

1. *Name it.*
2. *Look and see.*
3. *Listening:* Have one child be the baker with a plate of cookies or other baked goods. Have the baker close and cover his or her eyes. Point to a child, who asks, "Please may I have a cookie?" The baker says, "Yes, you may, _____" and guesses the child, who then takes a cookie. The baker guesses until he or she gets the name correct. The child whose name was guessed then becomes the baker. Continue until all children have had a cookie. VARIATION: Farmer with apples; squirrel with nuts.
4. Sorting and grouping by association.
5. *Guess what?*

Routine Times

1. At snack or meal times, feature foods that can be grouped or classified. For example:
   a. Fruits — apples, oranges, fresh pineapple, bananas, cherries, berries.
   b. Vegetables — carrots, green peppers, cauliflower, celery, peas, corn.
   c. Bread — enriched white, whole wheat, rye, raisin, pumpernickel.
   d. Milk — fresh, canned, powdered, buttermilk, chocolate.
   e. Meat/protein — fish, eggs, wieners, hamburger, pork chops, roast beef.
2. At snack or meal times, combine the serving of food with a dramatic play activity (see dramatic play centres, stories, songs, and poems earlier in this chapter).
3. Offer snacks with different flavours, such as salty pretzels, sour yogurt, sweet grapes, and vegetable crackers. Talk about putting food on the tongue to see how it tastes. Discuss how food tastes different when it is seasoned or when sugar is added.

Extended Experiences

1. Visit a bakery to buy some freshly baked rolls. Take them back to the centre to eat. Or bake your own bread at the centre. Let frozen dough rise and give each child a piece to twist into a design. Identify each child's roll by making a chart of the pan or by labelling the rolls with toothpicks.
2. Invite parents to come and help prepare nutritious snacks or food with the group. Make detailed preparations in advance for food and utensils needed, and simplify procedures for the youngest in the group.
3. Invite a dentist to come and show the children how to brush their teeth and to discuss ways to keep teeth clean and breath fresh.
4. Visit a local farm to see fruits and vegetables growing and being prepared before they are sent to wholesalers.
5. Visit a local fisherman to watch fish being caught before it is sent to stores and processors.
6. Visit a local restaurant for a tour (many fast-food chains offer excellent tours, as long as you do not go at meal times).

Teacher Resources
••••••••••••••••••••••••••••••

Books and Periodicals

Caplan, Theresa, and Frank Caplan. *The Early Childhood Years: The 2 to 6 Year Old.* Toronto: Bantam, 1983.

Cole, Joanna. *The Magic School Bus Inside the Human Body.* Richmond Hill, ON: Scholastic, 1989.

Cooper, Terry Touf, and Marilyn Ratner. *Many Hands Cooking: An International Cookbook for Boys and Girls.* New York: Crowell, 1974.

Ferrier, Shannon. *The Kids' Bakebook.* Toronto: Lorimer, 1986.

———. *Kids in the Kitchen.* Toronto: Lorimer, 1986.

———. *More Kids in the Kitchen.* Toronto: Lorimer, 1986.

Ferrier, Shannon, and Tamara Shuttleworth. *The Kids' Food Cookbook.* Toronto: Lorimer, 1986.

Liepmann, L. *Your Child's Sensory World.* New York: Dial Press, 1973.

Martin, Paul D. *Messengers to the Brain: Our Fantastic Five Senses.* Washington, DC: National Geographic Society, 1984.

Rivlin, Robert. *Deciphering the Senses: The Expanding World of Human Perception.* New York: Simon & Schuster, 1984.

Smith, Kathie B., and Victoria E. Crenson. *The Rand McNally Question Books: The Senses. New York: Macmillan, 1986.*

Sully, Nina. *Looking at the Senses.* Batsford, UK: David and Charles, 1982.

Suzuki, David. *Looking at Senses.* Don Mills, ON: Stoddart, 1986.

Wallace, Ian, and Angela Wood. *The Sandwich.* Toronto: Kids Can Press, 1985.

Films and Videos

NOTE: Check with your distributor about public performance rights.

Body Talking. National Film Board, 1983.

Frog Goes to Dinner. Evergreen/Firehouse Productions (released in Canada by International Tele-Film), 1985.

The Gingerbread Man. Perspective Films (released in Canada by Coronet Instructional Media), 1979.

The Mole and the Lollipop. Kratky Films, Prague (released in Canada by McGraw-Hill), 1971.

Pancakes with Surprises. Phoenix Films (released in Canada by International Tele-Film), 1977.

People Soup. Pangloss Productions (released in Canada by Marlin Motion Pictures), 1971.

Sandwich Stuff. British Columbia Provincial Educational Media Centre (released in Canada by Magic Lantern Films), 1979.

Stone Soup. Weston Woods, 1955.

Three for Breakfast. Walt Disney (released in Canada by Magic Lantern Films), 1947.

Community Resources and Organizations

☐   Home economist, dietitian.

☐   Eye, ear, nose, and throat doctors.

☐   Dentists, dental hygienists.

☐ Milk Marketing Board.
☐ Other food marketing boards.

Government Agencies

☐ Federal, provincial, and territorial ministries/departments of agriculture.

5 Smell

Basic Understandings
(concepts children can grasp from this subject)

- [ ] We smell odours through our noses.
- [ ] We learn about some things by the way they smell.
- [ ] Some things smell good (have a nice odour) and some things smell bad (have a bad odour).
- [ ] We take baths so that we will be clean and smell nice.
- [ ] The smell of smoke tells us something is burning.
- [ ] We can tell some foods by the way they smell; we can sometimes tell what we will be eating at the next meal by the way it smells while it is cooking.
- [ ] Most animals can find things by smelling for them. This helps them find food, their friends, and their enemies.
- [ ] Flowers have a nice odour (perfume) that attracts bees and helps them find the nectar (food) they like to eat.
- [ ] Skunks give off a bad (disagreeable) odour to protect themselves and to drive enemies away.

Additional Facts the Teacher Should Know

1. The senses of smell and taste are based on a sensitivity to chemicals. Different nerve endings are sensitive to particular chemical stimuli; for example, salt, sugar, acids. Because of the position of the olfactory nerve endings high in the inner back part of the nasal passages, it is sometimes necessary to sniff or smell closely to detect a delicate fragrance.
2. The tongue, like the fingers, has a higher number of nerve endings per square centimetre of surface than many other areas of the skin. Being sensitive to chemicals also makes it more highly sensitive to a variety of stimuli. The smell of food enhances its taste (if you hold your nose tightly you cannot taste what you are eating). If food smells bad, it may be a warning that the food is spoiled. Sometimes when children have a cold or are ill, their sense of smell may be hampered. The nostrils have fine hairs inside that help filter dust and particles and keep them from going into the lungs when we breathe.

143

3. Some children are born without a sense of smell, because the olfactory nerve endings located in the nose are not properly developed. Children who do not have a sense of smell also have a poor sense of taste and are unable to distinguish the differences between bland foods in particular. (See Chapters 4 and 16–20 for related activities.)

4. It is a myth that people who are blind or deaf have a better sense of smell. However, by learning to use an intact sense well, children with sensory impairments will have another means of compensating for an impaired sense. All the activities in this chapter are well-suited for use with children who have sight or hearing impairments.

Introducing This Subject to Children

1. Plan to bake gingerbread (use your own favourite recipe), and ask each child to smell the ingredients before they are added.
2. Children may smell an unpleasant odour, such as from a skunk, factory waste, or garbage, or a pleasant odour, such as from flowers or cooking. Discuss the different smells when children are playing outdoors.
3. Set out smelling tubes (see Teacher-Made Games and Materials later in this chapter).
4. Use a sleepmask (wrapped with fresh tissue for each child) to blindfold children, and then ask them to identify a variety of different objects by smell. Be sure to choose objects that can be easily distinguished by their smell.

Vocabulary

odour	aroma	fragrance	unpleasant
smell	scent	perfume	spicy
nose	sniff	delicious	sweet
musty	smoky	pleasant	tongue

Learning Centres

Discovery Centre

1. Take a smelling walk. Talk about the odours you smell and whether they are pleasant or unpleasant.
2. After the smelling walk, talk about smells that are specific to your community.
3. Cooking food is especially good for discovering smells. Bake bread, rolls, muffins, or cinnamon or peanut butter cookies, or make pancakes, waffles, or popcorn.
4. Set out a tray of fresh, washed fruits and vegetables. Identify the foods and let the children touch, smell, and taste them.
5. If possible, observe flowers or flowering trees or bushes nearby. Talk about how bees are attracted by the sweet-smelling scent and how they carry pollen from flower to flower. Watch out for bees.
6. Match smelling tubes (see Teacher-Made Games and Materials later in this chapter).

7. Burn scented candles or incense with different fragrances. Let children say what they think each fragrance smells like.

8. Bring in a vase of flowers or a potted flowering plant. (Make sure these have a distinctive scent. Lilacs and freesia are good choices.)

9. Encourage the children to explore the room to discover how different things smell, even those with no apparent odour, such as leather, rubber boots, wood, some flowers, polished furniture, an aquarium, pet cages, cedar chips, and painted objects.

10. Collect fragrant items for a smell tray. Include leather, fur, cedar, incense, a perfume sachet, foam rubber, a piece of carpet or linoleum, a magazine, newspaper, cotton, tissues, cork, soap, pine cones, and an evergreen twig.

11. Set up smelling boxes. Wash and dry 250 mL milk cartons. Place things with distinctive smells in each carton (for example, a cinnamon stick; pieces of cotton soaked in vanilla extract, perfume, or lemon juice; yeast; garlic; onion; dried mint; peanut butter; cloves; baby powder). Tape the cartons shut (if you wish, you can cover them with coloured contact paper). Use a pin to punch holes in the top of each carton. Encourage the children to explore the smells and then to identify and classify them. They can classify by different criteria; for example, smells that are sweet or sour, smells that are from things that people can or cannot eat, or smells that are pleasant or unpleasant. The materials should last about two weeks if you store them in a refrigerator when they are not in use. They should be set out about an hour before you plan to use them to bring them to room temperature and maximize the smells. [Source: Based on an idea in Debelak et. al. *Creating Innovative Classroom Materials for Teaching Young Children*, San Diego: Harcourt Brace Jovanovich, 1981.]

▼ **CAUTION: Remember that some children may be allergic or sensitive to some smells or foods. Before choosing items for centres, check on any allergies or dietary restrictions.**

Trying new foods is a multisensory experience that involves sight, smell, taste, and touch.

Dramatic Play Centres

Home-living centre

1. Encourage children to pretend to bake and cook. Have play dough available for baking in the housekeeping corner. You could comment on how good the baking smells.
2. Provide a dressing table with empty plastic bottles of perfume, lotion, and cream for playing dressup.

   ▼ **CAUTION:** Be sure containers are unbreakable and empty.

3. Put a bouquet of real flowers on the table.
4. Set out a small carton of scented tissues.

Block-building centre

1. Encourage fire-engine play by saying, "I smell smoke. I think there is a fire over here. Please come and put it out!"
2. Suggest that children build a fishing boat. Talk about how it smells.

Other dramatic play centres

1. Set up a florist shop with artificial flowers, plastic corsages, and plants (add a touch of perfume to these articles to make them more authentic). Provide a cash register, a pencil and pad, a telephone table, and chairs.
2. Set up a perfume store, adding appropriate fragrant items, or a spice store.

   ▼ **CAUTION:** *Make sure all items are unbreakable and all bottles are empty.*

3. Set up a bakery (see Dramatic Play Centres in Chapter 4, Taste).

Art Centre

1. Save coloured water from boiling brown onion skins (yellow) and red onion skins (purple) for the children to use as watercolour paints.
2. Make your own paste and add fragrant edible essences, such as almond extract or oil of wintergreen. Use in the art centre when paste is required.
3. Have the children make a collage of pictures of things they like to smell.
4. Printing with vegetables can be fun. Use inedible ends, rinds, or sections of vegetables with a distinct odour used by the cook in the past week; for example, green peppers, cabbage, and onions. Use a vegetable as you would any other printing tool, dipping it in paint and then stamping it on paper.

Learning and Language Materials Centre

Commercially made games and materials

Miscellaneous: Scratch and sniff stickers and scented washable markers.

   NOTE: Many of the items listed in Chapter 4, Taste, are also usable in this section as the two senses are so closely linked.

Teacher-made games and materials

   NOTE: For detailed descriptions, see Learning Games in Part 1.

1. *Sniff and smell.*
2. *Match-them:* Have two sets of smelling bottles filled with distinctive odours for the children to match. Include cloves, peppermint, coffee, cinnamon, garlic, chili, vanilla,

cocoa, perfume. Small, opaque plastic bottles obtained from a pharmacy or unbreakable film tubes are best. Puncture two or three holes in each lid. Glue a circle of nylon fabric inside the lid to keep ingredients from spilling out, but allowing the odour to rise.

3. *Name it:* Show a tray of fresh fruits and vegetables. Identify them by name, and allow children to hold and sniff them. Have children close and cover their eyes or use a sleepmask wrapped with fresh tissue for each child. The children identify the fruits or vegetables by odour alone.

Book Centre

- ••• Aliki. *My Five Senses.* New York: Crowell, 1962.
- •• Allington, Richard. *Smelling.* Milwaukee: Raintree, 1985.
- •• Berry, Joy. *Teach Me about Smelling.* New York: Grolier, 1986.
- • Curry, Peter. *I Can Smell, I Can Taste.* Surrey, UK: World's Work, 1982.
- •• Moncure, Jane B. *What Your Nose Knows!* Chicago: Children's Press, 1982.
- •• Parramon, J.M., and J.J. Puig. *Smell.* New York: Barron, 1985.
- •• Patrick, Denise. *Look Inside Your Body.* New York: Putnam, 1989.
- •• Pluckrose, Henry. *Smelling.* New York: Watts, 1986.
- ••• Polland, Barbara Kay. *The Sensible Book: A Celebration of Your Five Senses.* Millbrae, CA: Celestial Arts, 1974.
- •••• Rice, Melanie, and Chris Rice. *All about Me.* New York: Doubleday, 1987.
- ••• Showers, Paul. *Follow Your Nose.* Toronto: Fitzhenry & Whiteside, 1963.

 # Planning for Group Time

NOTE: All music, fingerplays, poems, stories, and games listed here may be used at other times during the session as appropriate.

Music

Songs

Please see "The Little Skunk" at the end of this chapter.

From *Piggyback Songs for Infants and Toddlers*, Warren
"Scrub a Dub Dub Song," p. 18
"This Is the Way We Take a Bath," p. 19
"Hair Washing Song," p. 19

From *Sally Go Round the Sun*, Fowke
"Oranges and Lemons," p. 31

Records and Cassettes

Bob Homme. *The Giant Concert of Concerts Presents the Friendly Giant. (A & M Records)*
"Seafood Concert"

Sandy Tobias Oppenheim. *If Snowflakes Fell in Flavours.* (Berandol Records)
"Don't Disturb My Olfactory Nerve"

Raffi. *The Corner Grocery Store.* (Troubadour Records)
"The Corner Grocery Store and Popcorn"

Fingerplays and Poems

From *Sally Go Round the Sun,* Fowke
"To Market to Market," p. 101
"Bubble Gum, Bubble Gum," p. 109
"Ink, Ink," p. 110

Stories

Stories about the sense of smell are difficult to find. When choosing stories, find ones that relate to other experiences the children have had in this theme. Curry's *I Can Smell, I Can Taste* is a good choice because it relates the senses of smell and taste and can be tied in with fragrant cooking experiences; for example, cooking cinnamon cookies.

Games

(See Learning Games in Part 1 and Teacher-Made Games and Materials earlier in this chapter for directions.)

1. *Name it.*
2. *Sniff and smell.*

Routine Times

1. Snack or meal time is a natural time to talk about the smell of foods. You might want to plan some foods with distinctive smells, such as popcorn, peanut butter, bacon, cinnamon toast, and chocolate milk.
2. When toileting, talk about the clean, soapy smell of washed hands.
3. When busing or walking, talk about the smell of the earth after rain, the smell of gasoline when stopping for a fill-up, the delicious smells from a bakery, the smell of new-mown hay or grass, or the perfume of flowers or flowering bushes.

Extended Experiences

1. Take a walk and look for things that have an odour. Talk about whether an odour is pleasant or unpleasant.
2. Visit a bakery to see and smell the baked goods. Buy something for a snack.
3. Visit a flower shop or greenhouse. Enjoy the many fragrances and talk about the colours that you see. If possible, buy some flowers to take back to the centre.
4. Make arrangements to visit a neighbour's flower or vegetable garden where the children would be welcome to explore.

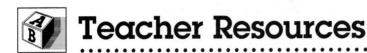 **Teacher Resources**

Pictures and Displays

☐ Put up pictures of noses (people's and animals') with pictures of good things to smell. Include pictures of flowers, perfume, and baked goods.
☐ Display smelling boxes.
☐ Put out fresh flower arrangements. Choose flowers with a characteristic fragrance, such as roses, carnations, and hyacinths.

Books and Periodicals

Caplan, Theresa, and Frank Caplan. *The Early Childhood Years: The 2 to 6 Year Old.* Toronto: Bantam, 1983.

Cole, Joanna. *The Magic School Bus Inside the Human Body.* Richmond Hill, ON: Scholastic, 1989.

Cooper, Terry Touf, and Marilyn Ratner. *Many Hands Cooking: An International Cookbook for Boys and Girls.* New York: Crowell, 1974.

Ferrier, Shannon. *The Kids' Bakebook.* Toronto: Lorimer, 1986.

———. *Kids in the Kitchen.* Toronto: Lorimer, 1986.

———. *More Kids in the Kitchen.* Toronto: Lorimer, 1986.

Ferrier, Shannon, and Tamara Shuttleworth. *The Kids' Food Cookbook.* Toronto: Lorimer, 1986.

Liepmann, L. *Your Child's Sensory World.* New York: Dial Press, 1973.

Martin, Paul D. *Messengers to the Brain: Our Fantastic Five Senses.* Washington, DC: National Geographic Society, 1984.

Rivlin, Robert. *Deciphering the Senses: The Expanding World of Human Perception.* New York: Simon & Schuster, 1984.

Smith, Kathie B., and Victoria E. Crenson. *The Rand McNally Question Books: The Senses.* New York: Macmillan, 1986.

Sully, Nina. *Looking at the Senses.* Batsford, UK: David and Charles, 1982.

Suzuki, David. *Looking at Senses.* Don Mills, ON: Stoddart, 1986.

Films and Videos

NOTE: Check with your distributor about public performance rights.

Body Talking. National Film Board, 1983.
The Clean Club. Churchill Films (released in Canada by McIntyre Media), 1989.
The Mole and the Lollipop. Kratky Films, Prague (released in Canada by McGraw-Hill), 1971.

Community Resources and Organizations

☐ Local florist.
☐ Local bakery.
☐ Fish store or market.
☐ Farmers' market.
☐ Farm.

- ☐ Milk Marketing Board
- ☐ Other food marketing boards.

Government Agencies

- ☐ Federal, and provincial, and territorial ministries/departments of agriculture.
- ☐ Local parks and recreation departments.

The Little Skunk

Traditional

1. Oh, I stuck my head in the lit-tle skunk's hole And the lit-tle skunk said, "Well

bless my soul! Take it out!   Take it out!   Take it out! Re - move it!"   (Oh, I)

2. Oh, I didn't take it out, and the little skunk said,
   "If you don't take it out you'll wish you had.
   Take it out! Take it out!" Pheeew! I removed it.

6 Touch

Basic Understandings
(concepts children can grasp from this subject)

- ☐ We feel with our skin.
- ☐ We may touch things with almost any part of our body (we can feel with our tongues, lips, feet, and arms) but we usually use our fingers.
- ☐ Some things feel soft, hard, smooth, rough, cold, hot, wet, or dry.
- ☐ Our skin helps keep us safe. It tells us when we are near something too hot, when we are too cold, and if we are hurt.
- ☐ We can "feel" happy or sad, sick or well, sleepy or wide awake, energetic or tired.
- ☐ We can feel the sun's rays, cool shade, wind, raindrops, snow, and hail.
- ☐ We can tell if we are moving or standing still. This is called the kinesthetic sense.
- ☐ We can feel pain or discomfort inside our bodies. This is called the organic sense.
- ☐ When people say hello or goodbye, they often touch, shake hands, kiss, or hug.

Additional Facts the Teacher Should Know

1. Touch is a broad term for several senses: those of temperature, pain, and pressure. The sense of touch is made possible by nerve endings scattered through the skin. Some nerve endings make our bodies sensitive to temperatures (cold or heat), others to pain, and still others to sensations from touch or pressure.

2. When stimulated, different nerve endings (receptors) send electrical impulses to the sensory area of the brain. The brain interprets what has happened by the kind of stimulus received and its source. In almost a reflex chain reaction, a message is sent back to the muscles to withdraw from or react to the stimulus, whether it involves extreme temperature, pain, pressure, or some other sensation. Receptors are also found in the mouth and inside the body, on muscles or organs, making possible sensitivity to pressure or internal distress, such as stomach pain, a sore throat, an earache, and so on. Fingers have a higher concentration of nerve endings per square centimetre of surface area and are therefore more sensitive to stimuli and have a better sense of touch than most other areas of the body.

   Some people do not have a sense of touch because of paralysis and may cut or burn themselves without knowing they are doing so. Some people have a very low threshold of pain, which means a little pain is very uncomfortable for them; others have a high threshold of pain, which means they can tolerate a good deal of pain.

3. This theme can provide an appropriate time for introducing streetproofing. While discussing touch, talk about proper and improper touching and help children understand the differences. It is important to prepare this material carefully and to send home complete information on what you have covered so that parents will understand what has been discussed with their children. The Teacher Resources section at the end of this chapter lists sources of information on this topic.

4. Young children with visual impairments are often wary of using their sense of touch. This is logical, as touching and being touched without the information received from visual input can be frightening. It is important that these children overcome their wariness (within reason), as touch is an important source of information about their environment. The activities in this chapter are useful for helping to develop the sense of touch. Remember the potential wariness of visually impaired children, and be sure that the activities are fully explained and do not frighten them.

5. Many children who are physically disabled will sit back and observe their world rather than explore it to the best of their abilities. The activities in this chapter encourage exploration and are well-suited to these children.

Introducing This Subject to Children

1. Fill a box or bag with items for children to feel and identify. Use a commercially made feel it box or make your own (see the instructions on p. 157).
2. While they play outdoors, encourage children to explore sand, rocks, bark, mud, water, ice, snow, twigs, fresh and dry leaves, sprouts, buds, seeds, roots, and shells through touch.
3. Make a feel book with different kinds of fabrics or materials, such as sandpaper, corduroy, satin, velvet, leather, and fur.

Vocabulary

rough, smooth	many, few	furry	soapy
hard, soft	big, little	bumpy	satin
cold, hot	sleepy, awake	finger	velvet
limp, crisp	tired, peppy	feel	fur
wet, dry	sick, well	touch	corduroy
happy, sad	sticky, slick	prickly	sandpaper
thick, thin	heavy, light	skin	cardboard

Learning Centres

Discovery Centre

1. Provide objects that have been warmed with a heating pad or cooled in a refrigerator for the children to feel.

2. Make or buy a feel book with animals or other figures made of such materials as silk, corduroy, sandpaper, smooth contact paper, and cotton. Identify the materials and help the children feel the differences and describe them. Use adjectives such as soft, furry, slippery, shiny, smooth, and rough.

3. Make or buy a feel it box. Place two each of 10 cm squares of various fabrics and materials in the box, and ask children to match the samples without looking. VARIATIONS: The task might be to retrieve two identical objects by feeling a concealed group of items; to match a concealed item with a visible item; to match a concealed item with one selected from a visible group.

4. Place a tub of warm water and a tub of cold water side by side. Have children put one hand in each tub of water. Add liquid detergent to the warm water for another feeling. Have towels available to dry hands. VARIATION: In season, add ice or snow to the cold water.

5. Let children explore a variety of items in a touch-and-feel tray to compare texture, size, mass, number, and consistency by touch. Encourage the children to discover how each item feels, first with bare hands and then wearing rubber or cotton gloves. Include:

fur (soft, furry)	brushes (bristly, soft)
coil (springy, cold)	pine-cone (prickly, rough)
bark (rough, bumpy)	fabrics (offer variety)
shells (smooth, hard)	wood (smooth, hard)
carpet (soft, stiff)	plastic (smooth, flexible)
cactus (prickly, sharp)	styrofoam (smooth, scratchy)
yarn ball (soft)	sandpaper (scratchy, rough)
cotton (soft, light)	foam rubber (spongy, soft)
feather (soft, light)	paper (crisp, soft, smooth)
rope/twine (scratchy)	metal (cold, smooth)
cellophane (crisp, thin)	

6. Encourage children to observe the different ways people greet one another, such as shaking hands, kissing, hugging, or nodding.

7. Allow children to explore a stringed instrument or a horn with valves. Demonstrate and talk about how instruments are played using fingers or the mouth. Note how musicians often "feel" for keys, strings, or valves without looking at them.

8. Conceal familiar objects in socks and have children feel and name them; for example, a pocket comb, a clothespin, a fork, etc.

Dramatic Play Centres

Home-living centre

1. Children can wash doll clothes in warm, soapy water and rinse them in cool, clear water. Talk about the temperatures of the tubs of water and how the soap feels. Hang the clothes up to dry, and ask how they feel before and after drying. Talk about the various fabrics.

2. Children can wash dolls and dry them with big bath towels.

3. Pretend the dolls are sick and have a fever. Do their foreheads feel hot? Take their temperature and call the doctor. Give sponge baths to lower their temperature.

4. Put blankets and sweaters on the dolls when they are cold.

Block-building centre

1. Set out wooden and plastic cars.

2. Provide props of different textures that could be added to the children's constructions (for example, pieces of carpet, foam packing chips, wood shavings, shredded paper).

3. Talk about how blocks feel — warm, smooth, curved, square.

After hiding a variety of objects in the picnic basket, the teacher invites the children to identify one object by touch. This activity develops problem-solving skills.

Other dramatic play centres

1. Provide woods of various textures at the woodworking bench. Talk about rough and smooth. Provide sandpaper for smoothing the various objects made by children.
2. Set up a clothing store. Hang dressup clothes on rolling clothes racks or clothes trees. Have a hat bar, a shoe department, and a glove and scarf counter. Talk about the various fabrics and textures of the clothes. A full-length mirror and small hand mirrors will encourage discussion of the clothes: How do they look and feel? A cash register, paper bags, and play money are needed, too. Boxes and shopping bags would also be useful.

Art Centre

- 1. Paint with tempera on corrugated paper or sandpaper to make textured paintings.
- 2. Paint eggshells with tempera. When dry, use a rolling pin to break them into chips to make a collage.
- 3. Make a sand painting: With fingers, a paintbrush, or cotton swabs, paint a design on paper with paste or white glue. Colour sand with tempera. When it is dry, place in containers with holes in the top. Shake sand onto the wet glue designs and then shake excess sand onto newspaper to reuse.
- 4. Fingerpaint with various media, such as liquid starch or whipped soapsuds. Add powered tempera for colour, and sawdust or salt for different textures.
- 5. Dip chalk in water or liquid starch, and colour on sandpaper.
- 6. Make play dough (see the recipes on pp. 30–31). Use rock salt for a grainier texture. Let children measure and feel the ingredients during preparation.

••• 7. With fingertips, draw designs in a tray of salt.

•• 8. Have children experiment with potter's clay.

••• 9. Gather leaves and other objects while taking a "feeling walk." Make a crayon rubbing by placing a sheet of thin white paper over one or more objects and rubbing the paper with the side of the crayon (remove paper from used crayons or use block crayons for this). Any interesting material, such as wire screen, coarse-grained wood, nylon mesh, coins, or paper clips, may also be used.

•• 10. Make a collage of textured materials, such as eggshells, yarn, corrugated cardboard, and buttons.

•• 11. Woodworking: Use hammer, saw, and sandpaper to make a wood design or just experience the feeling one gets when using these tools.

Learning and Language Materials Centre

Commercially made games and materials

1. *Construction and manipulative toys:* Montessori graded cylinders, tactile letters and letter cards, flannelboard cutouts, rocks, shells, and fossils.
2. *Outdoor toys:* Sandbox toys.
3. *Miscellaneous:* Sand and water-play tables.

Teacher-made games and materials

NOTE: For detailed descriptions, see Learning Games in Part 1.

1. Make a feel it box: Cut a hole in two sides of a sturdy cardboard box so a child cannot see in but can put a hand through each hole. Put pairs of fabric swatches of different textures, cut into 10 cm squares in the box; for example, two pieces of sandpaper,

Play dough (made by the teacher) is fun to use and helps children investigate the sense of touch (you will find recipes for play dough on pp. 30–31).

velvet, satin, corduroy, vinyl, cardboard, carpet, linoleum, and cork. Children reach in and match a pair by touch.

2. *Name it:* Use many different types of textured objects.

3. *Look and see:* Using a screen or a box, put several items that can be identified by touch out of sight, letting children see them first. Remove one item and have the children decide, by touching the remaining items, which one is missing.

4. *Sorting and grouping by association:* Provide several objects made of fur, leather, plastic, or cloth, and let children group them.

5. *Alike, different, and the same:* Use squares from *Match-them.* Put two alike and one different square together, and ask children to show you the one that is different. Talk about the differences. Ask children to do this with their eyes closed, or use a small screen or the feel it box. The squares can be alike in colour and shape, but should be different in texture.

Book Centre

- •• Aliki. *My Five Senses.* New York: Crowell, 1962.
- •• ———. *My Hands.* New York: Crowell, 1962.
- • Astrop, Caroline, and John Astrop. *Chatterbooks: Senses: Touch.* St. John's: Breakwater, 1991.
- •••• Baylor, Byrd, and Peter Parnall. *Everybody Needs a Rock.* New York: Aladdin, 1985.
- ••• Brighton, Catherine. *My Hand's World.* New York: Macmillan, 1984.
- • Ets, Marie Hall. *Talking without Words.* New York: Viking Press, 1970.
- •••• Gryski, Camilla. *Hand On, Thumbs Up.* Toronto: Kids Can Press, 1990.
- •• Hoban, Tana. *Is It Rough? Is It Smooth? Is It Shiny?* New York: Greenwillow Press, 1984.
- ••• Holzinthaler, Jean. *My Hands Can.* New York: Dutton, 1978.
- ••• Kline, Suzy, *Don't Touch.* Niles, IL: Whitman, 1985.
- • Kunhardt, Dorothy. *Pat the Bunny.* New York: Western, 1962.
- • Leninson, Riki. *Touch! Touch!* Markham, ON: Fitzhenry & Whiteside, 1987.
- ••• Littler, Angela. *What Can You Feel?* Englewood Cliffs, NJ: Messner, 1988.
- • Martin Jr., Bill, and John Archambault. *Here Are My Hands.* Markham, ON: Fitzhenry & Whiteside, 1987.
- •• McPhail, David. *The Bear's Toothache.* New York: Little, Brown, 1972.
- ••• Munsch, Robert. *50 Below Zero.* Willowdale, ON: Annick Press, 1986.
- ••• Parramon, J.M., and J.J. Puig. *Touch.* New York: Barron, 1985.
- •• Polland, Barbara Kay. *The Sensible Book: A Celebration of Your Five Senses.* Millbrae, CA: Celestial Arts, 1974.
- ••• Ryder, Joanne. *A Wet and Sandy Day.* New York: Harper & Row, 1977.
- ••• Showers, Paul. *Your Skin and Mine.* Toronto: Fitzhenry & Whiteside, 1965.
- ••• Stren, Patti. *Hug Me.* New York: Harper & Row, 1977. (Read–Tell)

Planning for Group Time

NOTE: All music, fingerplays, poems, stories, and games listed here may also be used at other times during the session as appropriate.

Music

Songs

Please see "Hot Potato" at the end of this chapter.

From *The Baby Beluga Book*, Raffi
"To Everyone in All the World," p. 21
"This Old Man," p. 32

From *Elephant Jam*, Sharon, Lois, and Bram
"Michael Finnegan," p. 13
"Arabella Miller," p. 45
"Head 'n' Shoulders, Baby," p. 52

From *Piggyback Songs for Infants and Toddlers*, Warren
"Never Play with Matches," p. 46
"One Blue Square," p. 48
"Toes are Tapping," p. 51
"Good Morning Song," p. 52

From *What Shall We Do and Alee Galloo!*, Winn
"My Hat It Has Three Corners," p. 54

Rhythms and Singing Games

1. Clapping: Use any suitable music with distinct rhythm patterns. Vary the patterns by striking the hands on the thighs or on the floor as well as clapping hands together.
2. Drums: Use fast and slow tempos, and vary the rhythms in patterned beats; for example, clap, clap, clap-clap; or clap, clap-clap, clap; or clap-clap-clap, clap, clap.

Records and Cassettes

Sandy Tobias Oppenheim. *If Snowflakes Fell in Flavours*. (Berandol Records)
"Let's Play a Statue Game"
"If Snowflakes Fell in Flavours"
"Peanut Butter"

Raffi. *The Corner Grocery Store*. (Troubadour Records)
"My Way Home"

Fingerplays and Poems

....

STICKY MAPLE SYRUP

by Robert Heidbreder

Sticky maple syrup
Dripping from your tree
You spread across the Prairies
                    the Maritimes
                         BC
You cover up all Canada
From sea to sticky sea.
Sticky maple syrup
Don't stick all over me.

You ooze right through my window.
You slosh around my bed.
You dribble down my pancakes
                     my waffles
                       and my bread.
You trickle through my hair
To my eyes, my ears, my nose.
You drip behind my knees
And run between my toes.
You fill my shoes with sticky stuff.
You soak my socks right through
My jeans, my shirt, my underwear
Are stuck to me with you.

Sticky maple syrup
I never want to meet
A grizzly bear who's hungry
For my maple syrup feet.
So — sticky maple syrup,
Wherever you may be,
I'll lick you up,
I'll lap you up,
Before you stick to me!

From *Don't Eat Spiders*, Heidbreder and Patkau
"Today and Yesterday," p. 48

From *Mischief City*, Wynne-Jones
"Holes," p. 24

From *Read-aloud Rhymes for the Very Young*, Prelutsky and Brown
"Showers," p. 12
"Little Wind," p. 12
"Mud," p. 13
"Cat Kisses," p. 18
"Slippery Sam," p. 45
"Pussy Willows," p. 57

From *Round and Round the Garden*, Williams
"Clap Clap Hands," p. 10
"Clap Your Hands," p. 45

From *Where the Sidewalk Ends*, Silverstein
"Hug o' War," p. 19
"Rain," p. 40
"Standing," p. 152

Stories

(To read, read–tell, or tell. See Book Centre earlier in this chapter for a complete list.)
The choice of stories to illustrate touch can be great fun, as it is possible to incorporate
movement and cognitive activities into storytime. Baylor's *Everybody Needs a Rock*
can stimulate thinking about how important the things we touch are to us.

Games

(See Learning Games in Part 1 and Teacher-Made Games and Materials earlier in this chapter for directions.)

1. *Together together:* Find your nose, clap your hands.
2. *Sally says/Sam says:* Touch your head, touch your toes.
3. *Did you ever see a lassie?* Pat your knees, rub your elbow.
4. *Follow the leader:* Touch parts of the body.
5. *Reach and feel:* Play this if your group is small enough to avoid a long wait for a turn.

Routine Times

1. At snack or meal times, talk about the coolness of the foods or beverages and the warmth of the cooked foods. A drink may feel cool to your hand when you lift the glass, and cool or warm when it touches your lips, tongue, and mouth.
2. At snack or meal times, provide several food textures and talk about how they feel — smooth like ice cream, rough like carrots and celery, or sticky like peanut butter.
3. When washing hands, talk about the temperature of the water and the slippery soap. Provide a few drops of hand lotion for children who want it.
4. When brushing teeth, talk about how brushing makes the teeth feel clean and smooth.
5. When dressing to go outside, talk about what is appropriate to wear and why. When coming inside on a cold day, talk about the warm room. When coming in on a hot day, talk about the cool air conditioning or the cool breeze from the fan.
6. When busing the children, talk about the use of the heater or air conditioner to make everyone feel as comfortable as possible. Also discuss the use of windows to keep out snow or rain or to let in cool breezes.

Large Muscle Activities

1. Take a feeling walk and have the children collect different objects for their texture. Describe how an out-of-reach object might feel — smooth, rough, shiny, furry, wet, or dry.
2. Allow outdoor water-play in an appropriate season (see Chapter 26, Water around Me, for ideas).
3. Encourage children to dig in the sand. Provide containers for filling. Allow children to dampen sand and use various containers as sand moulds.
4. Let children dig in the mud, make mud pies, or walk barefoot in the mud. Advise parents ahead of time to dress their children in old clothes.
5. Children can play in the snow (see Chapter 12, Winter, for ideas).
6. Children can run in the wind (see Chapter 13, Spring, for more ideas).
7. Take a walk in the rain, with or without umbrellas (see Chapter 13, Spring, for more ideas).
8. Encourage children to roll down a hill or on the grass.
9. Play ball with rubber, plastic, styrofoam, yarn, or nylon stocking balls.
10. Provide horseshoes or plastic, rubber, or rope rings for ring toss/quoits.
11. Play beanbag toss games.

Extended Experiences

1. Take the children to a petting farm or a petting zoo.

2. Bring an animal, such as a rabbit, a cat, a hen, or a turtle, for children to touch (see Chapter 17, Pet Animals, for more ideas).
3. Ask a blind person to visit and bring a book written in Braille. Ask the visitor to explain how Braille is read and how important the sense of touch is.

 # Teacher Resources
. . . .

Pictures and Displays

☐ Hang up pictures of hands doing things; people shaking hands, hugging, or kissing; and interesting things to feel.
☐ Have objects with different textures on a table for children to explore. Include a book written in Braille, if possible, and explain its use.

Games

There are commercial streetproofing games available that are not too alarmist in their presentation of the issues.

Books and Periodicals

NOTE: Check your local library for the latest books on streetproofing. New books are being published all the time, but attempt to choose books that are not too alarmist.

Caplan, Theresa, and Frank Caplan. *The Early Childhood Years: The 2 to 6 Year Old.* Toronto: Bantam Books, 1983.
Cole, Joanna. *The Magic School Bus Inside the Human Body.* Richmond Hill, ON: Scholastic, 1989.

NOTE: Cooking can be a tactile experience.

Cooper, Terry Touf, and Marilyn Ratner. *Many Hands Cooking: An International Cookbook for Boys and Girls.* New York: Crowell, 1974.
Ferrier, Shannon. *The Kids' Bakebook.* Toronto: Lorimer, 1986.
———. *Kids in the Kitchen.* Toronto: Lorimer, 1986.
———. *More Kids in the Kitchen.* Toronto: Lorimer, 1986.
Ferrier, Shannon, and Tamara Shuttleworth. *The Kids' Food Cookbook.* Toronto: Lorimer, 1986.
Liepmann, L. *Your Child's Sensory World.* New York: Dial Press, 1973.
Martin, Paul D. *Messengers to the Brain: Our Fantastic Five Senses.* Washington, DC: National Geographic Society, 1984.
Rivlin, Robert. *Deciphering the Senses: The Expanding World of Human Perception.* New York: Simon & Schuster, 1984.
Smith, Kathie B., and Victoria E. Crenson. *The Rand McNally Question Books: The Senses.* New York: Macmillan, 1986.
Sully, Nina. *Looking at the Senses.* Batsford, UK: David and Charles, 1982.
Suzuki, David. *Looking at Senses.* Don Mills, ON: Stoddart, 1986.

Films and Videos

NOTE: Check with your distributor about public performance rights.

Body Talking. National Film Board, 1983.
A Sense of Touch. National Film Board, 1983.

Community Resources and Organizations

☐   A school for the blind.
☐   Borrow some books in Braille.
☐   The Canadian National Institute for the Blind.

Government Agencies

☐   Federal, provincial, and territorial ministries/departments of social services for information and speakers on streetproofing.
☐   Local police officers (streetproofing).

Hot Potato

Traditional

Key of C Major

Activities

1. The children sit in a circle. One child holds a ball.
2. As the children start to sing, they pass the ball in one direction (decide before beginning whether it will be to the left or right).
3. The child holding the ball at the end of the song is "out."
4. The game is repeated until only one person is left.

Start with a large ball and pass it slowly.

As the children grow more proficient, sing faster and use a smaller and smaller ball.

Do the movements standing or kneeling in a circle, for variation and extra practice in co-ordination.

To train the various senses, use different objects instead of a ball. Have the children close their eyes and recognize the object by touch or smell or hearing alone:

Lumpy beanbag, pass it on. . .
Cold cold ice cube, pass it on. . .
Soft rubber ball, pass it on. . .
Hard rough ro-ock, pass it on. . .
Smooth smooth pla-ate, pass it on. . .

Props can be varied or children can be asked to imagine the feeling of the things they are singing about.

Part 3 **Families**

Introduction

Basic Understandings
(concepts children can grasp from this subject)

What is a family?

- [ ] A family is a group of people who may live together; they usually take care of one another.
- [ ] Some children are born into a family and some are adopted.
- [ ] Some families have several children, some have a few, some have just one, and some have none.
- [ ] Some families have two children born at the same time; these are called twins. Three such children are called triplets, four are called quadruplets, and five are called quintuplets.
- [ ] Some children live with only one parent, guardian, or other person. This could be a father, a mother, a grandparent, an aunt, an uncle, or a friend of the child.
- [ ] A person may live alone or with only a pet.
- [ ] Families may have other relatives besides those living *in* their family group, such as grandmothers, grandfathers, aunts, uncles, and cousins. Sometimes these relatives also live *with* the family.
- [ ] The family group may be changed for many reasons; for example, divorce, death, adoption, (re)marriage, when young people leave to marry, old age, separation caused by hospitalization, military service, term in prison, or job requirements.
- [ ] Each member of a family is special. In some ways family members are alike, and in some ways they are different from one another.
- [ ] Each family has a special beginning and way of life (culture); for example, native Canadian, Korean, Jamaican, Italian, Asian, European, Caribbean.
- [ ] A family is like some families but different from other families.
- [ ] A mother is a woman parent who has a child or children.
- [ ] A father is a man parent who has a child or children.
- [ ] Boys are called sons by their parents. Girls are called daughters.
- [ ] Boys and girls in the same family are called brothers and sisters.
- [ ] Children are called different group names at different ages; for example, infant, baby, toddler, preschooler, kindergartner, school-age child, preteen, teenager, adolescent, or young adult.

What is a home?

☐ A home is a place where a family lives, eats, sleeps, plays, and works.

☐ Families live in many different kinds of homes; for example, single house, apartment, row house, townhouse, condominium, duplex, cottage, igloo, mobile home, tent, houseboat, chalet, cabin, trailer, or penthouse.

☐ Homes may be made from many materials; for example, wood planks, logs, bricks, stones, mud, grass, leaves, branches, sheet metal, stucco, hides, canvas, ice blocks, or concrete blocks.

☐ Homes may be located in a city, town, or suburb; on a farm; in the country; on a river; on an island; in a valley; in a desert; on a mountain; on a reserve; or in the woods.

☐ The space or ground around a home differs in size and form. There may be much space, little space, or no space.

☐ The space around a house may be surfaced, may be bordered by water, or may have ground that allows for grass, flowers, shrubs, or bushes to grow depending on the climate, place, and cost.

☐ A group of homes where families live near one another is called a neighbourhood, settlement, community, commune, or subdivision.

☐ Most homes have one or more rooms, each named for how it is used; for example, bedroom, living room, bathroom, dining room, kitchen, recreation room, utility room.

☐ Often each room in a house has special furnishings to make the family more comfortable and the room more useful.

☐ Family members need a place to live, food to eat, clothes to wear, and people to care for them if they cannot take care of themselves.

Additional Facts the Teacher Should Know

1. The family is the core of the child's life. As teachers, we must remember that the family is the child's primary influence, and we must respect the family and its values. Our role as adults working with young children is to be a resource for the family. The traditional view of the family is changing, but we can still be with children and their families to help them celebrate the joy of family life in a wide variety of forms and cultural traditions.

2. In addition to presenting children with materials that will help them explore their own and other family traditions, teachers may also be called upon to help support children through family crises. The school or centre is often the second place children turn to when they face a crisis. Teachers need to be prepared to support children when they are facing stress in their lives. The section Books to Read with Children lists books that may be used to help children understand a stressful situation. They should be used with care and sensitivity. When possible, a short note should be sent home to the parents describing the content of the books used. This will help the parents answer questions that may arise at home after the children have been read these books. The Teacher Resources section lists books that may help you when you are working with children facing some crisis.

3. Chapters 7 and 8 focus on the enjoyment of varied family lifestyles. Obviously, crisis in the family is not an appropriate educational theme, but to deal effectively with family issues you will need resources for handling children's concerns that cover the entire spectrum of family life.

4. Canadians can be justifiably proud of the rich mixture of cultures that make up our backgrounds. Any educational setting may serve children and families from diverse

backgrounds ranging from people of the First Nations to newly arrived families from Sri Lanka. Children should be encouraged to be proud of their families and their cultures. Rather than pointing out differences from a dominant culture, educators should focus on similarities and celebrate the diversity in their groups. This necessitates a sensitivity to the assorted needs of all the children in your group.

 # Books to Read with Children

New Baby

- Alexander, Martha. *When the New Baby Comes, I'm Moving Out.* New York: Dial Press, 1979.
- Burningham, John. *The Baby.* New York: Crowell, 1974.
- •• Hazen, Barbara. *Gorilla Wants to Be the Baby.* New York: Atheneum, 1978.
- Hoban, Russell. *A Baby Sister for Frances.* New York: Harper & Row, 1964.
- •• Knotts, Howard. *Great Grandfather, the Baby and Me.* New York: Atheneum, 1978.
- von Königslöw, Andrea. *That's My Baby.* Willowdale, ON: Annick Press, 1986.
- ••• Wasson, Valentina. *The Chosen Baby.* Philadelphia: Lippincott, 1977.
- •• Wolde, Gunilla. *Betsy's Baby Brother.* New York: Random House, 1975.

Divorce and Separation

- ••• Brown, Laurene K. *Dinosaurs Divorce.* Boston: Atlantic Monthly Press, 1986.
- ••• Sharmat, Marjorie Weinman. *Sometimes Mama and Papa Fight.* New York: Harper & Row, 1980.
- ••• Steel, Danielle. *Martha's New Daddy.* New York: Delacorte Press, 1989.
- ••• Stinson, Kathy. *Mom and Dad Don't Live Together Anymore.* Willowdale, ON: Annick Press, 1984.
- •• Winthrop, Elizabeth. *Are You Sad, Mama?* New York: Harper & Row, 1979.
- Zindel, Paul. *I Love My Mother.* New York: Harper & Row, 1975.

Moving

- •• Cohen, Miriam. *Will I Have a Friend?* New York: Macmillan, 1967.
- ••• McCloskey, Robert. *Make Way for Ducklings.* New York: Viking Press, 1969.
- ••• Zolotow, Charlotte. *Janey.* New York: Harper & Row, 1973.

People with Special Needs

- ••• Aseltine, Lorraine. *I'm Deaf and It's Okay.* Niles, IL: Whitman, 1986.
- ••• Brighton, Catherine. *My Hands, My World.* New York: Macmillan, 1984.
- •• Brown, Tricia. *Someone Special Just Like You.* New York: Holt, 1984.
- ••• Cairo, Shelley. *Our Brother Has Down's Syndrome.* Willowdale, ON: Annick Press, 1985.
- •• de Paola, Tomie. *Now One Foot, Now the Other.* New York: Putnam, 1981.
- ••• Fassler, Joan. *Howie Helps Himself.* Niles, IL: Whitman, 1975.
- ••• Fox, Mem. *Wilfrid Gordon McDonald Partridge.* Brooklyn, NY: Kane Miller, 1985.
- ••• Lasker, Joe. *He's My Brother.* Niles, IL: Whitman, 1974.
- ••• Powers, Mary E. *Our Teacher's in a Wheelchair.* Niles, IL: Whitman, 1986.

··· Saxe, John Godfrey, and Paul Galdone. *The Blind Men and the Elephant.* New York: McGraw-Hill, 1963.
··· Smith, Lucia B. *A Special Kind of Sister.* New York: Holt, 1979.
··· White, Paul. *Janet at School.* New York: Crowell, 1978.
··· Wolf, Bernard. *Anna's Silent World.* Philadelphia: Lippincott, 1977.
··· ———. *Don't Feel Sorry for Paul.* Philadelphia: Lippincott, 1974.
··· Yolen, Jane. *The Seeing Stick.* New York: Crowell, 1977.

Hospitalization and Illness
• Bemelmans, Ludwig. *Madeline.* Harmondsworth, UK: Penguin, 1977.
···· Howe, James. *The Hospital Book.* New York: Random House, 1981.
·· Rey, M., and H.A. Rey. *Curious George Goes to the Hospital.* Boston: Houghton Mifflin, 1966.
··· Segal, Lore. *Tell Me a Mitzi.* Don Mills, ON: Collins, 1970.
··· Williams, Barbara. *Albert's Toothache.* New York: Dutton, 1974.
·· Wolde, Gunilla. *Betsy and the Chicken Pox.* New York: Random House, 1976.

Death
··· Aliki. *The Two of Them.* New York: Greenwillow Press, 1979.
··· Brown, Margaret Wise. *The Dead Bird.* Reading, MA: Addison-Wesley, 1965.
··· Buscaglia, Leo. *The Fall of Freddy the Leaf.* New York: Henry Holt, 1982.
··· de Paola, Tomie. *Nana Upstairs, Nana Downstairs.* New York: Putnam, 1973.
··· Doll, Elizabeth. *My Daddy Is a Policeman.* Englewood Cliffs, NJ: Prentice-Hall, 1973.
··· Viorst, Judith. *The Tenth Good Thing about Barney.* New York: Atheneum, 1971.

 # Teacher Resources

Child Psychology
Elkind, David. *The Hurried Child.* Reading, MA: Addison-Wesley, 1981.

Interviewing
Evans, D.R., M. Hearn, M.R. Uhlemann, and A.E. Ivey. *Essential Interviewing.* Monterey, CA: Brooks/Cole, 1979.
Garrett, Annette. *Interviewing.* New York: Family Service Association, 1972.
Stierlin, H., I. Rucker-Embden, N. Wetzel, and M. Wirsching. *The First Interview with the Family.* New York: Bruner Mazel, 1980.

Divorce and Separation
Despert, Louise. *Children of Divorce.* Garden City, NY: Doubleday, 1962.
Stuart, I., and E. Lawrence, eds. *Children of Separation and Divorce.* New York: Grossman, 1972.

Hospitalization and Illness

Petrillo, M., and S. Sanger. *The Emotional Care of Hospitalized Children.* Philadelphia: Lippincott, 1972.

Ramos, Suzanne. *Teaching Your Child to Cope with Crisis.* New York: David McKay, 1975.

Death

Furman, Erna. *A Child's Parent Dies.* New Haven, CT: Yale University Press, 1974.

Kübler-Ross, Elizabeth. *On Death and Dying.* New York: Macmillan, 1969.

Zeligs, R. *Children's Experience of Death.* Springfield, IL: Thomas, 1974.

7 Living in Families

Basic Understandings
(concepts children can grasp from this subject)

☐ Some families buy their homes, their food, and their clothes; others may build their homes, grow their food, and make their clothes.

☐ Homes and clothes may also be rented or borrowed.

☐ Some family members need to work to earn money to buy things the family needs, such as housing, food, and clothes (see Chapter 8, Families at Work).

☐ Family members can divide the work at home in many ways:

    a. Sometimes mother *takes care of the children.*

    b. Sometimes father *takes care of the children.*

    c. Sometimes both parents *take care of the children* at different times or at the same time.

    d. Sometimes a guardian, a family friend, or another member of the family, like grandma, *takes care of the children.*

    e. Sometimes a person is employed by the family to *take care of the children.*

    NOTE: Insert *takes care of the house, prepares the food, does the laundry,* and other tasks in place of italicized words above.

☐ Most families have tools and machines to help them work at home (see Chapter 28, Tools and Machines to Use in My World).

☐ Some families own a car that they use to go to work, to school, to shop, to visit friends and relatives, or to transport them to other places they wish to go.

☐ Some families use public transit or walk to get to places they wish to go.

☐ Some families own a truck, a motorcycle, a bicycle, a boat, an airplane, a snowmobile, a van, a motorscooter, a helicopter, or minivan that they use to carry themselves or other people or objects for work or fun.

☐ Families each do some things in their own way; for example, customs, dress, childrearing, and lifestyle. They have certain beliefs and ways of showing these beliefs in their worship and celebrations.

☐ Families celebrate certain days together, with special preparations and plans for things to do. These celebrations often include parties, gifts, and dinners to celebrate birthdays, weddings, Mother's Day, Father's Day, Valentine's Day, anniversaries, special religious days, and other occasions, both happy and sad.

☐ We should try to learn about other people's ways and what they believe so that we can understand and respect them as they are.
☐ Some families have pets that they care for.
☐ Families may do many things together at home; for example, eat, sleep, cook, clean, play, and work.
☐ Families can have good times together at home playing games, singing, or having barbecues.
☐ Families may do many things together away from home, such as shopping, riding, picnicking, walking, and visiting friends, relatives, parks, zoos, and other interesting places.
☐ Some children have two homes, one with their father and one with their mother.

Additional Facts the Teacher Should Know

1. Good early childhood centres encourage the family to share in the opportunities for learning they offer each child. At its best, the home is the primary educator of the child and programs at the centre are supplemental. Therefore, teachers should use interviews, home visits, and background information sheets to help them learn as much as possible about a child and his or her family that is relevant to their teaching job.
2. Canada is made up of many cultures and many lifestyles within these cultures. Divorce, remarriage, adoption, placement in a foster home resulting from death or illness of a parent, and child abuse are just a few of many events that may have far-reaching effects on your children. Children may not have the same last name as their parents. They may not have the same skin colour, culture, or religious background as the family with whom they are currently living.
3. The staff should always be supportive of children in helping them understand themselves, their relationship with their family or the group with whom they are living, their peers, and their need to identify with their own culture. (See Additional Facts the Teacher Should Know in Chapter 1, I'm Me, I'm Special, and the introduction to Part 4, Family Celebrations.)
4. The staff should know:
    a. Where each child lives and with whom.
    b. How many adults are in the home.
    c. How many children there are in the family and their approximate ages.
    d. The blood relationships of others in the family to the child.
    e. How the children in the family relate to one another.
    f. The child's level of skills.
    g. Whether the child is toilet-trained, able to feed himself or herself, able to dress, and able to communicate personal needs.
    h. The language(s) the child speaks.
    i. The ethnic and religious grouping to which the child and family belong.
       The purpose of acquiring this information is to help you assess a child's needs and to assist you with choices related to dealing with behaviour. This information may also help the staff to give support and understanding to a child when it is needed.
5. In your centre's newsletter for parents, include an activities column describing activities the children enjoy at school that can also be done at home. For example, list favourite songs, cassettes, and books; give the recipe for play dough; print the words of a song; describe a game that does not require equipment or several children.
6. Children should be encouraged to take pride in their culture and in their country. Provide opportunities for children to share knowledge and experiences. Accept each child and provide opportunities for each to express feelings, whether happy, sad, angry, hurt, dejected, or anxious.

7. Other chapters in this guide that include related topics are Chapter 1, I'm Me, I'm Special, and Chapter 8, Families at Work.

Introducing This Subject to Children

1. During an individual or group conversation, ask, "Who brought you to school today?" or, "Does your grandmother live nearby?"
2. Post pictures of families doing things together. Invite the children to help you. If this is not possible, take two or three children at a time on a picture walk around the room. Make sure that the pictures show different family groupings and people from the different cultures represented in your centre.
3. Invite further discussion when someone mentions that Mother's Day, Father's Day or a special family occasion is coming soon.
4. Talk about siblings when a brother or sister brings or picks up one of the children.
5. Read a story about a family or about mothers, fathers, babies, or grandparents.
6. Invite further discussion when a child announces that a new baby has been born in the family, or relates a family event.
7. Encourage children to talk about activities that they have done with their families; for example, going to a movie, watching television at home, having a barbecue, playing a game, going skiing, harvesting crops, going hiking.
8. When a child's family has a special visitor in the home, such as a grandparent, invite the visitor to bring the child to the centre and stay for a short visit.

Vocabulary

mother	grandmother	aunt	cousin
father	grandfather	uncle	care for
family	great-grandmother	great-aunt	live with
sister	great-grandfather	great-uncle	share
brother	children	baby	like
stepmother	mommy	home	belong to
stepfather	daddy	husband	love
stepsister	guardian	wife	adoption
stepbrother	foster mother	friend	divorce
godmother	foster father	babysitter	separation
godfather	housekeeper	nanny	foster home
twins			

Learning Centres

Discovery Centre

1. Invite a mother and an infant to visit. Observe the size of the baby's hands, feet, and mouth, and how it eats, sleeps, and is dressed. Encourage the children to ask questions and offer information. Allow touching of baby's feet rather than head or hands for

health and safety reasons. Talcum powder can be dusted on the baby's feet and hands to make prints on a dark piece of paper. Compare baby's prints with prints made of children's feet and hands.

2. Demonstrate the use of a baby bottle and food warmer. This would be especially appropriate when a mother comes to visit with a baby and feeds the infant during snack time. Children can be allowed to taste baby foods at this time. Many nursing mothers and babies are relaxed and natural even in a group setting. Invite a nursing mother to visit your centre to show an alternative to bottle feeding.

3. Compare the texture of puréed foods with the same foods when they are raw or cooked whole. You may wish to purée food in a blender or a simple hand-turned food mill that children can try.

4. Hang a simple map of your area showing where each child lives.

5. Borrow a pair of hamsters, guinea pigs, rats, mice, or gerbils for the children to observe. Let the animals mate and then raise a family.

   ▼ **CAUTION:** Do this only if you can later find a home for the pets. Also be aware that many of these animals eat their young.

6. Talk about animals that mate for life, such as foxes, and those that do not, such as cats or elephants.

   NOTE: Most large birds of prey keep the same mate each year unless one dies. Canada geese and swans do not remate if one mate dies.

7. Learn the names of some bird babies, such as:

chicken — chick	swan — cygnet	owl — owlet
duck — duckling	pigeon — squab	eagle — eaglet
turkey — poult	goose — gosling	

   Learn names of other animal babies (see Part 6, Animals. Children might especially enjoy the poem "The Guppy" in Chapter 17).

8. If a kitchen is available, let the children help make simple drop cookies or rolled cookies. If a kitchen is not available, supply plain cookies, several colours of frosting, and decorations, and let the children decorate the cookies. Eat during a party, snack time, or lunch time. Discuss favourite foods and who cooks in families.

Dramatic Play Centres

Home-living centre

1. Encourage adult/parent role playing by providing dressup clothes and dramatic play props. Consider the interchangeability of props and clothes for males and females.
   a. Parents/guardians: Include aprons, hats, purses, shoulder bags, wallets, wigs, vests, jewellery, shoes, jackets, ties, keys, briefcases, first-aid kit, sleepwear, evening wear, day clothes, lunch boxes, plastic-tool kits, gloves, coats, and boots.
   b. Grandparents: Include golf clubs, tennis rackets, gardening tools, books, eyeglass frames, wigs, sweaters, bedroom slippers, newspapers, magazines, magnifying glasses, and canes. Be careful not to stereotype grandparents as in need of chronic care — many grandparents are active, vibrant people.

   NOTE: All children should be allowed to dress up as they choose.

   c. Babies: Use life-size dolls representing all cultural groups. Dress them in real baby clothes (size 6 months to 1 year). Have lots of blankets. Include a few small hand towels for bathing babies. Allow children to bring a few baby items from the display table to use in the centre with supervision. A cradle, crib, bed, buggy, and rocking chair will also add to the dramatic play possibilities in this centre.

2. Allow children to give washable dolls a bath. Provide washcloths, bath towels, and talcum powder with puff.
3. Allow children to wash and dry doll dishes outdoors if the weather is nice. Provide tea towels, dishcloths, a rack, plastic dishpans, and liquid soap.
4. Encourage children to clean the cupboards, tidy the toy shelves, vacuum the carpet, dust the furniture, and sweep the floor in the home-living centre using dustpans, brooms, mops, dusters, and a toy vacuum.
5. Encourage the children to wash and dry doll clothes and pretend to iron them when they are dry.

> ▼ **CAUTION: Clothes and bedding may need a real washing and ironing by an adult after this.**

6. Allow a simple food to be prepared in the centre.
7. Play tea party. Have children take turns being hosts and visitors. For a special treat, pour water or fruit juice into cups. Cut bread, bananas, or other soft finger foods into small pieces to serve on dishes.

> ▼ **CAUTION: Be sure all dishes and utensils actually used for eating and drinking are sterilized. Paper cups and plates are recommended.**

■ Tea parties provide opportunities for children to socialize.
8. Provide food preparation tools commonly used at home; for example, eggbeater, rubber spatula, rolling pin, measuring cups and spoons. Add play dough to use with these tools.
9. Provide opportunities for children to use rulers, measuring tapes, and plastic hammers, wrenches, and saws to do parents' jobs around the house.

Block-building centre

1. Set out wooden, rubber, or plastic family figures. Try to find figures from different cultures.
2. Add a moving van or label a truck as one.
3. Encourage the use of blocks for building rooms and new houses.
4. Add a camper, a mobile home, a tent, and a variety of boats to encourage recreational play.

Other dramatic play centres

1. Set up a dollhouse adjacent to the block area with movable furniture and multicultural family figures.
2. Hand puppets of multicultural family figures can be used with a three-way play screen or a theatre made of blocks and planks.
3. Arrange for a hat bar with various types of hats to try on. An unbreakable hand mirror, a cash register, play money, and paper bags will encourage participation.
4. Set up a show store with men's, women's, and children's shoes for customers to try on. Add a cash register, play money, chairs, and shoeboxes.
5. Arrange a clothing store with mittens, gloves, shirts, skirts, scarves, purses, jewellery, and other items grouped into areas or on separate shelves. A small coat or hat tree is a helpful addition. Set up a check-out counter.
6. Set up a grocery store. Include shopping bags, a grocer's hat and apron, play money, plastic foods, and empty food cans and cartons among the props.
7. Encourage children to move the home-living centre or set up a second home. Provide cartons to pack, suitcases to carry clothes, and wagons to move the furniture.

> **NOTE:** Choose other family-related facilities, based on your children's experiences and your community; for example, a hamburger stand, a café, or a library (see Dramatic Play Centres in Chapter 8, Families at Work). What you highlight

Old tins have been reused to stock a home-living centre. The tins were carefully prepared by removing all sharp edges, but labels were retained. Boys and girls alike enjoy preparing "friendship soup."

may reflect the visitors your centre has had, trips you've taken, or the interests of the children.

8. Make a tabletop or floor terrain for building a community. Duplicate a terrain similar to one familiar to children. For instance, if you are located in an inner-city area, incorporate more concrete into your model. The illustration on p. 181 allows for play areas, a park, a farm, and a lake. Children will enjoy building homes and stores, driving with small cars or trucks on roads, and adding trees, boats, and animals around the lake, with endless variations. If roads are not too defined, children will have more alternatives in using the space. The terrain is easily stored when folded in half. This activity is best for older children who can work together.

   Cut out two sides of a stereo, desk, or other large carton. Tape the pieces together in the centre, and tape the edges for durability. Paint details with enamel.

   NOTE: Make the tape hinge with masking tape or paper mailing tape *before* painting the surface.

Art Centre

• 1. Doll blankets: With pinking shears, cut 30.5 cm squares from old sheets. Thumbtack to a square of white interior insulation board and let the children decorate them with coloured markers. When dry, remove them from the board and use with box cradles as blankets for dolls (or to take home).

•• 2. Play dough: Use rolling pins and cookie cutters with self-hardening play dough. Bake cookies in the play oven and use for tea parties in the doll corner when they become hard. See the recipe in Part 1.

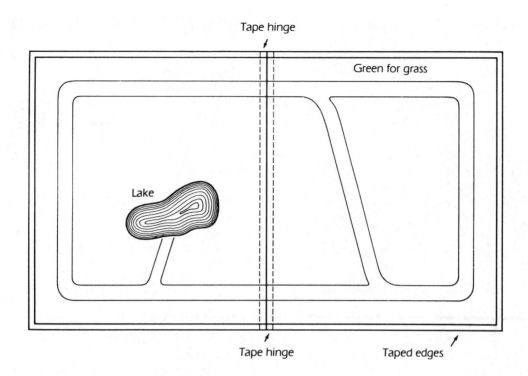

•••• 3. Cutting and pasting: Select many figures from old catalogues to represent mothers, fathers, and different-aged children. If possible, let the children cut around the figures they choose to represent their own family and paste them onto cardboard or another stiff backing. The figures will need to be precut for younger children.

   NOTE: An easy way for older children to cut them out is to outline the figures with felt pens and then to cut along the coloured lines.

•••• 4. Encourage the children to make a gift or a get-well card for a child or staff member when appropriate, as an expression of caring.

•••• 5. Children can make a gift and a greeting card for a special family occasion.

•••• 6. Have children make family albums. Provide sturdy white paper or bristol board (approximately 21.5 cm by 28 cm). Punch three holes along the long side of each sheet. Provide coloured felt cut and punched in the same way as the paper or bristol board, and felt scraps. Encourage the children to draw pictures of their families on one side of each page, leaving the other side blank. Ask the children to tell you about their pictures, and print their stories under the pictures. Then have the children decorate the felt covers. Tie the albums together with wool and send them home with the suggestion that the blank pages be used for family photos.

■ Children from unhappy homes may find this activity upsetting. Be especially aware of these children when completing the activity. Be sure to emphasize the diversity among families, and do not dwell on the media stereotypes of two-parent, financially comfortable families.

Learning and Language Materials Centre

Commercially made games and materials

1. *Puzzles:* Puzzles should include families of a variety of races, cultures, and colours. Be sure to include some puzzles with small knobs for younger children. It is acceptable

to use puzzles with animal families, but be sure to differentiate between the animals and humans.

2. *Dolls and puppets:* Dolls and puppets of people of various ages and cultures can be used to make up different family groupings. Be sure when using dolls in traditional costumes to make it clear to the children that the costumes are usually for special celebrations and are not everyday wear.

3. *Small toys for imaginative play:* Toys that are accurate models of household objects and materials can enhance imaginative play.

4. *Costumes:* Offer a wide variety of costumes and old clothes in the dressup centre. Try to have clothes that are suitable for people of different ages. Be sure the clothes are cleaned frequently and kept in good shape.

5. *Flannelboards:* Most commercial suppliers have excellent flannelboard sets showing different types of families and family activities.

6. *Posters:* Posters of family activities are available from most commercial suppliers. Make sure you are choosing posters that show a variety of families, diversity in family roles, and families having fun together.

Teacher-made games and materials

NOTE: For detailed descriptions, see Learning Games in Part 1.

1. *Name it:* Use diaper, bottle warmer, plastic baby bottle, and pacifier.
2. *Look and see:* Use rattle, pacifier, bath toy, and washcloth.
3. *Reach and feel:* Use plastic baby bottle, rattle, pacifier, soft rubber toy, and cotton ball.
4. *Who am I?* Have the children sit comfortably in a group. Describe a person to them and have them guess who the person is (for example: I have grey hair, my children all live in their own homes, I like to visit my children and grandchildren. Who am I?). After the children make their guesses, ask one or two to act out what the person is like.
5. *What would you do?* Find magazine pictures or sketches that show different family situations and paste them on bristol board (for example, a crying baby, or a mother and child in a kitchen with a broken dish on the floor). Hold up a picture and ask, "What would you do?"
6. *Sorting and grouping by association:*
   a. Set out dressup clothes. Ask children to separate them into various groupings: sleepwear, parents' clothes, baby clothes.
   b. Set out rubber or wooden farm animals and have children find the young that belong to the adult animals; for example, a cow and calf.
7. *Match-them:*
   a. Make sets of picture cards with two each of: family members, baby items, furniture.
   b. Use several pairs of mittens, shoes, socks. Divide into two piles, and let children find the match to the one they choose.
8. *Guess what?* Ask children, "What can a baby do? What can you do that a baby cannot? What can a grown-up do that you cannot?"

Book Centre

NOTE: In your library, look for books about families by Russell Hoban, Lois Lenski, and Joan Lexau, as each has several good books on this subject.

••• Alderson, Sue Ann. *Bonnie McSmithers You're Driving Me Dithers.* Edmonton: Tree Frog Press, 1974.
••• Andrews, Jan. *Pumpkin Time.* Toronto: Groundwood, 1990.

••• Bell, Bill. *Saxophone Boy.* Montreal: Tundra, 1980.

••• Bell, Caroline. *I Love My Dad.* Markham, ON: Fitzhenry & Whiteside, 1988.

••• Bonners, Susan. *The Wooden Doll.* New York: Lothrop, Lee & Shepard, 1991.

•• Bourgeois, Paulette. *Franklin Fibs.* Toronto: Kids Can Press, 1991.

••• ———. *Grandma's Secret.* Toronto: Kids Can Press, 1989.

••• Cairo, Shelly. *Our Brother Has Down's Syndrome.* Willowdale, ON: Annick Press, 1985.

•• Clifton, Lucille. *Don't You Remember?* Markham, ON: Fitzhenry & Whiteside, 1987.

••• de Paolo, Tomie. *Nana Upstairs, Nana Downstairs.* New York: Putnam, 1973.

•• Denton, Kady MacDonald. *Granny Is a Darling.* Toronto: Kids Can Press, 1988.

•• Dumas, Jacqueline. *And I'm Never Coming Back.* Willowdale, ON: Annick Press, 1986.

•• Fahlman, Ruth, and May Henderson. *All Together* (from the series *Hand in Hand: Multicultural Experiences for Young Children*). Don Mills, ON: Addison-Wesley, 1990 (text in Spanish, French, English, and Chinese).

••• Fernandes, Eugenie. *A Difficult Day.* Toronto: Kids Can Press, 1983.

••• Ferris, Sean. *Children of the Muskeg.* Windsor: ON: Black Moss, 1991.

• Flack, Marjorie, *Ask Mr. Bear.* New York: Macmillan, 1971.

•• Galloway, Priscilla. *When You Were Little and I Was Big.* Willowdale, ON: Annick Press, 1985.

••• Gilman, Phoebe. *Grandma and the Pirates.* Richmond Hill, ON: Scholastic, 1990.

••• Greenfield, Eloise. *Grandpa's Face.* New York: Putnam, 1988.

••• Griffith, Helen V. *Grandaddy's Place.* Toronto: Mulberry, 1991.

•• Hertz, Grete Janusz. *The Yellow House.* Willowdale, ON: Annick Press, 1991.

••• Hest, Amy. *The Ring and the Window Seat.* Richmond Hill, ON: Scholastic, 1990.

•••• Hutchins, Hazel. *Ben's Snow Song: A Winter Picnic.* Willowdale, ON: Annick Press, 1987.

••• Hutchins, Pat. *Titch.* New York: Macmillan, 1971.

•• Keats, Ezra Jack. *Peter's Chair.* New York: Harper & Row, 1976.

••• Khalsa, Dayal Kaur. *Tales of a Gambling Grandma.* Montreal: Tundra, 1986.

••• Krumins, Anita. *Who's Going to Clean Up This Mess?* Toronto: Three Trees Press, 1985.

••• Lasker, Joe. *He's My Brother.* Chicago: Whitman, 1974.

••• Laurence, Margaret. *Six Darn Cows.* Toronto: Lorimer, 1986. (Read–Tell)

••• Levinson, Rikki. *I Go with My Family to Grandma's.* New York: Dutton, 1986.

••• Lewin, Hugh. *Jafta.* Minneapolis: Carolrhoda, 1983.

••• Lewis, Robin Baird. *Aunt Armadillo.* Willowdale, ON: Annick Press, 1985.

•• Lim, John. *At Grandmother's House.* Montreal: Tundra, 1977.

••• Marton, Jirina. *Flowers for Mom.* Willowdale, ON: Annick Press, 1991.

•• McKay, Jed. *The Big Secret.* Willowdale, ON: Annick Press, 1985.

••• McPhail, David. *Something Special.* Boston: Little, Brown, 1988.

••• Morgan, Allan. *Daddy Care.* Willowdale, ON: Annick Press, 1986.

••• Munsch, Robert. *Love You Forever.* Scarborough, ON: Firefly, 1986.

••• Munsil, Janet. *Dinner at Auntie Rose's.* Willowdale, ON: Annick Press, 1984.

•• Obed, Ellen Bryan. *Little Snowshoe.* St. John's: Breakwater Press, 1984.

•• Ormerod, Jan. *Moonlight.* Markham, ON: Penguin, 1987.

••• Quinlan, Patricia. *My Dad Takes Care of Me.* Willowdale, ON: Annick Press, 1987.

•• Rockwell, Anne, and Harlow Rockwell. *Happy Birthday to Me.* New York: Macmillan, 1982.

••• Roe, Eilleen. *Con Mi Hermano/With My Brother.* Don Mills, ON: Bradbury Press, 1991.

••• Russo, Marisabina. *A Visit to Oma.* New York: Greenwillow, 1991.

••• Rylant, Cynthia. *The Relatives Came.* Don Mills, ON: Bradbury Press, 1985.

••• Schein, Jonah. *Forget-Me-Not.* Willowdale, ON: Annick Press, 1988.

••• Schwartz, David. *Supergrandpa.* New York: Lothrop, Lee & Shepard, 1991.

••• Stamm, Claus. *Three Strong Women.* Markham, ON: Penguin, 1987.

•• Staunton, Ted. *Simon's Surprise.* Toronto: Kids Can Press, 1986.

••• Steptoe, John. *Daddy Is a Monster . . . Sometimes.* New York: Harper & Row, 1980.

••• Tullock, Richard. *Stories from Our Street.* Toronto: Kids Can Press, 1989.

••• ———. *Stories from Our House.* Toronto: Kids Can Press, 1988.
••• von Königslöw, Andrea. *Catching Problems.* Willowdale, ON: Annick Press, 1990.
••• Waddell, Martin. *Grandma's Bill.* New York: Orchard, 1991.
  • Watanabe, Shigeo. *It's My Birthday!* New York: Putnam, 1988.
••• Watts, Bernadette. *David's Waiting Day.* Scarborough, ON: Prentice-Hall, 1978.
••• Wild, Margaret. *The Very Best of Friends.* Toronto: Kids Can Press, 1991.
 •• Zolotow, Charlotte. *William's Doll.* New York: Harper & Row, 1972.

 # Planning for Group Time

NOTE: All music, fingerplays, poems, and stories listed here may be used at other times
during the session as appropriate.

Music

Songs

Please see "Lots of Fish in Bonavist' Harbour" at the end of this chapter.

From *The Goat with the Bright Red Socks*, Birkenshaw and Walden
"This Is My City," p. 1
"What Makes a House a Home?" p. 20
"Who Is My Neighbour?" p. 21
"What Has this City Got?" p. 22 (substitute names and sites from your own city)

From *More Piggyback Songs*, Warren
"Happy Father's Day," p. 36
"Where Is Daddy?" p. 36

From *Singing Bee*, Hart
"Hush Little Baby," p. 12
"Bye Bye Baby Bunting," p. 14
"Lazy Mary," p. 62
"The Farmer in the Dell," p. 79
"Billy Boy," p. 111

From *Stepping Along in Music Land*, Murray
"My Grandpa," p. 3
"Shopping," p. 6 (Volume II)
"He's My Dad," p. 21 (Volume II)

Records and Cassettes

Anne Murray. *There's a Hippo in My Tub.* (Capitol Records)

Sandy Tobias Oppenheim. *If Snowflakes Fell in Flavours.* (Berandol Records)
"Clearing the Table Is My Job"

Fred Penner. *Special Delivery.* (Troubadour Records)
"My Grandfather's Clock"
"Mail Myself to You"

Raffi. *The Corner Grocery Store.* (Troubadour Records)
"My Way Home"

Bob Schneider. *When You Dream a Dream.* (Capitol Records)
"Grandpa's Song"
"Help Each Other"

Sharon, Lois, and Bram. *Elephant Show Record.* (Elephant Records)
"Go to Sleep Now My Pumpkin"
————. *Smorgasbord.* (Elephant Records)
"Father Papered the Parlour"

Fingerplays and Poems

From *Read Aloud Rhymes for the Very Young*, Prelutsky and Brown
"Mother Cat's Purr," p. 19
"The Old Woman," p. 24
"The Way They Scrub," p. 27
"My Sister Laura," p. 28
"Hamsters," p. 54 (if you have hamsters in the centre)
"Table Manners," p. 69
"Night Fun," p. 70
"Bedtime," p. 70

From *Mischief City*, Wynne-Jones
"Talking," p. 6
"I Must Be Talking Martian," p. 8
"Baby," p. 13
"I Wasn't Angry When I Thought About Maxine," p. 16
"They're Having a Party Downstairs," p. 19
"Monster Parents," p. 28

From *Finger Rhymes*, Brown
"Grandma's Spectacles," p. 7
"The Baby Mice," p. 14
"Five Little Mice," p. 16

From *Round and Round the Garden*, Williams
"My House," p. 14
"Here's a Ball for Baby," p. 39
"Here's the Lady's Knives and Forks," p. 43

From *A New Treasury of Children's Poetry*, Cole
"Rock, Rock, Sleep, My Baby," p. 44
"Two in a Bed," p. 53
"On Mother's Day," p. 163

From *Where the Sidewalk Ends*, Silverstein
"For Sale," p. 52
"What a Day," p. 118
"Me and God," p. 163
"Dreadful," p. 141

From *The New Wind Has Wings*, Downie
"Song for Naomi," p. 80

Stories

The choice of stories about families to read to children should reflect the current interests and concerns of the children and their families and should cover a wide range of feelings. Remember to include stories in which families have fun and also solve problems. For instance, Alderson's *Bonnie McSmithers You're Driving Me Dithers* gives children an opportunity to talk about solving problems related to rambunctious behaviour; Krumins's *Who's Going to Clean Up This Mess?* gives a humorous view of family roles and the sharing of jobs around the house.

Routine Times

1. Let children prepare the daily snack, such as pouring their own milk or juice, peeling and slicing bananas, scraping and cutting carrots, cutting up slices of bread, and washing grapes. All this must be done under close supervision. Use table knives.
2. One day, serve only baby food for a snack. Provide one jar of apricots, plums, peaches, or fruit dessert for each child. Save the jars for paint containers. You may wish to purée your own baby food.
3. For a snack, serve teething biscuits, milk, and baby food. A mother with a baby could be asked to bring some formula so the children could taste it. You may wish to demonstrate using the bottle warmer at this time.
4. Have the children wash off the tables with a damp sponge before and after snack or meal times. They could also straighten the chairs and sweep the floor.
5. When driving or walking with children, point out various homes you see.

Large Muscle Activities

1. Family play: Take or wear dressup clothes outdoors. Set up a house of hollow blocks or large cardboard cartons, a sheet over a jungle gym, or an arrangement of packing boxes. Tricycles and wagons can be family cars or public transit vehicles for going to work, shopping, or taking trips.
2. Encourage taking dolls for a walk in baby carriages or strollers.
3. Woodworking: Let children use the workbench in pairs. Provide play hammers, balsa wood, and large-headed plastic nails.
4. Sand play: In hot weather, use wet sand to bake cookies and cakes. Use orange crates or cardboard cartons for stoves. Have a mud picnic: bake mud pies in the sun and mix seeds and grass with mud for puddings. Sprinkle with sand or decorate with pebbles. Use leaves for sandwiches. Serve to one another or to dolls and pretend to eat.
5. Hang doll clothes washed in the home-living centre to dry outside.
6. Set up a car and truck wash. Use a bucket of water, rags, and lengths of hose.
7. Paint the outside of the centre. Provide large paintbrushes and small buckets of water (empty commercial paint cans with handles work well).
8. Set up a simulated bowling alley with plastic pins and balls.
9. See Dramatic Play Centres for activities that would be suitable to play outdoors when the weather permits.

Extended Experiences

1. Take a trip to visit a child's parent at work.
2. If your centre is in a residential area, take a walk around your block to look at and identify different kinds of housing. Talk about what the homes are made of, the number of floors, and the design, colour, and style. Contrast how they are different,

how some are similar or the same, and how the homes may differ inside — number of family members and their ages, number of rooms, furnishings, and so on.

3. Visit a store that sells clothes, shoes, furniture, kitchenware, appliances, or tools to see where things a family needs are purchased. Choose a store where children will be welcomed in small groups; go at a time when there will be few shoppers.

4. Occasionally it is possible to plan a trip to the home of a teacher or child. Select homes that are different in style or type, and plan a special activity related to the trip, such as exploring a backyard or seeing a pet.

5. Invite a parent with an infant to visit. Discuss what the baby can or cannot do. Does it have teeth? Hair? Fingernails? Why does it cry? What does it eat?

6. Invite grandparents to come and show pictures of themselves as children and recount interesting experiences or stories. Invite them to help with some of the centre activities: read a story; help with food preparations, creative arts, or woodworking; or repair or make a piece of equipment for the children.

7. Invite a parent, especially a father if you do not have a male on your staff, to share a special talent, such as playing a musical instrument, or to show an interesting hobby collection.

8. Have a family dinner at the centre. Invite all family members, including brothers and sisters. Ask each family to bring a favourite family food. Schedule the dinner to start a half hour before closing time for the centre, so that everyone can get to the dinner easily. Theme dinners can also be fun. For example, plan a red dinner. Invite everyone to wear something red and to bring food with red in it.

 # Teacher Resources

Pictures and Displays

☐ Select pictures of various family lifestyles from magazines, showing as many ethnic groups as possible. Mount these on coloured cardboard or construction paper and hang them around the room.

☐ Hang pictures of baby animals, their parents, and their homes.

☐ Show some hospital-made footprints of a baby; also the bracelet that babies and mothers wear for identification.

☐ Display some real baby items near the home-living centre. Include plastic baby bottles, rattles, pacifiers, baby food, diapers, ointments, powder, teething rings, spoons, bottle warmer, brush, plastic pants, soft rubber toys, and bath toys.

▼ CAUTION: Supervise closely so that the children do not actually put the nipples and spoons in their mouths. You will want to reserve the use of the bottle warmer for a demonstration by the teacher or a parent.

Books and Periodicals

Active Learning in the Early School Years. Toronto: Federation of Women Teachers' Associations of Ontario, 1986. (Sections on parents and community)

Parent magazine.

Today's Parent magazine.

Working Mother magazine.

Workshop Models for Family Life Education. New York: Family Service Association, 1977.

The You and Me Series. Scarborough, ON: Nelson, 1986.

Films and Videos

NOTE: Check with your distributor about public performance rights.

All about Me. The Canadian Filmstrip Company, 1987.

An American Tale. MCA Home Video, 1986.

Brave Irene. Weston Woods, 1989.

Cookie Goes to Hospital. Playing with Time, Inc. (released in Canada by Magic Lantern Films), 1981.

Get Ready, Baby's Coming! The Canadian Filmstrip Company, 1987.

Hush Little Baby. Weston Woods.

Learning about Families. The Canadian Filmstrip Company.

Learning about Myself. The Canadian Filmstrip Company, 1987.

Mary of Mile 18. National Film Board, 1981.

Mary Poppins. Walt Disney Home Video, 1964.

Pete's Chair. Weston Woods.

Smile for Auntie. Weston Woods, 1979.

The Tenth Good Thing about Barney. Canadian Learning Co., 1986.

Why Did You Have Dahl for Dinner? Manitoba Education and Training Instructional Resources Library, 1982.

Community Resources and Organizations

☐ Children's Aid Society or child welfare associations.
☐ Family service associations.
☐ Community health centres.
☐ Local cultural organizations.

Government Agencies

☐ Federal Department of Health and Welfare.
☐ Provincial or territorial ministries responsible for social services, such as health or welfare.
☐ Provincial and federal departments of multiculturalism.

Lots of Fish in Bonavist' Harbour

Newfoundland

Sharon, Lois, and Bram

Chorus

Catch a-hold this one, catch a-hold that one, swing a-round this one,

swing a-round she. Dance a-round this one, dance a-round that one,

did-dle-um this one, did-dle-um dee.

Oh!

2. Uncle George got up in the mornin',
   He got up in a wonderful tear.
   He ripped the seat right out of his britches,
   Now he's got no pair to wear,
   Chorus

8 Families at Work

Basic Understandings
(concepts children can grasp from this subject)

- [ ] Some family members need to work to earn money to buy things the family needs, such as food, clothes, and housing.
- [ ] Other family members sometimes work at home as full-time parents and home-makers.
- [ ] People sometimes have trouble finding a job or may lose their job.
- [ ] Some family members work as volunteers outside the home — perhaps even in your centre.
- [ ] Family members can divide the work at home in many ways (see Chapter 7, Living in Families).
- [ ] Some people have a special place to work at home (workshop, studio, office), while other people walk, drive, or commute to work by car pool, train, subway, bus, plane, boat, monorail, van, helicopter, or truck.
- [ ] Some people work at different times of the day and night. Sometimes their time to work changes from day to day, week to week, or month to month (shifts) or they may be on call depending on weather or need.
- [ ] Some people wear special clothes or uniforms when they work to protect their clothes, to keep them safe, or to tell who they are and what they do. Other uniforms are worn to carry tools or to keep workers or what they work with clean.
- [ ] Many people use tools or machines in their work.
- [ ] Some people use animals or work with animals in their jobs.
- [ ] Some people grow their own food, build their own houses, and make their own clothes; others pay someone else to do these jobs for them.
- [ ] Most people are paid for their work outside the home. Some are given money and some are given cheques, which they can cash for money.
- [ ] People can put money or cheques in the bank to keep it safe until they need it.
- [ ] Some people may trade work to get what they want done. One person may paint a house for someone in exchange for having a car fixed.
- [ ] Every worker and job is important. We need everyone to help in a personal way and do what he or she can do best.
- [ ] It is important that each person does a job as well as possible and that he or she tries to do a fair share of the work.

191

☐ We all depend on one another for the things or services we need.

☐ A person who does one kind of work very well is called a specialist.

☐ Jobs can be done by either men or women, if they choose to do those kinds of work and have the ability and training to do them.

☐ Often people have to go to school or take special training to learn how to do their job or to be licensed to do their work.

☐ Some people are taught how to do their job while they work at the job.

☐ Helpers in our community include:

   a. People who help to keep us well: doctors, dentists, nurses, pharmacists, public health officers, exercise instructors, paramedics, nutritionists.

   b. People who build things for us: carpenters, architects, bricklayers, construction workers, developers, engineers, and road, ship, and bridge builders.

   c. People who keep us safe: police officers, firefighters, crossing guards, weather watchers, emergency broadcasters, service-and-rescue patrollers, air traffic controllers, forest rangers, flight attendants, lifeguards, camp counsellors, and water, road, health, food, and equipment inspectors.

   NOTE: An inspector is a person who makes sure things are done or made the right way for our safety and protection.

   d. People who help us to know what is happening to others: teachers, writers, journalists, radio and television announcers, politicians, civil servants, librarians, legislators, ministers, rabbis, priests.

   e. People who fix things: appliance repair persons, utility maintenance workers, plumbers, carpenters, shoe repair persons, car mechanics, electricians, office equipment repair persons, piano tuners.

   f. People who sell or provide things we need: farmers, salespersons, clerks, realtors, grocers, clothiers, hardware merchants, shoe salespersons, retailers, manufacturers.

   g. People who provide entertainment or a place for us to play: park and recreation personnel, movie theatre owners, artists, musicians, actors, dancers, singers, clowns, circus performers.

   h. People who help us when we travel: service station attendants, tour guides, stewards, conductors, bus drivers, travel counsellors, flight attendants, taxi drivers, interpreters, tourist information officers, police officers.

   i. People who plan for food (grow, sell, cook, serve, deliver, prepare, or handle food or food products): farmers, grocery clerks, truckers, produce retailers, frozen food plant personnel, fishermen, harvesters, migrant workers, caterers, restaurant managers, servers, cooks, bakers, meat packers, food packagers, butchers.

   j. People who provide services for us: couriers, bookkeepers, bankers, caterers, drycleaners, laundry workers, tailors, carpet cleaners, car washers, babysitters, movers, taxi drivers, housekeepers, valets, luggage handlers, shippers, hairstylists.

   k. People who make new things: manufacturers of paper, rubber, cars, cards, toys, clothes, auto parts, furniture, plastic, glass, etc.; dressmakers, engineers, inventors, designers, artists, writers, sculptors, builders, carpenters, jewellers, chefs, architects.

Additional Facts the Teacher Should Know

1. People work for many reasons:

   a. To earn money to buy necessities and luxuries for themselves, their families, and their friends.

   b. As an outlet for creativity.

   c. To be of service to society.

    d. To enjoy varied activities.

    e. To produce goods.

    f. For adventure and discovery.

    g. To meet other people.

2. Both women and men are important to the labour force.

3. Many people have chosen to remain single and pursue a career; combine marriage with a career, combine marriage and parenthood; or combine marriage and parenthood with a career.

4. More and more husbands and wives work together as associates in business as lawyers, doctors, dentists, architects, and others. Some share jobs. Many share family responsibilities.

5. Some parents — writers, musicians, artists, educators, and those with businesses in their homes — share the work of the home and child care with their spouse or partner by mutual agreement for the satisfactions that come with closer relationships within the family. If a parent is a single parent, this combined role may be a necessity.

6. Since both sexes may now hold almost any job, the names of some jobs need to be modified or changed to eliminate sex differentiation. For example, remember to use:

firefighter for fireman	*logger* for lumberman
police officer for policeman	*newspaper carrier* for newspaper boy/girl
business executive / *business person* for businessman	*worker* for workman
civil servant / *politician* for statesman	*salesperson* for salesman, saleslady salesclerk
supervisor for foreman	*person* for man, woman
flight attendant for steward, stewardess; purser	*chairperson* for chairman
homemaker for housewife	*camera operator* for cameraman
maintenance crew member for maintenance man	*courier* for deliveryman
	letter carrier for postman

7. Preschool children can learn the names of various occupations and can understand a simple explanation of what each person does. It is wise to begin with jobs held by their parents or people with whom your children come into contact daily. You may choose to focus on one occupational grouping at a time. See the groupings listed in Basic Understandings.

NOTE: Many of the changes in today's lifestyles are reflected in current children's books, poems, fingerplays, and toys, but you will still need to edit and modify references that reflect sexism as you use otherwise suitable materials. Occasionally in telling a story you may simply change the leading character to the opposite sex to avoid stereotyping what boys are like or girls are like, reflecting instead what young children are like! You might also include a woman's or man's name in a list of workers in a story to suggest that *both* might exist in that situation. Father might be baking or fixing pancakes, bathing the baby, or doing the laundry. Mother may be repairing a chair or painting the house. We have tried to make these modifications in this book, but when referring to other books we have been limited in such editing and therefore leave this responsibility to you. Remember, too, that some parents may be unemployed. Be sensitive to these families when planning the section.

8. Children can learn something of our basic economic system — that we get paid for our work and can exchange our pay for services or for something we want or need, and that there is a basic interdependence in our society. If given play money to use in dramatic play centres, such as a service station, post office, or grocery store, *or* if given

real money in a real-life experience when buying a needed item at store when the group takes a trip, children get experience in purchasing goods or services.

▼ **CAUTION:** Coins are not suitable for children under three.

9. Many services are provided by volunteers, such as food-bank workers, hospital volunteers, distress-line operators, etc. Visits from volunteers with whom children may come into contact would add another perspective to your unit on work. Older children may be able to take on a volunteer project (for example, children may be asked to bring in a toy that they no longer use to be sent to a local children's hospital). Explain that often sick children cannot take their own toys into a hospital and that the hospital may need toys especially for these children.

10. Some occupations have been highlighted in other sections of this book. You may wish to refer to the following: Chapter 1, I'm Me, I'm Special; Chapter 7, Living in Families; Part 7, Transportation; Chapter 28, Tools and Machines to Use in My World.

Introducing This Subject to Children

1. On a table, display tools that highlight one occupation, such as doctor's/dentist's surgical mask, stethoscope, play thermometer, empty unbreakable pill bottle, hot water bottle, or ice bag.
2. Read a book about an occupation in the community (see Book Centre).
3. Invite a person, dressed in a uniform or professional garb, to come and show the children the tools of his or her occupation and how they are used.
4. Post pictures of one grouping of community workers on a bulletin board near the entrance or cloakroom.
5. Plan a trip to a workplace as part of developing an interest in another subject; for example, grocery store — food; pet store — pets.
6. The children may observe workers near the playground or seen when the children are on a walk.

Vocabulary

work	spend	cheque	cash
job	buy	bank	names of occupations
pay	sell	money	names of businesses
earn	trade	coins	task each person does
save	barter	change	

Learning Centres
••••••••••••••••••••••••••••••••

Discovery Centre

1. Find pictures of various jobs held by parents of your children. Put a photo of each child by pictures of his or her parents' jobs. Take instant camera pictures or cut them from business brochures or magazines. Encourage parents and children to help collect

pictures. Include in this display those who are jobless or who have nonpaying jobs, showing other kinds of jobs they do, such as caring for the family.

2. Set up an "our special visitor" or "work" discovery centre area where tools of a special kind of worker are displayed and can be explored and explained each day by a parent, community resource person, or teacher. This might be a bake centre, a special art centre, a workbench, or a sewing centre. Plan for opportunities for children to pursue the activity at their level of ability.

3. Display bankbooks, chequebooks, and unbreakable piggy banks.

4. Examine a stethoscope, simple microscope, and thermometer.

5. Borrow a real telephone from the telephone company (one that works but is not hooked up to a phone line) for children to explore.

6. Borrow a used typewriter or make available a computer for children to use. Encourage the children to type their names by finding and pressing the letters on the keys.

Dramatic Play Centres

Home-living centre

1. Place play money in purses and wallets so children are able to buy goods being sold in other dramatic play areas (don't give coins to children under three).

2. Provide lunch boxes or bags and laminated pictures of food or plastic foods to pack a lunch that a person might take to work.

3. Have tricycles, wagons, or ride-on cars for family members to drive to work or to go shopping.

4. For work-at-home suggestions, see Home-Living Centre in Chapter 7, Living in Families.

Block-building centre

1. Set out model accessories of community workers and family members and pictures of the job areas being emphasized to encourage the building of appropriate structures.

2. Set out toy trucks and machines. Encourage road building and building of structures to complement the occupations being emphasized.

3. Use hollow blocks or large brick blocks and ride-on cars, trucks, and machinery to encourage dramatic play on a different scale. Provide children with appropriate props (see Dramatic Play Props in Part 1).

4. When spotlighting animal doctors, set out toy animals that a veterinarian or zoo keeper might care for.

5. Set up a tabletop terrain (see the illustration on p. 181).

Other dramatic play centres

> **NOTE:** Suggestions for dramatic play materials to highlight various community helpers have been included in other sections of this book. Should a special visitor, trip, or opportunity make it desirable to use one of those listed below, you will find more detailed suggestions in the sections noted. The sections on dramatic play props and prop patterns in Part 1 may also be helpful.

1. With a three-way play screen, a cash register, paper bags, and play money you can set up a store. Vary the products sold each day, such as groceries, gifts, hats, shoes (see Chapter 7, Living in Families).

2. Doctor, baker, grocer, nurse (see patterns in Part 1).

3. Pilot, railroad engineer, post office worker, firefighter, ship captain (see Part 7, Transportation).

4. Grocer, truck driver, farmer.

5. Astronaut (see Chapter 22, Air Transportation).

Props have been provided to encourage dramatic play about firefighting. The "hose" is a cardboard tube that was used to ship drapery rods. The teacher models playfulness and facilitates the imaginary play.

6. Carpenter, painter, plumber, gas station attendant (see Chapter 28, Tools and Machines to Use in My World).
7. Veterinarian: Set up similarly to a physician's office, but have cages and pens to house animals that must remain to be cared for in the clinic.
8. Art museum or gallery: Let the children plan, arrange, and rearrange their artwork in a special corner in various ways. Hang pictures on a line, mount and tape to construction-paper mats, or thumbtack to a bulletin board. Display wood, paper, clay, and styrofoam sculptures in a kiosk made of stacked boxes.
9. Business office: Set up telephones, small tables and chairs (to serve as desks), a typewriter, staplers, paper, paper clips, pads, pencils, ink pads, rubber stamps, envelopes, and postage stamps. Be sure to monitor the use of staplers and small items like paper clips and elastic bands.
10. Play library: In the Book Centre, provide a long table for checking books in and out, file cards, an ink pad, and a date stamp. Small card rectangles with the children's names printed on them can be used as library cards.
11. Mail delivery route: Set out large brown envelopes with names or drawn objects identifying them to which the children can deliver matching postcards. Provide a hat and bag for the letter carrier to wear. For older children, the envelopes and cards could also have addresses for various locations around the room.

Art Centre

• 1. Play dough: Use rolling pins and baking pans from the home-living centre. Provide baker's hats (see patterns in Part 1). Encourage the decoration of baked goods. Have pictures of cakes, pastries, and colourful food on plates. Children may score clay with tongue depressors, potato mashers, or other utensils.

•••• 2. Make a book of families at work: Cut out pictures of workers at various jobs and mount on construction paper. Fasten together or place in a three-ring binder.

•• 3. Artist: Provide a variety of art media for several days. Expand special activities to correspond with a visit from an artist.

•• 4. Carpenter: Set out carpenter aprons, balsa wood in various shapes and sizes, and plastic tools at the woodworking centre.

•• 5. Use various objects and implements to create different painting effects; for example: spools of thread, old spatulas, pill-bottle lids, old movie reels, and old tools would all create interesting effects if used in place of fingers and paintbrushes.

•••• 6. Assemble job hats. Provide 5 cm wide bands of bristol board, stapled or glued to circle children's heads, glue, magazine pictures of people in different occupations, and assorted scraps for decorations. Suggest that the children choose a picture they like and glue it to the hatband. Then they can decorate the hat in any way they please. In group time; the hats can be worn for a hat parade, during which children can act out the job of the person on their hat.

Learning and Language Materials Centre

Commercially made materials

1. *Puzzles:* A variety of puzzles showing people working. Try to find puzzles that show men and women in atypical jobs. Be sure to include some puzzles that have small knobs on the pieces for younger children.
2. *Small toys for imaginative play:* A variety of small cars, trucks, and figures that are identified with various types of work. Canada Post has excellent models of postal trucks and mailboxes available in the main post offices and postal boutiques.
3. *Toys for riding:* Riding toys that are painted to look like various working vehicles; for example, a tractor, an ambulance, a fire engine.
4. *Dolls and puppets:* Puppets that represent a variety of careers.
5. *Costumes:* A variety of props and costumes that represent different occupations; for example, straw hats for farmers, slickers for fishermen, firefighter hats, white coats for doctors and nurses.
6. *Flannelboards:* Flannelboard sets that represent different occupations. Be sure to choose sets that show people from both sexes and a variety of races in many jobs.

Teacher-made games and materials

NOTE: For detailed descriptions, see Learning Games in Part 1.

1. *Name it:*
   a. Use community worker models or pictures of people at various jobs.
   b. Use hats: police officer, firefighter, baker, nurse.
   c. Use tools from various jobs: whistle, stethoscope, rolling pin, empty milk carton, wrench.
2. *Look and see:* Use materials listed in 1(a), (b), and (c).
3. *Which?* Use materials listed in 1(a), (b) and (c).
4. *Alike, different, and the same:*
   a. Two people wearing uniforms and one not.
   b. One male police officer, two female police officers.
   c. Doctor, nurse, and letter carrier.
5. *Sorting and grouping by association:*
   a. Group all those who wear uniforms on the job.
   b. Match the tool with the helper.

6. *Who am I?* Describe various jobs, mentioning what each person wears and does.
7. *Listen and hear:* Typewriter, hammer, whistle, eggbeater; sounds may be taped and replayed, leaving space on the tape for the child to think and guess before final answer is given.
8. *Let's tell a story:* Use a picture of someone at work; choose a picture with action to invite imaginative response.

Book Centre

••• Bauer, Judith. *What's It Like to Be an Airplane Pilot?* St. Catharines, ON: Troll Associates, 1990.

••• ———. *What's It Like to Be a Doctor?* St. Catharines, ON: Troll Associates, 1990.

••• ———. *What's It Like to Be a Nurse?* St. Catharines, ON: Troll Associates, 1990.

••• Bourgeois, Paulette. *Canadian Fire Fighters.* Toronto: Kids Can Press, 1991.

••• ———. *Canadian Garbage Collectors.* Toronto: Kids Can Press, 1991.

• Capdevila, Roser. *The City.* (Books about Us series). Willowdale, ON: Annick Press, 1986.

• ———. *Shopping.* (Books about Us series). Willowdale, ON: Annick Press, 1986.

• ———. *What We Do.* (Books about Us series). Willowdale, ON: Annick Press, 1986.

••• Craig, Janet. *What's It Like to Be a Newspaper Reporter?* St. Catharines, ON: Troll Associates, 1990.

••• ———. *What's It Like to Be a Ballet Dancer?* St. Catharines, ON: Troll Associates, 1989.

••• ———. *What's It Like to Be a Fisherman?* St. Catharines, ON: Troll Associates, 1989.

••• Daniel, Kira. *What's It Like to Be a Home Builder?* St. Catharines, ON: Troll Associates, 1989.

••• ———. *What's It Like to Be a Teacher?* St. Catharines, ON: Troll Associates, 1989.

••• Disalvo-Ryan, Dyanne. *Uncle Willie and the Soup Kitchen.* New York: Morrow Junior, 1991.

•• Florian, Douglas. *A Carpenter.* New York: Greenwillow, 1991.

•• ———. *A Potter.* New York: Greenwillow, 1991.

• ———. *People Working.* New York: Crowell, 1983.

••• Gaitskell, Susan. *Emily.* Toronto: Three Trees Press, 1986.

•• Graeme, Jocelyn. *C Is for Community* (from the series *Hand in Hand: Multicultural Experiences For Young Children*). Don Mills, ON: Addison-Wesley, 1990 (text is in Spanish, French, English, and Chinese).

•• Kovalski, Maryann. *Frank and Zelda.* Toronto: Kids Can Press, 1990.

••• Leines, Katherine. *Ask Me What My Mother Does.* Danbury, CT: Watts, 1978.

••• Lobel, Arnold. *On Market Street.* Richmond Hill, ON: Scholastic, 1986.

•••• Maas, Robert. *Fire Fighters.* New York: Scholastic, 1989.

••• Matthews, Morgan. *What's It Like to Be a Farmer?* St. Catharines, ON: Troll Associates, 1990.

••• ———. *What's It Like to Be a Postal Worker?* St. Catharines, ON: Troll Associates, 1990.

••• ———. *What's It Like to Be a Railroad Worker?* St. Catharines, ON: Troll Associates, 1990.

••• Morgan, Allen. *Matthew and the Midnight Tow Truck.* Willowdale, ON: Annick Press, 1984.

••• Poskanzer, Susan Cornell. *What's It Like to Be an Astronaut?* St. Catharines, ON: Troll Associates, 1990.

••• ———. *What's It Like to Be a Chef?* St. Catharines, ON: Troll Associates, 1990.

••• ———. *What's It Like to Be a Farmer?* St. Catharines, ON: Troll Associates, 1989.

••• ———. *What's It Like to Be a Puppeteer?* St. Catharines, ON: Troll Associates, 1989.

••• ———. *What's It Like to Be a Sanitation Worker?* St. Catharines, ON: Troll Associates, 1989.

••• Pellowski, Michael J. *What's It Like to Be a Police Officer?* St. Catharines, ON: Troll Associates, 1990.

••• ———. *What's It Like to Be a Fire Fighter?* St. Catharines, ON: Troll Associates, 1989.

••• ———. *What's It Like to Be a Forest Ranger?* St. Catharines, ON: Troll Associates, 1989.

••• Pinkwater, Daniel Manus. *Aunt Lulu.* New York: Aladdin, 1991.

•• Rockwell, Anne. *The Supermarket.* New York: Macmillan, 1979.

•• ———. *I Like the Library.* New York: Dutton, 1977.

•• Rockwell, Harlow. *My Doctor.* New York: Macmillan, 1973.

•• Scarry, Richard. *Nicky Goes to the Doctor.* New York: Western, 1972.

••• Schop, Janice. *Boys Don't Knit!* Toronto: Women's Press, 1986.

••• Shelby, Anne. *We Keep a Store.* New York: Orchard, 1990.

••• Stamm, Claus. *Three Strong Women.* Markham, ON: Penguin, 1987.

••• Stamper, Judith. *What's It Like to Be a Bus Driver?* St. Catharines, ON: Troll Associates, 1990.

••• ———. *What's It Like to Be a Dentist?* St. Catharines, ON: Troll Associates, 1990.

••• ———. *What's It Like to Be a Veterinarian?* St. Catharines, ON: Troll Associates, 1990.

••• ———. *What's It Like to Be a Truck Driver?* St. Catharines, ON: Troll Associates, 1989.

••• ———. *What's It Like to Be a Zoo Worker?* St. Catharines, ON: Troll Associates, 1989.

••• Tresselt, Alvin. *Sun Up.* New York: Lothrop, Lee & Shepard, 1991.

••• Udry, Janice. *What Mary Jo Shared.* Chicago: Whitman, 1966.

••• Wilks, Shelley. *What's It Like to Be a Grocer?* St. Catharines, ON: Troll Associates, 1990.

••• Yeoman, John. *The Wild Washerwomen.* Markham, ON: Penguin, 1986.

 # Planning for Group Time

NOTE: All music, fingerplays, poems, stories, and games listed here may also be used at other times during the session as appropriate.

Music

Songs

Please see "The Grocer" at the end of this chapter.

From *Do Your Ears Hang Low?*, Glazer
"Michael Row the Boat Ashore," p. 74

From *Elephant Jam*, Sharon, Lois, and Bram
"Dr. Knickerbocker," p. 72
"The Muffin Man," p. 79

From *Eye Winker, Tom Tinker, Chin Chopper*, Glazer
"Shoemaker, Shoemaker," p. 69
"When I Was a Shoemaker," p. 87

From *More Piggyback Songs*, Warren
"The Helpful O," p. 61
"Firefighters," p. 62
"I Am a Fireman," p. 62
"I Am a Policeman," p. 62

From *Piggyback Songs*, Warren
"Housework Song," p. 36
"To the Hospital," p. 46
"Community Helpers," p. 46
"The Policeman," p. 47

From *Sally Go Round the Sun*, Fowke
"Oats and Beans and Barley Grow," p. 14
"Miss Polly Had a Dolly," p. 40

From *Singing Bee*, Hart
"Doctor Foster," p. 41
"Simple Simon," p. 48
"Hippity Hop to the Barber Shop," p. 55
"Pat a Cake," p. 72
"To Market, To Market," p. 99

From *What Shall We Do and Alee Galloo!*, Winn
"Tommy Was a Soldier," p. 11

Records and Cassettes

Bob Homme. *The Giant Concert of Concerts by the Friendly Giant.* (A & M Records)
"Seafood Concert"
"Pretty Things Concert"

Raffi. *The Corner Grocery Store.* (Troubadour Records)
"The Corner Grocery Store"

Bob Schneider. *When You Dream a Dream.* (Capitol Records)
"A Computer Man"

Sharon, Lois, and Bram. *The Elephant Show Record.* (Elephant Records)
"Take Me Out to the Ballgame"

> **NOTE:** See also Music Centre in Part 1 for suggestions for music, music accessories, and rhythm band instruments to be used with dancing or a band. When using rhythm instruments, let children take turns being the conductor or leader.

Fingerplays and Poems

From *Don't Eat Spiders*, Heidbreder
"The Newfoundland Cod," p. 35

From *Read Aloud Rhymes for the Very Young*, Prelutsky and Brown
"My Father Owns a Butcher Shop," p. 79
"Ears Hears," p. 84

From *Round and Round the Garden*, Williams
"Pat a Cake," p. 38
"Here's the Church," p. 41

From *Where the Sidewalk Ends*, Silverstein
"Helping," p. 101
"Bang-Klang," p. 120

Stories

The choice of stories on the family or related areas should reflect the current interests and experiences of the children. The themes of the stories should cover a wide range of occupations and should include stories in which both men and women are successful and involved in a variety of jobs. Gaitskell's *Emily* describes the life of artist Emily Carr and helps children think about slightly unconventional ways of working. Scarry's *Nicky Goes to the Doctor* is useful for a discussion of doctors and hospitals, especially if one of the children has visited one recently.

Games

(See Learning Games in Part 1 and Teacher-Made Games and Materials earlier in this chapter for directions.)

1. *Together, together:* Act out jobs: paint a house, write a book, conduct an orchestra.
2. *Sally says/Sam says:* Be a painter, a carpenter, a dancer.

Routine Times

1. At snack or meal times, play restaurant. Allow children to take turns waiting on tables.
2. At snack or meal times, play flight attendant. Serve snacks or meals to passengers on a pretend airliner.
3. At pickup time, play moving van. Have children return toys to shelves using wagons, rolling platforms, or ride-on trucks as vans.
4. Have the children look for people at work — sanitation workers, painters, crossing guards, road crews, telephone maintenance crews, letter carriers.

Large Muscle Activities

1. Athletes: Play catch; toss a ball or rolled-up socks into a laundry basket.
2. Painters: Provide children with pails of water and large paintbrushes. Let children paint the outside of the centre or a fence with the water.
3. Carpenters: Move the woodworking bench and materials outside.
4. Bakers: Wet some sand. Encourage children to bake cakes and cookies by providing them with pans, spoons, and bowls. Decorate bakery products with dry sand, pebbles, and leaves.
5. Car wash: Provide sponges and pails of water near the tricycles and other wheel toys.
6. Crossing guards: This is a good opportunity to use safety signs with wheel toys.
7. Firefighters: Take firefighter hats, hoses, and hollow blocks outside for dramatic play.
8. Garage or service station: Provide rags, oil cans, hoses for gas, pumps for air in tires, and old credit cards.
9. Parking lot attendants: Set aside an area for parking toy cars.

Extended Experiences

1. Take a trip to visit a child's parent at work.
2. Take a walk and look for people doing different kinds of work.
3. Invite visitors to discuss what they do at work.
4. Help children discover nonsexist occupations by introducing them to women and men who hold similar jobs.

5. Ask parents to visit and to talk about their jobs. Ask them to dress as they would for their jobs and to bring one or more tools they use to share with the children.

6. Invite someone who comes to the centre on business to talk about his or her job — plumber, meter reader, letter carrier — or tape an interview with the person and let the children guess who it might be. Perhaps a few interested children could be allowed to look through the door of a delivery truck (it may not be possible for children to enter a Canada Post truck and some other kinds of trucks).

7. Plan to have letters delivered to children at the centre by the regular letter carrier. Address one manila envelope containing all the notes or picture postcards to the teacher so all will arrive on the same day. Let the carrier hand the teacher the envelop in front of the children; and invite him or her to stay a moment to meet the children. Used postcards could be recycled by pasting a new message over the previously written note. Choose special cards to fit the interests of individual children. Parents and friends could be encouraged to save their old postcards for your centre prior to this activity.

8. Show a film or filmstrip of a job that would be of interest to the children.

Teacher Resources

Pictures and Displays

☐ Put up pictures of various jobs. Be sure to include both men and women of various ethnic groups.

☐ Athletes: Display various kinds of balls — basketball, football, golf ball, baseball, tennis ball, bowling ball. Put up pictures of professional athletes near the display.

☐ Musicians: Display pictures of an orchestra, a band, and musical instruments.

☐ Writers: Display books, magazines, newspapers, paper, pencils or pens and a type-writer.

☐ Display a picture of a city scene.

☐ Display coins, dollar bill, bank cheques, bankbook, pay envelope, identification card.

☐ See Discovery Centre and Other Dramatic Play Centres for other suggestions.

☐ See related parts of this guide: Chapter 1, I'm Me, I'm Special; Part 7, Transportation; Chapter 28, Tools and Machines to Use in My World.

Books and Periodicals

Amato, Sheila, and Pat Staton. *Making Choices! Women in Non-Traditional Jobs.* Toronto: Green Dragon Press, 1987.

Films and Videos

NOTE: Check with your distributor about public performance rights.

Cold Pizza. National Film Board, 1972.
Doctor De Soto. Weston Woods.
The Mole as Chemist. Kratky Films, Prague (released in Canada by International Tele-Film), 1975.

Norman the Doorman. Weston Woods.
Police Officer. Encyclopedia Britannica (released in Canada by Visual Education Centre), 1981.
The Stonecutter. Weston Woods.

Community Resources and Organizations

- ☐ YMCA.
- ☐ YWCA.
- ☐ YMHA.
- ☐ An employment agency.
- ☐ A service club.
- ☐ Parents.
- ☐ Workers in the community.

Government Agencies

- ☐ Federal Department of Employment and Immigration.
- ☐ Ontario Women's Directorate.
- ☐ Provincial or territorial ministry responsible for labour and employment.

The Grocer

Laverne Warner

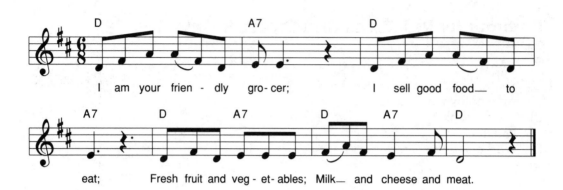

I am your frien - dly gro- cer; I sell good food___ to
eat;   Fresh fruit and veg - et- ables; Milk___ and cheese and meat.

Activity

Invite the children to collaborate in adding more verses about real or imaginary occupations.

Part 4 Family Celebrations

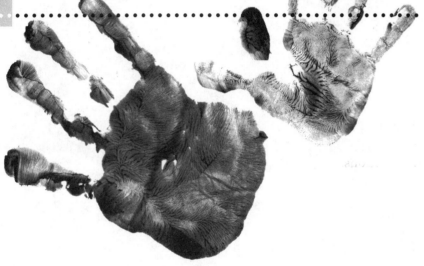

PART

4 Family Celebrations

Introduction

In Canada, we have many celebrations and holidays throughout the year. In addition, many families have celebrations that are unique to their culture or to their family practices. As educators, we can enhance the experience of the children with whom we work by inviting them to bring aspects of their family celebrations to the school.

Although many celebrations are standard across the country, there may be local variations in the way some are observed, such as in Vancouver, where Halloween is celebrated with backyard fireworks displays, or in Newfoundland, where mummers (people in disguises) visit homes at Christmas. There are also celebrations that are unique to a specific community, such as the Calgary Stampede, Kitchener's Oktoberfest, and Quebec City's Winter Carnival. The Teacher Resources section in each chapter will provide you with information about a particular holiday or special event in your area.

Each of the chapters in Part 4 begins with a Calendar of Events. The calendar identifies a selection of special events over a given period of months and lists their corresponding dates according to the solar calendar (Western tradition) rather than the lunar calendar (Eastern tradition). Most of these special events are featured in the chapters, some in greater depth than others. Those that are covered in depth should be used as models for planning celebrations with children.

When planning your program, it is important to remember that although celebrations may have interesting and important historical roots, some of these may be beyond the understanding of young children. Plan in a way that not only respects the origins of the celebration, but also acknowledges the children's level of understanding. (Remember, there are some religions and cultures that have very definite restrictions on how children participate in any celebration. It is wise to check with parents, perhaps during an initial interview, to ascertain whether a family has any specific practices. If they do, devise a plan for how the celebrations should be handled.)

It is also important to ensure that your celebrations reflect the backgrounds of the children in your program as well as the uniqueness of our country and its regions. Check with the children's parents to find out if there are any special holidays or celebrations that they would like to see included.

Finally, there are three basic concepts that children can take away from any celebration:

☐ Celebration is important and fun.

☐ There are many different kinds of celebrations and ways of celebrating, all of which are good.

☐ There are many different reasons for celebrating.

Books and Periodicals

Alder, D.A. *A Picture Book of Passover.* New York: Holiday House, 1981.

———. *The Picture Book of Jewish Holidays.* New York: Holiday House, 1981.

Baker, Donald, and James Last. "Celebration!" *Childhood Education.* January 1978, pp. 131–34.

Barber, Mary, and Flora McPherson. *Christmas in Canada.* Toronto: Dent, 1972. (Read–Tell)

Barer-Stein, T. *You Eat What You Are.* Toronto: McClelland & Stewart, 1979.

Casal, U.A. *The Five Sacred Festivals of Ancient Japan.* Rutland, VT: Tuttle, 1967.

Chud, Gyda, and Fahlman, Ruth. *Early Childhood Education for a Multicultural Society.* Vancouver: WEDGE, University of British Columbia, 1985.

Coffin, T.P. *The Book of Christmas Folklore.* New York: Seabury Press, 1973.

Crean, Patrick. *The Fitzhenry and Whiteside Fireside Book of Canadian Christmas.* Markham, ON: Fitzhenry & Whiteside, 1986.

Crystal, Frances H. "The Holiday Dilemma: Celebrating the Holidays in Preschool and Kindergarten." *Young Children.* November 1967, pp. 66–73.

Greenfeld, H. *Chanukah.* New York: Holt, Rinehart and Winston, 1976.

———. *Passover.* New York: Holt, Rinehart and Winston, 1978.

Hirsch, M. *I Love Hanukkah.* New York: Holiday House, 1984.

Joy, M. *Highdays and Holidays.* Boston: Faber & Faber, 1981.

Kalman, Bobbie, et al. *We Celebrate Family Days.* Toronto: Crabtree, 1986.

———. *We Celebrate Hanukkah.* Toronto: Crabtree, 1986.

———. *We Celebrate the Harvest.* Toronto: Crabtree, 1986.

———. *We Celebrate Valentine's Day.* Toronto: Crabtree, 1986.

———. *We Celebrate Winter.* Toronto: Crabtree, 1986. (and other titles in the *We Celebrate series*)

Kehoe, J. *A Handbook for Enhancing the Multicultural Climate of the School.* Vancouver: Western Educational Development Group, 1984.

Kessel, J.K. *St. Patrick's Day.* Minneapolis, MI: Carolrhoda, 1982.

Laurence, Margaret. *The Christmas Birthday Story.* Toronto: McClelland & Stewart, 1980. (Read–Tell)

Manning-Saunders, R. *Festivals.* London: Heinemann, 1973.

Montpetit, Raymond. *Les temps de fêtes au Québec.* Montreal: Les Éditions de l'Homme, 1978.

Moore, Sallie, and Phyllis Richards. *Teaching in the Nursery School.* New York: Harper, 1959, pp. 100–24.

Nickerson, B. *Celebrate the Sun.* Toronto: McClelland & Stewart, 1969.

Ontario Ministry of Community and Social Services. *Multicultural Early Childhood Education: Resource Kit.* Toronto: Ministry of Community and Social Services, 1990.

Ontario Ministry of Culture and Recreation. *Days to Remember: Observances of Significance in Our Multicultural Society* (Glyn P. Allen, ed.). Toronto: Government of Ontario, 1980.

Parry, Caroline. *Let's Celebrate: Canada's Special Days.* Toronto: Kids Can Press, 1987.

Ramsey, Patricia G. "Beyond Ten Little Indians and Turkeys." *Young Children* 34 (September 1979), pp. 28–51.

Ryan, Mary. *Multicultural Festivals.* St. Johns: New Brunswick Human Rights Commission, 1979.

Schmidt, V.E., and E. McNeill. *Cultural Awareness: A Resource Bibliography.* Washington, DC: National Association for the Education of Young Children, 1978.

Shepard, S.M. *Asian Food Treats.* Vancouver: Douglas & McIntyre, 1984.

Stephan, B. *Decorations for Holiday Celebrations.* New York: Crown, 1978.

Timberlake, Pat. "Classroom Holidaze." *Childhood Education.* January 1978, pp. 128–30.

Todd, Vivian E., and Helen Heffeman. *The Years before School.* Toronto: Macmillan, 1977, pp. 302–18.

U.S. Committee for UNICEF. *Joy through the World.* New York: Bragdon, 1985.

Wernecke, H.H. *Christmas Customs around the World.* Philadelphia: Westminster Press, 1979.

Wyndham, Robert. *Chinese Mother Goose Rhymes.* Cleveland: Collins-World, 1968.

Films and Videos

NOTE: Check with your distributor about public performance rights.

Chinese New Year

The Fire Flowers of Yet Sing Low. Sterling Educational Films (released in Canada by Marlin Motion Pictures), 1967.

Passover

Passover. Manitoba Education and Training Instructional Resources Library, 1982.

Easter

The Egg Cracker Suite. Castle Films (released in Canada by Magic Lantern Films), 1943.
The First Easter Rabbit. Perspective Films (released in Canada by Coronet Instructional Media), 1976.
Pysanka: The Ukrainian Easter Egg. Manitoba Education and Training Instructional Resources Library, 1975.
The Velveteen Rabbit. Random House, 1985.

Halloween

Dorothy and the Witch. Kratky Films, Prague (released in Canada by International Tele-Film), 1976.
Georgie. Weston Woods.
Halloween Dream. Phoenix Films (released in Canada by International Tele-Film), 1981.
The Trip. Weston Woods.

Christmas

NOTE: There are many films on this topic. Consult your local distributor.

Christmas at Moose Factory. National Film Board, 1971.
Christmas Customs Near and Far. Coronet Instructional Films, 1955.
The Christmas Tree. George Mendeluk (released in Canada by Magic Lantern Films). (Ukrainian story)

The Clown of God. Weston Woods.
The Little Drummer Boy. Weston Woods.
Max's Christmas. Weston Woods.
Miguel's Navidad. George Mendeluk (released in Canada by Visual Education Centre),
    1976.
Morris's Disappearing Bag. Weston Woods.
Zlateh the Goat. Weston Woods.

Community Resources and Organizations

- ☐ Chamber of commerce.
- ☐ Municipal offices.
- ☐ Tourist board or tourist information offices.
- ☐ Historical boards or associations.
- ☐ Service clubs.
- ☐ Public library.
- ☐ Cultural organizations or associations.
- ☐ Federal, provincial, or territorial ministries of culture, recreation, and multiculturalism.

Native Canadian Celebrations

Canadians are fortunate to have a rich and varied Native heritage. Yet we often overlook this wonderful aspect of our culture or treat it as an eccentric part of Canadian life. It is, therefore, important to include Native people's celebrations in any program that introduces children to Canadian celebrations.

When planning your program, it is important to remember that:

☐ There is no single Native culture in Canada; rather, there is a mosaic of cultures as varied and exciting as the many tribes and groups in the country.

☐ Celebrations in Native cultures tend to be tied to significant events, such as births, initiations, marriages, harvests, hunts, eclipses, etc. Most of these celebrations are religious ceremonies.

☐ Native people's celebrations are not as closely related to the calendar year as other Canadian celebrations.

Books and Periodicals

Campbell, Maria. *People of the Buffalo.* Vancouver: Douglas & McIntyre (How They Lived in Canada Series), 1976.

Cass, James. *Ekahotan, the Corn Grower: Indians of the Eastern Woodlands.* Toronto: D.C. Heath and the Royal Ontario Museum (Native Peoples of Canada Series), 1983.

———. *Mistatin, the Buffalo Hunter: Indians of the Plains.* Toronto: D.C. Heath and the Royal Ontario Museum (Native Peoples of Canada Series), 1983.

———. *Ochechak, the Caribou Hunter: Indians of the Subarctic.* Toronto: D.C. Heath and the Royal Ontario Museum (Native Peoples of Canada Series), 1983.

———. *Oyai, the Salmon Fisherman and Woodworker: Indians of the North Pacific Coast.* Toronto: D.C. Heath and the Royal Ontario Museum (Native Peoples of Canada Series), 1983.

Embree, J. *Let Us Live.* Don Mills, ON: Dent, 1977.

Harper, Kenn, ed. *Christmas in the Big Igloo.* Yellowknife: Outcrop, 1983.

Jennes, Diamond. *The Indians of Canada* (7th ed.). Toronto: University of Toronto Press, 1977.

Kirkland Lake Native People's Research Committee. *My People Anishnabe.* London, ON: Scholar's Choice, 1977.

Leechman, J.D. *Native Tribes of Canada.* Agincourt, ON: Gage, 1956.

Ridington, Jillian, and Robin Ridington. *People of the Longhouse.* Vancouver: Douglas & McIntyre (How They Lived in Canada Series), 1982.

———. *People of the Trail.* Vancouver: Douglas & McIntyre (How They Lived in Canada Series), 1978.

Siska, Heather Smith. *People of the Ice.* Vancouver: Douglas & McIntyre (How They Lived in Canada Series), 1980.

Steltzer, Ulli. *A Haida Potlatch.* Vancouver: Douglas & McIntyre, 1984.

Updike, R. Lee, and R.D. Symons. *The First People: An Artist's Reconstruction of Five Native Canadian Cultures.* Saskatoon: Western Producer Prairie, 1978.

Community Resources and Organizations

There are many Native friendship centres across Canada. The following organizations will be able to direct you to centres and Native celebrations in your area:

Aboriginal Friendship Centres of Saskatchewan
1440 Scarth St.
Regina, SK
S4R 2E9
(306) 525-5459

Alberta Native Friendship Centres Association
11445–124 St., Suite 201
Edmonton, AB
T5M 0K4
(403) 455-7185

British Columbia Association of Indian Friendship Centres
733 Johnson St., Suite 307
Victoria, BC
V8W 1M8
(604) 380-1447

Calgary Indian Friendship Centre
140–2nd Ave. SW
Calgary, AB
T2P 0B9
(403) 264-1155

Canadian Native Friendship Centre
1016–127 St.
Edmonton, AB
T5M 0T2
(403) 452-7811

Central Okanagan Indian Friendship Society
442 Leon Ave.
Kelowna, BC
V1Y 6J3
(604) 763-4905
(604) 861-5514 (FAX)

Hamilton Regional Indian Centre
712 Main St. E.
Hamilton, ON
L8M 1K8
(416) 548-9593

Ininew Friendship Centre
P.O. Box 1499
190–3rd Ave.
Cochrane, ON
P0L 1C0
(705) 272-4497

Manitoba Association of Friendship Centres
213 Notre Dame, Suite 605
Winnipeg, MB
R3B 1N3
(204) 943-8082
(204) 943-8674 (FAX)

Micmac Native Friendship Centre
2158 Gottlingen St.
Halifax, NS
B3K 3B4
(902) 420-1576

N'Amerind Friendship Centre
260 Colborne St.
London, ON
N6B 2S6
(519) 672-0131

National Association of Friendship Centres
396 Cooper St., Suite 204
Ottawa, ON
K2P 2H7
(613) 563-4844
(613) 594-3428 (FAX)

Native Canadian Centre
16 Spadina Rd.
Toronto, ON
M5R 2S7
(416) 964-9087

Ne-Chee Friendship Centre
152 Main St. S.
Kenora, ON
P9N 3S3
(807) 468-5440

Niagara Regional Native Centre
R.R. 4
Queenston and Taylor Road
Niagara-on-the-Lake, ON
L0S 1J0
(416) 688-6484

Northwest Territories Council of Friendship Centres
P.O. Box 470
Fort Simpson, NT
X0E 0N0
(403) 695-2577

North Bay Indian Friendship Centre
980 Cassells St.
North Bay, ON
P1B 4A6
(705) 472-2811

N'Swakamok Friendship Centre
110 Elm St.
Sudbury, ON
P3C 1T5
(705) 674-2128

Odawa Native Friendship Centre
396 MacLaren St.
Ottawa, ON
K2P 0M8
(613) 238-8591

Ontario Federation of Indian Friendship Centres
234 Eglinton Ave. E., Suite 207
Toronto, ON
M4P 1K5
(416) 484-1411
(416) 484-6893 (FAX)

Sault Ste Marie Indian Friendship Centre
29 Wellington St.
Sault Ste Marie, ON
P6A 2K9
(705) 256-5634

Skookum Jim Friendship Centre
3159–3rd Ave.
Whitehorse, YT
Y1A 1G1
(403) 668-4465

Thunder Bay Indian Friendship Centre
401 North Cumberland St.
Thunder Bay, ON
P7A 4P7
(807) 344-0706

Timmins Native Friendship Centre
170–2nd Ave.
Timmins, ON
P4N 1G1
(705) 268-6262

Union of New Brunswick Indians
35 Dedam St.
Fredericton, NB
E3A 2V2
(506) 458-9444

Union of Nova Scotia Indians
111 Memberton St.
P.O. Box 961
Sydney, NS
B1P 6J4
(902) 539-4107

Victoria Native Friendship Centre
533 Yates St., Penthouse
Victoria, BC
V8W 1K7
(604) 384-3211

Yukon Indian Cultural Education Society
22 Nisutlin Dr.
Whitehorse, YT
Y1A 3S5
(403) 667-7631
(403) 668-6577 (FAX)

POTLATCH

Potlatch, a Chinook word which means "to give," is the principal spiritual and social ceremony of the Pacific coastal nations. It is a festival of gift-giving that is held to celebrate the succession of a new chief upon the death of an old chief, an important marriage in the tribe, or a girl's initiation into womanhood or a boy's into manhood. During the celebration, there is much dancing and singing that conveys the meaning of the gifts or, if a name is being passed on, the history of the family name and its origins. Ceremonial gear includes hand-carved masks, rattles, and dance screens, headdresses, and totem poles. Some of the tribes that comprise the Pacific coastal nations include the Kwakiutl, Haida, Westcoast (Nootka), Tlingit, Tsimshian, Chinook, Bella Coola, and Coast Salish.

Extended Experiences

1. Masks, rattles, and headdresses can be made in the art centre. To make a headdress, paper feathers can be cut out, painted, and stapled to a paper headband. Plastic mustard squeeze bottles filled with pebbles make excellent rattles.
2. The children can also make special gifts in the art centre to be given during the celebration (see Steltzer, *A Haida Potlatch*).
3. Pictures of carved masks, totem poles, and other coastal Native art can be displayed throughout the centre.
4. Make salmon sandwiches for the celebration (salmon and berries are natural resources in the Pacific coastal region).

Teacher Resources

Cass, James. *Oyai, the Salmon Fisherman and Woodworker: Indians of the North Pacific Coast.* Toronto: D.C. Heath and Royal Ontario Museum (Native Peoples of Canada Series), 1983.

Johnson, Eve. "Masked Resurrection." *Equinox*, July/August 1982.

Ridington, Jillian, and Robin Ridington. *People of the Trail.* Vancouver: Douglas & McIntyre (How They Lived in Canada Series), 1978.

Steltzer, Ulli. *A Haida Potlatch.* Vancouver: Douglas & McIntyre, 1984. (Steltzer was invited to a potlatch and photographed the preparations, both the making of gifts and the gathering of food, and later the potlatch itself — the speakers, the singers, the dancers, and the spectators.)

POWWOWS

The largest powwow held in Canada each year is the Kainai Indian Days Celebration that takes place on the Blood Indian Reserve in southern Alberta. It is held in July to honour the end of the traditional sun-dance ceremony, which gives thanks to the spirits. During this massive powwow, which is open to all Canadians, there are dancing and dance competitions, a potlatch, performance art, a weekend rodeo, a parade, a baseball tournament, and a small midway replete with food and merchandise concessions (one of the food specialties is Indian fry bread). The dancers specialize in one of three dance styles: traditional dancing, which is a tap-step along the floor in slow, stately rhythm;

fancy dancing, which is twisting and spinning in rapid beats, blending Native movement with contemporary Canadian styles; and grass dancing, a sacred warrior-society dance in which the dancer wears a special costume that symbolizes grass. Some of the Plains tribes that participate in the powwow include the Assiniboine from Saskatchewan, the Shuswap and Kootenay from British Columbia, and the Cree, Blackfoot, Peigan, Sarcee, and Blood from Alberta. It is a celebration of Native Canadian culture and heritage.

Another annual powwow is held at the Wikwemikong Band Reserve on Manitoulin Island in Ontario. The celebration involves four days of tribal ceremonies by several Indian nations and presents Native artisans at work. The summer powwow usually takes place around the first weekend of August. All Canadians are welcome.

The Six Nations Indian Reserve in Brantford, Ontario, holds an Indian pageant each year. This is a re-enactment of Native history and culture. The annual event takes place throughout the month of August and is open to all Canadians. The six tribes that make up the Iroquois Nations are the Seneca, Cayuga, Oneida, Onondaga, Mohawk, and Tuscarora.

Extended Experiences

1. Water-based paints can be used to decorate the children's faces for the celebration.
2. Masks, rattles, and headdresses can be made in the art centre (see Potlatch).
3. Using a drum, encourage the children to try the different styles of dancing described above.
4. Display pictures of elaborate costumes, headdresses, Native people dancing, and teepees.

Teacher Resources

Campbell, Maria. *People of the Buffalo.* Vancouver: Douglas & McIntrye (How They Lived in Canada Series), 1976.

Cass, James. *Mistatin, the Buffalo Hunter: Indians of the Plains.* Toronto: D.C. Heath and the Royal Ontario Museum (Native Peoples of Canada Series), 1983.

Pringle, Heather. "Ceremonial Circuit." *Equinox*, July/August 1987.

9 Celebrations: January to March

Calendar of Events

(based on the solar calendar)

- ☐ New Year's Day — January 1
- ☐ Orthodox Christmas — January 7
- ☐ Chinese/Vietnamese New Year — varies from January 21 to February 19
- ☐ Ashura — sometime during February
- ☐ Groundhog Day — February 2
- ☐ St. Valentine's Day — February 14
- ☐ Basanth — late February or March
- ☐ Hina Matsuri — March 3
- ☐ St. Patrick's Day — March 17
- ☐ Purim — usually in March
- ☐ Basanta — usually in March
- ☐ Holi or Basaat — late March or early April

Included in this chapter are an example of a solar calendar New Year's Day celebration, a mainly Western tradition, and an example of a lunar calendar New Year's Day celebration, a mainly Eastern tradition.

NEW YEAR'S DAY

Basic Understandings

(concepts children can grasp from this subject)

- ☐ New Year's Day is celebrated by most Canadians on January 1. January 1 is the first day of the solar calendar year.
- ☐ People usually begin the new year with a resolution that the coming year will be happier and more prosperous than the one just ended.

☐ Many people celebrate the new year by giving a party with food, drink, dancing, and merriment. At midnight on New Year's Eve, whistles are blown, car horns are honked, bells are rung, and people shout "Happy New Year," kiss, and sing "Auld Lang Syne." The parties may be in homes, hotels, or public places such as Parliament Hill in Ottawa or the local city hall.

☐ Many families celebrate by attending a Watch Night service at church.

☐ Most businesses are closed on this holiday so that people can visit friends and relatives.

Additional Facts the Teacher Should Know

1. The custom of celebrating New Year's Day on January 1 began in the 1500s when the Georgian calendar was established. It is a solar calendar and is based on the time it takes for the Earth to travel around the sun — 365¼ days. Every four years, an extra day is added to February and that year is referred to as a leap year. The twelve months in our calendar have names, and most were taken from Roman gods. January, for example, was named for the god of doors and gates; Janus had two faces, one looking forward and the other backward.

2. Noisemaking is often a part of New Year's celebrations. This practice goes back to the ancient custom of driving out evil spirits. In Scotland, men and boys parade in the streets, circle friends' homes, and drown out the demons by shouting. In Denmark, they "smash in the New Year" by banging on the doors of friends' homes and "let in the New Year" by setting off fireworks. In Japan, dancers rattle bamboo sticks. In Nigeria, drums are beaten and ceremonial dances are performed.

3. The Germans believe that the way you live the first day of the year will affect the way you live the others, so homes are made spotless. In Spain, there is a similar belief applied to food; if you eat good food the first day, you will have plenty all year long.

4. Some New Year's customs involve children. In Belgium, children take wafers with raised crosses on them, called *nules*, to friends. In Italy, children receive gifts of coins and hang mistletoe on doors for luck. In Switzerland, children play hide-and-seek with their parents and shout "Happy New Year" when found. In Portugal, children sing songs in their neighbourhood, for which they receive coins and treats.

5. For young children, the New Year's celebration is often a disappointment, as it is essentially an adult celebration. All the talk and excitement lead children to expect something special, beyond a family or neighbourhood party. The concept of a new year is beyond the understanding of very young children. For most young children, the idea of a resolution is also incomprehensible. In your holiday newsletter to parents, include a few New Year's activities for children that can be done at home.

6. Many children's centres are closed for an extended holiday from before Christmas until after New Year's Day. Often, teachers of young children place little emphasis on this holiday in their curriculum planning because Canadian New Year's celebrations seldom involve children, except when they visit with relatives. However, when the children return to school, invite them to recall and discuss how *they* celebrated the New Year's holiday. Through sharing, they can learn more about the holiday and begin to recognize that children, and in fact everyone, celebrate New Year's Day with traditions that are sometimes similar, sometimes completely different, but always very interesting.

Extended Experiences

1. Display pictures of New Year's celebrations, including parties and parades.

2. Display a new calendar. Talk about the fact that it is the beginning of a new year. Children who can recognize numbers can be shown the numbers for last year and for this year. Include a lunar calendar, available from an Asian shop or import store.
3. Ask children to tell what they did on New Year's Day. Did they do something special with their families?
4. Read "They're Having a Party Downstairs" and "Mrs. Night" from *Mischief City* by Wynne-Jones in group time. They will help you talk about New Year's, parties, and changes in the calendar.

ORTHODOX CHRISTMAS

Many families celebrate Christmas on January 7 if they belong to one of the Orthodox Christian religions. In most cases, this is primarily a religious celebration, but it usually includes a special family meal. Check if there are any children in your program who celebrate Christmas on this date. Invite them to tell the other children about the special family and religious celebrations.

The celebration of Orthodox Christmas begins on January 6 — Christmas Eve — when the first star is sighted in the sky. Usually children will watch the sky for a star and will be in charge of letting the rest of the family know when to start the celebration. The meal on Christmas Eve consists of twelve courses, each representing one of the twelve apostles. After the super, the children receive gifts, traditionally nuts and apples. The family goes to church at midnight. A procession in the neighbourhood of the church is part of the celebration of the mass.

Basic Understandings
(concepts children can grasp from this subject)

☐ Some people celebrate Christmas in January. It is essentially the same holiday as other people celebrate in December.
☐ Some children call Santa Claus "St. Nicholas." He is a similar figure but has different names.
☐ Stars gradually appear in the evening as the clear blue sky darkens. We can watch the sky to see how many stars can be seen on different nights.

Extended Experiences

1. Serve a traditional Ukrainian, Serbian, Greek, Russian, or Croatian snack.
2. If your program runs until after the winter sunset, take the children outside to watch for the first star on January 6 or on a clear evening.
3. Arrange to visit an Orthodox church. The priest can tell the children about Orthodox Christmas and show them some of the special artifacts that are used in the celebration.
4. Arrange to have a visitor come from a local cultural organization whose culture celebrates Orthodox Christmas. The visitor can tell the children about the ways in which children participate in the celebration.

Teacher Resources

Barer-Stein, T. *You Eat What You Are.* Toronto: McClelland & Stewart, 1979.
Burke, M. *The Ukrainian Canadians.* Scarborough, ON: Nelson, 1982.

Chernin, H. *Letters to St. Nicholas.* Association of Ukrainian Writers, 1981.

Chimbos, P.D. *The Greek Experience in Canada.* Toronto: McClelland & Stewart, 1980.

Czuboka, M. *Ukrainian Canadian, Eh?* Winnipeg: Communigraphics, 1983.

Loeb, L., ed. *Down Singing Centuries: Folk Literature of the Ukraine.* Winnipeg: Hyperion Press, 1980.

Nickerson, B. *Celebrate the Sun.* Toronto: McClelland & Stewart, 1969.

Stechishin, S. *Traditional Ukrainian Cookery.* Winnipeg: Trident, 1984.

Symchych, V., and O. Vesey. *The Flying Ship and Other Ukrainian Folk Tales.* Toronto: Holt, Rinehart and Winston, 1976.

Wernecke, H.H. *Christmas Customs around the World.* Philadelphia: Westminster Press, 1979.

CHINESE/VIETNAMESE NEW YEAR

Basic Understandings

(concepts children can grasp from this subject)

☐ New Year's Day is celebrated by many Chinese or Vietnamese Canadians on the first day of the lunar calendar year. In terms of the solar calendar year, this takes place sometime between January 21 and February 19.

☐ The celebration of the Chinese/Vietnamese New Year once lasted as many as fifteen days; now it lasts for only a few days.

☐ The holiday, which has been celebrated for many, many years, begins with a special family dinner on New Year's Eve. The dinner includes fish (the symbol for prosperity and surplus), pork, eggs (the symbol for well-being and rebirth), and many vegetables (at least ten in a dish called *schu-chieng-tzi* [szhoo-jing-tsi] in Mandarin). Special foods (sweets and desserts) are baked and cooked for the occasion, such as watermelon seeds baked with cinnamon and salt, rice cakes, and dried fruit.

☐ Red is the symbol of happiness to all Chinese. This colour is always used for New Year's decorations, candles, and gift wrappings.

☐ On this holiday, children receive gifts of money from older relatives, such as grandparents, parents, aunts, and uncles. The gift money is given in red envelopes, often with gold lettering or pictures on them. If relatives live too far away, children may find their envelopes under their pillows when they awaken.

☐ Even numbers are considered lucky, especially the numbers two and ten. Therefore, two oranges, tangerines, or apples are often given and eaten on this day. Ten different dishes are often served for the New Year's feast.

☐ Homes are decorated with brightly coloured good-luck scrolls or banners that are usually hung in pairs on doorways or windows. These good-luck greetings are often written in couplets and hung in pairs on each side of the front doorway (see pp. 227, 232).

☐ It is important to Chinese children and their parents to wear new clothes, especially new shoes, on New Year's Day to bring them good luck.

☐ *Kung-Hi, Fot-Choy* (Cantonese), or *Kung-Hsi, Fah-Tsai* (Mandarin) is the most common New Year's greeting, meaning "Have a happy, rich, and prosperous New Year!" Sometimes children say *Kung-Hi* or *Kung-Hsi,* "I wish you joy" and adults then say "Sui Hi" or "Sui-Hsi," "May joy be yours!"

☐ The New Year's holiday usually includes a big parade the night of the first full moon of the New Year. Many firecrackers are fired. A lion dance or dragon dance performed by adults is an important part of this parade. Children often carry fish or flower lanterns. With drums, gongs, cymbals, and fireworks, the parade is very noisy and colourful. People cheer, set off fireworks, and tease the dragon, who pretends to bite the teasers. Dragons are make-believe animals, and to the Chinese they are friendly beasts and mean good luck.

☐ The Vietnamese celebration of New Year's is called *Tet*. This is a time for family reunions and the payment of outstanding debts.

☐ The heads of Vietnamese families light candles at family altars in remembrance of ancestors. Food and special papers decorated with herons are also placed at the family altar.

☐ Later in the day, fireworks are set off before a special family meal. Rice cakes are an important part of this meal.

Additional Facts the Teacher Should Know

1. In Canadian cities with a large Chinese/Vietnamese population (such as Vancouver, Toronto, Montreal, and Halifax), special holidays, festivals, and parades are held every year to which anyone is welcome. All children enjoy visits to these public celebrations. Children may also be welcome at Chinese or Vietnamese restaurants, where special festivities are often planned for customers.

2. Many Chinese and Vietnamese refer to an astrological calendar that is a combination of mathematical cycles and symbolic tradition. To record time, the Chinese developed a 600-year cycle based on shorter cycles of 60 years each. Within the smaller cycles, each "year" is given an animal's name as well as an element. (According to one legend, the twelve animals were selected on the basis of a cross-country race. The twelve, in order of finish, were: rat, ox, tiger, hare, dragon, serpent, horse, ram, monkey, rooster, dog, and boar.) The five elements symbolically connected to the calendar are: water, wood, fire, earth, metal. Many Chinese and Vietnamese call each year in this cycle by its animal name, such as the Year of the Horse; some believe that all people born in that year, and other years bearing that name, have traits in common. This is similar to the widespread belief in North America in the signs of the zodiac. The Chinese calendar, like the Hebrew, is lunar, and each month has 29 to 30 days. Every 30 months a double month is added; the calendar does not have the Christian BC and AD.

3. Recorded Chinese culture dates back over 4500 years. It is said that a primitive society on the Asian continent existed as far back as 600 000 years ago.

4. The Chinese New Year begins on *Yuan Tan*, the first day of the first moon, which can occur anywhere between January 21 and February 19. The festival once lasted until the full moon — about fourteen or fifteen days. Each day had its special activities, but today a family or community may shorten the celebration because of work and school schedules. On the Feast of Lanterns, or Feast of the Full Moon, a huge parade is staged with fireworks, gongs, drums, and people dressed in costumes carrying lighted lanterns; the parade features a golden dragon and a lion dance.

5. At one time, some Chinese believed their activities were ruled by the *Yang* and *Yin* principle: the positive and the negative, the male and the female, life and death, the rebirth of spring and the dormancy of winter. The noise and the light created on the Feast of the Lanterns are thought by some to demonstrate the *Yang* forces driving out the evil spirits that have accumulated during the past year.

6. The dragon is one of the four divine creatures that the Chinese believe dispel spirits. It is worshipped as the ruler of rivers, lakes, and seas. Its legendary appearance combines the head of a camel, horns of a deer, neck of a snake, claws of a hawk, belly

Chinese Fortune Calendar

Year of the					
Dragon		1988	2000	Dragon
Snake		1989	2001	Snake
Horse		1990	2002	Horse
Sheep		1991	2003	Sheep
Monkey		1992	2004	Monkey
Cock		1993	2005	Cock
Dog		1994	2006	Dog
Boar		1995	2007	Boar
Rat		1996	2008	Rat
Ox		1997	2009	Ox
Tiger		1998	2010	Tiger
Hare		1999	2011	Hare

of a frog, and scales of a fish. The dragon is the symbol of goodness and strength, and it virtually leads the way into a good year.

7. In preparation for the New Year holiday, homes are thoroughly cleaned, new clothes are purchased, and special sweets are baked. Doors or gates are often lacquered red to keep out evil spirits and to bring the family joy and happiness. Red is the featured colour of this holiday. Five signs of happiness are printed or written on red paper and hung by windowsills and door frames for luck. Two is considered the perfect number, so these scrolls are often hung in pairs, poems are written in couplets, double portions of food are served, and two presents are given at one time.

8. Characters representing Chinese words are written from top to bottom and right to left, although this is beginning to change. If you decide to make a scroll or card with the New Year's greeting *Kung-Hi, Fot-Choy*, be sure to write it in a single column with the character for *Kung* at the top.

9. The industry and science of silk weaving is attributed to the Chinese. They are also credited with inventing the compass, paper, printing, gunpowder, firecrackers, finger-plays, and the use of herbs as medicines. The Great Wall of China is an astonishing architectural and engineering feat. The Chinese have developed the arts of lacquering, calligraphy, painting, printing, weaving, knot tying (macramé), embroidery, paper folding, and paper cutting. They have also made outstanding use of bronze and porcelain chinaware. We have included in this guide suggestions for using some of these contributions, which will help the children have a broader knowledge of the Chinese culture.

	Good luck for the new Spring!	May you have prosperity!	Have a happy New Year!
MANDARIN:	Hsin-chwun-dah-jee	Kaw-ng hsee fah tsai	Hsin nee-an quai loh
CANTONESE:	Sahn chee-un dai-gaht	Gaw-ng hay faht choy	Sahn nee-in-fai lohk

Introducing This Subject to Children

1. Set up a display of Chinese and Vietnamese art or artifacts, such as chinaware, sculpture, jade, rings, greeting cards, paper cutouts, silk, fans, masks, Chinese or Vietnamese characters written on a banner, good luck symbols, and firecrackers.
2. Hang up a Chinese or Vietnamese calendar that has New Year's Day circled.
3. Collect news clippings, postcards, or a colour portfolio about the Chinese or Vietnamese New Year.
4. Display and show how to use an abacus or chopsticks.
5. Use the Chinese Fortune Calendar on p. 226 to determine which animals represent the years in which the children and the teachers were born. (If you cannot find the year you need, add 12 to or subtract 12 from the year in which the person was born until you find a date on the chart. For example, one of the authors was born in 1947. Adding 12, you have 47 + 12 = 59 + 12 = 71 + 12 = 83. Therefore, he was born in the Year of the Boar.)
6. Following the return of children after the New Year's holiday, talk about their celebration. Invite a Chinese or Vietnamese parent or student from a nearby university or college to come and make a New Year's treat that the children can eat. Encourage the visitor to demonstrate the use of chopsticks or to share some artifact or treasure.
7. Introduce a game like Chinese checkers, pickup sticks, or the seven-piece puzzle to the children. (See Teacher-Made Games and Materials, and talk about where the seven-piece puzzle originated.)

Vocabulary

Animals used to name years

Chinese	wind chimes	cake	above
holiday	lunar, moon	banner	fan
lantern	solar, sun	debt	tea
dance	calendar	red	rice
celebrate	parade	tease	jade
festival	almanac	lacquer	incense
feast	first	abacus	chow mein
fireworks	compass	embroidery	dragon
firecracker	gong	lucky	chinaware
chopsticks	sign	silk	

Chinese words used in English:
> *kowtow*, to bow down to another person
> catsup (*keh-chop*), tomato juice (sauce for meat)
> typhoon (*dai-fong*), big wind
> *chop suey*, bits and pieces (miscellaneous)
> *Kung-Hi, Fot-Choy* (Cantonese) pronounced Gaw-ng HAY, FAHT-choy =
>   "Have a happy and prosperous New Year!"
> *Kung-Hsi, Fah-Tsai* (Mandarin) pronounced Kaw-ng HSEE, FAH-tsai (as in
>   sigh) = "Have a happy, rich, and prosperous New Year!"
> *Kung-Hi* (Cantonese) pronounced Gaw-ng HAY = "I wish you joy"
> *Kung-Hsi* (Mandarin) pronounced Kaw-ng HSEE = "I wish you joy" and
>   usually followed by:
> *Sui-Hi* (Cantonese) pronounced soo-ee-HIGH = "May joy be yours!"
> *Sui-Hsi* (Mandarin) pronounced soo-AY-see = "May joy be yours!"
> *Yuan Tan* (Cantonese) pronounced Ywahn Dahn = New Year
> *Yuan Tan* (Mandarin) pronounced Yuhn DAHN = New Year
> *Hsin Nien* (Mandarin) pronounced SYIN nee-an = New Year
> *Hsien Nien* (Cantonese) pronounced SAHN nihn = New Year

NOTE: Chop suey is not a traditional Chinese food. According to one legend, it was first prepared from leftovers for a group of miners in California and means "bits and pieces." Now it is available in most Chinese restaurants. Fortune cookies are probably a commercialized product, too. Rice Krispies squares or crunchies made from marshmallows, butter, and Rice Krispies or Rice Krispies, syrup, brown sugar, and peanut butter are actually North American versions of an Asian confection called rice puff squares. In Korea and China, they are made from rice syrup and puffed (popped) rice. Sometimes roasted peanuts are added to the rice puffs or popped corn to add a nutty flavour. Soybeans are also popped and combined with rice syrup. Sesame seeds are browned and mixed with rice syrup to make a delicious chewy bar.

Learning Centres

Discovery Centre

1. Silkworms in their various stages of development are fascinating to children (some museums and science centres display silkworms).
2. Examine mulberry leaves, the food of silkworms, with a magnifying glass.
3. Display Chinese chinaware, a wok, and chopsticks. Compare similarities and differences with Western utensils. Notice that the chinaware is transparent when held up to the light.
4. Taste sweet-and-sour sauce and soy sauce. Smell ginger root and star anise. (The latter smells and tastes like licorice. It grows in southwest China on an evergreen tree and the fruits blossom into a star shape.)
5. Examine a block print and show children how it was made.
6. Burn incense so children can smell and experience what it is like.
7. Examine a compass: Let children hold it and move around the room with it in order to watch the needle move. Tell them the Chinese invented this instrument a very long time ago.
8. Experiment with sound: Tap gongs, finger cymbals, and bells of various sizes, listen to wind chimes, or hit blocks of wood. You might thumb-strike a piece of crystal to demonstrate the sound it makes (this is not an activity for children to try).
9. Explore authentic Chinese paper lanterns, kites, and paper cutouts to discover how they are made.
10. Let children examine Chinese scrolls, children's books, silk paintings, paper kites, greeting cards, pieces of jade, paper cutouts banners, fans, masks, costumes, and authentically dressed dolls. These may be borrowed from friends or purchased from an Asian or import store. Supervise closely, as these items are quite fragile.
11. Show the children bamboo brushes made of goat's or camel's hair.

    NOTE: There are camels in northern China.

12. Display a tea set from China and one from North America. Look for similarities and differences.
13. Make egg drop soup for the children to taste.

....

EGG DROP SOUP

(Egg Flower Soup)

15 mL/1 T cornstarch
25 mL/2 T cold water
1 egg
750 mL/3 cups clear chicken broth (can use bouillon cubes or strained chicken noodle soup)
Optional: 5 mL/1 tsp chopped parsley or scallion to suggest leaves.

Bring chicken broth to a boil in a metal saucepan. Add the water to the cornstarch in a baby food jar, cover with the lid, and shake vigorously. Open the jar and pour the cornstarch mixture into the broth; stir with a fork until smooth. Break an egg into a small bowl and beat with a fork. Slowly pour the beaten egg into the broth.

Allow children to watch and take turns helping to pour the egg into the broth. Then they can see the "flowers" form when the egg cooks in shreds as it is dropped into the broth: it sinks and then rises to float on the surface in bud-like pieces. Stir until all egg has been added and cooked; removed from heat, and serve. Make sure each child gets some flowers spooned into his or her cup.

Dramatic Play Centres

Home-living centre

1. Have two separate metre lengths of cotton or nylon with ties attached at each corner to wrap dolls to be carried on a child's back.
2. Appropriate dressup clothes include quilted jackets, mandarin collars, frog closings, and silk scarves.
3. Provide a low table or make one from a large carton.
4. Have a Chinese tea party (a red tablecloth would be especially appropriate).
5. Set out place mats of straw or woven paper.
6. Set out chopsticks and bowls on the cupboard shelves.

   NOTE: Allow spoons. Chinese children also use spoons until they are skilled in using chopsticks.

7. Set out plastic flowers in a simple wooden or metal vase.
8. Remove chairs and set out cushions.
9. Include a feather duster, feather hats, and feather fans.
10. Sturdy (or replaceable) lanterns or scrolls may be hung around the room by the children.

Block-building centre

1. Add a pagoda tower builder, available from educational suppliers.
2. Add boats and freeform shapes of blue construction paper for lakes, rivers, and ponds.
3. Discuss how sailors know in what direction to sail when they cannot see the land. Let children use the compass in this centre.

   NOTE: An inexpensive directional compass (available at variety stores) makes an ideal accessory in the block centre when children have assembled boats of large wooden or cardboard hollow blocks.

4. A large empty rectangular box makes a good boat. (For other suggestions, see Dramatic Play Centres in Chapters 24 and 26.)
5. Post pictures of Vietnamese or Chinese architecture, such as the Great Wall of China.
6. Set out toy animals representing the Chinese calendar years, such as a rat, ox, tiger, rabbit, dragon, snake, horse, sheep, monkey, cow, dog, and boar.
7. Set out proportional block arches.

Art Centre

•• 1. Blow art: Older children will enjoy blowing through a straw to push paint into a spidery, branchlike painting. Give children only brown or black paint. Then by sponge-daubing bright colours on these creations, they can be made to look like flower blossoms or leaves on a bush or tree. Blow art sometimes resembles rockets bursting in the air.

   ▼ **CAUTION: Children should be advised to hold the straw above the paper and should practise blowing through the straw. Children should not share straws for health reasons.**

• 2. Create a picture with shapes: Begin with Chinese puzzle shapes or small scraps of wood.

- 3. Clay work: Relate the beginning of all pottery and chinaware to the use of clay. Encourage the children to expand their use of clay by providing simple tools, such as tongue depressors, cuticle sticks, or coffee stir sticks.
- 4. Paper folding: Some simple plans for paper folding follow. (*Origami* is the Japanese term for paper folding.) Show children how to fold and pleat the paper, and let them make what they choose. Simple books on *origami* may suggest other possibilities.

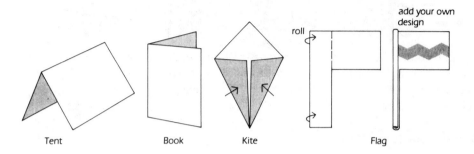

Tent   Book   Kite   Flag

- •• 5. Paper cutting: Try after seeing some examples of paper cutouts. Encourage the children to cut a picture or explore the use of paper and scissors. Give them paste or glue if they need it to complete their creations. Some may also wish to paint their cutouts.
- ••• 6. Make lanterns for decorations: Use lightweight construction paper. A piece of paper 22 cm x 30 cm or 21.5 cm x 28 cm can be folded lengthwise and slashed along the folded edge. When opened and rolled lengthwise into cylinder, it becomes a colourful lantern. Wallpaper makes an interesting patterned lantern, although children may wish to colour or paint a plain piece of paper and then cut as described, as the Chinese do. Rolling a piece of paper into a cylinder (without cutting) makes a different type of lantern. Add a strip of paper to form a handle as shown in the diagrams. Two paper cups attached mouth to mouth with paper clips makes another kind of lantern.

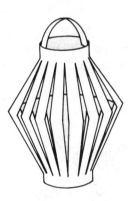 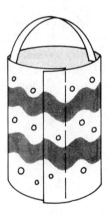 

- •• 7. Charcoal and chalk: It is interesting to discover that a Chinese ink stick rubbed in a porcelain dish with a drop or two of water forms ink for the brush that is used to write Chinese characters. The ink stick is made from charcoal and oil mixed into a kind of crayon.
- •• 8. Printing: Show children some wood-block prints. Let children print designs with blocks that you have made or ones that are commercially available.
- ••• 9. Weaving: The Chinese are masters in the use of bamboo, rattan, flax, and, of course, silk. Simple weaving may be done on a weaving frame with rug yarn, or on a slashed

piece of paper with coloured paper strips. Mesh bags or loosely woven pieces of drapery offer still other possibilities for weaving yarn. For a needle, use an inexpensive bodkin.

••• 10.   Make a good luck sign: Let the children design their own good-luck picture to hang like a scroll.

	Good Fortune	Prosperity	Long Life	Happiness
MANDARIN:	Foo	Loo	Hsiao	Hsi
CANTONESE:	Fulk	Luk	Sow	Hay

Other art projects to try

1.   Make an Asian kite: Below are several kites ranging from the very simple to the more complex. The carp kite is typically Japanese, hollow kites are also made by the Chinese. They are often made with silk or paper in many shapes, such as butterflies, boxes, and dragons. Note some of the pictures in the books listed in Book Centre.

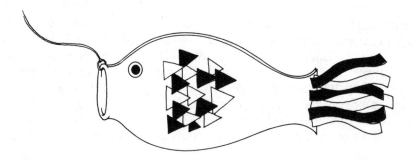

••   a.   Carp kite: Cut two matching fish shapes of lightweight paper, and glue them together along the outside edges to form a hollow fish. Glue a ring of pipecleaner around the mouth edge. Glue overlapping tissue triangles to the body of the fish and streamers to the tail. Attach a string to the mouth so that when the kite is pulled the wind will pass through the fish.

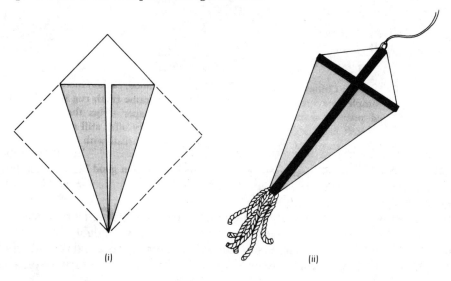

(i)   (ii)

••   b.   Paper-fold kite: Lay a square of lightweight paper flat, with one corner pointing up. Fold in the left and right corners to the centre, as in (i). Add tassels or tails to the lower corner. Attach a crosspiece of cardboard or wood for support, as in (ii).

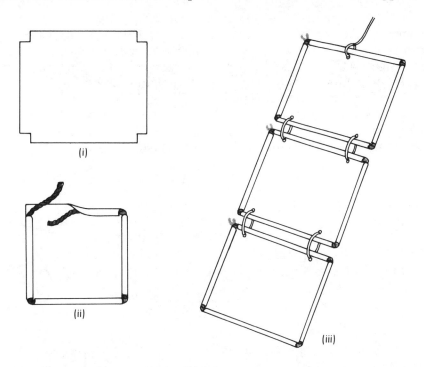

•••   c.   Flat kite: Begin with a rectangular piece of paper. Notch each corner as shown in (i). Roll each edge of the paper inward to form a tube. Thread a length of yarn through all four tubes and secure the ends with a knot. Punch four holes in the square, two on one side and two on the other. Make several of these squares, and connect them by slipping yarn through the holes. Each section of the kite can be decorated. Attach a string to one end.

Learning and Language Materials Centre

Commercially made games and materials

1. *Puzzles:* Many oriental gift shops have fascinating and inexpensive puzzles that can be used for this theme. Be sure that the puzzles are easy to assemble and contain pieces large enough not to present a choking hazard.
2. *Outdoor toys:* Kites are available in most toy stores and also in oriental gift shops. Be sure to choose a simple kite that will fly easily. There are some very attractive dragon kites that are easy to fly and are relevant to the New Year's celebration.
3. *Miscellaneous:* An abacus.

Teacher-made games and materials

NOTE: For detailed descriptions, see Learning Games in Part 1.

1. *Tic-tac-toe* (called Circles and Squares in China): Draw nine equal-sized squares on a piece of cardboard. Give each child five round counters or cubes to place on the carboard. Children take turns placing a counter in some of the squares. The object of the game is to get three counters in a row first. Each child should have a different colour or shape of counter.

NOTE: Children might be encouraged to make their own game if the squares of cardboard are precut for them.

2. *Match-them:* Make up sets of two pictures each of the twelve animals for which the Chinese years are named. Let children find matching pairs.

■ Matching can be challenging for some children. This is a very basic approach to matching. Be sure to allow children to handle the pictures to increase their involvement with the activity. It is also helpful to have children work in pairs to assist each other. A follow-up discussion of the ways the pictures match is a helpful extension for children developing advanced problem-solving skills.

3. *Alike, different, and the same:* Use the sets made in number 2 to compare other characteristics.

4. *I see something red:* Each child finds something red.

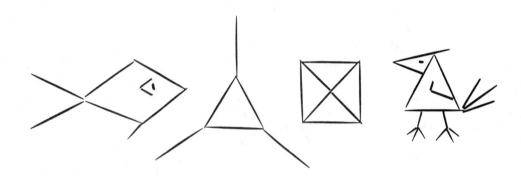

5. *Toothpick puzzlers:* Arranging coloured toothpicks in designs can be an interesting and challenging activity. Children may wish to glue their creations on a piece of paper after exploring the material on a piece of dark felt or paper. See the illustration above for ideas.

6. *Pickup sticks:* This is a rather difficult game for the very youngest that requires great patience. The pickup sticks need blunt or sanded ends. When this game is played with chopsticks it is much easier.

7. *Seven-piece puzzle:* Children fit the pieces together to make a square or other designs. You can make your own puzzle out of poster board. For the youngest children, draw a pattern on another piece of cardboard and let them match the shapes to it.

8. *Chinese checkers:* Older children may be able to grasp the concept of how this game is played. Supervise carefully, as marbles may be swallowed.

9. *Toteetum:* This game is played with a small cube that has a dowel inserted into one end and either numbers or pictures painted on each side. The child spins the toteetum and predicts what side will come up. Flipping coins is also a somewhat universal game. Spinning a wooden plate on its edge and predicting which side will come up is still another pastime. These games of chance may not be acceptable to some people.

Book Centre

•• Graeme, Jocelyn. *Celebrations.* Don Mills, ON: Addison-Wesley, 1990. (text is in Spanish, French, English, and Chinese)
•••• Kalman, Bobbie. *We Celebrate New Year.* Toronto: Crabtree, 1985.
••• Lattimore, Eleanor. *Little Pear.* New York: Harcourt Brace Jovanovich, 1968.
•••• Lim, John. *At Grandmother's House.* Montreal: Tundra, 1977. (Read–Tell)
••• Sendak, Maurice. *Chicken Soup with Rice.* New York: Scholastic, 1960.

••• Wallace, Ian. *Chin Chiang and the Dragon's Dance.* Vancouver: Douglas & McIntyre, 1984.
••• Waters, Kate, and Madeline Slovenz-Low. *Lion Dancer: Ernie Wan's Chinese New Year.* New York: Scholastic, 1990.

Planning for Group Time

NOTE: All music, fingerplays, poems, stories, and games listed here may also be used at other times during the session as appropriate.

Music

Songs

NOTE: Most of the songs that are appropriate for this section are difficult for non-Oriental children to sing. The "Oriental" songs in children's song books are often insulting to people of Oriental heritage. Songs of celebrations are very appropriate for this section. Songs such as "Puff the Magic Dragon" are very inappropriate for this section, in spite of the fact that it is a good song that may be used for other celebrations, such as Halloween.

Rhythms and Singing Games

1. Use drums and have a dragon dance: Make a dragon head out of papier-mâché or a paper bag; use a tablecloth or a bedspread to cover the dragon's body; attach a tail.
2. Play Asian music: Use finger cymbals, tone blocks, gongs, bells, or a guitar.

Fingerplays and Poems

NOTE: Tell children that the Chinese are credited with using fingerplays hundreds of years ago. Show children how to make shadow pictures with their fingers.

From *Let's Do Fingerplays*, Grayson
"Old Shoes, New Shoes," p. 18
"Shiny Shoes," p. 19

Stories

(To read, read–tell, or tell. See Book Centre for a complete list.)
Choose stories that introduce new ideas and customs to children who are not from a Chinese or Vietnamese background, but that respect the experience of children who are. Lim's *At Grandmother's House* is an excellent book for achieving this dual goal.

Games

(See Learning Games in Part 1 and Teacher-Made Games and Materials earlier in this chapter for directions.)

1. *Look and see:* Use animals of the Chinese Fortune Calendar year.
2. *Scramble:* Use animals of the Chinese Fortune Calendar year; also chopsticks, *daruma* doll, kite, fan, Vietnamese picturebook, and so on.
3. *I see something red.*

Routine Times

1. Serve rice and chicken, or pork or shrimp with broccoli for meal time.
2. Chinese and Vietnamese foods are offered in specialty stores or international food sections of supermarkets. Find out what is available in your community and plan to serve some samples at snack or mealtimes.

   NOTE: Travel by business people, students, and tourists has broadened the opportunities for tasting and learning about food that is prepared and eaten in different parts of the world. It has also nurtured a desire in many people to eat these foods as a regular part of their diets.

3. At snack or meal times, eat some of the food that has been prepared earlier by a Chinese or Vietnamese visitor or a parent. Have children observe how the food is made or help to make it.
4. Give each child two of everything at snack or meal time, since even numbers are considered lucky in the Chinese tradition. Two of anything means double happiness. Two sections of a mandarin orange or tangerine would be especially appropriate.
5. If possible, buy some dried fruits for the children for snack or meal times, such as dried apples. One student interviewed remembered a particular octagon-shaped tin that was always brought out for the New Year, with divided sections filled with different dried fruits and foods.

   ▼ **CAUTION:** Be aware of any food allergies or special diets in your group.

6. Play some Chinese music for rest time, or play it as background music when the children are using art materials and participating in free-choice activities.

Large Muscle Activities

1. Marble game (needs careful supervision): In China, children used to toss marbles, stones or seed pods into the air and catch them before they fell in a game similar to jacks. This is quite difficult, but it is interesting to note the origin of the North American game.
2. Chinese jump rope (a game with many variations): One variation involves raising an elastic rope higher and higher to see how high children can jump. Use waistband elastic for the rope.
3. Paper, scissors, and stone: On the count of three, two players show one of the following:

   Paper will cover a stone *(hand extended flat for paper)*
   Scissors will cut paper   *(index and middle finger extended to form V, wiggle as if cutting with scissors)*
   Stone will dull scissors *(hand makes a fist for a rock)*

   The child showing the most powerful subject wins or scores a point.

   NOTE: This is sometimes called Cloth, scissors, and stone.

4. Blowing game: Children in Asia make little folded paper frogs. They place them on a tabletop and blow them across the table to see whose frog gets there first. If the

tabletop has a ledge along the sides, ping-pong balls can be blown across the surface instead. See *origami* books for a frog pattern.

Extended Experiences

1. Visit a Chinese or Vietnamese restaurant with children.
2. Invite a Chinese or Vietnamese parent to visit and bring a traditional treat to share with the children. If the recipe is simple enough and there is no danger involved, the children might help to make it. Sometimes part of the preparation can be done beforehand and described to the children when completing the final steps.
3. Children will enjoy learning the skill of manipulating chopsticks. Soup crackers or miniature marshmallows make good items to be picked up and eaten by children.

   NOTE: Many Chinese children are nearly six before they can manipulate chopsticks adroitly. Younger children in China are given spoons.

# Teacher Resources

Pictures and Displays

1. Note display items suggested in the Discovery Centre. Consult the yellow pages of your phone book for your nearest import–export store.
2. Seek out and collect artifacts from parents, friends, or people who have travelled extensively. Teachers in the public school systems with a particular interest in cultural awareness may prove helpful. When possible, invite visitors to bring these artifacts so that they can be available to answer questions about them.
3. Obtain an Asian lunar calendar from an import–export store.

Books and Periodicals

Joy, M. *Highdays and Holidays.* Boston: Faber & Faber, 1981.
Manning-Saunders, R. *Festivals.* London: Heinemann, 1973.
Ontario Ministry of Culture and Recreation. *Days to Remember: Observances of Significance in Our Multicultural Society* (Glyn P. Ellen, ed.). Toronto: Government of Ontario, 1980.
Shepard, S.M. *Asian Food Treats.* Vancouver: Douglas & McIntyre, 1984.
U.S. Committee for UNICEF. *Joy through the World.* New York: Bragdon, 1985.
Wyndham, Robert. *Chinese Mother Goose Rhymes.* Cleveland: Collins-World, 1968.

Community Resources and Organizations

☐ Art museums for Chinese or Vietnamese artifacts.
☐ A Chinese or Vietnamese cultural or community centre.
☐ Parents, teachers, students, armed forces personnel, or other people who have lived in or visited an Asian country or who may themselves be Asian.
☐ An import–export store.
☐ A Chinese or Vietnamese restaurant and its staff.

☐ A group of Asian university students who may serve a traditional New Year's dinner or present an International Night, displaying artifacts and sharing dances, dress, or drama.

☐ Special celebrations, such as parades or festivities planned in restaurants for the Chinese/Vietnamese New Year.

ASHURA

(A-shoora)

This holiday of thanksgiving is celebrated in February by Muslims to commemorate their joy in Noah and his family's survival of the Flood and the sparing of humankind. According to legend, Noah asked his wife to prepare a special pudding on the day he was able to set foot on land after the flood. She gathered dates, figs, grapes, nuts, and currants in great quantities and prepared the largest pudding ever made, which was called *Ashura*. On this holiday, a similar pudding is prepared and eaten by Muslims as an expression of thanksgiving.

Extended Experiences

1. Provide a toy ark (houseboat) and pairs of toy animals in the block centre.
2. Allow children to make a simple pudding, adding any or all of the following fruits: dates, figs, grapes, nuts, currants, and so on.
3. A large cardboard box could also be set out for an ark. Hollow-block ramps can be used to march up into it.

GROUNDHOG DAY

Many towns and cities have a Groundhog Day celebration in a local park or zoo. This can be an informative trip for older children.

Groundhog Day can provide variety and diversion in the middle of winter's dreariness. Legend says that if groundhogs come out of their holes from winter hibernation on February 2 and see their shadows, they will return to their holes and we will have another two months of winter weather. If the day is cloudy and groundhogs do not see their shadow, then spring will come early. Canada's special groundhog lives in Wiarton, Ontario, and is named Wiarton Willy. The town of Wiarton has special celebrations on February 2 every year. Celebration of Groundhog Day could also be part of an exploration of the winter theme.

Basic Understandings

(concepts children can grasp from this subject)

☐ Some people believe that animals can help people find out about the weather.
☐ Groundhogs sleep or hibernate for most of the winter.
☐ Shadows are created when there is a strong light behind a person, an object, or an animal.

Extended Experiences

1. Tell children the story of the groundhog. Encourage them to check the playground to see if the groundhog would see his shadow in your area, by looking for the shadows of other children and their own shadows.
2. Provide scraps of brown nylon fur in the art centre so that children can make pictures of groundhogs with glue and stiff cardboard backing.
3. Serve raw vegetables at snack time as a special groundhog snack.

ST. VALENTINE'S DAY

St. Valentine's Day is a very commercial celebration, but its themes of kindness and love can be presented to children in a gentle manner that will help them appreciate the people whom they like and love. With the thematic colour for valentines being red, activities in Chapter 27, Colour in My World, can also be used or modified for use in this celebration. It is advisable to spend a very short time on this celebration; a maximum of two days is appropriate. If cards are being given out in the school, stress that every child should be given a card. It is helpful to parents to send home a description of the centre's plans for St. Valentine's Day and a list of all the children's names, but emphasize that it is not necessary to send cards.

Book Centre

••• Bond, Felicia. *Four Valentines in a Rainstorm.* New York: Harper Junior, 1990.
•• Greydanus, Rose. *Valentine's Day Grump.* Mahwah, NJ: Trail Associates, 1981.
•••• Kalman, Bobbie, et al. *We Celebrate Valentine's Day.* Toronto: Crabtree, 1986.
••• Prelutsky, Jack. *It's Valentine's Day.* New York: Scholastic, 1985.
•• Stock, Catherine. *Secret Valentine.* Don Mills, ON: Bradbury Press, 1991.

Songs

From *Elephant Jam*, Sharon, Lois, and Bram
"Skinnamarink," p. 58

From *More Piggyback Songs*, Warren
"Valentines Red," p. 23
"My Valentine," p. 23

From *Piggyback Songs*, Warren
"The Postman Brings a Valentine," p. 15
"Will You be My Valentine?" p. 16
"Valentine Game," p. 16
"Counting Valentines," p. 17
"Three Red Valentines," p. 18
"Heart Hopping," p. 18
"A Red Heart," p. 18
"I Love You," p. 18

From *Tunes for Tots*, Warner and Berry
"Be My Valentine," p. 34

Fingerplays and Poems

From *Don't Eat Spiders,* Heidbreder
"A Million Valentines," p. 32
"Valentine Helicopter," p. 33

Teacher Resources

Joy, M. *Highdays and Holidays.* Boston: Faber & Faber, 1981.
Manning-Saunders, R. *Festivals.* London: Heinemann, 1973.

BASANTH

(Buh-sahnth)

Usually this Muslim holiday for the first day of spring (lunar calendar) falls in late February or March (solar calendar) and is heralded by the new moon. It is celebrated in some parts of Eastern Europe and Africa as well as Asia. In Pakistan, Punjabi kites — special, elaborate, colourful kites without tails — are flown on this national holiday. Stout string stiffened or coated with starch and powdered glass allows boys to cut down each other's kites during competitions. Usually kites are flown from rooftops or high hills to avoid trees. Businesses and shops are often closed for the festivities.

Extended Experiences

1. The children might make a simple kite (see the patterns earlier in this chapter).
2. Prepare and serve a Pakistani treat. See Teacher Resources, below, for suggestions.

Teacher Resources

Hardwick, F.C., ed. *From Beyond the Western Horizon.* Vancouver: Tantalus, 1974.
Humayun, S.N. *Muslim Cookery.* Ottawa: Ottawa Muslim Women's Auxiliary, 1985.
Shepard, S.M. *Asian Food Treats.* Vancouver: Douglas & McIntyre, 1984.

HINA MATSURI

(HEE-nah MAT-soo-REE)

Traditionally, peach blossoms are a symbol of wedded happiness and also of the qualities of mildness, softness, and peacefulness. *Hina Matsuri,* the Japanese Doll Festival or Peach Festival, begins on March 3. It is a time when peach blossoms are usually in full bloom. Treasured heirloom dolls are exquisitely dressed in colourful embroidered silk costumes and are arranged very carefully on a tier-like platform in a special room or place in the home. Emperor and empress dolls are placed on the top shelf and ladies-in-waiting and their attendants are arranged on lower shelves. On the bottom shelf are placed lacquered miniature furniture and little musical instruments. Peach blossoms are arranged all around them.

The dolls (*hina ningyo*, pronounced HEE-nah NIN-GEE-yaw) are highly treasured, and because of the time it takes to produce them, they become almost priceless. They are handed down from generation to generation. During the festival, family friends are invited over to see the collections and to have special treats. Often soup, fish, rice boiled with beans, special diamond-shaped cakes, and fruit-shaped candies are served with tea.

This is a special day in Japan for girls. There is a complementary holiday for boys on May 8 called *Tan-Go-No-Sekku.*

Extended Experiences

1. Invite all children to bring in a doll or stuffed animal for this celebration. Tell them the story of *Hina Matsuri* and have a doll festival, displaying all the children's dolls or animals.
2. Serve fish and rice for lunch. Serve Japanese rice cakes for a snack.

Teacher Resources

Casal, U.A. *The Five Sacred Festivals of Ancient Japan.* Rutland, VT: Tuttle, 1967.

Kehoe, J. *A Handbook for Enhancing the Multicultural Climate of the School.* Vancouver: Western Educational Development Group, 1984.

Ontario Ministry of Culture and Recreation. *Days to Remember: Observances of Significance in Our Multicultural Society* (Glyn P. Allen, ed.). Toronto: Government of Ontario, 1980.

Takashima, R., and M. Haji. *The Art of Japanese Cooking for All Seasons.* Vancouver: Haji, 1985.

Takata, T. *Nikkei Legacy: The Story of Japanese Canadians from Settlement to Today.* Toronto: NC Press, 1983.

ST. PATRICK'S DAY

On March 17 each year, the Irish celebrate St. Patrick's Day by "wearin' of the Green." This holiday commemorates St. Patrick, who legend tells us went about Ireland as a missionary, preaching Christianity. St. Patrick is also credited with ridding Ireland of snakes. On St. Patrick's Day, Canadians of Irish origin wear shamrock pins or some articles of green clothing.

Songs

From *More Piggyback Songs,* Warren
"March 17th," p. 29
"Leprechauns," p. 29
"Do You Know What a Shamrock Is?" p. 30
"I'm a Little Leprechaun," p. 30
"Leprechaun's March," p. 30

From *Piggyback Songs,* Warren
"On St. Patrick's Day," p. 21
"Top of the Morning to You," p. 21

From *Tunes for Tots*, Warner and Berry
"The Leprechaun," p. 35

Extended Experiences

1. Learn about the colour green (see Chapter 27, Colour in My World).
2. The shamrock is the national symbol of Ireland. (The shamrock is a low-growing plant with three leaves, similar to the field clover that grows in the United States and Canada.) Shamrock plants are available from florists around St. Patrick's Day.
3. Several weeks before St. Patrick's Day, cut a large, flat, green sponge in the shape of a shamrock. Dampen the sponge and sprinkle it generously with grass seed. Keep moistened, and by St. Patrick's Day it will be covered with green grass.
4. Post pictures of Ireland and help children find it on the globe. Ireland is called the "Emerald Isle" because its land is covered with beautiful green grass.
5. Post pictures of a St. Patrick's Day parade.
6. Have a parade at music time.
7. Play "The Irish Washer Woman" and let the children dance or move to its fast tempo.
8. Display the Irish flag or a picture of one. Older children may be able to cut and paste, paint, or crayon one. The flag is rectangular with three equal vertical blocks of colour, which are, from left to right, green, white, and reddish orange.
9. Invite a parent to bring Irish linen, a Kerry cloak, a clay pipe, or a tall hat to show the children. English and Gaelic are spoken in Ireland. Perhaps this parent could teach the children a few words of Gaelic. (Gaelic is a very unusual and difficult language, so the words should be kept simple.)

Teacher Resources

Kane, A. *Songs and Sayings of an Ulster Childhood.* Toronto: McClelland & Stewart, 1983.

Ontario Ministry of Culture and Recreation. *Days to Remember: Observances of Significance in Our Multicultural Society* (Glyn P. Allen, ed.) Toronto: Government of Ontario, 1980.

· ·

PURIM

(POOR-ihm)

For Jewish families, *Purim* is *the* festival of merriment. There is an obligation to eat, drink, and be merry on this holiday. *Purim* a springtime religious festival that falls on the fourteenth day of the Hebrew month *Adar*, which usually falls in March. It is celebrated to mark the victory of the Jews in Persia, as written in the *Megillah* (Book of Esther).

The story of *Purim* tells of Esther, a Jewish woman who was married to the King of Persia. Haman, the Prime Minister of Persia, hated the Jews and tricked the king into agreeing that all the Jews in Persia should be killed. Esther heard of the plan and told the king how Haman had tricked him. When the king heard this, he had Haman put to death, and then gave the Jews their freedom. *Purim* is also called the Feast of Lots, because Haman drew lots to see which day would be best suited to enact his sinful plan.

The day before *Purim* is one of fasting. On the day of the holiday, the *Megillah* is read. Every time the name Haman is mentioned, the children yell, stamp their feet, and twirl a noisemaker called a *grager*.

Jewish children today have *Purim* parties and enjoy dressing up in biblical costumes and acting out the story of Esther. In Israel, children go from door to door singing loudly and reciting humorous poems.

Usually money and food are given to the poor. In the afternoon there is a feast with gifts of food for friends and relatives. *Hamantaschen* (Hah-mehn-tah-shen), which are three-cornered cakes with poppy seeds and honey or dried fruit fillings, are traditionally served. Some say the triangular shapes resemble Haman's hat (jailers wore tricornered hats in those days), and others say they are "Haman's pockets," because he had to pay out of his pocket for his wicked plan.

Extended Experiences

1. Read or tell a story from the following book: Adler, D.A. *A Picture Book of Jewish Holidays.* New York: Holiday House, 1981.
2. Sing a Jewish song or listen to a tape of Israeli music.
3. Invite a Jewish parent to bring a *grager* to show the children, or buy one at a Hebrew bookstore.
4. Display different kinds of noisemakers used at birthday parties, New Year's Eve, and Halloween. Also display a *grager*.
5. Make *hamantaschen* using the recipe below, or ask a Jewish parent to bake some and bring them for a snack, or to come and help the children make their own.

....

HAMANTASCHEN

Roll canned biscuits to 6 mm thick. Brush tops with melted butter. Place 15 mL of the chosen filling in the centre of each biscuit.

Pull up the edges to form a tricorner, pinching the corners to let some of the filling show. Brush the tops with honey or beaten egg. Bake on a greased cookie sheet for 20 minutes at 180°C/350°F.

Fillings:
a. *Poppyseed filling:*
   Melt 15 mL/1 T of butter with 15 mL/1 T of honey. Add 5 mL/1 tsp lemon juice, 125 mL/½ cup ground almonds, and 250 mL/1 cup poppyseeds. Stir until blended.
b. *Dried fruit filling:*
   In the top of a double boiler, mix 125 mL/½ cup each of raisins, pitted chopped prunes, chopped dried apricots, and fresh bread or cake crumbs. Add 125 mL/½ cup honey. Stir over boiling water until honey melts. If too thin, add more crumbs. Let cool.
c. *Plum jam filling:*
   Beat together 375 mL/½ cups plum jam, grated rind and juice of lemon, 125 mL/½ cup chopped almonds, and 125 mL/½ cup bread or cake crumbs.

Teacher Resources

Adler, D.A. *A Picture Book of Jewish Holidays.* New York: Holiday House, 1981.
American Association for Jewish Education. "Jewish Education: The Early Years." *Pedagogic Reporter* 24 (Fall 1972) p. 3.
Chanover, Hyman. *A Curriculum Guide for the Kindergarten.* New York: United Synagogue Book Service. n.d.

Edmonton Hadassah WIZO Association. *The Great Hadassah* WIZO *Cookbook.* Edmonton: Hurtig, 1982.

Temes, S.R. *Welcome to My Kitchen.* Toronto: Temes, 1985.

Weinfeld, W., ed. *The Canadian Jewish Mosaic.* Rexdale, ON: Wiley, 1981.

BASANTA

(Buh-SAHN-tah)

This is a spring Hindu holiday celebrated three weeks before Holi. In Sanskrit, *basanta* means yellow, which is the sacred colour of the Hindus. In India, this festival is held in recognition of *Saraswati*, the Hindu goddess of 64 arts and sciences and also the wife of the god *Brahma.*

Extended Experiences

1. If you have Indian friends, you might ask them to share some artifacts with the children, such as a beautiful silk sari; interesting pieces of silver or clay, possibly with mirrors embedded in them; or an exquisitely embroidered picture. Often wood is carved into elephants. Most young children are familiar with and fascinated by this animal and have seen it in picture books, if not in zoos or circuses.
2. At Christmas time, charming elephants, bells, and camels made of mirror-faceted clay are available as tree ornaments at import shops. Other such items are available during the rest of the year.
3. Prepare and serve an Indian dish. Consult the books listed in Teacher Resources for recipes.

Teacher Resources

Hardwick, F.C., ed. *From Beyond the Western Horizon.* Vancouver: Tantalus, 1974.

Nimji, N. *India Today: Traditional Cuisine with Western Convenience.* Calgary: Nimji, 1986.

Shepard, S.M. *Asian Food Treats.* Vancouver: Douglas & McIntyre, 1984.

HOLI OR BASAAT

(Hoh-lee or Buh-saht)

This is a spring festival and the gayest of the Hindu holidays. It usually occurs late in March or early in April before the monsoon (big rain) begins, on the fifteenth day of the light half of the moon in the Hindu month of *Phalguna.* Water games are often played during this holiday, sometimes involving teams of participants. Children squirt coloured water at each other; favourite Hindu colours — red, crimson, and saffron — are most often used in water pistols or large pumps. In India, wreaths are often made to place around cows' necks or to be hung near windows and doors.

In Bengal, India, gifts are given before eating special foods on this holiday, which is connected with worship of *Krishna,* a Hindu god. Coloured powders are thrown during the festivities. Indian children who live in North America enjoy throwing confetti when celebrating this holiday.

Extended Experiences

1. During this holiday, let children throw confetti, make simple wreaths or necklaces of coloured paper to hang near doors or windows, or squirt water at one another when dressed appropriately (in raincoats or swimsuits).
2. Children can squirt water and then sprinkle dry tempera on a large sheet of paper laid on the floor, and watch the colours run together.

Teacher Resources

Hardwick, F.C., ed. *From Beyond the Western Horizon.* Vancouver: Tantalus, 1974.
Nimji, N. *India Today: Traditional Cuisine with Western Convenience.* Calgary: Nimji, 1986.
Shepard, S.M. *Asian Food Treats.* Vancouver: Douglas & McIntyre, 1984.

10 Celebrations: April to September

Calendar of Events

(based on the solar calendar)

- ☐ Pesach (Passover) — late March or early April
- ☐ Easter — between March 22 and April 25
- ☐ St. George's Day (Newfoundland) — April 23
- ☐ Baisakhi — April or May
- ☐ Tan Go-No-Sekku — May 8
- ☐ Mother's Day — second Sunday in May
- ☐ Victoria Day — third Sunday in June
- ☐ St. Anthony's Day — second Sunday in June
- ☐ Father's Day — third Sunday in June
- ☐ Fête Nationale (former Fête de St. Jean Baptiste) (Quebec) — June 24
- ☐ Discovery Day (Newfoundland) — June 24
- ☐ Canada Day — July 1
- ☐ Memorial Day (Newfoundland) — July 12
- ☐ Civic Holiday (Manitoba, New Brunswick, Northwest Territories) — first Monday in August
- ☐ Simcoe Day (Ontario) — first Monday in August
- ☐ Saskatchewan Day — first Monday in August
- ☐ British Columbia Day — first Monday in August
- ☐ Heritage Day (Alberta) — first Monday in August
- ☐ Discovery Day (Yukon) — third Monday in August
- ☐ Labour Day — first Monday in September
- ☐ Rosh Hashanah — two days in September or early October
- ☐ Yom Kippur — late September or early October (ten days after Rosh Hashanah)

Historical and Political Holidays

From June 24 to the first Monday in September, there are many holidays that are of historical and political significance for Canadians. Most of these have little meaning for young children and take place on statutory holidays. Try to find out if there are any special activities in your community that would be of interest to young children, and make use of them in your program.

··

PESACH (PASSOVER)

(PES-ah)

A yearly festival celebrated by Jewish people for eight days every March or early April, Passover recalls the ancient Israelites' march to freedom from Egyptian slavery as told in the biblical book of Exodus. During Passover, Jews eat *matzo*, or unleavened bread, rather than bread made with yeast. This is in memory of the fact that the Israelites had no time to leaven their bread when they fled from Egypt. *Matzo* is made from potato starch and *matzo* meal instead of flour.

On the first or second night, a *Seder* (service) is held. At this service, special foods are eaten that are not eaten at any other time of the year. Orthodox Jews use a special set of dishes, cooking utensils, and silverware at this time, too. A traditional platter is always placed on the Passover table beside the *Haggadah*, the book containing the story of Passover. The platter contains parsley, saltwater, a hard-cooked egg, a horseradish root, a lamb shank, *moror* (bitter herbs or horseradish sauce), and *haroset* (chopped nuts and fruit), all symbolic in the Passover story, which is recited during the *Seder*. Close to this platter is a white napkin interleaved with three sheets of *matzo*. Two of the *matzo* are used in the ceremony, and the third one, called the *afikomen*, is hidden. Whoever finds it gets a reward, and then it is divided so everyone can eat a piece for good luck.

Wine is an important part of Jewish feasts. At the *Seder*, a glass of wine that no one touches is poured for the prophet Elijah, who is expected to appear one day to announce the coming of the Messiah. After dinner, the door of the home is opened and Elijah is invited to enter.

*V*ocabulary

freedom	*Seder*	*matzo*	cake
Pesach	supper	macaroons	fruit
Passover			

Book Centre

•• Adler, D.A. *A Picture Book of Passover.* New York: Holiday House, 1982.
  •• ———. *A Picture Book of Jewish Holidays.* New York: Holiday House, 1981.
•••• Corwin, Judith Hoffman. *Jewish Holiday Fun.* New York: Simon & Schuster, 1987.
   • de Paola, Tomie. *My First Passover.* New York: Putnam, 1991.
  •• Graeme, Jocelyn. *Celebrations.* Don Mills, ON: Addison-Wesley, 1990. (text is in Spanish, French, English, and Chinese)
 ••• Greenfeld, H. *Passover.* New York: Holt, Rinehart and Winston, 1978.
•••• Simon, Norma. *Passover.* New York: Crowell, 1965.
•••• ———. *My Family Seder.* New York: United Synagogue Book Service, 1961.

Extended Experiences

1. Invite a Jewish parent to visit the group and tell about the holiday, showing pictures or items of interest.
2. Prepare a Jewish food appropriate to the celebration.
3. Compare *matzo* and saltines: how they are alike and different in taste, colour, texture, and shape.
4. Compare *matzo* and sandwich bread made with yeast as to shape, colour, texture, and taste.
5. Compare two glasses of water, one of which has 5 mL of salt added. Give each child a hard-cooked egg. Let each child dip the egg in the plain water and take a bite, and then dip it in the saltwater and take a bite.
6. Compare dried fruits with fresh fruits. Soak dried fruits in water and compare with fresh fruits as to texture, size, and taste.
7. Make a compote of dried fruits: Simmer 750 mL/3 cups of soaked dried fruit in 375 mL/1½ cups water to which has been added 175 mL/¾ cup sugar, thin slices of lemon, a stick of cinnamon, and 3 or 4 whole cloves tied in cheesecloth. Cook for 20 minutes or until tender. Discard spices and add 250 mL/1 cup whole blanched almonds. Chill before serving.
8. Make Passover macaroons: Beat 3 egg whites until they hold a stiff peak. Beat in 25 mL/2 T superfine sugar until mixture is glossy. Fold in 150 mL/⅔ cup sugar mixed with 75 mL/6 T *matzo* meal and 250 mL/1 cup ground almonds or shredded coconut. Drop spoonfuls of the mixture on a cookie sheet lined with wax paper. Bake in 150°C/300°F oven for 20 minutes. Cool and peel off the paper.
9. Adapt the following games as noted:
   a. *I see something square:* Show *matzo*, and look for square things.
   b. *Chew, lick, and taste:* Use a variety of crackers, including *matzo*.
   c. *How many?* Count prune, peach, and apricot pits.
   d. *Match-them:* Use prune, peach, and apricot pits or pictures of these fruits.
   e. *Sorting and grouping by association:* Use items in (3).
   f. *Alike, different, and the same:* Use items in (d).

Teacher Resources

Adler, D.A. *A Picture Book of Jewish Holidays.* New York: Holiday House, 1981.

American Association for Jewish Education. "Jewish Education: The Early Years." *Pedagogic Reporter* 24 (Fall 1972) 3.

Chanover, Hyman. *A Curriculum Guide for the Kindergarten.* New York: United Synagogue Book Service. n.d.

Edmonton Hadassah WIZO Association. *The Great Hadassah WIZO Cookbook.* Edmonton: Hurtig, 1982.

Temes, S.R. *Welcome to My Kitchen.* Toronto: Temes, 1985.

Weinfeld, W., ed. *The Canadian Jewish Mosaic.* Rexdale, ON: Wiley, 1981.

• •

EASTER

Easter is the most joyous Christian festival. It commemorates the resurrection of Christ. Since this event is recorded in the Bible as occurring at the time of the Jewish Passover, it was originally celebrated at that time. But in 325 AD, the Council of Nicaea determined that Easter would be the first Sunday after the first full moon that appears after the spring equinox (*March 21*). Easter always occurs between March 22 and April 25.

Basic Understandings
(concepts children can grasp from this subject)

☐ Easter Sunday is a special, joyful day celebrated in the Christian churches and their church schools.

☐ Many children go to church or attend sunrise services outdoors on Easter Sunday with their parents.

☐ Churches are often decorated with white lilies, symbols of purity and light.

Additional Facts the Teacher Should Know

1. Many Easter traditions and customs come from ancient pagan celebrations. The word "Easter" comes from the name of an Anglo-Saxon goddess, *Eostre*, who represented light or spring. The Anglo-Saxon tribes held a festival in her honour every April. Just as the Earth is dressed in a new cloak of greenery, people often wear new clothes for Easter. In Europe, people take a walk through fields. In America, there are Easter parades. Probably this custom originated with Emperor Constantine, who had his leaders don their most elegant robes on Easter to honour Christ's resurrection. There was a belief that if a person wore a new article of clothing for the first time on Easter, he or she would surely have good luck for the rest of the year.

2. The legend of the Easter bunny is definitely not religious. After a long winter nap, the Easter bunny is supposed to hide brightly coloured eggs in the new green grass. He may bring dyed eggs, wooden eggs, even fancy sugar eggs. The idea of Easter eggs came to us from ancient Egypt and Persia; the eggs are symbols of new life. Newly born chicks, ducklings, and bunnies are also associated with spring.

3. Most child-related activities, including the Easter bunny, are not religiously oriented to this holiday.

Book Centre

••• Adams, Adrienne. *The Easter Egg Artists*. New York: Aladdin, 1991.

• de Paola, Tomie. *My First Easter*. New York: Putnam, 1991.

••• Friedisch, P. *The Easter Bunny That Overslept*. New York: Lothrop, Lee and Shepard, 1957.

•• Graeme, Jocelyn. *Celebrations*. Don Mills, ON: Addison-Wesley, 1990. (text is in Spanish, French, English, and Chinese)

•• Kalman, Bobbie, and Maureen Shaughnessy. *We Celebrate Easter*. Toronto: Crabtree, 1985.

•• Stock, Catherine. *Easter Surprise*. Don Mills, ON: Bradbury Press, 1991.

••• Williams, Margery. *The Velveteen Rabbit*. New York: Messner, 1983.

Songs

From *More Piggyback Songs*, Warren
"Did You Ever See a Bunny?" p. 31
"Easter Bunny," p. 31

From *Piggyback Songs*, Warren
"The Bunny Patch," p. 24
"Did You Ever See a Bunny?" p. 24
"Easter Bunny Hippity Hop," p. 25
"Down the Bunny Trail," p. 25

From *Singing Bee*, Hart
"Hot Cross Buns," p. 140
"The Easter Bunny," p. 141

From *A Treasury of Songs for Children*, Glazer
"Hot Cross Buns," p. 122

From *Tunes for Tots*, Warner and Berry
"I Wish I Was a Bunny," p. 37
"Easter Morning," p. 38

Fingerplays and Poems

From *Hand Rhymes*, Brown
"Little Bunny," p. 21

Teacher Resources

Joy, M. *Highdays and Holidays.* Boston: Faber & Faber, 1981.
Manning-Saunders, R. *Festivals.* London: Heinemann, 1973.
Patterson, L. *A Holiday Book for Easter.* Champaign, IL: Garrard, 1966.
Stephan, B. *Decorations for Holiday Celebrations.* New York: Crown, 1978.

BAISAKHI

(Bi-e-SAH-kee)

In India, the Hindu New Year, *Baisakhi*, comes in April or May. Hindus believe that bathing in the Ganges River will protect them from evil. Then they go to the temple and listen to the reading of the calendar of the New Year. Women and girls wear colourful saris on this day. Elaborate feasts are held, gifts are exchanged, and prayers are offered to family gods.

Extended Experiences

1. Display pictures or artifacts from India.
2. Invite a mother to show the children how to wrap a sari.
3. Ask a parent if he or she would play the sitar, bells, cymbals, or *tabla* for the children.
4. Invite a parent to demonstrate for the children how to prepare a traditional food for this holiday.

Teacher Resources

Hardwick, F.C., ed. *From Beyond the Western Horizon.* Vancouver: Tantalus, 1974.

Nimji, N. *India Today: Traditional Cuisine with Western Convenience.* Calgary: Nimji, 1986.

Shepard, S.M. *Asian Food Treats.* Vancouver: Douglas & MacIntyre, 1984.

TAN-GO-NO-SEKKU

(Tahn-goh-noh-seh-koo)

This holiday is celebrated in Japan on May 8. Historically, this was a day to celebrate military strength and to expel the evil spirits that caused poverty and misfortune. Today, it is a day to celebrate the beginning of summer and the warmth and good crops that it brings. This is a special day in Japan for boys: Japanese boys fly kites, fight mock battles with swords made of iris leaves, and display puppets. There is a complementary holiday for girls on March 3 called *Hina Matsuri.*

Extended Experiences

1. Set up a white sheet on a curtain rod and shine a bright light on the sheet from behind. Show the children how shapes can be seen as shadows on the screen. Provide them with bristol board, scissors, and sticks to assemble shadow puppets. They can stand behind the screen and move their puppets in time to music, while other children and teachers watch.
2. Serve fish and rice for lunch, and Japanese rice cakes for a snack.
3. Make and fly carp kites. Instructions are on p. 232 in Chapter 9.

Teacher Resources

Kehoe, J. *A Handbook for Enhancing the Multicultural Climate of the School.* Vancouver: Western Educational Development Group, 1984.

Ontario Ministry of Culture and Recreation. *Days to Remember: Observances of Significance in Our Multicultural Society.* (Glyn P. Allen, ed.). Toronto: Government of Ontario, 1980.

Takashima, R., and M. Haji. *The Art of Japanese Cooking for All Seasons.* Vancouver: Haji, 1985.

Takata, T. *Nikkei Legacy: The Story of Japanese Canadians from Settlement to Today.* Toronto: NC Press, 1983.

MOTHER'S DAY

Mother's Day is an important family celebration, to which teachers can contribute. In the week preceding Mother's Day, which is celebrated on the second Sunday in May, it is appropriate to sing songs about mothers, read stories about mothers, and prepare small gifts.

It is essential to be sensitive to the needs of children who do not live with their mothers or whose mothers are dead. Try to find out if there are any mother figures for whom these children would like to prepare a special card or gift, or suggest that they can do something special for their fathers on this day.

Songs

From *Elephant Jam*, Sharon, Lois, and Bram
"Skinnamarink," p. 58

From *Piggyback Songs*, Warren
"I Love You," p. 18

From *Tunes for Tots*, Warner and Berry
"Mother," p. 39

> **NOTE:** These songs are easy to learn, and children enjoy learning them to sing to their mothers on Mother's Day.

VICTORIA DAY

Victoria Day, which takes place every third Monday in May, is a holiday of historical importance for many Canadians, but it does not have great meaning for young children. For children, this holiday is usually important for its fireworks displays and because it is the beginning of many summer activities. It is useful to talk about fireworks and how they can be fun if they are used safely.

Extended Experiences

This is a good time to begin planting a garden inside or outside your centre.

Teacher Resources

Chickadee magazine.
Hardy, Ralph, et al. *The Weather Book.* Toronto: Little, Brown, 1982.
Owl magazine.

FATHER'S DAY

Father's Day, which takes place on the third Sunday in June, is an important family celebration, to which teachers can contribute. In the week preceding Father's Day, it is appropriate to sing songs about fathers, read stories about fathers, and prepare small gifts.

It is essential to be sensitive to the needs of children who do not live with their fathers or whose fathers are dead. Try to find out if there are any father figures for whom these children would like to prepare a special card or gift, or suggest that they can do something special for their mothers on this day.

Songs

From *Elephant Jam*, Sharon, Lois, and Bram
"Skinnamarink," p. 58

From *More Piggyback Songs*, Warren
"Happy Father's Day," p. 36
"Where's Daddy?" p. 36

> **NOTE:** These songs are easy to learn, and children enjoy learning them to sing to their fathers on Father's Day.

ROSH HASHANAH

(ROHSH-hah-shah-nah)

The Jewish New Year, *Rosh Hashanah*, is celebrated on two days in September or early October. The day is marked by the blowing of the *shofar* (ram's horn) calling the people to prayer. The *shofar* was blown when the people were called together to be told of the Ten Commandments by Moses. It is the opening of the most important time of the Jewish religious year, the ten-day period leading to the Day of Atonement, called *Yom Kippur* (Yohm Kip-POOR).

At sundown on New Year's Eve, the family eats a special meal. The *challah* (bread) for this meal is shaped like a ladder, symbolizing prayers ascending to God on its rungs or indicating that people can go up or down in the world (the braided *challah* is eaten on the Sabbath as well as on other Jewish holidays).

On this day, by tradition, the life of every person is judged by the Lord and is written in the Book of Life or the Book of Death. Therefore, it is the custom for friends to greet each other with the words, "May your life be inscribed for a happy New Year," or "May a good year be recorded for you." The ten days starting with *Rosh Hashanah* are known as the "days of repentance." It is a time to examine one's deeds for the last twelve months and resolve to do better. Those who are truly sorry can ask God's forgiveness and thereby be inscribed in the Book of Life on *Yom Kippur*. During the days of repentance, Jews call on those they have wronged and ask for forgiveness.

Extended Experiences.

1. Buy a loaf of *challah*. It is usually a braid-shaped loaf, but may be available in the shape of a ladder or round loaves that are more customary during this holiday. If neither is available, ask a Jewish friend or parent to bake several small loaves of the different shapes for you to share with the children. Have the children guess which spice is in the honey balls by smelling and tasting.
2. Invite a Jewish parent to visit and tell about *Rosh Hashanah* or bring a *shofar* to blow.
3. Visit a synagogue and see the *shofar* there.
4. Record the sound of the *shofar* on a tape-recorder as well as the sounds of other kinds of horns (e.g., car, trumpet, tuba, French horn.) Have pictures of instruments, or real

ones, to show as you play the tape. When children are familiar with the sounds, play the tape without the pictures and let the children guess which sound is which.
5. Read or tell either of the following stories:
•• Adler, D.A. *A Picture Book of Jewish Holidays.* New York: Holiday House, 1981.
••• Cone, Molly. *The Jewish New Year.* New York: Crowell, 1966.

Teacher Resources

Adler, D.A. *A Picture Book of Jewish Holidays.* New York: Holiday House, 1981.
Edmonton Hadassah WIZO Association. *The Great Hadassah WIZO Cookbook.* Edmonton: Hurtig, 1982.
Temes, S.R. *Welcome to My Kitchen.* Toronto: Temes, 1985.
Weinfeld, W., ed. *The Canadian Jewish Mosaic.* Rexdale, ON: Wiley, 1981.

YOM KIPPUR

(Yohm Kip-POOR)

Yom Kippur is the holiest day of the Jewish year. It is reverently called "The Sabbath of Sabbaths" and occurs ten days after *Rosh Hashanah*.

Nine days after *Rosh Hashanah* is the "Day of Atonement," which is marked by 24 hours of prayer, fasting, and asking God to forgive sins. At sundown the night before *Yom Kippur*, the family gathers for a special meal. Candles are lit (one is in memory of departed ones), and the family members ask one another to forgive any wrongdoings. After the meal, the family goes to the synagogue to pray. White, the symbol of purity, is worn by the officials, and white cloths cover the altar and the Ark, the holy chest that holds the scrolls of the *Torah*, a part of Jewish sacred scriptures. The men and boys wear white skullcaps. Often, white flowers are placed on the altar. From early morning the next day until sundown, a service is held at the synagogue. People fast, pray, and ask God's forgiveness. At sundown, a *shofar* (ram's horn) is blown, marking the closing of the gates of judgement for another year.

Extended Experiences

1. Read or tell the following story:
•• Adler, D.A. *A Picture Book of Jewish Holidays.* New York: Holiday House, 1981.
2. Invite a Jewish parent to visit and tell about *Yom Kippur* or bring a *shofar* to blow.
3. Visit a synagogue and see the *shofar* there.

Teacher Resources

Adler, D.A. *A Picture Book of Jewish Holidays.* New York: Holiday House, 1981.
American Association for Jewish Education. "Jewish Education: The Early Years." *Pedagogic Reporter* 24 (Fall 1972) p. 3.
Chanover, Hyman. *A Curriculum Guide for the Kindergarten.* New York: United Synagogue Book Service. n.d.

Edmonton Hadassah WIZO Association. *The Great Hadassah* WIZO Cookbook. Edmonton: Hurtig, 1982.

Temes, S.R. *Welcome to My Kitchen.* Toronto: Temes, 1985.

Weinfeld, W., ed. *The Canadian Jewish Mosaic.* Rexdale, ON: Wiley, 1981.

11 Celebrations: October to December

Calendar of Events

(based on the solar calendar)

- ☐ Sukkot — in September or October
- ☐ Thanksgiving — second Monday in October
- ☐ Halloween — October 31
- ☐ Remembrance Day — November 11
- ☐ Shichigosan — November 15
- ☐ Hanukkah — early December
- ☐ Christmas — December 25
- ☐ Boxing Day — December 26
- ☐ Kwanzaa — from December 26 to January 1

SUKKOT

(soo-cot)

Sukkot, a Jewish holiday observed in September or October, celebrates the harvest and commemorates the 40-year period after the Exodus from Egypt, during which the Jews wandered in the wilderness and lived in huts made of branches. A hut or booth called a *sukkah* is built of boards or canvas in the garden near the house or the synagogue. The top of the *sukkah* is made of pine branches through which the stars can shine at night. Flowers, vegetables, and fruits are woven into the branches or hung by children in the hut as decorations. During the festival, as many meals as possible are eaten in the *sukkah*, and they always include harvest fruits and vegetables. "Apple slice" and strudel are frequently served. It is customary to invite guests, especially those who do not have a *sukkah* of their own. Some people like to sleep in the *sukkah* at night. *Sukkot* is celebrated for eight days by Orthodox and Conservative Jews. On the last day of *Sukkot*, Jews thank God for the *Torah* in a ceremony called *Simhat Torah* ("rejoicing in the law"). Although associated with *Sukkot*, this is actually a separate holiday that comes after *Sukkot*. The sacred scrolls of the *Torah* are taken from the Ark and carried around the synagogue. Everyone joins in the parade. Boys and girls carry flags; on top of the flagstaffs are candles in hollowed-out apples. After the parade, the children are given nuts and candies.

NOTE: Apple slice is baked dough with apples, like a strudel.

Extended Experiences

1. See Discovery Centre and Learning and Language Materials Centre for the Thanksgiving celebration for suggestions on activities involving apples, nuts, and other harvest foods.
2. Taste Jewish apple slice or strudel.
3. Children might enjoy building a *sukkah* out of a large cardboard refrigerator box. Cut a door in one side and wide slits in the roof to appear like slats so that children can look up through the roof. Plastic flowers, fruits, and vegetables, and branches and leaves can be placed on the roof. Snacks of raisins, nuts, and fruits can be eaten inside.
4. Add the following books to your Book Centre to read–tell at story time:

 •••• Edelman, Lily. *The Sukkah and The Big Wind.* New York: United Synagogue Book Service, 1956.
 •••• Morrow, Betty, and Lewis Hartman. "Sukkot, A Double Thanksgiving," in *Jewish Holidays.* Champaign, IL: Garrard, 1967, pp. 33–45.
 •••• Simon, Norma. *Simhat Torah.* New York: United Synagogue Book Service, 1960.
 •••• ———. *Our First Sukkah.* New York: United Synagogue Book Service, 1959.

THANKSGIVING

Basic Understandings

(concepts children can grasp from this subject)

☐   Thanksgiving is a celebration of the end of the harvest.
☐   In the fall, some of the fruits and vegetables harvested include pumpkins, apples, and nuts.
☐   Families celebrate the end of the harvest with a special Thanksgiving dinner. The dinner usually includes a roasted turkey and pumpkin pie.
☐   In pioneer days, Native families and pioneer families sometimes celebrated together and shared the food they harvested.

Additional Facts the Teacher Should Know

1. Thanksgiving has its roots in Britain, where it was common to hold holidays of thanksgiving for any number of things, not only a bountiful harvest.
2. According to the *Canadian Encyclopedia*, the first Thanksgiving in the New World was celebrated in Newfoundland by explorer Martin Frobisher in 1578. He and his ship's crew gave thanks for having survived their dangerous venture into the Hudson Strait while in search of a northwest passage to China.
3. The first annual Thanksgiving Day was proclaimed by the Canadian Parliament on November 6, 1879, for "a bountiful harvest with which Canada has been blessed."
4. In 1957, Parliament permanently declared the second Monday in October as Canada's Thanksgiving Day.

Introducing This Subject to Children

1. Thanksgiving provides an opportunity to look at pioneer life. Rural teachers can celebrate the joys of life in a rural community with the children. Urban teachers can use this as an opportunity to introduce children to the satisfactions of life in a farming community. It is an ideal time to celebrate the importance of Canadian farmers for all Canadians.
2. Present a puppet show or flannelboard story of the first Thanksgiving in Canada.
3. Learn a Thanksgiving song.
4. Ask the children what they are thankful for.
5. Display pictures of pioneers, harvests, and Thanksgiving feasts.
6. Display a cornucopia with real or artificial gourds, vegetables, and fruits.

Vocabulary

Thanksgiving	harvest	feast	cranberry
give thanks	fruit	dinner	harvest
cornucopia	vegetable	food	pumpkin
pioneers	farm	turkey	crops
log cabin	apple		

Learning Centres

Discovery Centre

1. Examine turkey feathers and eggs, and note how they differ from those of a chicken. Scramble two turkey eggs.
2. Vegetable dyeing: Dip pieces of white cloth or white turkey feathers into solutions made by boiling the following plants in water and allowing the water to cool. Turkey feathers are available from some craft stores, butchers, and poultry farms.

   goldenrod stalks and flowers — yellow
   sumac leaves — yellow–brown
   onion skins — yellow or red
   beets — red–violet
   dandelion roots — magenta
   rhubarb leaves — light green

   spinach leaves — green
   blackberries — blue
   sunflower seeds — blue
   hickory bark — brown
   walnut hulls — brown
   cranberries — pink or red

   NOTE: If you can't provide adequate supervision of the children during this activity, boil the solutions in advance. If turkey feathers are used, wash them first in soap and water to remove oil, and then rinse.

3. Cooking: Prepare a food with the children that is related to Thanksgiving, using recipes from your favourite cookbook. Make cranberry salad, Waldorf salad, popcorn balls, pumpkin pie, pumpkin muffins, or baked potatoes. Use watercress or leeks in snacks or salads.
4. Examine dried fruits: Show samples of raisins and fresh grapes (include other dried and fresh fruits, such as apples, peaches, plums, and apricots, if available). What happens if raisins are put in water? What happens if grapes are put in the sun to dry?

Dramatic Play Centres

Home-living centre

1. Set out artificial fruits and vegetables. Encourage preparation of a big feast. You could mount pictures of turkeys, potatoes, or pies on heavy cardboard, or cut food sections from TV dinner boxes for children to use in preparing a Thanksgiving dinner.
2. Baking: Provide play dough, rolling pins, cookie cutters, and child-size pans or aluminum pot-pie pans for baking pies, cookies, or bread.
3. Dressup clothes: Add clothes and accessories worn by early settlers, such as ankle-length skirts, aprons, suspenders, calico dresses and shirts, and wide-brimmed hats.

Block-building centre

1. Encourage children to build houses to play in and to pretend that families are coming for a Thanksgiving Day visit.
2. Transportation toys: Trains, planes, buses that bring visiting grandparents.
3. Build farms: Set out toy animals, tractors, and trucks. Provide spools, small rocks, and other articles for crops to harvest and take to the market.
4. Toy logs: Older children may build log cabins. Flexible plastic and rubber family figures can be dressed in pioneer or Native Canadian clothing made from felt and imitation leather if you and your staff have the skill and time.

Art Centre

- 1. Sand drawing and painting: Show the children how to smooth sand in a sandbox or tray using a long, flat stick and then how to draw with a round stick or a finger in the smooth sand. Sand can also be washed and dried in an oven, mixed with dry tempera, and poured into shakers to be used in sand painting. After the children have drawn a picture with glue on lightweight cardboard or stiff paper, they sprinkle on sand from the shakers. Let paintings dry, and then tap to remove excess sand.
- • 2. Texture designs can be made by children by crayoning on newsprint over precut shapes of sandpaper or corrugated cardboard. Introduce other textures for interesting effects and designs.
- 3. Paste precut pieces of multicoloured tissue paper onto construction paper. Children may discover that, by overlapping pieces, tissue has the appearance of fall leaves.
- • 4. Collage: Glue dried seeds, sticks, or grasses onto paper.
- 5. Vegetable printing: Use fruits or vegetables you have prepared in advance. Cut 1 cm from the large end of a sturdy carrot or celery stalk for circles and crescent shapes, or half of a grapefruit shell. Dip the fruit or vegetable into paint and press onto paper.

  NOTE: Use parts of fruit or vegetables that are ordinarily discarded or inedible.

- • 6. Border designs: Describe a border as "shapes lying in a row." Give the children strips of coloured and white paper. Let each child select from a tray of assorted precut geometric shapes of construction paper the shapes he or she needs to design a border. Find examples in pictures or children's clothes. Allow the children to print a border using small spools, bits of wood-moulding scraps, dowels, plastic lids, rolls of corrugated paper, or bits of sponge cut into shapes, which have been dipped into shallow pans of thickened paint. Have several colours of paint from which to choose.
- • 7. Burlap pictures: Cut squares from burlap bags or colourful burlap material.
  a. String large-eyed, blunt embroidery needles with fine, bright-coloured yarn. Let children sew a design or picture onto a burlap square.
  b. Duplicate porcupine quill art by letting the children use coloured toothpicks instead of yarn.

8. Rugs (dollhouse or block accessory size) may be simulated by fringing loosely woven upholstery fabrics. Cut in rectangles and squares and show the children how to unravel the threads to make a fringe. See (i) below. Some children may be able to do simple weaving with loops on a frame or with yarn lengths on a homemade frame (ii). You will need to secure the edges of the fabric and the weaving by stitching them on a sewing machine so they will not fray.

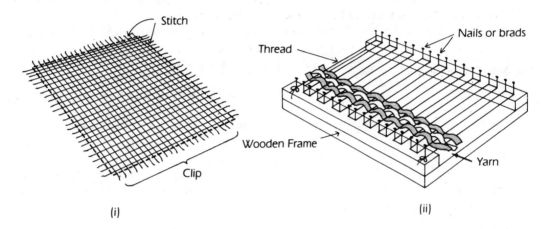

(i)   (ii)

Learning and Language Materials Centre

NOTE: See also Chapter 15, Fall, for other appropriate materials related to harvest time.

Teacher-made games and materials

NOTE: For detailed descriptions, see Learning Games in Part 1.

1. *Name it:* Identify fruits and vegetables and other Thanksgiving symbols.
2. *Look and see:* Use fall fruits and vegetables or other reminders of Thanksgiving.
3. *Reach and feel:* Use fruits, vegetables, or Thanksgiving symbols.
4. *Sniff and smell:* Use fruits and vegetables (see Chapter 5, Smell).
5. *Chew, lick, and taste:* Use fruits and vegetables (see Chapter 4, Taste).
6. *Match-them:* Use real objects or make cards using decorative seals.
7. *Sorting and grouping by association:* Use matching cards made for *Match-them* or real fruits and vegetables to mix and sort.
8. *Alike, different, and the same:* Use picture cards or real objects. Set out two cards or objects that are alike and one that is different; for instance, two green apples and one red. Vary the size, such as two big pumpkins and one small one.
9. *How many?* Count real objects or use pictures or flannel cutouts.
10. Count pictures of turkeys, pumpkins, and pioneers.
11. Make designs on small cards to be reproduced by matching with parquetry blocks.

Book Centre

••• Climo, Lindee. *Chester's Barn.* Montreal: Tundra, 1982.
•• Graeme, Jocelyn. *Celebrations.* Don Mills, ON: Addison-Wesley, 1990. (text is in Spanish, French, English, and Chinese)
•• Hellen, Nancy. *Old Macdonald Had a Farm.* New York: Orchard, 1990.
•••• Kalman, Bobbie, et al. *We Celebrate the Harvest.* Toronto: Crabtree, 1986.

•••• Kurelek, William, and Margaret Engelhardt. *They Sought a New World.* Montreal: Tundra, 1985. (Read–Tell)

• Roth, H. *Babies Love Autumn Days.* Markham, ON: Fitzhenry & Whiteside, 1986.

 # Planning for Group Time

NOTE: All music, fingerplays, poems, and games listed here may be used at other times during the session as appropriate.

Music

Songs

From *The Baby Beluga Book*, Raffi
"Biscuits in the Oven," p. 9
"Oats and Beans and Barley Grow," p. 12
"Thanks a Lot," p. 18

From *Elephant Jam*, Sharon, Lois, and Bram
"Sweet Potatoes," p. 103

From *More Piggyback Songs*, Warren
"Harvest Time," p. 41
"Thanksgiving Day," p. 47
"Let Us Give Thanks," p. 47

From *Piggyback Songs*, Warren
"A Thanksgiving Song," p. 43
"Ha Ha Turkey in the Straw," p. 44

From *A Treasury of Songs for Children*, Glazer
"Come Ye Thankful People Come," p. 53

From *Tunes for Tots*, Warner and Berry
"Turkey Gobbler," p. 26
"We Are Thankful," p. 27
"Pick a Big Pumpkin," p. 28

Rhythms and Singing Games

1. Dramatize different methods of going to grandmother's (or aunt's, cousin's, or friend's) house, such as walking, running, riding a trike, flying, or going by train, bus, or car.
2. Strutting: Children can strut like a turkey to appropriate music.
3. Hop, skip, jump: Use the tape *Rhythmic Activities*, Volume 1 (RCA).
4. Drums: Reproduce chants or poems to music or drumbeats; walk, jump, hop, or skip to drumbeats.
5. Dance: Toe-heel, toe-heel to Native music.

Fingerplays and Poems

....
MR. TURKEY

Mr. Turkey's tail is big and wide. *(spread hands wide)*
He swings it when he walks. *(swing hands back and forth)*
His neck is long, his chin is red. *(stroke chin and neck)*
He gobbles when he talks. *(open and close hand)*

Mr. Turkey is so tall and proud. *(straighten self up tall)*
He dances on his feet. *(make fingers dance)*
And on each Thanksgiving Day, *(hands in prayer)*
He's something good to eat. *(pat stomach)*

Games

(See Learning Games in Part 1 and Teacher-Made Games and Materials earlier in this chapter for directions.) Play traditional circle games similar to those that pioneer children might have played.

1. *Hokey pokey.*
2. *Mulberry bush.*
3. *Skip to my lou.*
4. *Oats, peas, beans.*
5. *Looby lou.*
6. *Did you ever see a lassie?*
7. *Go round and round the village.*
8. *A-hunting we will go.*
9. *Bluebird through my window.*
10. *London Bridge.*

Routine Times

1. At snack or meal time, use a cornucopia with real or artificial foods as a centrepiece.
2. Plan a Thanksgiving dinner the last day your group meets before Thanksgiving. Serve small portions if the meal is lunch or snack.
3. Talk about table manners, especially saying "thank you."
4. Talk about foods — their colour, texture, size, shape, taste, and odour as you are eating during snack or meal time.
5. At snack or meal time, use foods prepared by the children, such as popcorn, pumpkin pie, cranberry sauce, or Waldorf salad.
6. Serve foods for snack or meal time that Native people first introduced to the settlers.
   Snack-time foods: Popcorn, peanuts (use peanut butter on crackers), strawberries, pineapple chunks, cocoa, fresh or dried fruit (apples, figs, grapes, peaches).
   Lunch-time foods: Cornbread cakes with maple syrup, corn, sweet potatoes, nuts, squash, turkey, tomatoes, beans, pumpkin pudding, barbecued meat, fish, potato cakes, succotash. For salad: apples, raisins, nuts, and celery combined, carrot sticks. For dessert: fried bread, pudding, or fruit.
7. At lunch time, talk about what it would be like not to have forks — only hands or wooden spoons — with which to eat.

8. At pickup time, use a wagon to carry toys and equipment back to storage areas or shelves. Point out that this is how the early settlers moved their things. Show a picture of a covered wagon.

Large Muscle Activities

1. See Rhythms and Singing Games.
2. Catch the turkey: All the children are turkeys except one, who is a pioneer. The pioneer chases the turkeys until he or she catches one. The child who is caught becomes the pioneer. This game will probably interest only a few of the older children.
3. Skill games: Include games young pioneers or Native children may have played.
    a. Run to a destination and back.
    b. Walk a log, a balance beam, or a chalkline drawn on the ground or on the floor.
    c. Play follow the leader.
    d. Play with balls of various sizes.

Extended Experiences

1. Take a trip to the grocery store to look at or buy Thanksgiving foods — turkeys, pumpkins, apples, nuts, celery, onions, potatoes, cranberries.
2. Visit a turkey farm. Ask permission to make a loud noise, such as blowing a whistle or horn, to get turkeys to "gobble." Ask permission to collect turkey feathers or ask the owner to save some for you to use in the discovery, art, and learning and language materials centres.
3. Have a grandparent visit and tell about Thanksgiving Day when she or he was a child.

Teacher Resources

Joy, M. *Highdays and Holidays.* Boston: Faber & Faber, 1981.
Manning-Saunders, R. *Festivals.* London: Heinemann, 1973.
Stephan, B. *Decorations for Holiday Celebrations.* New York: Crown, 1978.

HALLOWEEN

Basic Understandings
(concepts children can grasp from this subject)

☐   In Canada and the United States, Halloween is celebrated on October 31.
☐   Pumpkins are commonly used to make jack-o'-lanterns.
☐   Halloween colours are orange, black, and white.
☐   On Halloween, children dress up to disguise themselves (hide who they are) from their friends and visit them to get a treat, or else they play a trick on their friends.
☐   Halloween is celebrated during the time of harvesting apples, pumpkins, and nuts, and when leaves change colour. These foods and materials are often used as decorations and in games at parties.

Additional Facts the Teacher Should Know

History of Halloween

1. The night of October 31 is Halloween. "Hallow" means "saint." November 1 is a church festival, All Saints' Day. Thus the word "Hallowe'en" is short for "All Hallows Evening." On November 1, the Roman Catholic Church celebrates the feast of all those who were known to have lived a good life but who were not included on the church's calendar of saints. October 31 was believed to be the one night during the year when ghosts and witches were most likely to wander about. In ancient Britain, October 31 was the last day of the year and celebrations were similar to those for New Year's Eve.

2. According to legend, November 1 was the date when the souls of the dead were liberated from purgatory, which according to Roman Catholic theology is a place or state after death for making amends or to atone for sins. It was believed the released souls were allowed to visit their homes, and thus the present-day custom has evolved of "trick or treaters" coming to neighbourhood homes dressed as skeletons. The carved pumpkin is another symbol of death.

3. Another legend says there was once a miserly man named Jack who was consigned to roam the earth until Judgement Day, because he was too stingy to get into heaven and too prone to playing practical jokes on the devil to go to hell. So, Jack carried his lantern (jack-o'-lantern) as he roamed.

4. Still another legend concerns a circle of dough, better known as the doughnut. According to this story, an English cook invented this "soul cake" to remind English beggars about eternity. The cook cut a hole out of a piece of dough and then dropped the dough into a pan of hot fat. Its circular shape was to be a reminder of the constancy of eternity. The people who received this doughnut were supposed to pray for the dead of the family who gave it to them.

5. Some say that the Halloween customs of bonfires, pranks, tricks, and jack-o'-lanterns were first introduced to Canada in the early 1900s by Irish immigrants. In recent years, schools, parents, and communities have encouraged parties and parades to discourage the pranks of the past, and now many children and teenagers collect funds for UNICEF on Halloween. Children dress up in costumes and masks and only ring doorbells where porch lights are lit to invite children to stop. Treats are prepared at such homes and given in return for the children's performing a trick or feat. Some communities, through the schools, encourage children to learn a trick to perform for a treat; for example, a poem, riddle, song, or physical feat, de-emphasizing malicious mischief and calling it a "trick *for* a treat."

About preschool celebrations of this holiday

1. Small children should be helped to realize that Halloween is a time for fun and surprises rather than a time for superstition and fright. For young children, perhaps the main emphasis should be on pumpkins and their uses, jack-o'-lanterns, tricks, and disguises (guess who?), with suggestions for painting faces and wearing hats or animal costumes, rather than wearing masks or portraying skeletons, witches, or goblins. A two-year-old feels disguised wearing a lampshade (as one author put it). Save the witches and ghosts for the older children who, it is hoped, are better able to tell what is fantasy and what is fact.

2. Many children enjoy making masks but refuse to wear them. For this reason, masks that can be held in front of them are often better. Stress the fun of guessing who is behind the mask.

3. In recent years, this holiday has been marred by vandalism as well as by the poisoning of children. Children should be encouraged to visit only the friends and neighbours that their parents suggest.

Introducing This Subject to Children

1. Take a trip to a farm where pumpkins are raised.
2. Take a trip to the store to buy apples, nuts, and several pumpkins.
3. Read or tell a story about Halloween or a pumpkin.
4. Hang pictures on the bulletin board of pumpkins growing, a jack-o'-lantern, or a pumpkin pie.
5. Bring several pumpkins to be cut and scooped out by the children (see Discovery Centre).

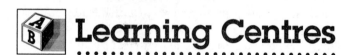

Vocabulary

pumpkins	orange	costume	ghost
jack-o'-lantern	black	riddle	joke
candle	pie	eyes	scare
trick	cat	nose	surprise
grin	owl	mouth	guess
seeds	mask	witch	harvest
treat			

Learning Centres

Discovery Centre

1. Bake sugar cookies, cutting pumpkins or other Halloween shapes. Children can frost these with orange frosting. Provide chocolate chips, raisins, or small marshmallows for decorating the cookies.
2. Make pumpkin custard. Use a recipe for pumpkin pie filling, and pour it into custard cups. Place custard cups in a baking pan filled with 2.5 cm of hot water. Bake at 180°C/350°F for 30 minutes (or until knife inserted comes out clean).
3. Make orange gelatin, chocolate pudding, or orange fruit drinks.
4. Observe pumpkins growing on the vine. Note variations in colour, size, shape, quality, and weight, and how pumpkins differ from squash.
5. Make jack-o'-lanterns from pumpkins. Let the children draw on the eyes, nose, and mouth shapes they want with a wax marking pen for you to cut out. Children can take turns scooping out the seeds. For a special treat, darken the room and light a candle inside a pumpkin. An adult should always be present and should be careful to watch children nearest the jack-o'-lantern. Short candles smoke less than tall ones. Drip candle wax into the pumpkin to secure the candle, or push a nail in from the underside of the pumpkin to hold the candle.
6. Wash and dry pumpkin seeds for planting, baking, frying, or dyeing for use in collages. When making jack-o'-lanterns, notice how the seeds grew inside the pumpkins.
7. Discover the differences between raw and cooked pumpkin by tasting some of each.
8. Discover the uses of pumpkins — puddings, pies, decorations, halloween jack-o'-lanterns.

9. Observe differences between cut apples and carrots that are dipped in lemon juice (which prevents browning) and those that are not.
10. Display masks used by community workers. Include picture books and mounted pictures that illustrate how and why these masks are worn. Include some of the following: oxygen mask, ski mask, football helmet with face guard, motorcycle helmet, face shields or goggles for welders or sanders, airpacks worn by firefighters, sleepmask, surgical mask, dark sunglasses, gas mask. Let children try on some of the masks and see if they can guess why each is worn.

■ Activities 1, 2, 3, and 7 can be used with children who have both sight and hearing difficulties. These activities will help all children enhance their use of the sense of taste. Some of the tasting may be done with eyes covered so that children can focus on using only their sense of taste to identify and describe the foods.

Dramatic Play Centres

Home-living centre

1. In this centre or behind a three-way play screen, have a costume shop with a mirror, or buy Halloween costumes and accessories, such as the following:
    a. Disguises for younger children:

    Hats (these are often enough for the youngest children).
    Mail carrier: Mail carrier's hat and bag.
    Police officer; Police officer's hat and tickets.
    Cowboy/cowgirl: Felt hat and stick horse.
    Mother or woman: Coloured or veiled hats, high-heeled shoes, purse, car keys.
    Father or man: Vest, tie, wallet, hat, shoes, car keys.

    b. Disguises for older preschoolers:

    Scarecrow: Patchy blue jeans and shirt; fringe sleeves, collar, and pant legs; battered hat; old pair of sneakers (cut so toes show).
    Bride: White dress (gathered or gored skirt with elastic waist), veil, lace curtain train, artificial flowers for hair and bouquet, rings.
    Animals: Dyed sleepers, stuffed tails with loop to fasten to belt, ears attached to skullcap.
    Ballerina: Tank top, sleeveless T-shirt top, or body suit; ruffled tutu to tie around waist; pipe cleaner tiara; ribbons to tie around shoes and ankles.
    Man: Black mustache (can be painted on with mascara), old hat, and black tie.
    Pirate or buccaneer: Bandana to tie around head, curtain rings to hang on ears with string; notched pair of old blue jeans, sash, short vest, and a cardboard or rubber knife.
    Clown: Pointed hat, crepe paper or cloth ruffles to tie around neck, wrists, and ankles or button onto a clown suit.
    Queen or king: Gilt cardboard crown or tiara covered with sequins and beads, old lace tablecloth or velvet curtain cloak or robe, cardboard sword or sceptre.

Block-building centre

1. Set out farm worker figures, tractors, trucks, and wagons.
2. Encourage farm play. Supply spools and coloured cubes or small plastic vegetables to be harvested, loaded into trucks, and driven to market.
3. Talk about how you get to the biggest city near you (if you live in a small town), such as up and down hills, over bridges, and through tunnels.

Art Centre

- 1. Provide orange and black paint to encourage Halloween art.
- 2. Fingerpaint in orange or make a monoprint. When dry, cut paintings or prints into pumpkin shapes.
- 3. Tint play dough with orange tempera. (For recipes for play dough, see Art Centre in Part 1.)

    VARIATION: Allow children to knead red and yellow powdered paint or food colouring into the play dough.

Other art projects to try

- 1. Create a paper jack-o'-lantern. Allow children to select a paper pumpkin from a variety of sizes and shapes and shades of orange (these may be precut or predrawn for the youngest children). Children attach scraps or precut geometric shapes for eyes, noses, and mouths. Identify shapes — crescents (moon-shaped), triangles, squares, circles, and half-circles — as you give them to the children. Features for the jack-o'-lantern may be precut from black gummed paper for the youngest to stick on. Talk about how many eyes, noses, and mouths we have, and show on a felt pumpkin a variety of faces possible by inverting and reversing the same shapes.

    NOTE: Do not post or make a sample as it may limit the children's creativity. Older children may be able to draw their own pumpkins, cut them out, and cut the desired features.

- 2. Make a "handle mask": Let the children cover a bent wire coat hanger with the foot of an old nylon stocking. Precover hangers for the youngest children. Have children create a face by gluing on scraps of felt, cloth, and yarn (see below). Children can hold these masks in front of their faces. For fun, make wild guesses as to who a child is; for example, Robbie the Rabbit or Freddie the Frog. Children are always identifiable behind the mask although they may think they're hiding.

    ▼ CAUTION: Be sure to bend the open hook back on itself to form the handle and eliminate a sharp point (see below).

- 3. Make a paper plate mask: Attach a tongue depressor or popsicle stick to the bottom of a paper plate with tape or staples and let children add a face.
- 4. Make a seed collage: Arrange pumpkin seeds on dark-coloured paper. To add variety, you may also dye seeds different colours using food colouring and 5 mL vinegar to 250 mL water. Spread seeds on paper towels to dry before using.
- 5. Make a trick or treat bag: Prefold a cuff around a large paper bag, inserting a thin strip of cardboard. Staple on an orange or black strip of bias tape, rope, string, ribbon, or cord for a handle. Encourage children to cut or tear Halloween shapes, such as pumpkins, owls, cats, cornstalks, or nuts, out of construction paper and glue them

onto the bag. Crepe-paper streamers, strips of black and orange paper, fringed borders, or yarn also make attractive decorations.

••• 6. Make Halloween banners for a parade: use crepe-paper streamers or tissue taped to the end of a cardboard tube. Glue or tape on the face of a jack-o'-lantern, clown, cat, or any other nonfrightening face.

••• 7. Make rattles or noisemakers out of small, empty boxes. Put in a few stones or spools, tape shut, paint or decorate, and fasten to stick or carry in hand.

• 8. Make paper bag pumpkins: Fill a small white or brown paper bag with torn newspapers (have some pretorn, as children tire of tearing). Twist the top and secure with a rubber band. Let children paint all sides of the bag orange and the twisted stem green. When dry, let older children add eyes, nose, and mouth by gluing on shapes to create a jack-o'-lantern. Some may wish to add a strip of green crepe paper on top for a gay stem. Younger children may leave their pumpkins plain.

•• 9. Make a pumpkin patch picture: This activity is fun following a trip to a pumpkin patch. Let the children paint a piece of brown or beige construction paper with glue. Give each child several cotton balls to roll in a shallow pan of dry orange tempera for use as pumpkins, and supply several lengths of green yarn to be twisted around among the pumpkins like a creeping vine.

▼ **CAUTION:** Be sure the children wear aprons for this activity.

••• 10. Make Halloween paper bag puppets (for the most mature young children): Paint paper bags orange for a pumpkin, black for a cat, or leave brown or beige for an owl. Precut appropriate shapes children might choose or need to make faces. You may let children snip their own features (see below).

Learning and Language Materials Centre

Teacher-made games and materials

NOTE: For detailed descriptions, see Learning Games in Part 1.

1. *Name it:* Use Halloween objects — mask, owl, black cat, pumpkin.
2. *Guess what?* Use hats, masks, or Halloween objects.
3. *I see something, what do you see?* Describe something about Halloween in the room. Let the children guess and describe something for you.
4. *Sorting and grouping by association:* Sort orange and black objects by colour.

5. *Guess who?* Describe a child in the group by saying, "I see someone who is wearing a blue dress and has brown eyes." Or, describe a community worker or a story character.

6. *Listening:* Tell the children that it is hard to guess who visitors are if they're dressed up, but sometimes we can tell who they are by listening to their voices. The child pointed to may say, "Hello," or "Trick or treat."

7. *Alike, different, and the same:* Cut several orange pumpkins and black cats out of felt, cardboard, or upholstery vinyl. Vary the sizes, shapes, and forms. Ask children to match two cutouts that are identical, to select one that is different, or to find several that are similar.

8. Make an orange felt pumpkin plus black felt triangles, circles, crescents, ellipses, and squares to arrange a variety of jack-o'-lantern faces. See p. 271 for shape suggestions.

9. Cut a pumpkin out of orange upholstery vinyl or heavy fabric. Use a zigzag stitch to secure the edges and make pumpkin crevice lines. Sew on buttons (at least 1 cm in diameter) where the eyes, nose, and mouth should be. Children can button on felt or plastic shapes to create their own jack-o'-lanterns. Leave a long shank when sewing on the buttons for easier buttoning. Sew buttons on both sides of the fabric to make it sturdier and reversible. For illustrations of pumpkin and face pieces, see p. 271.

   NOTE: The felt pumpkin invites the most creative use. The button-on pumpkin combines a learning skill with the child's creative use and is best for older children. Very young children will want to keep their pumpkins so explain that they belong to the centre but that children can make ones out of paper to take home.

10. *How many?* Talk about how many eyes, noses, and mouths are needed to make a face in the above activities or during creative experiences in the art centre.

Book Centre

••• Adams, A. *A Woggle of Witches.* New York: Scribner, 1971.
••• Asch, Frank. *Popcorn.* New York: Parents, 1979.
••• Balian, Lorna. *Humbug Witch.* Nashville: Abingdon Press, 1965.
•• Bell, Cathie, and David Bell. *Two Bears at the Party.* Toronto: Oxford University Press, 1991.
••• Bourgeois, Paulette. *Franklin in the Dark.* Toronto: Kids Can Press, 1986.
••• Calhoun, Mary. *Wobble the Witch Cat.* New York: Morrow, 1958.
••• Donnelly, Liza. *Dinosaurs' Halloween.* New York: Scholastic, 1987.
•• Graeme, Jocelyn. *Celebrations* (from the series *Hand in Hand: Multicultural Experiences for Young Children*). Don Mills, ON: Addison-Wesley, 1990 (text is in Spanish, French, English, and Chinese)
••• Howe, James. *Scared Silly.* New York: Morrow, 1989.
•••• Kalman, Bobbie et al. *We Celebrate Hallowe'en.* Toronto: Crabtree, 1985.
•• Keats, Ezra Jack. *Hi Cat!* New York: Macmillan, 1970.
••• Miller, Edna. *Mousekin's Golden House.* Englewood Cliffs, NJ: Prentice-Hall, 1964.
• Mueller, Virginia. *A Hallowe'en Mask for Monster.* Chicago: Whitman, 1986.
•••• Slobodkin, Louis. *Trick or Treat.* New York: Macmillan, 1967.
••• Smith, Maggie. *There's a Witch Under the Stairs.* New York: Lothrop, Lee & Shepard, 1991.

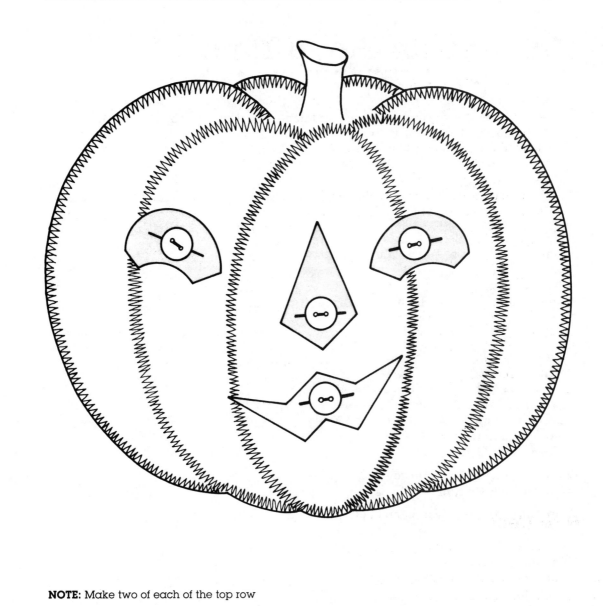

NOTE: Make two of each of the top row

EYE
shapes:

NOSE
shapes:

MOUTH
shapes:

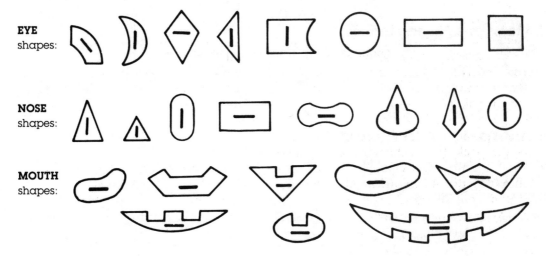

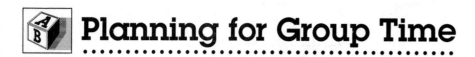

Planning for Group Time

NOTE: All music, fingerplays, poems, and games listed here may be used at other times during the session as appropriate.

Music

Songs

From *More Piggyback Songs*, Warren
"I'm Jack-O'-Lantern," p. 44
"Mr. Pumpkin," p. 45
"Sometimes I Like to Walk in the Dark," p. 46
"Ghosts and Witches," p. 46
"Ghosts and Goblins," p. 46

From *Piggyback Songs*, Warren
"Friendly Ghost," p. 40
"Do You Have the Spooky Ghost?" p. 40
"One Little Two Little Three Little Pumpkins," p. 41
"Jack-O'-Lantern," p. 41
"The Goblin in the Dark," p. 42
"Halloween Is Here," p. 42

From *Stepping Along in Music Land*, Murray
"Hallowe'en Is Coming," p. 49

From *Tunes for Tots*, Warner and Berry
"Boo," p. 21
"Hee, Hee, Hee," p. 23
"It's Halloween," p. 24
"Who Do You See on Halloween?" p. 25

Rhythms and Singing Games

Costume parade: Use any good marching record and parade around the room or through the building.

Fingerplays and Poems

From *Don't Eat Spiders*, Heidbreder
"Here Comes the Witch," p. 36
"Hallowe'en Night," p. 37

From *Hand Rhymes*, Brown
"Jack-O'-Lantern," p. 10
"Five Little Goblins," p. 12

....
MY PUMPKIN

by Darlene Hamilton

Here's my orange pumpkin *(have hands outspread)*
Big and fat and round *(make circle with hands)*
It's the very best one *(hold up one finger)*
I could find downtown. *(point in that direction)*

Now I need to make a nose *("cut" nose on your face)*
A mouth . . . Some eyes *(circle eyes like glasses)*
Or mother will use it *(motion to remove)*
To cook and bake some pies. *(act like stirring)*

....
JACK-O'-LANTERN

by Darlene Hamilton

See my jack-o'-lantern *(point)*
Smiling right at you *(smile)*
You don't need to be afraid *(look frightened)*
It can't holler **Boo!**

....
PUMPKINS

by Darlene Hamilton

A pumpkin is big *(circle hands over head)*
A pumpkin is round *(circle arms in front)*
A pumpkin has a great big smile *(outline smile on mouth)*
But doesn't make a sound. *(put finger over lips)*

....
MY JACK-O'-LANTERN FRIEND

Anonymous

(use appropriate actions)
All children have a happy friend, who comes just once a year.
He has two eyes, a nose, a mouth, and grins from ear to ear.
He has a light that's tucked inside. He's big and round and yellow.
An, when we light the candle bright, he's such a jolly fellow.
Now, who is he? Of course, you're right! He's jack-o'-lantern, big and bright!

....
PETER, PETER, PUMPKIN EATER
Use the traditional Mother Goose rhyme.

Games

(See Learning Games in Part 1 and Teacher-Made Games and Materials earlier in this chapter for directions.)

1. *Name it.*
2. *Who's missing?*

3. *I see something, what do you see?*
4. *Guess who?*
5. *Listening.*

Routine Times

1. At snack time, drink orange juice through black licorice straws (cut ends to open).
2. Cheese pumpkins can be served at snack or meal times.
   a. Cut cheese slices in the shape of pumpkins. Serve alone or on bread or crackers.
   b. Let children grate processed cheese and mould it into pumpkins. Eat immediately.

   NOTE: Wash hands first!

3. Jack-o'-lanterns made of a variety of foods may be served at snack or meal times during Halloween week:
   a. Apples with raisins for eyes, nose, and mouth. Use the end of the peeler to make holes in which to poke raisins.
   b. Cut out a face in an apple using a sharp knife. Dip in lemon juice to prevent browning.
   c. Use whole, peeled oranges for pumpkins. Make slices to insert a small apple wedge for a mouth, raisin eyes, and a miniature marshmallow nose. Use half an orange, placing the flat side down.
4. Carrot strips and raisins may be served at snack or meal times.
5. For snacks, eat Halloween cookies that the children have baked or decorated.
6. Play *Guess who?* while waiting for snacks or meals (see Teacher-Made Games and Materials, number 5).

Large Muscle Activities

(See also Rhythms and Singing Games earlier in this chapter.)

1. Costume parade: March around the room or through the building.
2. Beanbag game: Children can pass a beanbag around a circle or gently throw a beanbag to a partner.

Extended Experiences

1. Take a trip to the store to buy several pumpkins — one pumpkin per five children. Encourage children to select their favourite one, noting colour, weight, shape, flaws, size, and price. Each group of five children might choose their own and give the money to the cashier (with the supervision of a teacher, volunteer, or parent). This will give all the children an opportunity to participate in the total experience. If you can walk to the store, take a wagon to carry the pumpkins back to the centre.
2. Take a trip to a pumpkin farm: Select pumpkins for the centre and, if possible, one for each child.

Teacher Resources

Joy, M. *Highdays and Holidays*. Boston: Faber & Faber, 1981.
Manning-Saunders, R. *Festivals*. London: Heinemann, 1973.
Stephan, B. *Decorations for Holiday Celebrations*. New York: Crown, 1978.

SHICHIGOSAN

(Shee-CHI-goh-SAHN)

Shichigosan is the Japanese Feast of the Living Children. Celebrated on November 15, it is a day of thanksgiving honouring seven-year-old girls, five-year-old boys, and all three-year-old children, because they have survived three critical periods of childhood. The children are presented at a shrine by their parents. After their presentation, they have their picture taken and receive a gift of "candy for 1000 years." This consists of long sticks of red and white candy in a bag printed with pictures of a crane and a tortoise (symbols of good fortune and long life). The children are also given balloons.

Traditionally, this is the first time that a three-year-old girl wears her hair fully dressed in the fashion of her mother, the first time a five-year-old boy wears a long *kimono*, and the first time a seven-year-old girl puts on a stiff *obi*, or wide *kimono* belt. Japanese–Canadian children are more likely to wear bright-coloured clothes to reflect their joy and thankfulness.

Extended Experiences

1. Allow the children to play with balloons.
2. Display some Japanese dolls in traditional dress.
3. See the Chinese/Vietnamese New Year section (Chapter 9) for other information on Asian customs, toys, and games.
4. Include a tortoise or a crane in stories read or games played, mentioning their significance to Japanese people.

HANUKKAH

(HAHN-na-kuh)

Basic Understandings

(concepts children can grasp from this subject)

☐ *Hanukkah* is an eight-day festival of light observed by Jewish people.
☐ *Hanukkah* celebrates religious freedom for the Jews.
☐ Candles are lit each night in a special candleholder called a *menorah* (meh-NOR-ah). The candle known as the *shamash* (SHAH-mush) is lit every night. In addition, one candle is lit the first night, two the second, and so on, until there are nine in the *menorah* on the last night.
☐ Families enjoy eating potato pancakes called *latkes* (LOT-kuhs).
☐ Children like to play games with a *dreidel* (DRAY-dull).
☐ Gifts are generally given to children, one each night. Frequent *gelt* (coins) are given. Bags of chocolate coins covered with gold foil are in favour with Jewish–Canadian families.

Additional Facts the Teacher Should Know

1. *Hanukkah*, the festival of light, comes in late November or December and begins on the twenty-fifth day of the Hebrew month *Kislev*. The Hebrew calendar is a lunar one, so the exact date of *Hanukkah* varies each year. *Hanukkah* celebrates a great victory for the Jews approximately 2100 years ago.

2. Antiochus, a Syrian king, drove the Jews from their temple in Jerusalem and ordered them to worship Greek gods or be put to death. The Jews fought back, and under the leadership of the Maccabees, finally regained Jerusalem and set about purifying their temple, which the Syrians had defiled. When it was ready, they proclaimed a holiday and called it *Hanukkah*, which means "dedication." The celebration lasted eight days.

3. There is a legend about the first *Hanukkah* that relates how only one small jar of oil was found to light the holy lamp in the temple for the festival. It should have lasted only one day, but it miraculously lasted eight days until new oil was ready. This is probably why *Hanukkah* is celebrated for eight days.

4. Today, each family has a *menorah*, a candelabrum with eight branches made of wood, brass, silver, or gold. The first *menorahs* used little pots of oil, but today candles are used. There is also a place for a smaller candle called the *shamash*. It is usually in the centre and a little higher than the others, but can be in front of, behind, or to the right of the others if on the same level. It is lit first and then is used to light the other candles. The candles are placed in the *menorah* beginning on the right and moving to the left each day with the required number of candles. Then the candles are lit from left to right beginning with the new candle. Forty-four candles are needed for the eight-day festival, because each night new candles must be used.

5. Potato pancakes called *latkes* are frequently served during *Hanukkah*. They are dipped in sour cream or served with applesauce. Christians have a similar custom of eating pancakes on Shrove Tuesday.

6. Gifts are given to children at the beginning of the holiday or one each night. The intent is to spread light and joy. Although *Hanukkah* is celebrated during the same season as Christmas and gifts are given to children as part of both celebrations, *Hanukkah* is *not* the Jewish Christmas. Christmas is a Christian holiday; *Hanukkah* is a Jewish holiday. Each celebration is important to a child in his or her own faith for a very different reason. Also at *Hanukkah* time, Jewish children enjoy playing the *dreidel* game while adults play cards. The *dreidel* is a four-sided top with Hebrew letters on each side representing the words in the phrase "A Great Miracle Happened There," referring to the oil lasting for eight days during the first *Hanukkah*.

7. Very young children, whether Jewish or non-Jewish, do not always comprehend the history of their faith or the deeper meanings involved in their celebrations. But they can learn the name of the celebrations and begin to understand some of the outward symbols for the inner meanings.

Introducing This Subject to Children

1. Display *Hanukkah* candelabra, a *dreidel*, or pictures.
2. Sing a song or read a story about *Hanukkah*.
3. Discuss the festivals of various religions or national groups.
4. Discuss the fact that different people have festivals centring on the use of candles and other lights during the grey winter with its long, dark nights.
5. Invite a Jewish parent to bring *Hanukkah* decorations and a *menorah* to show the children.

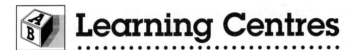

candle	*shamash* (SHAH-mush), helper candle
light	*ner tamid* (nehr-TAH-MEED), eternal light
first, eighth	*dreidel*
gelt	Maccabee (Jewish soldier-hero)
menorah	*latke*

Learning Centres

Discovery Centre

1. Make potato *latkes*:

....

LATKES

500 mL/2 cups raw, grated, peeled potato
1 small grated onion
5 mL/1 tsp salt
pinch of pepper
15 mL/1 T flour (matzo meal)
7 mL/1½ tsp baking powder
1 or 2 eggs (optional)

Add grated onion, salt, and pepper to grated potato. Mix flour and baking powder and add to potato mixture. One or two well-beaten eggs may be added. Drop mixture by spoonfuls onto a hot, well-greased frying pan. Spread thin with back of spoon. Turn pancakes when very brown. Place on paper towels to drain fat.

NOTE: A potato pancake mix may also be used. *Latkes* are especially good served with applesauce or dipped in sour cream.

2. Make *Hanukkah* cookies: Use your favourite sugar cookie recipe. Cookie cutters in the shapes of a candle, *dreidel*, lion, or Star of David (six-pointed star) are available in specialty stores or you might borrow some from a Jewish parent.
3. *Hanukkah* salad may be made by constructing a fruit candle as follows: Use a slice of canned pineapple for a base; stand half a banana in the pineapple for a candle; place a maraschino cherry on top of the banana for the flame (slit banana to insert).
4. Light: Candles and the light they give may lead to the discovery and discussion of many different kinds of light, such as electricity (lamp), fire (firelight), sun (sunlight), kerosene (lantern), and battery (flashlight). Help children find these in their environment or collect pictures illustrating these to put on the walls or in a scrapbook.
5. Post pictures or display often-used lights. Include small electric lamps, traffic lights, neon lights, flashlights, candles (teacher-supervised!), and porch lights. If you can give adequate supervision, light a candleholder with chimney, and demonstrate how the chimney keeps the candle from blowing out. Demonstrate how a candle snuffer is used to put out a flame.

Art Centre

•• 1. Paint and crayon: Make enough *dreidels* for each child in the group and let each paint or crayon every side of the cube. Put the letters on or let children use gummed letters.

••• 2. Pasting *menorahs*: Eight long strips of paper, straws, pipecleaners, yarn, or felt can be pasted on background paper to represent candles. One short one should be cut for the *shamash*. Pieces of cotton dipped in yellow paint, short lengths of yellow yarn, scraps of yellow paper, or cotton swabs dipped in yellow, red, or orange paint will offer a variety of possibilities for making flames. Gold or silver glitter can be used to cover a line of glue placed under the candles to represent a metal candleholder. Gold or yellow paper rectangles can be pasted on for bases.

• 3. Paper chains: Use royal blue and white construction paper for making chains in the traditional manner. Precut strips or let children with cutting experience cut their own strips.

Other art projects to try

1. Greeting cards:
•   a. Spatter-paint *Hanukkah* symbols using white paint on royal blue construction paper. Fold paper in half to form card before painting.
••   b. Use sponge stamps to print a combination of *Hanukkah* symbols on a card.
•••   c. Cut and paste two triangles to form a Star of David (six-pointed star) or paste precut *dreidels* to a folded card. Encourage children to make a border and, if they are able, to letter their names inside.

••• 2. Make candleholders of styrofoam or wooden spools mounted on a board and painted. Make eight places for candles, plus an extra one for the *shamash*.

Learning and Language Materials Centre

Teacher-made games and materials

NOTE: For detailed descriptions, see Learning Games in Part 1.

1. *How many?* Count candles on a flannelboard *menorah*.
2. *I see something, what do you see?* Find round things like a *latke*.
3. *Chew, lick, and taste:* Use a *latke* and a pancake.
4. *Dreidel game I:* Materials needed: *dreidel* (see pattern, p. 279) and tokens, nuts in the shell, or wrapped candies. Procedure: Everyone playing puts in a token. Children, in turn, spin the top and play for the tokens, nuts, or candies. If the letter *nun* (נ) faces up, the child gets nothing. If the letter *heh* (ה) appears, she or he gets half of the tokens. If the letter *shin* (ש) appears, she or he must put a token in the group pile from her or his stock. If the *gimel* (ג) appears, the child wins. (See also *Dreidel Game II*, p. 280.)

How to make a **dreidel:** use bristol board or a file folder to make a cube 5 cm square (or any size between 5 cm and 10 cm). Use the pattern and example shown on the next page. A dowel with one end pointed can be inserted through the holes in the top and bottom of the cube. Adjust cube up or down on dowel until it is balanced enough to spin easily. Wood or cardboard can be used if you have the necessary tools.

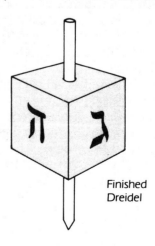

Finished
Dreidel

Dreidel Pattern

With paper cutout in front of you, fold on dotted lines so flaps are inside and Hebrew letters are outside.

Cut holes to suit the dowel diameter.

Reading from **right** to **left** the Hebrew characters from the four sides of the dreidel represent the following words:

Sham	**Hayah**	**Gadol**	**Nes**
THERE	WAS	GREAT	MIRACLE

"A GREAT MIRACLE WAS THERE!"

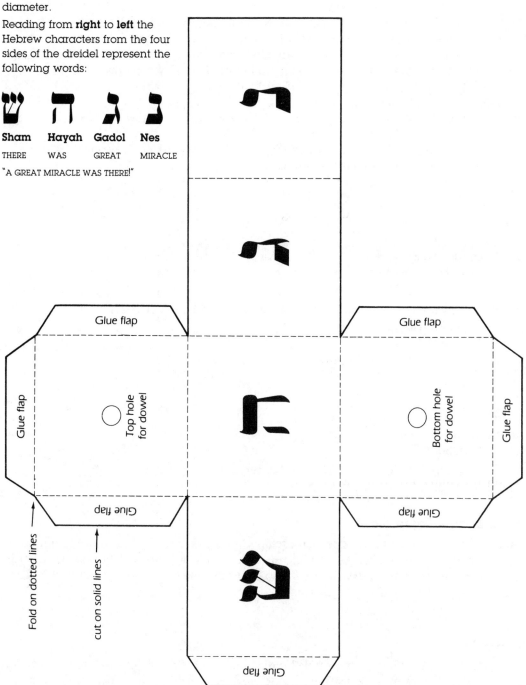

Glue flap

Glue flap

Glue flap

Glue flap

Top hole for dowel

Bottom hole for dowel

Glue flap

Glue flap

Fold on dotted lines

cut on solid lines

Glue flap

Book Centre

••• Adler, D.A. *A Picture Book of Jewish Holidays*. New York: Holiday House, 1981.
••• Chanover, Hyman, and Alice Chanover. *Happy Hanukkah Everybody*. New York: United Synagogue Book Service, 1954.
 • de Paola, Tomie. *My First Chanukah*. New York: Putnam, 1989.
••• Garvey, Robert. *Holidays Are Nice*. New York: Ktav, 1960.
•• Graeme, Jocelyn. *Celebrations*. Don Mills, ON: Addison-Wesley, 1990. (text is in Spanish, French, English, and Chinese)
••• Greenfeld, H. *Chanukah*. New York: Holt, Rinehart and Winston, 1976.
•••• Kalman, Bobbie, et al. *We Celebrate Family Days*. Toronto: Crabtree, 1986.
•••• ———. *We Celebrate Hanukkah*. Toronto: Crabtree, 1986.
••• Manushkin, Fran. *Latkes and Applesauce*. Richmond Hill, ON: Scholastic, 1990.
••• Morrow, Betty, and Lewis Hartman. "Hanukkah, Feast of Lights," in *Jewish Holidays* (Holiday Book Series). Champaign, IL: Garrard, 1967, pp. 41–47.
•• Shostak, Myra. *Rainbow Candles: A Chanukah Counting Book*. New York: Kar Ben, 1986.
••• Simon, Norma. *Hanukkah*. New York: Crowell, 1966.
••• ———. *Hanukkah in My House*. New York: United Synagogue Book Service, 1960.

 # Planning for Group Time
• •

> **NOTE:** All music and games listed here may also be used at other times during the session as appropriate.

Music

Songs

From *Singing Bee*, Hart
"Hanukkah Song," p. 144

From *A Treasury of Songs for Children*, Glazer
"Hanukkah Song," p. 108

Records and Cassettes

There are many lovely folk songs that are appropriate to the celebration of *Hanukkah*. Visit a local Jewish bookstore to pick up current tapes that will be useful for this celebration. Some community libraries also have suitable tapes, but go early as they are used a great deal in the *Hanukkah* season.

Games

Dreidel game II: Children form a circle holding hands. One child is chosen to be a *dreidel* in the centre. Children walk around a circle while the child in the centre spins in place for the first half of melody (use any Israeli music). Then both the circle and the *dreidel* stop. The child in the centre chooses another child to spin by holding hands and turning together in the centre while the circle moves again for the last half of the melody. The chosen child stays in the centre for the start of a new game and the first child rejoins the circle. Repeat until every child who wishes to can be a *dreidel*. Form a second circle if time will not allow everyone a turn.

Routine Times

1. During snack or meal times, serve *latkes*, candle salad, or sugar cookies in the shape of the Star of David, a lion, a candle, or a *dreidel*.
2. When walking or busing, look for a synagogue.

Large Muscle Activities

See Games on p. 280.

Extended Experiences

1. Visit a synagogue to see the eternal light (*ner tamid*).
2. Invite a Jewish parent, student, or friend to visit. Ask the visitor to share with the children any of the following:
   a. A *menorah*: Show how it is lit and explain how it is used.
   b. A *dreidel*: Show how to play the *dreidel* game, and explain the letters.
   c. *Hanukkah* cookies: Bring some, or bring *Hanukkah* cookie cutters and help the children make and bake cookies. Discuss the meaning of the shapes.
   d. *Latkes*: Bring some, or assist the children to make *latkes*.

 # Teacher Resources

Pictures and Displays

☐ Display a *menorah*, or make one with the children. Choose a special time each day to light the *menorah* candles, one each day in succession until the end of the eight-day period.
☐ Cut out Stars of David and suspend them from the ceiling.
☐ Make a mural showing the story of *Hanukkah*.

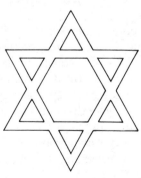

| Lion | Star of David | Menorah |

Books and Periodicals

Adler, D.A. *A Picture Book of Jewish Holidays.* New York: Holiday House, 1981.

Blumenthal, Paul H., et al. *Treasures of Chanukah.* Toronto: Doubleday, 1987.

Burns, Marilyn. *The Hanukkah Book.* New York: Four Winds Press, 1981.

Cavanah, Frances, and Lucy Pannell. *Holiday Round Up.* Philadelphia: Macrae Smith, 1968.

Corwin, Judith Hoffman. *Jewish Holiday Fun.* New York: Simon & Schuster, 1987.

Dobler, Lavinia. *Customs and Holidays around the World.* New York: Fleet Press, 1963.

Edmonton Hadassah WIZO Association. *The Great Hadassah WIZO Cookbook.* Edmonton: Hurtig, 1982.

Purdy, Susan. *Festivals for You to Celebrate.* Philadelphia: Lippincott, 1969.

Siegal, Richard, et al. *The Jewish Catalog.* Philadelphia: Jewish Publication Society of America, 1973.

Temes, S.R. *Welcome to My Kitchen.* Toronto: Temes, 1985.

United Synagogue Book Service, 155 Fifth Avenue, New York 10010. For storybooks, song books, and records and cassettes listed in Book Centre and Music Centre.

Weinfeld, W., ed. *The Canadian Jewish Mosaic.* Rexdale, ON: Wiley, 1981.

Community Resources and Organizations

- ☐ Jewish parents in your centre, students from a nearby college or university.
- ☐ Rabbi or director of Hebrew education.
- ☐ Hebrew bookstore.

CHRISTMAS

Basic Understandings

(concepts children can grasp from this subject)

- ☐ December 25 is Christmas Day and is a national holiday in Canada.
- ☐ Christmas is the Christian celebration of the birth of Jesus.
- ☐ Christians believe God sent His Son to Earth as a special gift of love, and like the Wise Men who brought gifts to him as a token of their love and respect, Christians give to others in Jesus's name.
- ☐ Christmas symbols are evergreen trees, stars, candles, crèches, bells, wreaths, holly, angels, sleighs, Christmas stockings, tree ornaments, reindeer, elves, and Santa Claus.
- ☐ Colours used at Christmas come from some of the symbols; for example, red for holly berries, cranberries, and Santa's suit; green for evergreen trees, wreaths, and holly; and silver or gold for the bright star the Wise Men followed.
- ☐ In Canada, traditional activities of the Christmas season include carol singing, special church services, gift making and giving, family gatherings at festive dinners and special parties, and sending greetings and cards to friends.
- ☐ Many children believe in Santa Claus.
  - a. Stories, songs, and poems suggest that Santa and Mrs. Claus live at the North Pole and that Santa spends the whole year making toys, which he delivers in a sleigh

pulled by eight reindeer, to good boys and girls while they are asleep on Christmas Eve.
b. We may see many people dressed like Santa Claus during the Christmas season.
c. Anyone can be a Santa's helper or play Santa to another person if he or she gives a gift to another person secretly (anonymously).

Additional Facts the Teacher Should Know

1. Christmas is a time set aside by Christians throughout the world to celebrate the birth of Jesus Christ. The word "Christmas" is derived from the early English term *Christes masse*, which means Christ's Mass. No one knows when it was first celebrated, except that it began with the early Roman Church.

2. It is important for teachers to be sensitive to the Christmas customs and practices that vary from family to family and from region to region. For some families, Christmas is solely a religious celebration, for others it is solely a secular celebration, for others it is a combination of the two, and for others it is not an occasion for celebration. Unless your program is based in a setting that teaches a particular religious philosophy, it is wise to focus on the secular aspects of Christmas and to leave the religious celebrations to each family. It is acceptable to present the religious aspects of Christmas as long as they are presented in the context of being the beliefs and stories of one group of people. This parallels the presentation of religious beliefs that has been recommended in other parts of the celebration chapters. It is critical to be aware of the children who do not celebrate Christmas in any form. It is equally important to be aware of the children for whom Christmas may be very stressful because of financial or family problems. Close consultation with parents before any holiday celebrations are begun will be helpful in designing a program that is acceptable to all families. The public media are other important influences in planning your Christmas program. Children are bombarded with the commercial celebration of Christmas for many weeks before the holiday. Counterbalance this by stressing the gentler aspect of Christmas and emphasizing the theme of kindness that underlies all Christmas history and legends.

3. Christmas is a statutory holiday in Canada. The secular and religious celebrations of Christmas have been strongly influenced by the practices of our ancestors from all over the world. Most Canadians celebrate Christmas in a similar way, but there are regional differences and traditions that are very important to the people of each region. Although you are likely aware of the main practices in your community, you may find that you can make the celebration of Christmas in your setting more personal by researching the particular practices of the children in your centre. There are some regional Canadian Christmas customs about which children enjoy learning. For example, in Vancouver, boats of all sizes are decorated with lights and sail around the harbours and inlets with people on board singing Christmas carols. In the Arctic, Inuit people will often have a community Christmas dinner of caribou, seal, or Arctic char and bannock. The dinner is usually followed by a tournament of traditional games such as archery, target shooting, and dog-team races. The last person to remain undefeated in the games is the champion of the Christmas games for the year. In Newfoundland, some communities continue the ancient European tradition of mummery, which has been becoming more popular in the past few years. Mummers dress in elaborate costumes and go from house to house performing short Christmas skits. They are usually given Christmas delicacies by their hosts. In larger communities, mummers perform in halls and theatres. In many communities across the land there are Santa Claus parades.

4. Many Christmas customs, celebrations, and legends have pagan roots. When the pagans of Northern Europe became Christians, they made their sacred evergreen trees a part of the Christian festival and decorated them with gilded nuts and candles to represent the stars, moon, and sun.

5. Mistletoe, holly, poinsettia plants, and evergreens are the most common plants used for decoration during the Christmas season. Mistletoe, holly, and poinsettia are poisonous to humans if eaten, so if you use these plants for decoration take proper precautions. Tell the children that "some plants are good to eat and some are not good to eat and will even make us sick."

6. The most popular legend about the first Christmas tree concerns Martin Luther, a German clergyman who found a small fir tree glistening with snow in the woods on a starry night. He took it home for his children and placed many lighted candles on it to represent the stars. To children, the Christmas tree represents much of the excitement and colour of the holiday season, and they may share in its decoration. The family usually gathers around the tree at Christmas to open their gifts. A Scandinavian legend loved by children is "The Friendly Beasts." According to this legend, all animals are able to speak at midnight on Christmas Eve.

7. Although Santa Claus is not a part of the religious celebration of Christmas, he is a very real part of the very young child's Christmas and is one of the most beloved figures in childhood legends. The modern, mythical Santa is said to have developed from a real person, St. Nicholas. This patron saint of schoolboys, dressed in his bishop's robes, brought gifts to them. Clement C. Moore's *A Visit from St. Nicholas* probably gives the best modern-day description of the saint. Reindeer also appear in this poem, which is probably based on a Scandinavian legend. Children seem to want to believe in Santa Claus even if they are not consciously taught this myth. This belief must be respected even if it is not encouraged. As children mature, they begin to realize that Santa Claus is the embodiment of the spirit of Christmas kindness and gift-giving.

8. Children should be encouraged to realize that Christmas is a time to share and to give gifts, not just to receive gifts. They can be helped to play Santa Claus by preparing gifts to be given to others. Surprises and secrets are especially fun (making gifts for parents, friends, or other special people). The Christmas season is the most exciting time of all for young Christian children. In many homes, children hang up stockings on Christmas Eve that they hope to find filled with treats in the morning.

9. It can be fun for children to explore the Christmas traditions of other countries. If children in your class were born outside Canada, examine the customs of their home countries and incorporate some of them into your program. Some customs from around the world follow.

Sweden

Christmas in Sweden begins on the morning of December 13, the Feast of St. Lucia, when the oldest daughter in the household, wearing a white robe and a crown of candles, awakens the family with food, drink, and a traditional song. St. Lucia is celebrated with candles and lights to drive away the darkness of midwinter. Candle making and gift-giving are an important part of the Swedish Christmas holiday. *Pepparkakor* (ginger cookies) trees, brass angel candle chimes, candles, and live Christmas trees are other Swedish Christmas traditions. Evergreen trees are decorated with intricate straw figures (stars, animals, sunbursts, snowflakes, and people) and always include at least one bird in a nest. Paper decorations include miniature Swedish flags of blue and yellow. Brightly painted wooden horses, pigs, goats, and figures, as well as straw mobiles and centrepieces in the form of crowns, are other decorations for this holiday.

Jultomte, an old gnome, is said to give gifts on Christmas Eve. Dipping Day, *doppa i grytan* (dip-in-the-pot), comes the day before Christmas. The custom recalls a famine winter when the only food available was black bread and broth. Today, the custom is an aid to parents who are busy baking and cooking for the family gathering. Dipping dark rye bread into the broth of simmering sausages calms appetites so that the family can more patiently wait for the evening meal. The Christmas Eve family dinner includes *lutfisk* (a white fish), saffron or caraway bread, and pork of some kind (sausage or ham). All are commonly eaten before the family goes to church services (most Swedes, however, attend *Julotta* services on Christmas morning). The holiday ends the day after Holy Kings' Day, January 6, with the burning of the Christmas tree or the replanting of the tree in the yard.

Denmark

Rye or wheat is placed on every gable and gateway in barns for the birds to eat. Rooms and windows in Danish homes are decorated with evergreen boughs. Trees are decorated with heart-shaped, woven paper baskets or baskets shaped like miniature hats that are filled with candy. Flat, linked paper chains, inverted cones, triple bells, and garlands of tiny flags are other tree decorations made from paper, using red and white, the Danish national colours, with a touch of gold. A *nisse*, a tiny bearded sprite, is said to deliver presents to children. On Christmas Eve, children walk around the Christmas tree singing carols. Then they all sit down to hear the Christmas story told to them by their parents. The legend of the Friendly Beasts (animals able to speak on Christmas Eve) is also told in Denmark. Goose and *grød* (rice pudding) are traditional foods served at Christmas.

Norway

Norwegians say there should be different kinds of cookies for every day of the Christmas season, fourteen in all! The Christmas season is considered to be Christmas Eve through the Twelfth Night festival (Little Christmas to Big Christmas).

The Christmas tree is usually topped with a replica of the aurora borealis. Cranberries, popcorn, and paper fishnets are other decorations. Sheaves of rye and wheat are tied on posts or high buildings to feed the birds. As in other Scandinavian countries, traditional church services are held on Christmas Day, with family dinners often on Christmas Eve.

England

England is credited with the first Christmas cards, yule logs, fruitcake, plum pudding, mincemeat pie, mistletoe, holly, and bells. Dickens's *A Christmas Carol* is commonly read during the holidays. Christmas trees are planted in tubs indoors to be returned to the garden after the holidays so they can be used again and again. Trees are topped with the British crown or an angel and may be covered with angel hair and artificial snow. Other decorations often include candy and sugarplums tucked into ribbon- and flower-decorated cornucopias or silver filagree doily baskets. Swags of red and gold ribbon and tiny packages wrapped in velvet, ribbons, or even brocade are also used. Father Christmas gives gifts to children on Christmas Day. These are placed by the fireplace, but gifts to others are given on Boxing Day, December 26. Bells are traditionally rung from every tower and church belfry at midnight on Christmas Eve, announcing Christ's birth. Carollers gather in town squares around Christmas trees. Earlier bells toll warnings to the Prince of Evil that the Prince of Peace's birth will soon be announced.

Wales

Carol singing is accompanied by the harp. Each town offers prizes for the best carols composed each year. Goose is a popular part of the Christmas meal. Taffy making is an important custom for the holidays, as well as the preparation of plum pudding.

Ireland

Candles burn brightly in windows to light the way of the Holy Family. All wanderers are given a meal and coins.

Greece

People sing carols while beating drums and striking triangles. Carollers are given figs, cookies, walnuts, almonds, oranges, tangerines, pomegranates, and money. *Christpsomo* (bread of Christ) is a simple cake decorated with nuts and covered with powdered sugar. When the cakes are soaked in diluted honey they are called *melomacaromas*. Christmas is primarily a religious festival with no Christmas trees or presents. Greeks give presents on St. Basil's Day, January 1, commemorating one of the four fathers of the Orthodox Church.

Italy

The crèche (or *presepio*) is the centre of the Italian Christmas celebration. *Presepios* include artistically crafted figures of the Holy Family, shepherds, and domestic animals. Gifts at Christmas are for the family and thought to be brought by *Gesù-Bambino*, the Christ Child, not by Santa Claus. Christmas letters or notes, written and decorated by little children as a surprise for their parents, include promises to be good, helpful, and obedient or are notes of praise. These are hidden under father's plate or tucked in his napkin or under the tablecloth, and read ceremoniously by him when the whole family is gathered and the meal is finished. Another form of *presepio*, equivalent in popularity to the Christmas tree in Canada, is the *ceppo*, a pyramid-shaped tripod fitted with three shelves. Candleholders for fat votive candles are fastened to the tripod sections at the corner of each shelf, making nine candleholders. The top shelf of the *ceppo* contains a star or an angel, and the middle shelf holds small gifts for the children, secretly placed there by their parents. On the bottom shelf are beautiful ceramic or hand-carved figures of the Holy Family and sometimes a few lambs, a donkey, and a cow. Sometimes fringes or tassels decorate the edges of the shelves. In some families, each child has his or her own small *ceppo*. On Christmas Eve, the candles are lit beside the *presepio* or on the *ceppo*, and the children dance around it with tambourines while singing. During the holidays, children go door to door reciting Christmas selections and receive coins to buy special treats.

Spain

A *nacimiento* or manger scene is found in almost every home. It is often lighted with candles, and children dance around it with tambourines while singing. Figures included in the nativity scene are a grey donkey, a Spanish bull, shepherds, and an angel. Some include a home for Herod and others have the Wise Men approaching from the East. Festivities end on the twelfth day of Epiphany, January 6. On this date the Magi (the Three Kings) are supposed to leave gifts for children on their way to visit the Christ Child. Children leave shoes on balconies with *cebada* (barley) for the tired camels. A favourite sweet served is *dulces de almend* (a sweet almond pastry). Elaborate parades are held in big cities on that day to honour the Three Kings.

Germany

Germany is credited with the first Christmas tree. Advent wreaths, candles, calendars, and other traditions are related to the religious celebration of Christmas. Crafting wooden toys and giving homemade gifts are still important customs. Such items are often used to decorate Christmas trees. Tree decorations also include *lebkuchen* (LAYB-koo-khen), gingerbread cookies shaped like men and women, animals, stars, hearts, and other handcarved ornaments. *Christkind* (Christ child, sometimes called Kriss Kringle) is the bearer of gifts — nuts, apples, and sweets — to children. Some homes give each other secret homemade gifts from the Christmas Angel once every week during Advent. *Stollen* (SHTUHL-len), a fruit-studded coffee cake, is often served at Christmas.

Netherlands

St. Nicholas Day is December 6, when St. Nicholas arrives in this country by ship. He wears a white bishop's robe, a scarlet cassock, a tall red mitre, and white gloves. He then mounts a white horse and delivers gifts to children. On Christmas Eve, inexpensive gifts are given, each one wrapped mysteriously and elaborately. Sometimes they are in a series of boxes, one within the other. Every gift is accompanied by a verse or rhyme.

Czechoslovakia

Christmas celebrations begin on December 6. The holiday ends with the visit of the *Tri Kralu* (Three Kings). The manger, the *jeslicky*, is always in the church or home. Young pig or goose is often served for Christmas dinner. "Good King Wenceslaus" is a traditional carol. Delicately dyed cornhusks are used to create nativity scenes. Sometimes tree ornaments are fashioned from bread dough and painted elaborately. Other ornaments are made from paper, straw, eggshells, and woven baskets; they can appear as little houses, heart-shaped windows, peasant dolls, clowns, birds, violins, or angels. Traditionally, children feed animals a portion of their Christmas dinner so the animals will give more milk, lay more eggs, and so on. It is said that *Svatej Nikulas* comes down from heaven on a golden rope and leaves gifts on December 5. On Christmas Eve (December 24), families gather around the trees and fortunes are told. Handcarved, heirloom crèches called Bethlehems or cribs have been placed under Christmas trees for generations. Originally, these were carved during long winter months by miners in their slack season and sometimes had as many as 100 pieces or more. These scenes were characterized by their inclusion of entire miniature villages, reflecting both the misery and the joy of the people.

France

Crèche is the French word for cradle and has come to be used for any manger scene including the figures of Mary, Joseph, and the baby Jesus. It can also include a donkey, cow, sheep, shepherds, and Magi. Crèches were popularized in the thirteenth century by monks who were concerned that people did not realize the true meaning of Christmas because they could not read and church services were held in Latin. Inspired after seeing shepherds sleeping in a nearby field with their sheep, the monks gathered live animals and asked people to take the parts of Mary, Joseph, and the shepherds in a living portrayal of the biblical story. They invited children to come to the manger and sing lullabies to the baby Jesus. The custom became very popular, and gypsies are said to have carried it throughout southern Europe. Churches in France often have a living crèche with real people and animals. Sometimes smaller crèches are decorated with holly, moss, laurel, and stones. *Santons*, or little saints, are added to miniature crèches in the home. They are painted terra cotta figures placed around the manger, representing families and tradespeople of a particular village. Trees are decorated with different-coloured stars. On Christmas Eve, toys, candies, and fruits are added to the tree. Most gifts are given on St. Nicholas Day, December 6, and then primarily to children. *Père Noël*, Father Christmas, is tall and slim and leaves gifts on Christmas Eve in shoes that have been placed before the fireplace. Drama and puppet shows are often part of the children's holiday. A special French treat is *bûche de Noël*, traditionally a yule log confection made of crushed chestnuts or cake moulded into a log and decorated with plenty of mistletoe and holly. Variations today may resemble a frosted cake like a jelly roll, but made with creamy filling and pistachio nuts. Baked ham and roast fowl are often served for the Christmas meal.

Romania

On Christmas Eve, boys carry long bags in which to pack gifts as they offer greetings to families, singing *colinde* (carols). A *steaua* (a star placed on a pole with little bells under it) announces the approach of the singers. Paper chains, cookies, pretzels, apples, and strings of cranberries decorate the Christmas tree, and straw is heaped beneath it.

Poland

Christmas is often called Little Star (*Gwiazdka*). No food is served on Christmas Eve until the appearance of the first star, in commemoration of the star of Bethlehem, a signal for the beginning of the festivities. Gilded nuts, sweets wrapped in coloured paper, frosted cookies, and bits of ribbon, straw, beads, eggshells, and even feathers are made into clowns, chickens, fish, pitchers, and stars to give Polish Christmas trees a special look. Straw is placed under the tablecloth because the Christ child was born in a manger. Sometimes villagers dressed as animals go about singing carols and are rewarded with food and drink. Boys, singing carols, often wander from house to house with small manger scenes in boxes or lighted stars mounted on poles.

South Africa

Christmas is a summer holiday in this country. Christmas greeting cards often show robins. There are open-air lunches of turkey or roast beef, mincemeat pie, suckling pig, and yellow rice seasoned with turmeric. The Christmas holiday is usually a week long carnival. People dressed in gay clothes sing, dance, and parade in the streets, often accompanied by pipe and string bands.

Ghana

Yam and rice festivals and tribal dances are part of the cultural celebrations before Christmas. Flowers and palm branches are used as decorations during Advent. Groups go together to buy cows, sheep, or goats to slaughter for the Christmas Day feast. Father Christmas does not come from the North Pole but from the jungles. *Egbona hee! Egbona hee! Egogo vo!* means "Christ is coming! Christ is coming! He is near!" and is a common greeting. The church has a decorated tree and candles, but usually individual homes do not. Foods eaten include rice and *fufu*, which is a dish of yams pounded into a kind of paste, stew-porridge, and bean or okra soup. Sheep, goats, cows, hogs, chickens, or fish are served on Christmas Day. Gifts are given, Christmas cards are sent, and enemies are reconciled. Love and forgiveness are emphasized.

Japan

Japanese Christmas trees are decorated with tinted Christmas cards, fine woodcuts, dolls, tangerines, paper fans, wind chimes, and tiny toys. Green and red paper balls, holly, red Japanese lanterns and glass wind chimes are other decorations. Christmas pageants are performed in Japanese dress. Party boxes or bags of Japanese cakes are shared. It is a church-centred holiday because seldom are all family members Christian. Christmas is often a day of caring for others in hospitals. The Japanese usually decorate a "back," which is a backdrop or cloth on which is fastened a scene of the shepherds or Wise Men with the Holy Family. Cardboard banners in assorted colours quote Bible verses about the birth of Jesus. A flat cake called *mochi* made from pounded, cooked rice is a favourite Christmas treat. It was once offered at shrines, but as a symbol of happiness it is now eaten during festive occasions.

Taiwan

Poinsettias bloom in this country from November to March. Streamers and paper chains are made. Big red and gold ideographs, messages written in Chinese characters, are also used as decorations. A candy that is like solid marshmallow is made of rice flour and sugar and decorated with Christmas symbols. Greeting cards are handpainted, often on fabric that is then glued to cards. Christmas is not a national holiday; therefore, it is usually celebrated on the weekend nearest December 25.

China

The Christmas tree is called the "Tree of Life." It is decorated with paper lanterns, fans, tassels, and chains. Glass ornaments lacquered with brilliant colours are also used for decorations, as well as Chinese lanterns, holly leaves and berries, tinsel, and lights. Sending postcards or greeting cards is more common than giving gifts. Gifts are given to Christian relatives, who may get silks, jewels, or more valuable gifts; to Christian friends or distant relatives, who might get food or cut flowers; and to the poor. *Lan Khoong* (nice old father) or *Dun Che Lao Ren* (Christmas old man) are Chinese Santa Claus equivalents. The Christmas meal is often shared with the church family, as usually not all members of a family are Christians. On Christmas Eve there is a lantern parade. The biggest feast is saved for New Year's Day, which is traditionally a more important holiday in China. Many Chinese greeting cards are exquisitely painted fabric pictures. Usually the Holy Family is painted with the features and dress of the Chinese.

Panama

Nacimientos (manger scenes) in churches and private homes are very elaborate and artistic. They often include houses, trees, waterfalls, and grass, duplicating a small Bethlehem scene. At school, gifts and greeting cards are made, and plays and pageants are given. Children send letters to the baby Jesus. Straw is woven into sunbursts, birds, fish, butterflies, people, and animals and used as tree decorations. The poinsettia, a native plant, is called *flor de la Noche Buena* (flower of the Holy Night).

Mexico

Houses are decorated with coloured paper lanterns, garlands, or wreaths of Spanish moss and evergreen. Pine branches and moss cover the area of the room where the crèche is located. The crèche, or *pesebre*, has shepherds, sheep, small huts, and trees. The figures of Mary, Joseph, and an empty cradle are placed in the stable. The baby Jesus figure is not set out until Christmas Eve. Santa Claus and Christmas trees are rare. Children receive toys and gifts on Epiphany; on the night of January 5 they put their shoes on a window ledge before going to sleep. On Christmas Eve, they receive candies and trinkets.

In many other Spanish-speaking countries of South and Central America or the West Indies, Bethlehem scenes, including the manger and Holy Family figures, are given similar emphasis during the Christmas holidays. For example, in Cuba such scenes are surrounded with eggs and cookies and decorated with fruit and flowers. In Costa Rica, a special small room known as a *portal* is filled with such a scene and visitors come to view each family's manger. In Honduras, *nacimientos* are set up in almost every home and are made from materials varying from very elaborate to very rustic, depending on the means or skill of the individual family. Families come to view *portals* much as they do in Costa Rica. In Ecuador, brightly painted *pesebre* figures are often made of bread dough and placed in simple cardboard box mangers. In most of these countries, each child places her or his most valuable possession near the *nacimiento* during this season, and it becomes a part of the scene.

Jamaica

In December, masked and brightly clad *Jonkunnu* dancers and musicians perform dances and sketches in the streets. Each character has a different name and costume; often, a dancer dressed in black tries to frighten children in the audience. Troupes of *Jonkunnu* dancers have been performing since the beginning of the eighteenth century.

On the Saturday before Christmas, the entire family goes to the Grand Market, which starts at five in the morning, to search out food and gifts for the Christmas celebration. The week before Christmas is spent cleaning up and fixing farms and yards. The home is decorated with flowers and branches of flowering shrubs, and a cactus makes a fine Christmas tree.

On Christmas morning, families attend performances involving song, dance, and comedy. And for luck, before the day is out, it is essential to consume twelve pieces of rich, dark Christmas pudding.

Syria

The Christmas holiday begins with St. Barbara's Day on December 4 and ends with the Epiphany celebration on January 6. St. Barbara is honoured for her goodness, faith, and love. The legend of St. Barbara says that her miserly father did not approve of her giving to the poor. When he caught her, he threatened her with a sword, and it is said that God turned the sword into a crochet hook. When her father demanded to see the food she had hidden in her lap, it had become roses. Parents hope this holiday and legend will teach children to be unselfish and to care for and share with those less fortunate. Children are encouraged to do this by sharing with others during Christmas. On the eve of this holiday, special sweets made from wheat, nuts, honey, and sugar are served. Wheat is cooked with sugar and flavoured with rosewater. These treats are taken to the poor or to homes where a family member has died recently. A party is given on St. Barbara's Day that includes dancing, singing, and games. In a special ceremony, girls go one by one to an elderly woman who anoints their eyes with a salve. Chicken, oranges, nuts, and pastries are special foods eaten during the Christmas holidays. Children save money to give to the poor. It is said that in southern Syria every tree bends its trunk and inclines its branches on Christmas Day in homage to the Christ Child. The gentle camel of Jesus is said to travel over the desert bringing presents to children. According to legend, this camel was the youngest camel of those that travelled with the Wise Men. Children customarily leave water and wheat for the camel on this night. Candles are also placed in windows to guide the camel over the hills. On January 1, presents are exchanged. It is also a day for the circumcision of male children. Children go from door to door to receive Turkish sweetmeats. January 2 is the women's visiting day.

India

Bundled branches of rice straw are soaked in water and then plastered with mud. Green pieces of oleander are added and candles put on the ends of the branches to form a Christmas tree. Paper chains and mica (a thin, sheetlike, fragile mineral) are scattered over the tree for decoration. Candles are put in candleholders in the windows of churches. Small candles are sometimes lighted and placed all along the roof.

Introducing This Subject to Children

1. Children can pin pictures of Christmas activities on bulletin boards, helped by a supervising adult who can discuss the pictures as they are chosen. (Use push-pins, which are much easier for children to manipulate than thumbtacks.)
2. Take a picture walk around the room. One teacher can accompany several children to look at and discuss what they see.
3. A child or teacher can share or talk about a Christmas picture, book, or object.

4. Children can make decorations for the room or the Christmas tree.
5. Take a shopping trip to buy a tree for the room or to see a decorated store window.

Vocabulary

Christmas	caribou	lights	Christmas Eve
gift	bells	twinkle	Santa Claus
turkey	merry	tinsel	St. Nicholas
bannock	wreath	candle	Père Noël
star	holly	Arctic char	reindeer
bell	night	candy cane	decorations
carol	glitter	elf/elves	stocking
sing	pine-cone	wrap	chimney
sleigh	evergreen	Christmas	tree present
mantel	snow	poinsettia	mummers
jingle	ornament	mistletoe	parade

Learning Centres

Discovery Centre

1. Collect different species of evergreen branches and pine-cones. Feel and smell them. Identify them and compare shape, size, and colour. Use a magnifying glass to note similarities and differences.
2. Remind children that the winter sky has particularly brilliant stars, to stimulate their sense of wonder.
3. Christmas ornaments and wrappings have delightful sensory appeal. Discuss colour, shape, size, and texture.
4. Cookies may be mixed, cut with cutters, baked, frosted, and decorated. Activities may depend on the maturity of your group or the time available.
5. Collect old Christmas cards, and encourage the children to sort them by colour, type of picture, shapes, etc.

Dramatic Play Centres

Home-living centre

1. Place a small Christmas tree in the centre.
2. Set out replicas of traditional Christmas foods from various cultures (laminated pictures or plastic foods). Encourage the children to prepare a family or community dinner.
3. Provide decorations (preferably made in the art centre) for the children to decorate the home-living centre.

Block-building centre

Provide large cardboard brick blocks to make chimneys and fireplaces.

Other dramatic play centres

1. Santa: A rocking boat is an excellent prop for a sleigh. Hollow blocks can be made into stalls for the reindeer or use stick horses as props. Provide children with a cloth sack to be filled with small toys for their sleigh. Add sleigh bells and a red stocking cap for anyone wishing to play Santa.

2. Jack-in-the-box: Children hide in a large cardboard box one at a time and pop out while you and the remaining group recite this poem:

> Down in the box there is a little man
> Who waits and waits as quiet as he can
> Until he opens the lid of his box
> A-n-n-n-n-nd (pause) . . . UP HE POPS!

NOTE: A box with a hinged top is the best. Paint or decorate the box.

Art Centre

- 1. Put out red and green paints only, to emphasize the basic Christmas colours.
- 2. Any art project can be made especially Christmas-like by using red and green paints or by sprinkling glitter from small shakers on the finished product.
- 3. Invite children to experiment with long sprigs of evergreen as paintbrushes. Let them use a dark-coloured paint on white paper or white paint on dark-coloured paper to make delicate paintings.
- 4. Fingerpaint with red or green on large sheets of paper. When these are dry, children can cut Christmas designs such as big bells and trees from their paintings as a second experience, if they wish. Fingerpaintings may also be matted with a tree-, bell-, or ball-shaped opening in the mat.
- •• 5. Spatter paint Christmas shapes: Use white paint on red or green paper, or vice versa.
- •• 6. Styrofoam sculptures: Invite children to use small precut pieces of styrofoam and coloured pipecleaners or telephone wire to make interesting decorations to hang on the tree, decorate the room, or decorate the tables at snack time.
- •• 7. Set out wooden toothpicks with styrofoam balls for children to make stars. Colour the toothpicks with food colouring, a box at a time. This is much cheaper than purchasing coloured toothpicks.
- ••• 8. If the children are cutting out Christmas trees at a cut-and-paste table, set out paper punches, pencils, cuticle sticks, or wooden skewers for those who wish to punch holes in their trees. Have available variegated tissue and metallic paper. Let children discover what happens when the punched trees are placed over other paper — they appear to have Christmas lights on them. Children may wish to paste coloured paper to the backs of their trees.
- •• 9. If folded blank cards and various scrap materials are available, children will enjoy designing their own cards or tree decorations.
- •• 10. Let children decorate green triangles or Christmas tree shapes with trimmings such as lace, yarn, ribbon, felt scraps, and buttons. Bits of coloured foil can also be added.
  VARIATIONS:
  a. Yesterday's fingerpaintings can be cut into tree shapes and decorated.
  b. An egg-carton lid can be used as a collage base. If children brush thinned white glue over its entire inside surface, they can add collage items to form a shadow-box picture. Dry and hang.
- 11. Children can print their own wrapping paper by using sponges or wood or cork shapes precut into Christmas designs by the teacher. Older children can print on tissue paper if stamp pads are used. Usually newsprint or a plain paper shopping bag works best. Use paint sparingly in shallow trays, or make a pad of paint-soaked paper towels.
  VARIATION: A child-size rolling pin can be covered with flocked vinyl wallpaper or a

piece of textured upholstery material secured with rubber bands. When rolled over a paint-soaked pad it can be used like a brayer to create printed wrapping paper. Hair rollers or spool brayers (see the instructions on p. 33) can be similarly used. Spool brayers can create striped or plaid wrapping paper, greeting cards, or gift tags. Offer the children a variety of quality paper scraps.

- 12. Provide a small artificial tree and durable decorations to be used by one or two children at a time. Allow them to decorate and redecorate the tree as they wish.

    NOTE: Move the tree when children need it to expand their dramatic play, such as into the home-living centre, or into the block-building centre when builders have completed a fireplace, room, or home and feel they need a tree to complete their furnishings.

Other art projects to try

Tree decorations

- 1. Small plastic lids can be used as bases on which to glue small Christmas stickers. Pictures cut from old greeting cards can also be used. Punch a hole for a ribbon or yarn hanger.
- 2. Tree garlands can be made from lengths of yarn with Christmas seals stuck back to back at intervals along the yarn.
- 3. Provide individual sections of egg cartons to make bells covered with a circle of aluminum foil, painted, or decorated with magic markers. Real jingle bells can be threaded on a pipecleaners through the bells. Several bells can be attached to a ribbon or a piece of yarn to hang on the tree.
- 4. Pipecleaners and coloured telephone wire can be twisted into candy canes and other tree ornaments.
- 5. Let children cut decorations from play dough with cookie cutters, or older children might mould some. When dry, these can be painted with tempera.
- 6. Invite children to roll, tear, cut, and crumple aluminum foil into free-form sculptures. Set out some dowels or pencils to wrap strips of foil around to make icicles.
- 7. Colour white glue by adding powdered paint. Let children pour the glue into any mould they choose that has been lined with plastic wrap. Allow to dry for four days, and then peel off paper. These ornaments can be hung by a piece of yarn if you drill a hole in each.
- 8. Children will enjoy stringing styrofoam packing chips on yarn or string for frosty garlands. Threaded bobby pins make good needles. VARIATION: Have children punch holes in bits of coloured construction paper or use precut lengths of plastic straw to alternate with the styrofoam and add colour to the garlands.
- 9. Cranberries and Cheerios can be strung and hung on trees to feed the birds. Popcorn is frustrating for young children to string because the kernels break.

    ▼ **CAUTION: Use blunt yarn needles. Allow adequate space between children and permit only one or two to string at a time.**

- 10. Flocked vinyl wallpaper can be cut into shapes for decorations. To make them sturdy, mount the shapes on heavy cardboard.

Gift ideas

- 1. Children can make handprints on art paper (a better-quality paper is more suitable for framing). If a kiln is available, make handprints in clay. Before firing, punch one or two holes at the top for a hanging loop of yarn or ribbon.
- 2. Show children how to place a photo of themselves face-down in a glass caster and cover it with a round piece of cardboard. Children can then fill the caster with plaster of Paris. When dry, glue felt over the plaster and use as a paperweight.

••• 3. Another paperweight can be made by filling the bottom of a milk carton with 2 cm of plaster of Paris. Children can choose different kinds of seeds, cones, and pods to push into the plaster as close together as possible. Gum-tree seeds, pine-cones, arborvitae cones, and acorns work well. When the plaster is dry, tear off the carton, spray with clear plastic or antique gold paint, and glue felt to the bottom.

NOTE: Felt helps protect wood surfaces against scratches.

••• 4. A simple candleholder can be moulded from an 8 cm ball of play dough (see recipes in Part 1). Show children how to flatten the bottom and use a real candle to make the candle hole. When dry, paint candleholders and sprinkle with glitter.

▼ **CAUTION:** Be sure the candle hole will hold a candle straight.

•• 5. Pine-cones are easily decorated by young children by brushing the tip of each scale with glue and then sprinkling with glitter and sequins. You might spray the cones with green, silver, or gold paint before the children decorate them.

•• 6. Centrepieces: Children will enjoy creating holiday centrepieces to share with their families if given a variety of materials, such as pine-cones, to be painted, sprinkled with glitter, or decorated. Children can use sequins, evergreen twigs or small branches, holly, discarded wrapping bows, bits of ribbon and doilies, containers. Cardboard fruit cartons or plastic berry boxes can be wrapped or woven with strips of yarn or ribbon. Crumpled aluminum foil or sturdy wrapping paper can also be used to cover containers.

••• 7. Abstract designs can be made by children either by dripping or squirting streams of thinned acrylic paint on a solid-coloured piece of upholstery fabric, or by placing shavings from crayon on the same kind of fabric and pressing with a warm iron under wax paper. If you plan the colour combinations and not too many colours are used, the results cannot fail and may be beautiful enough to be permanently stretched in a wooden frame.

Learning and Language Materials Centre

Teacher-made games and materials

NOTE: For detailed descriptions, see Learning Games in Part 1.

1. *Name it:* Use Christmas ornaments or models of symbols such as a tree, Santa, and a Christmas stocking.
2. *Look and see:* Use Christmas ornaments or symbols.
3. *Ponder posters:* Make posters using trees, Christmas balls, or stars with one or more different from the others in some way (see the illustration that follows).
4. *Alike, different, and the same:* Children can choose from felt shapes that are alike — all trees; different — trees of different sizes and shapes; or the same — two identical trees.
5. *Christmas tree:* Cut a large felt Christmas tree about 30 cm high. Use felt stars, balls, and bells to decorate. Yarn or trimming braid may be used for garlands. Children can decorate the tree as many times and in as many ways as they wish. The felt tree can be placed on a flannelboard or laid in a flat box with the trimmings placed in the lid (see Rhythms and Singing Games for a song that can be used with this tree).
6. *Match-them:* Count or match one, two, three, four trees, bells, pine-cones, sprays of evergreens, pictures or models of sleighs, dolls, or toys.
7. *Sorting and grouping by association:* Mount Christmas stickers on small squares or circles of cardboard to be sorted into a partitioned box or into separate, labelled boxes.
8. See also Games later in this chapter for other games two or three children can play with an adult at a table or on a mat.

Book Centre

> **NOTE:** When choosing books for this centre, try to respect the traditions of the children in your program.

••• Barry, Robert. *Mr. Willoughby's Christmas Tree.* New York: McGraw-Hill, 1963.

••• Baumann, Kurt. *Three Kings.* St. Catharines, ON: North–South, 1990.

••• Bierhorst, John. *Spirit Child: A Story of the Nativity.* New York: Mulberry, 1984.

••• Brett, Jan. *The Wild Christmas Reindeer.* New York: Putnam, 1987.

••• Cole, Joanna. *A Gift from Saint Francis: The First Crèche.* Toronto: Kids Can Press, 1989.

••• de Brunhoff, Jean. *Babar and Father Christmas.* New York: Random House, 1946.

•••• Delacre, Lulu. *Las Navidades: Popular Christmas Songs from Latin America.* Richmond Hill, ON: Scholastic, 1990.

•• Duvoisin, Roger. *Petunia's Christmas.* New York: Knopf, 1952.

••• Ets, Marie Hall. *Nine Days to Christmas.* New York: Viking Press, 1959.

•• Freeman, Don. *Corduroy.* New York: Viking Press, 1958.

•• Graeme, Jocelyn. *Celebrations.* Don Mills, ON: Addison-Wesley, 1990. (text is in Spanish, French, English, and Chinese)

•• Hoff, Syd. *Santa's Moose.* Markham, ON: Fitzhenry & Whiteside, 1986.

•••• Kalman, Bobbie, et al. *We Celebrate Family Days.* Toronto: Crabtree, 1986.

•••• ———. *We Celebrate Christmas.* Toronto: Crabtree, 1986.

••• Keats, Ezra Jack. *The Little Drummer Boy.* New York: Macmillan, 1968.

• Khalsa, Dayal Kaur. *Merry Christmas Baabee.* Montreal: Tundra, 1985.

•• Kovalski, Maryann. *Jingle Bells: An Adaptation of the Traditional Song.* Toronto: Kids Can Press, 1988.

••• Kroeber, Theodora. *A Green Christmas.* Berkeley, CA: Parnassus Press, 1967.

•••• Kurelek, William. *A Northern Nativity.* Montreal: Tundra, 1976. (Read–Tell)

••• Kusugak, Michael Arvaarluk. *Baseball Bats for Christmas.* Willowdale, ON: Annick Press, 1990.

••• Miller, Edna. *Mousekin's Christmas Eve.* Englewood Cliffs, NJ: Prentice-Hall, 1965.

•• Moore, Clement. *The Night Before Christmas.* New York: Random House, 1961.

• Peterson, Cheryl. *The Animal's Christmas: A Twelfth Century Christmas Carol.* New York: Random House, 1983.

••• Pilkington, Brian. *Grandfather Christmas.* St. John's: Breakwater, 1990.

•• Politi, Leo. *Pedro, the Angel of Olvera Street.* New York: Scribner's, 1972.

•• ———. *Rosa.* New York: Scribner's, 1964. (also available in Spanish)

••• Speare, Jean, and Ann Blades. *A Candle for Christmas.* Vancouver: Douglas & McIntyre, 1986.

••• Swede, George. *Dudley and the Christmas Thief.* Toronto: Three Trees Press, 1986.

•• Templeton, Bill. *How Mrs. Claus Saves Christmas!* Toronto: Collins, 1978.

••• Weinberg, Larry. *The Forgetful Bears Help Santa.* New York: Scholastic, 1988.

•• Woolaver, Lance. *Christmas with the Rural Mail.* Halifax: Nimbus, 1979.

Planning for Group Time

> **NOTE:** All music, fingerplays, poems, stories, and games listed here may be used at other times during the session as appropriate. In parodies, hyphenated words match music notes of the song used.

Music

Songs

There is a wealth of suitable Christmas songs. When choosing songs from among your favourites, remember that the most important criterion is the children's experience with music.

From *More Piggyback Songs*, Warren
"Christmas Time Is Here," p. 12
"Christmas Time Is Near," p. 13
"Christmas Time," p. 13
"The Merry Christmas Band," p. 15
"S-A-N-T-A," p. 16
"Santa's Coming," p. 16
"He'll Be Driving Eight Brown Reindeer," p. 17
"Rudolph's Light," p. 17
"Christmas Cookies," p. 18
"Merry Christmas Everywhere," p. 18
"Gingerbread Boy," p. 19
"Gingerbread," p. 19

From *Piggyback Songs*, Warren
"Ten Little Reindeer," p. 11
"On Christmas Day," p. 12
"Guess Who?" p. 12

From *Singing Bee*, Hart
"Santa's Chimney," p. 146
"Jingle Bells," p. 150
"Pat-a-Pan," p. 152
"We Wish You a Merry Christmas," p. 153

From *Stepping Along in Music Land*, Murray
"Christmas Presents on Parade," p. 51

From *A Treasury of Songs for Children*, Glazer
"Christmas Is Coming," p. 50

From *Tunes for Tots*, Warner and Berry
"Sleigh Bells," p. 30
"Christmas Bells," p. 31
"Santa," p. 32

From a book of traditional songs or sheet music in your own collection:
"Twinkle, Twinkle, Little Star"
"Jingle Bells"
"Up on the House Top"
"Here Comes Santa Claus"
"Santa Claus Is Coming to Town"
"Rudolph, the Red-Nosed Reindeer"
"Merry Christmas to You" (tune: "Happy Birthday to You")
"'Twas the Night Before Christmas"
"Away in a Manger"

Rhythms and Singing Games

Cut a felt Christmas tree about 25 cm wide by 35 cm high and tack it to a bulletin board or a heavy piece of cardboard. Also using felt, making the decorations that are mentioned in capital letters in the parody below. While you and the children sing the song, one or more children can add the decorations to the tree.

brush star with
glue and sprinkle
with glitter

glue rope tinsel
to length of felt

cut shape
of tree
from piece
of felt

candy cane:
stripe white felt
with marker
or paint

place gifts
and toys in front
of felt tree

HERE'S OUR LITTLE PINE TREE (a parody)

(tune: "I'm a Little Teapot")

adaptation by Darlene Hamilton

Here's our lit-tle pine TREE
    tall and straight.
Let's find the things
    so we can dec-o-rate
First we want to put
    a STAR on top!
Then we must be care-ful
    the BALLS don't pop
Hang on all the TIN-SEL
    shin-y and bright
Put on the CANES
    and hook them just right
Fin-ally put some PRES-ENTS
    for you and for me
And we'll be read-y
    with our CHRIST-MAS TREE!

Records and Cassettes

New Christmas recordings are issued every year and as many are taken out of circulation every year. As a result, a record and cassette list would be out of date before this book goes to print. Keep in mind that children enjoy listening to complex melodies and rhythms, but that recordings chosen for singing along must have songs that are within the range and ability of the children.

     NOTE: See also Large Muscle Activities for other musical participation games.

Fingerplays and Poems

From *Let's Do Fingerplays*, Grayson
"Christmas Is A-Coming," p. 92
"Santa Claus," p. 92
"Christmas Bells," p. 92
"Christmas Tree," p. 93
"Here Is the Chimney," p. 94

....

CHRISTMAS IS HERE

Here is the wreath that hangs on the door, (*make a circle with arms over head*)
Here is the fir tree that stands on the floor, (*make a triangle with thumbs and forefingers*)
Here is the book from which carols are sung, (*palms touching and facing upward like book pages*)
Here is the mantel from which stockings are hung. (*place one bent arm over the other bent arm in front of body, drop one arm like a hanging stocking*)

Here is the chimney that Santa comes down. (*make an upright rectangle with thumbs as the base and fingers for the sides*)
Here is the snow that covers the town, (*fingers flutter down*)
Here is a box in which is hid (*close right fist with thumb inside and place left hand on top*)
A Jack that pops up, when you open the lid. (*lift left hand up and pop out thumb*)

....

CHILDREN'S CHRISTMAS TREE

Here the children's Christmas tree (*make triangle with thumbs for the base and fingers forming the peak*)
Standing straight and tall.
Here's the pot to put it in (*cup hands together*)
So it will not fall.

Here are two balls bright and gay (*make circles with thumb and index finger of each hand*)
One ball — two balls — see? (*hold up to see*)
And two tall candles red! (*hold index fingers up straight for candles*)
To trim our Christmas tree. (*repeat triangle for tree*)

Stories

(To read, read–tell, or tell. See Book Centre for a complete list.)

A Candle for Christmas by Jean Speare and Ann Blades is a sensitive story about a family that is reunited for Christmas. The illustrations reflect the contrast between a northern winter landscape and safe and secure indoor family scenes. The story can be edited for younger children.

Games

(See Learning Games in Part 1 and Teacher-Made Games and Materials earlier in this chapter for directions.)

1. *Guess* what? (Christmas riddles): Describe a Christmas symbol or a toy and have the children guess what it is; for instance, "I'm brown and white, have four legs and antlers, and pull Santa's sleigh. What am I?"
2. *Merry Christmas* (variation of *Listening*): Children sit in a semicircle. Choose one child to close and cover his or her eyes. Point to one of the children in the semicircle, who says "Merry Christmas to you!" or "Hi Santa!" The child whose eyes are covered must guess the voice. The child who was the mystery voice guesses the next voice. This game requires that the children know one another well.
3. *Santa and his reindeer (or elves):* Children sit in a semicircle. Choose one child to be Santa. She or he closes and covers eyes. Point to another child to be a reindeer or an elf. This child hides. Santa looks at the remaining reindeer or elves to see who is missing. The hidden reindeer or elf then becomes the new Santa.

Routine Times

1. Use the fingerplays while the children are coming to the table for snack time. Milk may be coloured red or green with food colouring. (Let the children add the colour themselves.) Eat the cookies they have baked or decorated.
2. When washing hands, let children make thick soapsuds to make lovely Santa beards! Mirrors add to the fun.
3. Christmas carols may be played softly on the piano or tape-recorder during rest time.
4. When talking or busing, look for Santa and Christmas decorations.

Large Muscle Activities

1. "Santa's Pack": Let children all choose a toy to be and carry. The child who plays Santa calls out the name of a toy to be added to the pack in the invisible sleigh. Another child joins Santa in a follow-the-leader trip around the room, leaving toys where they belong on shelves. Adapt to suit your group and space. VARIATION: Can also be played like Fruit Basket Upset with piano or recorded music to signal a change (delivery) of toys. Santa may choose children to join him by touching them or motioning when the music stops. All go to their places and a new Santa is chosen.
2. "See the Puppets": Children pretend to be puppets and move to music rhythmically.
3. Adapt traditional tunes to a Christmas theme. For example:
   a. "Did You Ever See a Toy?" (adaptation of "Did You Ever See a Lassie?"): Children form a circle and watch a child in the centre act out the motions of any toy (truck, doll, or racing car). They try to guess the toy.
   b. "Here We Go Round the Christmas Tree" (adaptation of "Here We Go Round the Mulberry Bush": "This is the way to chop the tree, carry it home, stand it up, put on the lights."

Extended Experiences

1. Organ recital: If you know a church organist, perhaps the children can watch and listen for a few minutes while he or she practises Christmas music at a nearby church.
2. Visit Santa: Visit a department store to see Santa, or take the children to see interesting store windows decorated especially for children. Plan smaller groups for such an

excursion; extra adults will be necessary to help supervise. VARIATION: Have Santa visit your group. Plan for him or her to bring a treat that you provide.

3. Buy a living tree for your centre, and after the holiday plant it in your schoolyard or in a teacher's or parent's yard as soon as weather permits. (England)
4. Plan a display of Christmas cards from other countries. Check with parents, armed forces personnel, ministers, and students from other countries, all of whom might have such cards. Note how they are alike or different, and notice particularly the stamps on the envelopes.
5. Decorate a tree or potted branch with treats for the birds. Your favourite garden centre or tree nursery can help with seed suggestions.

>   NOTE: Let children fill containers with popped corn, cracked corn, cubes of cheese, doughnuts (stale or fresh), rolled oats, melon rinds, raisins, cranberries, pork fat, crumbs, cabbage or lettuce leaves, pumpkin or watermelon seeds, grain, peanut butter (if mixed with cornmeal so it will not choke the birds), and uncooked peas. (Scandinavia)

6. Make some Danish rice pudding. (Denmark)
7. Hang colourful Swedish Christmas wall hangings on your walls. (Sweden)
8. Make and decorate Christmas cookies. Select cookie cutters shaped like shepherds, sheep, Wise Men, donkeys, and other nativity figures. (Germany, Poland)
9. Invite children to share food, mittens, and other items with those less fortunate than themselves. St. Barbara's Day (December 4) would be a good day to collect donations. (Syria)
10. Display a hand-carved crèche borrowed from a friend. (Czechoslovakia)
11. Buy or borrow a few wooden, straw, or other unbreakable Christmas tree ornaments imported from another country. (Germany, Panama, or Scandinavian countries)
12. Invite a Japanese friend to fold some paper fish, stars, or butterflies (symbols of Christ) for your tree. (Japan)
13. Display pictures of trees showing decorations by different ethnic groups.
14. View a *nacimiento* (crèche that usually includes a whole village scene), a *pesebre* (manger), or a *ceppo* (group of shelves for gifts and crèche) in the home of a Spanish, Mexican, or Italian family during the *novena* of *Las Posadas* (*Las Posadas* marks the search of Mary and Joseph for shelter, a search that tradition says lasted nine days). You might try to prepare a *nacimiento* in a corner of your room with the children's help. (Spain, Mexico, Italy, South American countries)
15. Invite a harpist to play Welsh carols or other Christmas music. (Wales)
16. Share simple gifts on Twelfth Night, January 6 (see p. 293 for suggestions regarding gifts). (Many countries)
17. Encourage the children to draw picture letters for their parents. Older children might choose a piece of paper labelled "I love you because you . . ." or "I promise to help by . . ." to be folded up and sealed inside a decorated envelope to be placed by their parent's plate at dinner. (Italy)
18. Make small cone-shaped containers for treats from flocked wallpaper scraps to decorate a tree. Staple on small sprays of flowers as you attach ribbon or yarn handles. Staple silver or white plastic doilies into decorative baskets and attach twisted silver cord or braid for handles. (England)

Teacher Resources

Barber, Mary, and Flora McPherson. *Christmas in Canada.* Toronto: Dent, 1972. (Read–Tell)

Barer-Stein, T. *You Eat What You Are.* Toronto: McClelland & Stewart, 1979.

Coffin, T.P. *The Book of Christmas Folklore.* New York: Seabury Press, 1973.

Crean, Patrick. *The Fitzhenry and Whiteside Fireside Book of Canadian Christmas.* Markham, ON: Fitzhenry & Whiteside, 1986.

Harper, Kenn, ed. *Christmas in the Big Igloo.* Yellowknife: Outcrop, 1983.

Hunter, D., and J. Shipley. *Making Your Own Traditions: Christmas Fast and Easy Crafts and Recipes for Parents and Kids.* Lexington, SC: Traditions, 1984.

Joy, M. *Highdays and Holidays.* Boston: Faber & Faber, 1981.

Laurence, Margaret. *The Christmas Birthday Story.* Toronto: McClelland & Stewart, 1980. (Read–Tell)

MacDougall, S. *Christmas Cooking for Santa.* MacDougall, 1984.

Manning-Saunders, R. *Festivals.* London: Heinemann, 1973.

Nickerson, B. *Celebrate the Sun.* Toronto: McClelland and Stewart, 1969.

Ontario Ministry of Culture and Recreation. *Days to Remember: Observances of Significance in our Multicultural Society* (Glyn P. Allen, ed.). Toronto: Government of Ontario, 1980.

Stephan, B. *Decorations for Holiday Celebrations.* New York: Crown, 1978.

Wernecke, H.H. *Christmas Customs around the World.* Philadelphia: Westminster Press, 1979.

• •

KWANZAA

(Keh-WAHN-zah)

This special holiday, celebrated by some African families from December 26 to January 1, recognizes traditional African harvest festivals and stresses the unity of the family. In the African language Kiswahili, *Kwanzaa* means "first fruits." The holiday originally began as an alternative to the highly commercialized version of Christmas. It lasts for an entire week, with special parties on successive days, and often ends with a community-wide harvest feast and party on the seventh day. Small gifts are traditionally given on each day, often homemade or homegrown gifts, such as pecan pralines, molasses peanut brittle, molasses bread, and fruit.

Seven lessons associated with this holiday and a key word for each are listed below:

1. *umoja* (unity)
   We must stand together.
2. *kujichagulia* (self-determination)
   We must decide in our own way.
3. *ujima* (co-operation)
   We must work together.
4. *ujamaca* (sharing by all)
   We must share what we have.
5. *kuumba* (creativity)
   We need to use creativity in reflecting pride in and caring for our community.
6. *nia* (purpose)
   We must have a purpose in life to make a better world.
7. *imani* (faith)
   We need to have faith, which will result in works and action.

Customs of the traditional African holiday

1. Lighting candles called *mishumaas* to remind people to live and build together.
2. Placing candles in the *kinara* (candleholder) on a straw mat called the *mkeka* in the centre of the table.

3. Holding a feast on the last day of *Kwanzaa*, during which everyone drinks from a unity cup called the *kikombe*.
4. Giving each child an ear of corn called *mihindi*.
5. Giving gifts on the last day called *zawadi*.

The following recipe is a traditional African treat. It is associated with John Canoe, the celebration that African slaves held at Christmas time. It also can be enjoyed by children during *Kwanzaa*.

....

SWEET POTATO CANDY

500 g/1 lb sweet potatoes (500 mL/2 cups mashed)
500 mL/2 cups sugar (250 mL/1 cup brown, 250 mL/1 cup white)
5 mL/1 tsp lemon juice
250 mL/1 cup marshmallows (optional)

For flavouring, you may add:
15 mL/1 T orange juice or pineapple juice
5 mL/1 tsp vanilla
2 mL/½ tsp cinnamon

Wash and boil sweet potatoes. Cool, peel, and mash potatoes in a colander to remove strings. Place in a pan and add lemon juice, sugar, and marshmallows (optional). Cook over low flame, stirring constantly until very thick. Set aside to cool. Add vanilla or other flavouring. Spoon candy into paper cups. Dust with powdered sugar or sprinkle with candy beads.

Extended Experiences

1. Allow children to make gifts for a friend or family member.
2. Serve fruit or make sweet potato candy.
3. Mount pictures of African families doing things together for the holidays.
4. Eat corn on the cob at meal time, light candles, and have a *Kwanzaa* party.
5. For further information about this holiday, write: Institute of Positive Education, 7524 South Cottage Grove, Chicago, IL 60619.

Part 5 Seasons

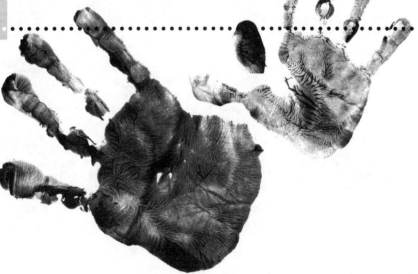

Introduction

Basic Understandings
(concepts children can grasp from this subject)

☐ In North America we have four seasons — winter, spring, summer, and fall.
☐ Each season has a different type of weather.
☐ In Canada, we can have different weather across the country in the same season. For example, in January (winter) flowers can be growing in the sun in Victoria, rain can be falling in Vancouver, warm winds (called chinooks) can be blowing down on the Prairies, wet snow can be falling in Toronto and Montreal, and heavy snow can be falling in the Maritimes.
☐ We do some things in specific seasons.
☐ We wear clothes that are comfortable and safe for each season.
☐ Our homes are built to keep us comfortable in different seasons.

Additional Facts the Teacher Should Know

It is difficult for children to comprehend the full significance of any of the seasons. The concepts are best introduced when there is some noticeable change in the weather or when there is some seasonally related local activity; for example, when the lawn outside the centre is reseeded, or the roads are repaired, or the last crops of the season are harvested.

Children hear lengthy discussions of weather, holes in the ozone layer, and changing weather patterns on the television and the radio. Some of this may be frightening to them. If you believe children have some concerns about these issues, try to explain the issues to them in simple terms. (For example: Pollution can ruin things. Pollution has eaten away at the natural sunshade in the sky so now it is easier to get a sunburn.) Follow up the explanation by talking about some of the things we can do to get rid of pollution.

Book Centre

•• Allen, Marjorie N., and Shelly Rotner. *Changes*. Toronto: Macmillan, 1991.
• Anno, Mitsumaso. *Anno's Counting Book*. New York: Crowell, 1977.

••• Aska, Warabé. *Who Hides in the Park?* Montreal: Tundra, 1986. (text is in English, French, and Japanese)

••• ———. *Who Goes to the Park?* Montreal: Tundra, 1984.

••• Aska, Warabé, and Alberto Manguel. *Seasons.* Toronto: Doubleday, 1990.

•• Baum, Arline. *One Bright Monday Morning.* New York: Random House, 1962.

•• Borden, Louise. *Caps, Hats, Socks, and Mittens.* Richmond Hill, ON: Scholastic, 1989. (also in a Big Book format)

•• Brown, Margaret Wise. *The Little Island.* New York: Doubleday, 1946.

••• Bunting, Eve. *Winter's Coming.* San Diego: Harcourt Brace Jovanovich, 1977.

•• Charles, Donald. *Calico Cat's Year.* Chicago: Children's Press, 1984.

••• de Paola, Tomie. *Four Stories for Four Seasons.* Englewood Cliffs, NJ: Prentice-Hall, 1977.

••• Freedman, Russell. *When Winter Comes.* New York: Dutton, 1981.

••• Gibbons, Gail. *The Seasons of Arnold's Apple Tree.* New York: Harcourt Brace Jovanovich, 1984.

••• Hall, Donald, and Barbara Cooney. *The Ox-Cart Man.* New York: Viking, 1979.

•• Hoban, Julia. *Amy Loves the Wind.* New York: Harper & Row, 1988.

•• Kuskin, Karla. *Sand and Snow.* New York: Harper & Row, 1965.

•• Lionni, Leo. *Mouse Days.* New York: Pantheon, 1981.

•• ———. *When?* New York: Pantheon, 1983.

••• Littlewood, Valerie. *The Season Clock.* Markham, ON: Penguin, 1986.

••• Lobel, Arnold. *Frog and Toad all Year.* New York: Harper & Row, 1978.

••• McNaughton, Colin. *Winter.* New York: Dutton, 1983.

••• Newman, Fran, and Claudette Boulanger. *Snowflakes and Sunshine.* Richmond Hill, ON: North Winds Press, 1979.

•• Oppenheim, Joanne, and Barbara Reid. *Have You Seen Birds?* Richmond Hill, ON: Scholastic, 1986.

••• Pienkowski, Jan. *Weather.* New York: Messner, 1983.

••• Provensen, Alice, and Martin Provensen. *A Book of Seasons.* New York: Random House, 1976.

•••• ———. *The Year at Maple Hill Farms.* New York: Atheneum, 1978.

• Rockwell, Anne. *First Comes Spring.* New York: Crowell, 1985.

•• Slote, Elizabeth. *Nelly's Garden.* Toronto: Tambourine, 1991.

• Spier, Peter. *Dreams.* New York: Doubleday, 1986. (a book about clouds)

• Tafuri, Nancy. *All Year Long.* New York: Greenwillow Press, 1983.

••• Turkle, Brinton. *Thy Friend, Obadiah.* New York: Viking, 1969.

• Wolff, A. *A Year of Beasts.* New York: Dutton, 1986.

• ———. *A Year of Birds.* New York: Dodd, Mead, 1984.

•• Zolotow, Charlotte. *Summer is . . . .* New York: Crowell, 1983.

NOTE: See the Book Centre sections in Chapters 12–15 for additional references.

12 **Winter**

Basic Understandings
(concepts children can grasp from this subject)

Winter is a season that comes after fall and before spring. There are many changes in nature in the winter.

Earth Changes

☐ When it gets very cold, water freezes (gets hard) and makes ice, such as snow, sleet, and icicles; also, materials that contain water freeze.
　　a.　Sleet is frozen raindrops.
　　b.　Snow is frozen crystals of water.
　　c.　Ice is a frozen mass of water.
☐ In many areas, the weather is warmer and it rains instead of snowing.
☐ We have blizzards when a strong wind blows for a long time during a heavy snowstorm. It causes deep snowdrifts and makes it hard for people to see or move around outside.
☐ Daylight hours get shorter in Canada in winter; in parts of the North, there are some days with no daylight at all.
☐ Children have a greater chance of seeing the moon and stars before going to bed or when they wake up early in winter (see Chapter 25, Day and Night).
☐ Usually, the winter weather is colder, chillier, and damper, and the wind is more likely to feel cold than in other seasons of the year.
☐ The length of the winter season depends on where we live.

Plants

☐ Where it is very cold, most plants stop growing for a while. (They seem to die, but their seeds, roots, or bulbs often live underground, protected from the frost by dirt and a blanket of snow.)
☐ Where it rains instead of snowing, flowers and trees continue to bloom and grow all year round.
☐ Some shrubs and trees grow and bloom all year round and are called "evergreens."
☐ Some trees lose their leaves and become bare when the weather gets cold.

☐   Some indoor plants seldom bloom except during the winter; for example, the Christmas cactus.
When frozen, plants wilt and turn brown.

Animals, Birds, and Insects
☐   Some animals hibernate (rest or sleep for a long time) during the winter.
☐   Animals hibernate in trees, underground, or in caves.
☐   Many birds migrate (fly away) to a warmer climate where they can find food during the winter months.
☐   Sometimes, animals grow thicker fur, down, or hair in winter to keep them warm.
☐   Some animals' fur changes colour in the winter to help camouflage and hide the animals when it snows.
☐   A few insects and animals, such as ants and squirrels, store food for winter.
☐   Some animals enjoy playing in the snow and on the ice.
☐   Special care must be taken of some animals in winter, such as sweaters for short-haired dogs, protection for livestock against blizzards, food for birds who do not migrate, or for those who return too early when there is a late snow in spring.

People
☐   Depending on how cold it is, children and adults need to wear heavier, warmer, or special clothes in winter for play and work, such as boots, sweaters, scarves, mittens, caps, hats, coats, thermal underwear, snowsuits, and parkas.
☐   Children and adults enjoy playing in the snow or on the ice, such as sledding, skating, skiing, tobogganing, snowmobiling, or ice fishing.
☐   Where it is very cold, people often spend more time indoors in winter baking, using fireplaces, giving parties, reading, playing games, or sipping hot chocolate.
☐   People need to clear snow from sidewalks and streets in order to walk or drive safely.
☐   Cold weather, rain, snow, and ice sometimes make it difficult to build or paint houses or to pour cement.
☐   Drivers have to put antifreeze in their cars to prevent the water in their radiators from freezing when it is very cold. Sometimes they need snow tires and chains, such as when driving on snow or on ice.
☐   People are more likely to catch colds and flu in winter.
☐   When it gets too cold outside, we need to heat the buildings where we live, work, or play, and turn on the heaters in buses, cars, and trucks.
☐   Fishermen often cannot work in the winter because of the cold weather. However, some people do go ice fishing.
☐   Farmers are not as busy with crops during the winter, but they must keep their animals warm, well-fed, and clean.

Additional Facts the Teacher Should Know
1. It is difficult for young children to comprehend the full significance of any of the seasons. However, they can understand that winter is a time when certain changes take place in our environment and certain events, activities, and holidays occur.
2. In most of Canada, winter extends from approximately December 21 to March 20. Winter in the southern hemisphere is from June 21 to September 22. These are the official dates determined by solar and lunar phases. It is easier for young children to understand changes in weather; such changes usually present better times to introduce the seasons.
3. The four seasons vary in time and length all over the world, as the sun's rays strike the earth differently at any one time. Because it gets dark early in this season, winter

is a good time to learn about day and night (see Chapter 25, Day and Night). The stars are visible in the winter while young children are still awake. Parents should be encouraged to help children find and enjoy the stars.

4. No two snowflakes are alike, although snowflakes are hexagonal (have six sides). You can help children appreciate their uniqueness and beauty by providing magnifying glasses and enlarged photographic reproductions. The exact way in which snowflakes form depends on what is happening in the atmosphere where they are formed. Snow that comes from very high and very cold clouds, where rapid freezing takes place, have simple crystals. Snow that falls from and through warmer air builds up more elaborate patterns.

5. Winter festivals are celebrated in many northern countries, including Canada. The most famous in Canada are held in Quebec City and Ottawa, but there are many local festivals. Check with your Chamber of Commerce or tourist board to find out if any special winter celebrations are planned for your area.

6. Ice-skating shows tour and perform in arenas. These shows are enjoyed by the whole family. Some children travel with their families to ski resorts and winter recreation parks for special winter activities. All children enjoy snow if it is a part of winter where they live.

7. If you live where it is too cold for plants to grow outside in winter, you may wish to plant bulbs or seeds indoors. This will give the children an opportunity to understand that plants need warmth and light to grow.

8. Most birds migrate in fall or early winter because food becomes scarce, not because it is cold. Birds grow an undercoating of down that keeps them warm. However, when ponds freeze and snow covers the ground, many insects die or hibernate, so birds have limited sources of food. Children might enjoy helping feed birds during the winter (see the illustration). However, if you start a bird-feeding station, you should maintain it all through the winter; otherwise, the birds who remain because of your efforts may be stranded and could die.

Make a bird feeder from a 3 L size bleach jug. Cut out two sides so the birds can fly through. Weight jug with coarse pebbles and fill it with birdseed. Wire it securely to a tree limb.

9. Suet or bacon fat can be melted and mixed with wild birdseed in equal proportions. This mixture can be poured into walnut shells, aluminum pie plates, margarine containers, paper cups, or on pine-cones; wires can be attached to the containers through punched holes and then tied to the tree.

10. Pour melted fat over birdseed mixture in small paper cups. Insert wire or pipecleaners into the mixture with 5 cm or so protruding. When hardened, peel away the paper and hang on a tree. Stale bread or doughnuts can be hung on branches or crumbled and thrown on the ground. Birds also like chicken scratch, livestock grain, and apple peels. If you do not have a suitable tree or bush, food can be spread out on the top of a box. A simple V-shaped roof nailed to the box provides protection from the wind while birds are eating. Dishes holding food should be nailed or tied down, because some birds push and shove while crowding around food.

11. Children may wish to help small animals by building a shelter for them. Dead branches heaped on an old stump or a pile of rocks, logs, or rail ties make good escape cover or winter dens. Old drain pipes buried under rocks and earth make artificial burrows. Children can put nuts and seeds out for squirrels, and leafy vegetables, beans, and carrots for rabbits. Develop children's interest in animals that live well with ice and snow be showing pictures of polar bears, penguins, and seals (see also Chapter 18, Woodland Animals).

12. Citrus fruits grown in Florida, Texas, southern California, and Mexico are the most prevalent during winter. Grapefruit, oranges, and tangerines are plentiful and make good snacks when peeled and sectioned or squeezed for juice. Many young children do not like grapefruit or its juice by itself, but will accept it in small amounts if it is combined with other fruit or juices.

13. Other sections of this guide that include related themes are Part 6, Animals, and Part 8, My World.

Introducing This Subject to Children

1. Note changes in weather, trees, birds, animals, etc.
2. Notice when it snows for the first time.
3. Take a pan of water outside on a freezing day. Observe the results.
4. Observe that some trees have bare branches and some don't.
5. Prepare a bird feeder or an animal shelter.
6. Read a story about winter or the four seasons.
7. Bring in a large dishpan or baby's bathtub filled with snow for the children to explore.

Vocabulary

winter	trees	temperature	snowflake
snow	bare	road salt	hockey
cold	evergreens	snow shovel	mistletoe
ice	birds	snowplow	holly
icicle	snowmobile	snowblower	poinsettia
rain	toboggan	ski	snow tires
fog	snowshoes	sled	parka
blizzard	animals	skate	longjohns
snowstorm	feeder	sleet	mittens
snow squall	hibernate	Jack Frost	ski jacket
freeze	migrate	igloo	snowsuit
			toque

Learning Centres

NOTE: Many of these suggestions are made for climates where there is snow. If you live in a milder climate, adapt each suggestion to rain (see Chapter 26, Water around Me), or use ice or frost from the freezer or refrigerator where feasible. If mountains are nearby, you could take a cooler and pack some snowballs, snow, or icicles for children to see when you return.

Discovery Centre

1. Take a pan of water outside when the temperature is below freezing. Observe what happens. After the water has frozen, bring the pan inside again and observe what happens.
2. Fill a juice can and a small milk carton with water. Staple the mild carton shut. Take both outside in freezing weather or place in a freezer. Observe what happens. VARIATION: Set out a small carton of milk to freeze. When almost frozen, give children a spoonful to taste.
3. Bring a pan of snow inside to measure and explore.
4. Bring icicles inside to observe as they melt.
5. Outside, observe snowflakes that fall on children's coat sleeves, or catch some on a dark velvet cloth. Use magnifying glasses if available.

A winter day provides the opportunity to explore patterns in the ice. This child is learning about some of the properties of ice.

6. Make snow cones by packing clean, crushed ice in paper cups and pouring fruit-fla-voured gelatin powder or syrup over the ice. Let children choose the flavour they want.

7. Store some snowballs or cartons of snow in a freezer so children can discover that the snow is still frozen in late winter or early spring when the snow outside has melted and disappeared.

8. Make ice cream using your favourite recipe. Talk about why the cream freezes.

9. Let children mix food colouring or paint with snow.

10. Look for animal or bird tracks in the snow.

11. Let the children observe, under supervision, indoor–outdoor thermometers. They can see that as it gets colder the mercury goes down.

12. Make a large cardboard thermometer using extra-wide cardboard (see Discovery Centre, number 5, p. 563). Provide old catalogues or magazines with pictures of children in clothes for different seasons. Encourage the children to cut out pictures that match different temperatures. Paste pictures at appropriate temperatures (for example, winter pictures under 10°C, spring and fall pictures between 10°C and 15°C, and summer pictures above 15°C).

13. Make Jack wax. Boil 500 mL of maple syrup until the softball stage is reached. Pour the hot syrup over crushed ice in a large bowl. Twirl the "wax" onto forks.

14. Go outside on a cold day to see water vapour when children breathe and talk.

15. To show that plants need sunlight, force hyacinth bulbs. In the fall, plant bulbs outside in a buried pot. Dig up the pot in January, bring it inside, and put it in a warm, dark place. Soon, yellow leaves will appear. Move the pot to a sunny ledge and watch the plant grow and blossom.

NOTE: See also Discovery Centres in Part 6, Animals, and Chapter 26, Water around Me.

Dramatic Play Centres

Home-living centre

1. Set out blankets, sweaters, jackets, hats, snowsuits, and parkas for the dolls, suggesting the need for warmer clothes in winter.

2. Put up pictures of snow and rain, and activities related to each. Include pictures of children dressed for freezing temperatures or rainy weather, using some that are appropriate to your area's climate.

Block-building centre

1. Set out animal figures and suggest that unit blocks be used to build a barn, a stable, or another animal shelter.

2. A bulldozer can be a make-believe snowplow, and dump trucks can be used to haul away the snow.

3. Toy logs can be set out for older children to build houses as the first settlers did for their first winter.

4. Blocks can be used to build igloos.

Art Centre

1. Feature white paint for painting snow pictures.

2. Provide white chalk and coloured construction paper for making snow pictures.

3. Paint pine-cones white or green and glue to styrofoam bases. Use as decorations on tables, or to add a winter effect to block-building constructions. Bare twigs stuck in styrofoam could be used as deciduous trees in the block-building centre.

• 4. Mix soap flakes and water into a thick paste using an eggbeater or electric mixer. Add a small amount of liquid starch and white powdered tempera for a more permanent, attractive product. Let children create designs by painting the thick mixture on paper with a brush or rubbing it on with a tongue depressor.

••• 5. Children who have had a great deal of experience with clay and dough may discover they can make snow sculptures.

••• 6. When outdoors, encourage children to sculpt snow into freeform figures.

•• 7. Paste cotton balls on construction paper to make a snowy day picture.

•• 8. Cut a star shape out of sponge or cut a green pepper in half around the middle to get an unusual star shape. Let children dip the star in white paint and print snowflakes on coloured construction paper.

•• 9. Make styrofoam sculptures using precut scraps of styrofoam, styrofoam balls, toothpicks, bits of yarn and leather, and feathers. Use toothpicks and pipecleaners with glue to assemble the sculptures.

Learning and Language Materials Centre

Commercially made games and materials

1. *Puzzles:* Snowflake puzzles and other puzzles with winter themes.
2. *Small toys for imaginative play:* Snowplows, snowmobiles, and sleds made of vinyl, plastic, or metal.
3. *Outdoor toys:* Dogsleds and model snowmobiles; plastic child-size snow shovels and pails for digging and playing in the snow; child-size hockey sticks and vinyl hockey pucks.

   NOTE: Choose a sturdy plastic that is less likely to crack in the cold.

4. *Dolls and puppets:* Glove puppets; winter clothes for dolls.
5. *Flannelboards:* Weather cutouts; for example, storm clouds, snowflakes, etc.
6. *Posters:* Weather charts.

   NOTE: Choose boards that can be changed each day, preferably by one of the children.

7. *Miscellaneous:* Large indoor–outdoor thermometer in an unbreakable case.

Teacher-made games and materials

NOTE: For detailed descriptions, see Learning Games in Part 1.

1. *What's missing?* Use a styrofoam snowball, plastic or paper snowflake, pair of mittens, pair of earmuffs, ski mask.
2. *Match them:* Show children a styrofoam snowball. Say, "This snowball is round. Find me something else that is round," or, "This snowball is white. Find me something else that is white." Or, show children a pair of mittens and say, "These mittens are red. Find me something else that is red."
3. *Match them:* Scramble several pairs of mittens and have children find a matching pair.
4. *Reach and feel:* Use objects similar to those in number 1.
5. *Show me:* Use objects similar to those in number 1, and ask, "Show me the one we wear on our hands," or, "Show me the one that keeps our ears warm."
6. Make a calendar for one or all of the winter months, making each day a 5 cm square. Use decorative seals to mark the special holidays, birthdays, and other events that will have meaning for the children at your centre. Surround the calendar with paper snowflakes. As each day goes by, cover it with one of the snowflakes. In areas where there is no snow, mark off the days with poinsettias, evergreen trees, raindrops, or clouds.

Book Centre

- •• Bell, Cathie, and David Bell. *Two Bears in the Snow.* Toronto: Oxford University Press, 1991.
- •• Blades, Ann. *Winter.* Toronto: Groundwood, 1989.
- ••• Branley, F.M. *Snow Is Falling* (rev. ed.). Markham, ON: Fitzhenry & Whiteside, 1986.
- •• Breinburg, P. *Sally Ann in the Snow.* London: Bodley Head, 1977.
- ••• Brett, Jan. *The Mitten: A Ukrainian Folktale.* New York: Putnam, 1990.
- •• Burningham, John. *Seasons.* New York: Bobbs-Merrill, 1970.
- •••• Carrier, Roch. *The Hockey Sweater.* Montreal: Tundra, 1984. (also available in French as *Le chandail de hockey*) (Read–Tell)
- ••• Craig, Janet. *Here Comes Winter.* St. Catharines, ON: Troll Associates, 1988.
- ••• Egvindson, Peter. *The Wish Wind.* Winnipeg: Pemmican, 1987.
- ••• Hartley, Deborah. *Up North in Winter.* Markham, ON: Fitzhenry & Whiteside, 1986.
- •• Hasler, Eveline. *Winter Magic.* Toronto: Kids Can Press, 1989.
- •• Hoff, Syd. *When It Snows!* New York: Harper & Row, 1971.
- •• Hutchins, Hazel. *Norman's Snowball.* Willowdale, ON: Annick Press, 1989
- ••• ———. *Ben's Snow Song: A Winter Picnic.* Willowdale, ON: Annick Press, 1987.
- ••• Kalman, Bobbie, et al. *We Celebrate Winter.* Toronto: Crabtree, 1986.
- • Keats, Ezra Jack. *The Snowy Day.* New York: Viking Press, 1962.
- •••• Kidd, Bruce. *Hockey Showdown.* Toronto: Lorimer, 1986. (Read–Tell)
- •••• Kurelek, William. *A Prairie Boy's Winter.* Montreal: Tundra, 1973. (Read–Tell)
- •• Lemieux, Michèle. *What's That Noise?* Toronto: Kids Can Press, 1989.
- ••• Maestro, Betsy C. *Snow Day.* New York: Scholastic, 1989.
- ••• McKee, David. *Snow Woman.* London: Arrow, 1987.
- ••• Mendez, Phil. *The Black Snowman.* New York: Scholastic, 1989.
- ••• Miller, Edna. *Mousekin's Woodland Sleepers.* Englewood Cliffs, NJ: Prentice-Hall, 1970.
- ••• Morgan, Allan. *Sadie and the Snowman.* Toronto: Kids Can Press, 1986. (also available in French)
- ••• Munsch, Robert. *50 Below Zero.* Willowdale, ON: Annick Press, 1986.
- ••• ———. *Thomas's Snowsuit.* Willowdale, ON: Annick Press, 1985.
- •• Paré, Roger. *Winter Games.* Willowdale, ON: Annick Press, 1991.
- • Podendorf, Illa. *The True Book of Seasons.* Chicago: Children's Press, 1972.
- ••• Priest, Robert. *The Short Hockey Career of Amazing Jany.* Toronto: Aya Press, 1986.
- •• Scheidl, Gerda Marie. *Flowers for the Snowman.* St. Catharines, ON: North-South, 1988.
- •• Tibo, Gilles. *Simon and the Snowflakes.* Montreal: Tundra, 1988. (also available in French as *Simon et les flocons de neige*)
- ••• Waldren, K.C. *A Winter's Yarn.* Red Deer, AB: Red Deer College Press, 1986.
- ••• Zolotow, Charlotte. *Hold My Hand.* New York: Harper & Row, 1972.

Planning for Group Time

NOTE: All music, fingerplays, poems, stories, and games listed here may also be used at other times during the session as appropriate.

Music

Songs

From *Elephant Jam*, Sharon, Lois, and Bram
"The Wind," p. 28

From *More Piggyback Songs*, Warren
Songs about Winter, pp. 11–24

From *Piggyback Songs*, Warren
Songs about Winter, pp. 11–18

From *Sally Go Round the Sun*, Fowke
"The Wind the Wind," p. 65

From *Singing Bee*, Hart
"The North Wind Doth Blow," p. 33
"Over the River and Through the Wood," p. 142

From *Stepping Along in Music Land*, Murray
"Seasons," p. 52
"Winter Won't You Go," p. 53

Rhythms and Singing Games

1. Snowflakes: Give children white scarves, white crepe-paper streamers, or precut white paper snowflakes.
   a. Play fast-tempo music, and let children pretend to be snowflakes on a windy day.
   b. Play slow-tempo music, and let children pretend to be softly falling snowflakes.
2. Ice-skating: Play the "Skater's Waltz" and let the children pretend to be ice-skaters.
3. Sleigh ride: Using a rope as a harness and stick horses, have children pretend to be horses pulling a sleigh through the snow. Six horses could pull at a time and the rest of the children could be sitting in the sleigh (line up several rows of three chairs each). Those in the sleigh can shake bells in time with the music.

Records and Cassettes

Sandy Tobias Oppenheim, *If Snowflakes Fell in Flavours*. (Berandol Records)

"If Snowflakes Fell in Flavours"

> **NOTE:** The songs on this recording are difficult for young children to sing, but this is an excellent recording for listening.

Fingerplays and Poems

From *Don't Eat Spiders*, Heidbreder
"Vancouver," p. 18
"Sticky Maple Syrup," p. 29 (also in Chapter 6 in this book)
"Polar Bear Snow," p. 31

From *Hand Rhymes*, Brown
"Snowflakes," p. 17
"The Snowman," p. 18

From *Let's Do Fingerplays*, Grayson
"Mittens," p. 18
"My Zipper Suit," p. 18
"The Mitten Song," p. 20
"Big Hill," p. 23
"Snowflakes," p. 48
"Snow Men," p. 48
"Shiver and Quiver," p. 58

From *Read Aloud Rhymes for the Very Young*, Prelutsky and Brown
"Little Wind," p. 12
"The Moon's the North Wind's Cooky," p. 51
"The Wind and the Moon," p. 51
"The More It Snows," p. 74
"The Mitten Song," p. 74
"Winter Sweetness," p. 74
"Jack Frost," p. 75
"It Fell in the City," p. 75
"First Snow," p. 76
"January," p. 76
"Icy," p. 76
"Snowman," p. 77
"Snow," p. 77

Stories

(To read, read–tell, or tell. See Book Centre for a complete list.)

When you are choosing stories in the wintertime, choose a combination of stories that reflect the weather in your region and also teach children about weather in other parts of the country. For example, if your centre is in Victoria you may want to read Scheffler's *A Walk in the Rain* (see Book Centre in Chapter 13, Spring) and contrast it with stories from Kurelek's *A Prairie Boy's Winter*. If children in your group were born in or have visited a tropical or subtropical country, you might extend the discussion of different winter weather to include their experience.

Games

(See Learning Games in Part 1 and Teacher-Made Games and Materials earlier in this chapter for directions.)

1. *What's missing?*
2. *Match-them.*
3. *Reach and feel.*
4. *Show me.*

Routine Times

1. At snack or meal times, serve fruits that are available in winter, such as oranges, grapefruit, and tangerines. Talk about the fact that these are grown in areas where it is warmer and that they are brought by ship, train, or truck to stores in your area.

2. At snack or meal times, serve foods that are white, such as milk, marshmallows, enriched white bread, popcorn, potatoes, or rice. Talk about how the colour of snow and the colour of the food are similar.
3. At rest time, pretend to be hibernating animals sleeping through the cold winter.
4. When walking or busing the children to and from the centre, call attention to any signs of winter: frost, snow, bare trees, evergreens, people dressed warmly, frozen ponds, and seeing one's breath.
5. When dressing to go outside, talk about the weather. Look at the outdoor thermometer and decide how cold it is and what you and the children need to wear. If you made a cardboard thermometer with pictures of children in appropriate clothing at various temperatures, this might help them decide. Set the cardboard thermometer beside the outdoor thermometer and see which picture is closest to the outdoor temperature. You might recite "The Mitten Song," "Mittens," or "My Zipper Suit," from Grayson's *Let's Do Fingerplays* as the children are putting on these articles of clothing.

Large Muscle Activities

1. Provide children with child-size snow shovels and let them shovel the playground walks and other paved surfaces. Show them where to put the snow. It could be loaded into wagons and carried to another part of the yard for snow sculptures, or it could be used for the activities suggested in number 2.
2. Provide children with some of the toys and utensils that would be appropriate for using with snow as they would with sand — pails, shovels, spoons, moulds, pie plates, and measuring cups.
3. If the snow is the wet kind that sticks together, have children make a snow sculpture, moulding it into interesting shapes as they would with clay or dough.
4. Show children how to make angels by lying down on their backs in the snow and moving their arms up and down.
5. If you have a hill in your playground and the snow is good for sledding, provide the children with cardboard squares from packing boxes, flying saucers, old trays, or sleds. Establish traffic patterns for going up and coming down. It is ideal to have one adult at the top and one at the bottom of the hill to help regulate traffic. However, if only one adult is available, she or he should be stationed at the bottom of the hill to direct those who have completed their slide on where to climb back up. The adult could instruct the children at the top of the hill to wait until called to avoid collisions.
6. Throwing snowballs at others should be discouraged. Provide a suitable target for children who wish to throw snowballs. The target should be away from the general play area.
7. Children's snowshoes are fun to wear outside after a new snow.
8. *Follow the leader* can be played in fresh snow, with children following the footprints made by the leader. If you are the leader, remember to take small steps, especially if the snow is deep. Try hopping and jumping as well as walking.
9. Snowball toss: Make snowballs and see how many children can toss into a basket, box, or wastebasket. If no snow is available, use styrofoam balls or white nylon balls made from discarded white pantyhose.

Extended Experiences

1. Take a walk and look for things that tell us it is winter — snow, ice, bare trees, icicles, a frozen pond, evergreen trees, and people dressed warmly.
2. Visit a site where your children can safely go sledding if your facility does not have a suitable slope.

3. Visit a frozen pond where the ice is thick enough for the children to walk on. Sleds and flying saucers pull easily over frozen ice, so bring them along.
4. If you know someone with a horse and sleigh, you might be able to arrange a ride for the children.
5. Show the video *The Snowy Day* (Weston Woods).
6. Have a picnic in the snow.

 # Teacher Resources

Pictures and Displays

☐ Set out winter issues of or mount pictures from *Owl, Chickadee, Canadian Geographic,* and *Equinox* magazines.
☐ Post pictures of snow, frozen ponds, bird or animal feeders and shelters, hibernating animals, and winter sports like skiing, skating, and hockey.
☐ Make a mobile of plastic snowflakes (available where Christmas tree decorations are sold), or cut your own from folded paper. When opened, these can be covered with glitter or artificial snow. Snowflakes can also be cut from heavy-duty foil wrap. When opened, flatten these foil snowflakes between the pages of a book. Remember — no two snowflakes are alike, so make yours different.

> **NOTE:** Snowflake stencils can be cut from cardboard and designs stencilled on windows using sponges and a thick paste of soap flakes. Commercial stencils are available at Christmas time.

☐ Decorate windows and walls with snowflakes cut as suggested above.
☐ Make mats to put under each cup at snack or meal times from 1 cm thick sections of pine-cone. Glue each section of pine-cone to a larger, thin circle of wood or cork.
☐ Make a snow scene: A mirror makes a good frozen pond. Surround the pond with cotton batting and pine-cone trees painted green or white, if you wish. Bare twigs can be deciduous trees. Add small plastic skiers, skaters, toboggans, birds, rabbits, and other small animals to the winter wonderland.

Books and Periodicals

Barrett, Norman. *Snow Sports.* New York: Franklin Watts, 1989.
Biene, Susanna. *Sing through the Seasons: Ninety-Nine Songs for Children.* Ulster Park, NY: Plough, 1972.
Canadian Geographic magazine (winter issues).
Chickadee magazine (winter issues).
Cleary, Val. *Seasons of Canada.* Willowdale, ON: Hounslow Press, 1979. (good for pictures of all the seasons in all parts of the country)
Equinox magazine (winter issues).
Hardy, Ralph, et al. *The Weather Book.* Toronto: Little, Brown, 1982.
Holford, Ingrid. *The Guinness Book of Weather Facts and Feats* (2nd ed.). Enfield, UK: Guinness Superlatives, 1982.
Markle, Sandra. *Exploring Winter.* New York: Macmillan, 1984.
Owl magazine (winter issues).
Stokes, Donald W. *A Guide to Nature in Winter.* Camden East, ON: Equinox, 1986.

Whitfield, Philip, and Joyce Pope. *Why Do the Seasons Change? Questions on Nature's Rhythms and Cycles Answered by the Natural History Museum.* New York: Viking Penguin, 1987.

Films and Videos

NOTE: Check with your distributor about public performance rights.

Chickens in a Tree. Insight Productions (released in Canada by Viking Films), 1971.
Chicken Soup with Rice. Weston Woods.
The Snowman. Weston Woods.
The Snowy Day. Weston Woods.
Time of Wonder. Weston Woods.
Zlateh the Goat. Weston Woods.

Community Resources and Organizations

☐ Natural history museums: Often exhibits are changed to reflect the change in season, or there are exhibits that show winter habitats.
☐ A frozen pond in a park nearby.
☐ Snow sculptures created by university or civic groups.
☐ A local television or radio weather reporter.
☐ Local winter fairs.
☐ Local skating rink.

Government Agencies

☐ Federal, provincial, and territorial ministries of the environment.

13 Spring

Basic Understandings
(concepts children can grasp from this subject)

Spring is a season that comes after winter and before summer. There are many changes in nature in the spring.

Earth Changes
- ☐ In areas where there is ice and snow, these both melt.
- ☐ Days are longer (sunrise is earlier and sunset is later than in winter).
- ☐ The temperature is usually warmer, the wind blows hard, and there are often thunderstorms.
- ☐ East, west, and central parts of Canada have very different types of weather in spring. In some areas it may still be cold; in others it may be rainy, windy, and warmer.
- ☐ The ground thaws as the rain warms and softens it. Spring showers and warm sunshine help seeds to sprout and begin to grow.
- ☐ There may be many storms, such as late snowstorms, in the spring when warmer weather suddenly becomes colder.
- ☐ The length of the spring season depends on where we live.

Plants
- ☐ Seeds sprout and plants begin to grow.
- ☐ Leaf buds turn into leaves on trees and on bushes.
- ☐ Blossoms appear on some plants (fruit trees, spring bulbs, dandelions, and pussy willows).
- ☐ Grass turns green and starts to grow.
- ☐ Some indoor plants can be planted outdoors for the summer months, such as geraniums, ivies, and begonias.

Animals, Birds, and Insects
- ☐ Animals that hibernate (sleep during the winter) wake up and come out of their sleeping places.
- ☐ Most animals have babies in the spring.

☐   Birds migrate to their summer homes and build nests.
☐   Birds and animals often grow new coats of feathers or fur to adjust to the weather and to the new colours of their surroundings.

People
☐   We begin to wear lighter clothing in spring.
☐   Farmers prepare their fields for planting.
☐   City workers clean the streets and prepare parks and gardens for new plants and flowers.
☐   Road workers begin to repair roads and highways.
☐   Children and animals play outdoors.
☐   Spring is a time of beginning — housecleaning, planting.

Festivals
☐   Spring festivals are celebrated all over the world. Some are related to religious holidays and others to the arrival of spring and the planting of crops. One special, nonreligious festival is the Tulip Festival held in Ottawa. Many cities and towns have a celebration called Earth Day. Earth Day celebrates the spring and reminds people to protect nature.

Additional Facts the Teacher Should Know

1. In the northern hemisphere, spring is the period from March 21 to June 20 (in the southern hemisphere, it is the period from September 23 to December 20). These are the official dates determined by solar and lunar phases. It is easier for young children to understand changes in weather; such changes usually present better times to introduce the seasons.

2. An equinox is a time of year when the centre of the sun is directly over the equator. The word "equinox" means equal night. During an equinox, the days are the same length as the nights all over the world. The sun crosses the equator twice a year, so there are two equinoxes. The spring, or vernal, equinox occurs around March 20 as the Earth tilts its northern hemisphere toward the sun. The autumnal equinox comes about six months later, around September 23, as the earth tilts back and the sun "moves" south. These changes in the earth's position produce variations in the patterns of warm and cold air masses, to such a degree that storms are frequent at the time of the equinoxes. As the sun "travels" north, its rays strike the northern countries more directly each day, and the weather grows steadily warmer. The time from the end of the vernal equinox to the beginning of the autumnal equinox is longer than the time from the autumnal equinox to the following vernal equinox. This difference amounts to seven days each year, or six days in leap years. It is caused by the elliptical shape of the earth's path around the sun — the earth must move faster when it is nearer the sun.

   NOTE: See Additional Facts the Teacher Should Know in Chapter 25, Day and Night, for an illustration of the equinoxes.

Introducing This Subject to Children

1. Talk about what happens in the spring — new leaves sprout, flowers bloom, seeds sprout, baby animals are born, and birds return and build nests.
2. Read a story about the change of seasons or about spring (see Book Centre).

3. Let the children select pictures of spring and spring activities and put them on the bulletin boards (they can do this more easily with push-pins rather than thumbtacks).
4. Set up a discovery table with a bird's nest or broken eggs, a blooming potted crocus, or sprouting seeds.
5. Force a flowering shrub or tree branch (such as forsythia or flowering almond). Bring the branch indoors in late February or March, once there have been a few days of mild temperatures. Put the branch in warm water, and invite the children to watch for leaf and flower development over a period of a few weeks.
6. Begin in the fall if you want to try forcing spring bulbs such as daffodils, hyacinths, tulips, or crocuses. Look for bulbs marked "suitable for forcing." Plant the bulbs in potting soil or gravel according to the directions from the nursery, and water thoroughly. The bulbs then require a six- to eight-week period of cold (small bulbs such as paperwhite narcissus are often pre-chilled; you need only bury them in gravel and keep them well watered for them to flower). If you chill the bulbs in the refrigerator, the children can watch for root and leaf development. After the cold period, bring the bulbs into the light and watch for shoots.
7. Encourage children to watch for signs of spring — the first robin, a bulb sprouting, leaf or flower buds unfurling, the first dandelion, frogs croaking, grass turning green, a crocus blooming, and snow melting.

Vocabulary

kite	plant	born	blossom
crocus	robin	dandelion	wind
bulb	tulip	bouquet	seed
sprout	tadpole	garden	flower
daffodil	polliwog	rain	leaf
earth	spring	showers	bloom
migrate	hatch	bud	

Learning Centres

Discovery Centre

Plants

1. Provide child-size gardening tools (real garden tools of small size are much more sturdy and satisfactory than toys) and, if yard space allows, plant a vegetable or flower garden. This can be a most educational and rewarding experiment. If you plan extended experiences, children will be able to: observe plants' gradual growth; learn how to care for the plants; harvest, cook, and eat their crop, if vegetables, or pick and arrange, if flowers. Ideally, a plot in the playground that can be easily cared for routinely by the children when they are outdoors is far better than a garden that must be maintained by you. Allow children to care for their garden by watering and weeding it. Radishes and lettuce are rewarding to grow because they mature quickly. Marigold seeds are fairly dependable for quick flowers.

▼ **CAUTION:** Careful supervision is necessary as tools have sharp edges.

2. Discover how seeds grow. Line the inside of a large, straight-sided jar with brown blotting paper. Dampen this paper and place a variety of seeds of different sizes about halfway down the side of the jar between the jar and the blotting paper. The seeds will sprout at different times, which will help to maintain the children's interest. Radish seeds seem to sprout almost immediately. Bean sprouts are more likely than other seeds to turn mouldy before they have a chance to sprout. Carrot, lettuce, and corn seeds also sprout quickly. Keep just enough water in the jar to touch the bottom of the blotting paper. If the paper dries out, the sprouts will die quickly.

3. Place seeds in shallow pans and display the corresponding vegetables or fruits so that the children can see what grows from each seed; for instance, grapefruit seeds, a tiny grapefruit tree newly sprouted, and a grapefruit. The real vegetable or fruit is better than a picture. VARIATION: Plant seeds or seedlings in peat pots. These can be taken home and planted directly in the ground. If you use paper or plastic cups without making holes in the bottom, roots are more likely to rot from being overwatered.

4. Provide a magnifying glass for the close examination of buds, new leaves, seeds, and insects.

5. Force a hyacinth bulb: This can be done in late October or November. Set several bulbs in soil in a large pot and bury the pot outdoors so that the tops of the bulbs are about 20 cm below the surface of the ground. After ten or twelve weeks, bring the pot inside and place it in a cool, dark place until the sprouts are about 10 cm high; keep watered. Bring the pot into the light occasionally and observe that the yellow sprouts quickly turn green and the buds and blooms soon appear. Fertilize in the sprout stage. You should have hyacinths blooming in February.

▼ **CAUTION:** Be sure to store fertilizer away from the children.

6. If children plant bulbs in the fall, they can watch the plants develop and bloom naturally in April. For instance, a lily bulb forced to bloom is more satisfactory than just buying a plant that has already bloomed.

7. Watch a sweet potato sprout. It is interesting to observe that the part of the potato in the water makes roots while the top produces sprouts with leaves.

8. Plant seeds in eggshells. Marigold or pumpkin seeds produce very gratifying results and may be taken home and planted by the children by gently crushing the eggshell before putting it in the ground. The seeds are easily tended by placing the eggshells in an egg carton and keeping the lid on until the seeds sprout. Water with a teaspoon.

9. Take a spring walk to find and observe new and growing things. Take a magnifying glass and paper bags in which to collect treasures.

Animals

1. Care for a baby animal such as a gerbil, guinea pig, or rabbit. Be sure there is a home that will welcome this creature when you no longer wish to keep it in the classroom. (See Chapter 17, Pet Animals, for care and feeding.)

2. Incubate and hatch an egg. Make a calendar to check off days — 21 days for chicks and 28 days for ducklings. Quail eggs are another possibility.

3. Prepare and observe an ant farm (available from science supply companies).

4. Earthworms may be housed in a jar of loose, damp earth and fed on a small amount of minced lettuce.

▼ **CAUTION:** Do not drown the worms with too much water. Use as little as possible.

5. Provide insect cages for insects the children may catch. Observe for a day or so and then turn the insects loose. Many children seem to feel that "a bug is to squash"; careful handling and concern for these small creatures must be emphasized constantly (see Chapter 20, Insects and Spiders).

6. Visit a farm to see new baby animals.
7. Go to a pond or stream to find frog eggs or tadpoles. You must be just in time to watch the eggs hatch into tadpoles. Spring peeper tadpoles turn into frogs in one season and into bullfrogs in two seasons. The huge bullfrog tadpoles are wonderful to observe. Be sure to keep these creatures in pond water and return them to their natural environment, since they are becoming an endangered species.

   ▼ CAUTION: Make sure you can supervise the children closely when you are near a pond or stream.

Weather

1. Fly a kite on a windy day (see Chapter 9 for patterns), or blow bubbles outdoors. The children could let milkweed seeds out of their pods. Make paper pinwheels or fly paper airplanes or helicopters (see Chapter 22 for patterns). Release fluffy feathers into the air.
2. Go for a walk during a spring shower, and look for a rainbow.
3. Make a rainbow (see Chapter 27, p. 536).
4. Use a cardboard thermometer (see Chapter 29, p. 563).
5. Make a weather calendar: Each day in March, have a child check the weather and paste an appropriate symbol on the day — sun, clouds, rain, or snow. There is usually quite a variety of weather in this month.

Senses

1. Listen for sounds of spring — bird and animal calls, thunder, wind, raindrops, insects buzzing.
2. Uniquely spring smells are fresh air, flower fragrances, spring rain, the smell of soil, and fresh-cut grass.
3. Provide opportunities to feel pussy willows, new grass, animal fur, blossoms, wind and air currents, seeds.
4. Look for all signs of spring (see Introducing This Subject to Children).
5. If you have access to a spotlight or a filmstrip projector, let children experiment with making shadow pictures.
■ Sensory activities are helpful to children with cognitive delays, who may have trouble understanding some of the concepts related to changing seasons.

Dramatic Play Centres

Home-living centre

1. Replace some winter articles such as hats, scarves, and mittens with spring hats, gloves, stoles, and rainwear.
2. Suggest that the house could be spring-cleaned or rearranged.
3. Doll clothes could be washed and hung outside to dry.
4. Provide real or artificial flowers to make bouquets.

Block-building centre

1. Set out toy chicks, ducks, and rabbits and suggest building pens, hutches, and fences. Include sets of mother animals and their young.
2. Small plastic flowers could be used to lay out a park or garden by letting children insert them into flat pieces of styrofoam to hold them upright as if growing.

Other dramatic play centres

1. Locate rabbit, duck, chicken, or baby animal Halloween costumes for children to pretend to be animals. A tail, wings, or ears will suffice. Appropriate masks can be

made from wire coat hangers, paper bags, or paper plates (see the Halloween section in Chapter 11).

2. Commercial or homemade sock puppets can be used for a puppet show behind a box, three-way screen, or puppet stage. Children's white socks make nice puppets.

3. Hand puppets can be made from small paper bags, and the children can either paste on ears and faces or mark them with felt-tip pens.

4. Arrange a hat store from hats children make in the art centre or hats you have in the house-living centre.

Art Centre

•• 1. Provide paints in pastel colours by adding colour to white paint.

•• 2. Spatter paint animal or flower shapes. Children can make their own stencils by choosing and arranging geometric shapes cut from plastic lids or vinyl upholstery scraps.

•• 3. Pastel soap painting: Colour soap flakes with tempera to make pastel shades for painting. A little liquid starch added to this stiff mixture makes it less fragile when dry.

•• 4. Blow painting (to illustrate wind): Show children how to place a spoonful of paint on paper and, using half a drinking straw, blow on the paint to make a splatter picture.

••• 5. Sponge paint blossoms on crayoned tree trunks drawn on construction paper.

• 6. Mud paint outdoors with bare feet.

•• 7. Drawing with large kindergarten chalk on pastel construction paper creates lovely effects.

••• 8. Take kindergarten chalk outside and have the group create a picture on a piece of concrete sidewalk. The children can then observe how the chalk is gradually washed away by rain and foot traffic.

These children have found a comfortable spot for visiting and chatting on an early spring day.

■ This activity encourages children to co-operate. It is particularly useful for children who require more experience in socializing.

•• 9. Dipping pastel chalk in water before applying it to construction paper makes a more permanent product.

••• 10. Make rainbows using flat sides of crayon stubs.

•• 11. Use animal- or flower-shaped cookie cutters with play dough.

••• 12. Cut and paste pictures from flower and seed catalogues, wallpaper books, and old greeting cards.

••• 13. Tear large, free form shapes from white construction paper and paste them on blue paper. Suggest that the children tell you what the pictures look like when they are finished. Make up their own *It Looked Like Spilt Milk* book with these pages (see Book Centre).

•• 14. Colour sawdust or rice with tempera or food colouring. Sprinkle on construction paper that has been brushed or squirted with white glue.

•• 15. Make collages from seeds, twigs, and soft maple and elm pods.

•• 16. Pastel styrofoam from egg cartons makes a lovely spring collage material.

•• 17. Vegetable prints: Save sliced ends of green peppers, celery, cabbage, lemons, limes, or apples. Dip in tempera and print on paper. Sponge or corrugated cardboard shapes can also be used for printing.

••• 18. Pressed flowers: Use on a spring mural or on greeting cards.

••• 19. Draw two posts on paper, and paste a piece of string or yarn between them. Children like to paste pieces of cloth on this line to look like clothes hanging on a clothesline in the wind.

•• 20. Precut tissue-paper circles: Children can wad these up, dip them in paste, and fasten them to coloured paper to represent crocuses in green grass or blossoms on a tree.

••• 21. Individual pussy willows make tiny animals. Let children design their own pussy willow creatures using collage materials, crayons, or paint.

••• 22. Make egg-carton caterpillars painted green or another colour. Add toothpicks with balls of play dough or small pipecleaners for antennae. Children can decorate their caterpillars with gummed paper shapes.

••• 23. Make butterflies from cylindrical clothespins: Provide precut rectangles of tissue paper for wings. Children can decorate butterflies with bits of gummed paper or other collage materials. Birds can be made from small paper bags stuffed with tissue; attach paper wings and tails with tape. Encourage children to explore insect, bird, and butterfly books.

••• 24. Make pinwheels or paper gliders (see Chapter 22 for directions and patterns).

•• 25. Make kites (see Chapter 9 for patterns).

• 26. Paste precut, coloured paper ovals in the centre of a sheet of construction paper. Let children finish the picture by adding eyes, wings, bills, tails, and feet to make chicks and other animals.

•• 27. Make rabbits, clouds, and lambs by pasting cotton balls on paper.

Learning and Language Materials Centre

Commercially made games and materials

1. *Puzzles:* Rainy day, flower, farm, and fishing puzzles.
2. *Construction and manipulative toys:* Fishing games with magnets or loops, sewing cards of fish and flowers.
3. *Outdoor toys:* Soft foam balls, plastic bats, skipping ropes, perforated plastic balls, plastic hoops, pogo sticks, beanbags, rubber quoits or rings, wagons, model road signs.
4. *Flannelboards:* Cutouts of flowers, sun, clouds, baby animals, farm equipment, fishing equipment.
5. *Posters:* Weather charts.

6. *Miscellaneous:* Cardboard thermometer (see Chapter 29, p. 563), small plastic watering can insect cages, butterfly and fish nets, ant farms (available from science supply companies), magnifying glasses and viewers.

Teacher-made games and materials

NOTE: For detailed descriptions, see Learning Games in Part 1.

1. Children can cut out and paste spring pictures onto pages to be assembled into a book about spring, or tack the pictures on the bulletin board. Provide pictures from seed and flower catalogues.
2. Make *Match-them* cards by mounting large, gummed seals of birds, animals, flowers, butterflies, or rabbits on cardboard. Make match-themes of animals and their young, or of animals and what they eat.
3. *How many?* Make circle counters for counting or sorting colours and other subjects by mounting gummed seals on cardboard discs.

Book Centre

•• Atkinson-Keen, S. *Fun Times.* Toronto: Greey de Pencier, 1986.

••• Birnbaum, A. *Green Eyes.* New York: Western, 1973.

•• Burningham, John. *Seasons.* New York: Bobbs-Merrill, 1970.

••• Burton, Virginia Lee. *The Little House.* Boston: Houghton Mifflin, 1969.

•• Clifton, L. *The Boy Who Didn't Believe in Spring.* New York: Dutton, 1978.

••• Donnelly, Liza. *Dinosaur Garden.* New York: Scholastic, 1990.

••• Gans, Roma, and Franklyn M. Branley. *Flash, Crash, Rumble and Roll.* New York: Crowell, 1964.

••• ———. *It's Nesting Time.* New York: Crowell, 1964 (filmstrip, record, cassette).

••• Gordon, Sharon. *First Day of Spring.* St. Catharines, ON: Troll Associates, 1981.

• Hines, Anna. *Taste the Raindrops.* New York: Greenwillow Press, 1983.

• Hutchins, P. *The Wind Blew.* New York: Macmillan, 1974.

••• Jordan, Helene. *How a Seed Grows.* New York: Crowell, 1960.

••• Krauss, R. *The Carrot Seed.* New York: Harper & Row, 1945. (available in Spanish and in a Big Book format)

• Leonard, Marcia. *Little Puppy's Rainy Day.* New York: Bantam, 1987.

••• Lifgren, Ulf. *The Wonderful Tree.* New York: Delacorte Press, 1970.

••• McCloskey, Robert. *Make Way for Ducklings.* New York: Viking Press, 1969.

••• Parker, Mary Jessie. *City Storm.* Richmond Hill, ON: Scholastic, 1990.

•• Rey, Margaret. *Curious George Flies a Kite.* Boston: Houghton Mifflin, 1958.

•••• Rosen, Mike. *Spring Festivals.* New York: Franklin Watts, 1991.

•• Scheffler, Ursel. *A Walk in the Rain.* New York: Putnam, 1986.

• Shaw, Charles G. *It Looked Like Spilt Milk.* New York: Harper & Row, 1947.

••• Shulevitz, Uri. *Rain Rain Rivers.* New York: Farrar Strauss & Giroux, 1969.

• Spier, Peter. *Peter Spier's Rain.* Garden City, NJ: Doubleday, 1982.

• Stock, Catherine. *Sophie's Bucket.* New York: Lothrop, Lee & Shepard, 1985.

•• Tresselt, Alvin. *Hide and Seek Frog.* New York: Lothrop, Lee & Shepard, 1965.

•• ———. *Rain, Drop, Splash.* New York: Lothrop, Lee & Shepard, 1965.

••• ———. *Follow the Wind.* New York: Lothrop, Lee & Shepard, 1950.

••• ———. *Hi, Mr. Robin.* New York: Lothrop, Lee & Shepard, 1950.

•• Zolotow, Charlotte. *When the Wind Stops.* New York: Abelard-Schuman, 1962.

••• ———. *The Storm Book.* New York: Harper & Row, 1952.

Planning for Group Time

NOTE: All music, fingerplays, poems, stories, and games listed here may also be used at other times during the session as appropriate.

Music

Songs

From *Elephant Jam*, Sharon, Lois, and Bram
"The Wind," p. 28

From *More Piggyback Songs*, Warren
"Songs about Spring," pp. 25–32

From *Piggyback Songs*, Warren
"Songs about Spring," pp. 19–30

From *Sally Go Round the Sun*, Fowke
"The Wind the Wind," p. 65

From *Singing Bee*, Hart
"Rain, Rain," p. 49
"Nuts in May," p. 80
"Over the River and Through the Woods," p. 142

From *Stepping Along in Music Land*, Murray
"Butterfly, Butterfly," p. 47
"Seasons," p. 52
"New Day in Spring," p. 54

From *A Treasury of Songs for Young Children*, Glazer
"It's Raining, It's Pouring," p. 132

Rhythms and Singing Games

1. Using appropriate music listed under Songs, above, children can pretend to be waddling ducks, hopping rabbits, pecking chickens, and so on.
2. Bunny Hop: Make headbands with paper rabbit ears attached, and bunny tails made of yarn or old pantyhose.
3. Easter Parade: Use hats the children have made in the art centre.

Records and Cassettes

Bob McGrath. *If You're Happy and You Know It*, Volume I. (Kids Records)
"Mr. Sun"
"Take Me Out to the Ballgame"

Anne Murray. *There's a Hippo in My Bathtub*. (Capitol Records)
"You Are My Sunshine"

Sandy Tobias Oppenheim. *If Snowflakes Fell in Flavours*. (Berandol Records)
"Hey Little Bird"
"Muck"

Raffi. *Baby Beluga*. (Troubadour Records)
"Over in the Meadow"

Fingerplays and Poems

From *Don't Eat Spiders*, Heidbreder
"Sun, Sun," p. 9
"Vancouver," p. 18
"Bird's Nest," p. 25
"Sticky Maple Syrup," p. 29 (also in Chapter 6 in this book)

From *Hand Rhymes*, Brown
"The Caterpillar," p. 28

From *Let's Do Fingerplays*, Grayson
"Animal Antics" section, pp. 30–38
"Kitty, Kitty," p. 42
"Chickens," p. 42
"My Garden," p. 46
"Pitter-Pat," p. 46
"Raindrops," p. 47
"Five Little Froggies," p. 62
"Five Little Kittens," p. 64
"Two Little Ducks," p. 71
"Two Little Blackbirds," p. 73

From *Read Aloud Rhymes for the Very Young*, Prelutsky and Brown
"Showers," p. 12
"Little Wind," p. 12
"The Rain," p. 12
"Rainy Day," p. 13
"Mud," p. 13
"Sun after Rain," p. 13
"Little Seeds," p. 14
"A Spike of Green," p. 14
"Singing in the Spring," p. 23
"A Kite," p. 33
"The Butterfly," p. 33
"Ode to Spring," p. 56
"The Spring Wind," p. 56
"Pussy Willows," p. 57
"April," p. 61
"Umbrellas," p. 61

From *Round and Round the Garden*, Williams
"Round and Round the Garden," p. 6
"The Apple Tree," p. 12
"I Hear Thunder," p. 37
"The Cherry Tree," p. 46

Stories

(To read, read–tell, or tell. See Book Centre for a complete list.)
As spring is a season of contrasts, it is fun to choose stories in pairs that will show the contrasts; for example, Zolotow's *The Storm Book* and Baum's *One Bright Monday Morning*.

Games

(See Learning Games in Part 1 and Teacher-Made Games and Materials earlier in this chapter for directions.)

1. *Name it:* New leaf, bud, blade of grass, bird's nest, pussy willow, daffodil.
2. *I see something, what do you see?* Choose things that tell it's spring, outdoors or in the room.
3. *Reach and feel:* Bag of spring items.
4. *Listen and hear:* Sounds of spring outdoors or with window open.
5. *Who am I?* Riddles, simple descriptions of baby animals.
6. *Alike, different, and the same:* Use plastic models or flannelboard cutouts of young animals, eggs, or flowers.
7. *Listening: Play Hen and chicks.* The mother hen (chosen child) leaves the room and then one or more children are chosen to be chicks. When the mother hen returns, the hidden chicks peep softly until she finds them by the sound.
8. *Pin the tail on the bunny:* Use circles of masking tape to stick the bunny tail on, or sew a magnet on a yarn pom-pom and put the bunny picture on a metallic board, cookie sheet, or magnetized flannelboard.

Routine Times

1. Decorate the snack table with garden flowers or potted spring bulbs that have been forced.
2. Eat snacks or meals outside; have a picnic.
3. Eat vegetables the children have grown for snacks or at meal times.
4. Use spring fingerplays at snack or meal times.
5. Eat eggs in different ways, such as devilled eggs and egg salad.
6. Use spring placemats that children have made and decorated.
7. When dressing, talk about the weather and what clothing is needed.
8. Look for signs of spring while walking or busing.
9. Rest outside in suitable weather. Look at clouds, and listen for birds, wind, thunder, and insects.

Large Muscle Activities

1. Play shadow tag.
2. Play leap frog.
3. Play follow the leader.
4. Fly a kite (see patterns in Chapter 9).
5. Play with balloons.
6. Encourage water play (see Chapter 26, Water around Me).
7. Encourage dirt and sand play (see Chapter 26, Water around Me).
8. Have a treasure hunt, outdoors if possible.
9. Paint cement walks or walls and equipment outside using large paintbrushes and buckets of water.

Extended Experiences

1. Visit a local greenhouse to see Easter lilies and other spring blooming plants.
2. Visit a local farm to see newborn animals, spring planting, or beehives.
3. Visit a hatchery to see newborn chickens or ducks.
4. Visit a zoo that may have newborn animals or a petting farm.

5. Go on a nature walk in a park.
6. Fly a kite in an open field.
7. Visit a feed and seed store or a farm implement company.
8. Explore a "magic circle." Give each child or group a 1m length of string or yarn to outline a circle on the ground. Let them use magnifying glasses to see what can be found in the circles. Encourage children to look carefully under stones and in grass for insects, plants, and other life.
9. A small, shallow stream is a safe place to observe water creatures like tadpoles, frogs, crayfish, and minnows.

 # Teacher Resources

Pictures and Displays

☐ Make a tree for all seasons: Stand a bare tree branch in sand or pebbles in a large coffee can. Children can hang tissue-paper blossoms on it in the spring; tree leaves in the summer; fruit, nuts, coloured leaves, or seed pods in the fall; and leave the branch bare or paint it white in the winter.

☐ Make an insect motel to use on a collecting trip or for a temporary display by cutting a 5 cm by 10 cm rectangular window from the side of a small round ice-cream carton. Roll a piece of wire screen to fit inside and cover the window. A string may be attached to the lid for carrying. This will save insect guests from too much handling. Nylon hose pulled over a milk carton from which two large windows have been cut can also be used. Another insect keeper can be made from a piece of screen rolled into a cylinder, with empty tuna cans placed on each end.

☐ Make frames for children's paintings by cutting ovals or rectangles from large pieces of white mat board or cardboard. Reuse for other art projects.

Books and Periodicals

Biene, Susanna. *Sing through the Seasons: Ninety-Nine Songs for Children.* Ulster Park, NY: Plough, 1972.

Canadian Geographic magazine (spring issues).

Chickadee magazine (spring issues).

Cleary, Val. *Seasons of Canada.* Willowdale, ON: Hounslow Press, 1979. (good for pictures of all the seasons in all parts of the country)

Cooper, Terry Touff, and Marilyn Ratner. *Many Hands Cooking: An International Cookbook for Boys and Girls.* New York: Crowell, 1974. Tofu Toss (Japan), p. 4; Holiday Date Bits (Israel), p. 37; Ancient Day Salad (Egypt), p. 38; Kaju (India), p. 39.

Equinox magazine (spring issues).

National Geographic magazine (spring issues).

Owl magazine (spring issues).

Peterson, Roger Tory, and Margaret McKenny. *A Field Guide to Wildflowers.* Boston: Houghton Mifflin, 1968.

Seed catalogues.

Spring issues of garden and farm magazines (for example, *Organic Gardening* and *Harrowsmith*).

Whitfield, Philip, and Joyce Pope. *Why Do the Seasons Change? Questions on Nature's Rhythms and Cycles Answered by the Natural History Museum.* New York: Viking Penguin, 1987.

Films and Videos

NOTE: Check with your distributor about public performance rights.

The Amazing Bone. Weston Woods.
Chicken Soup with Rice. Weston Woods.
Glory of Spring. International Film Bureau, 1950.
Time of Wonder. Weston Woods.

Community Resources and Organizations

☐   Local dairy council.
☐   Parks or public gardens.
☐   Greenhouses or garden centres.
☐   Florist shops.
☐   Hardware stores for small, sturdy garden tools (not toys).
☐   Local television or radio weather reporters.

Government Agencies

☐   Federal, provincial, and territorial ministries of the environment.

14 Summer

Basic Understandings
(concepts children can grasp from this subject)

Summer is a season that comes after spring and before fall. There are many changes in nature in the summer.

Earth Changes
- ☐ In some areas there is not much rain; it can be hot or warm every day.
- ☐ Sometimes, ponds, streams, and lakes dry up or become smaller.
- ☐ When it gets very dry, there is a risk of forest fires.
- ☐ In the summer, there are often thunder and lightning storms.
- ☐ On very windy days, dust storms may form.
- ☐ Breezes blowing across ponds, oceans, lakes, or rivers help to keep people and animals cool.
- ☐ Cement, sand, and brick hold the heat from the sun and are hot to touch, walk on, or live by.
- ☐ In Canada, the daylight hours in summer are longer and there are fewer hours of darkness.
- ☐ In some parts of Canada, summer weather lasts a long time, while in other parts, the hot weather period is very short.

Plants
- ☐ Many trees, flowers, and shrubs bloom and grow in the summertime.
- ☐ Fruits, nuts, and vegetables grow best in summer and ripen enough to eat.
- ☐ Often grass, trees, flowers, and other plants need to be watered if there is not enough rain.
- ☐ Some plants wither and dry up in the hot sun.
- ☐ Leafy bushes, trees, and vines offer shade for people, homes, and animals.

Animals, Birds, and Insects
- ☐ Some animals shed their heavy coats of fur in summer. Sometimes people help their pets by cutting their hair to make them cooler; for example, sheep and dogs.

☐ Some animals change from lighter to darker colours in summer to match the colours where they live; examples are birds and rabbits.

☐ In summer, animals need water to drink and in which to bathe. They also need shade and places in which to cool off (ponds, streams, and lakes).

☐ In summer, some animals and birds raise their young, feed them, protect them, and teach them to find food and defend themselves.

People

☐ Because it is often hot, we need to wear less clothing in summer.

☐ Some children go barefoot.

☐ People often lie in the sun to get suntanned. We must be careful, however, to wear a sun protection lotion so as not to get sunburned and damage our skin.

☐ Children and adults like to swim, go boating, water-ski, and play in the sand in summer.

☐ We often go to parks, have picnics, go on hikes, and play games outdoors, such as baseball, tennis, and miniature golf, in the summer.

☐ Some foods ripen and can be canned, preserved, frozen, stored, or eaten by people in summer.

☐ Many families go camping, go on vacations, or have more time to do things together in summer.

☐ We often need to turn on fans and air conditioners in the buildings where we live, work, and play in order to keep cool.

☐ We may turn on air conditioners in cars, trucks, and buses in order to be more comfortable when travelling in the summer.

☐ Some communities in which we live have special programs or activities at schools, parks, pools, churches, or community centres. Families often go to county fairs that are usually held in late summer.

☐ Many schools close for the summer. Others stay open and offer special classes.

☐ Farmers are very busy planting and caring for their crops.

☐ Families with gardens must care for their plants and flowers in the summer.

☐ We should not waste water in summer.

☐ Fishermen spend a great deal of time at sea catching fish.

Additional Facts the Teacher Should Know

1. In most of Canada, summer is the period from June 21 to September 20. These are the official dates determined by solar and lunar phases. It is easier for young children to understand changes in weather; such changes usually present better times to introduce the seasons.

2. Summer weather is not the same for all the regions. The North does not have as high temperature readings for such a prolonged time as does the South, where temperatures of 21°C and above occur almost daily from the middle of May to the middle of September. Keep in mind the uniqueness of your area when teaching about this season. It is difficult for young children to grasp the full meaning of summer, but they can begin to understand some of the changes that take place at this time of year. They can also learn about some of the most common activities families enjoy together at this time.

3. Children can be very easily burned in the hot summer sun. Make sure they do not spend too much time in the direct sun; have them wear sun hats or visors and play in shaded areas.

4. Other parts of this guide that are related to the subject of summer are Part 6, Animals; Part 7, Transportation; Chapter 26, Water around Me; and Chapter 27, Colour in My World.

Introducing This Subject to Children

1. Take a walk and look for some of the signs that tell us it is summer, such as lawn sprinklers turned on, dogs panting, people dressed in lightweight clothes, trees covered with leaves; flowers blooming, and noisy crickets.
2. Read a story about summer.
3. Invite children to talk about vacations or special activities their families are planning.
4. Talk about how hot it is.
5. Make lemonade to drink outside in the shade of a tree.
6. Display pictures of summer activities; for instance, at the beach, in the swimming pool, boating, and picnicking.

Vocabulary

summer	fan	parade	hose
sprinkler	fireworks	lemonade	cool
air conditioner	lawns	plant	water
hot	leaves	flower	shells
ice	march	fruit	beach
dry	flag	ripe	sand
ice-cream cone	holiday	shade	swim

Learning Centres

Discovery Centre

1. Discovery table: Display things children have found, such as flowers, shells, fruits and vegetables, a bird's nest, and insects.
2. If you planted a garden in the spring, continue to care for it. Check to see if the soil is hard or damp. If it is hard, it should be hoed and watered. If you don't have a garden, check seed packages and see if there is still time to start a garden in your yard.
3. Melon-tasting feast: Bring in a watermelon, a honeydew melon, and a cantaloupe. Cut the melons, and compare colour, odour, taste, texture, and seeds. Invite children to state which melon is their favourite and to explain why.
■ This activity encourages problem solving and independence. All children will benefit, but this will especially help children to socialize.
4. Berry-tasting party: Set out bowls of whole, washed blackberries, blueberries, raspberries, and strawberries. Compare size, colour, shape, odour, and taste.
5. Set out a vegetable tray: Include potato, carrot, onion, tomato, celery, radish, cucumber, or whatever is available and in season. Let children explore. Talk about colour, shape, taste, odour, and texture. Let children help wash, slice, and peel the vegetables.
6. Listen for cicadas; they make a noisy, shrill sound when it gets hot. Try to find one.
7. Look for a rainbow after a sudden summer shower.
8. After several hours of rain, look for worms on the sidewalks.

9. Insects and spiders are plentiful in summer, and the children will discover many, especially butterflies and fireflies. Look under rocks. (See Chapter 20, Insects and Spiders, for related activities.)

10. Plant and care for some flowers: Geraniums and zinnias are very hardy and will grow in a sunny spot; you might try wax begonias or impatiens in the shade.

11. Set up a composting area to create compost for the plants. Contact your local municipality for instructions on setting up a composter. Include the children in dumping kitchen scraps into the composter. Explain how compost becomes food for plants and how it helps reduce the amount of garbage we generate.

12. Borrow or purchase several types of plants. Help children discover that different plants need different amounts of water and begin to understand the phrase "No plant likes wet feet!" by allowing them to water and observe plants.
    a. Cactus or rubber plant: Water once a week or every ten days.
    b. Boston fern: Water every other day (needs to be root-bound).
    c. Philodendron: Water every other day.
    d. Azalea (planted in peat moss): Water daily.

    NOTE: Plants should never stand in water. Water the plants when the soil feels dry to the touch. Make a chart to remind children when to check the plants.

13. Make or buy a birdbath, and put it in a quiet part of the playground. Make sure the children can observe it from their classroom window.

14. Make strawberry or peach ice cream: Use your favourite recipe.

15. Make lemonade from squeezed lemons. Taste with and without sugar.

16. Display a shell collection: Provide a magnifying glass for closer viewing, or hide some shells in a small box of sand and let the children find and arrange them.

17. If feasible, allow children to remove their shoes to walk in the grass, step on a cement walk or on blacktop, or step on dirt or on a smooth board. Which is warmer? Cooler? Smoother? Rougher? Softer? Harder? VARIATION: Ask children to touch and compare the temperature of a metal bar, a piece of wood and the ground, all in the sun. Which is cooler? Touch the same objects in the shade. What is different? Why?

    ▼ **CAUTION:** Make certain there is no glass or sharp objects where children will be walking.

18. If you have flowers or flowering bushes, such as lilacs, in the schoolyard, allow children to pick some stems with buds and place them in a container of water. Set them in a sunny window and observe what happens.

19. If some equipment, such as a tire, a wooden box, or a board, has been left sitting on a grassy area for several days, move it and let the children discover what happened to the grass underneath that was without sun and air. Leave the area uncovered and observe what happens over a few days.

20. When busing children for an excursion in the summer, turn on the air conditioner (if you have one) and talk about what happens to the air in the bus if the windows are closed.

Dramatic Play Centres

Home-living centre

1. Set out beach hats, hats with visors, straw hats, beach towels, terry robes, thongs, and sandals.
2. Place travel folders, brochures on local parks, and road maps on shelves to encourage planning of family trips.
3. Set out boxes of artificial flowers with a variety of containers so children can make floral arrangements.

The teachers have moved the sand from a sand table to a "beach" in a corner of the centre. Children can test the qualities of the sand and develop their creativity. A beach umbrella and appropriate toys can extend the summer theme.

Block-building centre

1. Set out cars, campers, trains, ships, and planes to encourage travel play.
2. Set out farm equipment to encourage planting, cultivating, and harvesting of crops. Provide small plastic foods to carry to market.

Other dramatic play centres

1. Set up a tent on the playground for the children to use for camping out.
2. Set up a water-play table, large tub of water, or tractor tire cut in half into two circular troughs for sailing boats or water play.
3. Add new equipment to the sandbox to increase interest in this area; for example, sieves, funnels, pails, and shovels.

Art Centre

- 1. Summer is all colours! Move art media outdoors whenever possible and feature a wide choice of paint colours.
- •• 2. Sponge paint blossoms on crayoned tree trunks; trunks and branches can be drawn by using the broad side of short crayons that have their paper wrappings removed.
- •• 3. Blow painting: Show children how to blow drops of bright-coloured paint across paper with a straw.
- •• 4. Sand painting: Mix sand with dry tempera. Children draw designs on paper with glue and sprinkle on coloured sand. When paintings are dry, shake off the excess sand.
- •• 5. Make wet-sand sculptures by using various containers as moulds or hand-moulding.
- ••• 6. Glue crumpled tissue paper to green construction paper to simulate flowers in the grass; also let children tear, cut, or slash paper for grass.

•••• 7. Burlap pictures: Cut squares from burlap bags or colourful burlap material. Thread wide-eyed, blunt embroidery needles with brightly coloured yarn, and let children sew designs on the burlap.

•• 8. Simulated porcupine quill art: Children can weave coloured toothpicks into burlap squares.

• 9. Make drawings in sand or damp earth with a stick.

Learning and Language Materials Centre

Commercially made games and materials

1. *Puzzles:* Rainy day, flower, farm, and fishing puzzles.
2. *Construction and manipulative toys:* Fishing game with magnets or loops, sewing cards of fish and flowers.
3. *Outdoor toys:* Soft foam balls, plastic bats, skipping ropes, perforated plastic balls, plastic hoops, pogo sticks, beanbags, rubber quoits or rings, wagons, model road signs. Pails, sifters, shovels for sand play. Light plastic garden hose, spinning lawn sprinkler, and small garden tools that can be used by children. Rugged outdoor play tunnel. Child-size wheelbarrows.
4. *Flannelboards:* Cutouts of flowers, sun, clouds, farm equipment, fishing equipment.
5. *Posters:* Weather charts.
6. *Miscellaneous:* Cardboard thermometer (see Chapter 29, p. 563), small plastic watering can.

Teacher-made games and materials

NOTE: For detailed descriptions, see Learning Games in Part 1.

1. *Look and see:* Use differently shaped and coloured sea-shells, a variety of plastic foods, and transportation toys.
2. *Reach and feel:* Use a swim mask, bathing cap, and sand shovel.
3. *Summer fun:* The children can make a picture book of summer by cutting out appropriate pictures and mounting them on paper, punching holes in the pages, and fastening them together.

Book Centre

••• Atkinson-Keen, S. *Unexpected Wonders.* Toronto: Greey de Pencier, 1986.

•• Bell, Cathie, and David Bell. *Two Bears at the Seaside.* Toronto: Oxford University Press, 1991.

• Burningham, John. *Seasons.* New York: Bobbs-Merrill, 1970.

•• Carlstrom, Nancy White. *Wild Wild Sunflower Child Anna.* New York: Aladdin, 1991.

•••• Cole, S. *When the Tide Is Low.* New York: Lothrop, Lee & Shepard, 1985. (Read–Tell)

• Cristini, E., and L. Puricelli. *In My Garden.* New York: Picture Book Studio, 1985.

••• Hughes, S. *Lucy and Tom at the Seaside.* London: Victor Gollancz, 1976.

•••• Kessler, Leonard. *Last One in Is a Rotten Egg.* New York: Harper & Row, 1969. (Read–Tell)

•••• Kurelek, William. *A Prairie Boy's Summer.* Montreal: Tundra, 1975. (Read)

••• Lobel, A. *The Rose in My Garden.* Toronto: Methuen, 1986.

• Loree, Kate. *Pails and Snails.* New York: Hale, 1967.

•• Lund, Doris. *The Paint Box Sea.* New York: McGraw-Hill, 1972.

••• O'Donnell, Elizabeth Lee. *The Twelve Days of Summer.* New York: Morrow, 1991.

••• Orange, A. *The Flower Book.* New York: Lerner, 1975.

• Paré, Roger. *Summer Days.* Willowdale, ON: Annick Press, 1989.

••• Plantos, Ted. *Heather Hits Her First Home Run.* Windsor, ON: Black Moss Press, 1986.

- ••• Podendorf, Illa. *The True Book of Seasons*. Chicago: Children's Press, 1972.
- •• Rockwell, Anne. *At the Beach*. New York: Aladdin, 1991.
- •••• Rosen, Mike. *Summer Festivals*. New York: Franklin Watts, 1991.
- •• Ryder, J. *A Wet and Sandy Day*. New York: Harper & Row, 1977.
- • Schick, Eleanor. *City in the Summer*. New York: Macmillan, 1969.
- •• Tresselt, Alvin. *Sun Up* (rev. ed.). New York: Lothrop, Lee & Shepard, 1991.
- ••• Vaughn, Marcia. *Goldsworthy and Mort in Summer Fun*. Toronto: HarperCollins, 1990.
- •• Zion, Gene. *The Plant Sitter*. New York: Harper & Row, 1976.
- •• ———. *Harry by the Sea*. New York: Harper & Row, 1965.
- ••• Zolotow, Charlotte. *Summer Is . . . .* New York: Crowell, 1983.

Planning for Group Time

NOTE: All music, fingerplays, poems, stories, and games listed here may be used at other times during the session as appropriate.

Music

Songs

From *More Piggyback Songs*, Warren
"Songs about Summer," pp. 33–38

From *Piggyback Songs*, Warren
"Songs about Summer," pp. 31–36

From *Singing Bee*, Hart
"Nuts in May," p. 80
"Over the River and Through the Wood," p. 142

From *Stepping Along in Music Land*, Murray
"Butterfly, Butterfly," p. 47
"Seasons," p. 52

From *A Treasury of Songs for Young Children*, Glazer
"It's Raining, It's Pouring," p. 132

Rhythms and Singing Games

A parade can provide a change of pace in the summer program — choose any excuse for a parade. Have the children choose their costumes, what they wish to carry, and the songs they will sing in the parade (from choices offered by you). Parade around the room, the halls, the offices, and the playground. Warn other people working in your centre that you are planning a parade.

Records and Cassettes

Anne Murray. *There's a Hippo in My Bathtub*. (Capitol Records)
"Teddy Bears Picnic,"
"You Are My Sunshine"

Bob McGrath. *If You're Happy and You Know It*. Volume I. (Kids Records)
"Mr. Sun"

"Take Me Out to the Ballgame"

Sandy Tobias Oppenheim. *If Snowflakes Fell in Flavours.* (Berandol Records)
"Hey Little Bird"
"Muck"

Raffi. *Baby Beluga.* (Troubadour Records)
"Dayo"
"Over in the Meadow"

————. *The Corner Grocery Store.* (Troubadour Records)
"Going on a Picnic"

Fingerplays and Poems

From *Don't Eat Spiders*, Heidbreder
   "Sun, Sun," p. 9 (also in Chapter 27 in this book)
   "Bird's Nest," p. 25

From *Hand Rhymes*, Brown
"The Caterpillar," p. 28

From *Let's Do Fingerplays*, Grayson
"An Airplane," p. 22
"The Train," p. 22
"The Bus," p. 25
"Row, Row, Row Your Boat," p. 26
"My Turtle," p. 32
"There Was a Little Turtle," p. 33
"My Garden," p. 46
"Who Feels Happy?" p. 76
"The See Saw," p. 78
"The Window," p. 78

From *Read Aloud Rhymes for the Very Young*, Prelutsky and Brown
"Little Wind," p. 12
"Mud," p. 13
"Sun after Rain," p. 13
"Little Seeds," p. 14
"A Spike of Green," p. 14
"Shore," p. 30
"We Build a Castle Near the Rocks," p. 31
"The Picnic," p. 31
"Picnic Day," p. 32
"Joyful," p. 32
"August Heat," p. 32
"Wouldn't You?" p. 33
"A Kite," p. 33
"The Butterfly," p. 33
"In the Summer We Eat," p. 58

From *Round and Round the Garden*, Williams
"Round and Round the Garden," p. 6
"The Apple Tree," p. 12
"I Hear Thunder," p. 37
"The Cherry Tree," p. 46

Stories

(To read, read–tell, or tell. See Book Centre for a complete list.)
There are many children's activities that are specific to the summer. Children enjoy hearing stories about these activities and then planning how they may do similar things. Plantos's *Heather Hits Her First Home Run* is a good example of a story that serves this purpose. This book also provides an example of a girl succeeding in what has been considered a boy's sport and offers a positive role model for girls. Some boys may react to it by saying, "Girls shouldn't play baseball — it's for boys." This will allow discussion of role stereotyping and exploration of nontraditional activities and occupations.

Games

(See Learning Games in Part 1 and Teacher-Made Games and Materials earlier in this chapter for directions.)

1. *Guess what?* Describe what you like to do outside in summer — swim, go on picnics, go to the zoo. Together, think of summer-related activities.
2. *I'm taking a vacation:* Describe something you will put into your suitcase. "I need it after I eat and before I go to bed . . . I use it in my mouth, with toothpaste" (toothbrush). Continue to give other hints until children guess the answer. VARIATION: "I am going in something that . . ." (describe airplane, car, bus).

Routine Times

1. At snack or meal times, use foods harvested from the children's garden. Also offer special summer treats like watermelon, strawberries, tomatoes, corn on the cob, and cherries.
2. At meal time, have a picnic outside.

Large Muscle Activities

1. Children can walk a balance beam, log, or chalk mark drawn on the floor.
2. Have children run to a destination and back.
3. Take a hike with the children.
4. Toss and catch a beach ball.
5. Have a parade (see Rhythms and Singing Games).
6. Let children run in the spray from a lawn sprinkler (warn parents to send bathing suits along with the children).
7. Add some new sand toys and tools to the sandbox, such as sand combs, sifters, measuring cups and spoons, watering cans, and boats.

Extended Experiences

1. Have a picnic in a park.
2. Watch a parade.
3. Visit the zoo or a circus.
4. Visit a county fair.

Teacher Resources

Pictures and Displays

Hang pictures of parades, the beach, summer flowers, and summer activities.

Books and Periodicals

Biene, Susanna. *Sing through the Seasons: Ninety-Nine Songs for Children.* Ulster Park, NY: Plough, 1972.

Canadian Geographic magazine (summer issues).

Chickadee magazine (summer issues).

Cleary, Val. *Seasons of Canada.* Willowdale, ON: Hounslow Press, 1979. (good for pictures of all the seasons in all parts of the country)

Coleman, Mary Jane. *Foliage Plants for Modern Living.* Kalamazoo, MI: Merchants, 1974.

Equinox magazine (summer issues).

Hardy, Ralph, et al. *The Weather Book.* New York: Little, Brown, 1982.

National Geographic magazine (summer issues).

Owl magazine (summer issues).

Whitfield, Philip, and Joyce Pope. *Why Do the Seasons Change? Questions on Nature's Rhythms and Cycles Answered by the Natural History Museum.* New York: Viking Penguin, 1987.

Films and Videos

NOTE: Check with your distributor about public performance rights.

Chicken Soup with Rice. Weston Woods.

Snowman in July. Stratford Productions (released in Canada by Almanac Films), 1952.

Time of Wonder. Weston Woods.

Community Resources and Organizations

☐ Cherry or peach orchard; farm.
☐ Television or radio weather reporter.

Government Agencies

☐ Federal, provincial, and territorial ministries of the environment.

15 Fall

Basic Understandings
(concepts children can grasp from this subject)

Fall is a season of the year that comes after summer and before winter. Autumn is another word for fall. There are many changes in nature in the fall.

Earth Changes
- ☐ The daylight hours become shorter and the night (hours of darkness) becomes longer because the sun rises later and sets earlier.
- ☐ The temperature slowly drops and the weather becomes cooler, especially at night.
- ☐ Frost may appear at night or in the early morning. We can see our breath outside.
- ☐ The soil gets harder and sometimes freezes.
- ☐ There are usually more rainy or cloudy days than in summer.

Plants
- ☐ Most leaves begin to change colour; some trees remain green and are called "evergreens."
- ☐ Parts of some plants fall to the ground, such as leaves, apples, nuts, pine-cones, and seeds.
  - a. Some leaves change colour but do not drop until replaced by new leaves in the spring; for example, pin oak.
  - b. Evergreen trees remain green all year round, but they stop growing in the fall and won't grow again until spring.
- ☐ In some areas, grass and plants turn brown and wither.
- ☐ Some bulbs are dug up and stored and others are planted for spring blooming.
- ☐ Some plants are brought inside to prevent freezing, such as geraniums, ivies, and plants in hanging baskets.
- ☐ In fall, many foods ripen and are picked. This is called "harvesting." Examples are pumpkins, apples, cranberries, squash, potatoes, and nuts.

Animals, Birds, and Insects

☐ Some birds and butterflies fly (migrate) south where they can find food more easily.
☐ Some animals get ready to sleep or rest a long time (hibernate) by eating much food or storing it in their homes.
☐ Some animals grow thicker fur or a special undercoating to help keep them warm.

People

☐ We begin wearing warmer clothes, such as sweaters and heavy jackets, hats, and mittens.
☐ People need to build fires or turn on heaters or furnaces to keep their homes warm.
☐ Many people set out bird feeders and food for the birds once it begins to snow.
☐ In many areas, farmers harvest many foods and sow winter crops.
☐ Fall activities include raking leaves, football, Thanksgiving, and Halloween.

Additional Facts the Teacher Should Know

1. It is difficult for young children to grasp the full meaning of fall because it is not something that can be seen, touched, or held. However, children can learn that fall is a time of year when various changes take place in our environment.
2. In Canada, fall is the period between September 21 and December 20. These are the official dates determined by solar and lunar phases. It is easier for young children to understand changes in weather; such changes usually present better times to introduce the seasons.
3. The four seasons do not occur at the same time all over the world because the sun's rays are striking the earth differently at any one time, resulting in very different climates. Also, countries with large geographic areas, such as Canada, have a wide range of climates during a given season.
4. Squirrels can be found in many parts of the world and in most parts of Canada, in woods and city parks. Their obvious activity of collecting seeds and nuts for the winter has long been a sign of fall.
5. Chipmunks are like small squirrels, but they live in cleverly hidden burrows 15 to 20 cm underground. They make several passageways, storage areas, and a large sleeping area. There are several kinds of chipmunks in North America and Asia. In Canada, they are usually seen in the woods. The most common are reddish- or greyish-brown with black and white stripes down their backs. They are about 25 cm long with flat, bushy tails. Chipmunks eat seeds, nuts, berries, insects and grubs. They hibernate from November until spring; however, they may come out of hibernation at intervals. Three to five chippers are born by April.
6. In the fall, the monarch butterfly, which is orange and black, hatches from a caterpillar that has black, yellow, and white stripes around its body. The monarch's larva can be found in the fields near milkweed, which it likes to eat and which, incidentally, gives the caterpillar a bad taste to birds. If you find a caterpillar and wish to observe it, put it in a container with a screen over the top for ventilation. Place a stick in the container at a 45-degree angle for it to use to suspend its chrysalis. Provide it with fresh milkweed leaves daily. The caterpillar will eat a good deal just before it spins a chrysalis of a lovely apple-green colour, edged at the large end with gold. A monarch butterfly will emerge in less than two weeks and should be allowed to fly away. These butterflies migrate after they emerge, and return in the spring to lay their eggs. The change from caterpillar to butterfly is called "metamorphosis." (See Chapter 20, Insects and Spiders.)

7. Woolly bears are the caterpillars of the Isabella tiger moth and are found in many parts of Canada. They are black and reddish-brown. They hibernate through the winter, then spin their cocoons in April or May. Near the end of May, the moths hatch. Some people say they are weather predictors: the thicker the fur or the wider the black bands, the colder the winter is supposed to be, but no one has ever proved this. Do not bring a woolly bear inside if you want to see it change into a moth; it is too warm inside. Build a wire cage about the size of a large coffee can out of window screening, leaving it open at one end. Place the open end down over a patch of clover or dandelions and put the woolly bear inside the cage. The children will then be able to watch without losing or disturbing the caterpillar. (See Chapter 20, Insects and Spiders.)

8. Migration is the movement of animals from one place to another. Birds, fish, and butterflies migrate. In the fall, birds migrate from the north to the south, where they can find food. Some birds that migrate are Canada geese, robins, swallows, and mallards. Not all birds migrate when it turns cold; cardinals, English sparrows, chickadees, juncos, and nuthatches are examples of birds that remain during the winter months. Some birds (such as Canada geese) have stopped following their natural migration patterns because they are being fed and cared for by people. This is an unfortunate example of people interfering with nature. These birds have a special covering of soft down, which they grow when it turns cold to help keep them warm through the winter.

9. Hibernation is a sleeping or half-sleeping state many animals remain in during the winter months. At this time, the animal's body functions slow down, and it is able to live through the cold winter when it would not be able to find food. Some lie in a deep sleep and others move around on warm days. Animals do not grow during hibernation and may lose as much as one-third of their weight. Only those animals that can store up enough food to last through the winter are able to hibernate. Bears are said to hibernate, but their body temperature does not drop as much as it does in a true hibernating animal. Certain frogs, turtles, toads, and lizards bury themselves in the earth below the reach of frost. The horseshoe crab sinks in the mud beneath deep water until May or June. Spiders and snails hibernate under rocks. The woodchuck (groundhog), raccoon, and praying mantis also hibernate. (See Chapter 18, Woodland Animals, and Chapter 19, Zoo Animals, for more information about some of these animals.)

10. Trees in Canada are divided into two main groups. Those that lose their leaves in the fall are called "deciduous" trees. Conifers or cone-bearing trees remain green all year round and are called "evergreens."

11. Fruits that ripen in the fall include purple grapes, apples, and cranberries.

12. Flowers that bloom in the fall are chrysanthemums, goldenrod, purple asters, barberry, heather, thistle, and wild sunflower.

Introducing This Subject to Children

1. Take a walk and look for things that tell us it is fall, such as coloured leaves, ripe nuts, milkweed pods, woolly bears, and birds flying south.
2. If a child brings in a pretty leaf, an apple, a pine-cone, or a chrysanthemum, say, "This is one of the signs that tell us it is fall." Let the children take turns holding the item, and help them to observe, describe, and compare it with other items.
3. Read a book about fall or the four seasons to the children.
4. Set out a new fall puzzle or flannelboard kit.

Vocabulary

fall	chrysalis	high, low	evergreen
autumn	change	warm, cool	red
hibernate	birds	frost	orange
migrate	squirrel	thermometer	yellow
harvest	chipmunk	tree	green
caterpillar	woolly bear	leaves	brown
butterfly	chrysanthemum	nuts	
cocoon	temperature	pine-cone	

Learning Centres

Discovery Centre

1. Have a table where children can put signs of fall they bring in. There should be small boxes, an insect cage, a magnifying glass, pictures of fall, and resource books. October and November issues of *Owl* and *Chickadee* magazines are especially suitable. Help a child identify the object she or he has brought in and discover its outstanding characteristics, such as colour, shape, size, weight, texture, name, and use. If it is an animal or insect, add habits, what it eats, what it does, how it moves, sounds it makes, and safety precautions. Find these things in the pictures or resource books you have provided.

2. Display fall pictures with the book *Fall Is Here* (see Teacher Resources).

3. Display a poster or pictures of the life cycle of a monarch butterf y.

4. Display a poster or pictures of how seeds spread from mature plants and germinate.

5. Find a milkweed pod and open it. Talk about how seeds travel — by wind, on clothing, on animals' fur.

6. Cut apples in half crosswise to reveal a star-shaped seed case with seeds. Talk about the various parts, colours, textures, and shapes. Buy yellow, red, and green apples and compare how they are alike and how they are different. Have the children taste the different apples and compare the different flavours and textures.

   ▼ **CAUTION: Make a cardboard sheath for the paring knife and keep it in the sheath and out of the children's reach when not in use.**

7. Make applesauce: Pare, core, and cut the apples in advance. Using your favourite recipe, cook apples, water, and sugar on a stove or hot plate, or in an electric skillet. The children can help with measuring, stirring, and mashing. A dash or two of nutmeg, cinnamon, or ginger can be added. Serve applesauce warm or cool with cookies or crackers or save until meal time. Have whole apples available to compare texture and appearance.

   ▼ **CAUTION: High heat is required for cooking the apples, so extra supervision is necessary. Try to have extra help and then limit this centre to three or four children at a time, or use a microwave oven to cook the apples.**

8. Buy and compare several kinds of corn — popcorn, corn on the cob, canned, frozen, and cream style. Compare sizes, tastes, and textures. Pop some corn to serve as a snack;

use an electric popper with a glass lid or a wire basket popper so children can see the corn popping. (See Chapter 2, Sight, for songs and other related experiences with popcorn.)

▼ **CAUTION: High heat is required to pop corn. Close supervision will be necessary.**

9. Buy as large and as accurate a thermometer as you can. Indoor–outdoor models are excellent as children can compare the temperatures between the two. They can see that as it gets colder the mercury goes down, and vice versa. (See also Teacher-Made Games and Materials, number 11.)
10. Obtain a kitchen food scale or balance pans so children can weigh nuts, apples, or pumpkins. Which has a greater mass, an apple or a nut? A pumpkin or five apples? Children may want to weigh themselves or other objects in the classroom on a bathroom scale.
11. When outdoors, watch for birds flying south if you live along a migration route. As a beginning experience, you might simply announce, "Look, the birds are flying south, where it will be easier for them to find food." With children who have had more experience, use a compass to find north and then draw a directional cross on the sidewalk in chalk or paint it on a block of wood. Label the four points N, E, S, W. On a sunny day, help children decide which direction is south from where they are. On a windy day, tie a scarf to a stick and hold it over the compass cross to see which way the wind is blowing.
12. Help children discover that wet leaves leave prints on the sidewalk.
13. Falling leaves, nuts, and apples may lead to an interest in gravity.

Dramatic Play Centres

Home-living centre

Set out sweaters, coats, and blankets for dolls to indicate the change in the weather.

Block-building centre

1. Set out farm animals. Encourage children to build barns or other buildings for the animals.
2. Make a barn of large hollow blocks or large cardboard boxes. Sing "Ha Ha Turkey in the Straw" from *Piggyback Songs* by Warren (p. 44).

Art Centre

1. Feature the fall colours seen in your area in paints, fingerpaints, chalk, crayons, and play dough.
2. Spatter painting: Let the children spatter paint over leaves they have found. Allow children to arrange various leaves, twigs, nutshells, and dried grasses on a piece of construction paper and then spatter paint the arrangement.
3. Make a leaf stencil by tracing around a leaf on cardboard and then carefully cutting it out. The stencil can be used to make leaf designs by spatter painting or sponge painting. Upholstery vinyl or pieces of innertube make washable, reusable stencils.
4. Roll-on painting: Wrap heavily textured fabric swatches around small rolling pins and fasten in place with two rubber bands. Drop small amounts of fingerpaint or thick poster paint on a piece of paper. Let the children choose the roller designs and colours they wish. There will be interesting blends of colour. If they are ready, help the children to see the relationship between the colours put on and the ones resulting from the blending.

•• 5. Crayon rubbings: Cover a leaf with a good vein pattern with a sheet of newsprint. Have a child rub firmly over the leaf with the flat side of a crayon from which the paper has been removed.

• 6. Pasting leaves: Have children paste real or precut paper leaves on sheets of paper.

• 7. Tearing leaves: Children can make their own leaves by tearing them out of tissue paper.

•• 8. Hand printing leaves: Children dip each hand, palm down, in a different colour of paint and then press their palms down on paper in different positions. Hands may be washed and two other colours chosen. When finished, the effect is like multicoloured leaves.

• 9. Leaf printing: Use any of the following methods to make leaf prints:

•   a.   Cut flat sponges into leaf shapes to be dipped in paint and pressed onto paper.

•   b.   Cut sponges into any small shape and let children daub paint with sponges on paper. Use a separate sponge for each fall colour. The result looks like multi-coloured leaves.

•••   c.   Place real or precut paper leaves on blueprint paper. Expose to the sun for five to ten minutes. The outlines of the leaves will remain when the leaves are removed.

••• 10. Caterpillar: Remove the lid from an egg carton and cut the bottom part in half lengthwise to make two caterpillars. Children can paint their caterpillars and add pipecleaner or toothpick antennae. Cotton balls can also be dipped in powdered paint and glued to the humps to give the caterpillars a fuzzy appearance.

••• 11. Fall mural: Children first draw tree trunks with the side of a crayon from which the paper has been removed. Branches can be added with a few upward strokes fanning out from the top of the trunk. Leaves can then be added by using any of the methods suggested in numbers 6 to 9. A ground cover can be made by pasting on dried grass, nutshells, and twigs.

Learning and Language Materials Centre

Commercially made games and materials

1. *Puzzles:* Puzzles of leaves, wind, rain, and harvest time.
2. *Outdoor toys:* Child-size rakes, kites.

> ▼ **CAUTION:** Only use kites if you can take the children to an area where they can fly them away from power and telephone lines

3. *Flannelboards:* Cutouts of leaves, clouds, umbrellas, kites, and warm clothing.
4. *Posters:* Weather charts.
5. *Miscellaneous:* Thermometer (see Discovery Centre, number 9), small plastic watering can.

Teacher-made games and materials

NOTE: For detailed descriptions, see Learning Games in Part 1.

1. *What's missing?* Use several objects from the discovery table, such as a pine cone, nut, or leaf.
2. *Show me:* Use a nut, yellow leaf, and apple and ask, "Show me the one you eat. Show me the one that is round."
3. *Match-them:* "This leaf is yellow; each of you (or name one child) find me something in this room that is yellow." "This nut is round; find me something in this room that is round." Use sets of two cards with identical pictures of fall objects to match.
4. *What am I?* "I am thinking of something that is tall and green and has needles; what is it?" "I am thinking of something that has grey fur and likes to eat nuts; what is it?" "I am thinking of something that is big and round and orange; what is it?"

5. *Reach and feel:* Use fall objects.
6. *Sorting and grouping by association:*
   a. Buy several kinds of nuts in quantity, or use those you find. Identify the nuts for the children and compare the sizes, colours, and textures. Mix the nuts together in a large bowl or container, and provide as many smaller bowls or containers as there are kinds of nuts. Let the children sort the nuts.
   b. Sort leaves by colour or by shape. Use leaves you find or precut some from coloured construction paper.
   c. Sort pine-cones by size or type.
7. *Alike, different, and the same:* Make sets of cards with pictures of leaves, trees, birds, squirrels, chipmunks, fall fruits, and fall vegetables. Put out two cards that are alike and one that is different.
8. Count nuts, seeds, pine-cones, or leaves. Start with one to three; experienced children may count to ten.
9. Division: Apples can be cut in halves or quarters for a snack.
10. Make a calendar for September, October, or November with 5 cm squares for the days. Paste appropriate pictures on the squares for holidays you are planning to celebrate. Remember to highlight trips and birthdays. Add to the decoration of the room and to the children's understanding by cutting a large tree from brown construction paper and putting it beside the calendar. Cut enough leaves of various colours to put on the tree to correspond with the number of days on the calendar. Each day, take one of the leaves off the tree and cover up the day that is on the calendar. When the month is over the tree will be bare, coinciding with the way trees will look in your community. Do this during the fall month when leaves usually drop in your area.
11. Make a large cardboard thermometer with movable elastic or ribbon mercury (see Chapter 29, p. 563). Talk about the kinds of clothes we wear when the temperature is at various positions, or degrees, on the thermometer. Pictures of children wearing appropriate clothes can be cut from catalogues and pasted around the thermometer. You could also set the temperature on the cardboard thermometer at the same degree as on the real outdoor thermometer. The next day, look at the outdoor thermometer again, compare it with the cardboard thermometer, and help children decide if it is warmer or colder than yesterday.

Book Centre

••• Allington, Richard L., and Kathleen Krull. *Autumn*. New York: Raintree, 1985.
• Bacon. *Wind*. Toronto: Methuen, 1986.
• Bancroft, Henrietta. *Down Come the Leaves*. New York: Crowell, 1961.
• Burningham, John. *Seasons*. New York: Bobbs-Merrill, 1970.
• Fisher, Aileen. *I Like Weather*. New York: 1963.
• Hines, A. *Taste the Raindrops*. New York: Greenwillow Press, 1983.
• Hutchins, P. *The Wind Blew*. New York: Macmillan, 1974.
• Leonard, Marcia. *Little Puppy's Rainy Day*. New York: Bantam, 1987.
•••• Locker, T. *Sailing with the Wind*. New York: Dial Press, 1986. (Read–Tell) (notable for its beautiful pictures)
••• Marino, Dorothy Bronson. *Buzzy Bear's Busy Day*. New York: Franklin Watts, 1965.
•• Miles, Betty. *A Day of Autumn*. New York: Knopf, 1965.
••• Podedorf, Illa. *The True Book of Seasons*. Chicago: Children's Press, 1972.
• Zion, Gene. *All Falling Down*. New York: Harper & Row, 1951.

Planning for Group Time

NOTE: All music, fingerplays, poems, stories, and games listed here may also be used at other times during the session as appropriate.

Music

Songs

From *Elephant Jam*, Sharon, Lois, and Gram
"The Wind," p. 28

From *More Piggyback Songs*, Warren
"Songs about Fall," pp. 39–48

From *Piggyback Songs*, Warren
"Songs about Fall," pp. 37–44

From *Sally Go Round the Sun*, Fowke
"The Wind the Wind," p. 65

From *Singing Bee*, Hart
"The North Wind Doth Blow," p. 33
"Rain, Rain," p. 49

From *A Treasury of Songs for Young Children*, Glazer
"It's Raining, It's Pouring," p. 132

Rhythms and Singing Games

Dramatize falling leaves, migrating birds, or shaking down apples while singing the songs above. Other activities might include crawling or tunnelling to music, to simulate animals burrowing underground to hibernate for the winter.

Records and Cassettes

Bob McGrath. *If You're Happy and You Know It*, Volume I. (Kids Records)
"Take Me Out to the Ballgame"

Raffi. *Baby Beluga*. (Troubadour Records)
"Over in the Meadow"

Fingerplays and Poems

From *Don't Eat Spiders*, Heidbreder
"Falling Leaves," p. 10
"Vancouver," p. 18

From *Let's Do Fingerplays*, Grayson
"This Little Squirrel," p. 35
"Little Bird," p. 37
"Falling Leaves," p. 47
"October," p. 47
"Whirling Leaves," p. 47

From *Read Aloud Rhymes for the Very Young*, Prelutsky and Brown

"Showers," p. 12
"Little Wind," p. 12
"The Rain," p. 12
"Rainy Day," p. 13
"Mud," p. 13
"Sun after Rain," p. 13
"A Kite," p. 33
"The Moon's the North Wind's Cooky," p. 51
"The Wind and the Moon," p. 51
"Umbrellas," p. 61

From *Round and Round the Garden,* Williams
"Round and Round the Garden," p. 6
"The Apple Tree," p. 12
"I Hear Thunder," p. 37
"The Cherry Tree," p. 46

BABY SEEDS

In a milkweed cradle, snug and warm, (*close fingers into fist*)
Baby seeds are hiding safe from harm,
Open wide the cradle, hold it high, (*open hand and hold it up in the air*)
Coming along wind, help them fly. (*wiggle fingers*)

WHISKY FRISKY

Whisky Frisky
Hippity hop,
Up he goes
To the tree-top.

Whirly, twirly,
Round and round
Down he scampers
To the ground.

Furly, curly
What a tail!
Tall as a feather,
Broad as a sail!

Where's his supper?
In the shell;
Snappy, cracky,
Out it fell.

WALKING AROUND THE BLOCK

We went walking around the block together
Leaves were scarlet, leaves were brown
It was fun in sunny weather
Squirrels darting — squirrels scampering
Acorns dropping — brown birds chattering
Leaves were crunching with our feet
Smell of pine was sharp and sweet
We held pine-cones in our hand

It was fun when we walked together
Walked around the block in autumn weather
Walked around the block in sunny weather
All of us liked it
All of us thought it was fun!

CRUNCHY LEAVES

We make such a crunchy sound
In the leaves upon the ground
Crunchy, crunchy, hear the noise
Made in leaves by girls and boys.

LITTLE SQUIRREL

I saw a little squirrel
Sitting in a tree;
He was eating a nut
And wouldn't look at me.

ROLY-POLY CATERPILLAR

Roly-poly caterpillar (*walk finger across left palm*)
Into a corner crept, (*fold up fingers of left hand over caterpillar*)
Spun around himself a blanket, (*make winding motion around hand*)
Then for a long time slept. (*pretend to sleep, close eyes*)

Roly-poly caterpillar (*pretend to wake; open eyes*)
Wakening by and by,
Found himself with beautiful wings, (*put thumbs together; flutter fingers like wings*)
Changed to a butterfly. (*fly the butterfly away*)

GREY SQUIRREL

Grey squirrel, grey squirrel,
Whisk your bushy tail,
Grey squirrel, grey squirrel,
Whisk your bushy tail.

Wrinkle up your funny nose,
Hold a nut between your toes,
Grey squirrel, grey squirrel,
Whisk your bushy tail.

Stories

(To read, read–tell, or tell. See Book Centre for a complete list.)
There are many fall stories about the wind. Try reading Bacon's *Wind* or Zion's *All Falling Down* to your group, and follow this by having them imitate the wind's sound and movement.

Games

(See Learning Games in Part 1 and Teacher-Made Games and Materials earlier in this chapter for directions.)

1. *What's missing?*
2. *Show me.*
3. *Match-them.*
4. *Reach and feel.*
5. *What am I?*
6. *Alike, different, and the same.*

Routine Times

1. During snack or meal times, feature foods made from foods that are harvested in fall — popcorn, apple wedges (spread peanut butter on them for variety), nuts, applesauce, corn, squash, sweet potatoes, pumpkin pie. Use your favourite recipes.

   NOTE: Children who are not getting enough to eat at home may find it difficult to use food as a cognitive medium as suggested in Discovery Centre and Teacher-Made Games and Materials. For these children, these activities might best be carried out in combination with snack or meal times, with the idea that the food will be consumed immediately afterward. Sorting nuts or other similar use of foods may also be successfully offered as cognitive media after meal time. Otherwise, use pictures of food or plastic models.

2. While busing or walking children to and from school, look for signs that it is fall.
3. Before dressing to go outside, talk about the weather. Look at the indoor–outdoor thermometer and talk about what you and the children need to wear today.
4. During rest time, suggest that children pretend to be hibernating animals getting ready to sleep through the cold winter.

Large Muscle Activities

1. Raking leaves: Rake leaves into a pile and let children run and jump in them. Child-size leaf rakes are desirable, or shorten handles of adult-size leaf rakes by cutting and sanding the edges. If your playground does not have trees that drop their leaves, plan a trip to a nearby park. Children enjoy scuffling through leaves to hear the crunchy noise. Sing songs about leaves at this time.
2. Kicking football or soccer ball: To develop large muscle control, children might kick a football off a tee. Use a ball that is *slightly* underinflated or a whiffle football (a plastic ball with holes in it). Show the children how to place the ball on the tee, and demonstrate kicking. Ensure that both boys and girls participate in this activity.

   ▼ **CAUTION: Be sure to place the tee so that the ball will be kicked away from where other children are playing.**

Extended Experiences

1. Take a walk to look for things that show us it is fall. Collect leaves, nuts, milkweed pods, pine-cones, caterpillars, and other items. Bring them back to the centre for the discovery centre, art activities, and learning games. Take bags to collect pebbles, twigs, dry grasses or flowering weeds, or seeds. Also look for chipmunks or squirrels collecting nuts, and try to spot migrating birds.

A variety of playground equipment gives children choices of activities and allows them to develop skills in a variety of areas.

2. Take a trip to an apple orchard to pick apples.
3. Take a trip to a grocery store to buy apples, gourds, nuts, popcorn, or pumpkins for the various planned activities.
4. Visit a farm or an agricultural museum to see harvesting and planting equipment.
5. Visit a natural history museum with fall exhibits.

 # Teacher Resources
• •

Pictures and Displays

☐ Mount and display pictures of trees in fall, squirrels, chipmunks, monarch butterflies, harvest fruits and vegetables, children in sweaters and coats, animals hibernating, birds migrating, Halloween, Thanksgiving, and other fall holidays and celebrations.

☐ Place a bowl or vase of plastic or real fall flowers on a windowsill for the children to enjoy.

☐ Place a basket or cornucopia of plastic or real fruits that ripen in the fall on a low table for the children to enjoy and talk about.

Books and Periodicals

Biene, Susanna. *Sing through the Seasons: Ninety-Nine Songs for Children.* Ulster Park, NY: Plough, 1972.

Brockman, C. Frank. *Trees of North America.* New York: Golden Press, 1979.

Canadian Geographic magazine (fall issues).

Chickadee magazine (fall issues).

Cleary, Val. *Seasons of Canada.* Willowdale, ON: Hounslow Press, 1979. (good for pictures of all the seasons in all parts of the country)

Equinox magazine (fall issues).

Glover, Susanne, and Georgeann Grewe. *A Splash of Fall.* Carthage, IL: Good Apple, 1987.

Hardy, Ralph, et al. *The Weather Book.* New York: Little, Brown, 1982.

Holford, Ingrid. *The Guinness Book of Weather Facts and Feats* (2nd ed.). Enfield, UK: Guinness Superlatives, 1982.

National Geographic magazine (fall issues).

Owl magazine (fall issues).

Reader's Digest. *Birds: Their Life, Their Ways, Their World.* New York: Abrams, 1976.

Sterling, Dorothy. *Fall Is Here.* Garden City, NY: Doubleday, 1966.

Venino, Suzanne. *What Happens in Autumn?* Washington: National Geographic Society, 1982.

Whitfield, Philip, and Joyce Pope. *Why Do the Seasons Change? Questions on Nature's Rhythms and Cycles Answered by the Natural History Museum.* New York: Viking Penguin, 1987.

Films and Videos

NOTE: Check with your distributor about public performance rights.

☐ *Animals in Autumn.* Encyclopedia Britannica Educational Corp. (released in Canada by Visual Education Centre), 1957.
☐ *Autumn.* Centron Films (released in Canada by Magic Lantern Films), 1980.
☐ *Chicken Soup with Rice.* Weston Woods.
☐ *Time of Wonder.* Weston Woods.

Community Resources and Organizations

☐ Department of agriculture at a local college or university.
☐ Farmers' market.
☐ Orchard or fruit farm.
☐ County fair.
☐ Natural history museum.

Government Agencies

☐ Federal, provincial, or territorial ministries of the environment.
☐ Provincial agricultural representative.

Part 6 Animals

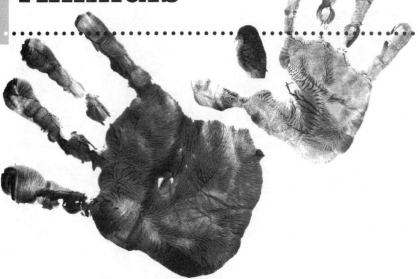

Introduction

Basic Understandings
(concepts children can grasp from this subject)

☐ Anything that is alive and is not a plant is an animal.
☐ There are many different kinds of animals in the world (at present, approximately 3 million).
☐ Some of the different kinds of animals are birds, fish, insects, worms, shell creatures, reptiles, amphibians, and mammals.
☐ All animals need food and water to live. Some animals eat plants; some eat other animals (meat); some, like people, eat both meat and plants.
☐ Animals get their food in many different ways and places:
   1. Out of the air — frogs catch flying insects.
   2. In the water — ducks catch fish.
   3. On the ground — cows eat grass.
   4. Out of the ground — birds eat worms.
   5. Above the ground, off bushes, plants, or trees — rabbits eat lettuce, raccoons eat berries.
   6. From the keeper or owner — lions in a zoo, pets in a home, chickens on a farm are given food.
   7. From their mother or father (parents) — kittens nurse from their mother.
☐ Some animals are born alive, while others are hatched from eggs.
☐ Most animals do not look like their parents at birth, but they change and grow up to look like them later.
☐ Animals differ from one another in colour, size, body covering, and body parts, but they are similar to one another within family groups.
☐ Each animal moves about in its own special way. Some of the ways animals move are:

swim, float	jump, leap, hop	walk, run, trot, gallop
fly	swing	slither, slide, creep, crawl
climb	burrow, tunnel	

☐ Each animal makes a different sound. Some of the sounds animals make are:

bark	growl	chatter	chirp
whinny	snort	squeal	whistle
grunt	bleat	honk	hiss
crow	quack	moo	purr
roar	mew	trumpet	cluck

     NOTE: Try to imitate actual sounds for the children. See Additional Facts the Teacher Should Know.

☐ Animals have different kinds of coverings, such as:

fur	hair	skins (hides)	feathers
shell	scales	plates	down

☐ Animals can provide people with many things:
  1. Pleasure, comfort, and companionship — as pets to love and play with.
  2. Assistance — to help physically challenged.
  3. Protection — as watchdogs and guard dogs.
  4. Labour — to help people carry, push, pull, or lift something.
  5. Wool and feathers — for clothing, hats, and decorations.
  6. Food — eggs, honey, and milk.
☐ Some animals we hear about are make-believe, such as dragons and unicorns.
☐ Some animals, such as dinosaurs and dodo birds, are extinct.
☐ Each kind of animal is given a different name for the male, the female, the offspring, and the group (see animal charts under Additional Facts the Teacher Should Know in each chapter).
☐ Some animals need people to help them:
  1. By caring for them in captivity in zoos, homes, animal hospitals, or on farms.
  2. By helping them to live in their natural homes:
     a. By assisting wild animals to find food and water, especially in times of hardship.
     b. By protecting them from other animals, from machines, from people, from enemies, and from weather.
     c. By building or fencing off special places for them to live.
     d. By setting rules for fishermen and hunters.
☐ Sometimes animals are referred to by the place where they live — farm animals, animals of the woods, zoo animals, and pets (animals we have at home).
☐ Many animals, especially birds, insects, and wild animals, are coloured to look like the place where they usually live; because they match tree bark, leaves, ground, rocks, or grass, other animals or hunters cannot find them easily, and they are safe.
☐ Animals live in different kinds of homes — water, burrow, nest, or tree.
☐ A veterinarian is a doctor for animals.
☐ An animal hospital or clinic is a place where sick and injured animals can be taken to get help.
☐ The Humane Society (animal shelter) is a place where lost animals or animals without owners are cared for until they are claimed or a home is found for them; some will not be claimed and may have to be killed.

Additional Facts the Teacher Should Know

  1. Most animals have backbones and are called "vertebrates."
  2. Animals without backbones are called "invertebrates." Examples are insects and spiders.

3. Mammals are warm-blooded vertebrates that are born alive and are covered with fur or hair. They nurse their babies with milk from their own bodies. The duckbill platypus and the spiny anteater produce their young as eggs, but they, too, nurse the young once they are hatched.

4. Reptiles and amphibians are cold-blooded vertebrates. Reptiles such as snakes crawl on their bellies, while others, such as lizards, turtles, alligators, and crocodiles, crawl on very short legs. Reptiles are covered with dry scales and are *not* slimy, and most lay eggs on dry land. Four groups of reptiles now living are lizards, snakes, turtles, and alligators and crocodiles. Amphibians live both in water and on land. Their skins are bare and moist, with no scales, fur, or feathers. Frogs, toads, and salamanders are amphibians. Cold-blooded animals must bury themselves underground or hibernate in caves in cold weather (see Chapter 12, Winter, and Chapter 15, Fall).

5. Most baby animals are cared for by their parents when young; some must take care of themselves from birth. Some baby animals eat the same kind of food that their parents eat; others get milk from their mother's body.

6. To avoid misconceptions while teaching the sounds animals make, try to imitate the real sounds. If possible, listen to good recordings that reproduce these sounds accurately (see the animal charts in each chapter).

7. Do not forget that it is great fun for children to try to imitate animals. A rousing chorus of animal sounds can add a great deal to animal stories.

8. When reading or telling stories in which animals have human qualities, ensure that the children understand the stories are imaginative and are allegories for real situations. Asking questions such as, "What would you do if you were this animal?" or, "What would it be like if your dog actually could talk and wear your clothes?" will remind children that the stories are fanciful without spoiling the fun.

Teacher Resources

Durrell, Gerald. *The Stationary Ark.* London: Collins, 1976.
Forsyth, Adrian. *Mammals of the Canadian Wild.* Camden East, ON: Equinox, 1986.
Grey Owl. *The Adventures of Sajo and the Beaver People.* Toronto: Macmillan, 1973.
Headstrom, Richard. *Suburban Wildlife.* Camden East, ON: Equinox, 1986.
Hendrikson, Robert. *Animal Crackers.* Markham, ON: Penguin, 1983.
The Larousse Encyclopedia of Animal Life. London: Hamlyn, 1967.
Seton, E.T. *Wild Animals I Have Known.* Ottawa: University of Ottawa Press, 1977.
Tremain, Ruthven. *The Animal's Who's Who.* New York: Scribner, 1982.
Whitaker, Muriel, ed. *Great Canadian Animal Stories.* Edmonton: Hurtig, 1978.

16 Farm Animals

Basic Understandings
(concepts children can grasp from this subject)

☐ A farm is a piece of land, usually larger than a city lot, that is used to raise crops or animals. It is ordinarily located outside a city or town.

☐ There are many kinds of farms — poultry, grain, dairy, livestock, fruit, and vegetable. At one time, farmers used to raise crops *and* animals; some farmers still do. But more often, only one main crop or one kind of animal is raised — wheat, corn, potatoes, beans, peaches, berries, sheep, turkeys, ducks, hogs, etc.

☐ Horses and cattle are sometimes raised on ranches. The people who work on ranches are called ranch hands or ranchers.

☐ Animals usually raised on a farm are cows, horses, sheep, goats, pigs, chickens, ducks, turkeys, and geese.

☐ Most farm animals need to be fenced into fields, so they do not stray into a roadway or into another farmer's field. Fences prevent animals from escaping to other fields where they might eat the wrong foods.

☐ To protect them from bad weather, farm animals usually have special houses, such as barns, sheds, stables, coops, or pens, to sleep in at night.

☐ Sometimes the farmer raises food for the farm animals — hay, alfalfa, corn, oats, and barley.

☐ The farm family and employees work long hours to care for their animals and their crops. At certain times of the year (during planting, cultivating, irrigating, harvesting, butchering, breeding, and marketing), they are much busier than at other times.

☐ A herd is a group of one kind of animal living together.

☐ There are ways in which farm animals help the farmer:
  1. Horses provide transportation and pull wagons.
  2. Chickens lay eggs.
  3. Cows and goats give milk.
  4. Cats catch mice.
  5. Dogs guard other animals.
  6. Sheep grow wool.
  7. Bees make honey.

☐ The farmer uses many tools and machines to take care of farm animals (see Chapter 28, Tools and Machines to Use in My World).

- ☐ Many farm families show their best animals at fall fairs or exhibitions. Sometimes they win ribbons or prizes.
- ☐ At rodeos, ranch hands show how well they can rope (lasso) calves and ride horses.

Additional Facts the Teacher Should Know

Chickens
- ☐ Brood (family group).
- ☐ Hen (female).
- ☐ Rooster (male).
- ☐ Chick (young).
- ☐ They are covered with feathers that vary in colour depending on the breed; two pieces of red flesh called wattles hang behind and below their bills.
- ☐ Hens communicate through clucks; roosters crow.
- ☐ Chickens eat corn, grains, and gravel (which they need to digest their food).
- ☐ Although they have wings, they can fly only short distances.
- ☐ The average hen lays 218 eggs a year.
- ☐ The average life span is eight to fourteen years.

Cattle
- ☐ Herd (family group).
- ☐ Cow (female).
- ☐ Bull (male).
- ☐ Heifer (young female).
- ☐ Calf (young male).
- ☐ They are covered with coarse hair that varies in colour depending on the breed; both cows and bulls have horns; cows have large udders with teats, which hold their milk.
- ☐ Cattle communicate through moos and bellows.
- ☐ They eat grass, hay, corn, and grains, and they lick salt.
- ☐ The average life span is twenty years.

Hogs
- ☐ Herd (family group).
- ☐ Sow (female).
- ☐ Boar (male).
- ☐ Piglet or shoat (young).
- ☐ Their long, heavy bodies are covered with short, bristly hair that varies in colour depending on the bread; they have large snouts and short, curly tails.
- ☐ Hogs communicate through squeals, grunts, snorts, and oinks.
- ☐ They eat almost anything.
- ☐ The average life span is nine to fifteen years.

Horses
- ☐ Herd or band (family group).
- ☐ Mare (female).
- ☐ Stallion or gelding (male).
- ☐ Filly (young female).
- ☐ Colt (young male).
- ☐ Foal (newborn).
- ☐ They are covered with a coat of hair that varies in colour; they have long manes and tails.
- ☐ Horses communicate through whinnies or neighs.

☐ They eat oats, hay, grass, clover, barley, and carrots, and they lick salt.
☐ The average life span is 20 to 30 years.

Sheep
☐ Flock (family group).
☐ Ewe (female).
☐ Ram (male).
☐ Lamb (young).
☐ They are covered with a thick coat of wool that varies in colour depending on the breed; some rams have horns.
☐ Sheep communicate through bleats and baahs.
☐ They eat grain, grasses, and corn.
☐ The average life span is thirteen years.

Goats
☐ Herd or band (family group).
☐ Nanny (female).
☐ Billy (male).
☐ Kid (young).
☐ They are covered with thick, coarse hair that varies in colour depending on the breed.
☐ Goats communicate through bleats.
☐ They eat a variety of grains and grasses.
☐ The average life span is eight to ten years.

Introducing This Subject to Children

1. At meal time, discuss animal-food products from farms.
2. Take children on a trip to a farm.
3. Read a farm storybook such as *Barn Dance* (see Book Centre).
4. On walks, look for a truck or cattle car full of farm animals.
5. Make a picture display of farm scenes.
6. Have a veterinarian or a farmer visit.
7. Make egg-salad sandwiches or an omelette. Talk about the original source of eggs, milk, butter, and cream.

Vocabulary

saddle	trough	pasture	ranch
cowboy/cowgirl	stable	corncrib	hay
cattle	pigpen	field	silo
sheep	poultry	dairy	stall
brand	livestock	fence	barn
hayloft	harness	farm herd	
feeder			

Add words that pertain to farm animals observed by your group. Include the names, body parts, sounds, and foods eaten by animals you observe.

Learning Centres

Discovery Centre

1. Make butter using a butter churn, if available, or an electric mixer. Whichever tool is used, begin with cold whipping cream and cold containers.
2. Make ice cream. Small handcranked ice-cream makers are inexpensive and make ice cream very quickly. Mix together whipping cream and flavourings. Following the manufacturer's directions, fill the outer container with salt and ice. Invite children to take turns cranking the handle until the mixture solidifies.
3. Examine raw eggs, and then poach, scramble, soft boil, hard boil, and bake them. Compare the different forms eggs can take.
4. Make cottage cheese:

   1 L milk
   1 rennet tablet

   Heat milk to lukewarm. Dissolve rennet tablet in a small amount of the milk. Stir rennet mixture into remaining milk, and then let stand in a warm place until set. Drain through a strainer lined with cheesecloth; bring corners of cloth together and squeeze or drain mixture. Rinse mixture with cold water and drain again. Add a little butter and salt.

5. Make pudding: Pour hot milk into a plastic container. Add instant pudding mix. Seal the container, and then shake. Let the pudding cool before eating.
6. Take a pony ride at a farm or in a park.

   NOTE: Make sure you have adequate adult supervision and that the animals are used to children. Do not insist any child ride who does not wish to.

7. Explore wool: Examine wool clippings, lanolin, dyed yarn, yarn spun into thread, wool cloth, sheepskin, and wool articles (mittens or scarves). Order a folder of samples from a wool company.
8. Explore a loom or other spinning and weaving equipment. A parent who weaves as a hobby may be able to give a demonstration.
9. Examine feathers: Note differences between tail or wing feathers and down. See if feathers will float in water, and talk about why they float. Ask, "What are feathers for?" (to keep birds warm or cool, and to help ducks float on water). Use a magnifying glass to examine feathers.
10. Examine blown-out or hard-boiled eggs: Compare sizes and colours of chicken, duck, and goose eggs. Put feathers with each kind of egg in a box with a picture or model of the bird so that children can make the correct association.
11. Examine various grains that farm animals eat under a magnifying glass or in a sealed pill bottle.
12. Examine leather. Identify a leather article's source, such as pigskin gloves, snakeskin belt, calfskin shoes, horsehide baseball, or sheepskin coat or collar. Point out that some endangered animals are now protected by law.
13. Taste goat milk, cream, skim milk, whole milk, cottage cheese, sour cream, butter, margarine, and buttermilk. Smell sour milk.

Dramatic Play Centres

Home-living centre

1. Post pictures of baking, showing eggs and milk next to mixing bowls.
2. Post pictures of chickens with eggs or cows being milked.
3. Find pictures of foods that are familiar to children — foods that are commonly eaten in their homes and at your centre. Mount the pictures on cardboard and either cover them with clear adhesive plastic or have them laminated at a photocopy shop or an educators' resource centre. Have the pictures available in the centre so that children can use them with the cooking utensils. (Refer to Part 2 for further ideas on choosing foods that are appropriate for the children in your program.)
4. Display marble or plastic eggs (unbreakable plastic eggs are available through toy companies. Coloured plastic eggs are available at stores at Easter). Put eggs in the refrigerator or cupboard.
5. Add empty milk cartons and evaporated milk or pudding cans to the centre (tape can edges for safety). If possible, choose containers with labels that show the whole food in its natural state.
6. Add pie plates, frying pans, spatulas, and muffin tins for cooking.
7. Collect colour pictures from grocery store flyers to make food cards or notebooks for grocery lists.

Block-building centre

1. Set out model farm animals (including cats and dogs), tractors, dump trucks, farm fences, trees, troughs, and people.

After a trip to the farm, these children are playfully mixing together plastic zoo animals and farm animals and talking about which animals they saw at the farm. The children saw many animals with their young at the farm. They have set up some of their animals nursing their young.

2. Hang pictures of farm activities, including a farmer milking cows or harvesting crops. Also include pictures of chickens, goats, pigs, and other farm animals.
3. Set out a shoebox filled with shredded paper hay to feed farm animals.
4. Add some blue paper cut in freeform shapes to use as lakes and ponds.
5. Set out coloured cubes and spools to be used for loading and unloading trucks and wagons.
6. Encourage the use of large hollow blocks for building barns. Children can pretend to be animals.
7. Make a silo from a cardboard cylinder wrapped with coloured paper or foil.
8. Provide buckets, work gloves, an old saddle or a child harness, dishpans for feeding chickens, work hats, and short stepladders (to go to the hayloft).

Other dramatic play centres

1. Set out clothes and props for a farmer or ranch hand (see Dramatic Play Props in Part 1).
2. Make paper-bag puppets of farm animals; provide costumes of farm animals, such as ducks, chicks, and rabbits; or make coat-hanger masks (see Halloween in Chapter 11).

Art Centre

- 1. Offer clay for modelling animals.
  2. Collages:
- a. Geometric paper collage: Let children experiment with felt or magnetic shapes for several days prior until they get the idea that everything is a shape or a combination of shapes.
- b. Yarn collage: Provide clipped yarn, yarn pom-poms, and various lengths and colours of yarn.
- c. Texture collage: Offer children materials of different textures and encourage them to create a collage using as many textures as possible.
- d. Grain and seed collage: Use grains, seeds, or other products gathered from a farm, if possible.
- e. Scrap collage: Dye eggshells to use in collages.
- 3. Cut farm animal shapes out of paper or felt. Suggest that the children use crayons to draw a picture of a farm and then suggest that they glue the shapes on to their pictures. Ask the children to tell you about their pictures. Encourage them to make up stories about their pictures.

Learning and Language Materials Centre

Commercially made games and materials

1. *Puzzles:* Puzzles with a variety of farm animals. Make sure some of the puzzles have knobs for younger children.
2. *Small toys for imaginative play:* Durable plastic or wooden animals and farm buildings made of non-toxic materials. Choose models with pieces that are of a good size to fit into children's hands. Try to find models of animals that children are likely to see in your area. Miniature animals could be used to make a farm diorama.
3. *Toys for riding:* Tractors and wagons.
4. *Dolls and puppets:* Dolls in farm work clothes and farm animal puppets. Remember that farmers can be both men and women and that male and female farm costumes and puppets should be available.
5. *Miscellaneous:* Animal dominoes.

Teacher-made games and materials

> **NOTE:** For detailed descriptions, see Learning Games in Part 1.

1. *Match-them:* Match farm animals with what they provide; or animal parents with their babies.
2. *Match-them:* Use homemade animal-word identification cards. Cut several cardboard rectangles about 12 cm by 12 cm. Glue a picture of an animal on the upper half of each card. Letter the name of each animal beneath its picture. Cut several more cardboard rectangles 3 cm by 10 cm, and label each with an animal's name. Children can match the names on the small cards with those on the large cards. For younger children, use animal pictures on the small cards instead of animal names. Look for sticker books on farms or animal homes to use in making game cards, or buy packages of gummed animal seals.
3. *Look and see:* Farm animal shapes cut from felt or pictures mounted on felt can be used on a flannelboard. Use food with the animal it comes from, mothers with their young, and so on.
4. Make cardboard classification cards at least 25 cm by 30 cm on which to place pictures of animals as children classify them. Decorate each card with a different picture or drawing in the centre (house, lake, grass, or barn). VARIATION: Paste pictures of houses, cages, or barns on the ends of shoeboxes.
5. Offer a box of geometric felt shapes with a flannelboard for children to make animal shapes.
6. Count animal parts in pictures of animals or in live animals in the discovery centre.
7. *Sorting and grouping by association:* Classify plastic animals by their outer coverings, by their food products, or by their homes. Sort into boxes labelled with pictures of the animals.
8. Have the children tell a story about a farm or what they saw on a visit to a farm. Then, write it down and post it with farm pictures.

Book Centre

- Anastasiou, S. *The Farmyard.* Toronto: Lorimer, 1985.
- •• Anderson, C.W. *Blaze and the Gray Spotted Pony.* New York: Macmillan, 1968.
- ••• Borenstein, Ruth. *Of Course a Goat.* New York: Harper & Row, 1980.
- •• Bourgeois, Paulette. *Too Many Chickens!* Toronto: Kids Can Press, 1991.
- • Chase, Edith N., and Barbara Reid. *The New Baby Calf.* Richmond Hill, ON: Scholastic, 1984.
- ••• Climo, Lindee. *Chester's Barn.* Montreal: Tundra, 1982.
- •••• Laurence, Margaret. *Six Darn Cows.* Toronto: Lorimer, 1986.
- • Lloyd, David. *Duck.* Willowdale, ON: Annick Press, 1988.
- ••• Lobel, A. *A Treeful of Pigs.* New York: Greenwillow Press, 1979.
- ••• ———. *How the Rooster Saved the Day.* New York: Greenwillow Press, 1977.
- •••• Locker, T. *The Mare on the Hill.* New York: Dial Press, 1985. (beautiful pictures for use with telling the story)
- ••• Lunn, Janet. *Amos's Sweater.* Toronto: Groundwood, 1988.
- •• Lyon, G. *A Regular Rolling Noah.* New York: Bradbury, 1986.
- •••• Martin Jr., Bill, and John Archambault. *Barn Dance.* New York: Henry Holt, 1986. (Read–Tell)
- •• McCloskey, Robert. *Make Way for Ducklings.* New York: Viking Press, 1969.
- •• McMillan, B. *Here a Chick, There a Chick.* New York: Lothrop, Lee & Shepard, 1983.
- • McPhail, D. *Farm Morning.* New York: Harcourt Brace Jovanovich, 1985.

- Miller, J. *A Farm Alphabet Book.* Englewood Cliffs, NJ: Prentice-Hall, 1984.
- ••• Myers, Bernice. *The Millionth Egg.* New York: Lothrop, Lee & Shepard, 1991.
- •• Pienkowski, Jan. *Farm.* London: Heinemann, 1985.
- •••• Provenson, A., and M. Provenson. *Our Animal Friends at Maple Hill Farm.* New York: Random House, 1984. (Read–Tell)
- ••• Robart, Rose. *The Cake that Mack Ate.* Toronto: Kids Can Press, 1986.
- •• Roffey, M. *Home Sweet Home.* New York: Coward, 1983.
- • Schmid, Eleonor. *Farm Animals.* St. Catharines, ON: North-South, 1986.
- ••• Scott, Mary. *A Picture Book of Farm Animals.* St. Catharines, ON: Troll Associates, 1991.
- • Tafuri, N. *Early Morning in the Barn.* New York: Greenwillow Press, 1983.
- ••• Weiss, Nicki. *An Egg Is an Egg.* New York: Putnam, 1990.
- ••• Wildsmith, Brian. *Goat's Tail.* New York: Knopf, 1986.
- ••• ———. *Daisy.* New York: Pantheon, 1984.

Planning for Group Time

NOTE: All music, fingerplays, poems, and stories listed here may be used at other times during the session as appropriate.

Music

Songs

Please see "The Farmer's in the Barn" at the end of this chapter.

From *Do Your Ears Hang Low?* Glazer
"The Horse Stood Around," p. 37
"I Had a Little Rooster," p. 43

From *The Goat with the Bright Red Socks*, Birkenshaw and Walden
"The Goat with the Bright Red Socks," p. 25

From *More Piggyback Songs*, Warren
"I Hear the Animals," p. 73
"All around the Barnyard," p. 80
"Farm Sounds," p. 80
"I Like Baby Animals," p. 81
"Farm Animals," p. 81
"Are You Listening to the Animals?" p. 82
"Can You Guess What I Am?" p. 82

From *Singing Bee*, Hart
"All the Pretty Horses," p. 11
"This Little Pig," p. 26
"Baa, Baa, Black Sheep," p. 47
"Goosey, Goosey Gander," p. 57
"Bingo," p. 82
"See the Pony Galloping, Galloping," p. 98

From *A Treasury of Songs for Children*, Glazer
"The Farmer in the Dell," p. 82
"Go Tell Aunt Rhody," p. 99

"The Gray Goose," p. 102
"Mary Had a Little Lamb," p. 161
"Turkey in the Straw," p. 226

From *Tunes for Tots*, Warner and Berry
"Farm Sounds," p. 80
"Oink, Oink," p. 81

From *What Shall We Do and Alee Galloo!*, Winn
"The Little Pony," p. 53
"Wake Up You Lazy Bones (Hunt the Cows)," p. 74

Records and Cassettes

Bob McGrath. *If You're Happy and You Know It*, Volume I. (Kids Records)
"Baa, Baa, Black Sheep"
"Home on the Range"
"The Farmer in the Dell"

Raffi. *The Corner Grocery Store.* (Troubadour Records)
"Cluck, Cluck Red Hen"

Sharon, Lois, and Bram. *Smorgasbord.* (Elephant Records)
"Did You Feed My Cow?"
"Riding Along"

Fingerplays and Poems

From *Finger Rhymes*, Brown
"Five Little Pigs," p. 8

From *Hand Rhymes*, Brown
"Quack, Quack, Quack!" p. 22

From *Let's Do Fingerplays*, Grayson
"When a Little Chicken Drinks," p. 36
"This Little Calf," p. 38
"Two Little Ducks," p. 71
"Two Mother Pigs," p. 72

From *Oranges and Lemons*, King and Beck
"The Scarecrow," p. 36

From *Read Aloud Rhymes for the Very Young*, Prelutsky and Brown
"Higglety, Pigglety, Pop!" p. 5
"The Pigs," p. 36
"Mary Middling," p. 36
"There Was a Small Pig Who Wept Tears," p. 36
"Chook, Chook," p. 42
"Five Little Chickens," p. 42
"Quack, Quack!" p. 43
"A Little Talk," p. 43
"Ducks in the Rain," p. 43
"The Donkey," p. 46

From *Round and Round the Garden*, Williams
"Piggy on the Railway," p. 12
"This Little Pig," p. 36

From *Where the Sidewalk Ends*, Silverstein
"The Farmer and the Queen," p. 32

Stories

(To read, read–tell, or tell. See Book Centre for a complete list.)
Margaret Laurence's *Six Darn Cows* is an excellent example of a story to read or tell to children, as it captures the flavour of farm life for urban children and will be familiar and fun for rural children.

Routine Times

1. Serve animal cookies and milk at snack time.
2. At snack or meal times, have the children eat scrambled, devilled, or hard-boiled eggs that they prepared earlier in the discovery centre.
3. Serve cheese wedges, cottage cheese, milk, and a variety of juice drinks at snack time.
4. Talk about sources of foods, and play a guessing game about them at snack or meal times.
5. During rest time, encourage the children to curl up like a cat or dog.
6. When dismissing children to leave the room or go outside, say, "You can gallop like a horse, hop like a bunny, waddle like a duck. . . ."

Large Muscle Activities

1. Allow wagons and trikes to be used as tractors for hauling (children could clean up twigs on the farm).
2. Large hollow blocks, cylinders, cardboard packing boxes, or laundry barrels can be used for farm animal houses, barns, and silos.
3. Children can pretend to be goats and butt large balls (such as beach balls) with their heads.

■ If children in your group have special mobility needs, arrange the group of children around a large round table and have them butt a ball back and forth across the table. Be sure to allow space around each child so that children do not butt one another's heads.

■ 4. Encourage children to imitate the movements of farm animals: head movements, walking, or arm and leg movements. All children can participate in this activity, whether or not they are mobile.
5. Add water to sand and dirt, and encourage the exploration of these elements that are so important to growing things.
6. Let the children pretend to ride horses by providing them with stick horses.

Extended Experiences

1. Take children on trips to:
   a. A dairy.

   ▼ CAUTION: There may be too much machinery for very young children.

   b. An ice-cream shop.
   c. The dairy section of a grocery store.
   d. A fair or exhibition (visit the farm section to see the most common farm animals).
   e. Farms (turkey, sheep, dairy, horse, or chicken).

2. Bring a farm animal pet to school (turkey, lamb, or young goat).
3. Show a filmstrip about farm animals.

 # Teacher Resources

Pictures and Displays

☐ Hang a mobile of shapes with pictures of animals on one side and their products on the other. Mount pictures on circles, squares, or triangles.
☐ Hang pictures of food and farm animals.
☐ Display pictures on a bulletin board divided into the following sections:
   a. Ranch, ranch hand, cattle.
   b. Poultry farming.
   c. Grain fields.
   d. Dairy farm, swine farm, beef farm.
   e. Fruit orchards.

   NOTE: Vary the number of sections depending on the pictures available, the size of the bulletin board, and your focus of interest.

Books and Periodicals

Durrell, Gerald. *The Stationary Ark.* London: Collins, 1976.
Farm journals.
Harrowsmith magazine.
Hendrikson, Robert. *Animal Crackers.* Markham, ON: Penguin, 1983.
The Larousse Encyclopedia of Animal Life. London: Hamlyn, 1967.
Tremain, Ruthven. *The Animal's Who's Who.* New York: Scribner, 1982.

Films and Videos

   NOTE: Check with your distributor about public performance rights.

Apryl and Her Baby Lamb. Atlantis Productions (released in Canada by Viking Films), 1956.
Big Red Barn. Moreland-Latchford Productions, 1973.
Charlie Needs a Clock. Weston Woods.
Charlotte's Web. Paramount Home Video, 1979.
Chick, Chick, Chick. Mick'nbob Productions (released in Canada by Gordon Watt Films), 1975.
Farmyard Babies. Coronet Instructional Media, 1978.
Make Way for Ducklings. Weston Woods.
The Most Wonderful Egg in the World. Weston Woods.
Petunia. Weston Woods.
Rosie's Walk. Weston Woods.
The Story about Ping. Weston Woods.
Suho and the White Horse. Weston Woods.

Community Resources and Organizations

☐   Veterinarian.
☐   Farmer.
☐   Fairs and exhibitions.
☐   Marketing boards for various farm products.

Government Agencies

☐   Federal, provincial, and territorial ministries of agriculture.

The Farmer's in the Barn

Donna Wood

1. The far - mer's in the barn, the farm - er's in the barn,
2.   far - mer has a cow, the far - mer has a cow,

hi   ho   the der - ry oh, the far - mer's in the barn.   The
hi   ho   the der - ry oh, the far - mer has a cow.   (The)

Formation: A circle in the middle of a *large* room. Choose the farmer.

1. The farmer's in the barn etc. (the farmer stands in the middle of the circle).
2. The farmer has a cow etc. (the farmer chooses a cow to stand beside him or her).
3. The farmer has a duck etc. (the farmer chooses a duck to stand beside him or her).
4. The farmer goes to sleep etc. (lies down, hiding face) and the animals "hide" at opposite ends of the room.
5. The farmer wakes up (stands up). The farmer calls out "Where is my cow?" The cow answers "moo" from hiding place. The farmer listens and then decides where to go to get the cow.
6. The farmer's found the cow etc. (farmer brings back cow to circle). The farmer calls out "Where is my duck?" (continue as with cow).
7. The farmer's found the duck etc.

NOTE: This game could be extended to include other farm animals.

17 Pet Animals

Basic Understandings
(concepts children can grasp from this subject)

☐ Any tame animal that is kept just for fun as a special friend is called a pet.

☐ Children should choose pets carefully because:
   1. Pets have special needs due to their size, diet, need for exercise, and need for protection.
   2. Some pets are more playful than others and therefore make better companions.
   3. Some pets need more care than a child can give, and parents may not wish to assume the responsibility.

☐ Sometimes you cannot keep a pet where you live.
   1. Big pets, such as ponies, lambs, and goats, need large, fenced areas in which to exercise.
   2. Some pets may be noisy or dangerous and should live where they will not need to be confined.
   3. Some pets are more dangerous than others (they may bit or scratch).
   4. Some pets need special equipment, such as cages or tanks, in order to be kept in a house.
   5. Sometimes apartments and condominiums do not allow people to keep pets.
   6. An animal should not be kept in a cage if it cannot be happy there.
   7. Some pets cost more money than others to feed and care for, because their food may be hard to get or may be expensive.
   8. We need permission from our families for most pets.

☐ All pets need to be loved and cared for.

☐ Sometimes pets get sick or injured. Doctors for pets are called veterinarians.

☐ Some common house pets are dogs, cats, gerbils, goldfish, parakeets, hamsters, guinea pigs, and canaries.

☐ Other pets include rabbits, crickets, chameleons, horned toads, white mice, rats, and guppies.

☐ Pets need to be handled gently and carefully.

☐ Pets often need baths, their hair brushed, their toenails clipped, and their eyes washed out. These should always be done with the help of a grown-up. Pets also need opportunities to eat, sleep, and play, much like children do.

☐   Some pets, like dogs and cats, have to wear a licence tag, so if they are lost they can be returned to their owners.

☐   Some pets need to be immunized (have shots) so they cannot give or get diseases from other animals or from people.

☐   Sometimes children and parents exhibit their pets at pet shows. Prizes and ribbons are given for pets that are well-mannered and well-groomed (prepared for showing).

Additional Facts the Teacher Should Know

■ Pets and animals may be used to extend children's experiences in your program. Some programs adopt pets to live at the centre. Before you adopt a pet for your program, ensure that the local public health office approves of it. In addition, confirm that children in your program are not allergic to the pet you plan to bring in. Childhood asthma and allergies are being identified and treated early, but an allergic reaction may interfere with successful treatment.

Cats

☐   Queen (female).
☐   Tom (male).
☐   Kitten (young).
☐   They are covered with a thick fur coat of either long hair or short hair; the coats vary in colour depending on the breed.
☐   Cats communicate by meowing and purring, hissing and growling.
☐   They eat milk, fish, and cat food; they may also eat mice or birds.
☐   The average life span is sixteen years.

Dogs

☐   Bitch (female).
☐   Dog (male).
☐   Pup (young).
☐   They are covered with coats of either long or short hair; the coats vary in colour depending on the breed.
☐   Dogs communicate by barking and howling, whimpering and growling.
☐   They eat meat, fish, and dog food.
☐   The average life span is fourteen years.

Gerbils

☐   Gerbil (female, male and young).
☐   They are covered with a coarse, light brown, black-tipped fur coat; they have slightly protruding eyes and large ears.
☐   Gerbils are usually silent; as babies, however, they may issue a sound like a whispering squeak or sniff.
☐   They eat lettuce and rabbit pellets.
☐   The average life span is one to two years.

Hamsters

☐   Hamster (female, male, and young).
☐   They are covered with short, smooth, golden-brown and white fur; they have black eyes, a big bulge behind the cheek for storing food, large ears, poor eyesight, and almost no tail.
☐   Hamsters communicate through squeaks and growls.
☐   They eat bread, raw vegetables, grain, seeds, lettuce, and a few drops of cod-liver oil.

☐ The average life span is two to three years.

NOTE: Gerbils and hamsters move quickly and can easily get away from small children. They should be handled only under adult supervision.

Rabbits

☐ Doe (female).
☐ Buck (male).
☐ Fawn (young).
☐ They are covered with a fur coat that may be long or short, depending on the breed; the colour of the coat also depends on the breed.
☐ Rabbits are usually silent; however, they may squeak to show fear or affection, and growl to show anger or fear.
☐ They must have hard foods, such as rabbit pellets or carrots, to keep their front teeth from growing too long (unlike human teeth, these regenerate constantly). Rabbits enjoy all kinds of fruits, vegetables, and grains.
☐ The average life span is four to eight years.

Guinea pigs

☐ Sow (female).
☐ Boar (male).
☐ Piglet (young).

A pet in the centre gives children the opportunity to learn about the growth and care of small animals. This rabbit frequently becomes the focus of socializing. The friendly older child is telling the younger children about the rabbit's exploits.

■ Unusually shy or quiet children may find that an animal helps them build friendships with other children by giving them something to talk about or show to their peers. Encourage this by asking questions, such as, "Why don't you show the others where the rabbit is hiding?"

☐ Some have long-haired coats and others have short-haired coats; the colour of the coat varies depending on the breed; they have no tail.
☐ Guinea pigs communicate through squeals, grunts, whistles, or squeaks.
☐ They eat fresh greens with grain, apples, cauliflower, celery tops, corn, tomatoes, and other vegetables.
☐ The average life span is eight years.

Parakeets
☐ Clutch (family group).
☐ Hen (female).
☐ Cock (male).
☐ Chick (young).
☐ They have green and yellow feathers, although some have blue, grey, and white feathers, depending on the breed.
☐ Parakeets communicate with chirps and whistles.
☐ They eat birdseed, fresh spinach, carrots, celery tops, or dandelion greens. They also need gravel to digest their food.
☐ The average life span is ten years.

Introducing This Subject to Children
1. A child might bring in a new or favourite pet to share with the group.
2. Encourage children to discuss pets they see on the way to school.
3. Invite a child to tell about the birth of pet babies at home.
4. Take a trip to a pet shop to purchase a pet and its food for the classroom.
5. Display pictures of children with pets playing, sleeping, or eating, or pictures of children caring for pets.
6. Read a new pet story or poem, or teach a song about a pet.
7. Present a new puzzle or game about pets (see Learning and Language Materials Centre).
8. Introduce a new classroom pet.

Vocabulary

pet	biscuit	whiskers	born
cage	water bottle	feathers	home
bone	exercise wheel	fur	house
bed	love	coat	indoor
tail	care	claws	outdoor
supplies	pellets	paws	feed
feeding dish	drink		

Include the names, sounds, body parts, and foods of the pets you are observing.

Learning Centres

Discovery Centre

1. Questions to ask while observing a pet in the classroom:
    a. What kind of animal is it?
    b. What does it look like?
    c. What does it eat?
    d. How does it eat?
    e. How does it sleep?
    f. When does it sleep?
    g. What is it doing?
    h. What sounds does it make?
    i. How does it move?
    j. How could it best be handled? Why?
2. Compare this pet with another kind of pet. How are they different? How are they the same? Why?

    ▼ CAUTION: Be sure that when animals are brought to school they are used to children and are known to be friendly to them. If the animal will be staying for half or all the day, have a place for it to be safe from the children for periods of time. Also provide food, water, and a place to eliminate. Someone who knows the animal should be present to help handle it. If baby animals are considered, try to provide at least two of them — this prevents the overtiring of just one well-discovered and enjoyed baby animal. It also means less waiting for a turn by the children.

3. Set out a variety of foods — plants, meat, and human food — to discover which the animal will choose. Talk about why it chooses a certain food. What body parts does the animal need to eat that food? What body parts would it need to eat other food?
4. Compare animals by using toy animals or pictures, and by grouping them into categories (big/brown/furry/hoofed, or pets/farm/zoo/forest).
5. Make cookies shaped like cats, bunnies, and other pets. Let children experiment with making their own shapes. Decorate cookies with coloured frosting, or paint them with egg yolk and 15 mL water with food colouring added to desired intensity. Use new, clean watercolour brushes to apply. Give each child 15 mL to 25 mL of frosting in a plastic cup with a spreader. A coffee stir stick works well.

    ▼ CAUTION: Do not use the same bowl of frosting or spreader for everyone. Children will want to taste.

6. Set up a display of common pet supplies: an unbreakable pet feeding dish, pet toys (rubber bone, ball, or mouse), leash, licence tags, brush, empty cage, cedar chips, and empty containers of cat, dog, fish, or bird food. Ask children which pet uses the various supplies (pictures on boxes will provide hints). Post pictures above the display of appropriate pets eating and sleeping, or of children caring for pets.

Dramatic Play Centres

Home-living centre

1. Provide stuffed animals for pets, or invite children to bring in their favourite ones.

2. Include a pet bed, box, or basket with a blanket or cushion in it. You may make it large enough for a child to pretend to be a pet.
3. Add a few pet toys — ball, rubber bone or mouse, or ball on a string. Use unbreakable pet feeding bowls and plastic baby bottles for feeding toy pets.
4. Set up a pet store using stuffed toys and empty pet-food containers.

Block-building centre

1. Set out rubber, wooden, cardboard, or unbreakable plastic models of pets.
2. Hang pictures showing pets' homes to encourage an interest in building homes or fences for pets.

Art Centre

- 1. Play dough: Set out play dough and coffee stir sticks or tongue depressors for cutting or marking forms.
- 2. Use potter's clay to sculpt pet animals.
••• 3. Finish the picture: Provide sheets of paper with circles or ovals drawn or pasted on them, and encourage children to use crayons to finish the pictures. Ask them what a shape makes them think of (this activity is more successful when it follows activities with felt shapes).

   ■ Some children will find this activity very challenging, because they have difficulty identifying shapes and associating them with real animals. Introduce the activity by asking the children to think of an animal that has a body with the same shape as the one on their paper. Ask volunteers to tell about their animal. After children have heard a few suggestions, all of them will have an idea. After the children have completed their drawings, invite them to tell you about their animals. Have them print the name of the animal on the picture if they know how, or label the pictures for them. This review process helps all the children build their knowledge of associations between actual objects and abstract shapes.

••• 4. Some five-year-olds can make picture books of animal drawings using crayons. Label the pictures with the names children supply in talking about them so that their parents can identify the animals.
••• 5. Cut and paste: Make a pet book. Add a storyline for a group book, or have children mount pictures they like until they have enough for their own books. Staple pages together.
   6. Make an animal picture collage.
•••   a. Geometric paper collage: Encourage children to make a picture of their favourite pet or a pet they would like to own (provide precut geometric shapes for inexperienced cutters).
•••   b. Yarn collage: Have children paint with thinned glue on a page. They can "draw" with yarn lengths, securing them as they go, and then fill in the outline with clipped yarn. Provide yarn in the colours of most pets (black, brown, white, grey, and beige), so that the children will have available the colours of pets they know. You could also provide yarn pom-poms.
•••   c. Texture collage: Be sure to include trays of clipped yarns, scraps of felt, fur, textured cloth, bits of rope or yarn for tails, and buttons for eyes.
•• 7. Styrofoam sculpture: Provide an assortment of precut styrofoam pieces (curved and square), styrofoam balls of various sizes, and decorations, such as pieces of yarn, leather, and felt, buttons, and coloured toothpicks, for children to make their favourite pet animal (real or imagined).

Other art projects to try

•• 1. Encourage children to make a *Match-them* game that they can keep, using gummed animal seals and pictures of foods they eat, or pairs of the same animals. Mount pictures on cardboard cut into geometric shapes.

•• 2. Bookmarks: Children can cut out small pictures of pets outlined with a magic marker, or they can stick gummed labels of pets on strips of cardboard for bookmarks to share with the group or give as gifts to parents or older brothers or sisters.

•• 3. Pull-toy pets:
   a. Tie colourful bread wrappers or tissue into pom-poms; attach about 1 m of string to make a kitten pull toy.
   b. Dye spools with vegetable dye; thread with string for a pull-toy pet.

•• 4. Stick puppets: Children can cut out pictures of pets outlined with magic marker to avoid cutting difficult details. Glue these to cardboard ovals or circles. Slip a tongue depressor between the picture and the cardboard for a handle. Younger children can make puppets if you precut cardboard and pictures.

••• VARIATION: Children make a face on a paper plate using styrofoam scraps, yarn, and buttons. Use paper strips or straws for whiskers and tails. Melt crayon pieces into bottle caps to use as eyes, noses, or mouths; use ruffled crepe paper for manes, and circles of construction paper, tissue, or fabric for scales or feathers. Glue or staple plastic or cardboard handles to backs of plates. These puppets can also be used as masks.

Learning and Language Materials Centre

Commercially made games and materials

1. *Puzzles:* Puzzles with a variety of pet animals. Make sure some of the puzzles have knobs for younger children.
2. *Small toys for imaginative play:* Model animals made of durable plastic or wood. Choose models with pieces that are of a good size to fit into children's hands. Try to find models of animals that are similar to animals the children are likely to see in your area.
3. *Dolls and puppets:* Stuffed animals such as dogs, cats, mice, etc. Puppets that are models of a variety of domestic animals.
4. *Miscellaneous:* Animal dominoes.

Teacher-made games and materials

NOTE: For detailed descriptions, see Learning Games in Part 1.

1. *Name it:* Use models or pictures of pets.
2. *Who am I?* Describe various pets.
3. *Which?* Compare which is larger, or use some other adjective with pictures or toy animals.
4. *Look and see:* Use pet pictures or models.
5. *Match-them:* Use flannelboard cutouts to match pets with foods they eat, parents with their young, or pets with their homes. Use commercial game cards, such as Snap, Animal rummy, or Kiddie cards, for matching cards. Modify games to suit your group or a child's ability.
6. *Guess what?* Use recordings of animal sounds.
7. Count pets in a picturebook — how many cats? Count body parts of pets in the classroom. Make cardboard counting discs or squares with gummed seals of pets.

Book Centre

- Aliki. *At Mary Bloom's.* New York: Greenwillow Press, 1983.
- ••• Anderson, C.W. *Billy and Blaze.* New York: Macmillan, 1964.
- ••• Asch, F. *Here Comes the Cat!* Richmond Hill, ON: Scholastic, 1989.
- •• ———. *The Last Puppy.* Englewood Cliffs, NJ: Prentice-Hall, 1983.
- •••• Atwood, M., and J. Barkhouse. *Anna's Pet.* Toronto: Lorimer, 1986. (Read–Tell)
- •• Bell, Cathie, and David Bell. *Two Bears Find a Pet.* Toronto: Oxford University Press, 1991.
- •• Bliss, C., and A. Bliss. *The Dog Melley.* New York: Hastings, 1981.
- • Bonsall, C. *Mine's the Best.* New York: Harper & Row, 1984.
- ••• Brandt, Hanne. *The Cat's Night Out.* St. John's: Breakwater Press, 1989.
- ••• Calhoun, Mary. *High-Wire Henry.* New York: Morrow, 1991.
- ••• Chalmers, M. *Six Dogs, Twenty-Three Cats, Forty-Five Mice and One Hundred and Sixteen Spiders.* New York: Harper & Row, 1986.
- ••• Cohen, M. *Jim's Dog Muffin.* New York: Greenwillow Press, 1984.
- •••• Cole, Joanna. *My Puppy Is Born.* New York: Morrow, 1991.
- • De Regniers, B.S. *It Does Not Say Meow.* Boston: Houghton Mifflin, 1972.
- •• Feldman, Barbara. *Stephen's Frog.* Willowdale, ON: Annick Press, 1991.
- • Flack, Marjorie. *Angus and the Cat.* Garden City, NY: Doubleday, 1971.
- ••• Gackenbach, D. *A Bag Full of Pups.* Boston: Houghton Mifflin, 1981.
- • Ginsburg, Mirra. *Three Kittens.* New York: Crown, 1973.
- ••• Gise, Joanne. *A Picture Book of Horses.* St. Catharines, ON: Troll Associates, 1991.
- ••• ———. *A Picture Book of Dogs.* St. Catharines, ON: Troll Associates, 1990.
- • Grindley, Sally. *Four Black Puppies.* Toronto: Walker, 1991.
- ••• Hearn, E. *Race You Fanny!* Toronto: Women's Press, 1986.
- • Hellen, Nancy. *Pets.* St. Catharines, ON: Vanwell, 1991.
- • Hoban, Tana. *One Little Kitten.* New York: Greenwillow Press, 1979.
- ••• Holl, A. *One Kitten for Kim.* Reading, MA: Addison-Wesley, 1969.
- •••• Holmes, E.T. *The Christmas Cat.* New York: Crowell, 1976. (Read–Tell)
- ••• Keats, Ezra Jack. *Pet Show.* New York: Macmillan, 1972.
- ••• ———. *Hi Cat!* New York: Macmillan, 1970.
- ••• ———. *Whistle for Willie.* New York: Viking Press, 1964.
- ••• Kerr, J. *Mog, the Forgetful Cat.* London: Collins, 1970.
- ••• Khalsa, Dayal Kaur. *I Want a Dog.* Montreal: Tundra, 1987.
- ••• Kovalski, Maryann. *Brenda and Edward.* Toronto: Kids Can Press, 1984.
- ••• Lee, Dennis. *Lizzy's Lion.* Don Mills, ON: Stoddart, 1984.
- ••• Mattern, Joanne. *A Picture Book of Cats.* St. Catharines, ON: Troll Associates, 1991.
- ••• Miles-Cadman, Margaret. *Little Fan and the Fountain Fairy.* St. John's: Breakwater Press, 1989.
- •• Muir, Mary Jane. *Gynn.* Richmond Hill: Scholastic, 1985.
- •••• Noble, C. *The Day Jimmy's Boa Ate the Wash.* New York: Dial Press, 1980.
- ••• Ohuigin, Sean. *Pickles: Street Dog of Windsor.* Willowdale, ON: Black Moss, 1985.
- • Ormerod, Jan. *Kitten Day.* Toronto: Walker, 1991.
- ••• Parish, Peggy. *Too Many Rabbits.* New York: Macmillan, 1974.
- • Paulin, Stéphane. *Could You Stop Josephine?* Montreal: Tundra, 1988.
- • ———. *Can You Catch Josephine?* Montreal: Tundra, 1987.
- • ———. *Have You Seen Josephine?* Montreal: Tundra, 1986.
- • Rison, Ole. *I Am a Kitten.* New York: Western, 1970.
- • ———. *I Am a Puppy.* New York: Western, 1970.
- ••• Schaffer, Marion. *I Love My Cat.* Toronto: Kids Can Press, 1980.
- •• Selsam, M. *How Kittens Grow.* New York: Four Winds Press, 1975.
- •• ———. *How Puppies Grow.* New York: Four Winds Press, 1972.
- •• Simon, Norma. *Where Does My Cat Sleep?* Chicago: Whitman, 1982.
- •• Titus, Eve. *The Kitten Who Couldn't Purr.* New York: Morrow, 1991.

•••• Waber, Bernard. *The House on East 88th Street.* New York: Houghton Mifflin, 1975. (fun
   to read and contrast with other stories about conventional pets)
•• Wheeler, Bernelda. *A Friend Called Chum.* Winnipeg: Pemmican, 1984.
• Wheeler, C. *Marmalade's Yellow Leaf.* New York: Knopf, 1985.
• ———. *Marmalade's Nap.* New York: Knopf, 1983.
• ———. *Marmalade's Picnic.* New York: Knopf, 1983.
• ———. *Marmalade's Snowy Day.* New York: Knopf, 1982.
••• Wildhelm, H. *I'll Always Love You.* New York: Crown, 1985.
•• Wildsmith, Brian. *Cat on the Mat.* Toronto: Oxford University Press, 1986.
•• ———. *Give a Dog a Bone.* New York: Pantheon, 1985.
•• ———. *Pelican.* New York: Pantheon, 1983.
• ———. *Fishes.* New York: Franklin Watts, 1970.
• ———. *Birds.* New York: Franklin Watts, 1968.
•• Wilkon, Piotr. *The Brave Little Kittens.* St. Catharines, ON: North-South, 1991.
••• Wooding, Penny. *Naughty Scamper Meets the Bush Monster.* St. John's: Breakwater Press,
   1991.
••• Yashima, Mitsu, and Taro Yashima. *Momo's Kitten.* New York: Viking Press, 1961.
•• Zion, Gene. *Harry the Dirty Dog.* New York: Harper & Row, 1956.

Planning for Group Time

> **NOTE:** All music, fingerplays, poems, and stories listed here may be used at other times
> during the session as appropriate.

Music

Songs

From *Elephant Jam,* Sharon, Lois, and Bram
"Little Peter Rabbit," p. 55
"Alison's Camel," p. 66 (the words can be changed to include other pets and, of course,
   other children)
"Tingalayo," p. 89 (pets in other countries)
"Candy Man, Salty Dog," p. 118

From *Singing Bee,* Hart
"I Love Little Pussy," p. 46
"Pussy Cat, Pussy Cat," p. 50
"Three Little Kittens," p. 72
"Bingo," p. 82
"Where Oh Where Has My Little Dog Gone?" p. 115

Rhythms and Singing Games

From *Songs for the Nursery School.* MacCarteney
Use appropriate actions with songs, pp. 25, 27, 30, 35, 36.

From *Music Resource Book,* Lutheran Church Press
"Six Little Ducks," p. 62

Rhythmic activity: Pretend to move like various pet animals.

Records and Cassettes

Bob McGrath. *If You're Happy and You Know It.* Volume I. (Kids Records)
"My Dog Rags"

Fingerplays and Poems

....

THE GUPPY

by Ogden Nash

Whales have calves,
Cats have kittens,
Bears have cubs,
Bats have bittens,
Swans have cygnets,
Seals have puppies,
But guppies just have little guppies.

From *Hand Rhymes*, Brown
"There Was a Little Turtle," p. 4
"Kittens," p. 24

From *Let's Do Fingerplays*, Grayson
"Kitten Is Hiding," p. 32
"There Was a Little Turtle," p. 33
"My Rabbit," p. 34
"Golden Fishes," p. 35

From *Mischief City*, Wynne-Jones
"I'm Collecting Monsters," p. 4

From *Read Aloud Rhymes for the Very Young*, Prelutsky and Brown
"The House Cat," p. 18
"Cat Kisses," p. 18
"At Night," p. 18
"Mother Cat's Purr," p. 19
"The Puppy Chased the Sunbeam," p. 40
"How a Puppy Grows," p. 40
"Chums," p. 40

Stories

(To read, read–tell, or tell. See Book Centre for a complete list.)
Read stories about pets who are well cared for by their owners. Wheeler's *A Friend Called Chum* and Muir's *Gynn* are good examples of this type of story.

Routine Times

1. Serve commercial animal cookies or those baked and frosted by children at snack or meal times.
2. If you have a pet in your program, either permanently or as a visitor, its care may be built into the daily routine. Encourage the children to think about what care the pet will need (they may need some guidance from you to ensure that the pet's needs are properly met). Make up a chart using both words and pictures to outline the pet's care

routine. Discuss the chart with the children. Although most children in your program will not be able to read the chart, the association between the words and the pictures is useful.

■ This type of problem solving around routines is very helpful for children who need support in controlling their behaviour. The group problem-solving exercise gives them a model for problem solving and for developing their own routines and solutions. The group exercise can then be used as a reference point with a child who is challenged by routines.

Large Muscle Activities

1. Set out boxes and barrels for children to crawl into and through to imitate animal behaviour.
2. Play ball (roll or toss two or more).
3. Play *Follow the leader:* The group follows the leader, imitating ways pets move — hopping, crawling, leaping, running, walking, climbing, and slithering. The children can take turns being leader; suggest actions as necessary. This activity is best done with a small group.

Extended Experiences

1. Take a trip to a teacher's home or a child's home to see a pet.
2. Visit a pet store to view supplies as well as pets.
3. Visit a pet farm, pet library, or petting zoo.
4. Invite a representative of the Humane Society or a veterinarian to bring an animal and talk to the children about the care of pets. Alert the visitor to what the children may be able to understand or need to hear.
5. View a filmstrip about a pet.

 # Teacher Resources

Pictures and Displays

☐ Encourage children to bring in pictures of their favourite pets or to share books with pictures of pets. Display pictures on a bulletin board. Set books in the book centre, or share them at group time.

☐ Group pictures of a specific kind or family of pets; for example, all kinds of cats, black pets, furry pets, or caged pets. Use coloured paper or yarn circles to help group pictures on a bulletin-board or wall display.

☐ Snapshot display: Make a display of "Our Pets at Home." Encourage the children to bring in snapshots of pets they have or have had. Label photos with child's name, name of pet, and kind of pet. You may need to begin the display with pictures of pets you have had. Put the display near the group-time area so children can point and share at that time. VARIATION: Let children select pictures of pets they would *like* to have. Have children cut and mount the pictures and label each with child's name.

▼ CAUTION: When returning photos to children, put them in envelops and pin them to children's clothing to avoid loss.

Books and Periodicals

Alday, Gretchen P. *Devoted Friends: Amazing True Stories about Animals Who Cared.* Crozet, VA: Betterway, 1990.

Canadian Geographic magazine.

Chickadee magazine.

Chinery, Michael, ed. *Dictionary of Animals.* New York: Arco, 1984.

Equinox magazine.

Hendrikson, Robert. *Animal Crackers.* Markham, ON: Penguin, 1983.

National Geographic magazine.

Owl magazine.

Pugnetti, Gino. *The Great Book of Dogs: An International Anthology.* New York: Galahad, 1973.

Settel, Joanne, and Nancy Baggett. *Why Do Cats' Eyes Glow in the Dark? And Other Questions Kids Ask about Animals.* New York: Ivy, 1990.

Seuling, Barbara. *Elephants Can't Jump and Other Freaky Facts about Animals.* New York: Ivy, 1988.

Tremain, Ruthven. *The Animal's Who's Who.* New York: Scribner, 1982.

Films and Videos

NOTE: Check with your distributor about public performance rights.

Angus Lost. Evergreen Productions/Firehouse Productions (released in Canada by International Tele-Film), 1982.

A Boy and a Boa. New York State Education Department (released in Canada by International Tele-Film), 1975.

Goggles. Weston Woods.

Harry and the Lady Next Door. Weston Woods.

John Brown, Rose and the Midnight Cat. Weston Woods.

Let's Give Kitty a Bath. Evergreen Productions/Firehouse Productions (released in Canada by International Tele-Film), 1985.

Madeline's Rescue. Billy Snyder Films (released in Canada by Marlin Motion Pictures), 1959.

Millions of Cats. Weston Woods.

The Perils of Priscilla. Manitoba Education and Training Instructional Resources Library, 1969.

The Puppy Who Wanted a Boy. Ruby-Spears Productions (released in Canada by Coronet Instructional Films), 1978.

What Mary Jo Wanted. Bernard Wilts Films (released in Canada by Gordon Watt Films), 1982.

Community Resources and Organizations

☐ Veterinarian.
☐ Animal clinic.
☐ Pet owners and breeders associations.
☐ Pet store.
☐ Family with a pet at home.

18 Woodland Animals

Basic Understandings
(concepts children can grasp from this subject)

- ☐ A woodland or forest is an area of ground with many trees and bushes. It often has streams or a pond.
- ☐ Wild animals who live in this area are called animals of the woods or forest animals.
- ☐ The most common forest animals are beavers, skunks, deer, foxes, bears, raccoons, porcupines, chipmunks, moose, and birds.
- ☐ Most animals of the woods are coloured or marked to match the leaves, bark, rocks, or grass where they live.
- ☐ Small forest animals are often frightened by loud noises and people.
- ☐ Some animals, like snakes, may eat only once a week. Other animals, like birds, hunt and eat almost all day long.
- ☐ A wild animal often feeds and rests in its home.
- ☐ We should not throw glass, cans, paper, or other garbage in streams and ponds because this pollution kills woodland animals.
- ☐ We can sometimes see some animals of the woods in a zoo or a park.
- ☐ Woodland animals often found in city parks are squirrels and birds.

> **NOTE:** Include basic understandings listed in the Introduction, p. 369, as appropriate. See Chapters 12 to 15 on the seasons for information on hibernation, migration, and other seasonal habits of forest animals.

Additional Facts the Teacher Should Know

1. When teaching this subject, encourage children to observe and protect animals in their own surroundings. Frogs and toads have not been included as animals to be captured and observed because pollution is decreasing their numbers. Also, bringing the eggs or tadpoles into the classroom further decreases their chances of survival. Animals that have been in captivity for even a short time stand little chance of survival when returned to their natural habitat.
2. Snakes are not included in this chapter because they are difficult to feed, and because it is difficult for the average person to tell harmless snakes from poisonous ones.

3. Trying to catch wild animals is dangerous, as most animals will bite when they feel trapped or threatened, and they may carry rabies.
4. Many television programs feature endangered species. Children may raise questions about pollution and hunting after seeing these programs. This offers an opportunity to ensure that the children understand the problems and to talk about the things we can all do to help save endangered animals. Be aware of family values concerning hunting. For many rural families, hunting is a necessity of life. It is also a part of the cultural heritage of many Native–Canadian families.

Beavers

☐ Beaver (female and male).
☐ Kit (young).
☐ They have a coat of soft, dense, waterproof fur that is dark brown in colour; a long, paddle-shaped tail that is used as a balance on land and as a rudder in the water; and powerful, web-footed hind legs.
☐ Beavers communicate by making crying sounds; they slap their tails on the water to warn of danger.
☐ They eat leaves and bark, and store large amounts of food for the winter.
☐ The average life span is nine to twelve years.

Deer

☐ Doe (female).
☐ Buck (male).
☐ Fawn (young).
☐ Herd (family group).
☐ They have a thick, reddish-brown coat of fur with a white underbelly, and antlers.
☐ Deer are usually silent; however, if frightened, they utter loud, hoarse, high-pitched shrieks and snorts.
☐ They eat leaves, twigs, fruits, grasses, and farm crops in the summer, and nuts, acorns, mosses, lichens, and seeds in the winter.
☐ The average life span is 15 years in nature, 25 years in captivity.

Foxes

☐ Vixen (female).
☐ Fox (male).
☐ Kit (young).
☐ Skulk (family group).
☐ They have a pointed muzzle, large ears, and a long, thick fur coat that varies in colour depending on the breed; they also have a long, bushy tail.
☐ Foxes are generally silent; however, during the mating season a male will respond to a female's shrill calls with a few short barks.
☐ They eat rabbits, small rodents, wild birds, poultry, insects, turtles, snakes, fruits, frogs, and fish.
☐ The average life span is twelve years.

Raccoons

☐ Raccoon (female).
☐ Buck (male).
☐ Cub (young).
☐ They have a pointed muzzle; a black mask; a long, striped, bushy tail; thick, dense, brownish-grey fur tipped with black; and dexterous fingers.
☐ When annoyed, raccoons snarl or growl; otherwise, they have a shrill, whistling night cry.

☐ They eat fruits, nuts, grains, mice, frogs, lizards, fish, birds, eggs, insects, larvae, clams, crayfish, and grasshoppers, and always wash their food before they eat it.
☐ The average life span is eight to thirteen years.

Skunks

☐ Skunk (female and male).
☐ Kitten (young).
☐ They have a thick, black fur coat with a white stripe down the middle of the back to the tip of the tail, sharp teeth, small eyes, and a blunt nose.
☐ Skunks communicate with growls, screeches, purrs, sniffs, coos, and whistles. When they are annoyed, they stamp their front paws — this is a warning that they are about to spray their strong, repulsive scent.
☐ They eat insects, worms, grubs, mice, turtle eggs, rodents, small plants, fruit, and berries.
☐ The average life span is eight to ten years.

Bears

☐ Sow (female).
☐ Boar (male).
☐ Cub (young).
☐ Stock (family group).
☐ The grizzly bear averages a mass of 400 kg to 500 kg.
☐ They have a massive head, a large muzzle, huge paws with long claws, and thick, long, shaggy fur of varying colours depending on the breed and the season.
☐ Black-bear cubs hum and moan, older black bears whine and grunt; grizzly bears cough and roar.
☐ They eat plants, animals, grass, mice, lizards, insects, worms, honey, fish, and larvae.
☐ The average life span is 20 years in nature, 40 years in captivity.

Introducing This Subject to Children

1. Observe a bird, squirrel, toad, or turtle while on a walk or when these animals come to a feeding station.
2. If your centre is in the country, you may see a fox, raccoon, or small deer near a stream in the woods.
3. Occasionally, in a small town or a city, you may see a skunk or smell its characteristic odour after a rain.
4. In winter, point out footprints of animals in the snow.

Vocabulary

forest	fur	claws	cave
woods	hide	footprint	log
stream	hoofs	hibernate	lodge
burrow	odour	pollution	trees
nest	wild	den	rocks
hole			

Include the names, sounds, body parts, and foods of the most common forest animals that you observe.

Learning Centres

Discovery Centre

1. Find issues of *Canadian Geographic, National Geographic, Owl, Chickadee,* and *Equinox* magazines that have features on forest animals. Put paperclips on the relevant pages and place them in the discovery centre so children can look at the pictures of the animals.
2. Display foods that forest animals eat — acorns and other nuts, eggs (hollow), seeds, berries, and fruit (use artificial berries and fruit).
3. Borrow a caged squirrel, a de-scented skunk, a raccoon, a snake, or any other animal for a short visit accompanied by its owner.
4. Take a walk to a park, a pond, a field, or a forest to see what animals live there. Observe them from a respectful distance. Older children can use binoculars or a telescope. Take a paper bag for collecting litter.
5. Bring a pet rabbit to school.

Dramatic Play Centres

Block-building centre

1. Add unbreakable models of forest animals to the centre.
2. Provide small twigs and branches to use in building animal homes or environs.
3. Set out unbreakable plastic trees or bushes.
4. Children can tear or cut abstract shapes of blue construction paper for lakes, ponds, or streams.
5. Provide pieces of green carpet or upholstery fabric for grass.
6. Papier-mâché rocks or crumpled tan or grey construction paper can simulate rocky areas without the dangers presented by real rocks and stones.

   NOTE: Additional suggestions can be found in the following chapters: squirrels — Chapter 15; birds — Chapters 12, 13, and 15; rabbits — Chapter 13.

Other dramatic play centres

Animal puppets can be used by older children with verbal skills. See Chapter 11, p. 269, for instructions for paper-bag puppets.

Art Centre

- 1. Offer green, yellow, black, tan, and brown paints and crayons.
- 2. Provide play dough or potter's clay for modelling animals.
- •• 3. Collages: Provide yarn, paper, geometric cloth or paper shapes, scraps of fur, feathers, and other materials for creating animals.
- •• 4. Collage turtle: Precut turtle shapes for green, brown, or black construction paper. Set out walnut shells, individual egg-carton sections, paints, and glue. Children can

choose the materials they wish to use to make their turtles. The dotted lines on the pattern to the right indicate the position of the shell on the top side. Walnut shells can be cut in half with a sharp knife along the seam line. Save the meats for cooking.

•• 5. Geometric shape arrangements: Set out magnetic, felt, or paper geometric shapes for creating animals.

Learning and Language Materials Centre

Commercially made games and materials

1. *Puzzles:* Puzzles with a variety of forest animals. Make sure some of the puzzles have knobs for younger children.
2. *Small toys for imaginative play:* Durable plastic or wooden animals made of non-toxic materials. Choose models with pieces that are of a good size to fit into children's hands. Try to find models that are similar to animals the children are likely to see in your area.
3. *Dolls and puppets:* Puppets that are models of a variety of forest animals.
4. *Miscellaneous:* Animal dominoes, animal lotto games, and animal card games; bird feeders; children's binoculars.

Teacher-made games and materials

NOTE: For detailed descriptions, see Learning Games in Part 1.

1. *Match-them:* Use mounted forest-animal seals or stamps.
2. *How many?* Use felt animal cutouts flannel-backed pictures of animals, or plastic models of animals.
3. *Sorting and grouping by association:* Group animals by their coverings (fur, fins, feathers), their actions (flies, runs, swims), or their body parts (no legs, two legs, four legs).
■ For some children, sorting and grouping may be challenging. Provide concrete cues for the associations to assist children in the abstract processes of sorting and grouping. For example, if you are asking children to identify animals that swim, provide pictures of children swimming and then have the children act out swimming. Then show a series of pictures of animals in and out of the water. Ask the children to find the animals that can swim. The concrete cues (the pictures and the acting out of human swimming) will help children associate with the abstract idea of animals swimming.
4. Adapt games in Chapters 16, 17, or 19 to forest animals.

Book Centre

••• Abolafia, Yossi. *Fox Tale.* New York: Greenwillow Press, 1991.
••• Allix, Hereward. *The Maladjusted Jungle.* Toronto: Oxford University Press, 1991. (poems)
• Bartoli, J. *In a Meadow, Two Hares Hide.* Chicago: Whitman, 1978.
••• Bauman, H. *Chip Has Many Brothers.* New York: Philomel, 1985.
••• Brinklol, J. *Fireflies.* New York: Macmillan, 1985.
••• Burke, M. *Tales from the Beechy Woods.* Burlington, ON: Hayes, 1983.

•• Burningham, John. *Harquin, the Fox Who Went Down to the Valley.* Don Mills, ON: Academic Press, 1979.

• Caldone, P. *Over in the Meadow.* Englewood Cliffs, NJ: Prentice-Hall, 1986.

••• Cleaver, Elizabeth. *The Enchanted Caribou.* Toronto: Oxford University Press, 1985.

• Crisitini, E. *In the Woods.* New York: Picture Book Studio, 1985.

•••• Dorros, Arthur. *Rain Forest Secrets.* Richmond Hill, ON: Scholastic, 1990.

•• Flack, Marjorie. *Ask Mr. Bear.* New York: Macmillan, 1932.

••• Gise, Joanne. *A Picture Book of Forest Animals.* St. Catharines, ON: Troll Associates, 1990.

•• Hazen, Barbara. *Where Do Bears Sleep?* Reading, MA: Addison-Wesley, 1970.

••• Kassian, O. *Slip the Otter Finds a Home.* Toronto: Greey de Pencier, 1984.

• Keats, Ezra Jack. *Over in the Meadow.* New York: Four Winds Press, 1971.

••• Lane, M. *The Beaver.* New York: Dial Press, 1982.

•• Lemieux, Michèle. *What's That Noise?* Toronto: Kids Can Press, 1989.

••• McCloskey, Robert. *Blueberries for Sal.* New York: Viking Press, 1948.

•••• Murphy, Jim. *The Call of the Wolves.* New York: Scholastic, 1989.

••• Nicoll, Helen. *Meg and Mog.* Markham, ON: Penguin, 1976.

• Obed, E.B., and W. Ritchie. *Little Snowshoe.* St. John's: Breakwater, 1984.

••• Oppenheim, Joanne, and Barbara Reid. *Have You Seen Birds?* Richmond Hill, ON: Scholastic, 1986.

•• Paul, A.W. *Owl at Night.* New York: Putnam, 1985.

••• Potter, Beatrix. *The Tale of Peter Rabbit.* London: Warne, 1972. (see also other books by Potter)

•• Rockwell, Anne, and Harlow Rockwell. *Toad.* Garden City, NY: Doubleday, 1972.

••• Sillers, Patricia, and Karen Patkau. *Ringtail.* Toronto: Oxford University Press, 1987.

••• Spier, P. *The Fox Went Out on a Chilly Night.* Garden City, NY: Doubleday, 1961.

••• Strauss, Susan. *Coyote Stories for Children.* Pickering, ON: Silvio Mattacchione, 1991.

• Tafuri, N. *Rabbit's Morning.* New York: Greenwillow Press, 1985.

• ———. *Have You Seen My Duckling?* New York: Greenwillow Press, 1984.

••• Tejima, Keizaburo. *Fox's Dream.* New York: Sandcastle, 1990.

••• Tresselt, Alvin. *Beaver Pond.* New York: Lothrop, Lee & Shepard, 1970.

•••• Wallace, I. *The Sparrow's Song.* Markham, ON: Penguin, 1986. (Read–Tell)

••• Waterton, B. *A Salmon for Simon.* Toronto: Groundwood, 1990.

•• Wheeler, Bernelda. *I Can't Have Bannock, but the Beaver Has a Dam.* Winnipeg: Pemmican, 1984.

••• Yolen, Jane. *Owl Moon.* New York: Putnam, 1987.

••• Young, Ed. *Lon Po Po: A Red-Riding Hood Story from China.* New York: Putnam, 1989.

Planning for Group Time

NOTE: All music, fingerplays, poems, stories, and games listed here may also be used at other times during the session as appropriate.

Music

Songs

Please see "All the Little Ducklings" at the end of this chapter.

From *The Baby Beluga Book*, Raffi
"Over in the Meadow," p. 28

From *More Piggyback Songs*, Warren
"Crawl, Crawl Little Snake," p. 74
"Little Tadpole," p. 75
"Birds Fly High," p. 75

From *Singing Bee*, Hart
"Over in the Meadow," p. 44
"El Coquito," p. 136

From *A Treasury of Songs for Young Children*, Glazer
"The Frog Went a Courtin'," p. 92

From *Tunes for Tots*, Warner and Berry
"The Owl," p. 78
"Down in the Meadow," p. 83
"Guess the Animal (Turtle)," p. 86
"The Birds," p. 88

Rhythms and Singing Games

Choose appropriate piano or recorded music for movements of animals, such as bunnies, squirrels, bears, foxes, mice, and birds. Use scarves for wings and tails. Sew a loop of elastic to a small chiffon square; it can be worn on the wrist or fastened to a strap or belt.

Records and Cassettes

Sandy Tobias Oppenheim. *If Snowflakes Fell in Flavours.* (Berandol Records)
"Hey Little Bird" (good for singing to children)

Fred Penner. *Special Delivery.* (Troubadour Records)
"The Fox"

Raffi. *Baby Beluga.* (Troubadour Records)
"Over in the Meadow"
————. *The Corner Grocery Store.* (Troubadour Records)
"Les Loups-Garous"
"Y un Rat"

Fingerplays and Poems

From *Don't Eat Spiders*, Heidbreder
"A Big Bare Bear," p. 5
"How to Catch a Bird," p. 11
"Bird's Nest," p. 25

From *Finger Rhymes*, Brown
"There Was a Little Turtle," p. 4
"The Baby Mice," p. 14
"Five Little Mice," p. 16
"Two Blackbirds," p. 19
"The Squirrel," p. 25

From *Hand Rhymes*, Brown
"Little Bunny," p. 21

From *Let's Do Fingerplays,* Grayson
"Animal Antics," pp. 30–37
"My Rabbit," p. 34
"This Little Rabbit," p. 35
"Chickadees," p. 60
"Five Little Froggies," p. 63
"Five Little Squirrels," p. 63
"Telegraph Poles," p. 66
"Two Little Blackbirds," p. 73
"Little Mousie," p. 80

From *Oranges and Lemons,* King and Beck
"Five Little Speckled Frogs," p. 32
"Goldilocks and the Three Bears," p. 40

From *Read Aloud Rhymes for the Very Young,* Prelutsky and Brown
"The Snail and the Mouse," p. 4
"A Frog and a Flea," p. 4
"The Little Turtle," p. 20
"A Big Turtle," p. 20
"The Toad," p. 21
"The Frog on the Log," p. 21
"Humming Birds," p. 23
"Singing in the Spring," p. 23
"The Swallow," p. 23
"Squirrel in the Rain," p. 60

From *Round and Round the Garden,* Williams
"Foxy's Hole," p. 9
"Two Little Dicky Birds," p. 31
"The Little Bird," p. 47

....

THE TURTLE

Anonymous

The turtle crawls on the ground and makes a rustling sound.
He carries his house wherever he goes,
And when he is scared, he pulls in his nose and covers his toes!

....

FIVE LITTLE TURTLES

by Bonnie Flemming

One little turtle all alone and new,
Soon it finds another and then there are two.
Two little turtles crawl down to the sea,
Soon they find another and then there are three.
Three little turtles crawl along the shore,
Soon they find another and then there are four.
Four little turtles go for a dive,
Along swims another and then there are five!

NOTE: Use felt or flannelboard turtles.

HERE IS A BUNNY

Here is a bunny with **ears** so funny. (*bend two fingers over thumb*)
And here is a **hole** in the ground. (*make hole by putting left hand on hip*)
When a noise he hears, he pricks up his **ears** (*hold "ears" straight*)
And **hops** into his hole so round. (*hop bunny over and pop in hole*)

Stories

(To read, read–tell, or tell. See Book Centre for a complete list.)
Most of the stories written on this subject are fanciful. Try to choose stories with interesting illustrations and plausible characters. Wheeler's *I Can't Have Bannock, but the Beaver Has a Dam* is an interesting and untraditional choice.

Games

(See Learning Games in Part 1 and Teacher-Made Games and Materials earlier in this chapter for directions.)

1. *Look and see:* Use flannelboard cutouts of forest animals.
2. *Alike, different, and the same:* Use materials prepared for *Match-them.*
3. *Reach and feel:* Use fur, feather, acorn, twig, and grass.

Routine Times

1. At snack or meal times, offer nuts, peanuts in the shell (for children over four only), sunflower seeds, toast squares, carrot or celery sticks, lettuce or cabbage leaves, raisins, apples, bananas, berries, and animal crackers.
2. At rest time, encourage children to curl up like sleeping animals.

Large Muscle Activities

1. Caves: Packing boxes or barrels placed on their sides can be used by children to pretend to be animals in caves.
2. Children can use fabric tunnels as animal burrows.
3. Beaver dams: Show pictures of beaver dams or the film *The Beaver Family* (see Films and Videos). Suggest that children build a beaver dam in the sandbox. Have them think about what they need to build a beaver home. If you have a park nearby, go hunting for sticks and twigs. Use a garden hose set at a slow flow to create a running river in the sandbox. The children may need help in figuring out the "engineering" of the dam; ask them what they think they need to stop the water.
4. Nests: Allow children to use twigs and small branches in the sandbox to build other animal homes.
5. Gopher or rabbit holes: turn shallow cardboard boxes upside down and cut a hole in the top of each one. Make up games for using these on rainy days.
6. Nuts: Collect acorns or other nuts that have fallen from trees, or wad brown tissue paper for children to use when pretending to be squirrels.
7. Forest animal models: Place models in or near the sandbox to help children develop creative play involving forest animals.
8. *Follow the leader:* Suggest that children imitate the ways various animals move or walk.

Extended Experiences

1. Take a trip to a natural history museum.
2. Take a trip to a zoo or a park that has forest animals.
3. Take a trip to an aquarium or marina if your group is interested in fish.
4. Take a trip to see a beaver dam. Avoid going after a heavy rain, as the dam may be damaged. A naturalist or taxidermist may be able to advise you on where to find one, or where to find squirrels, raccoons, and foxes.
5. Explore a shallow stream or wooded area if one is nearby.
6. Woodland party or picnic: Make name tags using forest animal stickers. Have children bring stuffed animals or puppets, if they wish. Serve foods listed in Routine Times, number 1.
7. Invite a provincial or national parks staff member or a forester to tell children how they can help forest animals; two or three suggestions are best. Perhaps the visitor could share a poster on preventing forest fires.

 # Teacher Resources
••••••••••••••••••••••••••••••••

Pictures and Displays

☐ Look for forest animal pictures in forest product companies' magazine advertisements.
☐ Display plastic animal models in a forest scene. Use as a centrepiece for a woodland party.
☐ Display stuffed forest animals children share, such as teddy bears, rabbits, skunks, squirrels, chipmunks, and deer.
☐ Obtain wildlife stamps from the Canadian Wildlife Federation.

Books and Periodicals

Canadian Geographic magazine.
Chickadee magazine.
Chinery, Michael, ed. *Dictionary of Animals.* New York: Arco, 1984.
Durrell, Gerald. *The Stationary Ark.* London: Collins, 1976.
Equinox magazine.
Facklam, Marhery. *Do Not Disturb: The Mysteries of Animal Hibernation and Sleep.* Boston: Little, Brown, 1989.
Forey, Pamela. *An Instant Field Guide to Mammals.* New York: Crown, 1986.
Godfrey, E.W. *The Birds of Canada.* Ottawa: Queen's Printer, 1966.
Grey Owl. *The Adventures of Sajo and the Beaver People.* Toronto: Macmillan, 1973.
Hall, Tom W., and David Black. *The Wildlife of Canada.* Guildford, UK: Bramley, 1987. (excellent photographs)
Hendrikson, Robert. *Animal Crackers.* Markham, ON: Penguin, 1983.
The Larousse Encyclopedia of Animal Life. London: Hamlyn, 1967.
National Geographic magazine.
Owl magazine.
Ranger Rick magazine.
Reader's Digest. *North American Wildlife.* Pleasantville, NY: Reader's Digest, 1982.
Seton, E.T. *Wild Animals I Have Known.* Ottawa: University of Ottawa Press, 1977.

Settel, Joanne, and Nancy Baggett. *Why Do Cats' Eyes Glow in the Dark? And Other Questions Kids Ask about Animals.* New York: Ivy, 1990.

Seuling, Barbara. *Elephants Can't Jump and Other Freaky Facts about Animals.* New York: Ivy, 1988.

Tremain, Ruthven. *The Animal's Who's Who.* New York: Scribner, 1982.

Whitaker, Muriel, ed. *Great Canadian Animal Stories.* Edmonton: Hurtig, 1978.

Your Big Backyard magazine.

Films and Videos

NOTE: Check with your distributor about public performance rights.

Adventures. National Film Board, 1968.

The Adventures of Willie the Skunk. Contemporary Films (released in Canada by McGraw-Hill), 1966.

A Badger's Bad Day. Grover-Jennings Productions (released in Canada by the National Film Board), 1959.

Bambi. Walt Disney Home Video (based on the 1942 original).

A Bear Called Paddington. FilmFair Inc. (released in Canada by International Tele-Film), 1975.

The Beaver Family. Encyclopedia Britannica Films (released in Canada by Visual Education Centre), 1982.

Blueberries for Sal. Weston Woods.

Corduroy. Weston Woods.

Fire! Manitoba Education and Training Instructional Resources Library, 1975.

Frederick. Lionni & Gianini Productions (released in Canada by International Tele-Film), 1970.

The Jungle Book. Walt Disney Home Video, 1990.

Community Resources and Organizations

- [ ] Parks and wildlife director or forester.
- [ ] Department of biology or zoology at a university.
- [ ] Taxidermist (to borrow specimens).
- [ ] Museum curator.
- [ ] City or provincial park director.
- [ ] Zoo keeper.

Government Agencies

- [ ] Canadian Wildlife Service.
- [ ] World Wildlife Fund.
- [ ] Environment Canada.
- [ ] Federal, provincial, or territorial ministries of the environment, forestry, or natural resources.

All the Little Ducklings

Donna Wood

LINE 1: Children all squat and waddle forward like ducks.
LINE 2: Follow words — heads down and tails up.

19 Zoo Animals

Basic Understandings
(concepts children can grasp from this subject)

☐ A zoo is a place where people can safely see wild animals in captivity.

☐ At a zoo, animals from all over the world are kept in cages, in fenced-off areas, or in special houses that are like their former homes (caves, hillsides, woods, or waterways).

☐ At zoos, certain families of animals may be grouped near one another.
   1. Cats (tigers, panthers, lions, cheetahs, leopards).
   2. Monkeys and apes (gorillas, orangutans, chimpanzees, spider monkeys).
   3. Bears (black, brown, grizzly, polar, panda).
   4. Birds.
   5. Reptiles and snakes.
   6. Fish.

☐ Animals found in most zoos are giraffes, elephants, lions, tigers, monkeys, apes, zebras, bears, and hippopotami.

☐ Other animals sometimes included in zoos are alligators, crocodiles, rhinoceroses, camels, goats, deer, seals, foxes, wolves, peacocks, ostriches, panthers, leopards, and tortoises.

☐ It is necessary to cage wild animals because most of them are not safe to play with. Also, a cage offers protection for the animals and keeps them from straying.

☐ Tame animals are usually safe to play with, except when they are eating or sleeping. Wild animals are *not* safe to play with except by owners who have tamed and trained them.

☐ It is not safe to feed zoo animals, as they may bite and seriously injure children and adults.

☐ We pay money to go into some zoos. This money helps to pay for the feeding, care, and purchase of the animals.

☐ Many people work in a zoo to keep the animals healthy, safe, fed, and exercised. Other people sell tickets, food, and rides, or care for the walks, roads, plants, and flowers.

☐ Some zoos have a petting or children's zoo where children can pet, hold, feed, or ride the animals.

411

NOTE: Include basic understandings listed in the Introduction, p. 369, as appropriate.

Additional Facts the Teacher Should Know

NOTE: Typical zoo animals in Canada may be animals that children in another country see daily. For example, an Indian child may see elephants on a daily basis. If you have children in your group who have recently moved to Canada, find out the animals that are familiar to them. These children will then be a resource when you are talking about some Canadian zoo animals.

Elephants
- Cow (female).
- Bull (male).
- Calf (young).
- Herd (family group).
- They have wrinkled grey skin; long, powerful trunks; two ivory tusks; a thin tail with coarse hairs at the tip; and huge, flapping ears.
- Elephants roar when they're enraged, trumpet when they're warning intruders, purr or squeal when content, and thump the ground with their trunks when suspicious.
- They eat leaves, roots, fruit, bark, tubers, twigs, grasses, and bamboo shoots. In captivity, an elephant eats 20 to 90 kg of hay per day as well as 300 kg of fresh greens, and drinks 135 to 230 L of water.
- The average life span is 50 to 60 years (maximum 70).

Giraffes
- Cow (female).
- Bull (male).
- Calf (young).
- Corps or herd (family group).
- They have buff-coloured coats with patterns of various shades of brown, long necks, horns, and long legs.
- Giraffes communicate by making gurgling whimpers, cries, moos, or snores; the bull's mating call is a snorting cough.
- They eat shoots of acacia and mimosa, and favour legumes.
- The average life span is 20 years in nature, 28 years in captivity.

Lions
- Lioness (female).
- Lion (male).
- Cub (young).
- Pride (family group).
- They have tawny yellow-brown fur; powerful front legs; sharp, retractable claws; excellent hearing and sight; and the males have a long mane.
- Lions roar frequently.
- They eat meat, which they hunt singly or in groups.
- The average life span is 20 to 25 years in nature, and up to 30 years in captivity.

Monkeys
- Monkey (female, male, young).
- Troop or colony (family group).

☐ They have dark-brown, grey, or red fur coats with black faces and underparts of grey or buff; well-developed colour vision; slender bodies; small heads; and long limbs.
☐ Monkeys communicate with chatters, shrieks, and howls.
☐ They eat plants, fruits, shoots, leaves, eggs, insects, small animals, and sometimes nuts, depending on the breed.
☐ The average life span is 25 to 30 years in captivity.

Zebras

☐ Mare (female).
☐ Stallion (male).
☐ Foal (young).
☐ Herd (family group).
☐ They have black-and-white striped hides, black noses, and short, bushy manes.
☐ Zebras' honking and barking is loud and shrill.
☐ They eat grasses and herbs in the wild, and carrots, potatoes, oats, and apples in captivity.
☐ The average life span is 20 to 30 years in captivity.

Tigers

☐ Tigress (female).
☐ Tiger (male).
☐ Cub (young).
☐ Ambush (family group).
☐ They have coarse, short-haired coats that are tawny yellow with black vertical stripes, large paws, and large heads.
☐ Tigers roar; they also make a strange, bell-like noise called "titting" when hunting.
☐ They eat meat — up to 4.5 kg per day in captivity.
☐ The average life span is 12 to 19 years in captivity.

Introducing This Subject to Children

1. Set model zoo animals on shelves or on a table.
2. Read or tell a story about a zoo or zoo animals.
3. Show pictures of zoo animals in magazines or newspapers.
4. Make a bulletin-board display of zoo animals.

Vocabulary

wild	watch	claws	fence
tame	circus	hoofs	arena
keeper	zoo	fur	striped
tricks	tour	mane	spotted
cage	gate	cave	protect
sharp	pool	tank	veterinarian

Include sounds, body parts, and foods of zoo animals observed by your group.

Learning Centres

Discovery Centre

1. Display some nonperishable models of foods that wild animals not in captivity eat: hay, grass, leaves, bark, and bananas.
2. Show a film, filmstrip, or video about zoo animals (see Films and Videos later in this chapter).

Dramatic Play Centres

Home-living centre

1. Post pictures that suggest a family going to the zoo. Ensure that the families pictured reflect the families who use your program, for example, single-parent families, Native-Canadian families, etc.
2. Set out souvenir pennants, made in the art centre, to carry to the zoo.
3. Provide stuffed zoo animal toys, such as teddy bears, tigers, and pandas.

Block-building centre

1. Set out unbreakable models of zoo animals.
2. Place hay or shredded paper in a box for children to feed or bed down animals.
3. Hang pictures of animals in a zoo. These may suggest building enclosures for wild animals with hollow or unit blocks.

Other dramatic play centres

Set up a zoo materials centre using some of the following suggestions:
1. Use cartons as cages or caves for children to crawl inside. Cut barred windows.
2. Tour train: Set up rows of chairs to make a train. Post large pictures of zoo animals or outdoor scenes for passengers to see. Sell tickets. (See Chapter 23, p. 472, for more ideas.)
3. Laminate pictures of raw meat for pretend feeding of zoo animals.
4. Have small buckets available for feeding and watering the animals.
5. Set out work gloves and a large ring with keys for opening cages (a toy sheriff's lock and keys work well).
6. Allow children to use short lengths of rubber hose for washing elephants and cages.
7. Souvenir stand: Sell pennants made in the art centre, or balloons.
8. Popcorn stand: Sell bags of popcorn for a snack. Provide a cash register, play money, a vendor's hat and an apron (see Dramatic Play Props in Part 1).

Art Centre

• 1. Make pennants for zoo visitors. Provide large paper triangles for children to staple to cardboard handles and decorate as they wish.
• 2. Make place cards with zoo animal stickers to use at a zoo party. Children can use magic markers to add stripes, polka dots, and their names, if they can.
•• 3. Encourage children to draw or paint a picture of their favourite zoo animal.
••• 4. Make caged animal pictures: Children cut out and paste animal pictures on a plain piece of paper, and then cut strips to glue on as bars. Offer precut pictures to the youngest children. Old wallpaper books and discarded picture books are good sources of pictures.

- 5. Collages: Provide spotted, striped, and fur fabric scraps, leather scraps, shredded papers, yarn, rope, and cotton balls.
- 6. Yarn collages: Provide yarn of various sizes and colours.
••• 7. Box sculpture: Have children make zoo animals from small boxes. Fasten boxes together with masking tape. Supply rope or yarn for tails, buttons for eyes, scrap leather or felt for tongues.

Other art projects to try

1. Puppets:
- a. Stick: see Chapter 17, p. 393.
••• b. Sock: Glue on bits of felt for eyes, ears, manes, and tails using white glue.
•• c. Paper-bag: See illustration, p. 269.
••• 2. Zoo cages: Paint shoeboxes. Paste, glue, or draw a zoo animal picture on the inside bottom of each box. Then glue construction-paper strips over the top of the box, or thread pipecleaners through holes punched along two opposite edges. Put straw or shredded paper in the bottom of the cage and glue bottle caps for feeding dishes to the floor of the cage. Plastic discs or bottle caps can be added to cages as wheels.
••• 3. Decorate halved wooden barrels that are sturdy enough to climb and stand on. These can be used in dramatic play areas as platforms when children are imitating wild animals performing in a circus.

Learning and Language Materials Centre

Commercially made games and materials

1. *Puzzles:* Puzzles with a variety of zoo animals. Be sure some of the puzzles have knobs for younger children.
2. *Small toys for imaginative play:* Durable plastic or wooden animals made of non-toxic materials. Choose models with pieces that are of a good size to fit into children's hands. Try to find models of animals that are similar to animals the children are likely to see in your area.
3. *Dolls and puppets:* Puppets and stuffed animals that are models of a variety of zoo animals.
4. *Miscellaneous:* Animal dominoes, simple board and matching games with animals.

Teacher-made games and materials

NOTE: For detailed descriptions, see Learning Games in Part 1.

1. *Match-them:* Match zoo animal models with pictures of the animals. Large animal gummed seals may be glued to the backs of old playing cards for this purpose.
2. *Alike, different, and the same:* Name animals that have similar characteristics, such as claws, teeth, tails, and fur. Have children separate model animals into groupings of zoo, pet, and farm animals. Compare animals by size, colour, and family to designate which are alike and which are different.
3. *Sorting and grouping by association:* Group animals by outer covering (fur, feathers, or fins) or by action (swims, flies, crawls, walks) using models or pictures.
■ See Chapter 18, p. 403, for a modification of this activity for children who need more support in sorting and classifying.
4. a. *Guess the animal 1:* Cover 7.5 cm x 12.5 cm file cards with synthetic fur and feathers (available at a craft store). Ask children to close their eyes, and have them guess the animals that the cards represent. Ask them to tell the group the reasons for their choices.

■ This is an excellent activity for children who have visual or auditory problems, and children who have problems in classifying. All children benefit from this activity; so it is well-suited to programs that integrate children with special needs.

b. *Guess the animal 2:* Find a recording of animal sounds. Have children cover and close their eyes and guess the animals that the sounds represent (closing eyes reduces distractions and adds a sense of mystery to the game, but is not a necessity). Ask children to tell the group the reasons for their choices.

■ This is an excellent activity for children who have visual problems and children who have problems in classifying. All children benefit from this activity, so it is well-suited to programs that integrate children with special needs.

Book Centre

•••• Blanchet, M. Wylie. *A Whale Named Henry.* Madeira Park, BC: Harbour, 1983. (Read–Tell)

••• Bottner, Barbara. *Zoo Song.* New York: Scholastic, 1987.

••• Bowen, E. *The Good Tiger.* New York: Knopf, 1965.

•• Browne, A. *Gorilla.* New York: Knopf, 1985.

• Campbell, R. *Dear Zoo.* New York: Macmillan, 1984.

•• Cantiene, B. *Little Elephant and Big Mouse.* New York: Picture Book Studio, 1981.

•• Carle, E. *1, 2, 3 to the Zoo.* New York: World, 1968.

•• Freeman, Don. *The Seal and the Slick.* New York: Viking Press, 1974.

• ———. *Dandelion.* New York: Viking Press, 1964. (filmstrip and record also available)

•• Gantschev, I. *Journey of the Storks.* New York: Picture Book Studio, 1983.

• Hellen, Nancy. *A Visit to the Zoo.* St. Catharines, ON: Vanwell, 1991.

••• Himmelman, John. *Ibis: A True Whale Story.* Richmond Hill, ON: Scholastic, 1990.

• Hoban, Tana. *A Children's Zoo.* New York: Greenwillow Press, 1985.

••• Isenberg, B., and S. Wolf. *The Adventures of Running Bear.* Boston: Houghton Mifflin, 1982.

••• Johnson, Crockett. *Ellen's Lion: Twelve Stories.* Markham, ON: Fitzhenry & Whiteside, 1984. (read)

••• Kipling, Rudyard. *The Elephant's Child.* St. John's: Breakwater Press, 1990.

••• Lee, Dennis. *Lizzy's Lion.* Don Mills, ON: Stoddart, 1984.

••• Lester, Helen. *Tacky the Penguin.* Boston: Houghton Mifflin, 1990.

••• Lewis, R.B. *Aunt Armadillo.* Willowdale, ON: Annick Press, 1985.

••• Mahy, M. *The Boy Who Was Followed Home.* New York: Dial Press, 1986.

••• Morgan, A. *Barnaby and Mr. Ling.* Willowdale, ON: Annick Press, 1984.

•• Munsil, Janet. *Zach at the Zoo.* Willowdale, ON: Annick Press, 1984.

••• Ormerod, Jan. *When We Went to the Zoo.* New York: Lothrop, Lee & Shepard, 1991.

•• Paré, Roger. *Circus Days.* Willowdale, ON: Annick Press, 1988.

•••• Patterson, Dr. Francine. *Koko's Story.* New York: Scholastic, 1987.

••• Peet, B. *Pamela Camel.* Boston: Houghton Mifflin, 1984.

• Pienkowski, Jan. *Zoo.* London: Heinemann, 1985.

• Rajankovsky, Feodor. *Animals in the Zoo.* New York: Knopf, 1962.

••• Rice, E. *Sam Who Never Forgets.* New York: Greenwillow Press, 1977.

•• Schwartz, Roslyn. *Rose and Dorothy.* Toronto: Kids Can Press, 1990.

••• Seuss, Dr. *If I Ran the Zoo.* New York: Random House, 1950.

•• Slobodkina, Esphry. *Caps for Sale.* Reading, MA: Addison-Wesley, 1957.

••• Wildsmith, Brian. *Python's Party.* Toronto: Oxford University Press, 1991.

Planning for Group Time

NOTE: All music, fingerplays, poems, stories, and games listed here may be used at other times during the session as appropriate.

Music

Songs

Please see "One Elephant, Deux Éléphants" at the end of this chapter.

From *The Baby Beluga Book*, Raffi
"Baby Beluga," p. 5
"Joshua Giraffe," p. 41

From *Elephant Jam*, Sharon, Lois, and Bram
"Elephant and Giraffe: A Game," p. 12
"Elephant Rhyme," p. 42
"Five Little Monkeys," p. 48
"Three Little Monkeys," p. 49
"Alison's Camel," p. 66
"Monte sur un Éléphant," p. 95

From *More Piggyback Songs*, Warren
"I Know a Bear," p. 79

From *Singing Bee*, Hart
"Eletelephony," p. 124

From *Tunes for Tots*, Warner and Berry
"The Monkey," p. 82
"Giraffe," p. 84
"Camel," p. 85
"Penguin," p. 87

Rhythms and Singing Games

1. From your own rhythm recordings: Select appropriate music for elephants, bears, monkeys, etc., and have children act out the animals' movements in time to the music.
2. From your own favourite music book: Choose appropriate music for a giraffe stretching, a kangaroo hopping, and so on, and have children pretend to be these animals.
3. Adapt "This is the Way We Wash Our Clothes" to: This is the way the elephant walks, the lion stalks, the monkey climbs, and so on.

Records and Cassettes

Anne Murray. *There's a Hippo in My Tub*. (Capitol Records)
"There's a Hippo in My Tub"
"Animal Crackers"

Raffi. *Baby Beluga*. (Troubadour Records)
"Baby Beluga"
"Joshua Giraffe"

Sharon, Lois, and Bram. *Elephant Show Record.* (Elephant Records)
"One Elephant Went Out to Play"

———. *Smorgasbord.* (Elephant Records)
"Three Little Monkeys

Fingerplays and Poems

From *Don't Eat Spiders*, Heidbreder
"Hippopotamus," p. 6
"Ellie the Elephant," p. 21

From *Hand Rhymes*, Brown
"Two Little Monkeys," p. 9

From *Read Aloud Rhymes for the Very Young*, Prelutsky and Brown
"The Elephant Carries a Great Big Trunk," p. 10
"Holding Hands," p. 11
"Wild Beasts," p. 16
"I Can Be a Tiger," p. 17
"When You Talk to a Monkey," p. 22
"Before the Monkey's Cage," p. 22
"Way Down South," p. 46
"Giraffes Don't Huff," p. 58

From *Round and Round the Garden*, Williams
"The Ostrich," p. 13

TWO LITTLE MONKEYS

Two little monkeys, jumping on the bed, **jump, jump, jump.** (*use two index fingers making jumping motion*)
One fell off and bumped his head. (*one index finger falls, other hand is placed on head*)
We took him to the doctor, and the doctor said: (*walk index fingers to doctor*)
That's what you get, for jumping on the bed. (*shake one index finger, pointing at group*)

Stories

(To read, read–tell, or tell. See Book Centre for a complete list.)
Use stories about zoo animals in their natural habitat for this subject, such as Gantschev's *Journey of the Storks.*

Games

(See Learning Games in Part 1 and Teacher-Made Games and Materials earlier in this chapter for directions.)

1. *Guess who?* A child who is chosen to be "it" makes a zoo animal sound. The other children guess what the animal is.
2. *Reach and feel:* Use model zoo animals in a bag.
3. *Who am I?* Describe a zoo animal.
4. *Which?* Compare sizes of model zoo animals or pictures of animals, and ask "Which is larger?" For more accurate comparison, select models and pictures that are to scale.
5. *Look and see:* Use model zoo animals, pictures of animals, or flannelboard cutouts.

This bulletin board was prepared by the teachers for the children's parents. It keeps parents informed about activities and provides a reminder of a successful school trip.

Routine Times

At snack or meal time:
1. Have a zoo party with centrepieces of stuffed zoo animal toys.
2. Eat animal crackers.
3. Let older children "sell" real popcorn at the zoo as a snack.

> ▼ CAUTION: Encourage children to chew popcorn carefully and wash it down with a drink of water.

4. Popsicles: Freeze juice in ice-cube trays with coffee stir sticks inserted as handles. Children can "buy" these as treats.

Large Muscle Activities

1. Provide large cartons to make zoo train cars.
2. Encourage "monkeys" to do tricks on climbing gyms using the monkey grip for safety (thumbs under, fingers over the bar).
3. Play *May I?* — children may take three elephant steps, two lion leaps, three alligator glides, one kangaroo hop, and so on.
4. Play *Teddy bear:* "Teddy bear, teddy bear turn around."
5. Pantomime a walk through a zoo: Children choose an animal to pantomime. Cages can be backs of chairs that children crouch behind. The piano can provide magnificent sound effects to accompany the children's pantomimes, or use recorded sound effects.

Extended Experiences

1. Plan a trip to a:
   a. Zoo or circus.
   b. Natural history museum.
   c. Petting farm.

Teacher Resources

Pictures and Displays

☐ Display a group of stuffed toy zoo animals.
☐ Display pictures of a circus.

Books and Periodicals

Canadian Geographic magazine.
Chickadee magazine.
Chinery, Michael, ed. *Dictionary of Animals.* New York: Arco, 1984.
Durrell, Gerald. *The Stationary Ark.* London: Collins, 1976.
Equinox magazine.
Hendrikson, Robert. *Animal Crackers.* Markham, ON: Penguin, 1983.
The Larousse Encyclopedia of Animal Life, London: Hamlyn, 1967.
Metropolitan Toronto Zoo. *ZooBook* series. Toronto: D.C. Heath, various dates. (sixteen-page booklets of information and photographs concerning various species found at the Metro Zoo)
National Geographic magazine.
Nayman, Jacqueline. *Atlas of Wildlife.* London: Heinemann, 1972.
Owl magazine.
Page, Jake. *Zoo: The Modern Ark.* Toronto: Key Porter, 1990.
Seton, E.T. *Wild Animals I Have Known.* Ottawa: University of Ottawa Press, 1977.
Settel, Joanne, and Nancy Baggett. *Why do Cats' Eyes Glow in the Dark? And Other Questions Kids Ask about Animals.* New York: Ivy, 1990.
Seuling, Barbara. *Elephants Can't Jump and Other Freaky Facts about Animals.* New York: Ivy, 1988.
Tremain, Ruthven. *The Animal's Who's Who.* New York: Scribner, 1982.

Films and Videos

NOTE: Check with your distributor about public performance rights.

About Zoos. National Geographic (released in Canada by Visual Education Centre), 1971.
Andy and the Lion. Weston Woods.
Balthazar the Lion. Desta Film Studio for Animation, Berlin (released in Canada by International Tele-Film), 1973.
Caps for Sale. Weston Woods.
A Day at the Calgary Zoo. National Film Board, 1965.
Dumbo. Walt Disney Home Video (based on the 1941 original).

How the Elephant Got His Trunk. Learning Corporation of America (released in Canada by Marlin Motion Pictures), 1971.

Sharon, Lois, and Bram at the Zoo. Golden Book Video, 1985.

Tillie, the Unhappy Hippopotamus. Learning Corporation of America (released in Canada by Marlin Motion Pictures), 1979.

The Zoo. King Screen Productions (released in Canada by Holt, Rinehart & Winston), 1970.

Community Resources and Organizations

☐ Natural history museum curator.

☐ Zoo keeper or zoo personnel.

☐ Instructors of zoology at a nearby university.

One Elephant, Deux Éléphants

Singing game

Sharon, Lois, and Bram

2. Deux éléphants allaient jouer
   Sur une toile d'araignée.
   Ils s'amusaient tellement bien
   Qu'ils appelaient à un autre, viens!

3. Three elephants went out to play
   Upon a spider's web one day.
   They had such enormous fun
   That they called for another elephant
      to come.

4. Quatre éléphants allaient jouer
   Sur une toile d'araignée.
   Ils s'amusaient tellement bien
   Qu'ils appelaient à un autre, viens!

5. All the elephants were out at play
   Upon a spider's web one day.
   They had such enormous fun
   But there were no more elephants left
      to come.

Choose one person to be the first elephant, with the rest of the "herd" sitting on the floor. With one arm extended forward to make the trunk and the other extended back for the tail, the first elephant walks around the herd while the first verse is sung. At the end of the verse, elephant Number 1 selects a second elephant to join him or her by linking his trunk to Number 1's tail. Both walk around as the second verse is sung. The song and actions continue until there are no more elephants left to come. With a large group, add more than one elephant at a time.

20 Insects and Spiders

Basic Understandings

(concepts children can grasp from this subject)

☐ There are many kinds of insects (over half a million).

☐ Insects are found in nearly all parts of the world. Some even live in ice and snow.

☐ Insects differ in many ways — size, shape, colour, kinds of eyes and mouths, and number of wings, as well as the food they eat.

☐ They have six legs (three pairs) and, if winged, four wings (two pairs).

☐ Bees, wasps, butterflies, moths, flies, grasshoppers, ants, dragonflies, ladybugs, mosquitoes, beetles, crickets, bugs, and fireflies are insects we often see.

☐ A spider is not an insect. It is an arachnid.

☐ Spiders have eight legs (four pair) and no wings.

☐ Most spiders spin webs for their homes, for their young, or to help catch insects for food.

☐ Insects and spiders live all around us in the grass, in the trees, on the flowers, and in the earth.

☐ Some insects (bees, ants, termites, and certain wasps) live in colonies.

☐ All insects and spiders come from eggs.

☐ When some insect babies hatch out of their eggs, they are called larvae (caterpillars in the case of butterflies). Others, like grasshoppers, look like grown-up insects when they hatch; only smaller.

☐ Young spiders are called spiderlings.

☐ Some insects and spiders are beautifully coloured (morpha butterfly, golden garden spider, harlequin cabbage bug).

☐ Some insects spread disease.

☐ Insects sometimes eat our food while it is growing in fields and gardens. Farmers and gardeners do not like this.

☐ Some insects help us by making honey (bees) and pollinating fruits and flowers.

☐ Spiders help us by eating insect pests.

☐ Birds, snakes, frogs, and toads eat great numbers of insects.

NOTE: Include basic understandings listed in the Introduction, p. 369, as appropriate.

Additional Facts the Teacher Should Know

Insects

1. There are more kinds of insects than any other kind of animal. Insects are invertebrates — they have no backbone. They have a segmented body, jointed legs, and an external skeleton (exoskeleton). Insects outgrow their exoskeletons — they shed the one that is too small and grow a new, larger one. An insect's body is divided into three parts (head, thorax, and abdomen), and the adults usually have two pairs of wings. Some insects are harmful — they may eat crops or spread disease. Many insects are helpful — they help pollinate fruits and flowers. Insects are food for birds, frogs, toads, snakes, and some large insects (dragonflies and praying mantises). They provide us with many products, including honey and medicinal substances.

2. Insects have two sets of jaws, but they do not move as ours do. They grind or move sideways. Some insects use their mouths for chewing and others for piercing and sucking. Some insects use their legs for more than walking — they also use them for swimming, jumping, or digging. Some have forelegs that are adapted for grasping and holding prey. Others have legs with hairs or suction discs to help them walk on water. Other special leg structures are: combs for cleaning antennae or eyes; hearing organs and other special sensory structures, such as taste, smell, and chemical receptors; noisemaking organs; and silk glands.

3. Insects breathe, although they require very little oxygen. They absorb oxygen through the body or through special openings for breathing. They can also get oxygen from their food.

4. An insect's blood can be colourless, pale yellow, green, or red, depending on what it has eaten. One part of a tube that carries its blood pulsates and is called the heart. Insects have a central nervous system and a primitive kind of brain. They are more sensitive to touch than people are. They have touch receptors all over their bodies, as well as two feelers. Insects can also hear — some can hear sounds that humans cannot. They can taste. Insects have a keen sense of smell and use it to recognize other insects of their own kind, to find their way, to find a mate, and to locate food. Most insects have two kinds of eyes and in some ways can see better than humans. They mate to reproduce, and their reproductive organs are named similarly to humans: testes, ovaries, vagina.

5. Insects do not have voices, but they do make sounds with other parts of their bodies. Some tap their heads against the sides of their burrows. Others hum or buzz by vibrating their wings or their thorax, or they squeak by forcing air out through their breathing holes. Some crickets and grasshoppers rub a "scraper" on one wing cover across a "file" on another wing cover.

6. Insects come from eggs, many of which can be seen with the human eye. Baby insects are usually called larvae. Most insects go through a pupal stage. The pupa of a butterfly is called a chrysalis because it is studded with bright, metallic spots. The pupae of many species are enclosed in a cocoon that the larvae make before they enter this stage. Most cocoons are made of silk, often with bits of leaves, wood, earth, or excrement worked into them. Some are waterproof and airtight, but others have valves, or openings, with lids at one end to help the adult emerge. Cocoons may be found in soil, under tree bark, beneath stones, rolled up in leaves, hanging from twigs, or tucked into crevices. When an insect struggles free of the cocoon, it may have to wait until its wings dry before it can fly away.

7. In order to observe the opening of a cocoon or a chrysalis in your centre, make a cage from a rectangular piece of wire screen and two shallow round cans or pans. Select a piece of screen large enough to overlap 6 cm when rolled inside one of the two cans

or pans. Use the second can or pan as a lid. Large tuna cans and cake pans work well. A twig with the cocoon or chrysalis attached should be placed vertically inside the cage. A cocoon found during the cold months of the year and brought into a warm room will develop a month ahead of the regular season. It should be kept in a cool place, and then in the spring placed in the cage for observation. Sprinkle the cocoon occasionally with a little water to keep it pliable. If several moth cocoons of the same mother are placed in the cage at the same time and allowed to develop into adult moths, the eggs they lay may hatch and grow into small caterpillars.

8. Any insect developed from a cocoon or chrysalis should be set free after a few days. Otherwise, when they try to fly they will break their wings on the cage and die.

Caring for caterpillars

1. Children often find caterpillars at various times during the spring, summer, and early fall months. If found on a tree or bush, put some of the leaves of the plant in the cage with the caterpillars. Different caterpillars eat the leaves of different kinds of plants. When caterpillars are ready to spin a cocoon, they will leave the food alone and hunt for a suitable place.

   NOTE: Children tend to destroy every insect and spider they see. This can be because of fear, because of a sense of adventure, or because they see adults killing these small creatures. Children can be taught to handle insects appropriately. See Introducing This Subject to Children in this chapter for some suggestions.

2. If the caterpillar of the tomato sphinx (tomato worm) is brought in, put it in a fruit jar with some dirt, as it burrows into the ground to pupate. The caterpillar of the polyphemus moth should be put into a glass jar containing twigs and leaves. Clean out the jar daily. When the caterpillar is ready to spin its cocoon, it will use the twigs and side of the jar as the foundation and spin the leaves into its cocoon. After it is spun, the cocoon may be removed from the jar and put in a cool place. It should be dampened from time to time. If the cocoon is placed in a warm place and kept moist, you can force its development and a full-grown moth will emerge.

3. Twigs should be placed in the jar with the cecropia and monarch caterpillars. The leaves from a milkweed plant should be placed in the jar with a monarch caterpillar. The caterpillar spins a pad of silk on a leaf or twig, hangs from it, and sheds its larval skin, leaving the green chrysalis. This is an extremely interesting stage of development to observe. Some woolly bear caterpillars hibernate in the larval stage under dead leaves and bark. They will spin a cocoon in the spring and a tiger moth will emerge in late May. Other varieties spin their cocoons in the fall (see Chapter 15, Fall, for further information).

   NOTE: Silkworms are wonderful to observe. The entire metamorphosis takes less than two months from hatching eggs to laying eggs. Earthworms are *not* a stage of insect development. They are annelids.

Spiders

1. Spiders are not insects. They have no backbones and do not have antennae and they have only two body sections: the cephalothorax and the abdomen. They have four pairs of legs instead of three. The pair of legs nearest the head is used primarily for holding and moving things, the other three pairs are used for walking. Like insects, spiders shed their exoskeleton. Spiders are found in almost all parts of the world. They usually spin silk webs.

2. Most spiders have poison glands and fangs, which they use for defence or for killing prey. Generally, however, spiders are not dangerous to people, because they usually do not attack human beings unless they are provoked or cornered. If they do bite, the wound is usually not serious.

3. Silk is made in abdominal glands inside the spider's body and comes out of tubes called spinnerets. The silk hardens and forms strands that are fine but very strong and elastic. This silk is used to make webs to preserve food, to protect the spider's eggs, and to trap prey.

4. A spider's blood is clear. Its heart is like that of insects. It can breathe through body openings like those of insects or through book lungs, so called because they look like an open book.

5. All spiders come from eggs. Many spiders lay eggs in a cocoon fastened to a twig, a stone, or a web. The baby spiders or larvae grow very rapidly and become spiderlings. If the temperature is warm, they may tear their way out of the cocoon and almost immediately begin feeding.

6. Adult spiders spend much of their time seeking food. Some chase the insects they will eat, some spit sticky material on their victims to immobilize them, some wait in holes for the insects to fall in and be trapped, and some spin webs to catch the insects.

7. All spiders spin a dragline behind them. Using the dragline, a spider drops from a surface, hangs suspended in midair, and then climbs back up or floats gently down. Draglines are also used to lay down the framework of webs, which can take many shapes.

8. Spiders can be put in a jar with holes in the lid (not big enough for them to get out of). Cover the bottom of the jar with soil. Place leaves and twigs on the soil, or lean a small branch with smaller branches growing from it against the jar. These will provide food and will be a centre of interest for the children to observe how this animal handles its food. Supply water by putting a piece of moist blotting paper or sponge in the jar.

Introducing This Subject to Children

1. Many children will bring in insects and spiders that they have found. Introduce ways of handling insects so that they will not be hurt. The best way to handle insects is to ease them into a container with holes in the top so that the insect is not cut off from fresh air. Talk about insects that help us and insects that may hurt us, so that irrational fears are addressed.

2. Pictures of insects and spiders and their homes should be prominently displayed to encourage discussion about them.

3. An ant farm could be prepared and displayed. While outside, the children could look for ant hills and make closer observations with a magnifying glass.

4. In the appropriate season, the children could collect insects or spiders and keep them as described earlier or in a plastic bug-keeper for a day.

5. Go on a walk to look for insects or spiders and their homes.

6. Follow a child's discovery of a water bug or other insect with other discovery activities.

7. Locate a cricket by its sound (in season).

8. Look up in a book how to care for the insects the children bring in.

Vocabulary

insect	grasshopper	moth	antennae (feelers)
larva	spider	wasp	butterfly
pupa	pollinate	beetle	ladybug
cocoon	spiderling	cricket	ant
caterpillar	mosquito	firefly or	bee
hatching	dragonfly	lightning bug	fly

Include the names, sounds, body parts, and foods of the insects you are observing.

Learning Centres

Discovery Centre

1. An insect or spider collection could be brought to school, as well as books that help to identify these animals.
2. Parents should be notified about the insects and spiders theme, and that they can do much to stimulate their children's interest and to answer their questions.
3. Present a honeycomb and let the children taste the honey it contains.
4. Observe an ant farm (available from science supply companies).
5. Find a caterpillar, care for it, and observe its behaviour.
6. Compare a moth and a butterfly.
7. Observe a dead fly or other insect under a microscope or magnifying glass (giant tripod magnifiers are available commercially).
8. Listen to a cricket (you have captured) during rest time.
9. Observe an insect in a cage.
10. Watch films and videos about insects.

Art Centre

- 1. Cut paper in the shape of butterfly wings for the children to paint.
- 2. While children are fingerpainting, play a recording of "Flight of the Bumblebee." Suggest that they pretend their fingers are bumblebees buzzing around bushes or chasing an animal or a person.
- 3. Suggest that children fingerpaint creepy-crawly pictures.
- •• 4. Mould insect bodies of clay or play dough. Use sticks, straws, pine needles, pipe-cleaners, or paper for legs and wings.
- ••• 5. Let children arrange crayon shavings on a butterfly- or insect-shaped piece of wax paper, cover with another piece of wax paper, and press with an iron set at low heat (use iron with caution). VARIATION: Mount melted-crayon pictures under mats with a butterfly- or insect-shaped opening.

•••• 6. String beads, paper circles, or styrofoam packing pieces to make caterpillars or other insects.

•• 7. Insects and spiders can be made from circles or ovals of corrugated cardboard and decorated. Insert pipecleaners through holes for legs. Individual egg-carton sections can be similarly used for insect bodies. Children can stick gummed shapes on their insects or paint them.

•• 8. Provide half-lengths of egg-carton sections for the children to paint. Short pieces of pipecleaners can be used as feelers.

•• 9. Make thumbprint insects. Have children add details with crayons.

Learning and Language Materials Centre

Commercially made games and materials

Miscellaneous: Insect cages, butterfly and insect kites, and butterfly nets.

Teacher-made games and materials

NOTE: For detailed descriptions, see Learning Games in Part 1.

1. *Match-them:* Use sets of insects and the foods they eat; include flowers for bees. Make *Match-them* cards with insect or spider stickers. These can be used for counting and sorting as well.

Book Centre

•••• Aardema, Verna. *Why Mosquitoes Buzz in People's Ears: A West African Tale.* Markham, ON: Fitzhenry & Whiteside, 1978.

••• Batulla, Barbara. *Insects.* New York: Sterling, 1990.

•• Brinckloe, Julie. *The Spider's Web.* Garden City, NY: Doubleday, 1974.

•• Carle, Eric. *The Very Hungry Caterpillar.* Cleveland: Collins and World, 1970.

••• Caudill, Rebecca. *A Pocketful of Crickets.* New York: Holt, Rinehart & Winston, 1964.

••• Craig, Janet. *Amazing World of Spiders.* St. Catharines, ON: Troll Associates, 1990.

••• Freschet, Bernice. *The Web in the Grass.* New York: Scribner, 1972.

• Garelick, May. *Where Does the Butterfly Go When It Rains?* Reading, MA: Addison-Wesley, 1961.

•••• Goor, Ron, and Nancy Goor. *Insect Metamorphosis: From Egg to Adult.* New York: Macmillan, 1990. (Read–Tell)

•• Graham, Margaret Bloy. *Be Nice to Spiders.* New York: Harper & Row, 1972.

• Hellen, Nancy. *Bugs.* St. Catharines, ON: Vanwell, 1991.

••• Heller, Ruth. *How to Hide a Butterfly.* New York: Grosset & Dunlap, 1986.

• Lionni, Leo. *Inch by Inch.* New York: Astor-Honor, 1962.

•••• Losito, Linda, et al. *Insects and Spiders.* New York: Commerce Clearing House (Facts on File), 1989.

••• Martin, C.L.G. *Three Brave Women.* Don Mills, ON: Macmillan, 1991. (a book about spiders)

••• Mattern, Joanne. *A Picture Book of Insects.* St. Catharines, ON: Troll Associates, 1991.

••• Mizumura, Kazue. *If I Were a Cricket.* New York: Crowell, 1973.

•• ———. *Way of the Ant.* New York: Crowell, 1970.

••• Parker, Nancy Winslow, and Joan Richards Wright. *Bugs.* New York: Greenwillow, 1987.

••• Ryder, J. *When the Woods Hum.* Toronto: Morrow, 1991.

•• ———. *Fireflies.* New York: Harper & Row, 1977.

••• Sabin, Francene. *Amazing World of Ants.* St. Catharines, ON: Troll Associates, 1982.

••• Sabin, Louis. *Amazing World of Butterflies and Moths.* St. Catharines, ON: Troll Associates, 1982.

••• Selsam, M. *Backyard Insects.* New York: Scholastic, 1983.

•••• ———. *A First Look at Insects.* New York: Walker, 1974.

••• ———. *Terry and the Caterpillars.* New York: Harper & Row, 1962. (Tell)

••• Waber, B. *A Firefly Named Torchy.* Boston: Houghton Mifflin, 1970.

••• Wagner, J. *A Story about a Spider.* New York: Bradbury, 1978.

Planning for Group Time

NOTE: All music, fingerplays, poems, and stories listed here may also be used at other times during the session as appropriate.

Music

Songs

From *More Piggyback Songs*, Warren
"Pretty Butterfly," p. 75
"Bugs," p. 75

From *Piggyback Songs*, Warren
"Butterfly, Butterfly," p. 27
"Fly Fly Butterfly," p. 27

From *Singing Bee*, Hart
"Caterpillar," p. 22

From *Stepping Along in Music Land*, Murray
"Wiggly Worm," p. 27
"Butterfly, Butterfly," p. 47
"How Many Bees?" p. 57

From *A Treasury of Songs for Children*, Glazer
"The Blue Tail Fly," p. 41
"Eency Weency Spider," p. 76
"Shoo Fly," p. 201

From *Tunes for Tots*, Warner and Berry
"Bees," p. 74
"Butterfly, Fly," p. 76

Rhythms and Singing Games

....

THE LITTLE CATERPILLAR

by Jean Warren

(tune: "Itsy, Bitsy Spider")

       F   C7   F
The little caterpillar crawled up into a tree,
F   C7   F
Spun his cocoon and slept so quietly,
F   C7   F
All through the winter he didn't make a sound,
      F   C7   F
He dreamt of his new life when he'd be flying all around.

F   C7   F
While he was sleeping the snow did gently fall,
F   C7   F
Winter came and went, then he heard the robin's call,
F   C7   F
"Come on Mr. Butterfly, out of your cocoon —
F   F   C7   F
Spread your wings and fly for me, while I sing my tune."

This song is easy for children to act out. Have all the children lie on the floor and move like a caterpillar. Suggest that they make themselves as small as possible to fit into the cocoon. Then have them move around the room, flying as butterflies.

■ If some children in your group are limited in their ability to move or if you do not have enough room for "flying," this activity can be done while seated. Have the children move one hand or arm like a caterpillar crawling. Then have them make themselves as small as possible, while seated. Finally, have them move their hands like flying butterflies.

Records and Cassettes

Bob Homme. *The Giant Concert of Concerts by the Friendly Giant.* (A & M Records)
"The Buzzy Concert"

Bob McGrath. *If You're Happy and You Know It*, Volume I. (Kids Records)
"The Incey Wincey Spider"

Anne Murray. *There's a Hippo in My Tub.* (Capitol Records)
"Inchworm"

Sandy Tobias Oppenheim. *If Snowflakes Fell in Flavours.* (Berandol Records)
"Did You Ever Hear an Ant Say Can't?"

Fred Penner. *Special Delivery.* (Troubadour Records)
"There Was an Old Lady"

Fingerplays and Poems

From *Don't Eat Spiders*, Heidbreder
"Don't Eat Spiders," p. 23
"The Giant Snail," p. 41

From *Hand Rhymes*, Brown
"Here Is the Beehive," p. 14
"The Caterpillar," p. 28

From *Let's Do Fingerplays*, Grayson
"Five Little Ants," p. 63
"Grasshoppers," p. 65
"Bumblebee," p. 73

From *Read Aloud Rhymes for the Very Young*, Prelutsky and Brown
"Snail's Pace," p. 20
"The Butterfly," p. 33
"Wings," p. 39
"Fuzzy Wuzzy Creepy Crawly," p. 62
"Only in My Opinion," p. 62
"Ants," p. 62
"Ants Live Here," p. 62
"Grasshopper Green," p. 63
"Dragonfly," p. 63
"But I Wonder . . .," p. 63
"Firefly," p. 65
"An Explanation of the Grasshopper," p. 72
"Under the Ground," p. 73
"The Underworld," p. 73
"Tell Me Little Wood Worm," p. 79

From *Round and Round the Garden*, Williams
"The Incy Wincy Spider," p. 17

From *Where the Sidewalk Ends*, Silverstein
"One Inch Tall," p. 55

EENSIE WEENSIE SPIDER

adaptation of southern folksong

The tiny, tiny spider went up the water spout. (*"walk" first and second fingers up arm*)
Down came the rain and washed the spider out. (*brush hand down arm*)
Out came the sun and dried up all the rain. (*make circle with arms overhead*)
And the tiny, tiny spider went up the spout again. (*"walk" two fingers up arm*)

THE ANT HILL

(*The right hand with the thumb closed inside is the ant hill. The fingers will be the ants. Lift each finger as it is counted, beginning with the thumb*)

Once I saw an ant hill, with no ants about
So I said, "Little ants, won't you please come out?"
Then as if they had heard my call, one, two, three, four, five came out.
And that was all.

Stories

(To read, read–tell, or tell. See Book Centre for a complete list.)
Stories chosen for this subject should help children get rid of any fears they may have
of insects, such as Aardema's *Why Mosquitoes Buzz in People's Ears*. Stories can also

give children information about insects, such as Garelick's *Where Does the Butterfly Go When It Rains*?

Routine Times

1. Use fingerplays, poems, and songs about insects or spiders while children are coming to the table for lunch or snacks.
2. Serve honey and biscuits at snack or meal times.

Extended Experiences

1. Go for a walk in a nearby park, around the block, or around your playground to find insects. Look under rocks, in cracks in sidewalks, and in bushes — shake bushes into an open umbrella.
2. Ask someone to bring in a butterfly collection to show.

Teacher Resources

Pictures and Displays

☐ Display magazines with articles on insects:
   a. *Canadian Geographic.*
   b. *National Geographic.*
   c. *Owl.*
   d. *Chickadee.*
   e. *Equinox.*
☐ Use the insects made in the art centre to decorate tables.
☐ Hang pictures of spiders, caterpillars, moths, and butterflies.

Books and Periodicals

Bailes, Edith G. *But Will It Bite Me? A Reference Book of Insects for Children and Their Grownups.* Richmond, ME: Cardamom, 1985.

Canadian Geographic magazine.

Carr, Anna. *Rodale's Color Handbook of Garden Insects.* Emmaus, PA: Rodale Press, 1983.

Chickadee magazine.

Equinox magazine.

Horton, Casey, et al. *Amazing Fact Book of Spiders.* Mankuto, MN: Creative Education, 1987.

Klots, Alexander B., and Elsie B. Klots. *One Thousand One Questions Answered about Insects.* New York: Dover, 1977.

———. *Insects of North America.* Garden City, NY: Doubleday, 1972.

Your Big Backyard magazine.

Films and Videos

NOTE: Check with your distributor about public performance rights.

Anansi the Spider: A Tale from the Ashanti. Landmark Educational Media Corp./Gerald McDermott Films (released in Canada by International Tele-Film), 1969.

Backyard Bugs. National Geographic, 1990.

The Bear and the Fly. Weston Woods.

Caterpillar. Kresleny Films Learning Corporation of America (released in Canada by Marlin Motion Pictures), 1971.

The Cricket and the Hand-Saw. Kratky Films, Prague (released in Canada by International Tele-Film), 1979.

Dog and the Bees. Phoenix Films (released in Canada by International Tele-Film).

Incy Wincy Spider. Nursery Rhyme Joint Venture/David Yates, Media Home Entertainment (released in Canada by McNabb Films), 1983.

Why Mosquitoes Buzz in People's Ears. Weston Woods.

Community Resources and Organizations

☐ Invite a beekeeper or an entomologist to visit the classroom.

☐ Visit a natural history museum or a zoo.

Part 7 Transportation

7 Transportation

21 Many Ways to Travel

Basic Understandings
(concepts children can grasp from this subject)

- [ ] Transportation means moving people or things from one place to another.
- [ ] People can move from one place to another:
    - a. By their own movements — walking, running, swimming, or crawling.
    - b. By riding an animal or being pulled by one in a wagon or carriage.
    - c. By riding in or on a machine — car, train, plane, ship, or bus.
- [ ] Some machines that move or carry us need motors, wind, water, steam, gas, oil, or people to make them go.
- [ ] When we travel or transport things:
    - a. We first decide what we need to move — people or things.
    - b. We think about where we need to move them or ourselves.
    - c. We decide the best way to move them or ourselves.
    - d. We buy a ticket, pay a fare, or give instructions to the person or animal that is going to take us.
    - e. We may turn a key or a switch or pull a throttle to start the machine in which we are travelling.
- [ ] Machines most often used for moving people or things are cars, trucks, buses, streetcars, taxis, trains, airplanes, ships, and boats.
- [ ] The person who steers most transportation machines is called the driver.
- [ ] A driver must have a licence and follow certain rules. Drivers who break the rules may get a ticket from a police officer, pay a fine (money), or have their licences taken away.
- [ ] We usually must pay money to transport people or things:
    - a. People buy tickets to ride on trains, airplanes, ships, or buses.
    - b. People pay fares (money) to ride in a taxi, bus, subway, ferry, or streetcar.
    - c. People who own their own car (or other machine) must take care of it and buy gasoline and oil for it.
    - d. Sometimes drivers must pay a toll (money) to drive on roads or drive in tunnels or over bridges. The money collected is used to help build and care for the roads, tunnels, and bridges.

☐ We can travel or carry things on the ground, in the air, or through the water.

☐ When people walk on the sidewalks we call them pedestrians; when pedestrians cross streets they must be careful and obey the crossing guard, police officer, or traffic lights.

☐ People can do many things while travelling as passengers: eat, sleep, rest, talk, read, and sometimes stand, walk, or use rest rooms.

☐ Drivers must pay attention to their driving and passengers must be careful not to disturb or distract them.

☐ All drivers must follow signs and signals for safety:
   a. Railroad engineer: semaphores, flags, and whistles.
   b. Pilot: windsocks, radar, and radio signals.
   c. Ship captain: whistles, buoys, flags, and radio signals.
   d. Crossing guard and police officer: road signs and traffic lights.

☐ There are many specially trained people who help us with transportation, such as train conductors and flight attendants.

Additional Facts the Teacher Should Know

1. This chapter will deal with concepts and activities that involve all methods of moving people or things from one place to another. It will deal with movement of people, use of animals for transportation, and transportation by air, road, rail, or water, or in space. Subsequent chapters dealing specifically with transportation by air, road, rail, or water, and in space have been developed for use where children show a special interest in one form of transportation.

2. First experiences with transportation should begin with ways the children can move and carry things. Use of wheel toys that can be pushed, pulled, or pedalled enlarge the concepts of moving things and people. Cars or buses used for transporting the children to and from the centre provide additional experiences with transportation. If your centre is near a railroad track, beneath a flight pattern, near a river, or near an ocean, you will have natural exposure to these means of transportation.

3. The basic concepts listed are understandably broad and are not intended to be taught outside of the children's opportunities to experience them. For example, you would not suggest activities involving toll booths, ferries, or streetcars if they do not exist in your community, unless a child in your group has had experience with them. Select those concepts that will have the most meaning for your group.

Introducing This Subject to Children

1. Discuss a trip a child or teacher at the centre has taken.
2. Read a story about transportation.
3. Put up pictures or display scale models of trains, airplanes, ships, boats, cars, trucks, buses, or spaceships.
4. If a parent works for a transportation agency, have him or her visit the classroom, dressed in working attire, and talk about the job. If possible, the visitor could bring something that he or she uses on the job to show the children. Many transportation companies have representatives in their public relations departments who will visit centres.

Vocabulary

transportation	fare	suitcase	go
passenger	toll	baggage	start
schedule	taxi	boat	car
airplane	tourist	pack	run
move	travel	ride	crawl
carry	driver	walk	drive
trip	train	ship	truck
bus	carry	stop	streetcar
ticket			

Learning Centres

Discovery Centre

1. Help children discover that there are many ways to move things or people — carry by hand, animal, car, train, truck, airplane, or ship. Discuss the methods by which a product, like milk, is carried by people, animals, cars, trains, planes, and ships. If possible, have pictures of each mode of transportation.
2. Encourage children to observe signs, crossing guards, police officers, and traffic lights when taking a trip and crossing streets. Provide picture books, films, or driving manuals to help children discover some of these signs and signals.
3. Display hats and pictures of people at work to help children discover that some people wear uniforms or special clothes when they work at their transportation job, and some do not.
4. Display a model train, car, truck, bus, ship, boat, and airplane on a table. Encourage discussion about transportation. Discuss similarities and differences between modes of transportation and why each is necessary.
5. Display pictures or models of animals used to carry people or things, such as horses, elephants, donkeys, dogs, and camels.

Dramatic Play Centres

Home-living centre

1. Have several overnight bags available so they can be packed for a trip with dressup clothes or doll clothes.
2. Have several travel brochures with colourful pictures and timetables on a shelf for the children to look at.
3. Put play money in purses so tickets can be purchased or fares or tolls paid.
4. Hang travel posters here and in the block-building centre.

Block-building centre

1. A steering wheel or dial panel, planks, and hollow blocks all provide opportunities for many kinds of transportation play. A dial panel (see illustration, p. 472) can be made

out of wood or a heavy cardboard box. See other transportation chapters for specific suggestions for its use.

2. Set out items to be transported in trucks, such as animals, blocks, cars, and containers full of buttons, beads, spools, twigs, and pebbles.
3. Commercial materials that will add to dramatic transportation play include:
   a. Unit blocks to build roads, bridges, stations, garages, docks, and airports.
   b. Unit-block transportation vehicles — cars, trucks, planes, taxis, boats, and ships.
   c. Unit-block people to transport, and to be transportation workers.
   d. Unit-block animals to transport.
   e. Hollow blocks and building boards for large scale building.
   f. Toy traffic light.
   g. Traffic signs — unit-block size and wheel-toy size.
   h. Wheel toys — doll carriage, wagons, trikes, and wheelbarrows.
   i. Oversize vehicles — trucks, planes, trains, and boats.
   j. Ride-on vehicles.
   k. Cash register and play money.
4. Post pictures of highways, bridges, docks, airports, railroad stations, or launching pads in the block-building centre to encourage the use of unit blocks in transportation play.

Other dramatic play centres

1. Two rows of chairs with an aisle between can suggest a bus, a train, a subway, a streetcar, or an airplane. If space is limited, one row is sufficient. Provide play money, tickets, and a conductor's hat, or make a hat using the pattern on p. 473.
2. Ask parents and staff to bring in used airline or rail tickets to use in the mock vehicles.
3. Empty cardboard cartons from large appliances make excellent buses, fire engines, trains, etc. The children can decorate them using paint and large pieces of construction paper.

Art Centre

••• Pasting: Children could help make a picture book of transportation for the book centre by cutting pictures out of magazines, catalogues, or brochures and pasting them on coloured construction paper. These pages could then be punched and placed in a three-ring binder.

> NOTE: Cut one side and the bottom rectangle out of six large grocery bags. When all six are cut, stack and fold them to form a book. Staple at the folded edge to make a large, flat scrapbook of twelve pages.

Learning and Language Materials Centre

Commercially made games and materials

1. *Puzzles:* A variety of puzzles with transportation themes.
2. *Construction and manipulative toys:* Wooden steering wheels and wheels that match large wooden blocks encourage the construction of a variety of transportation vehicles.
3. *Small toys for imaginative play:* Plastic models of various vehicles for younger children. Metal models of various vehicles for older children. A printed vinyl play mat that represents the layout of a town that can be used in conjunction with model vehicles and blocks.
4. *Toys for riding:* A variety of toys for riding both indoors and outdoors. Be sure to choose toys that are replicas of vehicles the children are likely to see, not models of vehicles

on television. Choose vehicles that are sturdy and that do not have sharp edges. Make sure they are easy to steer and that you have a variety of sizes to fit different children.

5. *Costumes:* Hats and coats that represent various employees of the transportation industry.

Teacher-made games and materials

NOTE: For detailed descriptions, see Learning Games in Part 1.

1. *Look and see:* Use sturdy models of various transportation vehicles.
2. *Reach and feel:* Use sturdy models of various transportation vehicles.
3. *Can you remember?* Use transportation toys.
4. *How many?* How many ways can you get from one side of the room to the other? Get to school? From one city to another? Get a car across the river? Get across the ocean?
5. *Who am I?* Describe someone who works for an airline, a railroad, a bus company, or a trucking firm; for example, "I fly an airplane; who am I?"
6. *Sorting and grouping by association:* Place several models of each type of transportation vehicle in a box or on a tray. Let children sort them into appropriate groups. Label boxes, or make an appropriate garage, hangar, or harbour into which vehicles can be sorted.
7. *Alike, different, and the same:* Use scale models or sets of picture cards of the various transportation vehicles. Toy catalogues or model catalogues available from some hobby stores may provide you with the pictures for this game. Have children find two pictures that are alike. As children gain experience, add one picture that is different to pairs that are alike, and ask children to find the one that is different; for example, two cars and a bus.
8. *Colour, shape, size, and number:* When observing real transportation vehicles or when using scale models, talk about the colour, shape, size, and number characteristics as appropriate; for example, "What *colour* is the caboose?" "Put away the *big* truck." "How *many* propellers does your airplane have?" "*Count* the wheels on the car."

Book Centre

••• Baer, Edith. *This Is the Way We Go to School: A Book about Children around the World.* New York: Scholastic, 1990.
••• Bauer, C. *My Mom Travels a Lot.* Markham, ON: Penguin, 1985.
•• Curry, Peter. *Trucks, Planes, Boats, Trains.* New York: Price Stern, 1984.
••• Douglas, Barbara. *The Great Town and Country Bicycle Chase.* New York: Lothrop, Lee & Shepard, 1984.
• Feldman, Barbara. *Going, Going.* Willowdale, ON: Annick Press, 1989.
•• Graeme, Jocelyn. *Many Ways to Travel.* Don Mills, ON: Addison-Wesley, 1990. (text is in Spanish, French, English, and Chinese)
•• Hall, Donald. *Ox-Cart Man.* New York: Viking Press, 1979.
•• Hartman, Gail. *As the Crow Flies: A First Book of Maps.* New York: Bradbury Press, 1991.
••• Helldorfer, M.C. *The Mapmaker's Daughter.* New York: Bradbury Press, 1991.
• Hutchins, Pat. *Rosie's Walk.* New York: Macmillan, 1971.
• Keats, Ezra Jack. *Skates.* New York: Franklin Watts, 1973.
• Lenski, Lois. *Davy Goes Places.* New York: Walck, 1961.
••• Mitsumasa, Anno. *Anno's Journey.* New York: Putnam, 1987.
••• Poulin, Stéphane. *Travels for Two: Stories and Lies from My Childhood.* Willowdale, ON: Annick Press, 1991.
• Prater, John. *You Can't Catch Me.* London: The Bodley Head, 1986.
• Rockwell, Anne. *My Travel Book.* Burlington, ON: Hayes, 1986.

• ———. *Things that Go.* New York: Dutton, 1986.

••• Shannon, George. *The Piney Woods Peddlar.* New York: Greenwillow Press, 1981.

•• Wildsmith, Brian. *Daisy.* New York: Pantheon, 1984.

 # Planning for Group Time

NOTE: All music, fingerplays, poems, stories, and games listed here may also be used at other times during the session as appropriate. In parodies, hyphenated words match the music notes of the tune used.

Music

Songs

TAKE A TRIP (a parody)

(tune: "Twinkle, Twinkle, Little Star")

adaptation by Wendy Flemming

Take a bus or take a train,
Take a boat or take a plane.
Take a tax-i, take a car,
May-be near or may-be far.
Take a spaceship to the moon,
But be sure to come back soon.

NOTE: To add interest, use pictures, flannelboard cutouts, or models.

From *The Baby Beluga Book*, Raffi
"Morningtown Ride," p. 46

From *More Piggyback Songs*, Warren
"Buckle Up," p. 67
"When I Cross the Street," p. 67
"Safety," p. 67
"Choo Choo Train," p. 89

From *Piggyback Songs*, Warren
"We Sail a Ship," p. 31
"Off We Go — A Travelling Song," p. 33
"Twinkle Twinkle Traffic Light," p. 47

From *What Shall We Do and Alee Galloo!*, Winn
"Run Children, Run," p. 70

NOTE: There are many songs that may be used in this section — see the following chapters for further suggestions.

Rhythms and Singing Games

1. Hoofbeats can be imitated by using walnut or coconut shells or tone blocks when songs about horses or donkeys are played.

2. Play a variety of tempos on the piano or segments of recordings that will encourage the children to walk, run, tiptoe, and jump.
3. The sounds made by airplanes, trains, cars, trucks, buses, or boats can be suggested by certain music or appropriate rhythms. Allow children to respond to these creatively.
4. Allow children to use stick horses when galloping or trotting music is played.

....
LET'S ALL MARCH DOWN THE STREET

by Jean Warren

(tune: "If You're Happy and You Know It")

    C   G7
Let's all march down the street, down the street,
    G7   C
Let's all march down the street, down the street.
    F
Let's all march down the street,
        C
Smile at everyone we meet.
    G   C
Let's all march down the street, down the street.

(Repeat, using "skip, run, crawl, hop," etc.)

....
ROUND AND ROUND THE VILLAGE

NOTE: Sing this song using different ways of moving around a village.

Let's fly a-round the vil-lage. *(pretend to be an airplane)*
Let's walk a-round the vil-lage. *(walk)*
Let's drive a-round the vil-lage. *(pretend to be cars, trucks, or buses)*
Let's swim a-round the pool. *(pretend to do the crawl)*
Let's row a-round the lake. *(pretend to row a boat)*
Let's pad-dle down the riv-er. *(pretend to paddle a canoe)*

....
AS I WAS WALKING DOWN THE STREET

(adaptation of "Rig-a-Jig-Jig")

As I was walk-ing down the street, down the street, down the street
A lit-tle friend I went to meet, hi-ho, hi-ho, hi-ho.
Skip-pet-y-skip and a-way we go, a-way we go, a-way we go
Skip-pet-y-skip and a-way we go, hi-ho, hi-ho, hi-ho!

NOTE: Change verse to include running, jumping, hopping, flying in the sky, rowing down a stream, and other action verbs.

Records and Cassettes

Bob Homme. *The Giant Concert of Concerts by The Friendly Giant.* (A & M Records)
"Railroad Concert"

Bob McGrath. *If You're Happy and You Know It*, Volume I. (Kids Records)
"The Wheels on the Bus"
"Little Wheel a-Turnin'"
"She'll Be Comin' Round the Mountain"

Fred Penner. *Special Delivery.* (Troubadour Records)
"Car Car Song"
"En Roulant"

Raffi. *The Corner Grocery Store.* (Troubadour Records)
"Swing Low, Sweet Chariot"
"Jig Along Home"
"Sur le pont d'Avignon"

Sharon, Lois, and Bram. *Smorgasbord.* (Elephant Records)
"Mango Walk"
"Riding Along (Singing a Cowboy Song)"

Fingerplays and Poems

From *Let's Do Fingerplays*, Grayson
"Things that Go," pp. 22–26
"Big Hill," p. 23

From *A New Treasury of Children's Poetry*, Cole
"The Sidewalk Racer," p. 135

From *The New Wind Has Wings*, Downie
"Donkey Riding," p. 15

From *Rhymes for Fingers and Flannelboards*, Scott and Thompson
"The Airplane," p. 21
"Five Little Sailors," p. 23

From *Where the Sidewalk Ends*, Silverstein
"Where the Sidewalk Ends," p. 64
"Traffic Light," p. 121

Stories

(To read, read–tell, or tell. See Book Centre for a complete list.)
The choice of stories for introducing the transportation section should reflect the children's experiences. Although they may have been exposed to most modes of transportation through television, they will become more interested in the subject if you start with stories that relate to their direct experiences.

Games

(See Learning Games in Part 1 and Teacher-Made Games and Materials earlier in this chapter for directions.)
1. *Look and see.*
2. *Reach and feel.*
3. *Can you remember?*
4. *How many?*
5. *Who am I?*
6. *Sorting and grouping by association.*

Routine Times

1. During snack or meal times, talk about how the various foods you are eating were brought to the centre.
   a. How does the food get from the kitchen to the tables?
   b. How does the food get from the store to the kitchen?
   c. How does the food get from the farm, dairy, or canning factory to the store?
2. At snack or meal times, ask children to help by *transporting* food, dishes, silverware, water, and other food or utensils as needed.
3. At pickup time, point out to the children that carrying things in our hands and walking are forms of transportation. Suggest also the use of wagons and rolling platforms as means of transporting blocks and toys to shelves to be put away.
4. While riding or walking, look for different kinds of vehicles.
5. When riding in a bus or car, talk about safety: Use safety belts, lock the doors, and be considerate of the driver. Talk about traffic signals and rules.

Large Muscle Activities

1. An old, discarded steering wheel from a car, boat, or tractor, remounted on a large wooden box big enough for three or four children to stand in, makes an excellent dramatic play vehicle. If it does not look like a particular kind of vehicle it will be more versatile. A couple of hooks mounted on the side will allow for hanging a hose when the box is being used as a fire engine, or for hanging a coil of rope for a lifeline or an old bicycle tire for a life preserver when it is being used as a boat.

   NOTE: Set the box on cement blocks outside and drill a few drain holes in its bottom so it will weather without rotting.

2. Encourage the use of wheel toys for transporting children or things around the playground. Add traffic signs and signals.
3. Remind children of traffic rules and boundaries where wheel toys cannot go.

Extended Experiences

1. Visit a railroad station, a bus terminal, or an airport. Time your visit to see arrivals and departures.
2. Ride on a bus, trolley, train, or boat (whatever is possible in your area that would interest your group).
3. Visit a park or other public site that may have a ship, a locomotive, or an airplane as a permanent display that children are free to explore.
4. Visit a hobby shop that has a model car racetrack or model train on display.

Teacher Resources

Pictures and Displays

☐ Mount and display pictures of trains, cars, trucks, buses, boats, ships, wheel toys, or children walking or running.

Books and Periodicals

Billout, Guy. *By Camel or by Car: A Look at Transportation.* Englewood Cliffs, NJ: Prentice-Hall, 1979.
Hancock, Ralph. *Supermachines.* Don Mills, ON: General Publishing, 1978.
Milsome, John. *Machines and Roads.* London: Burle, 1976.

Films and Videos

NOTE: Check with your distributor about public performance rights.

The Boy and the Airplane. Japiri (released in Canada by Films Francais), 1969. (no narration)
The Little Engine that Could. Coronet Instructional Films, 1983.
Little Tim and the Brave Sea Captain. Weston Woods.
The Mole and the Car. Kratky Films, Prague (released in Canada by International Tele-Film), 1977. (no narration)

Community Resources and Organizations

☐ Travel agencies for posters, brochures, and timetables.
☐ A travel agent.
☐ Public relations personnel of airlines, steamship lines, or railway companies for pictures, calendars, brochures, and timetables.
☐ A VIA Rail agent.
☐ An airline representative.
☐ Hobby stores, for models and catalogues.
☐ Public transit company.
☐ Societies interested in transportation; for example, a model train club, a flying club, a train buffs club, a motor sport club, a hang-gliding club, a shipping and ship travel club.
☐ Railway, marine, or other transportation museum.

Government Agencies

☐ Federal, provincial, and territorial ministries of transportation and communication.

22 Air Transportation

Basic Understandings
(concepts children can grasp from this subject)

- [ ] Airplanes carry people and things from one place to another by flying in the sky.
- [ ] Some airplanes are small and carry one or two people, and some are very big and carry many, many people.
- [ ] Some people own their own private airplanes.
- [ ] People can buy tickets (pay money) to ride in an airplane.
- [ ] Most airplanes take off and land on runways at an airport.
  - a. Seaplanes can take off and land on water.
  - b. Ski planes can take off and land on snow.
  - c. Some planes land in fields.
  - d. Helicopters land on fields, parking lots, and buildings.
- [ ] The person who flies the airplane is called the pilot; his or her assistant is called the co-pilot.
- [ ] Flight attendants ride in the cabin on a passenger plane to help make the passengers comfortable and serve them snacks or meals.
- [ ] The air terminal is the building at the airport where people buy tickets and wait for airplanes. It often has a lounge, rest rooms, a restaurant, a snack bar, telephones, car rental and ticket agents, gift shops, and newsstands.
- [ ] The control tower is a tall building where an air-traffic controller can view all the runways. The tower has radar, which helps the controller guide pilots to make safe takeoffs and landings.
- [ ] Hangars are buildings at the airport that house airplanes when they are not in use. They are like huge garages.
- [ ] Some small towns have small, but important, airports with sheds for buildings; they usually have limited equipment.
- [ ] There are many different kinds of aircraft — passenger planes (airliners), cargo planes (for freight only), jets, seaplanes, ski planes, helicopters, and gliders.
- [ ] Each aircraft has a number, symbol (logo), or flag painted on it so we know who owns it. International aircraft have the flags of their countries painted on the sides.
- [ ] Airplanes have seat belts for safety, just as cars do.

☐ People depend on airplanes to travel long distances quickly, to bring them food, to carry mail, and to bring them other goods.

☐ Most aircraft travel from one place to another on the earth. There are craft called space ships, satellites, and space shuttles that travel to other planets.

☐ Satellites and space shuttles help us receive telephone calls and television programs.

Additional Facts the Teacher Should Know

1. How can something that is heavier than air fly? An airplane flies because of the work done by the propellers, the wings, and the engine. A glider does not have an engine but is towed into the air by another airplane to which it is attached by a cable. When the glider is at the proper height, the cable is released and the glider flies back to earth. Airplanes are powered by gasoline engines, turbine engines, jet engines, or rockets. These engines provide power to turn the propellers or provide forward thrust for the airplanes. Forward thrust causes air to flow over the wings, which are curved on top and flat on the bottom. As airplanes are thrust forward, air flowing over the curved part of the wings has farther to go than air flowing across the flat undersides. The air that has to go farther moves faster to meet the slower air beneath. Because the air goes faster, it does not push down as much as the slower air pushes up. The faster airplanes go forward, the greater the lift.

2. Gases from burning fuel in jet engines rush out from a hole in the rear of each engine (these can be seen in the pods under the wings) with terrific force, and the plane is pushed forward. Forward thrust can be demonstrated by blowing air into a balloon and then letting the balloon go. As the air rushes out the open end, the balloon goes in the opposite direction. Jet engines use the oxygen from air, but rockets must carry their own oxygen supply. The first plane to fly faster than the speed of sound was a jet. When a plane or rocket flies faster than the speed of sound, a loud boom is heard, and the plane or rocket is said to be "breaking the sound barrier." Vibrations from the sonic boom may cause houses to shake, windows and dishes to break or rattle, and objects to fall.

3. Three controls are used in flying an airplane. They are the control stick, the rudder pedals, and the throttle. In smaller, older planes, the control stick has a knob on the end for the pilot to grasp, but larger and newer craft have a small steering wheel. There are two ways to turn an airplane to the right and to the left — by moving the stick or turning the wheel to the left or right, and by pushing the rudder pedals down. Usually a pilot works both the stick and rudder pedals together. There are two ways to make an airplane go up or down. When the control stick is pushed forward, the airplane descends; if the stick is pulled back, the airplane climbs. The second way involves the throttle, which controls the speed of the engine. Pushing the throttle in makes the engine go faster, increasing the lift, so the airplane goes higher. If the throttle is pulled back, the engine slows down, increasing the downward force, so the plane descends.

4. Most takeoffs and landings are made by pilots with permission obtained by two-way radio communication with an air-traffic controller. In good weather with good visibility, pilots land planes under their own control. However, the controller in the tower can bring in an airplane with the use of radar and other instruments when visibility is poor. Bringing a plane in by radar is called a ground control approach (GCA), and instrument landing systems (ILS) means a radio highway approach.

5. Airports range in size from small landing fields with one runway, a windsock, and no landing lights (no night service) to huge international airports serving several airlines. The largest airports are virtually mini-cities.

6. At the larger airports, each airline has its own ticket counter, baggage-claim centre, boarding gates, and customer-service staff. Tickets are printed and confirmed by computer. Tickets are presented by passengers at customer-service stations near boarding gates, where they receive boarding passes. When it is time for boarding a plane, passengers must go through a security checkpoint. Because of the risk of hijackings and hidden bombs, everyone must walk through a magnetometer or scan-screen, which detects the presence of metal. All coats, purses, and hand luggage are checked by security guards or placed in a scan-ray machine that detects metal. Once through the security checks, passengers walk through tunnels called gangways or telescopic gangways to waiting planes.

7. Baggage is placed on a conveyor belt that takes it out to a service area where it is placed on baggage tugs or luggage carts and taken to waiting planes. A ramp with a conveyor belt carries it up into the baggage compartment.

8. Airplanes have many parts — wings, propellers, engine, control stick or steering wheel, tail, rudder, and wheels. The cockpit is where the pilot sits to fly the plane. The cabin is where the passengers sit. Transcontinental planes have galleys, rest rooms, and lounges. Some planes have seats that can be converted to sleeping berths.

9. All food and drink served on an airplane is catered by food service companies. The food is prepared in advance and brought to the airplane before takeoff. The small kitchens, or galleys, on the airplane are used for preparing drinks and setting up trays that are taken to passengers in their seats by flight attendants. Special meals can be ordered by passengers with special diets if the airline has been alerted to their specific needs.

10. Helicopters cannot fly as fast as airplanes, but they can take off and land straight up and down, as well as hover, making them excellent for rescue work in mountains and valleys where runways do not exist. In place of propellers and wings, helicopters have two rotors, which look like very large propellers. Most have one big rotor overhead and a smaller one on the tail. One rotor turns clockwise and the other turns counterclockwise, keeping the helicopter in balance.

11. Ski planes are equipped with giant skis that allow them to glide over snow. Seaplanes are equipped with pontoon that allow them to land and float on water. Both kinds of planes also have sets of wheels that can be lowered to land on runways. Some seaplanes can land on their bellies.

12. As the concepts of space and space exploration are often beyond their comprehension, many children find the discussion of space transport either boring or frightening. Be sure that the children are interested before introducing the material in this section. Often, children will be most interested in imaginative and nonscientific play in relation to space. Many of the activities and resources relating to space travel will be most successful if you do not take them too seriously and focus on having fun rather than worrying about how much the children are learning about space exploration. Often, children are interested in the sun, the moon, and the stars.

Introducing This Subject to Children

1. Discuss an airplane trip a child or one of the teachers has taken.
2. Put up pictures or display scale models of various kinds of planes.
3. Read a story about airplanes.
4. If a parent works for an airline, have him or her visit and tell about the job, or arrange for a representative of an airline or a travel agent to visit.
5. Observe planes or helicopters from the playground.

Vocabulary

aircraft	space ship	helicopter	astronaut
airplane	space shuttle	satellite	fasten
airport	terminal	cockpit	windsock
airline	baggage	wing	takeoff
runway	hangar	fly	landing
flight attendant	tower	jet	air-traffic
glider	ski plane	propeller	controller
pilot	seaplane	seat belt	

Learning Centres

Discovery Centre

1. Display model airplanes of various kinds. Help children identify the airplanes and discover the uses made of each kind. Compare similarities and differences. Look for symbols (logos), numbers, and flags for identification. Demonstrate how airplanes take off and land.
2. Help children understand how a propeller works by providing pinwheels, either commercial or homemade (see the pattern in Large Muscle Activities).
3. Help children understand how a jet engine works by blowing up a balloon and letting it go. The escaping air pushes the balloon forward.
4. Make a windsock to take outside to find out which way the wind is blowing. Sew a tube of material or the sleeve of a shirt to a circle of wire or an embroidery hoop. Fasten the hoop to a stick to be used as a handle or stuck in the ground. Airplanes must take off and land into the wind. The windsock tells the pilot which way the wind is blowing.

Dramatic Play Centres

Home-living centre

1. Have airline schedules and travel brochures in this centre to encourage the planning of a trip by airplane. Provide suitcases to pack and play money in the purses to purchase tickets.
2. Collect airline tickets and travel posters from travel agents and government tourist offices for this centre.

Block-building centre

1. Build a runway with long planks or unit blocks. Have unbreakable model airplanes available for takeoffs and landings.
2. Add toy cars, people, and baggage to the model airplanes. These will suggest building an airport terminal, runway, tower, or hangar.
3. Hang pictures of terminals, airplanes being loaded and boarded, or airplanes flying to encourage an interest in air transportation.
4. Provide cylindrical and cone-shaped blocks for children who wish to build space stations and rocket ships. Display authentic space pictures on walls in this centre.

5. Styrofoam cones, balls, wreaths, and sheets can provide short-term exploration.
6. When block buildings fall, talk about gravity.

Other dramatic play centres

1. A plank laid across a wooden box or sturdy cardboard carton makes an airplane. Add a steering wheel or dial panel (see the illustration on p. 472). Propellers can be cut out of cardboard and taped to the plank. Steps can be pushed up to the plane for passengers to get on or off the plane. A wagon or rolling platform can be used to take passengers' luggage to and from the plane.
2. Set up two rows of chairs with an aisle between. Section off a galley with a three-way play screen or other room divider. Provide TV dinner trays with laminated food cutouts and paper cups for the flight attendants to serve to the passengers.
3. Set up two short rows of chairs with an aisle between for an airport limousine or a minibus. The driver can wear a chauffeur's cap and a skycap can manage the luggage.
4. Boxes and bags of various sizes can be used as airplane cargo. They can be packed and delivered to a mock terminal or stores.
5. Make binoculars or telescopes for the children to use. Materials needed:
   cardboard rolls from paper towels, wax paper, plastic wrap, or aluminum foil to make telescopes
   cardboard rolls from toilet paper to make binoculars

   Procedure: Find pairs of cardboard rolls that fit one inside the other so they can telescope. Let the children paint or decorate them. Fasten the toilet-paper rolls together in pairs for binoculars after they have been painted by the children.
6. Construct a space ship for the children to use indoors.
   Materials needed:
   cardboard cone or pyramid
   cardboard fins
   spools
   wires
   two large cardboard boxes of different sizes (large enough for a child to get into)
   wooden or metal knobs, old dials

   Procedure: Using the illustration that follows as a guide, cut a door in the biggest box and a hole in the top of it. Tape the smaller box on this, open side down. Make a cone

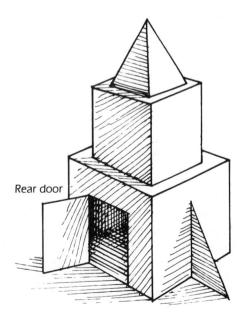

Rear door

or pyramid from a large sheet of posterboard and tape it on top. Cut two fins from posterboard and attach them to the sides of the lower box. Attach spools, wires, knobs and dials inside the boxes wherever you want. The children can paint each section with tempera, or the whole space ship can be covered with silver paper or painted with grey or aluminum paint. Instead of standing upright, the space ship could lie on its side. A space ship for the playground can be made by arranging large packing boxes and adding a nose cone, fins, and instruments in the same way.

7. Make a space helmet for the children to use.

    Materials needed:

    round ice-cream cartons, plastic bleach or water jugs, or a carton or paper bag large enough to go over a child's head

    discarded garden or vacuum-cleaner hose

    shoe box, paper cups, wire, electrical cord, pipecleaners, small boxes, leather straps, canvas webbing, and other scrap materials

    Procedure: Using the illustration as a guide, cut the bottom and a face hole or eye holes from a plastic jug and smooth the edges, then cut a hole for the hose. Let children decorate helmets any way they choose. They can be painted with tempera or coloured with felt pens. Thread the hose through a hole in the shoebox and tape it in place. This is worn on the child's back and secured over the shoulders with straps. Children can add details to their "oxygen packs" with scrap materials.

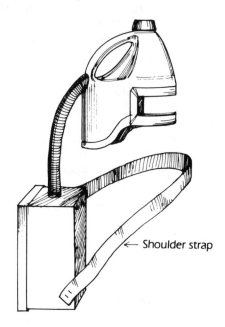

← Shoulder strap

Art Centre

•• 1. Make several different kinds of airplane stencils. Let children spatter paint airplanes on blue construction paper.

•   2. Children could make a picture book of airplanes by pasting precut pictures of different kinds of airplanes onto construction paper. The pictures could then be put in a photo album with magnetic pages, or they could be punched and put in a three-ring binder.

••• 3. At the woodworking table, set out wheels (discs cut from dowels, bottle caps, and plastic caps) and precut shapes of balsa that children can nail together to make airplanes. Propellers can be precut from plastic lids or bottles.

••• 4. Have children decorate large paper grocery bags with paint, scraps of tissue paper, and crayons. Attach a 2 m to 3 m length of string to one corner of the open end of each bag to make kites.

5. Fold some paper gliders (see the illustration). Show the children how to make the folds. Once the children have the idea, they will design their own gliders.

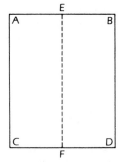

Start with paper 21.5 cm x 28 cm. Fold in half lengthwise. Unfold and label with letters.

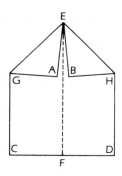

Fold A and B to within 1 cm of centre line E-F.

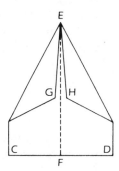

Fold G and H over A and B to within 1 cm of centre line E-F.

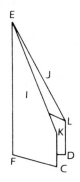

Fold E-K-C over E-L-D.

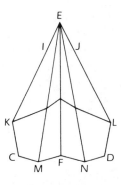

Fold E-K-C and E-L-D back to centre line E-F, forming fold lines E-M and E-N.

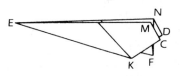

Turn glider over. Fold E-K and E-L back to E-F.

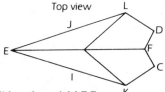

Holding glider along fold E-F, lift up wings I and J. Use a paperclip to hold glider together (optional).

Learning and Language Materials Centre

Commercially made games and materials

1. *Puzzles:* A variety of puzzles with air transportation themes.
2. *Construction and manipulative toys:* Wooden steering wheels and wheels that match large wooden blocks encourage the construction of a variety of transportation vehicles.

3. *Small toys for imaginative play:* Plastic models of vehicles for younger children. Metal models of vehicles for older children. Replicas of airports.
4. *Toys for riding:* A variety of toys for riding both indoors and outdoors. Be sure to choose toys that are replicas of vehicles the children are likely to see, not models of vehicles on television. Choose vehicles that are sturdy and that do not have sharp edges. Make sure they are easy to steer and that you have a variety of sizes to fit different children.
5. *Costumes:* Hats and coats that represent various employees of the airline industry.

Teacher-made games and materials

NOTE: For detailed descriptions, see Learning Games in Part 1.

1. *Look and see:* Use unbreakable models of different kinds of airplanes that show detail.
2. *Can you remember?* Use different airplane models.
3. *Alike, different, and the same:* Make matching pairs of each type of model airplane available. Mix the models and have children find the pairs that match. Put two matching planes and a different one together. Ask children to point to the one that is different.
4. *Colour, shape, size, and number:* When observing real planes or working with models or pictures, talk about size, colour, shape, and number. Count wheels, pontoons, propellers, jets, wings, and tails.

■ Children who need extra support in sorting and classifying will find all of the above activities easier to understand after a trip to a local airport. While at the airport, point out categories of airplanes using simple vocabulary. When you return to the centre, refer to the trip and present the above activities. The references to the concrete experience will help children with categorizing.

Book Centre

•• Assanthiany, Sylvie, and Louise Pelletier. *Grandma's Visit.* Toronto: Lorimer, 1987. (also available in French as *Grand-maman*)
• Barton, Byron. *Airport.* New York: Crowell, 1982.
• Bruna, Dick. *Miffy Goes Flying.* New York: Price Stern, 1984.
•• Crews, Donald. *Flying.* New York: Greenwillow Press, 1986.
• Florian, D. *Airplane Ride.* New York: Crowell, 1984.
• Gay, Michael. *The Little Helicopter.* New York: Macmillan, 1986.
••• Gelman, Rita Golden, and Jack Kent. *Why Can't I Fly?* Richmond Hill, ON: Scholastic-TAB, 1985.
••• Hines, Norman D. *My Brother the Helicopter.* Willowdale, ON: Annick Press, 1991.
• Khalsa, Dayal Kaur. *Bon Voyage, Baabee.* Montreal: Tundra, 1983.
•• Munsch, Robert. *Angela's Airplane.* Willowdale, ON: Annick Press, 1988.
• Rockwell, Anne. *Planes.* New York: Dutton, 1986.
••• Wilson, Sarah. *Three in a Balloon.* New York: Scholastic, 1990.

Books about space travel

•••• Bentley, Roy. *Shuttleburn.* New York: Deutsch, 1984.
•••• Branley, F.M. *Journey into a Black Hole.* Markham, ON: Fitzhenry & Whiteside, 1987.
•••• Ciupik, Larry. *Space Machines.* Milwaukee, WI: Raintree, 1979.
•••• Marshall, James. *Merry Christmas Space Case.* New York: Dial Press, 1986.
•••• Marzallo, Jean. *Jed's Junior Space Patrol.* New York: Dial Press, 1982.
••• Sadler, M. *Allistair in Outer Space.* Englewood Cliffs, NJ: Prentice-Hall, 1984.
•• Wildsmith, Brian. *Professor Noah's Spaceship.* New York: Oxford University Press, 1980.
•• Young, Ruth. *A Trip to Mars.* New York: Orchard Books, 1990.

Planning for Group Time

NOTE: All music, fingerplays, poems, stories, and games listed here may also be used at other times during the session as appropriate. In parodies, hyphenated words match the music notes of the tune used.

Music

Songs

From *The Goat with the Bright Red Socks*, Birkenshaw and Walden
"The Transportation System," p. 30

From *Musical Games for Children of All Ages*, Nelson
"Two Twin Airplanes," p. 8

From *Piggyback Songs*, Warren
"My Kite," p. 22
"I Wish I Were a Windmill," p. 23
"My Bubble Flew Over the Ocean," p. 34

From *Singing Bee*, Hart
"Twinkle Twinkle Little Star," p. 64
"Hey Diddle Diddle," p. 67
"Sally Go Round," p. 87

....

I'M A LITTLE AIRPLANE

(tune: "I'm a Little Teapot")

adaptation by Bonnie Flemming

I'm a lit-tle air-plane; *(raise arms to side at shoulder height)*
I can fly, *(turn right arm in front for propeller)*
Here is my throt-tle; *(reach hand out to instrument panel)*
Give me a try. *(push throttle in)*
When I get all revved up *(make engine noises)*
Then I fly *(move forward down runway)*
Off the run-way *(keep moving forward)*
To the sky! *(go up on tiptoe running forward)*

Rhythms and Singing Games

From *Move, Sing, Listen, Play*, Wood
"Aeroplane Game," p. 136

Records and Cassettes

Bob McGrath. *If You're Happy and You Know It*, Volume I. (Kids Records)
"Mr. Sun"

Anne Murray. *There's a Hippo in My Bathtub*. (Capitol Records)
"Stars Are the Windows of Heaven"

Fred Penner. *Special Delivery.* (Troubadour Records)
"Stars"

Sharon, Lois, and Bram. *Sing and Play with Balloons.* (Elephant Records)
"Follow the Clouds"

Fingerplays and Poems

INVASION FROM PLANET PIZZA

by Tim Wynne-Jones

I've seen them in the sky at night,
Shed their bright and cheesy light,
Skimming low across the trees,
Low enough to grab a bite —

But DON'T!

Beware them and their sneak attacks,
Aliens disguised as snacks.
They laugh at us behind our backs,
Those pizzas from outer space.

You say, no thanks, but they insist,
And then they start to twist your wrist.
You turn away, you try to leave,
But — oh, that smell — you can't resist —

But DO!

Beware them and their sneak attacks,
Aliens disguised as snacks.
They laugh at us behind our backs,
Those pizzas from outer space.

ARRRGGGGHHHHH!

You've got one all over your face!

From *Don't Eat Spiders*, Heidbreder
"Rockets," p. 44
"Space," p. 45
"Creature from Outer Space," p. 47

From *A New Treasury of Children's Poetry*, Cole
"I Can Fly," p. 132

From *Read Aloud Rhymes for the Very Young*, Prelutsky and Brown
"A Kite," p. 33
"Wouldn't You?" p. 33
"Wings," p. 39
"Moon Boat," p. 71
"I See the Moon," p. 71
"Moon-Come-Out," p. 71
"The Star," p. 71

From *Where the Sidewalk Ends*, Silverstein
"The Flying Festoon," p. 80

Stories

(To read, read–tell, or tell. See Book Centre for a complete list.)
Assanthiany and Pelletier's *Grandma's Visit* is an excellent story for introducing the subject of air travel.

Games

(See Learning Games in Part 1 and Teacher-Made Games and Materials earlier in this chapter for directions.)
1. *Look and see.*
2. *Can you remember?*
3. *Alike, different, and the same.*

Routine Times

1. At snack or meal times, have children arrange chairs in two double rows. Have "flight attendants" put food on trays and serve it to the passengers" on the plane. Use finger foods for this snack or meal. Omit liquids with younger children, or fill glasses only half full.
2. When walking or riding to and from the centre, listen for airplanes.
3. At rest time, suggest that the children be very quiet and listen for an airplane.

Large Muscle Activities

1. Use a packing box or sturdy carton with a plank across it for an airplane. Add a steering wheel or dial panel (see illustration, p. 472). Steps pushed up to the packing box can be used for passengers to get on or off the plane. A wagon or wheeled platform can be used for a baggage cart.
2. Outdoors is the perfect place for action songs (see Music).
3. Provide the children with paper pinwheels (see illustrations). They can pretend the pinwheels are propellers and they are airplanes.

Pinwheel pattern

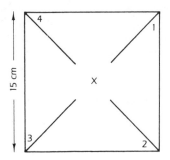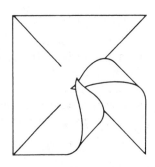

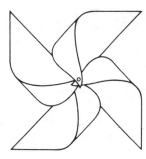

Pinwheel: From each corner, cut 7 cm toward the centre. Place each numbered corner over the X and hold with thumb. Fasten pinwheel to a dowel 15 cm to 25 cm long with a large-headed pin or thumbtack. Very young children should not be sent home with pins or tacks.

4. Paper gliders are fun to run with or fly (see pattern, on p. 457).
5. Paper helicopters are fun to drop from the top of a jungle gym, a climber, or a packing box (see illustration).

Helicopter pattern

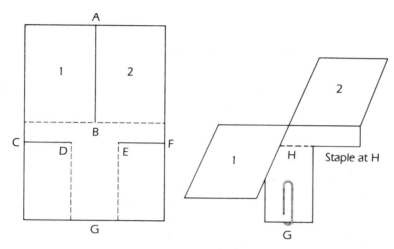

Helicopter: Cut a 2.5 cm x 28 cm piece of construction paper into quarters. Each quarter sheet will make one helicopter. Following illustration, fold each in half and cut from A to B. Cut C-D and F-E. Fold F to D and C to E. Paperclip at G, and staple at H. Fold down wings 1 and 2. Hold high and let go.

Extended Experiences

1. Visit an airport to see airplanes take off and land. For very young children, a first visit to a small, private airfield might be best — jet engines are very noisy and may frighten them. At a smaller airport there might be a greater opportunity to take a closer look at the airplanes and visit a hangar. Perhaps permission could be obtained for the children to board one of the planes to see what it looks like inside. Older children may be able to understand the various parts that make up a large airport.
2. Invite a pilot or a flight attendant to come to the centre and talk briefly about his or her job. Ask the visitor to wear his or her job uniform and to bring the seat belt and oxygen mask that is used in safety demonstrations and the earphones for the inflight movie.
3. Show slides of various airplanes and different buildings found at your local airport or one in a nearby community. Contact a local flying school or the manager or public relations director of a nearby airport or airline company for slides.

Teacher Resources

Pictures and Displays

☐   Display travel posters, airline tickets, baggage-claim checks, airline schedules, and models of several kinds of planes.

☐ Display model airplanes made by a model enthusiast out of the reach of children.
☐ Use sturdy model airplanes as a table centrepiece to encourage discussion about air transportation while children are eating.
☐ Hang pictures of different kinds of aircraft, an airport, a pilot, a flight attendant, a control tower, and a windsock.

Books and Periodicals

Lambert, M. *Jane's All the World's Aircraft 1990–1991.* Alexandria, VA: Janes Information Group, 1990.
Mondey, David. *Aircraft.* New York: Octopus, 1973.
Tryckare, Tre. *The Lore of Flight.* Göteborg, Sweden: Cagner, 1970.

Films and Videos

NOTE: Check with your distributor about public performance rights.

The Boy and the Airplane. Japiri (released in Canada by Films Francais), 1969 (no narration)
The Mole and the Rocket. Kratky Films, Prague (released in Canada by International Tele-Film), 1977. (no narration)
The Sky Is Blue. National Film Board, 1969.

Community Resources and Organizations

☐ Transportation companies.
☐ Societies interested in transportation; for example, a flying club or a hang-gliding club.
☐ A travel agent.
☐ An airline representative.
☐ Hobby stores, for models and catalogues. Obtain the names of people who have collections of model airplanes and who may be willing to lend them for display. These people may also have collections of slides that could be borrowed.
☐ Flying school: Contact the director about an instructor coming to the centre to talk to the children, or about a visit to the flying school for a closeup view of an airplane, with permission to board one.
☐ Airlines: Contact public-relations directors for literature.
☐ Airport: Contact the manager of your local airport to arrange a visit.

Government Agencies

☐ Federal, provincial, or territorial ministries of transportation and communication.

23 Ground and Road Transportation

....

Basic Understandings

(concepts children can grasp from this subject)

> **NOTE:** The word "car" in the following statements is used to represent all road vehicles. If your group interest at the moment is trucks, then use only that term in the statements. When "car" is used it would then refer only to automobiles.

- [ ] Cars (and trucks, buses, and campers) are machines that we drive on roads to get people or things from one place to another.
- [ ] The person who steers a car is known as the driver, and those who ride with him or her are known as passengers.
- [ ] Cars are made in different shapes, sizes, and colours.
- [ ] Cars have motors that run on gasoline, diesel fuel, and batteries.
- [ ] Many families own a car, which they use to drive to and from many places, such as work, school, shopping centre, doctor, laundry or dry cleaner; to visit friends or relatives; or to take trips to see interesting things.
- [ ] Cars are usually parked in garages or carports; buses and trucks are parked in larger garages.
- [ ] Cars get gasoline, diesel fuel, oil, and air at a service station or a self-serve pump. Trucks get gasoline or diesel fuel at a truck stop.
- [ ] Cars are repaired in garages, body shops, and some service stations.
- [ ] Cars can be washed in an automatic car wash.
- [ ] Cars have safety belts and door locks to help keep us safely inside.
- [ ] The driver must pay attention to his or her driving, and the passengers must not distract the driver.
- [ ] A driver has to take special tests to get a driver's licence.
- [ ] A driver must obey (follow) certain traffic rules or else she or he may get a ticket from a police officer and have to pay a fine (money) or have her or his driver's licence taken away.
- [ ] Road signs, traffic lights, and police officers help drivers drive safely.
- [ ] When we travel by car, we can eat:
    a. By taking a bag lunch and eating it in the car as we ride.
    b. By taking a picnic lunch and stopping at a roadside park.
    c. By stopping at a restaurant and buying food.

465

☐ When we travel by car, we can sleep:
   a. At a roadside rest area or campground and sleep in the car, a camper, a trailer, or in a tent.
   b. In a hotel or a motel.

☐ If a car is damaged in an accident, it is towed to a garage by a tow truck.

☐ There are different kinds of cars — sedans, convertibles, station wagons, sports cars, dragsters, jeeps, racing cars, and vans.

☐ Some cars are built and equipped to do special jobs:
   a. Police cars have sirens and two-way radios.
   b. Fire engines carry ladders, hoses, and firefighters to fires.
   c. Ambulances are usually white and have sirens. They are equipped with first-aid equipment and stretchers. They carry people who are sick or hurt to the hospital.
   d. Taxis have meters and two-way radios. People can pay the driver to take them where they wish to go.

☐ Trucks are specially built to carry things, animals, or people; for example, garbage, building supplies, firefighting equipment, furniture, concrete, milk, mail, animals and gasoline.

☐ There are different kinds of buses — school, city, and transcontinental (these travel across the country).

☐ Cars can tow many things — trailers, campers, boats, horse vans, or other cars.

☐ A ferry carries cars and people across a river, a lake, or an ocean channel.

☐ Tunnels are dug under rivers and through mountains for cars.

☐ Bridges are built so cars can get across rivers and deep valleys.

☐ Sometimes drivers have to pay a toll (money) to cross some bridges or drive through some tunnels.

☐ Other names for a road are street, avenue, boulevard, drive, court, crescent, lane, freeway, thruway, expressway, and highway.

☐ There are two-wheeled vehicles, such as bicycles, scooters, and motorcycles.

☐ Many people travel on bicycles. Some packages and letters are delivered by people riding on bicycles (couriers).

☐ Some drivers like to enter car races, such as drag racing, stock-car racing, and grand prix races.

☐ In parts of the country, sleighs and snowmobiles are used to transport people and things from one place to another.

☐ In the North, sleighs and snowmobiles run on the snow using skis instead of wheels. Sleighs can be pulled by dogs or horses.

☐ Tractors, combines, and other farm vehicles are used to plant and harvest crops on farms and ranches.

☐ Some transportation machines run on rails; for example, railway trains, subway trains, streetcars, and monorail trains.

☐ Most trains and streetcars run on two rails called tracks; monorail cars run on one rail.

☐ You may find rails or tracks in many places:
   a. Railway and monorail tracks are laid on top of the ground.
   b. Streetcar tracks are set into city roads.
   c. Subway tracks are laid underground.

☐ Streetcars are like city buses; they take people from one part of the city to another part. However, they can move only where tracks are laid.

☐ There are different kinds of trains:
   a. Passenger trains carry people from one place to another.
   b. Commuter trains carry people into and out of cities.
   c. Subway trains carry people in tunnels under the ground from one part of a city to another.

       d. Freight trains carry things from one location to another. Some things they carry are animals, cars, food, furniture, lumber, and oil.

       e. Work trains (maintenance-of-way trains) carry workers and machines to help repair tracks and trains.

☐ The locomotive or diesel engine pulls the train. Two or more engines are needed if the train is very long.

☐ There are different kinds of cars on a passenger train — coach, sleeping car, dining car, vistadome car, lounge or club car, baggage car, and observation car.

☐ There are different kinds of cars on a freight train — tank car, boxcar, flatcar, cattle car, gondola car, hopper car, autoveyor, refrigerator car, and caboose.

☐ Many people work for railway companies — ticket agents, engineers, brakemen, conductors, porters, cooks, servers, and dispatchers.

☐ The trains stop at various stations so that passengers can get on and off and freight can be loaded and unloaded.

☐ A railway station or terminal is a large building where passengers can buy tickets to ride on the train. Most stations have a snack bar or restaurant, newsstands, waiting room or lounge, and rest rooms.

☐ Many of the things you do at home may be done on a train:

       a. Sit, talk, read, look out the window, walk, or eat.

       b. Eat a meal in the dining car.

       c. Sleep in a pullman car in bunk-type beds called berths, or in a small compartment.

       d. Wash your hands and use a toilet in the rest room.

       e. You may take your pets, but they must ride in the baggage car.

☐ There are special signals for drivers on roads that tell them a train is coming — two flashing red lights, a bell, or sometimes crossing gates are dropped across the road.

☐ The train blows its whistle when it is ready to start, is going to cross a road, or is coming into a station.

Additional Facts the Teacher Should Know

1. Many books, songs, fingerplays, and poems still use old titles for the community workers now called letter carriers, firefighters, and police officers. Simply substitute the correct names as you use these materials with the children. (See Chapter 8, Families at Work, for a complete list.)

2. This chapter deals with transportation vehicles that travel on roads or the ground. There are many different kinds of cars, trucks, and buses being designed and manufactured today.

3. Two-wheeled vehicles that can be driven on roads are powered both by pedalling and by motor. All bicycles, except those with training wheels, can be ridden in the streets, and cyclists must follow the same rules as those for car drivers. Some bikes have hand brakes and special gear mechanisms that allow the cyclist to pedal at various speeds with less effort. If two-wheeled vehicles are driven at night, they must have headlights and rear reflectors. Most communities have a licence requirement for motorized two-wheeled vehicles. In addition, there is a national law requiring all motorcyclists to wear helmets while riding.

There are many different kinds of cars

Familiarize yourself with the different kinds of cars to identify them correctly for the children. Cars carry one to six people and may have two or four doors. Most cars have a trunk in the back where a spare tire is stored under the floor. Most cars have heaters, radios, clocks, and seat belts. Some seats recline or have headrests.

1. *Convertibles* are similar to sedans or coupes but have roofs that fold back, retract, or can be removed.
2. *Station wagons* are similar to sedans but longer, with larger floor areas instead of trunks for carrying things. Usually there are luggage racks on the roof.
3. *Racing cars* are small, one-seated cars that are designed to go very fast for a long period of time.
4. *Four-wheel-drive* vehicles have good traction; they are used primarily for driving in open country, and on rough or snowy roads.
5. *Vans or minibuses* are larger than sedans but smaller than buses. They may have three or four rows of seats and carry up to twelve people.
6. *Taxis* are sedans with meters and two-way radios or computers that are used for transporting people for a fare based on kilometres travelled and time spent in the taxi.
7. *Ambulances* are specially designed to transport sick or injured people. Stretchers, cots, or rolling tables can be put into the back section. Ambulances carry emergency medical equipment. A siren and flashing red light warn of its coming.
8. *Limousines* are long, comfortable sedans used for transporting up to nine people to and from rail and air terminals. Some businesses provide free limousine service for their customers. Limousines are also used to carry people to special events, such as weddings.
9. *Police cars* are sedans with sirens, flashing lights, and two-way radios.

There are many different kinds of trucks

Trucks are used to transport goods and people. The part of the truck that the driver sits in is called the cab. The cab and the motor are usually mounted over the front wheels of the truck. Smaller trucks are moulded onto a single frame like a car, but most larger trucks are in two or more sections. The section that pulls is called the tractor, and the section that is being hauled is called the trailer. A flatbed trailer is a platform on wheels. Containerized freight can be lifted onto it using a crane, while some machines, like tractors and other farm equipment, can be driven up on ramps. Cylindrical or oval-shaped trailers are called tank trailers and rectangular, enclosed trailers are vans. Most trucks are powered by gasoline, propane, or diesel fuel. Those burning diesel fuel can be recognized by the vent pipe behind the cab.

1. *Pickup trucks* are small trucks with open beds and short sides that are used for carrying small equipment, tools, and materials.
2. *Dump trucks* are larger than pickups and have higher sides. They are built with hydraulic lifts so the beds can be tilted to allow the contents to slide out through the hinged tailgates or through special openings. They are used to haul dirt, coal, and gravel.
3. *Tank trucks* carry liquids, such as milk, chemicals, oil, or fuel.
4. *Moving vans* come in various sizes and are large, enclosed rectangular trailers used for moving household goods or office equipment.
5. *Garbage trucks* are used to haul garbage to landfill sites.
6. *Cement mixers* have mixers mounted on the trailers that simultaneously transport and mix concrete.
7. *Freight trailers* have rectangular vans that are used for carrying food, clothes, equipment, tools, and other goods.
8. *Automobile carriers* are designed to carry cars. The cars are driven on and off the trailers on tracks called skids.
9. *Livestock trucks* have rectangular trailers with slats that let air in for transporting cattle, horses, pigs, chickens, and other animals.
10. *Fire engines* carry firefighters and ladders, hoses, and other equipment for fighting fires.
11. *Canteen trucks* are designed like small kitchens and transport prepared foods to job sites for workers.

Small cars and trucks extend the transportation theme into all activities in the centre.

12. *Delivery trucks* are small, enclosed trucks used to deliver commercial products to homes and businesses. They are often operated by bakeries, florists, diaper services, department stores, and courier services.
13. *Mail trucks* are used by Canada Post to transport mail and packages.
14. *Campers* are small trailers for camping in parks.

There are many different kinds of buses

1. *School or church buses* (usually painted yellow) have centre aisles with eighteen to twenty rows of seats arranged on each side. They are used to transport people to and from school or churches or for special outings.
2. *City buses* carry people from one part of a city to another, stopping at bus stops.
3. *Transcontinental buses* are sometimes called scenic cruisers or motorcoaches. These buses are air conditioned and frequently have two levels of seats and domed windows for viewing scenery as passengers travel across the country.
4. *Buses for physically disabled people* are available in many towns and cities. These buses are designed to accommodate wheelchairs and to be accessible to people who use crutches and canes. Some children in your program may use these special buses, or they may have a relative, neighbour, or friend who uses these services.

Basic facts about trains

1. Diesel or steam engines are called locomotives. Diesel engines have almost entirely replaced steam engines. Therefore, the coal-shovelling job has become obsolete, and the diesel engineer is now assisted by a front brakeman who helps to check the road signals and other safety controls.
2. There are different kinds of trains and different kinds of cars used in making them. It is not appropriate to teach detailed definitions. If children are interested in the types of cars they see in trains, label them by their purpose.

3. There are many different jobs involved in operating a train. Again, detail is not really necessary for young children unless they display curiosity. Describe the duties performed by the workers in whom they show an interest.

4. Each railway has its own symbol, logo, or herald; for example, VIA Rail has yellow and blue stripes for its logo.

5. Canadian history is closely tied to the history of railways in our country. Until recently, Canada has had two major railway companies and a few small, local rail services. Canadian National and Canadian Pacific provided passenger and freight services across the country. All passenger services have been taken over by VIA Rail. The freight industry is flourishing, but passenger service has declined. Many small towns have lost their passenger services, and much of the equipment used by VIA Rail is old. In contrast, Canada has some efficient, high-speed passenger trains in the busy Windsor to Montreal corridor. Some large cities also have commuter train services, subway or métro trains, elevated or "sky" trains. These trains are designed for short trips. For most children, these will be their first experience of a train. Many people still consider rail service of all sorts to be very important to Canada.

Introducing This Subject to Children

1. Relate your experience of a trip taken by bus, car, streetcar, subway, or train, or invite children to relate their experiences.

2. Read a story about cars, trucks, buses, or trains.

3. Hang pictures of cars, trucks, buses, or trains, or display models of all kinds of road vehicles.

4. If one of the children's parents drives a taxi, bus, or other vehicle, have him or her visit the centre and tell about the job.

5. Take a trip to a nearby train station.

6. Have someone who works for a railway visit the centre and talk about his or her job.

Vocabulary

traffic	service station	key	park
light	police officer	drive	parking meter
road sign	firefighter	driver	steer
tow truck	letter carrier	speed	bridge
toll booth	parking lot	ticket	tunnel
attendant	gas	licence	garage
car wash	oil	race	ferry
restaurant	air	haul	taxi
motel, hotel	tow		
whistle	subway	berth	switch
freight	locomotive	upper	track
passenger	conductor	lower	tank car
monorail	engineer	coach	flatcar
station	streetcar	train	boxcar
engine	dining car	signal	cattle car
caboose	sleeping car		

kinds of cars, trucks, and buses   parts of cars   names of roads

Learning Centres

Discovery Centre

1. Set up a display of toy cars, trucks, trains, and buses. Help children understand that each vehicle is specifically designed to do a special job.
2. Show maps of your area, your province, and Canada. Include maps of local bus routes. Talk about how different maps are used by drivers. Discuss different ways to ride around your city, your province, and the country. Talk about how the children got to the centre — by car (kind), taxi, bus, van, truck, subway, or train.
3. If the playground or windows in the centre overlook a busy street that the children can see easily, in safety, talk about the different kinds of vehicles on the road. If the centre gets special mail or package deliveries, have children watch for the delivery truck.
4. Help children discover that every vehicle that drives on the road must have a licence. Trucks that drive in many provinces have several. Start a collection of licence plates from all the provinces and display them so that children can see the similarities and differences. They sometimes have mottos or emblems on them. Talk about the special features of your province's plates.
5. On a table, display a driver's licence; a licence plate from your province; road maps of your city and province; a model car, station wagon, camper, and trailer; and brochures of parks or well-known landmarks in or near your community. Encourage conversation about how families use their cars for fun.
6. To help children understand how brakes are used, make a gently sloping hill and a steep hill from several blocks and two planks. Provide cars for the children to roll down the hills. Which hill makes cars go faster? Which driver would need to use the brakes the most?

Dramatic Play Centres

Home-living centre

1. Make bus and train schedules and travel brochures available so children can plan a trip by bus, car, or train. Suitcases and play money in purses will increase the amount of travel play.
2. Fill a lunchbox for an auto mechanic, a truck driver, or a bus driver to take to work.
3. Provide toy tools to fix a tricycle, ride-on truck, or car.
4. Set out hats for different kinds of transportation workers.
5. Set out overnight bags and suitcases. These can be packed with dressup clothes and doll clothes for a trip.

Block-building centre

1. Feature road accessories, such as cars, people, and road signs, to encourage the building of roads and transportation play. Have cans of small materials, such as buttons, pebbles, and twigs, for children to use as freight.
2. Encourage children to build bridges, tunnels, toll booths, garages, or bus stations.
3. Children may wish to make a network of roads, several structures (restaurants, motels, a bus station, traffic signals, bridges, and tunnels), or a whole city. This kind of activity can last several days if structures can remain standing from day to day.
4. Occasionally, when the children name a structure they have built, you may wish to fasten a sign to it, such as "Miguel's Motel" or "Semareh's Service Station."

5. Gasoline pumps of the correct scale for use with unit blocks are commercially available, or you can make your own with scraps of wood and paint, using plastic clothesline or rope for gas hose.

6. Build roads for larger trucks and cars by using blocks and ramps. Encourage the road builders to make a garage, station, or parking lot. A child-size gasoline pump could be made from wood and garden hose. Two large cardboard cylinders set in a wooden box or a sturdy carton with rope or garden hose attached make usable gas pumps. children can help paint them. Weight two tall, corrugated boxes by placing rocks in the bottom, paint them, and attach rope or garden hose to make pumps. These are only sturdy enough for short-term use.

7. Encourage interest in trains by hanging pictures of stations and trains in this centre.

8. Set out an interlocking train set.

9. Make miniature traffic signs out of cardboard.

Other dramatic play centres

1. To simulate a train station, set up a three-way play screen with tables, or build a ticket counter with hollow blocks and boards. Use ride-on train, or set up two rows of chairs with an aisle between. Provide engineer and conductor hats (see patterns on pp. 26 and 473), bandanas to wear around the neck, paper punches, coloured paper scraps for tickets, and train schedules. A simple lantern (no glass) and a dial panel (see illustration) are other dramatic play accessories children can use. Encourage children to share hats. You may need to use a timer or set a reasonable time limit for a treasured prop.

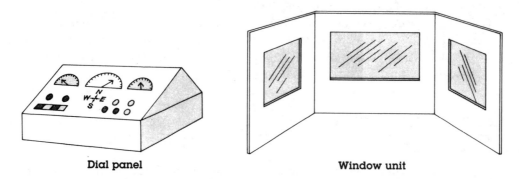

Dial panel   **Window unit**

Cut out "windows" or paste or paint pictures of appropriate scenery for the driver. Place around dial panel or a steering wheel unit. (Contributed by Janice Bailey.)

2. Set up two rows of chairs with an aisle between for a bus. A commercial or homemade steering wheel or dial panel can be added for the driver to use.

3. A car or taxi can be made by putting two rows of three chairs one behind the other. Add a steering wheel or dial panel and traffic signs.

4. Encourage playing firefighters by providing hats (see pattern), ladders, and short lengths of garden hose. A bicycle handle grip makes a good nozzle for the hose. A wagon or a long, sturdy cardboard box makes a good fire engine. If you have a ladder box or a climbing house, children could pretend that it is the building that is on fire.

5. Obtain discarded hats and uniform shirts from police officers, bus drivers, or letter carriers. Less durable hats can be made of construction paper. (See patterns.)

6. In the winter sleds and toy snowmobiles can provide fun in the snow. Children can volunteer to pull sleds around the playground.

NOTE: See Large Muscle Activities for additional ideas.

Letter carrier or conductor's hat pattern

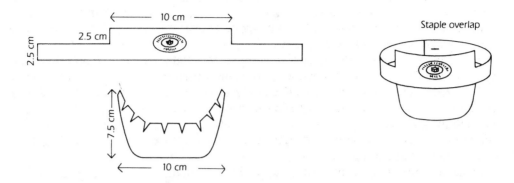

Letter carrier or conductor's hat: Cut a rectangle of blue construction paper 53 cm long and 5 cm deep. As shown in the top left diagram, cut away 21.5 x 2.5 cm at each side to leave a peak 10 cm x 5 cm at centre of hat. Notch visor as indicated in bottom left diagram. Staple ends of headband together. Glue visor to headband.

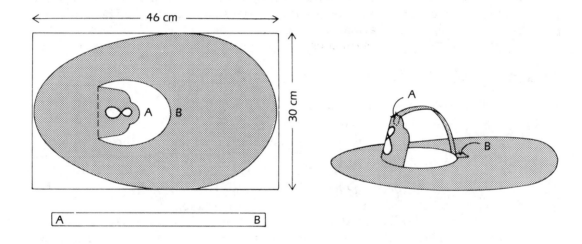

Firefighter's hat pattern: Cut hat shape out of a 30 x 46 cm piece of red or black construction paper. Cut out the unshaded area. Cut strip A-B to define the crown of the hat and staple it as shown.

Art Centre

•• 1. Provide children with coloured construction paper and precut rectangles, squares, and circles of various sizes to make designs. Some will discover that they can make trucks, wagons, and other vehicles.

••• 2. At the woodworking bench, set out wheels cut from dowels, bottle caps, plastic lids, and precut shapes of balsa that children can use to make a vehicle.

   NOTE: Do not direct children as to what they should make, but instead offer assistance as needed to help them make what they have in mind. Shapes cut from coloured plastic bottles (heat in hot water before cutting with scissors or use a utility knife) make colourful bumpers and stripes that are easily punctured by nails.

•••   3. A shoebox train can be made by combining several shoeboxes in various ways, painting them, and tying them together with nylon twine, plastic clothesline, or thin rope.

••   4. Children can help make a picture book of trains. Pictures can be cut out of magazines or model catalogues or precut, mounted on construction paper, and put in a three-ring binder photo album with magnetic pages.

•••   5. Make a mural of the inside of a special train car for your centre (plan on taking three to four days to complete this activity). Cover a bulletin board that can easily be reached by children with light-coloured paper. Outline the shape of a train car on the board. Put a banner at the top of the board that says "(your centre or school's name) Train Car." Read the group the story *Jesse on the Night Train* by Richard Thompson (see Book Centre). Then suggest that the children make their own train car for a night train trip. Work with the group to decide what they need to make the train car special and comfortable. Then, as the group decides on each element of the car, make a list. Once all the components are identified, send the children on a hunt to find the materials they will need to make their car. Have them work together on the mural.

■   This activity encourages co-operation. It is particularly useful if you have children in your group who need to improve their socializing skills. The activity also encourages problem solving. By working in a group to plan the car, good problem solving is modelled for children. Be sure to use open-ended questions when working with the group. Encourage the children to review the decisions they have made. This will model the problem-solving process for everyone.

Learning and Language Materials Centre

Commercially made games and materials

1. *Puzzles:* A variety of puzzles with transportation themes.
2. *Construction and manipulative toys:* Wooden steering wheels and wheels that match large wooden blocks encourage the construction of a variety of transportation vehicles.
3. *Small toys for imaginative play:* Plastic models of various vehicles for younger children. Metal models of various vehicles for older children.
4. *Toys for riding:* A variety of toys for riding both indoors and outdoors. Be sure to choose toys that are replicas of vehicles the children are likely to see, not models of vehicles on television. Choose vehicles that are sturdy and that do not have sharp edges. Make sure they are easy to steer and that you have a variety of sizes to fit different children.
5. *Costumes:* Hats and coats that represent various employees of the trucking, mail, bus, and railway industries.

Teacher-made games and materials

NOTE: For detailed descriptions, see Learning Games in Part 1.

1. *Look and see:* Use toy cars, trucks, taxis, buses, and campers.
2. *Reach and feel:* Use small, sturdy models of a station wagon, a tank truck, a pickup truck, and other vehicles.
3. *Can you remember?* Use model vehicles and pictures of various drivers, such as police officer, cab driver, bus driver, and mail-truck driver.
4. How many?
   a. How many ways can children get to school using machines that drive on the roads?
   b. How many wheels does a bicycle have? A car? A bus? Supply models of these vehicles so children can count them.
   c. How many ways can a car get across a river? (bridge, tunnel, ferry)

■   These activities are useful for helping children develop problem-solving methods. Children with cognitive delays will need a model for this type of problem solving.

Break the problem into steps, and give them clues to the solution for each step. After they have solved the problem, review how they arrived at the solution. Using props may help.

Encourage advanced or gifted children to think of alternative answers to the standards. For example, "How would you get to school if the buses were not working, the subways were broken down, and your parents' car wasn't working?" Encourage fantastic answers. If children invent a way of getting to the centre, suggest that they draw a picture of the vehicle they have invented.

5. *Who am I?* Describe drivers of various vehicles, such as: "I drive a truck that carries oil to gas stations, who am I?"
6. *Match-them:* Make card sets of pairs of different kinds of cars, trucks, and buses and pairs of drivers, such as taxi drivers, bus drivers, police officers, and sanitation workers. Mix the pairs up and have children find pairs that match.
7. *Sorting and grouping by association:* Use the card sets from number 6 and have children group them into cars, trucks, or drivers. Children could also match a driver with the kind of vehicle she or he drives.
8. *Alike, different, and the same:* Use the card sets from number 6.
9. *Colour, shape, size, and number:* When observing real road vehicles or when using scale models, talk about colour, shape, size, and number. For example: "See the *big* truck." "What *colour* is the car?" "The *cylindrical* tank truck carries gas."

■ Ask children to identify vehicles they see; for example: "What kind of truck is that?" "What do you think it might be carrying?" After they answer, ask them, "Why?" This will help all children develop problem-solving and thinking skills.

Book Centre

••• Aylesworth, Jim. *Country Crossing.* New York: Atheneum, 1991.
• Barton, Byron. *Trains.* New York: Crowell, 1986.
• ———. *Trucks.* New York: Crowell, 1986.
•• Borden, Louise. *The Neighborhood Trucker.* Richmond Hill, ON: Scholastic, 1990.
• Bruna, Dick. *Miffy's Bicycle.* New York: Price Stern, 1984.
• Burningham, John. *Mr. Gumpy's Motorcar.* London: Jonathan Cape, 1973.
••• Cossi, Olga. *Gus the Bus.* New York: Scholastic, 1989.
••• Crews, Donald. *School Bus.* New York: Penguin, 1985.
••• ———. *Freight Train.* New York: Greenwillow Press, 1978.
••• Ehrlich, Amy. *The Everyday Train.* New York: Dial Press, 1977.
•• Gibbons, Gail. *Fill It Up, A Book about Service Stations.* Markham, ON: Fitzhenry & Whiteside, 1986.
••• Greene, Carla. *Truck Drivers: What Do They Do?* New York: Harper & Row, 1967.
••• Greene, Graham. *The Little Train.* Markham, ON: Puffin, 1977.
••• Greve, Andreas. *Christopher's Dream Car.* Willowdale, ON: Annick Press, 1991.
••• Harvey. *Gilbert and the Bicycle.* Richmond Hill, ON: Scholastic, 1987.
••• Hines, Gary. *A Ride in the Crummy.* New York: Greenwillow Press, 1991.
• Hoban, Tana. *Dig, Drill, Dump, Fill.* New York: Greenwillow Press, 1975.
••• Howard, Elizabeth Fitzgerald. *The Train to Lulu's.* New York: Bradbury Press, 1988.
•••• Italiano, Carlo. *Sleighs: The Gentle Transportation.* Montreal: Tundra, 1974. (Read–Tell)
•• Kesselman, Wendy. *There's a Train Going By My Window.* Garden City, NY: Doubleday, 1982.
••• Kovalski, Maryann. *The Wheels on the Bus: An Adaptation of the Traditional Song.* Toronto: Kids Can Press, 1987.
••• Lyon, George Ella. *A Regular Rolling Noah.* New York: Aladdin, 1991.
•••• Maas, Robert. *Fire Fighters.* Richmond Hill, ON: Scholastic, 1989.
• Magee, Doug. *Trucks You Can Count On.* New York: Dodd Mead, 1985.

••• Morgan, Allen. *Andrew and the Wild Bikes.* Willowdale, ON: Annick Press, 1990.

••• ———. *Matthew and the Midnight Tow Truck.* Willowdale, ON: Annick Press, 1984.

••• Munsch, Robert. *Jonathan Cleaned Up, Then He Heard a Sound.* Willowdale, ON: Annick Press, 1981. (subway trains)

••• O'Young, L. *Mike and the Bike.* Toronto: Lorimer, 1986.

••• Pierce, J. *The Freight Train Book.* Minneapolis, MN: Carolrhoda, 1980.

•• Price, Matthew. *The Working Wheels Series: (Tractors, Special Engines, Diggers, Trucks).* Toronto: Kids Can Press, 1986.

• Retan, Walter. *The Big Book of Real Trucks.* New York: Grosset & Dunlap, 1986.

•• Rey, H.A. *Curious George Rides a Bike.* New York: Sandpiper, 1973.

• Rockwell, Anne. *Bikes.* New York: Dutton, 1986.

• ———. *Fire Engines.* New York: Dutton, 1986.

• ———. *Things That Go.* New York: Dutton, 1986.

•• Ross, Diana. *The Little Red Engine and the Rocket.* Albuquerque: Transatlantic Arts, 1978.

•• ———. *The Little Red Engine Goes to Town.* Albuquerque: Transatlantic Arts, 1978.

•• ———. *The Story of the Little Red Engine.* Albuquerque: Transatlantic Arts, 1978.

••• Sattler, Helen R. *Train Whistles.* New York: Lothrop, Lee & Shepard, 1985.

••• Siebert, Diane. *Train Song.* New York: Crowell, 1990.

• ———. *Truck Song.* New York: Crowell, 1990.

• Slater, Teddy. *The Big Book of Real Fire Trucks and Fire Fighting.* New York: Gosset & Dunlap, 1986.

•• Stevenson, James. *Are We Almost There?* New York: Greenwillow Press, 1985.

••• Thompson, Richard. *Jesse on the Night Train.* Willowdale, ON: Annick Press, 1990.

Planning for Group Time

••

NOTE: All music, fingerplays, poems, stories, and games listed here may be used at other times during the session as appropriate. In parodies, hyphenated words match the music notes of the tune used.

Music

Songs

··

THE WHEELS ON THE BUS

by Jean Warren

      F   F
Oh, the wheels on the bus go round and round,

    C   F
Round and round, round and round.

      F   F
Oh, the wheels on the bus go round and round,

    C   F
All through the town. *(make circling motions with hands)*

      F   F
Oh, the wipers on the bus go swish, swish, swish,

C   F
Swish, swish, swish; swish, swish, swish.

         F   F
Oh, the wipers on the bus go swish, swish, swish,

C   F
All through the town. *(move hands back and forth like windshield wipers)*

         F   F
Oh, the people on the bus go up and down,

C   F
Up and down, up and down.

         F   F
Oh, the people on the bus go up and down,

C   F
All through the town. *(move body up and down)*

(Additional verses: The horn on the bus goes toot, toot, toot; The baby on the bus goes waa, waa, waa; The mother on the bus goes shh, shh, shh; etc.)

From *The Baby Beluga Book*, Raffi
"Morningtown Ride," p. 46

From *The Best Singing Games for Children of All Ages*, Bloy
"Down the River," p. 74

From *Elephant Jam*, Sharon, Lois, and Bram
"A Peanut Sat on a Railway Track," p. 13
"Sur le pont d'Avignon," p. 82

From *Eye Winker, Tom Tinker, Chin Chopper*, Glazer
"Down by the Station," p. 21
"This Train," p. 84

From *The Goat with the Bright Red Socks*, Birkenshaw and Walden
"How Do I Get from Here to There?" p. 6
"Transportation System," p. 30

From *More Piggyback Songs*, Warren
"Jimmy Jones Built a Car," p. 55
"Buckle Up," p. 67
"When I Cross the Street," p. 67
"Safety," p. 67
"Choo Choo Train," p. 89

From *Sally Go Round the Sun*, Fowke
"Going to Chicago," p. 26
"Going to Boston," p. 39

From *Singing Bee*, Hart
"The Bus Song," p. 130

From *Stepping Along in Music Land*, Murray
"Rolling Down the Highway," p. 43
"Traffic Signs," p. 55
"On My Way to School," p. 56

From *A Treasury of Songs for Children*, Glazer
"Down by the Station," p. 71
"I've Been Working on the Railroad," p. 133
"Pat Works on the Railroad," p. 186
"She'll Be Comin' Round the Mountain," p. 199

From *What Shall We Do and Alee Galloo!*, Winn
"Chug-a-lug-a-lug," p. 20

....

WATCHING TRAFFIC (a parody)

(tune, "Frère Jacques")

adaptation by Bonnie Flemming (verse 1: Romona Ware)

Watch the cars go, watch the cars go,
Whiz-zing by, whiz-zing by.
Beep, beep, beep, beep, beep, beep,
Beep, beep, beep, beep, beep, beep,
That's like mine! That's like mine!

Watch the bus go *(repeat)*
Roll-ing by *(repeat)*
Stop for all the peo-ple *(repeat)*
Get on board! *(repeat)*

See the trucks go, see the trucks go
Down the street, down the street.
Gas and oil and milk trucks,
Mail and trash and dump trucks,
On their way, on their way.

....

THE FIREFIGHTER (a parody)

(tune: "The More We Get Together")

adaptation by Bonnie Flemming

Oh, hear the warn-ing si-ren
The si-ren, the si-ren
Oh, hear the warn-ing siren;
Get out of the way!

Oh, see the big red pump-er
The pump-er, the pump-er
Oh, see the big red pump-er
Go off to the fire!

Oh, see the brave firefighters
Firefight-ers, firefight-ers
Oh, see the brave firefighters
Put out the big fire!

Rhythms and Singing Games

1. Play piano or recorded music that has a distinct two-beat rhythm, a repetitive tune, and a variable tempo (a two-beat rhythm can sound like the engine of a car). Suggest that the children listen to the music and move around the room like cars. As the music gets faster, they should move faster, and as it slows down, they should slow down. When the music stops, tell them they are out of gas or that they have arrived at home.
2. Sand blocks rubbed together can be used with songs or recordings to accent the rhythm of train wheels.
3. Talk about how the children might form a train, such as putting their hands on the shoulders of the child in front of them. Let children suggest ways. Use music about a train on a recording or on the piano.

NOTE: It is better to let the children imaginatively imitate a train than to make rhythm time a structured activity.

4. A wooden whistle would be another effective sound to accompany either number 1 or 2 (wash it between uses if it is used by more than one person).

Records and Cassettes

Raffi, *Baby Beluga.* (Troubadour Records)
"Morningtown Ride"

————. *The Corner Grocery Store.* (Troubadour Records)
"Swing Low Sweet Chariot"

Sharon, Lois, and Bram. *Elephant Road.* (Elephant Records)
"Chugga, Chugga"
"The Wheels on the Bus"

Bob Homme. *The Giant Concert of Concerts by the Friendly Giant.* (A & M Records)
"Railroad Concert"

Bob McGrath. *If You're Happy and You Know It*, Volume I. (Kids Records)
"She'll Be Comin' Round the Mountain"
"The Wheels on the Bus"
"A Little Wheel a-Turnin' "

————. *Smorgasbord.* (Elephant Records)
"Rain Is a-Comin' "

Fred Penner. *Special Delivery.* (Troubadour Records)
"Car, Car Song"
"En roulant"

Fingerplays and Poems

From *Let's Do Fingerplays*, Grayson
"The Train," p. 22
"The Big Train," p. 22
"Choo Choo Train," p. 23
"The Windshield Wipers," p. 24
"Auto, Auto," p. 24
"Driving Down the Street," p. 25
"The Bus," p. 26
"The Steam Shovel," p. 26

From *Where the Sidewalk Ends*, Silverstein
"Bang Clang," p. 120
"Traffic Light," p. 121
"The Little Blue Engine," p. 158

From *A New Treasury of Children's Poetry*, Cole
"Songs of the Train," p. 34
"Steam Shovel," p. 187

From *The New Wind Has Wings*, Downie
"Windshield Wipers," p. 78

From *Read Aloud Rhymes for the Very Young*, Prelutsky and Brown
"The Modern Dragon," p. 35

From *Round and Round the Garden*, Williams
"Piggy on the Railway," p. 12

From *Sally Go Round the Sun*, Fowke
"Engine Engine Number 9," p. 110

....

THE ENGINEER

I ride in the engine (*point to self*)
The whistle I blow (*pull cord*)
I do all the things
That will make the train go. (*Pull throttle, turn dials*)

Whoo! Whoo! Goes the whistle (*Put hands to mouth*)
Clickety-clack go the wheels (*roll arms in wheel motion*)
I'm chief engineer (*pat chest*)
'Til I'm called for my meals! (*pretend to eat*)

....

FREIGHT TRAIN

by Bonnie Flemming

As the big locomotive moves slowly down the track
I wonder where it goes to and when it's coming back.

The engine needs a braker, it needs an engineer
It pulls so many cars of freight that come from far and near.

See the big red boxcar and there is an orange one too
Now see an autoveyor with cars of green and blue.

Next there are two long flatcars with tractors for the farm
You see, the wind and weather will do them little harm.

Refrigerator, tank, and flatcars go rolling down the track
All these cars have wheels of steel that go clickety-clickety-clack.

Look now at the very end, a red caboose I see
And there is the friendly braker waving back at me.

NOTE: Use model railroad cars or pictures to illustrate the poem. If pictures are found, they could be mounted on construction paper and put in a three-ring binder to make a picture book.

....

WINDSHIELD WIPER

I'm a windshield wiper (*bend arm at elbow with fingers pointing up*)
This is how I go. (*move arm to left and right, pivoting at elbow*)
Back and forth, back and forth (*continue back and forth motion*)
In the rain and snow. (*continue back and forth motion*)

Stories

(To read, read–tell, or tell. See Book Centre for a complete list.)
The choice of stories in this area is simple, as there are so many good ones. It is fun to choose a story that can be enhanced by the addition of sound effects that the children

can imitate; for example, Sattler's *Train Whistles* or Burningham's *Mr. Gumpy's Motorcar.*

Games

(See Learning Games in Part 1 and Teacher-Made Games and Materials earlier in this chapter for directions.)

1. *Look and see.*
2. *Can you remember?*
3. *Who am I?*
4. *Alike, different, and the same.*
5. *Sorting and grouping by association.*
6. *Reach and feel.*

Routine Times

1. Use toy cars, trucks, and buses with scale-model people, animals, and road signs as a centrepiece at meal time to encourage conversation about road transportation.
2. During snack or meal time, talk about which truck or car brought the food.
3. At pickup time, have children use ride-on trucks, wagons, or rolling platforms to carry toys back to shelves.
4. While walking or riding to and from the centre, look for cars, trucks, and buses. Talk about how to cross a street safely when walking.
5. When riding to and from the centre, talk about safety in a car or bus:
   a. Always wear seat belts.
   b. Always lock the doors, and do not lean against them.
   c. Be considerate of the driver — do not disturb him or her.
   d. Talk about traffic signals and rules as you see them on the street.
6. At rest time, have the children pretend that they have been travelling for a long time and have decided to stop at a motel or hotel for the night.

Large Muscle Activities

1. Encourage the use of trikes, wagons, and ride-on cars and trucks. Provide short ropes or chains so that a trike can tow a wagon. Supervise very carefully.
2. Make or buy some traffic signals and road signs. Set up traffic patterns, draw lines on the playground with chalk, or use a length of rope for a highway divider. Have a police officer check on drivers and issue tickets to those who break rules. Provide the officer with a hat, a whistle, and an emergency road kit (for the police to help cars with engine trouble).

   ▼ CAUTION: Whistles should be washed if shared.

3. Set up a garage or a service station next to the pretend highway where drivers can get gas, oil, and air. Provide gasoline pumps (see Dramatic Play Centres), oil can, bicycle-tire pump, tool box with toy tools, and a pail (can be empty) and rag to wash windshields.
4. Set up a parking lot where trikes can be parked while drivers go shopping. Provide stiff pieces of paper as tickets, and play money and a cash register for the attendant.
5. Set up a restaurant or a roadside stand by the highway where drivers can stop for a snack or a meal. Chefs can wear white aprons and hats (see patterns, pp. 26 and 27)

in the kitchen, while those waiting on tables can wear aprons and carry trays. If possible, take tables and chairs outside or use packing boxes.

Extended Experiences

1. Take a walk to a nearby mailbox to mail a letter and to watch the mail truck arrive.

   NOTE: Time your walk to coincide with regular pickup.

2. Visit a post office to see the mail trucks unloading and mail being cancelled, sorted, and loaded.
3. Visit a fire station to see where the firefighters eat, sleep, and care for the fire engines. Find out when they wash the engines. If the station has a pole, ask for a demonstration of sliding down the pole or jumping into a net. If the station has a hook and ladder, ask for a demonstration of how the ladder is put up.

   ▼ CAUTION: One adult for each two children is required on this trip, because if an alarm sounds while you are visiting, the children must be kept out of the way of the firefighters and trucks. Explain to the children in advance that the alarm is very loud so all the firefighters can hear it.

4. Visit a grocery store to see delivery trucks bringing food to the store. Check with the store manager in advance, and find out when most deliveries are made and where is a safe place to stand and watch. Arrange with the store manager to allow the children to go into the storeroom afterward, so they can make the association between the delivery and the items on the shelves. Of course, plan to buy something that is needed at the centre, such as milk or bread.
5. If delivery trucks come to the centre, allow the children to watch the unloading. Perhaps the driver will allow the children a closer look inside the door of the truck.
6. Take a bus ride or visit a bus terminal to see arrivals and departures of buses. If you cannot take a trip, make arrangements with a bus company for children to board a scenic cruiser that is temporarily idle.
7. Ride a city bus. Allow each child to deposit his or her own fare.
8. Invite a police officer to come to the centre in a patrol car. Have the officer talk about the uniform and what things are carried or worn. He or she can show the children how one talks to the control centre and how the siren and flashing light are activated.
9. If one of the children or a staff member comes to the centre in a taxi, ask whether the children might look inside. Ask the driver to show the children the meter and the radio or computer.
10. Invite a letter carrier to come to the centre in uniform in a mail truck, so the children may have a look inside the door of the truck. Perhaps they could have a get-well card, an invitation to parents, or a Mother's Day card for the letter carrier to take to the post office. The children might send valentines or letters to one another to be delivered to the centre, or you could put a letter, Christmas card, or valentine for each child in a large manila envelope and address it to the centre so that all will arrive together.
11. Invite a firefighter to bring a fire engine to the centre. This is especially good for younger children and for those who show a fear of fire engines or fire halls. There is also no worry about an alarm being sounded, and the children will be more free to explore the fire engine. Show the children what the firefighters wear to put out a fire and where the axes and tools are kept. Listen to the siren. If possible, let the children try on fireboots or hats.
12. Take a train ride: Unfortunately, most local passenger-train service has been discontinued, but if short trips are still available in your area, take one. Commuter and subway trains are also possibilities.

13. Some steam-engine runs and narrow-gauge railroads are maintained for recreational or historical purposes. You might consider these for special excursions.
14. Ride a miniature train or a monorail train in a nearby park or recreation area.
15. Inquire whether a roundhouse with turntable is available in your area and whether the children could watch it operate.

   ▼ CAUTION: Locomotives are very noisy when they are running, and very big. Children may be frightened by them. Adult supervision on these trips should be one adult to two children, one for each hand!

16. Take a small group of mature children who show an avid interest in trains to visit the home of a model railroader. He or she can demonstrate how a freight or passenger train is made up, how a slower train is put on a siding to allow a faster train to pass.
17. If parents of some of the children work for a railroad, you might invite them to come and talk about their jobs. If possible, they should wear what their jobs require and bring something of interest that is job-related to show the children.

Teacher Resources

Pictures and Displays

☐ Hang road maps of your area, your province, and Canada.
☐ Hang pictures of trains, stations, crossings, and train personnel. Most railroad companies put out calendars that are available on request. They usually have large pictures of trains on them.
☐ Make a table display using model trains. If possible, have a passenger train, freight train, work train, streetcar, and subway train. Include timetables and brochures with the display. A train crew hat, a conductor's hat, a rail spike, tickets, and a lantern may be obtainable.
☐ Hang pictures of cars from automotive dealers.

Books and Periodicals

Hollingsworth, Brian. *An Illustrated Guide to Modern Trains*. New York: Simon & Schuster, 1985.
Howarth, William. *Traveling the Trans-Canada: From Newfoundland to British Columbia*. Washington: National Geographic Society, 1987.
Johnson, Brian D. *Railway Country: Across Canada by Train*. Toronto: Key Porter, 1985.
Marshall, Ray, and John Bradley. *The Train: Watch It Work*. New York: Viking Penguin, 1986.
The Time-Life Book of the Family Car. Chicago: Rand McNally, 1975.
Wolfe, Robert. *The Truck Book*. Minneapolis, MN: Carolrhoda, 1981.

Films and Videos

   NOTE: Check with your distributor about public performance rights.

Alexander and the Car with the Missing Headlight. Weston Woods.
Blackberry Subway Jam. National Film Board, 1984.

Curious George Rides a Bike. Weston Woods.
Hercules. Weston Woods. (about a fire engine)
The Little Engine that Could. Coronet Instructional Films, 1983.
The Mole and the Car. Kratky Films, Prague (released in Canada by International Tele-Film), 1977. (no narration)

Community Resources and Organizations

☐ Transportation companies.
☐ Societies interested in transportation; for example, a model train club, a train buffs club, a car-racing club.
☐ A VIA Rail representative.
☐ Railroad companies serving your city: Ask for timetables, calendars, and brochures.
☐ Commuter services — rail, bus, subway, streetcar, etc.
☐ Cab companies.
☐ Fire department: A safety director or public-relations officer can provide you with information about firefighters and help arrange a visit to a fire hall or for a firefighter to visit the centre.
☐ Post office: A public-relations director will help explain the workings of the post office, arrange for a letter carrier to visit your centre, or help arrange a visit to the post office. Many post offices do not allow children under six inside the post-office working area. Postal boutiques and substations can be visited.
☐ Bus company: A public-relations director will help arrange a bus trip or a tour of a terminal and a bus.
☐ Trucking firms in your community may co-operate in letting the children have a closer look at the trucks they use. They may have calendars with pictures of trucks on them.
☐ Travel agents: Ask for posters, brochures, and schedules.
☐ Hobby shop: model train catalogues are a good source of pictures. The manager may also give you the names of some model railroaders who would be willing to lend or demonstrate model trains.

Government Agencies

☐ Federal, provincial, and territorial ministries of transportation or communication.

24 Water Transportation

Basic Understandings
(concepts children can grasp from this subject)

☐ People or things can be carried across (through) the water in a boat or in a ship.
☐ The boat or the ship is made to float on the water.
☐ The boat or the ship moves through the water in different ways:
    a. Wind blowing the sails.
    b. People paddling, rowing, or poling.
    c. Motors or engines propelling.
☐ There are many different kinds of boats — rowboats, canoes, kayaks, motorboats, lifeboats, sailboats, fishing boats (trawlers), ferries, houseboats, tugboats, barges, and steamboats.
☐ There are many different kinds of ships — ocean liners, tankers, cabin cruisers, lakers, freighters, and schooners.
☐ People can travel the oceans in passenger ships (cruise ships or ocean liners) that have many stores and service personnel:
    a. Each family has its own rooms, as in a hotel or a motel.
    b. The passengers eat in a dining room, as in a restaurant.
    c. There are places to buy clothes, food, flowers, shoes, and medicine.
    d. The ship has a doctor, nurse, dentist, and hospital (infirmary).
    e. It has a dry cleaner, laundry, barber shop, and beauty salon.
    f. It has a ballroom, a movie theatre, game rooms, lounges, one or more swimming pools, children's playrooms, and gymnasiums.
☐ The captain and the crew manoeuvre the boat or the ship through the water.
☐ A dock or a pier is a platform where people can get on or off a ship.
☐ People get from the dock to the ship by walking up a ramp (gangplank) or steps.
☐ Ships and boats are given names, such as the *Pacific Princess*, the *Queen Mary*, and the *Bluenose*.
☐ The crew of a boat or a ship can talk to or signal the crew of another boat or ship by using whistles, flags, or lights.
☐ Buoys and lighthouses help the crew to know where to safely sail (steer) the ship.

☐ Most boats and ships move on the surface of the water.
☐ Ferries carry people and cars across rivers, lakes, channels, or bays.
☐ Many people enjoy boating, boat racing, or fishing from boats.
☐ Some people own their own boats; others rent them.
☐ Fishermen are people who go out in boats to catch fish, lobsters, and crabs. They sell their catch to canneries, markets, or the public.
☐ Some people live on houseboats.
☐ Some people own or rent cabin cruisers for vacations on the water. People can eat and sleep in cabin cruisers.

Additional Facts the Teacher Should Know

All boats may be known as ships and all ships may be known as boats. However, the term "boat" is usually used when referring to a small craft, and "ship" is usually used when referring to a large craft. A boat floats because of the way it is built. Much of the boat is filled with air, which is much lighter than water. If the boat is constructed correctly, it will weigh less than the water that would take up the same space even when the boat is loaded with people and cargo.

> **NOTE:** There are many different kinds of boats with which you should be familiar so that you can use the correct terms when identifying them for the children.

Boats and ships have many parts

1. The *bow* is the front of a ship.
2. The *stern* is the rear of a ship.
3. *Starboard* is the right side of a ship, as you face the bow.
4. *Port* is the left side of a ship, as you face the bow.
5. The *deck* is the flat surface on the upper part of a ship where people can walk. Passenger ships have several decks.
6. The *hull* is the lower part of a ship.
7. The *screw* is the propeller that turns, pushing a ship through the water.
8. The *galley* is the kitchen on a ship.
9. The *hatch* is the door on a ship.
10. The *anchor* is the heavy weight at the end of a long rope or steel cable that is dropped when a ship wishes to remain in one place and does not have a dock at which to tie up.
11. The *hold* is the large area in the lower part of a ship where cargo is stowed.
12. The *mast* is the slender vertical pole used to hold up the sails on a sailboat.
13. The *boom* is the horizontal pole used to hold the sail on a sailboat or is the pole on a cargo ship that sticks up and out and holds the ropes and pulleys used in loading cargo onto the ship.
14. The *wheelhouse* is located in the front, top part of a ship. It has windows all around to provide the crew with a view for steering the ship. The wheelhouse is equipped with many instruments that help sail the ship, such as compasses, very accurate clocks, weather instruments, radios, and radar. There is also communication equipment to connect the wheelhouse with the chief engineer in the engine rooms down inside the ship.

Many people are needed to run a ship

1. The *captain* is in charge of the ship.
2. The *first mate* or executive officer is the second in command.

3. The *helmsman* steers the ship.
4. The *chief engineer* is in charge of the engines.
5. *Deckhands* look after the ropes, keep the decks clean, and ensure that equipment is in working order. These workers are also known as sailors or crew.

The captain and crew can communicate with other ships and with land in many ways

1. *Telephones* can be used and *telegraph* and *radio* messages can be sent while at sea.
2. *Flags* are used to represent letters and numbers to spell out messages.
3. *Morse code* can be used by opening and closing the shutters on a large lamp.
4. Ships have whistles that can be blown in certain patterns of long and short blasts that have special meanings: one short toot: turning to the right; two short toots: turning to the left; three short toots: backing up; four short toots: danger, one long toot: leaving the pier; three long toots: hello.
5. On board ship, time is designated by bells. There are six tours of watch duty of four hours each, starting at 8:00 PM. Each half hour of the watch is struck by the bells: one bell: 8:30; two bells: 9:00; three bells: 9:30; and so on, until eight bells are struck at midnight, ending the first watch. At 12:30, one bell is struck, and the pattern repeated for each four-hour watch.
6. Smaller craft are moved through the water by use of oars, paddles, sails, or small motors. Larger craft have diesel engines, steam engines, or nuclear reactors to turn the large propellers known as screws. When the propellers turn one way, they push the water behind and the ship goes forward. When the propellers turn the other way, they push the water ahead and the ship goes backward. The rudder is turned to make the ship turn left or right.
7. Lighthouses and buoys help the captain and crew of a ship avoid shallow water, rocks, or other obstructions. The markers have both lights and bells on them, so they can be seen and heard at night or in a fog.
8. Fishing is a very important business, especially for people living by rivers and oceans. Some commercial fishing is still done by hook and line, but trawling and seining have largely replaced this method. Fishing boats either drag nets through the water (seining) or set out main lines to which shorter lines with baited hooks are attached (trawling). As many as 5000 hooks may be baited and set, and the main line can run for kilometres. The line is marked with buoys or floats so it can be found. Salmon, tuna, red snapper, and halibut are usually caught this way.
9. Lobsters and crabs are caught in slotted wooden traps called lobster pots, which are baited with fish. The lobsters and crabs can get in but cannot get out. Lobsters are found in the Maritimes, especially off the shores of Nova Scotia. Shrimp are found primarily in the waters between Vancouver Island and the British Columbia mainland.

Introducing This Subject to Children

1. Hang pictures of boats and ships near dramatic play centres and on bulletin boards.
2. Read a story about boats or ships.
3. Take the children to see boats on a river or lake.
4. Invite a parent who catches fish or works for a shipping company to tell the children about his or her work.
5. Ask a parent or a staff member to tell about his or her vacation on a ship.
6. Parents or staff members may own a boat. Invite them to bring in pictures of the boat and to tell the children about their hobby.

Vocabulary

boat	captain	life preserver	shore
ship	sailor	lifeboat	steer
dock	crew	lighthouse	cargo
oars	cabin	water	row
sails	deck	float	tow
paddles	anchor	sink	rope

Learning Centres

Discovery Centre

1. Obtain realistic, sturdy models of different kinds of ships and boats. Identify them, and tell how they are useful and how they move through the water.
2. Some children may wonder how something as big and heavy as a boat can float. You might help them understand by telling them the shape is important. The boat or ship must be made to hold a lot of air, which is lighter than water. The following demonstration might help: Cut two pieces of aluminum foil the same size. Have a child wad one of the pieces into a ball and place it in water; it should sink. Help the children make a little rowboat out of the other piece by turning up the edges and putting it on the water; it should float.
3. Show the children how sailboats move. Float a toy sailboat in a tub of water and let children blow on the sails. Ask what would happen if they were sailing and the wind stopped.
4. Submarines and floating boats may lead to an interest in water (see Chapter 26, Water around Me, for related activities).

Dramatic Play Centres

Home-living centre

1. Hang pictures of boats and ships used for pleasure and travel. Set out brochures on travelling by ship to encourage the planning of a cruise.
2. Have suitcases available for packing.
3. Put play money in purses for purchasing tickets.

Block-building centre

1. Encourage children to make a dock with unit blocks. Set out model ships and boats to encourage water transportation play.
2. Have cans or boxes of small materials, such as sticks, stones, buttons, and cloth scraps, to use as cargo.
3. Suggest that children build a boathouse with unit blocks.
4. Outline a rowboat on the floor with hollow blocks lying on their edges. Provide sailor hats.

Other dramatic play centres

1. A rocking boat makes a good boat to row or paddle. Sing "Row, Row, Row Your Boat" as children rock. Make paddles or oars out of cardboard, and provide sailor hats.
2. The rocking boat can also be a fishing boat. Give the children cardboard-roll poles with strings tied to magnets. Stock the "water" with paper fish that have paperclips put on for mouths. Supervise carefully so no one gets hit with a pole or a magnet.
3. Ask a florist to save heavy, waxed cardboard boxes in which flowers are delivered. These make fine boats, although almost any sturdy box can be used.
4. Piers for larger toy boats can be made from hollow blocks. Piers can also be used for fishing activities.

Art Centre

- 1. Children can make a picture book by pasting precut pictures of boats and ships on construction paper. The mounted pictures could be put in a three-ring binder. Children with cutting experience could help with the cutting.
••• 2. Precut a sailboat stencil. Let children spatter paint the stencil on blue construction paper. Allow paintings to dry, and then spatter paint white sails or paste on triangles cut from cloth or paper.
••• 3. Precut hulls and sails of different sizes and colours from fabric scraps or construction paper, and let children paste them on blue construction paper.
••• 4. At the woodworking centre, provide precut wooden shapes and scraps to allow children to make boats and ships. Masts could be made of wooden dowels or plastic straws. Float boats in water when finished.

   NOTE: Hand drills should be provided for drilling mast holes.

- 5. Styrofoam can be precut in the shape of a ship's hull. Provide toothpicks, straws for masts, and styrofoam scraps to make a cabin or a wheelhouse. Paper or cloth sails can be glued to the masts. Let children float the boats in a tub of water.

Learning and Language Materials Centre

Commercially made games and materials

1. *Puzzles:* A variety of puzzles with transportation themes.
2. *Small toys for imaginative play:* Plastic models of various boats for younger children. Metal models of various boats for older children. Make sure that the toy boats you choose will float in a water table or a small pool.
3. *Costumes:* Hats and coats that represent various employees of the fishing, shipping, and cruise industries.

Teacher-made games and materials

   NOTE: For detailed descriptions, see Learning Games in Part 1.

1. *Look and see:* Use models of different kinds of boats and ships.
2. *Can you remember?* Use models of different kinds of boats and ships.
3. *Alike, different, and the same:* Make sets of pairs of the different kinds of boats and ships. Mix them up and let the children find pairs that match. Use a matching pair and one that is different, and ask children to point to the one that is not like the others.
4. *Sorting and grouping by association:* Take one each of boats and ships and mix with one each of trucks, airplanes, and railway cars. Ask children to find all the ones that go on water, on rails, on roads, or in the sky.

5. *What am I?* After the children are familiar with some of the boats and ships and their uses, describe one and ask children to identify, it such as, "I am a boat that carries cars and people across a river. What am I?"

Book Centre

- ••• Agell, Charlotte. *The Sailor's Book.* Willowdale, ON: Firefly, 1991.
- ••• Ardizzone, Edward. *Little Tim and the Brave Sea Captain.* New York: Walck, 1972.
- • Bruna, Dick. *Lifeboat.* London: Methuen, 1984.
- • Burningham, John. *Mr. Gumpy's Outing.* New York: Penguin, 1984.
- •• Crews, Donald. *Harbor.* New York: Greenwillow Press, 1982.
- ••• Haley, Gail. *Noah's Ark.* New York: Atheneum, 1971.
- ••• Maestro, Betsy. *Big City Port.* New York: Macmillan, 1983.
- ••• Gramatky, H. *Little Toot.* New York: Putnam, 1989.
- ••• Morgan, Allen. *Nicole's Boat.* Willowdale, ON: Annick Press, 1986. (good for reading before rest time)
- ••• Murphy, Shirley R. *Tattie's River Journey.* New York: Dial Press, 1983.
- •••• Pfanner, Louise. *Louise Builds a Boat.* New York: Orchard, 1990.
- ••• Quinlan, Patricia. *Emma's Sea Journey.* Willowdale, ON: Annick Press, 1991.
- ••• Randall, Beverly. *Aboard Lucy Lee.* Richmond Hill, ON: Scholastic-TAB, 1987.
- •••• Robbins, Ken. *Boats.* New York: Scholastic, 1989.
- ••• Spier, Peter. *The Erie Canal.* Garden City, NY: Doubleday, 1970.
- ••• Staunton, Ted. *Miss Fishley Afloat.* Toronto: Kids Can Press, 1990.
- ••• Swift, Hildegarde. *The Little Red Lighthouse and the Great Gray Bridge.* New York: Harcourt Brace Jovanovich, 1974.
- ••• Williams, Vera. *Three Days on a River in a Red Canoe.* New York: Greenwillow Press, 1981.
- ••• Wynne-Jones, Tim. *Zoom Away.* Toronto: Groundwood, 1985.
- ••• ———. *Zoom at Sea.* Toronto: Groundwood, 1983.
- •• Young, Ruth. *Daisy's Taxi.* New York: Orchard, 1991.
- ••• Zander, Hans. *My Blue Chair.* Willowdale, ON: Annick Press, 1985.

 # Planning for Group Time

NOTE: All music, fingerplays, poems, stories, and games listed here may also be used at other times during the session as appropriate.

Music

Songs

Please see "Lightly Row" and "Michael Row the Boat Ashore" at the end of this chapter.

From *The Best Singing Games for Children of All Ages*, Bloy
"Four in a Boat," p. 22
"Down the River," p. 74

From *Elephant Jam*, Sharon, Lois, and Bram
"Long Legged Sailor," p. 16
"Lots of Fish in Bonvist' Harbour," (see Chapter 7, p. 189)

From *Eye Winker, Tom Tinker, Chin Chopper*, Glazer
"Charlie Over the Water," p. 18
"Sailing at High Tide," p. 68
"There's a Hole in the Bottom of the Sea," p. 78

From *Musical Games for Children of All Ages*, Nelson
"A Sailor Went to Sea, Sea, Sea," p. 62

From *MusicPlay*, Burton and Hughes
"Row, Row, Row Your Boat," p. 89
"Fish Pole Song," p. 151

From *Piggyback Songs*, Warren
"We Sail a Ship," p. 31
"I'm a Fish," p. 32

From *Sally Go Round the Sun*, Fowke
"The White Ship Sails," p. 37

From *Singing Bee*, Hart
"Merrily We Roll Along," p. 59
"The Gallant Ship," p. 84
"Lightly Row," p. 138
"I Saw Three Ships," p. 139

From *A Treasury of Songs for Children*, Glazer
"Erie Canal," p. 79

Rhythms and Singing Games

Row, row, row your boat: Have children sit on the floor in pairs, facing each other. Have them join hands and spread their legs in the shape of a V, with the soles of their shoes touching. As you sing the song together, have the children pull each other back and forth in time to the music.

Records and Cassettes

Raffi. *Baby Beluga.* (Troubadour Records)
"Baby Beluga"
"Water Dance" (good for movement)

Sharon, Lois, and Bram. *Elephant Show.* (Elephant Records)
"Jack Was Every Inch a Sailor"
"Rig a Jig Jig"

———. *Smorgasbord.* (Elephant Records)
"Newfoundland Jig Melody"
"Long Legged Sailor"

Bob Homme. *The Giant Concert of Concerts by the Friendly Giant.* (A & M Records)
"Seafood Concert"

Fingerplays and Poems

....

THE BOATS

This is the way, all the day long
The boats go sailing by,
To and fro, in a row,
Under the bridge so high.

(form a bridge with one arm and move the other hand back and forth under it)

....

ROW, ROW, ROW YOUR BOAT

Row, row, row your boat
Gently down the stream,
Merrily, merrily, merrily, merrily,
Life is but a dream.

(put fists together in front of you and pretend to row)

Pittman's *Down by Jim Long's Stage* and *One Wonderful Day for a Sculpin Named Sam* are exceptional books of poetry to read for this subject.

From *Don't Eat Spiders*, Heidbreder
"The Newfoundland Cod," p. 35

From *Finger Rhymes*, Brown
"Fish Story," p. 12

From *Let's Do Fingerplays*, Grayson
"The Boats," p. 26

From *A New Treasury of Children's Poetry*, Cole
"Where Go the Boats," p. 130

From *The New Wind Has Wings*, Downie
"The Ships of Yule," p. 12
"Noah," p. 45

From *Read Aloud Rhymes for the Very Young*, Prelutsky and Brown
"Fish," p. 44
"I'd Like to Be a Lighthouse," p. 78

From *Where the Sidewalk Ends*, Silverstein.
"Homemade Boat," p. 12
"Captain Hook," p. 18
"The Unicorn," p. 76
"Pirate Captain Jim," p. 144

Stories

(To read, read–tell, or tell. See Book Centre for a complete list.)
There are many interesting stories on this theme. Wynne-Jones's *Zoom at Sea* and *Zoom Away* offer fun and fantasy with a Maritime theme. In contrast, Gramatky's classic *Little Toot* stories are diverting, but also contain many interesting facts.

Games

(See Learning Games in Part 1 and Teacher-Made Games and Materials earlier in this chapter for directions.)

1. *Look and see.*
2. *What am I?*
3. *Can you remember?*
4. *Alike, different, and the same.*

Routine Times

1. At snack or meal times, serve chocolate, cocoa, bananas, pineapple, or coconuts. Explain that these foods probably came to our country by freighter. Serve fish, lobster, or crab, and talk about how they are caught in nets from fishing boats.
2. At snack or meal times, have a captain's table. Each day, choose one child to be captain, who in turn selects those who will dine at the captain's table. Make sure everyone gets included!
3. At rest time, tell the children you will ring the ship's bell four times when it is time to get up. Use a bell with a clapper, and ring as follows: strike bell twice, pause, and strike bell twice more.
4. While busing children to and from the centre or on other trips in the community, you may cross rivers, go round lakes, or go by the ocean, where boats or ships may be seen. Talk about the kinds of boats you see and what they do.

Large Muscle Activities

1. A packing box or other large, sturdy carton could be used for boat play. Use cleated walking board as a gangplank to the packing-box ship.
2. Put a real rowboat on the playground. Combine with a steering wheel or a dial panel (see illustration, p. 472) and provide sailor hats.
3. Float boats in a water table or another large container filled with water.
4. Have water available to fill canals in the sandbox. Provide small boats to encourage water transportation play.
5. See Dramatic Play Centres for additional suggestions involving large muscles.
6. Slice a tire around its circumference to make two boat canals.

Extended Experiences

1. Watch boats or ships on a nearby river, lake, or ocean.
2. Take a ferry ride.
3. Ride an excursion boat.
4. Go out in a sailboat, rowboat, or motorboat.

  ▼ CAUTION: All children should wear life jackets, and one of the adults in the boat should have a current senior lifesaving certificate. In addition to the person handling the boat, there should be one adult for every two children.

5. Watch a trawler, freighter, or laker unload.
6. Watch a boat race or a regatta.
7. Invite a Chinese parent or friend to visit and tell about the Dragon Boat festival in China. Perhaps this person could bring a picture of one of these boats.
8. Invite a sailor to come in uniform and tell the children about living and sailing at sea.

9. Invite a person who fishes commercially or for a hobby to tell the children about commercial or hobby fishing (this could be arranged just before the spring fishing season and could be followed up with a visit to a local fishing dock).

Teacher Resources

Pictures and Displays

☐ Hang pictures of different kinds of boats, people who work with boats, buoys, a lighthouse, boat races, docks, fishermen, fishing nets, and lobster pots.

☐ Ask someone to bring in a model ship or a ship in a bottle.

Books and Periodicals

Blocksma, Mary, and Dewey Blocksma. *Easy-to-Make Water Toys that Really Work.* Englewood Cliffs, NJ: Prentice-Hall, 1985.

Parry, J.H. *Romance of the Sea.* Washington: National Geographic Society, 1981.

Rutland, Jonathan. *Amazing Fact Book of Ships.* Mankato, MN: Creative Education, 1987.

The Sea. New York: Time-Life, 1977.

Wall, Robert. *Ocean Liners.* London: Chartwell, 1977.

Ships and Submarines. Los Angeles, CA: Price Stern, Sloan, 1987.

Williams, Brian. *Ships and Other Seacraft.* New York: Franklin Watts, 1984.

Films and Videos

NOTE: Check with your distributor about public performance rights.

Little Tim and the Brave Sea Captain. Weston Woods.

Tuktu and the Big Kayak. National Film Board, 1967.

Community Resources and Organizations

☐ Transportation companies.

☐ Societies interested in transportation; for example, a model boat club, a shipping and ship travel club.

☐ A travel agent.

☐ A fishery.

☐ Fishing companies or fishermen for permission to watch the unloading of fish.

☐ Shipping companies may have calendars or brochures with pictures of ships.

☐ A marina, for rental of boats.

☐ Sailing clubs for schedules of races or names of people who may be willing to give the children rides in their boats.

Government Agencies

☐ Federal, provincial, and territorial ministries of transportation or communication.
☐ Federal Ministry of Fisheries and Oceans.

Lightly Row

(Alles Neu Macht Der Mai)

Traditional Tune ("Fahrathen")

German Folk Song

NOTE: Two lines (verses 2 and 3) have been omitted in this adaptation of the original tune to simplify it for use with young children.

Michael Row the Boat Ashore

Traditional

Adapted by Bonnie Flemming

3. Pe-ter pad-dle the can-oe, etc.
4. Mar-y fly the plane a-round, etc.
5. Moth-er drive the car to town, etc.
6. Fath-er ride the train to work, etc.

NOTE: The "Hallelujah" is optional. Phrases can be completed by repeating preceding refrain. For example, "row the boat!" "set the sail!"

Part 8 My World

25 Day and Night

Basic Understandings
(concepts children can grasp from this subject)

☐ The sun gives off light and heat.
☐ It is lighter and warmer during the day, because at that time our part of the earth is turned toward the sun.
☐ At night it is darker and colder, because at that time our part of the earth is turned away from the sun.
☐ When it is day in our half of the world, it is night in the other half of the world.
☐ A whole day lasts 24 hours and consists of both day (light) and night (dark).
☐ Sometimes the daylight lasts longer than the darkness (in summer), and at other times the darkness lasts longer than the daylight (in winter).
☐ Night is nice (stress pleasant aspects of night). It is a good time to sleep and rest.
☐ The sun is a big star. Stars shine (give off light and heat) all the time.
☐ Clouds may hide the sun and stars from our view.
☐ Fog is caused by clouds forming close to the earth. It may hide the sun and stars from our view.
☐ The sun and the stars shine all the time. We do not see the stars in the daytime because the sunlight is so bright we cannot see them.
☐ Most stars are so far away we see them as tiny dots of light.
☐ Some of the stars appear grouped together. These groups are called constellations.

Additional Facts the Teacher Should Know

1. The earth turns counterclockwise (from west to east) on its imaginary axis, which runs from the north to the south pole as it travels on an elliptical path around our sun. It takes 24 hours, or one calendar day, for the earth to make a complete turn on its axis.
2. A moon is a heavenly body that revolves around a planet. We have one moon that is about 149 000 km away. It is 1305 km wide, and about 80 times lighter than the earth. Therefore, its force of gravity is much less and people weigh less on the moon. The moon's gravity exerts some pressure on our earth and causes large bodies of water to move, resulting in tides. The moon rotates on its imaginary axis as it orbits around

the earth. It takes the moon 27 days and 8 hours to orbit around the earth, and about the same time to make a complete turn on its axis.

3. The moon gives off no light of its own; what we see is a reflection of the sun's rays off its surface. One-half of the moon is always lighted by the sun, but when the moon is almost between the earth and the sun, we do not always see the lighted half. The sun's rays are so bright, we do not often see the moon during the day. When we can see all of the lighted half we say it is a full moon. As the moon changes its position, less and less light is reflected off it toward the earth, so it becomes less and less visible to us. This is why the moon sometimes appears to be only a crescent or half-moon shape, although its size does not actually change. The different positions of the moon are called phases.

4. An eclipse of the moon occurs when the earth is between the sun and the moon and the sunlight cannot shine on the moon. The moon gets very dull, and we can barely see it. An eclipse of the sun occurs when the moon is between the sun and the earth and we cannot see the sunlight.

> ▼ CAUTION: It is dangerous to look directly at an eclipse of the sun. Permanent eye damage can result.

5. At certain times of the year, particularly in the autumn, the moon rises early and shines for a long time. This is called a harvest moon. It sometimes appears large and orange in colour if there is dust in the air.

6. Twice during the year in Canada, we have approximately twelve hours each of daylight and darkness. One time is the vernal equinox on March 20, 21, or 22, and the second is the autumnal equinox on September 20, 21, or 22. The exact date is officially determined each year when the sun crosses the equator at noon. In the summer, our part of the earth is tipped toward the sun and we have longer days. In the winter, our part of the earth is tipped away from the sun and we have shorter days (see illustration).

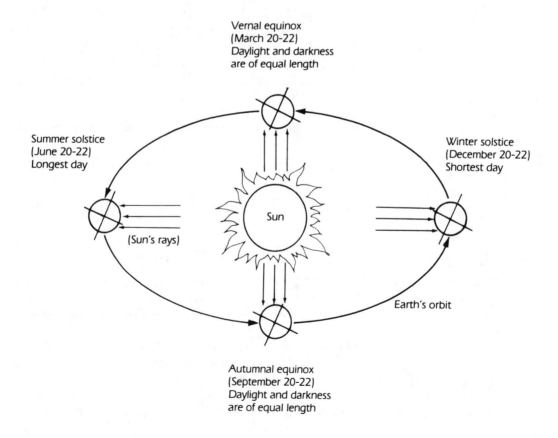

Vernal equinox
(March 20-22)
Daylight and darkness
are of equal length

Summer solstice
(June 20-22)
Longest day

Winter solstice
(December 20-22)
Shortest day

Sun

(Sun's rays)

Earth's orbit

Autumnal equinox
(September 20-22)
Daylight and darkness
are of equal length

7. Many children are afraid of nighttime and the dark. Often, between the ages of four and five, children who have been willing to go to bed will begin to cry and want a light left on. Children should learn facts about light and dark but also be encouraged to talk about their fears related to darkness or being away from home at night. They should learn about the beauty, goodness, and necessity of night. Dreams become important to children at about three-and-a-half years of age. Be prepared to listen to what the children say about their dreams and to offer them reassurance.

Introducing This Subject to Children

1. Display pictures showing daytime and nighttime activities.
2. Say "good morning" when children arrive and "good night" if they leave in late afternoon.
3. Darken the room to simulate night at rest time.
4. Hang a mobile of our solar system.
5. Read a story about night, such as Margaret Wise Brown's *Goodnight Moon* (see Book Centre).

Vocabulary

sun	dark	awake	nightmare
day	light	dream	sundial
night	moon	shadows	sunny
hot	cold	prism	cloudy
fog	sleep	sunglasses	shine
stars	rest	flashlight	earth

Learning Centres

Discovery Centre

1. Call attention to the children's shadows and those of objects on the playground. Help children discover that shadows are caused by light.
   a. Measure children's shadows in the morning, at noon, and before they leave in the afternoon, all at the same spot.
   b. Have the children put one hand in the sunlight and one in the shade on a sidewalk. Discuss which is warmer, and why.
   c. Pound a 1.5 m long stick into the ground in an open spot. Measure the length of its shadow from time to time during the day, and discuss.

A sunny playground invites games that allow children to experiment with their shadows. Such concrete experiences outdoors can be followed up indoors through discussion, stories, and art.

    d. Have the children look for their shadows indoors. Use a flashlight as the sun and a stand-up doll as a person. Let each child discover how to make long and short shadows on all sides of the doll.

    e. Use a bright light on a movie screen, sheet, or light-coloured wall, and let the children make hand shadow pictures.

    f. Make shadow silhouettes (see Games, number 3).

    g. Display Chinese paper cuts (buy at a local Oriental gift store).

2. Make a sundial and mark the hours (check an encyclopedia for instructions). Explain that this is how people told time before clocks were invented.

3. Day and night: On a globe, tape a small paper figure on your centre's city. Tape another figure on the opposite side of the globe. Darken the room, and use a flashlight to represent the sun. Turn the globe slowly — the children will observe what causes day and night. If you have no globe, use a ball instead.

4. Clouds can keep us from seeing the sun, the stars, and the moon. Cut paper clouds or use cotton balls to place between children's eyes and the sun (outdoors) or a lamp (indoors).

5. Heat of the sun: Discuss how the sun burns us. Have children stand in the sun and then in the shade. Which is warmer? Use a thermometer to show changes of temperature in sun and shade.

    ▼ **CAUTION: Watch children closely when doing the last activity.**

6. Absence of light: Have children take brightly coloured objects into a closet and slowly close the door. The colours disappear.

7. Reflected light: In a dark closet, shine a flashlight on a circle cut from white material. The circle will appear to shine too. That is how the moon shines at night with the sun's reflected light. Our earth is especially bright when the sun shines on it because so many things reflect the sun's light, especially the dust in the air.

8. Use a prism to demonstrate how light is made up of many colours (see Chapter 27, Colour in My World).

9. Cut cookies in the shapes of stars, moons (crescents), and suns (circles). Frost with yellow or white icing. Add silver candy beads to moons and stars.

Dramatic Play Centres

Home-living centre

1. Darken this centre, if possible, by turning off the lights or closing off the area with screens and covering the windows with dark material.

2. Set out night clothes and blankets for dolls.

3. Provide nightgowns, pyjamas, robes, and slippers for dressup.

4. Add boxes big enough for children to use as beds or cots; also provide some stuffed animals and crib blankets.

5. Simulate sunrise by lighting the area and removing coverings from windows. Family members can get up and get ready for breakfast, school, and work.

Block-building centre

1. Children can build a house without a roof using unit blocks. Provide sturdy doll house furniture for children to arrange as they wish for eating, sleeping, and so on.

2. Set out commercial or homemade doll houses with open sides or tops for children to arrange furniture and people in various day and night activities.

Art Centre

1. Spatter paint: Precut star and moon stencils. Have children spatter paint the stencils with dark blue or black tempera paint on white paper.

2. Starry night: Use an old dark-coloured window shade or a night shade.

   a. Have children draw the night sky on the dark side of the shade with white crayons or chalk.

   b. Find some sturdy cardboard boxes that are at least 40 cm x 30 cm on each side. Cut holes no larger than 16 cm x 20 cm in the sides of the boxes. Tape pieces of black construction paper over each hole. Provide each child with a push-pin to make "constellations" in the paper. Shine a flashlight into the box so the children can see their constellations. The constellations can be taken home to be taped to the window.

   ▼ CAUTION: Ensure that the children use the push-pins only under direct adult supervision.

3. Precut phases of the moon from pale yellow construction paper or silver or white gummed paper. Children can paste these on sheets of black paper and add gummed stars.

4. Night and day pictures: Join a light and a dark piece of construction paper end to end or back to back. Children can cut night and day pictures from magazines and paste them on the appropriate side, or draw pictures on each side.

5. Mural: Make a large orange or yellow sun in the centre of a long sheet of brown paper. The children can draw or paint people, houses, trees, and animals on either side of the

sun. Then they can add black shadows on their figures to show the relationship of light and shadow (this is best done after Discovery Centre number 1d).

Learning and Language Materials Centre

Commercially made games and materials

1. *Puzzles:* Variety of puzzles showing sun, moon, bedtime, bathtime, clock, etc. Be sure to have some puzzles with knobs for younger children.
2. *Dolls and puppets:* Doll clothes and accessories, including night clothes and cribs.
3. *Costumes:* A variety of night clothes for dramatic play.
4. *Miscellaneous:* A large teaching clock with movable hands and a large digital clock; a large, durable globe that shows your community well or on which you can mark your community easily; a rechargeable flashlight with a handle that young children can hold; a 15 cm prism available from science stores or educational suppliers.

Teacher-made games and materials

NOTE: For detailed descriptions, see Learning Games in Part 1.

1. *Look and see:* Use flannelboard cutouts of sun, moon, and stars.
2. *I see something, what do you see?* Say, "I see something round like the moon; black like the night; yellow like the sun; pointed like a star," and so on.
3. *Who's missing?* Change to "Who went to bed?"
4. *Match-them:* Use pictures of the sun, stars, and phases of the moon.
5. *Alike, different, and the same:* Use pictures of two suns and a star, or two stars and a moon.
6. Make a calendar for the month. Each day, paste paper sun or cloud on the appropriate square. Count the cloudy and sunny days.

Book Centre

••• Asch, F. *Moon Bear.* New York: Scribner, 1978.
•• Bennett, David. *Day and Night.* New York: Bantam, 1988.
•• Bourgeois, Paulette, and Brenda Clark. *Franklin in the Dark.* Toronto: Kids Can Press, 1986.
••• Branley, Franklyn M. *What Makes Day and Night?* New York: Crowell, 1986.
• Brown, Margaret Wise. *Goodnight Moon.* New York: Harper & Row, 1947.
•••• Cole, Joanna. *The Magic School Bus Lost in the Solar System.* Richmond Hill, ON: Scholastic, 1990.
••• Dayrell, Elphinstone. *Why the Sun and the Moon Live in the Sky: An African Folktale.* Boston: Houghton Mifflin, 1968.
• de Regniers, Beatrice S., and Isabel Gordon. *The Shadow Book.* New York: Harcourt Brace Jovanovich, 1962.
••• de Regniers, Beatrice S., and Leona Pierce. *Who Likes Sun?* New York: Harcourt Brace Jovanovich, 1961.
•• Dickson, Barry. *Afraid of the Dark.* Toronto: Lorimer, 1986.
•••• Dorros, Arthur. *Me and My Shadow.* New York: Scholastic, 1990.
••• Fleishman, Paul. *Shadow Play.* New York: Harper & Row, 1990.
•• Hearn, Emily. *Good Morning Franny/Good Night Franny.* Toronto: Women's Education Press, 1984.
•• Heckman, Philip. *The Moon Is Following Me.* New York: Atheneum, 1991.
•• Hoban, Russell. *Bedtime for Frances.* New York: Harper & Row, 1965.
••• Hort, Lenny. *How Many Stars in the Sky?* New York: Tambourine, 1991.

••• Horwitz, Elinor L. *When the Sky Is Like Lace.* Philadelphia: Lippincott, 1975.
•• Hurd, Edith T. *The Day the Sun Danced.* New York: Harper & Row, 1965.
•• Ipcar, Dahlov. *The Song of the Day Birds and the Night Birds.* Garden City, NY: Doubleday, 1967.
•• Jam, Teddy. *Night Cars.* Toronto: Groundwood, 1991.
•• Jennings, Sharon. *Jeremiah and Mrs. Ming.* Willowdale, ON: Annick Press, 1990.
••• King, Christopher. *The Boy Who Ate the Moon.* New York: Putnam & Grosset, 1988.
•• Leonard, Marcia. *Little Kitten Sleeps Over.* New York: Bantam, 1987.
•• Mayer, Mercer. *There's a Nightmare in My Closet.* New York: Dial Press, 1968.
••• Mollel, Tololwa. *The Orphan Boy.* Toronto: Oxford University Press, 1990.
• Morgan, Allen. *Nichole's Boat: A Good-Night Story.* Willowdale, ON: Annick Press, 1986.
••• Munsch, Robert. *The Dark.* Willowdale, ON: Annick Press, 1986.
••• Obed, Ellen Bryan. *Borrowed Black: A Labrador Fantasy.* St. John's: Breakwater Press, 1988.
••• Rice, E. *Goodnight, Goodnight.* New York: Greenwillow Press, 1980.
•• Rylant, Cynthia. *Night in the Country.* New York: Aladdin, 1991.
•• Sara. *Across Town.* New York: Orchard, 1991.
••• Sendak, Maurice. *Where the Wild Things Are.* New York: Harper Collins, 1988.
••• Shulevitz, Uri. *Dawn.* New York: Farrar, Straus & Giroux, 1974.
••• Stevenson, J. *We Can't Sleep.* New York: Greenwillow Press, 1982.
••• Wynne-Jones, Tim. *Architect of the Moon.* Toronto: Groundwood, 1988.
• Zolotow, Charlotte. *Wake Up and Good Night.* New York: Harper & Row, 1971.

 # Planning for Group Time

NOTE: All music, fingerplays, poems, stories, and games listed here may also be used at other times during the session as appropriate.

Music

Songs
Please see "Sally Go Round the Sun" at the end of this chapter.

From *Elephant Jam*, Sharon, Lois, and Bram
"Skinnamarink," p. 58
"Bye 'n' Bye," p. 127

From *Sally Go Round the Sun*, Fowke
"No Bears Out Tonight," p. 42

From *Singing Bee*, Hart
"Twinkle Twinkle Little Star," p. 64
"Oh, How Lovely Is the Evening," p. 134

From *A Treasury of Songs for Young Children*, Glazer
"Au claire de la lune," p. 23
"Sleep Baby Sleep," p. 55
"Frère Jacques," p. 89
"Go to Sleep," p. 100
"Hush Little Baby," p. 124

"Lazy Mary," p. 151
"Oh, How Lovely Is the Evening," p. 174

From *What Shall We Do and Alee Galloo!*, Winn
"When Ducks Get Up in the Morning," p. 26

Rhythms and Singing Games

Play thematic music: marches, lively dance music from various cultures, or rock songs for day, and lullabies, waltzes, or other quiet music for night. Have the children move in time to the music.

Records and Cassettes

Anne Murray. *There's a Hippo in My Tub.* (Capitol Records)
"Stars Are the Windows of Heaven"
"Sleepytime"
"You Are My Sunshine"
"Lullaby Medley"

Bob Schneider. *When You Dream a Dream.* (Capitol Records)
"In the Morning"
"When You Dream a Dream"

Fred Penner. *Special Delivery.* (Troubadour Records)
"Bon soir, mes amis"

Raffi. *Baby Beluga.* (Troubadour Records)
"Dayo"
"Morningtown Ride"

Sharon, Lois, and Bram. *Elephant Show.* (Elephant Records)
"Go to Sleep Now My Pumpkin"

———. *Smorgasbord.* (Elephant Records)
"Hobo's Lullaby"

Fingerplays and Poems

From *Finger Rhymes*, Brown
"Sleepy Fingers," p. 30

From *Let's Do Fingerplays*, Grayson
"Good Morning," p. 80

From *Mischief City*, Wynne-Jones
"I Like Drawing Pictures," p. 14
"Don't Drink the Bathwater," p. 18
"They're Having a Party Downstairs," p. 19
"After the Lights Go Down Low," p. 20
"Mrs. Night," p. 21
"The Arrangement," p. 36

From *The New Wind Has Wings*, Downie
"After Midnight," p. 71
"The Sun," p. 110

From *Read Aloud Rhymes for the Very Young*, Prelutsky and Brown
"Swinging Time," p. 3
"Swimming," p. 9
"Before the Bath," p. 26
"Naughty Soap Song," p. 26
"The Way They Scrub," p. 27
"Wish," p. 27
"Happy Winter Steamy Tub," p. 27
"Night Fun," p. 70
"Bedtime," p. 70
"Moon Boat," p. 71
"I See the Moon," p. 71
"Moon Come Out," p. 71
"The Star," p. 71
"Wide Awake," p. 82
"Silvery," p. 87
"Good Night, Good Night," p. 88

Stories

(To read, read–tell, or tell. See Book Centre for a complete list.)
When choosing stories that are about day and night, remember that some children may be afraid of the dark. Dickson's *Afraid of the Dark* is very helpful to read with children who are anxious. If your children are relaxed in the dark, it can be fun to turn off the lights, close the curtains, and tell a story with a flashlight shining on the pictures.

Games

1. *World game:* Play this after Discovery Centre, number 3. Darken the room, and put a lamp or flashlight at one end of the room. Have the children form a circle to represent the earth. Divide the earth into two halves. The half facing the sun (light) does daytime activities, such as eating, jumping, and running. The half facing away from the sun (night) pretends to go to sleep. Then the circle re-forms, the earth rotates halfway around, and the halves switch from day to night activities, and vice versa.
2. *Night and day:* Tell the children to close their eyes, then call on a child to tell about one thing that happens at night. Tell the children to open their eyes and call on another child to tell about one thing that happens in the day. Repeat for as long as there is interest or every child has participated.
3. *Whose shadow?* Hang a sheet, and place a light behind it. Have children cover their eyes and put their heads on their knees. Tap one child, who goes behind the screen, The other children open their eyes and guess whose shadow is on the sheet.

Routine Times

1. At snack or meal times, eat day and night cookies — stars, moons, suns — baked by the children.
2. At rest time, always darken the room slowly. Pretend night is coming and the sun is going down. Also, brighten the room as slowly as possible at the end of rest time to simulate sunrise.

Large Muscle Activities

1. Play shadow tag or just try to step on one another's shadows outdoors. Show children how to avoid getting their shadows stepped on by squatting quickly or hiding it in the shadow of a building or a tree.
2. Play *Sally go round the sun.*

Extended Experiences

1. Send home notes requesting that parents take children out at night to see the stars, the moon, and a sunset, or get them up early to watch a sunrise.
2. Ask a parent who works at night to visit and talk about his or her job.

 # Teacher Resources

Pictures and Displays

☐ Hang pictures that show day, night, or activities that go on during the day or night.
☐ Make two dioramas, one of a day scene and one of a night scene.

Books and Periodicals

Baker, David. *Flight to the Stars.* Vero Beach, FL: Rourke, 1989
Berry, Richard. *Discover the Stars: Star Watching Using the Naked Eye, Binoculars, or a Telescope.* New York: Crown, 1987.
Chickadee magazine.
Darling, David J. *The Sun: Our Neighborhood Star.* Minneapolos: Dillon, 1984.
Owl magazine.
Paten, John. *Astronomy.* New York: Warwick Press, 1982.
Sneider, Cary I. *Earth, Moon, and Stars.* University of California, Berkeley: Lawrence Science, 1986.

Films and Videos

NOTE: Check with your distributor about public performance rights.

A Dark Dark Tale. Weston Woods.
Happy Birthday, Moon. Weston Woods.
Moon Man. Weston Woods.
The Napping House. Weston Woods, 1985.
Owl Moon. Weston Woods, 1989.
Where the Wild Things Are. Weston Woods.
Wynken, Blynken and Nod. Weston Woods.

Community Resources and Organizations

☐ A planetarium.
☐ A university department of astronomy.

Sally Go Round the Sun

Traditional

Sal - ly go round the sun, Sal - ly go round the moon,

Sal - ly go round the chim - ney top Ev - ery af - ter - noon.

26 Water around Me

Basic Understandings

(concepts children can grasp from this subject)

> NOTE: Most statements below refer to water as a liquid unless identified by another term, such as ice, snow, fog, or mist.

- [ ] Water is necessary to all living things.
- [ ] Water is all around us, in the air and in the ground. It is in milk, vegetables, fruit, and meat; leaves, trunks, and branches of a tree; it is even in stones.
- [ ] Water is used for many things:
  a. To drink — toads drink through their skin, birds tip their heads back, horses suck, cats and dogs lap, and other animals drink in their own ways.
  b. To wash things — dishes, cars, clothes, ourselves.
  c. To cook things in (eggs, vegetables), or use in things we cook (cakes, soup).
  d. To put out fires.
  e. To play in — pools, ponds, lakes, oceans; or to play with when using hoses.
  f. To water plants, lawns, trees, and bushes.
  g. To transport cargo and people on ships or boats.
- [ ] Water is wet when it is a liquid. Water is dry when it is ice or vapour.
- [ ] Pure water is colourless. It often appears blue in ice or in a clear lake, or green or brown in a river, because it contains or reflects other matter.
- [ ] Water that contains mineral salts (calcium and magnesium) is called "hard water." Rainwater is most often soft water. Well water or water from streams flowing over gypsum, limestone, or dolomite is more likely to be hard.
- [ ] Water is heavier than air.
- [ ] Ocean water is salty.
- [ ] More plants and animals live in water than on land, some in saltwater and some in freshwater.
- [ ] There is much more water than land on the earth's surface.
- [ ] Water flows; it will run from a higher place to a lower place and seek the lowest possible level.
- [ ] Water takes three forms:
  a. It is a liquid in lakes, oceans, or when it comes from taps.
  b. It is a solid when it is ice or snow.
  c. It is a gas when it is steam, clouds, air, fog, mist, or vapour.

☐ Water comes to the earth as rain or snow. Most of it goes back into the air. Fog or mist is a cloud on the ground.

☐ Ice is very strong. It holds you up when you skate on it if it is thick enough. Some Inuit used to build winter houses from blocks of snow and ice. If water gets into bottles, iron pipes, or cracks in rocks or pavement, it can break them when it turns into ice because it expands when frozen.

☐ Cold water from taps comes from many sources — surface run-off stored in reservoirs behind dams, deep wells, springs, streams, and rainwater collected in concrete basins.

☐ Hot water from taps is the same water as the cold, but it is heated in a hotwater tank in our homes before we use it.

☐ Water needs to be saved if we are to have enough. We can help by turning off dripping taps and by pouring excess drinking water on plants or in the garden instead of down sink drains.

▼ CAUTION: Do not overwater plants.

☐ Many things mix with water, such as sugar, salt, and soap. Some things do not, such as sand or oil.

NOTE: See Chapters 16 to 20 for uses of water by animals and Chapter 24, Water Transportation, for information about uses of water by people. See Indoor Large Muscle Activities Centre in Part 1 for rainy-day ideas.

Additional Facts the Teacher Should Know

1. Pure water is composed of the elements hydrogen and oxygen (two parts hydrogen to each part oxygen). When these two invisible gases combine to form a liquid (water) or a solid (ice), we can see them. When they remain in a gaseous form, such as steam or vapour, they are not always visible.

2. The earth's surface is about 75 percent water and 25 percent land. The human body is about 70 percent water. Many compounds contain water. Foods hold a lot of water: milk, 87 percent; peaches, 89 percent; eggs, 74 percent; steaks, 60 percent; watermelons, 92 percent.

3. Water is used in great quantities in industrial and power applications, such as electricity and steam power. This level of information is usually difficult for very young children to understand, so it has not been mentioned in the basic concepts.

4. Water is the most precious material on earth, more than gold, diamonds, or oil. One-quarter of all water is used for industry. It takes 45.5 L of water to prepare one can of lima beans and 2273 L to make 4.5 L of gasoline! One-quarter of the earth's water is used to make electricity with steam power. Two-fifths is used for irrigation, and less than one-tenth for houses and public buildings. We are using so much water that, unless we learn to reuse it, there will not be enough for the next generation.

5. The four worst sources of water pollution are:
   a. Acid rain.
   b. Sewage poured by communities into major streams.
   c. Industrial wastes loaded with chemicals dumped into streams.
   d. Agricultural pesticides washed into streams that kill fish and poison birds and animals that eat fish.

6. Four ways to stop water pollution include:
   a. Building treatment plants for sewage.
   b. Having industries treat their waste before dumping it.
   c. Controlling or banning the use of dangerous pesticides.

d. Cleaning up leaking dump sites, such as those polluting the Niagara River and Lake Ontario.

7. To control erosion by rain and water, we can:
   a. Build dams and reservoirs.
   b. Build irrigation ditches.
   c. Build canals.
   d. Reforest logged areas.

8. Clouds are water vapour that contains billions of tiny droplets of water. They can be several kilometres high. Rain occurs when these droplets combine and get too heavy to float, so they fall to earth. Water keeps travelling from sky to earth to ocean and back again to sky. This constant movement is called the "water cycle," and it has been going on for billions of years. Water gets into the sky by evaporation and transpiration from the leaves of plants. An apple tree will lose as much as 182 L of water from its leaves on a hot day. As raindrops ("soft" or nearly pure water) fall to earth, they pick up tiny particles from the air and ground to become impure or "hard." Boiled water becomes clean again. Water becomes a solid when it is frozen into ice at 0°C. Hailstones are frozen raindrops. When water freezes, it expands. Ice floats on water and fish can live below it. Water becomes a gas when it boils into steam at 100°C.

   NOTE: Some children will know about soft and hard water because they have water conditioners in their homes, and their parents may require that they drink water only out of a specific faucet.

9. Water is a natural air conditioner. Water in the thick layer of air around the earth absorbs the hot rays of the sun; if it were not there, it would be too hot on earth for life. At night, the damp air holds in the heat that has been absorbed during the day. Otherwise, the earth would freeze every night. Air is never completely dry; there is always a blanket of moisture around the earth.

10. Water and many other liquids weigh approximately 1 kg/L. Water is colourless. The deep blue or green colour of lakes or oceans comes from light. The blue of the sky also comes from light rays reflected by water molecules. In space, the sky is black because there is no moisture.

11. All plants and animals began as simple forms in the ocean. The ocean has always been a great source of food. Our ancestors speared fish before they killed land animals. Amphibians, such as frogs and turtles, can get oxygen from the water through their skins and from the air by means of their lungs. Warm-blooded animals and people cannot breathe without mechanical assistance under water. The average adult loses about 2.5 L of water everyday through her or his skin, lungs, and body wastes. It is replaced by eating and drinking. The water lost in perspiring cools you off by evaporation.

12. For years, explorers used water routes for transportation, and later added canals for this purpose.

Introducing This Subject to Children

1. When children notice the weather on a rainy, snowy, or foggy day, relate it to water.
2. On a cold day, the children might notice their breath outdoors; they are making their own clouds, but these fade quickly.
3. In the discovery centre, have a world globe and two pitchers of water, one salty and one fresh. Point out the oceans on the globe and let the children taste the saltwater.

Then point out the lakes and rivers and let them taste the freshwater. Notice how much of the earth's surface is covered with saltwater.

4. Have picture books available showing children playing in water and animals in or near water.
5. Hang pictures of lakes, rivers, and oceans around the room.
6. Set up an aquarium in a prominent place.

Vocabulary

water	rain	ocean	melt
wet	lake	cloud	drip
pond	stream	mist	damp
swim	river	moist	wash
ice	drops	dew	spray
snow	vapour	freeze	sprinkle
fog			

Learning Centres

Discovery Centre

1. Water is very inexpensive and readily available as a material for play. If you don't have water in the classroom, place a large metal or plastic tub, tank, plastic baby bath, or small wading pool on an old throw rug, blanket, bedspread, or towels on the floor. Older children could help to partly fill the container by carrying pitchers, buckets, or cups of water from the nearest source. Have lots of wiping-up materials handy, such as mops, sponges, and rags. If plastic aprons are available, have children wear them. When weather permits, have water play outdoors.
2. Pouring and measuring: Start by providing plastic or metal measuring cups. Each day, add something else, such as spray bottles, funnels, plastic or rubber tubing, straws, short lengths of hose, sponges, eggbeaters, strainers, wire whisks, cooking spoons (metal and wooden), measuring spoons, shakers. Be sure all utensils are unbreakable and will not rust. Use plastic eye droppers of different sizes and have children count how many drops they hold. Also do this with a baster. Use measuring spoons and cups to count how many of each smaller size it takes to fill a larger size.
3. Floating and sinking: Have children try floating and sinking objects, such as nails, rocks, wood, cork, styrofoam, plastic objects, spools, cups, and soaps. Try a small plastic bottle with the lid off; then screw the lid on tightly and try again. Next put some sand in the bottle, cap it, and try it again. Keep adding more sand until it sinks. Do the same with water. Explain that when a submarine's air tanks are full of air, it floats; but when filled with water it sinks. As the water is pumped out and replaced with air again, it rises to the surface. Air helps things float, such as balloons, corks, wood, and our lungs.

4. Washing: Add detergent or soap to the water and let children use it to wash toys that are dirty *and* washable, such as cars, trains, doll furniture, and doll clothes. Wash tabletops and shelves. Experiment to see whether hot or cold water dissolves soap more quickly.

5. Mixing: Let children mix different things with water, such as soap powder, sand, salt, flour, sugar, oil, baking soda, and cornstarch. Using three jars of water, put sand in one, soil in one, and salt in one. Shake all three and notice how fast the water clears.

6. Evaporation: Pour water to the same level in two similar jars. Put a rubber band around the outside of both at the water level. Cap one but leave the other uncapped. Observe the change in level from day to day. Notice the residue. Put saltwater in a flat dish. Note the residue after evaporation; taste it. Iron a damp cloth until dry (do not let children do this). To watch evaporation, pour some water on a warm sidewalk on a sunny day. Soon the sidewalk will be dry. Indoors, wipe a blackboard with a wet sponge and watch it become dry. Blow on it or turn a fan on it and observe.

7. Hot and cold: Fill one jar with water, one with packed snow, and one with ice cubes or chips. After they have all become water, compare volumes and cleanliness of contents. Suggest that children use a magnifying glass to see snowflakes, and then watch them turn into water in their warm hands. Blow on a cold window to see the water vapour from your breath. Heat a small piece of ice to water and then to steam. Heat water to steam, then turn it back into water on a mirror or a metal pan. Water will take the shape of any container it is put into. Freeze water in a balloon, milk carton, pie pan, or paper cup (cone-shaped, if possible). Notice the shapes when the containers are removed. Spill some water on a flat table and notice the shape it takes. Fill a glass with hot water and another with cold. Measure the temperature with a thermometer, if you wish. Have children put a finger in each glass. Put some water from each glass into a third glass. Feel it and measure the temperature. Put some ice

Water play is both relaxing and fun for children. It helps them learn about concepts such as floating and sinking. This child has chosen to play with foam letters in the water and is also practising the words she has learned.

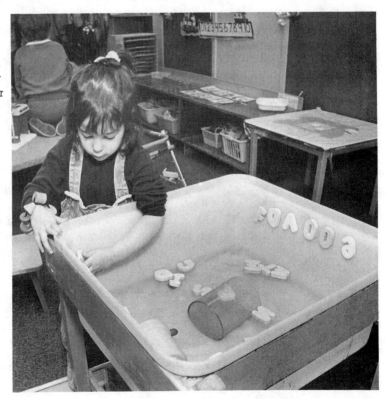

cubes into a glass of water. Feel its temperature. Also observe drops of water that form on the outside of the glass.

8. Absorption and displacement: Weigh a dry sponge; soak it with water and weigh it again. Show how water soaks into a paper towel but forms drops or runs off wax paper. Show how water magnifies by dropping a penny into a glass of water. Suck on a straw in a glass of water to show how you can lower the water level. Put your finger on the top end of the straw full of water, then release your finger. Observe what happens. Partly fill a jar with water. Put a rubber band at the water level. Lower several nails on a thread to the bottom, one at a time, and notice the water level.

9. Put some cut flowers or pussywillows in a jar of water and some in a jar with no water. Observe what happens. Keep a green plant watered and a similar one unwatered.

10. Punch holes in a vertical line from the top to the bottom of a can. Fill with water and observe how the water spurts farther from the bottom holes.

11. Put the top end of a dry towel in a pan of water on a table and the bottom end in a pan on the floor. See what happens.

12. Demonstrate how a siphon works with rubber tubing or hose.

13. Have children make small waves by blowing on a flat pan of water.

14. Demonstrate the use of a level. Children can check to see whether tables and shelves are level or not.

15. In the summer, supply a bowl of soap bubbles (see the recipe for Iridescent Soap Bubbles in Basic Resources) for each child and plastic straws for each. Let the children blow bubbles. Bubbles will show rainbow colours in the sun and be blown around by the wind.

16. Fill one pan each with soil, clay, sand, coarse sand, pebbles. Slowly pour water on each and notice in which pan the water sinks fastest.

17. Make rainbows in the sun with water from a hose. Notice how water drops sparkle on grass.

18. Watch a street sweeper, if possible, to see how water is used in its operation.

19. On a hot day, wear swimsuits and run through a sprinkler or have a water fight with spray bottles and hoses, if possible. If no hose is available, use a large water cooler with rubber tubing and a pinch clamp on the spigot.

20. Let each child put out a lighted candle using a spray bottle filled with water.

21. While it is raining, listen for the thunder, watch for lightning, and listen for the sounds of cars going by and of rain on the windows or on the roof. Go outdoors in the rain (if it is not an electrical storm) in raincoats and boots, or if it is warm enough, in swimsuits.

22. See Chapter 12, Winter, for related snowy-day activities.

23. After a rain, look for worms and rainbows and how clean the leaves, grass, and streets have become. See how dust has settled, how birds are bathing from a puddle, and how clouds are blowing away. Look for a deep groove where rainwater came off a roof or washed out from a downspout. Measure the amount of rain in a transparent tube or gauge. Watch water evaporate from wet sidewalks after rain.

24. Spray a hose straight up. Also spray it on the ground, turned on full force, to show what water pressure can do. Spray it on a metal roof or barrel, on the sidewalk, the grass, a tree, or a window. Listen to the different sounds and watch the different ways it dissipates.

▼ CAUTION: Make sure no one will be hit by the water from the hose or from water bouncing off a surface.

NOTE: Draw no conclusions from the above activities. Observe and comment only — *let the children discover.*

Dramatic Play Centres

Home-living centre

1. Let children bathe washable dolls in a plastic tub. Provide soap and lots of towels.
2. Let children wash and dry play dishes in this centre.
3. Let children wash doll clothes and hang them to dry. This activity can take place outdoors if the weather is nice.
4. Ask the children to do some of the actual cleaning in the classroom, such as mopping up spills and cleaning paintbrushes and other art materials. If you have a glass door, a child on each side washing it at the same time can be hilarious. Washing a mirror can also be fun.
5. Provide rainy- or snowy-day dressup clothes, such as rain hats, raincoats, boots, umbrellas, and mittens; also firefighter hats (see pattern on p. 473), boots, and hoses.
6. Let children practise pouring. Use real water, coloured with food colouring if you wish, for tea parties.

    NOTE: Disposable paper cups should be used unless dishes are washed with soap after a party.

Block-building centre

1. Suggest using blocks to build canals, bridges, and dams for toy boats to use.
2. Show how a marina is made.
3. Suggest a car wash for toy cars to go through.
4. Suggest building fire hall for toy fire engines and houses that have pretend fires to put out.

Other dramatic play centres

1. Sandbox: Use a hose to make a stream, dams, or a reservoir. Suggest that children make a channel and let water from the hose flow in it. They can sail wooden boats made from scraps in the woodworking centre.
2. Set up a car wash outdoors. Use a hose and wash wagons and tricycles. Supply rags and sponges.
3. Use wet sand for "cooking" with jelly moulds, muffin pans, custard cups, and other aluminum or wooden utensils.
4. After a heavy rain, notice how water pushes aside fine sand, exposes coarse pebbles, and leaves trails of dirt.
5. Flood the sandbox and watch the rivers running off, the ponds that are left, and the sand and sticks that are washed into a pile on the side.
6. Outdoors, arrange packing boxes like a boat or a fleet of boats. Add cardboard-roll fishing poles with magnets and paper fish with paperclips for fishing. Supervise so that a magnet or pole does not hit anyone.
7. Paint outdoors with water: Provide buckets, large paintbrushes, old paint rollers and trays, and spray bottles for spray painting. Also supply painters' hats and overalls. Paint playground equipment, sidewalks, toys, and walls with water.
8. Make mud pancakes and cookies. Sprinkle sand on the products for sugar, or add leaves and grass. Let dry and bake in the sun.

Art Centre

- 1. Have children paint with dry tempera on wet paper.
- ••• 2. Let the children mix their own tempera with water. Note how the colour gets lighter with additional water and darker with additional paint.

•• 3. Provide water colours as a change from more opaque tempera.
•• 4. Wet sheets of light-coloured construction paper. Have children drip paint from a brush or squeeze bottle.
•• 5. Drip paint onto a sheet of paper and blow through a straw to create abstract designs.
• 6. Make prints by blotting paint between two pieces of paper.
• 7. Children can crayon with bright colours on a large sheet of white construction paper. Then they can paint a wash over the entire paper with thin grey, blue, or purple tempera or water colour.
••• 8. Suggest that children try crayon on wet paper and then try chalk on wet paper.
••• 9. Have children draw with coloured chalk and then decorate with drops of water from en eyedropper or a squeeze bottle.
• 10. Show how dry water-soluble felt pens can be used again if dipped into water.
• 11. Paint on a blackboard with wet brushes, sponges, or rags.
••• 12. Let children mix dry, powdered clay with water to a modelling consistency.
•• 13. Rain and clouds collage: Use blue construction paper and have children paste on cotton balls for clouds, gold or silver rickrack for lightning. Christmas-tree icicles for rain, or other appropriate collage materials.
•• 14. Wet and dry paper collage: Provide construction-paper scraps of varied colours, bowls of warm water, sheets of painting paper, and glue. Suggest that the children experiment with tearing dry paper and damp paper (paper that has been dipped in the water) into shapes to glue on the painting paper. Have them glue each shape as soon as they have torn it. After the collages are dry, have the group discuss the effects of gluing damp paper with dry paper. They will see that the wet paper formed much softer shapes and that the wet paper's colours ran together with the dry paper's colours.

   ■ Children with co-ordination problems will find it easier to tear the wet paper. If a child in your group has severe co-ordination problems, have the children work in pairs; they can assist each other with tearing the paper. Children may need some direction in how to help each other without taking over the task completely and leaving their partners to watch.

•• 15. Make walnut-shell boats: Stick a round toothpick through a white paper sail. Attach the other end of the toothpick to the bottom of the walnut shell with any kind of play dough that dries hard (see the recipe in Part 1). Let harden before using.
•• 16. Make wooden boats at the woodworking centre out of scraps of balsa.

Outdoors

• 1. Paint with water on sidewalks and playground equipment. Use buckets of water and old paintbrushes and paint rollers.
• 2. Draw in wet sand with sticks.
• 3. If you have a muddy place on the playground after a rain, make mud handprints and footprints. When fairly dry, make plaster casts of them.
• 4. Model with mud dough; also try mud and sand mixtures.
•• 5. Draw on a dry sidewalk with a spray bottle of water.

Learning and Language Materials Centre

Commercially made games and materials

1. *Puzzles:* Variety of puzzles showing boat and water scenes. Make sure some puzzles have knobs for younger children.
2. *Construction and manipulative toys:* Water and sand play materials, large indoor water-play table, pails and containers in a variety of sizes, scoops, shovels, funnels, flour sifters, etc.
3. *Small toys for imaginative play:* Plastic and wooden boats in a variety of sizes; make sure they float.

4. *Outdoor toys:* Large indoor water-play table, pails and containers in a variety of sizes, scoops, shovels, funnels, flour sifters, etc. Provide a variety of bubble blowers. Make your own bubble solution (one part soap to twenty parts water).
5. *Posters:* Seaside scenes, scenes of fishermen and their catch, and posters of rain and rainwater.
6. *Miscellaneous:* Small fishing rods with magnetic bait or plastic hooks. Fish with large loops made of metal.

Teacher-made games and materials

NOTE: For detailed description, see Learning Games in Part 1.

Name it: Use objects we use with water, such as a toy boat, a plastic glass, a straw, a scrub brush, an ice-cube tray, and a hose. VARIATION: Use objects we use with water to get ready for bed, such as soap, a washcloth, a toothbrush, and a towel.

Book Centre

••• Bains, Rae. *Wonders of Rivers.* St. Catharines, ON: Troll Associates, 1982.
•• Bang, Molly. *Yellow Ball.* New York: Morrow, 1991.
•• Bell, Cathie, and David Bell. *Two Bears Go Fishing.* Toronto: Oxford University Press, 1991.
•• Blades, Ann. *By the Sea: An Alphabet Book.* Toronto: Kids Can Press, 1986.
••• Branley, Franklyn. *Floating and Sinking.* New York: Crowell, 1967.
•••• Cole, Joanna. *The Magic School Bus at the Waterworks.* Richmond Hill, ON: Scholastic, 1986.
• Cristini, E. *In the Pond.* New York: Picture Book Studio, 1985.
••• Curran, Eileen. *Life in the Pond.* St. Catharines, ON: Troll Associates, 1985.
••• ———. *Life in the Sea.* St. Catharines, ON: Troll Associates, 1985.
••• Gantschev, Ivan. *Walk Under the Rainbow.* New York: Silver, 1986.
••• Grace, Theresa. *A Picture Book of Underwater Life.* St. Catharines, ON: Troll Associates, 1990.
•• Henkes, K. *Clean Enough.* New York: Greenwillow Press, 1982.
• Hughes, S. *Bathwater's Hot.* New York: Lothrop, Lee & Shepard, 1985.
••• ———. *An Evening at Alfie's.* New York: Lothrop, Lee & Shepard, 1985.
•• Jones, Rebecca C. *Down at the Bottom of the Deep Dark Sea.* New York: Bradbury Press, 1991.
•• Kalan, Robert. *Rain.* Toronto: Mulberry, 1991.
••• Kessler, Deirdre. *Lobster in My Pocket.* Charlottetown: Ragweed Press, 1987.
•• Koch, Michelle. *By the Sea.* New York: Greenwillow Press, 1991.
••• Larsen, John. *Captain Carp Saves the Sea.* Willowdale, ON: Annick Press, 1983.
•• Leonard, Marcia. *Little Raccoon Goes to the Beach.* New York: Bantam, 1987.
• ———. *Swimmy.* New York: Pantheon, 1963. (also available in French as *Nageat* and in Spanish as *Suimi*)
•• Lionni, Leo. *On My Beach There Are Many Pebbles.* New York: Ivan Obelensky, 1961.
•••• Maestro, Betsy. *A Sea Full of Sharks.* Richmond Hill, ON: Scholastic, 1990.
••• Maestro, Betsy, and Delvecchio, Ellen. *Big City Port.* New York: Four Winds, 1984.
••• Marzollo, J. *Amy Goes Fishing.* New York: Dial Press, 1980.
••• McCloskey, R. *Time of Wonder.* New York: Viking Press, 1957.
••• Munsch, Robert. *The Mud Puddle.* Willowdale, ON: Annick Press, 1982.
••• Nelson, Audrey. *Michael's Saturday Surprise.* Willowdale, ON: Black Moss Press, 1988.
• Patkau, Karen. *In the Sea.* Willowdale, ON: Annick Press, 1989.
••• Peacock, David. *The Sea Serpent in Grenadier Pond.* Willowdale, ON: Hounslow Press, 1986.

- - - Pittman, Al. *Down by Jim Long's Stage*. St. John's: Breakwater Press, 1988.
- - - ———. *One Wonderful Fine Day for a Sculpin Named Sam*. St. John's: Breakwater Press, 1983.
- Rockwell, A., and H. Rockwell. *Nice and Clean*. New York: Macmillan, 1984.
- - - Rounds, G. *Washday on Noah's Ark*. New York: Holiday, 1985.
- - - Saltman, Judith. *Goldie and the Sea*. Toronto: Groundwood, 1987.
- Shulevitz, Uri. *Rain, Rain, Rivers*. New York: Farrar, Straus & Giroux, 1969.
- Spier, Peter. *Peter Spier's Rain*. Garden City, NY: Doubleday, 1982.
- - - Staunton, Ted. *Simon's Surprise*. Toronto: Kids Can Press, 1986.
- - - Thompson, Richard. *Effie's Bath*. Willowdale, ON: Annick Press, 1989.
- - - ———. *Gurgle, Bubble, Splash*. Willowdale, ON: Annick Press, 1989.
- - - Warner, Rachel. *Going Fishing*. London: A & C Black, 1990. (photographs from Bangladesh)
- - - Waterton, Betty. *A Salmon for Simon*. Toronto: Groundwood, 1986.
- - - Wynne-Jones, Tim. *Zoom at Sea*. Toronto: Groundwood, 1983.
- - - Zolotow, Charlotte. *The Storm Book*. New York: Harper & Row, 1952.

 # Planning for Group Time

NOTE: All music, fingerplays, poems, stories, and games listed here may also be used at other times during the session as appropriate.

Music

Songs

Please see "Here We Go Looby Loo" at the end of this chapter.

From *A Treasury of Songs for Young Children*, Glazer
"The E-RI-E," p. 77
"Erie Canal," p. 79

From *Singing Bee*, Hart
"Merrily We Roll Along," p. 59
"Polly Put the Kettle On," p. 60
"Little Drops of Water," p. 63
"The Gallant Ship," p. 84
"Sur le pont d'Avignon," p. 108
"Lightly Row," p. 138

From *Elephant Jam*, Sharon, Lois, and Bram
"Charlie Over the Ocean," p. 36

Rhythms and singing games

Reproduce tone:
a.   Add water in different amounts to a set of eight identical glasses. With care you can get a one-octave range of notes when the glasses are tapped with a rhythm stick. Let the children experiment with the pouring also. Try to play simple tunes, such as "Mary Had a Little Lamb."

b. Hang up a set of various-shaped bottles by their necks, add water in different amounts, tap with a rhythm stick.

c. Put different amounts of water in stemware. If you wet a finger and run it around the rim of a glass, a clear note will be produced. Close supervision is necessary for this activity! If you look closely at the surface of the water, you can actually see tiny ripples that the sound vibrations make.

d. Put different amounts of water in bottles and blow across the tops. Listen to the variations.

e. Dramatize: Wash doll clothes, scrub tables, wash hands, or fingerpaint to music.

Records and Cassettes

Bob Homme. *The Giant Concert of Concerts by the Friendly Giant.* (A & M Records)
"Seafood Concert"

Raffi. *Baby Beluga.* (Troubadour Records)
"Baby Beluga"
"Water Dance"

Sharon, Lois, and Bram. *Elephant Record.* (Elephant Records)
"London Bridge"
"Noah's Old Ark"
"Jack Was Every Inch a Sailor"

———. *Smorgasbord.* (Elephant Records)
"Long Legged Sailor"
"Newfound Jig Medley"
"Sur le pont d'Avignon"

Fingerplays and Poems

NOTE: Pittman's *Down by Jim Long's Stage* and *One Wonderful Day for a Sculpin Named Sam* are filled with wonderful poems for this subject.

From *Mischief City*, Wynne-Jones
"Drink the Bathwater," p. 18

From *Oranges and Lemons*, King and Beck
"Noah's Ark," p. 16
"The Big Ship Sails in the Alley, Alley O," p. 44

From *Round and Round the Garden*, Williams
"Row, Row, Row Your Boat," p. 19
"I Hear Thunder," p. 37

From *Read Aloud Rhymes for the Very Young*, Prelutsky and Brown
"Swimming," p. 9
"Home," p. 30
"Shore," p. 30
"Chums," p. 40
"Fish," (#1) p. 44
"Fish," (#2) p. 44
"Belly and Tubs Went Out in a Boat," p. 45
"Drinking Fountain," p. 85

Stories

(To read, read–tell, or tell. See Book Centre for a complete list.)

Stories for this subject should be chosen on the basis of children's experience. For example, Leonard's *Little Raccoon Goes to the Beach* would be excellent for children in Manitoba who are more likely to have visited lakes and rivers than oceans. Maestro and Delvecchio's *Big City Port* would be a good option for children living in St. John's, Halifax, Quebec, Montreal, Toronto, or Vancouver.

Games

(See Learning Games in Part 1 for directions.)

1. *Mulberry bush:* Play using such variations as wash our hands, face, teeth; wash the car; scrub the floor, stairs.
2. *Row your boat:* Have children sit in pairs on the floor facing each other with feet together and holding hands. They rock back and forth in time with the tune as you sing.
3. *London bridge:* Sing and play with older children.
4. *Six little ducks:* Follow the actions suggested in the song. Give each child a feather to hold in his or her hand for a tail.
5. *Musical stars:* Play using puddles instead of stars.

Routine Times

Snack or lunch

1. Let children mix a powdered drink with water or make their own lemonade.
2. Let children make gelatin, measuring the water and the powder and stirring.
3. Taste different kinds of water — distilled water, well water, tap water, rainwater, saltwater, and sugar water.
4. Invite children to drink cold, warm, and hot water.
5. Demonstrate what happens when you boil an egg, spaghetti, or a carrot. Taste the food before and after cooking.
6. Eat fish at snack time and discuss where it came from.
7. Bake a cake mix to which you add only water, such as gingerbread. See how the batter changes in cooking.
8. Lick ice cubes.
9. In the summer, make juice popsicles in the freezer. Cover and try to freeze them outdoors in the winter.
10. Make snow cones (see Discovery Centre in Chapter 12).
11. Float a flower (or candle) in a clear bowl for a centrepiece at snack time.

Toileting

1. Notice how much water is used in the bathroom, where it comes from, and where it goes. Follow the water pipes to their source, if possible.
2. Find the hot-water tank.
3. Stress the importance of water for cleanliness and the importance of not wasting it.

Cleanup

1. Wash tables with a sponge before and after eating. Wash dishes used for snacks.
2. Wash easels and shelves with sponges.
3. Water plants, add water to the fish tank, and be sure any small pets such as gerbils have enough water. Talk about the exact amounts of water needed.

4. Wipe up spills with mops or sponges.

Rest time

On hot days, try damp washcloths on foreheads.

Large Muscle Activities

1. Use a rocking boat both indoors and outdoors as a fishing boat.
2. Sail all the boats made in the art centre in a play pool or water table, or cut a tire around its circumference to form two circular troughs in which to sail boats.
3. On hot days, set up a play pool.
4. Let a hose trickle for drinks.
5. Let children run through a sprinkler.
6. Blow bubbles outdoors.
7. Plant a garden and water it regularly with a watering can or a hose.
8. On a hot day, when the children are in swimsuits, run the hose down a slippery slide. Supervise carefully.
9. Fill balloons with water and drop them from a height, such as a slide or a jungle gym. Discuss how the heavy water breaks the balloons. Do not use children as targets!
10. Dig up earth, and turn it over. Notice that it is more damp underneath.
11. Set out a chunk of damp earth to dry in the sun. Feel and look at it later.
12. Water the grass.
13. Wash a car.
14. Play firefighter and put out a pretend fire with water.
15. Make wet footprints on a dry sidewalk.
16. Crawl through or climb over large sewer pipes in the playground.
17. Play *Jump the brook:* Lay two ropes on the ground parallel to each other. Children take turns jumping over the "brook." After each child has had a turn, increase the distance between the ropes.
18. Have a digging spot or hole where mud can be made. You will need shovels that really dig, big rocks to push around for stepping-stones, boards for bridges, boxes or tubs for boats and houses, and a hose or tap nearby to rinse off with. If children are allowed to go barefoot, be sure there are no sharp objects, such as glass, tin cans, or pointed rocks, in the hole.

Extended Experiences

1. Go for a walk to find sources of water outdoors, such as hoses, fire hydrants, puddles, drainage canals, and sewers. Notice clothes drying on a clothesline.
2. Take a walk indoors to try to locate water pipes, sewer pipes, and the hot-water tank.
3. If possible, visit a house or other building under construction to see how the plumbing is installed. Get permission and plan for adequate supervision.
4. Visit a plumbing shop or a laundromat, or take a group in a car through a car wash.
5. Watch a road construction site where underground sewer pipes are exposed or are being laid.
6. Go to see a water tower or a water storage tank on the ground.
7. If you visit a farm, notice the water tanks for livestock, the windmills to pump water, and a hand pump, if one is still in use.
8. Take the children on a trip to a local aquarium.
9. If snorkel or scuba diving is taught in your area, arrange to have the children watch a demonstration.
10. Visit an indoor and an outdoor swimming pool.

11. Watch a street-sweeping machine.
12. If you are lucky enough to live near a lake, a river, or an ocean, take a trip to watch boats of all kinds, water-skiing, and sailing. Extra supervision will be necessary if the children are allowed to wade or play in the sand at the water's edge.
13. Visit a park or other area where there are fountains, waterfalls, swans, ducks, boating, a water lily pond, or fish ponds.
14. Stand on a small bridge and watch the water flow under it on one side; cross to the other side and watch the water flow out from under it. Drop a small floating object (stick, or pine-cone) over the first side and watch it come out on the other side. Try a nonfloating object, such as a small rock.
15. Visit a small pond on a still day. Look at the reflections in the water, then disturb the water and look at it again (this can be done in a play pool in the yard).
16. Throw pebbles into water and notice how they form concentric circles. On a hot day, take off shoes and socks and wade to see the ripples made in the water.
17. Encourage children to play in dry and wet sand. Offer them a water source and sand toys.
18. Invite the owner of a pet shop to visit and bring a pet turtle or fish and explain its care.
19. Ask a plumber to visit your centre.
20. Invite a scuba diver to visit.
21. Borrow a globe and maps for finding water bodies and streams.

Teacher Resources

Pictures and Displays

- ☐ Hang travel posters that show lakes, ski areas, or the seashore.
- ☐ Some calendars have excellent water pictures.
- ☐ Make large posters to show clothing that is worn on rainy days, on snowy days, or for playing in the water on hot days.
- ☐ Float a flower (or a candle) in a clear bowl.

Books and Periodicals

Ardley, Neil. *Working with Water*. New York: Franklin Watts, 1983.
Blocksma, Mary. *Easy-To-Make Water Toys that Really Work*. New York: Simon & Schuster, 1985.
Fish. New York: Time-Life, 1979.
Heslewood, Juliet. *Earth, Air, Fire and Water*. New York: Oxford University Press, 1989.
Ontario Science Centre. *Scienceworks*. Toronto: Kids Can Press, 1986.
Powledge, F. *Water*. New York: Farrar, Straus & Giroux, 1982.
The Sea. New York: Time-Life, 1977.
Twist, Clint. *Rain to Dams: Projects with Water*. New York: Franklin Watts, 1990.

Films and Videos

NOTE: Check with your distributor about public performance rights.

Burt Dow: Deep-Water Man. Weston Woods.

Come See the Dolphin. Coronet Instructional Films, 1975.
Swimmy. Lionni & Gianini (released in Canada by Connecticut Films), 1968.

Community Resources and Organizations

☐ A fishing or anglers club.
☐ A sailing club.
☐ Harbour Police.
☐ A scuba-diving club or school.
☐ Canadian Power Squadron.
☐ A swimming club.
☐ Canadian Red Cross (Lifeguard and Swimming Division).
☐ Royal Lifesaving Society of Canada.
☐ Marina or aquarium.
☐ Fish hatchery.
☐ Plumber.

Government Agencies

☐ Federal, provincial, or territorial ministry of the environment.

Here We Go Looby Loo

Donna Wood

(3-4-5) l s f m r d

2. You put your left hand in.
3. You put your right foot in.
4. You put your left foot in.
5. You put your head right in.
6. You put your whole self in. *(just one step)*

Formation: A stationary, standing circle. A dramatic introduction adds interest — the circle is a bath, ready for Saturday night. When you put your hand "in," the water is very hot, so you quickly take it out again, as the song tells you.

Game: While singing the chorus, pick up the beat with clap, stamp, or finger snap. While singing a verse, the action follows the words.

27 Colour in My World

Basic Understandings
(concepts children can grasp from this subject)

- [ ] Colour is a word used to describe an object.
- [ ] Colours are everywhere that we can see — in flowers, clothes, food, cars, and so on.
- [ ] Colours have names — red, orange, yellow, green, blue, and purple.
- [ ] We cannot see colours without light (in a dark place). If we cover our eyes, we cannot see colours.
- [ ] Some rocks, minerals, and paints change colour under special lights (fluorescent, ultraviolet, and "black" light) or glow in the dark.
- [ ] Sunlight (which we see as yellow or white) can be split into a rainbow.
- [ ] Some colours are used to depict certain things: yellow for sunshine, green for grass, blue for sky, and so on. However, this does not mean that these colours must always be used for these things.
- [ ] Colours are used for road safety symbols that everyone recognizes, such as stop signs, traffic lights, school zones, and railroad crossings.
- [ ] Some colours (or pigments) can be mixed together to make other colours:

  blue + red = purple
  blue + yellow = green
  red + yellow = orange
  red + yellow + blue = brown
  white + colour = tint
  colour + black = shade

- [ ] We cannot make red, yellow, blue, black, or white by mixing paints.
- [ ] Each person has a skin, a hair, and an eye colour that are just right for him or her. Each colour may differ from ours.
- [ ] Sometimes we have favourite colours or consider some colours prettier than others, and so we prefer to use these more often than other colours.
- [ ] Almost everything has a colour, except clear glass, clear plastic, pure air, and pure water.
- [ ] If we can see through something clearly, it is transparent.
- [ ] Colours look bright on a sunny day and dull on a cloudy day or in the shade.

☐   There are paint colours that look like some metals we use — gold, silver, copper, and brass.

☐   Wood comes in different colours and has different names. Wood is usually named for the tree from which the lumber comes: maple, walnut, oak, white or yellow pine, cedar, ebony, and redwood.

Additional Facts the Teacher Should Know

1. Light, the source of all colour, is white when it reaches us from the sun. Each colour wave in the white ray of light has a different wavelength, and each wavelength, as it passes through a prism, is deflected at a different angle due to its velocity (rate of speed) in passing from one medium to another. Thus, the complex white ray of light is dispersed into its many-coloured wavelengths (a rainbow). The longest ray is red; the shortest is violet. The longer wavelengths of light are called warm colours — red, orange, yellow. The shorter wavelengths are called cool colours — blue and violet. Green falls between the warm and the cool colours.

2. The primary colours are red, yellow, and blue. The secondary colours orange, green, and purple are produced by mixing two primary colours. The easiest way for children to make brown is by mixing red, yellow, and blue. Brown can also be obtained by mixing orange and black. Children may discover this method at the art centre when using these paints for Halloween activities.

3. "Hue" is the name of a colour. "Value" is the lightness or darkness of a colour. "Intensity" is the saturation or purity of the colour. A hue may vary in intensity when it is mixed with white to make a tint (be sure to add the colour to the white); mixed with black to make a shade (add black to the colour); mixed with black and white to make a tone; and mixed with its complement to make gradations of grey tones.

4. The primary colours of light are red, green, and blue. They are used in stage lighting and window displays. If we take red, green, and blue spotlights into a darkened room and shine them on a white screen, we will get the following secondary colours: red light + green light = yellow; red light + blue light = magenta or red-violet; blue light + green light = cyan blue or blue-green. Red, green, and blue light shining on the screen together produce white.

5. Colour may transmit an emotion or a symbolic meaning to the viewer of an artwork.

6. We often use colour to express emotions. For example, we see "red" when we are angry, we are "green" with envy, we are "yellow" when we lack courage, we have the "blues" when we are sad. These concepts are on an adult level and only produce confusion in preschoolers.

7. Some young children seem much more colour-conscious than others. Children tend to be aware of colour distinctions and to be able to classify objects by colour before they can attach names to their groupings. Understand that children can experience colour activities and enjoy them, but may not be ready for real recognition of the concepts involved. Avoid forcing these concepts on a child who is not ready.

8. When introducing colour in the centre, begin with the three primary colours. As any two or all three of these are mixed, secondary colours are produced. Secondary colours may be added to primary colours later for variety and for more brilliant hues. Pastel tints are delightful for a change of pace in the spring. Be sure to offer a choice of colours when children wish to depict skin colours in their artwork. Remember that dark colours are attractive and pleasant to look at and are associated with good things (such as chocolate pudding), just as brighter colours are.

9. Colour blindness could be the cause of persistent colour confusion by a child. There are simple tests to detect this condition; consult an eye doctor for assistance. More boys show this tendency than girls.

10. Colours have symbolic value in every culture. Be aware of the meanings of colours for the children in your program. If a colour has a special (either negative or positive) meaning for a child, give him or her an opportunity to talk about the meaning.

■ 11. Obviously, colour is a difficult topic for children who are visually impaired. Avoiding the topic will not assist these children. Instead, try to develop associations between different colours and concepts the children will understand; for example, a fire often has yellow and red flames in it. These are warm colours that a child can associate with a sensation of warmth.

Introducing This Subject to Children

1. Go for a walk to observe colours.
2. Read a simple story about single colours, such as *Red Is Best* (see Book Centre).
3. Explore a colour saturation module (see Discovery Centre, number 15).
4. A seasonal activity will suggest certain colours; for example: red, Valentine's Day; orange and black, Halloween; white, winter.
5. Discuss the colours of food at meal times; colours of skin, hair, and eyes at routine times; or colours of cars, trucks, houses, trees, and flowers while in transit.
6. Have colour days for a total experience with colour (see Discovery Centre, number 1).

Vocabulary

colour	orange	dark	transparent
shadow	red	gold	reflection
silver	blue	white	violet
maple	yellow	black	shiny
brown	copper	rainbow	glow
iron	walnut	prism	rust
sun	green	pink	ebony
bright	light	purple	ivory
dull	brass		

Learning Centres

Discovery Centre

1. Colour days: Explore a colour for a certain time period. We recommend one week per colour for a beginning experience, three to five days for children with previous experience, and one to three days for those with much colour experience. The following is an example of a red day:

   On the day preceding the first red day, send each child home with a note explaining the colour days or week attached to a square of pure red paper pinned to the child's clothing. Ask children to come to school wearing some article of red clothing or to bring an object or a picture showing the colour red. Both parents and children can become very involved in this project. Teachers, of course, should wear the colour of the day. You may add a surprise element at special times during the day by pinning a colour book on your smock or jacket. (Fold pages of appropriately coloured paper into a small book 10 cm by 12 cm. Paste coloured objects on each page.)

NOTE: Have scarves, handkerchiefs, or coloured yarn loops for children who forget to bring or wear something for the colour day. Display a poster of red objects at the door or in a conspicuous place, and put red objects on the discovery table. Feature red media in the art centre. Use a fingerplay about red and read stories or books that emphasize the colour red. Serve red foods at snack or meal times. Sing red songs and use red games and other activities. Feature firefighters in dramatic play. After all the colour days have been presented, all colours are stressed and rainbows are considered. A suggested colour sequence is red, yellow, blue, green, orange, and violet. After violet could come brown, then black and white, and finally rainbow days featuring all the colours.

2. Make or look for rainbows:
   a. Place a small mirror in a glass of water, with the mirror tilted against the glass.
   b. Hold a prism close to the eyes on a bright day to see everything outlined in rainbows. Look for prisms in beads, chandelier pendants, diamonds, and bevelled glass.
   c. The sun shining directly through the water in an aquarium makes a rainbow.
   d. Observe how a drop of oil in a puddle produces a rainbow.
   e. Observe how a fine water spray with the sun shining through it produces a rainbow.

   NOTE: Always have the sun behind the child holding the hose. The sun must fall on the water to make a rainbow.

   f. Look for a real rainbow after a rain.
   g. Soap bubbles have rainbows.
3. Observe differences in the brightness of colours in sun and in shade.
4. Let children experiment with making the colour brown by squeezing drops of primary food colouring into water in a clear plastic glass.
5. Encourage children to mix primary colours to obtain secondary colours:
   a. Overlap pieces of tissue paper in primary colours and hold them against a window.
   b. Overlay sheets or cut out shapes of coloured plastic or cellophane.
   c. Mix tempera or fingerpaints.
   d. Brush water colours on a sheet of white paper.
   e. Use a commercial colour paddle, rainbow box, or tricolour viewer.
6. Try on tinted glasses of different hues to observe same-coloured items.
7. Set out kaleidoscopes for examination.
8. Explore a mirror to see how it reflects images.
9. Set out objects you can see through and those you can't — glasses, binoculars, fish bowl, clear plastic tumblers, magnifying glass; rocks, wood, metal, china, construction paper.
10. Children can explore a coloured flashlight (some have two or three colours).
11. Older children may enjoy dyeing materials and seeing how objects of the same colour differ in shade.
12. Dye white hard-boiled eggs.
13. Have samples of different kinds of wood and, if possible, pictures of the trees from which they come. Let children sand wood to make it smooth. Notice the different grains.
14. Display rocks and minerals of various colours. Provide hand-held and tripod magnifying glasses. Look at fluorescent minerals under a "black" light if one is available.

15. Colour saturation modules: Furnish a large carton or wooden box big enough to crawl inside with nature items, food, upholstery fabric and textured cloth, toys, and equipment of the same colour. You could also set up a corner or enclose an area with a three-way play screen. Appeal to all of the children's senses. Invite children to interact with this special colour environment. Be sure to make the outside intriguing enough to entice children inside. Prints of paintings focussing on the colour, windows to peek through, and a rug leading to the door will enhance this area. Equip your module in such a way that props can be changed to introduce new colours. Use hooks on the walls to hang a roller drop of drapery material, wallpaper, vinyl, or carpeting. For example, a yellow module might contain bananas, daffodils, yellow velvet, lemon incense, bamboo bug-keeper, balloons, yellow cab, sponges, low-watt yellow bulb, straw hat, lemon-scented soap, and yellow plastic or cellophane on the windows.

Dramatic Play Centres

Home-living centre

1. Make available a full-length mirror and as many brightly coloured objects, toys, and dressup clothes as possible. Reinforce colour awareness in conversation; for example: "The firefighters that we visited had red hats; ours are red too."
2. Dress dolls or paper dolls in different-coloured clothing. Use scraps of material or construction paper to make clothes.
3. Emphasize colour in foods and dishes.
4. Talk about metals — copper and aluminum pots and pans, stainless steel utensils, silverware, and iron.

Block-building centre

1. Emphasize colour in cars, trucks, road signs, and other block-building accessories.
2. Draw property lines on the floor with coloured chalk.
3. Identify each child's construction with a colourful sign.

Other dramatic play centres

1. Set out traffic signs and signals for use with wheel toys. Make your own from cardboard or construction paper. A traffic light can be made by pasting red, green, and yellow circles on an egg-carton lid.
2. Go fishing: Cut out paper fish of various colours. Attach paperclips for mouths. Let children fish with cardboard-tube poles that have string lines with magnets attached.
3. Dramatize *Caps for Sale* by Slobodkin (see Book Centre). You will need red, green, yellow, and blue caps for the monkeys and one brown cap for the peddler.

Art Centre

NOTE: Substitute other colours as you wish in the activities that follow.

• 1. Feature a particular colour at the easel. If a secondary colour is being featured, also offer the two primary colours that produce it.

▼ CAUTION: To keep paints from getting muddy, use small amounts in unbreakable paint pots. Change as needed. Use one brush for each jar.

•• 2. Blotto prints: press paint between two sheets of paper.
•• 3. Blue: Sponge paint on light-blue paper.
•• 4. Violet: Let children sprinkle dry red tempera on wet paper and paint with it for awhile. Then sprinkle on blue tempera to discover violet.

•• 5. Brown: Spatter paint brown animals on pastel paper, or make brown crayon rubbings over pennies.

••• 6. Make a rainbow using either water colours brushed onto a large sheet of white paper with a wide brush or the long side of peeled crayons.

•• 7. Scribble paintings: Children scribble many colours on a large sheet of white paper, pressing hard with brightly coloured wax crayons. Then they paint over the entire paper with either black water colour or thin black tempera.

•• 8. Offer tempera paint and brushes for painting woodworking creations. Liquid detergent added to paint makes it stick better.

•• 9. Roller painting: Use small rolling pins or heavy cardboard tubes covered with textured upholstery fabric, and roll across drips of paint.

• 10. Use spool brayers to make stripes and plaids of different colours (see p. 33).

• 11. Sort out crayons for the colour of the day.

• 12. Use big kindergarten chalk for writing on the blackboard. Vividly coloured chalk can be used on dark paper.

• 13. Orange: Start with uncoloured play dough. Have children sprinkle dry yellow tempera in a depression in the dough and work in with fingers, then add red tempera to discover orange. Children may want to make pumpkins or carrots.

• 14. Yellow: Crumple precut yellow tissue circles and paste them on green paper to represent yellow flowers in the grass.

••• 15. Children can cut or tear multicoloured tissue paper into irregular shapes to be overlapped and glued on rice paper with thinned white glue. Hang pictures in windows.

• 16. Black and white: Make a collage by gluing shavings of white styrofoam on black paper, or make shadow pictures of the children's heads.

17. Multicolour days:

••• a. Decorate eggs dyed in the discovery centre.

•• b. Make a collage of crushed, dyed eggshells by gluing them on black paper with thinned white glue.

• c. Mix sawdust with thick tempera paint and spread it out to dry. Sawdust can be glued to paper later in a collage.

• d. Rock salt or coarse pickling salt, dyed and sprinkled with glue and glitter, give a sparkling effect.

e. Sponge painting or stamp printing allows children to explore overlapping colours.

• 18. Make a collage from coloured yarns, ribbons, sequins, and glitter.

• 19. Collages can be made from thin wood scraps glued together. These can be painted.

• 20. Sponge printing: Dip sponges cut in different shapes into dark-coloured paint; press them on light-coloured paper of the same hue.

••• 21. Fingerprints: Use sponges in flat dishes as stamp pads. Use one colour (red, blue, yellow, green) per dish. Children use two fingers on each hand (one finger for each colour) to print on white paper (requires co-ordination).

••• 22. Make multicoloured wire sculptures from coloured plastic wires.

••• 23. Try origami with different-coloured paper (only for older children). (See p. 231 for examples.)

Learning and Language Materials Centre

Commercially made games and materials

NOTE: Set out puzzles and other cognitive materials featuring the colour of the day.

1. *Puzzles*: Puzzles with large coloured shapes that give children the opportunity to match the shapes and the colours.

Puzzles that associate shapes with
particular colours add to the children's
exploration of colour.

2. *Construction and manipulative toys:* Large coloured pegs and coloured pegboard.
   Wooden mosaic tiles that can be formed into a variety of patterns.
3. *Miscellaneous:*
   a. Montessori colour tablets.
   b. Kaleidoscope with changeable coloured screens.
   c. A large plastic stand that can be used with reusable plastic shapes to create
      designs.
   d. Prisms, colour paddles, colour pyramids.

   ▼ **CAUTION: Ensure that all prisms, paddles, and similar equipment are made of unbreakable
   materials.**

   e. Board games: Games for colour matching.
   f. Coloured magnetic letter and number sets.
   g. Coloured washable markers.

Teacher-made games and materials

NOTE: For detailed descriptions, see Learning Games in Part 1.

1. Many inexpensive, unbreakable, small coloured objects can be used in interesting
   colour sorting games. For example, small plastic cars can be parked in matching
   coloured construction-paper parking lots. Cars or airplanes can be sorted into milk-
   carton garages or hangars that have been painted different colours.
2. Spools can be painted pure colours and used as beads to string on long boot strings, or
   sorted on lengths of dowel.
3. *Match-them:* Match paint chips, spools of thread, rug samples, or swatches of fabric.

4. *Match-them:* Make two or more colour envelopes. Enclose in each a red square, a yellow circle, a green triangle, and a blue rectangle. Ask children to take an envelope and match their shapes with yours.

5. *Match-them:* Match coloured paper to pictures or objects in the room.

6. Coloured rubber bands of various widths and lengths can be stretched between pegs on a pegboard.

7. *Colour lotto:* Make two sets of coloured cardboard squares. Glue one set to lotto cards, making sure that same-colour squares are placed in a variety of positions on various cards.

8. *How many?* Use coloured geometric paper shapes, colour chips, or other small coloured objects.

9. *Sequence:* Make a row of coloured squares or objects.

10. *Alike, different, and the same:* Children select the coloured piece that does not belong with a group of like-coloured objects or pieces of paper.

> NOTE: Any conversation with a child about colour helps to make the child more colour-conscious. Always include the colour of an object you are distinguishing; for example, "Do you want the red paint?" Otherwise, the child may think "red" is the object if you only say, "Do you want red?"

Book Centre

> NOTE: Additional books for use in this section can be found in Chapter 2, Sight.

•• *Colours* (First Discovery Series). Toronto: Moonlight, 1991.

• Crews, Donald. *Freight Train.* New York: Greenwillow, 1968.

•• Ehlert, Lois. *Planting a Rainbow.* New York: Harcourt Brace Jovanovich, 1988.

••• Emberley, Ed. *Green Says Go.* Boston: Little, Brown, 1968.

•• Freeman, D. *The Chalk Box Story.* New York: Harper & Row, 1976.

•• ———. *A Rainbow of My Own.* New York: Viking Press, 1966.

•• Gill, Bob. *What Colour Is Your World?* New York: Astor-Honor, 1962.

•• Hoban, Tana. *Is It Red? Is It Yellow? Is It Blue?* New York: Greenwillow, 1978.

•• Johnson, Crocket. *Harold and the Purple Crayon.* New York: Harper & Row, 1955.

•• Leonard, Marcia. *Paintbox Penguins: A Book about Colors.* St. Catharines, ON: Troll Associates, 1990.

•• Lionni, Leo. *Little Blue and Little Yellow.* New York: Astor-Honor, 1959.

• Ormerod, Jan. *My Little Book of Colours.* Toronto: Walker, 1991.

••• Pinkwater, Daniel Manus. *The Big Orange Splot.* Toronto: Methuen, 1986.

•• Silsbe, Brenda. *Just One More Colour.* Willowdale, ON: Annick Press, 1991.

•• Slobodkin, Esphyr. *Caps for Sale.* Reading, MA: Addison-Wesley, 1947.

•• Stinson, Kathy. *Those Green Things.* Willowdale, ON: Annick Press, 1985.

•• ———. *Red Is Best.* Willowdale, ON: Annick Press, 1982.

• Testa, F. *If You Take a Paintbrush: A Book of Colours.* New York: Dial Press, 1976.

••• Winik, J.T. *Fun with Colours.* Burlington, ON: Hayes, 1985.

•• Zacharias, Thomas, and Wanda Zacharias. *But Where Is the Green Parrot?* New York: Delacorte Press, 1968.

•• Zimmerman, H. Werner. *Alphonse Knows — The Colour of Spring.* New York: Oxford University Press, 1990.

•• Zion, Gene. *Harry, the Dirty Dog.* New York: Harper & Row, 1956. (black and white)

••• Zolotow, Charlotte. *The Sky Was Blue.* New York: Harper & Row, 1963.

Planning for Group Time

NOTE: All music, fingerplays, poems, stories, and games listed here may also be used at other times during the session as appropriate.

Music

Songs

....

SUN, SUN

by Robert Heidbreder

"Sun, Sun overhead,
What's your colour?"

"I am red."

"Sun, Sun, fiery fellow,
What's your colour?"

"I am yellow."

"Sun, Sun in sky of blue,
What's your colour?"

"Orange too.
I'm golden yellow,
Orange and red,
A burning fire above your head."

Prepare large circles of Bristol board in yellow, red, and orange, and a square of blue. Give the shapes to children in the group and encourage them to hold up their colour when they hear it. This activity builds familiarity with colours. You might also introduce this poem to children as part of a discussion of seasons.

From *The Colours of My Rainbow*, Wayman
All the songs in this excellent activity book are useful for the colour theme. When choosing songs from this book, use the criteria discussed on pp. 41 and 42 to decide which are best for singing with or to children.

From *The Goat with the Bright Red Socks*, Birkenshaw and Walden
"The Goat with the Bright Red Socks," p. 25

From *Elephant Jam*, Sharon, Lois, and Bram
"Jenny Jenkins," p. 122

From *Stepping Along in Music Land*, Murray
"Little Green Man," p. 42
"Rolling Down the Highway," p. 43
"Colour Song," p. 44
"Make a Rainbow," p. 46

Rhythms and Singing Games

Use good marching music. Children could carry brightly coloured flags of solid colours.

> **NOTE:** Balloons, chiffon scarves, felt ribbons, and crepe-paper streamers of different colours make good dance props.

Records and Cassettes

Bob Homme. *The Giant Concert of Concerts by the Friendly Giant.* (A & M Records)
"Ribbon Concert"

Raffi. *The Corner Grocery Store.* (Troubadour Records)
"Cluck, Cluck Red Hen"

Bob Schneider. *When You Dream a Dream.* (Capital Records)
"Over the Rainbow"

Sharon, Lois, and Bram. *Elephant Show.* (Elephant Records)
"Five Brown Buns"
——. *Smorgasbord.* (Elephant Records)
"Father Papered the Parlour"

Fingerplays and Poems

From *The Colours of My Rainbow,* Wayman
"Urple Purple," p. 41

From *Read Aloud Rhymes for the Very Young,* Prelutsky and Brown
"Grasshopper Green," p. 63
"Crayons," p. 86
"Silvery," p. 87

MY PUSSY WILLOW

I have a little pussy
Her coat is soft and grey;
She lives down in the meadow
And she never runs away.

Although she is a pussy,
She'll never be a cat;
For she's a pussy willow!
Now what do you think of that?

COLOURS IN MY FOOD

by Bonnie Flemming

Colours, colours, what colours do I see
In the food the farmer grows for me?
Orange carrots and ripe, red tomatoes,
Green string beans and nice brown potatoes.
Yellow butter is to spread on my bread,
Cold, white milk and an apple so red,
Yes, these are the foods that are best, I know,
Because they help me to grow and grow!

NOTE: Use flannelboard cutouts of foods. You or children can place foods on the flannelboard as the poem is read. Use real foods at snack time, and allow children to eat them when the poem is finished.

Stories

(To read, read–tell, or tell. See Book Centre for a complete list.)
Any book with colourful illustrations could be used with a story that emphasizes the colours. The illustrations in Brian Wildsmith's books are very good.

Games

(See Learning Games in Part 1 and Teacher-Made Games and Materials earlier in this chapter for directions.)

1. *Name it.*
2. *I see something, what do you see?*
3. *Look and see.*
4. *Guess what?*
5. *What am I?*
6. *Match-them.*
7. *Alike, different, and the same.*
8. *Colour lotto.*

Routine Times

1. Snack or meal times: Have a conference with the school cook to get his or her ideas about foods to match your colour days. The following are some suggestions:

Yellow days
pineapple juice
lemonade
yellow apple slices
half a banana
scrambled eggs
custard
lemon gelatin

Red days
cranberry juice
tomatoes
red apple slices
cherry gelatin
cherry tarts
bing cherries (pitted)

Purple days
grape juice
purple grapes
purple plums
grape jelly
grape gelatin

Blue days
blue popcorn balls
blue milk (use food colouring)
blue cream cheese spread on crackers
    (use food colouring)
blueberries

Green days
lime gelatin
lime drink
lettuce
green grapes
celery
green peppers
pickles

Brown days
chocolate pudding
peanut butter
brown bread
hot chocolate
graham crackers
gingerbread children

Orange days	*Black-and-white days*
carrot coins	chocolate/vanilla cookies
orange juice	milk
cheese crackers	white bread
orange wedges	popcorn
orange gelatin	marshmallows
mandarin oranges	prunes
	raisins

a. Let children colour their milk with drops of food colouring. Use coloured straws to match the colour of the day. Children can choose a favourite colour of straw on multicolour days or make fruit-based milk shake to achieve different colours.

b. Use real or artificial flowers or fruits in appropriate colours to decorate the tables.

c. Make place mats from shelf paper or paper towels in the colour of the day.

2. Rest time: Designate which child should get up from rest time by saying, "Anyone who has on red shoes may get up now." When it is time for older children to get up from rest time, print their names on the blackboard with chalk in the colour of the day.

3. In transit: Look for the day's featured colour along the way to and from the centre.

Large Muscle Activities

1. Use balls of different colours for ball play.
2. *Beanbag toss:* Use beanbags of different colours.
3. Blow and chase bubbles: Make wire loops for giant bubbles. Dip loops into a shallow cake or pie pan filled with soap bubbles.
4. Colour songs: Give each child a small object of red, blue, yellow, or green. Children stand up or sit down as their colour is sung, or when the colour of their clothing is called.
5. *A tisket, a tasket:* Use green and yellow berry baskets placed behind children, instead of a handkerchief.
6. *Two little blackbirds:* Children sit on the floor in two rows. First pair gets up, "flys" around, and comes back to sit down at the end of the row as the song is sung. Repeat until all have had a turn.
7. *Hot potato* (for brown days).
8. *Fly little bluebird.*

Extended Experiences

1. Visit a paint, fabric, or carpet store.
2. Visit a furniture store. Notice different woods, metals, and fabrics.
3. A lapidary or rock hound may visit and bring colourful rocks and minerals to show, especially those that change colour under black light.
4. An artist might enjoy showing the children how to mix paints on a palette and several ways to use the paint.
5. If you know people who do stage lighting, perhaps they would demonstrate how lights and gels are used for different effects (try a college or university drama department).

Teacher Resources
....

Pictures and Displays

☐ A bulletin board can be sectioned off into colour areas for pictures. Objects that the children bring in can be displayed on a colour table.

☐ Pictures that illustrate fingerplays add interest. Be sure to include pictures of rainbows, grasshoppers, foods, crayons, and purple items such as grapes.

☐ Grocery stores will often give teachers big pictures of fruits and vegetables.

☐ Make large posters from pictures that are all one colour, including objects that are familiar to children. These posters can be used to show the featured colour of the day. Mount them on the classroom door or in a conspicuous place where children can discuss them.

☐ Display artwork made during the colour week.

☐ Display clear plastic glasses or vases of water tinted with food colouring on window sills.

Books and Periodicals

Chickadee magazine.

Hill, Julie, and Julian Hill. *Looking at Light and Color.* North Pomfret, VT: Trafalgar Square/David & Charles, 1986.

McKinnon, Elizabeth S., and Jean Warren. *One-Two-Three Colors: Activities for Introducing Color to Young Children.* Bothell, WA: Warren, 1988.

Owl magazine.

Films and Videos

NOTE: Check with your distributor about public performance rights.

Le ballon rouge. Films Montsouris (released in Canada by Marlin Motion Pictures), 1959. (no narration)

The Day the Colors Went Away. Film Polski (released in Canada by Visual Education Centre), 1971.

Harold and the Purple Crayon. Weston Woods.

The Mole as a Painter. Kratky Films, Prague (released in Canada by International Tele-Film). (no narration)

Patrick. Weston Woods.

Rainbow War. Manitoba Educational and Training Instructional Resources Library, 1985.

The Red Carpet. Weston Woods.

Community Resources and Organizations

☐ Drapery, upholstery, and rug dealers for colour samples.

☐ Paint stores for paint chips and formica samples

☐ Grocery stores for posters of floods, flowers, and butterflies.

☐ Lapidary in a jewellery store.

- [ ] Rock hound.
- [ ] Geologist in a nearby college or university.
- [ ] A community theatre group (for stage lighting demonstrations).
- [ ] A fabric shop.
- [ ] Museums that have displays on colour and light.

28 Tools and Machines to Use in My World

Basic Understandings
(concepts children can grasp from this subject)

- [ ] A tool is an instrument held in the hand and used to make a job easier and faster.
- [ ] A machine is an object that is used for doing some kind of work; it may or may not be operated by hand.
- [ ] A machine usually makes work easier.
- [ ] Tools and machines cannot work by themselves; they need people or some kind of power (heat, air, water, chemicals, or electricity) to make them work.
- [ ] A power tool is a kind of tool that was once operated by hand and is now operated by electricity, batteries, gas, or other sources of energy. We often need to turn a switch or control the tool by hand.
- [ ] A tool can also be a machine.
- [ ] Some tools are not machines; for example, pencils, erasers, rulers, drinking straws, cups, bowls, and magnifying glasses.
- [ ] Some of the tools we use at home are screwdrivers and screws, hammers, saws, pliers, scissors, brooms, eggbeaters, can openers, pulleys, ladders, and files.
- [ ] Tools we may use in the garden are rakes, hoes, spades, and trowels.
- [ ] Some machines used in our homes are run by electricity, such as vacuum cleaners, mixers, can openers, washing machines, clothes dryers, and sewing machines.
- [ ] Some machines used outdoors use fuels, electricity, or motors to make them run, such as cars, lawn mowers, trains, and airplanes.
- [ ] Farm machines help farmers do their work. These include corn shellers, tractors, combines, seeders, cultivators, balers, and milking machines.
- [ ] Transportation machines help us get from one place to another (see Part 7, Transportation).
- [ ] Tools and machines are used in factories to make cars, furniture, toys, and other products.
- [ ] Tools and machines are used in offices to help do work. Office tools often include pencils, pens, erasers, rulers, staplers, and hole punches. Some office machines used are calculators, typewriters, telephones, photocopiers, and computers.
- [ ] Machines and tools that are used to help build houses and buildings include screwdrivers, saws, hammers, nails, drills, cement mixers, bulldozers, and power saws.

☐ Machines used for road building and heavy construction are trenchers, steam-rollers, road graders, steam shovels, bulldozers, augers, and cement mixers.

☐ Some tools and machines make loud noises, such as power mowers, electric drills, and hammers.

☐ Some tools and machines are quiet, such as pencils, screwdrivers, clocks, wrist-watches, and tape measures.

☐ Although machines can help do work, they can also be dangerous if we get in their way or use them the wrong way.

☐ Most musical instruments are kinds of machines.

☐ Computers help bankers, taxi drivers, sales clerks, librarians, teachers, and many other workers do their work more quickly and easily.

Additional Facts the Teacher Should Know

1. A machine is any device, simple or complex, by which the intensity of an applied force is increased, its direction changed, or one form of motion or energy is changed into another form. It may be made of two or more fixed or movable parts. All complex machines are combinations of six simple machines, which are divided into two classes:
   a. Primary: Lever, pulley, inclined plane, and wedge.
   b. Secondary: Wheel and axle, block and tackle, and screw.

2. A tool is a machine that is operated by hand. Complex machines may run on various kinds of energy — heat, chemicals, electricity, nuclear, oil, gas, and steam. In machines, a small force can be applied to overcome a much larger resistance or load.

3. A screw is actually an inclined plane wound around a straight central core. A wedge is another example of an inclined plane. A needle, a nail, and a door wedge are examples of wedges. Tongs, scissors, and crowbars are simple lever machines.

Introducing This Subject to Children

1. Display pictures of tools and machines.
2. Read a story about a community worker and the tools or machines he or she uses.
3. Let children prepare soap flakes for soap painting using different tools (see Discovery Centre, number 18).
4. Have a display of simple tools and machines in the discovery centre.
5. Visit a construction or road-building site or any similar work going on nearby and watch the workers using tools and machines. Talk about the machines being used and how they make the work easier.

Learning Centres

Discovery Centre

1. Toss scraps of paper on the floor. Have children pick up the scraps by hand or by using a broom, a hand vacuum, or an electric vacuum cleaner. Talk about how the tool or machine helps. While children are assisting with tidying the centre, give them the opportunity to use vacuum cleaners and hand vacuums. Then have them compare these with brooms.

Vocabulary

Tools

Workbench	*Household*	*Office*	*Gardening*
tool	scissors	stapler	rake
nail	brush	hole punch	hoe
hammer	can opener	pen	shovel
screw	rolling pin	pencil	spade
screwdriver	nutcracker	eraser	trowel
pliers	hand eggbeater	paperclip	wheelbarrow
wrench	spoon	ruler	
ruler	broom		
tape measure	tongs		
saw	needle		
crowbar			
drill			

Machines

Construction	*Household*	*Office*	*Transportation*
cement mixer	grinder	typewriter	bicycle
road grader	sewing machine	telephone	car
auger	refrigerator	computer	train
truck	electric saw	photocopier	bus
bulldozer	vacuum cleaner	electric pencil	boat, ship
trencher	electric drill	sharpener	airplane
electric motor	electric mixer	tape recorder	wagon
gear	blender	postage meter	truck
switch	shaver	fax machine	
	dryer	calculator	*Yard*
Farm	washer		electric
disker (harrow)	clock		lawn mower
baler	microwave oven		snowblower
combine	food processor		electric hedges
milking machine	stove		clippers
tractor	refrigerator		fertilizer spreader
seeder	curling iron		sprinkler
cultivator	hair dryer		
mower	television		
harvester	VCR		
	freezer		
	iron		

2. Make a feel it box (see p. 157) of simple tools to identify. Include a hammer, a screwdriver, pliers, and scissors. Talk about how these tools help us.
3. Let the children beat an egg with a fork, a hand eggbeater, or an electric mixer. Discuss the work involved in each.
4. Put blocks in a big box. Have the children try to lift it and push it; then put it on a dolly or a wagon and move it. Discuss.
5. Use a single pulley fastened to a ceiling, or a rope over a tree. Ask a child to lift a tricycle; then tie it on the rope and have him or her pull the other end. Ask, "Which way is easier?"

6. Tie a string around a heavy box, and have the children try to lift it. Then put a broomstick through the string; put the broomstick across a chair or sawhorses and have children push down on one end. This illustrates the principle of the lever.

7. Have screws started in soft wood. Let children use screwdrivers to drive them in farther. Do the same with nails and hammers.

8. Let the children explore and use an old typewriter.

9. Let the children examine an old windup clock to see the wheels and gears.

10. Wind a music box and let the children watch the gears move (see-through music boxes are available from many gift stores).

11. Provide a science table with tools and machines (old radios, clocks, and other machines of any kind).

12. Let the children find as many wheels as they can in the room. Help them identify dials and tape as wheels and to note gear wheels in toys and clocks.

13. Identify the number of wheels on various vehicles.

14. Have children use a magnet to pick up nails.

15. Have children use a battery and wires to ring a buzzer or light a bulb.

16. Encourage the children to explore musical instruments. Talk about how they help a person change sound to music.

17. Tell the children they can help make whipped soap flakes for painting. (See recipes, p. 32.) Give some of the children a fork, some a hand eggbeater, and let some help operate an electric mixer (with supervision). Talk about the time and work needed in each case. Ask the children to think of other machines and tools that help us.

18. Use tools and machines when cooking and preparing food. Here are some specific suggestions.

Machines

Electric blender:

a.   Make milk shakes or eggnog.

b.   Make applesauce. Cook apples, beat in blender, and add sugar.

The pump on the playground is used to teach children about machines. Although this may be unusual on an urban playground, a pump is something that many rural children have seen.

Electric mixer:
a. Whip gelatin.
b. Make meringue or frosting.
c. Make cookies or cupcakes.
d. Make marshmallows: Combine 1 package of gelatin, 150 mL/⅔ cup boiling water, 250 mL/1 cup sugar, and 45 mL/3 T light corn syrup. Dissolve gelatin in water, stir in sugar, and blend in corn syrup. Chill until slightly thickened. Beat on highest speed until soft peaks form (15 minutes). Pour into pan lined with wax paper and greased with butter. Refrigerate overnight. Dust pastry board with powdered sugar. Cut into squares and roll in powdered sugar.

Hand Tools
Hand egg beater:
a. Make meringues.
b. Whip flavoured gelatin.
c. Make scrambled eggs.

Can opener:
Open a can of juice or other food.

Hand grinder:
Make cranberry relish. Combine 500 mL/2 cups cranberries and 2 whole oranges (including rind). Purée in a food mill and add about 500 mL/2 cups sugar. Serve with crackers for a snack.

Dramatic Play Centres

Home-living centre
1. Provide housekeeping tools, such as cleaning brushes, dustpans, dustcloths, brooms, mops, and spray bottles. Supervise. Children may also be allowed to clean mirrors, windows, or sinks.
2. Let children beat soap flakes in water.
3. Encourage children to use rollers, cookie cutters, and tongue depressors with play dough.
4. Encourage the use of doll carriages, strollers, or wagons to take dolls on an outing.
5. Talk about tools used in preparing, cooking, and eating foods, such as bowls, rolling pins, spatulas, potato mashers, measuring cups, knives, forks, and spoons. Discuss how tools make work easier.

Block-building centre
1. Call attention to uses of ramps (inclined planes), cranes, pulleys, levers, wheels, and gears.
2. Provide rubber or plastic tools for use in this area.
3. Have some hard hats, tool aprons, and tool kits available.

Other dramatic play centres
1. Carpenter's workshop: Set up a workbench and provide nails, screws, hammers, sanding blocks, and tool aprons.
2. Painter's workplace: Encourage children to pretend to paint using dry paintbrushes, and empty paint cans and wearing painter's caps. Caps are often free at a paint store. Supply the painters with sample paint chips or swatches to show to customers. VARIATION: Outdoors, allow water to be used for paint. Invite painters to paint walls and toys.

3. Plumbing centre: Set out real plumbing parts (elbows, nipples, T's, taps with adapter couplings, and lengths of pipe) for children to fit together. Include a wrench. Use plastic pipes, which are readily available in building supply stores. Used pipe is often available from plumbing companies, but it needs to be cleaned with steel wool and lubricated before joining.

   NOTE: Children will enjoy connecting their plumbing pipes to an outdoor faucet. This quickly becomes a discovery experience when water does or does not flow as expected.

Art Centre

1. Painting: Offer brushes of different widths.
2. Gadget printing: Use gears, toy-car wheels, nuts and bolts, and other parts of tools, or items such as sponges, corks, pieces of wood moulding, or rolled cardboard to make prints.
3. Paint with rollers: Use small painting rollers or foam hair rollers.
4. Use tools, such as rollers, sticks, or cookies cutters, with clay or play dough.
5. Use spool brayers to make stripes and plaids.
6. Use empty roll-on deodorant dispensers filled with thinned paint as markers.
7. Use glue sticks, brushes, cotton swabs, or squeeze bottles to apply glue.
8. Cut paper with scissors. Children might like to cut and paste a book of tools and machines.
9. Let children hammer, saw, sand, and paint wood sculptures.

Learning and Language Materials Centre

Commercially made games and materials

1. *Puzzles:* Puzzles showing tools, machines, and musical instruments.
2. *Construction and manipulative toys:* Plastic tools for imaginative play; wooden or plastic bolts, screws, etc.; child-size tools that can be used with careful supervision; sheets of styrofoam to be used in place of wood, balsa wood, wood scraps (available from local lumberyards and contractors); and child-size washable hard hats (these can be worn in a building centre. Control the number of children in the centre by establishing a rule that to play in the centre a hard hat must be worn); child-size household tools (for example, brooms, and mops); models of simple machines that can be taken apart; simple boards with interlocking gears that can be turned by manipulating a variety of knobs; toy levers, cranes, and pulleys that are accessories for block sets.
3. *Outdoor toys:* Child-size gardening tools.
4. *Music boxes:* Be sure boxes can be operated by children. See-through music boxes are very interesting for children.
5. *Miscellaneous:* Musical instruments; see pp. 41 and 42 for a discussion of choosing suitable instruments.

Teacher-made games and materials

   NOTE: For detailed descriptions, see Learning Games in Part 1.

1. *Name it:* Use vocabulary list for suggestions for pictures or objects.
2. *Sorting and grouping by association:* Sort pictures or models of tools and machines into boxes labelled with pictures relating to farms, houses, buildings, offices, transportation, and road work.

3. *How many?* Count the number of wheels on vehicles.
4. *Match-them:* Pair tools with association pictures of their uses, such as a rake with leaves, an eggbeater with eggs or a bowl, or a hammer with a board. VARIATION: Pair tools with workers who use them from flannelboard cutouts or picture cards.

Book Centre

••• Alexander, M. *Marty McGee's Space Lab. No Girls Allowed.* New York: Dial Press, 1981.
••• Allen, Jeffery. *Mary Alice, Operator, Number Nine.* Markham, ON: Penguin, 1978.
••• Althea. *What Makes Things Move?* St. Catharines, ON: Troll Associates, 1991.
•• Barton, B. *Machines at Work.* New York: Harper Junior, 1987.
• ———. *Building a House.* New York: Greenwillow Press, 1981.
••• Bell, Bill. *Saxophone Boy.* Montreal: Tundra, 1980.
••• Branley, Franklyn, and Eleanor Vaughn. *Mickey's Magnet.* New York: Crowell, 1956.
•• Burton, Virginia Lee. *Katy and the Big Snow.* Boston: Houghton Mifflin, 1959.
•• ———. *Mike Mulligan and His Steam Shovel.* Boston: Houghton Mifflin, 1959.
• Domanska, J. *Busy Monday Morning.* New York: Greenwillow Press, 1985.
• Douglass, B. *Good as New.* New York: Lothrop, Lee & Shepard, 1982.
•••• Fleisher, Paul, and Patricia Keeler. *Looking Inside: Machines and Constructions.* New York: Atheneum, 1991.
••• Geringer, Laura. *Molly's New Washing Machine.* New York: Harper & Row, 1986.
•• Gibbons, Gail. *Fill It Up, A Book about Service Stations.* Markham, ON: Fitzhenry & Whiteside, 1986.
• Haddad, H. *Truck and Loader.* New York: Greenwillow Press, 1982.
• Hoban, T. *Dig, Drill, Dump, Fill.* New York: Greenwillow Press, 1975.
••• Hutchins, H. *Leanna Builds a Genie Trap.* Willowdale, ON: Annick Press, 1986.
•••• Isadora, Rachel. *Ben's Trumpet.* Toronto: Macmillan, 1979. (Read)
•••• Krumins, Anita. *Who's Going to Clean Up This Mess?* Toronto: Three Trees Press, 1985. (Read–Tell)
••• Kumin, Maxime. *The Microscope.* New York: Harper & Row, 1987.
•••• Lauber, Patricia. *Get Ready for Robots.* New York: Crowell, 1986.
••• Morgan, A. *Matthew and the Midnight Tow Truck.* Willowdale, ON: Annick Press, 1984.
•• Rockwell, Anne, and Harlow Rockwell. *Machines.* New York: Macmillan, 1972.
• ———. *Tool Box.* New York: Macmillan, 1971.
•• Schick, E. *A Piano for Julie.* New York: Greenwillow Press, 1984.
••• Spier, Peter. *Bored, Nothing to Do.* Garden City, NY: Doubleday, 1978.
••• Staunton, Ted. *Simon's Surprise.* Toronto: Kids Can Press, 1986.
•• Strickland, Paul. *Machines as Big as Monsters.* Toronto: Kids Can Press, 1989.
•• ———. *Machines as Tall as Giants.* Toronto: Kids Can Press, 1989.
••• Williams, V. *Music, Music, for Everyone.* New York: Greenwillow Press, 1984.

 # Planning for Group Time

NOTE: All music, fingerplays, poems, and stories listed here may also be used at other times during the session as appropriate.

Music

Songs

From *Elephant Jam*, Sharon, Lois, and Bram
"Monday Night the Banjo," p. 29
"The Very Best Band," p. 120

From *Eye Winker, Tom Tinker, Chin Chopper*, Glazer
"Shoemaker, Shoemaker," p. 38
"Peter Hammers," p. 41
"When I Was a Shoemaker," p. 87

From *Tunes for Tots*, Warner and Berry
"The Brass Band," p. 100
"Making Music," p. 101

From your own traditional songbook:
"Johnny Works with One Hammer"
"I've Been Working on the Railroad"
"Round and Round the Village" (see parody, p. 447)

Fingerplays and Poems

....

LITTLE ROBOT

by Robert Heidbreder

I'm a Little Robot,
  Wires make me talk.
I'm a Little Robot,
  Wires make me walk.
I'm a Little Robot,
  Wires bend my knees.
I'm a Little Robot,
  Wires make me sneeze.
    AAAACHOOOOOO!

I'm a Little Robot,
  Wires make me work.
So if you cross them,
  I'll probably go BERSERK!

ZOING ZOING BOINK!
ZOING ZOING BOINK!
ZING!

Have the children walk like robots around the room while you recite the poem. When you say "ZOING," allow them to go "BERSERK!"

From *Don't Eat Spiders*, Heidbreder
"Rockets," p. 44

From *Let's Do Fingerplays*, Grayson
"Cobbler, Cobbler," p. 18
"I Have a Little Watch," p. 27
"The Windshield Wipers," p. 24
"Driving Down the Street," p. 25
"The Bus," p. 25

....

THE DIGGER

I'm a digger, big and strong *(puff out chest and pat)*
Here's my arm, it's very long. *(extend both arms out straight)*
Here's my scoop, and with a spurt *(form scoop with hands and scoop arms to floor)*
I clutch the ground and bring up dirt. *(scoop up dirt and raise arms)*
I turn and drop it in the truck *(turn whole body and open hands, letting dirt fall)*
Then start all over — chuck, chuck, chuck. *(swing body back to starting position)*

....

THE CLOCK

Tick-tock, tick-tock,
Tick-tock says the clock.
Little boy, little girl
Time to wash our hands.
     (put the blocks away)
     (go outside)
     (ride the bus)

Stories

(To read, read–tell, or tell. See Book Centre for a complete list.)
Stories for this subject can range from the fanciful (for example, Krumins's *Who's Going to Clean Up This Mess?*), to stories in which children safely and successfully use tools (for example, Staunton's *Simon's Surprise*).

Routine Times

1. Eat food prepared earlier at snack or meal times.
2. Use a rolling cart to bring food to tables at snack or meal times.
3. Call attention to tools and machines as you use them — doorknobs, light switches, levers, stairs, utensils, tops, brushes.
4. At pickup time, use a wagon or a rolling platform to return toys to shelves.
5. When out walking or riding, watch for uses of machines and tools by others.
6. At meal time, talk about utensils as tools, including those used to prepare food.

Large Muscle Activities

1. Use wheeled toys and ramps (inclined planes).
2. Use wheelbarrows for moving blocks.
3. Use pulleys for lifting pails of sand.
4. Oil the tricycles and wagons.
5. Bring out garden tools in the spring.
6. Water the lawn with sprinkler or hose in the summer.
7. Shovel snow in the winter.
8. Rake leaves, and use wagons to collect them in the fall.
9. Add a variety of sand toys to the sandbox, such as sand combs, sifters, sand wheels, scoops, and scrapers.

Extended Experiences

1. Visit a construction site if the builder will allow children there.
2. Attend a school band rehearsal.
3. Visit a service station that has a lift and car wash.
4. Go to a hardware store to show the children where tools and small appliances are sold. Buy some nails or screws, a pulley, a hammer, a screwdriver, some garden tools, or pipe fittings.
5. Invite parents to come on different days and show children the tools they use at work, how to use them, and when and why their tools are necessary. For example, a visitor might actually repair a playground vehicle while children watch, or a carpenter might build a bird feeder or a simple tote tray to be used at school. Encourage children to help sand, stain, or paint.

   NOTE: If the carpenter has a crosscut section from a tree or a piece of lumber that shows an edge of bark, children can better associate the source of lumber to trees.

6. Let children watch when a plumber comes to fix the plumbing. VARIATION: Watch the custodian using tools to clean the school building.
7. Children will enjoy attaching their plumbing pipes and fittings to an outdoor tap so that they can see what happens. This is an excellent cause-and-effect discovery experience.

8. Some centres may have access to personal computers with programs that are appropriate for young children. Computers are also available at some libraries and community centres. For further information on the use of computers with young children, see the book list under Teacher Resources.

Teacher Resources

Pictures and Displays

☐ Display mounted pictures of kitchen tools and machines in the home-living centre.
☐ Display mounted pictures of construction machines and tools in the block-building centre.
☐ Set out catalogue sections showing gardening or other tools and machines to be used around the home. Sale catalogues or flyers are excellent sources of coloured pictures that can be cut out to make picture books, games, and puzzles.

Books and Periodicals

Blocksma, Mary. *The Marvelous Music Machine: A Story of the Piano.* Englewood Cliffs, NJ: Prentice-Hall, 1984.
Blocksma, Mary. *Action Contraptions: Easy-to-Make Toys that Really Move.* Englewood Cliffs, NJ: Prentice-Hall, 1988.
Canadian Tire and other hardware catalogues.
Carpentry tool catalogues or woodworking magazines.
Chickadee magazine.
Farm journals and farm equipment catalogues.
Lear, Peter. *Let's Look at Computer Play.* Burlington, ON: Hayes, 1985.
────── . *Let's Look at Computers.* Burlington, ON: Hayes, 1985.
Mackie, David. *Let's Look at BASIC.* Burlington, ON: Hayes, 1985.
Mail-order catalogues.
Marine suppliers' catalogues.
Office-supply company catalogues.
Owl magazine.

Films and Videos

NOTE: Check with your distributor about public performance rights.

The Cricket and the Engine. Kratky Films, Prague (released in Canada by International Tele-Film), 1978.
The Doughnuts. Weston Woods.
Mike Mulligan and His Steam Shovel. Weston Woods.

Community Resources and Organizations

☐ A neighbouring building site; make sure it is safe to visit.
☐ Parents who work with tools and machines, such as a carpenter, a plumber, or a secretary.

- ☐ Automobile dealers, hardware dealers, television and radio dealers, and others who sell tools or machines might give you out-of-date catalogues or posters to be used for flannelboard cutouts, games, or pictures for children to cut and paste.
- ☐ A local music school or school band.
- ☐ Community cable television channels will arrange tours of their studios.
- ☐ A college or university early childhood education program that offers courses on the use of computers with young children.

Government Agencies

- ☐ Federal, provincial, and territorial ministries of labour.
- ☐ Provincial or territorial workers' compensation boards have excellent safety posters that would be very useful for this section.

29 Mathematics in My Everyday World

Basic Understandings
(concepts children can grasp from this subject)

- [ ] A group of objects is called a "set," such as a set of blocks or a set of dishes.
- [ ] We count to find how many objects we have in a set — one to three, one to five, or one to ten.
- [ ] Objects can be grouped in sets in many ways, such as by kind (family), size, colour, use, weight, and shape (*classification*).
    1. Objects can be grouped together because they are similar, alike, or the same.
    2. Objects that are not like the others in some way are not alike, or are different.
    3. Two objects that are alike or are used together are known as a pair (socks, mittens, shoes) or twins (girls, boys, lambs, squirrels).
- [ ] We compare objects (*comparison*):
    1. By size — small, large, big, little, tall, short, fat, thin, wide, narrow.
    2. By location — near, far, in front of, behind, over, under, in, out, up, down, above, below, inside, outside.
    3. By quantity — few, many, a lot, a little, more, less, some, none.
    4. By weight — heavy, light.
- [ ] We can arrange objects in order (*seriation*):
    1. By size — smallest to largest, largest to smallest, shortest to tallest, thinnest to thickest.
    2. By location — nearest to farthest, farthest to nearest.
    3. By position — first, second, third, next to last, last.
- [ ] If we add an object to a set we have more than we did before (*addition*).
- [ ] If we take an object away from a set we have less than we did before (*subtraction*).
- [ ] If we remove all the objects in a set we have none left or an empty set.
- [ ] Objects or sets can be divided into subsets or parts (*division*).
    1. Sets can be divided into two equal parts, or in half.
    2. If we have more chairs or cookies than children, we have more than enough, or too many.
- [ ] Objects have different shapes.
    1. Two-dimensional:
        a. Circle — round

     b. Triangle — three sides.

     c. Rectangle or square — four corners and four straight sides.

  2. Three-dimensional

     a. Spherical — ball, globe, orange.

     b. Triangular — triangular block, musical triangle.

     c. Rectangular — rectangular blocks, boxes, books.

     d. Conical — funnel, party hat.

  3. Other shapes include stars, cylinders, arches, crescents, hearts, and diamonds.

☐ Many things help us measure.

  1. A clock tells us what time it is (the hour of the day).

  2. A thermometer tells us the temperature (how hot or cold the weather or something is).

  3. A ruler (metre stick, measuring tape) tells us how long, high, or wide something is.

  4. A calendar tells us what day (week, month, year) it is.

  5. Scales tell us how much something weighs.

  6. Measuring cups and spoons help us measure food or other materials.

☐ A numeral represents a number rather than a letter or other symbol or character. Children can learn the correct names for numerals, such as one, 1; two, 2; three, 3. Children who speak other languages have other words for these numerals.

☐ We use numbers in many ways:

  1. On our house so our friends or the letter carrier can find us.

  2. On the telephone so we can call someone.

  3. On a cash register to find out how much we should pay the store clerk.

  4. On money so we know how much it is worth.

  5. On stamps to tell us how much they are worth.

  6. On book pages so we can tell someone where to find a story or a picture.

  7. On licence plates so we can tell who owns a car.

☐ We use money to buy things such as food, clothes, a house, a car, and toys.

  1. We have coins and bills to use as money.

  2. Our coins have names — penny, nickel, dime, quarter, and dollar. Many children do not have a clear concept of exact value and are confused by the lack of relationship between size and value.

☐ We use the word "time" to talk about when things happen. Children begin to understand:

  1. Today or day is the time between when we get up in the morning and when we go to bed at night.

  2. Night is the time when it is dark and we go to sleep.

NOTE: See Chapter 25, Day and Night, for additional concepts.

  3. Tomorrow is the time it will be when we wake up after we go to bed tonight.

  4. Yesterday is the day it was before we went to bed last night.

  5. Morning is between breakfast and lunch.

  6. Afternoon is between lunch and dinner (supper).

  7. Evening is between dinner and the time you go to bed.

  8. The days have names, such as Sunday and Friday (children do not always know the correct order).

  9. Several days make a week (children do not know how many).

  10. The months have names, such as January and June (children do not always know the correct order).

  11. A year is a very, very long time. Children do not know how many days or weeks.

Additional Facts the Teacher Should Know

1. Mathematics, which involves concepts about numbers, measuring, money, spatial relationships, time, and problem solving, can be presented to young children in some form that is understandable to them; math, therefore, belongs in the curriculum for young children. The activities and materials suggested in this chapter will direct your attention to some of the potential in the classroom environment for teaching mathematical concepts. You will find many ways of helping children discover some of the basic understandings.

2. Very young children can discover that we use numbers in many ways, have many ways of measuring, can classify things in many ways, and can compare things in many ways. They can begin to understand some of the mathematical skills of counting, adding, subtracting, and dividing. However, very young children have difficulty realizing that objects can have more than one property and can belong to several classes; for example, a red pencil can be grouped with red things, hard things, long things, and wooden things. This realization is acquired by grouping and regrouping according to different traits. At first young children may need to group by traits suggested by you, but children with more experience should be encouraged to decide for themselves the traits that make certain groupings. Grouping in different ways encourages flexible thinking.

3. Very young children's concepts of money are mainly confined to the knowledge that we earn it by working and then use it to buy the things we need or want (see Chapter 8, Families at Work). They are beginning to know the names of some of the coins but do not know their exact value. Very young children will most likely think a nickel is worth more than a dime because it is bigger in size.

4. Time is one of the most difficult things for young children to understand. They can learn that a clock tells us what time it is, but they will be much older before they can tell the actual time for themselves. In the meantime, it is helpful if you verbalize the use of the clock to familiarize the children with telling time. For example, point to the clock on the wall and say, "It is ten o'clock; time for juice," or, looking at a wristwatch, say, "My wristwatch says it is eleven-thirty; time to go outside." The understanding of the passage of time from one day to the next, one week to the next, and one year to the next develops slowly. Through conversation and the use of the calendar in the classroom, children can come to understand that days of the week have names, that several days (one line of numbers on most calendars) make a week, several weeks (several lines or one page of the calendar) is a month, that the months have names, and that a year is a very long time. Children become most aware of the concept of a year when they hear much discussion about this around New Year's Day and on their birthdays. Children are usually five before they realize that holidays and birthdays recur on a regular basis. Some calendars read vertically and some put Monday in the first space. It is best to use those that read horizontally.

5. Many different approaches to teaching math to very young children are being used today, and many commercial materials are now available. This chapter includes a little bit of everything. A brief explanation of some of the methods follows to help you understand why they were included.

6. The math being taught in most public schools today emphasizes understanding of how and why the mathematical processes work rather than demanding rote learning or acceptance on faith for many of the steps in problem solving. This basic philosophy of seeing, doing, and understanding has long been used at the preschool level. This method, however, has a new vocabulary with "set" (a group of one or more) as its basic unit. It is appropriate to use this term with young children, as they are already familiar with a set of dishes or a set of blocks. However, use the term when referring to other things not normally referred to as sets, such as a set of hats.

7. The extensive study done by Piaget of children's understanding of mathematical concepts is being given renewed attention in many early-childhood centres. While his labels of "equivalence," "conservation," and "seriation" are not widely used, the activities basic to understanding the concepts are appropriate. It is imperative that you review Piaget's materials in his texts or in child development texts (see the book list under Teacher Resources).

8. Montessori's major contribution to the teaching of math to young children is her ingenious self-teaching materials. They are all designed on the metric system and are self-teaching in that they vary in only one dimension at a time. Thus, if children order them incorrectly, the errors will be obvious and can be corrected. Montessori's sets of graded cylinders that vary in only one dimension (length, diameter) are excellent materials for teaching Piaget's concept of seriation. Thus, in these statements, we are suggesting the blending of many different approaches to the teaching of math to young children.

9. Canada uses the metric measuring system. The metric system uses centimetres, metres, and kilometres as units of length, and grams and litres as units of volume. The following table shows metric/Imperial equivalents.

Metric		Imperial	Metric		Imperial
25.4 millimetres	=	1 inch	1 millimetre	=	0.039 inch
2.54 centimetres	=	1 inch	1 centimetre	=	0.394 inch
0.914 metre	=	1 yard	1 metre	=	1.094 yards
1.6 kilometres	=	1 mile	1 kilometre	=	0.621 mile
28.35 grams	=	1 ounce	1 gram	=	0.035 ounce
453.6 grams	=	1 pound	1 kilogram	=	2.2 pounds
0.94 litres	=	1 quart	1 litre	=	1.06 quarts

Introducing This Subject to Children

1. Use cooking activities that involve measuring ingredients and using various-sized utensils and pans.
2. Dramatic play: Set up a grocery store where children can talk about and handle different-sized containers, bags, and play money.
3. Tell a flannelboard story that emphasizes quantity and size, such as "The Three Bears" (great big daddy bear, middle-sized mother bear, wee little baby bear; various-sized bowls, chairs, and beds).
4. Introduce number readiness materials (see Learning and Language Materials Centre).

Vocabulary

numbers	thermometer	less	set
count	metre stick	more	pair
measure	calendar	enough	twin
shape	birthday	none	both
scales	same	add	circle
ruler	alike	divide	square
clock	different	half	triangle
time	match	empty	star

Learning Centres

Discovery Centre

1. Make cookies, pudding, no-cook candy, gelatin, or other dishes that require the use of measuring spoons and cups and various sizes of pans, bowls, and utensils. Talk about full, half full, empty, big, little, in, out, and measuring.
2. Measure and weigh children: If you do this at the beginning of the year, repeat at a later time or at the end of the year to tell them how much they have grown. Who is shorter, taller, heavier, lighter, or the same? Tape plain paper, a tree, or a giraffe picture chart to the wall and mark off in centimetres. Write children's names by the marks for their height.
3. Balance scales: Let children experiment with how many beans will balance a bolt or how many acorns will balance a pebble (in terms of many or few). Talk about heavy and light.
4. Thermometers: Have a large, accurate one in the room and on the playground. Talk about the weather and whether it is hot or cold. Help children to see that as the weather gets warmer, the mercury goes up, and as it gets colder, the mercury goes down. An indoor–outdoor thermometer is nice to have so the children can see the similarity or difference between the two temperatures.
5. Make a large cardboard thermometer with markings from –40°C to 50°C. Make two horizontal slots 12 mm wide at the highest and lowest markings. Cut a length of 1 cm wide elastic that is twice the distance between the slots, plus 6 mm for overlap. Thread the elastic through the slots from the front and overlap it 6 mm on the back and sew securely. Run the overlap down to the bottom slot. Colour all the elastic that is showing on the front of the thermometer with a red felt-tip marker. To lower the "mercury," pull the elastic down. To raise the mercury, pull it up. The elastic can be moved up or down by you or a child to help children understand the concept of temperatures rising and falling.
6. At a water or sand table or in a large pan, provide plastic measuring cups, containers of various sizes and shapes, measuring spoons, pitchers, and funnels. Let children experiment with pouring water or sand into the various containers and making comparisons. Watch for opportunities to help children who are ready to discover that objects or liquids do not change in amount (number and quantity) when they are put in a smaller or larger container (conservation). Have a child fill a 250 mL measuring cup to the 250 mL mark. Then have the child pour the contents into a tall, narrow container. Notice that the contents go higher. Ask whether there is more water in the new container than in the old one. Let the child pour the water back into the measuring cup to check the answer.
7. Count body parts on animals: "How many feet? Ears? Tails?"
8. Count trees, leaves, flowers, petals, and seeds.
9. Count pebbles, pieces of coal, or seashells.
10. Classifying: Children can group items of various kinds by type, colour, shape, mass, or texture. Use real objects from nature or pictures. Beginning experiences should include two or three different types of items with three to five in each group. Increase number and types as children gain skill. Let children decide on the groupings and explain their reasons for choosing them.
11. Look for and identify shapes, indoors and out.

Dramatic Play Centres

Home-living centre

1. Talk about sets of dishes and flatware and their sizes; sort by size and shape — saucers, cups, plates, glasses, knives, forks, and spoons.
2. Include plastic or metal measuring cups, spoons, mixing bowls, and beaters to bake with. Now and then, allow water or sand for measuring.
3. Talk about equivalence or one-to-one correspondence: "Are there enough cups and saucers for everyone? Too many? Too few? How many do we need?"
4. Put a discarded telephone book by a toy telephone to encourage looking up a number and calling someone. Underline the names of families in your centre. Remind children that they need parental permission to use the phone at home.
5. Put a bathroom or kitchen scale in this centre so children can weigh food, themselves, or their dolls. If possible, obtain a baby scale.
6. Hang a calendar on the wall in this centre.
7. Put out a toy clock with movable hands or an old alarm clock.
8. Talk about portions of food being served. Talk about more or less. Have child put food in two dishes. "Your doll is very hungry; will you give him/her more?"

Block-building centre

1. Call attention to tall or short buildings, long or short roads. If a metre stick is handy, you could help children measure their constructions. Ask, "Who has more blocks? Do you need more blocks to make yours as tall as Joan's?" Count blocks used in a construction. State numbers as many and few: "Jimmy used many blocks to build a tower."
2. Call attention to shapes of blocks used — rectangular, triangular, or square. Help children see spatial relationships — up, down, above, below, under, and beside. Help children discover that two triangles can make a square, two squares make a rectangle, and two rectangles equal one longer rectangle. Use a good set of unit blocks and ask for a specific number of blocks by name. "Please give me one square block and two arches."
3. Encourage older children to build a parking lot. Have one child park the cars and another collect the fees.
4. Encourage older children to add bridges and tunnels to their constructions.

Other dramatic play centres

Set up a grocery store. Emphasize pricing by putting up signs, such as "2 for 50¢." Provide scales for weighing produce. Emphasize such concepts as sizes and shapes of containers, a dozen is twelve, the use of a cash register (or a divided box for coins), paying for food, and making change.

Art Centre

- 1. When painting, give children a choice of one or two colours. Talk about the paint pots being empty or half full.
- 2. When moulding and sculpting, talk about the size of the ball of clay or dough being worked. A large ball can be divided into two small balls.
- •• 3. Paste geometric shapes of various sizes on coloured construction paper to make different designs. VARIATIONS: Use gummed paper or pieces of fabric.
- •• 4. Cut geometric shapes out of sponges. Let children use them to print designs on coloured construction paper.

••• 5. At the woodworking table provide a ruler for measuring the boards to be cut. Provide nails of different lengths. Show children how to measure and how to decide the right-length nail to use.

••• 6. Cutting: Show children with cutting skills how to cut a heart shape. Fold a square of paper in half (this paper could be one of their paintings). Starting at the fold, draw half a heart on the paper with a magic marker. Children should be instructed to start cutting at the bottom point of the fold and to cut up, around, and back to the top point of the fold.

Learning and Language Materials Centre

Commercially made games and materials

1. *Puzzles:* All puzzles are useful, but shape and number puzzles are particularly relevant.
2. *Construction and manipulative toys:* Montessori materials — cylinder blocks, shapes and templates, tower, long stair, broad stair, number rods; weaving mats — to teach over and under; sorting boxes — for sorting by shape and size; scales — simple balance-beam scales with containers that can hold a variety of media, liquids, solids, etc; simple spring-balance scales with large dials that are easily read; a sturdy, simple bathroom scale with the readout in kilos; a variety of clear and coloured plastic containers that can be used to pour and compare liquids, cornmeal, sand, etc. Include measuring containers that are clearly marked with metric measures.

Unit blocks help children learn about numbers. The teacher is extending the experience by asking the children to experiment with their constructions. She asks questions about length, shape, and colour.

3. *Outdoor toys:* A large outdoor thermometer to place in the playground. A variety of clear and coloured plastic containers that can be used to pour and compare liquids, sand, etc. Include measuring containers that are clearly marked with metric measures.

4. *Games:* Beginning board games with spinner dials that will teach the children how to count and move objects a corresponding number of spaces; traditional and picture dominoes; pegboards; an abacus.

5. *Miscellaneous:* A large, easily read clock, a large teaching clock with both analog and digital readout, a simple wind-up egg timer; play money — make sure it is a facsimile of Canadian money; a play cash register — make sure you choose one that is sturdy and that will work when the children push the keys; a teaching thermometer with sliding colour for mercury.

Teacher-made games and materials

NOTE: For detailed descriptions, see Learning Games in Part 1.

1. Counting: Encourage rational counting of any objects a child is using during free-choice period, such as blocks, beads, feathers, pegs, or scissors.

2. Classification: Children can be given objects to group or classify, such as beads, cubes, buttons, and plastic lids of various sizes.

- Children are asked to put objects together that are alike.
- • Children decide how objects should be grouped, such as by colour, size, or texture.
- • • After the first groupings by children, ask whether they can group objects another way. This encourages flexible thinking and the understanding that there is more than one way to do things.

3. Talk about shape, size, mass, and location of objects that children are working with during their free-choice activity.

4. Use a flannelboard with geometric or animal cutouts, allowing children to group things by shape that may be different in size or colour. Later, children can regroup by size or colour, illustrating that objects can belong to different groups.

5. To establish one-to-one correspondence or equivalence (just enough for everyone), use spools to represent people and pop-bottle caps for hats; let children pick out enough hats for all the people. Discover the meaning of just enough, not enough, too many, and too few.

6. Look for meaningful ways to use a calendar, clocks, scales, a thermometer, a telephone, money, stamps, and metre sticks.

7. *Look and see:*
   a. Use different coins and bills.
   b. Use different stamps.
   c. Use thermometers, alarm clocks, metre sticks, measuring cups, desk calendars, and measuring tapes.

8. *Reach and feel:* Use items in 7c, above.

9. *Match-them:* Match objects by shape, size, mass, and location.

10. *Alike, different, and the same:* Use geometric shapes, coins, or stamps.

11. *Which comes first?* Use items of current interest.

12. *How many?* Set out varying numbers of objects.

13. Block form board: On a large piece of cardboard, trace around one of each of the shapes in your set of unit blocks. Let children match blocks with the shapes on the form board.

14. Object form board: Trace around familiar objects and let children find the matching objects and place them on the form board.

15. Make sandpaper, felt, or flocked number cards.

Book Centre

Numbers

•• Anno, Mitsumasa. *Anno's Counting Book*. New York: Crowell, 1977.

• Children of la Roche and Friends. *Bryan and His Balloon: An English Chipewyan Counting Book*. Edmonton: Tree Frog Press, 1984.

•• Cowther, Robert. *The Most Amazing Hide and Seek Counting Book*. Markham, ON: Penguin, 1986.

••• Crews, D. *Ten Black Dots*. New York: Greenwillow Press, 1986.

••• Feelings, Muriel. *Mojo Means One: Swahili Counting Book*. New York: Dial Press, 1971. (East African)

•• Graeme, Jocelyn. *One Nose, Two Hands*. Don Mills, ON: Addison-Wesley, 1990. (text is in Spanish, French, English, and Chinese)

• Gretz, S. *Teddy Bears 1–10*. New York: Macmillan, 1986.

••• Hoban, Tana. *Count and See*. New York: Macmillan, 1972.

••• Langstaff, John. *Over in the Meadow*. New York: Harcourt Brace Jovanovich, 1956.

•• Lewin, B. *Cat Count*. New York: Dodd Mead, 1981.

••• Lottridge, Celia. *One Watermelon Seed*. Toronto: Oxford University Press, 1986.

••• Mack, Stan. *Belmont the Bat Catcher and Other Nutty Number Stories*. Toronto: Methuen, 1986.

• Magee, D. *Trucks You Can Count On*. New York: Dodd Mead, 1985.

•• McGee, Barbara. *Counting Sheep*. Willowdale, ON: Annick Press, 1991.

•• O'Halloran, Tim. *Know Your Numbers*. Burlington, ON. Hayes, 1986.

• Peppe, Rodney. *Circus Numbers: A Counting Book*. New York: Delacorte, 1986.

• Pienkowski, Jan. *Numbers*. New York: Simon & Shuster, 1981.

••• Sendak, Maurice. *Chicken Soup with Rice*. New York: Harper & Row, 1962.

••• Testa, Fulvio. *If You Take a Pencil*. New York: Dial Press, 1982.

•••• Viorst, Judith. *Alexander, Who Used to Be Rich Last Sunday*. New York: Macmillan, 1978. (Read–Tell)

••• Wadsworth, Olive A. *Over in the Meadow*. Toronto: Methuen, 1986.

• Wildsmith, Brian. *Brian Wildsmith's 1, 2, 3's*. New York: Franlin Watts, 1965.

• Winik, J.T. *Fun with Numbers*. Burlington, ON: Hayes, 1985.

•• Wood, A. *Kids Can Count*. Toronto: Kids Can Press, 1976.

Time

•• Barrett, Judith. *Benjamin's 365 Birthdays*. New York: Atheneum, 1974.

••• Spier, Peter. *Fast-Slow, High-Low*. Garden City, NY: Doubleday, 1972.

••• Watson, Nancy Dingman. *When Is Tomorrow*? New York: Knopf. 1955.

Space, shape, and size

••• Allen, Pamela. *Who Sank the Boat*? New York: Coward, 1983.

•• Bruna, Dick. *I Know about Shapes*. New York: Price Stern, 1984.

••• Fisher, L.E. *Look Around! A Book about Shapes*. Markham, ON: Penguin, 1986.

••• Galloway, P. *When You Were Little and I Was Big*. Willowdale, ON: Annick Press, 1984.

•• Hoban, Tana. *Circles, Triangles and Squares*. New York: Macmillan, 1974.

••• Hutchins, Pat. *Changes, Changes*. New York: Macmillan, 1971.

• Pienkowski, Jan. *Sizes*. New York: Simon & Shuster, 1983.

• ———. *Shapes*. New York: Simon & Shuster, 1981.

••• Stinson, Kathy. *Big or Little*. Willowdale, ON: Annick Press, 1985.

•••• Walter, Marion. *Make a Bigger Puddle, Make a Smaller Worm*. Philadelphia: Lippincott, 1971. (discovering the concepts of big and little with a mirror)

Planning for Group Time

NOTE: All music, fingerplays, poems, stories, and games listed here may also be used at other times during the session as appropriate.

Music

Songs

Please see "Ten Red Apples" at the end of this chapter.

From *Elephant Jam*, Sharon, Lois, and Bram
"One Elephant, Deux Éléphants" (see also Chapter 19, p. 422)
"Five Little Monkeys," p. 48
"Three Little Monkeys," p. 49
"One Finger, One Thumb," p. 50

From *The Goat with the Bright Red Socks*, Birkenshaw and Walden
"Echo Clock," p. 5
"I Can Count," p. 8
"Let's Do the Numbers Rumba," p. 10

From *Stepping Along in Music Land*, Murray
"Coloured Sticks," p. 33
"Shapes," p. 34
"Five Toes," p. 35
"Incubator," p. 36
"Hop Little Bunny," p. 37

From *Tunes for Tots*, Warner and Berry
"Counting Songs," pp. 89–97

From *What Shall We Do and Alee Galloo!*, Winn
"The Clock Song," p. 36
"My Hat It Has Three Corners," p. 54

Records and Cassettes

Bob McGrath. *If You're Happy and You Know It*, Volume I. (Kids Records)
"Five Little Ducks"
"Six Little Monkeys"

Anne Murray. *There's a Hippo in My Tub*. (Capitol Records)
"Inchworm"

Fred Penner. *Special Delivery*. (Troubadour Records)
"My Grandfather's Clock"

Bob Schneider. *When You Dream a Dream*. (Capitol Records)
"Computer Man"

Sharon, Lois, and Bram. *Elephant Show*. (Elephant Records)
"One Elephant Went Out to Play"
"Five Plump Peas"
"Noah's Old Ark"
"Ten in the Bed"

Fingerplays and Poems

NOTE: Many fingerplays in the other sections of this book involve number concepts. Select those that are of current interest to your group.

From *Don't Eat Spiders*, Heidbreder
"Count on Me," p. 15
"Counting's Easy," p. 17

From *Finger Rhymes*, Brown
"Five Little Pigs," p. 8
"Five Little Mice," p. 16
"Two Blackbirds," p. 19
"Ten Little Candles," p. 26

From *Hand Rhymes*, Brown
"Five Little Babies," p. 6
"Two Little Monkeys," p. 9
"Five Little Goblins," p. 12

From *Let's Do Fingerplays*, Grayson
The section "Counting and Counting Out," pp. 60–74, is very useful.
"Ten Fingers," p. 3
"Right Hand, Left Hand," p. 9
"Point to the Right," p. 11
"Five Fingers," p. 11
"Two Little Hands," p. 12
"Five Little Girls," p. 20
"Clocks," p. 27
"I Have a Little Watch," p. 27
"The Metronome Song," p. 28
"People," p. 50
"The Stilt Man," p. 50
"Five Years Old," p. 101

From *Oranges and Lemons*, King
"Five Brown Teddies," p. 6
"Noah's Ark," p. 16
"Five Little Speckled Frogs," p. 32
"The Wheels on the Bus," p. 38 (see also Chapter 23, p. 476)

From *Read Aloud Rhymes for the Very Young*, Prelutsky and Brown
"Ten to One," p. 37
"Just Three," p. 54
"Three Tickles," p. 79
"It's Eleven O'Clock," p. 80
"Ten Fingers," p. 82

From *Round and Round the Garden*, Williams
"Five Fat Sausages," p. 8
"Ten Little Men," p. 16
"Ten Little Fingers," p. 18
"Two Fat Gentlemen," p. 22
"Five Fat Peas," p. 29
"Five Little Soldiers," p. 42

....

GREAT BIG BALL

A great big ball (*arms make circle over head*)
A middle-sized ball, (*make ball with both hands in front*)
A little ball I see. (*make ball with thumb and forefinger*)
Now let's count the balls we've made, 1 — 2 — 3. (*make each ball again as you count*)

....

HICKORY, DICKORY, DOCK

Hickory, dickory, dock, (*stand, swing arm like pendulum*)
The mouse ran up the clock. (*bend over, run hand up body*)
The clock struck one, (*clap hands over head once*)
The mouse ran down, (*run hand down to feet*)
Hickory, dickory, dock. (*stand, swing arm like pendulum*)

....

TWO LITTLE BLACKBIRDS

Two little blackbirds sitting on a hill, (*place a fist on each knee*)
One named Jack and one named Jill. (*move each fist a little*)
Fly away Jack, fly away Jill, (*fling each hand over your shoulder*)
Come back Jack, come back Jill. (*bring each hand back to knee*)

Stories

(To read, read–tell, or tell. See Book Centre for a complete list.)
Exercise care when choosing stories to read aloud or tell in this area, as many books that children enjoy on their own become repetitive when read aloud. Books with a story and characters are well-suited for use in this area, such as Wadsworth's *Over in the Meadow* or Mack's *Belmont the Bat Catcher and Other Nutty Number Stories*. Many books in this area have simple vocabulary, but are conceptually beyond the young child. Be sure to assess stories for conceptual as well as linguistic suitability.

Games

(See Learning Games in Part 1 and Teacher-Made Games and Materials earlier in this chapter for directions.)
1. *Look and see:* Use thermometer, clock, timer, measuring cup, and ruler.
2. *How many?* Count objects.

Routine Times

1. At snack or meal times, talk about whether there are enough napkins, cups, plates, or spoons for all the children.
2. At snack or meal times, talk about the size of a serving. Ask, "Would you like a big serving or a small serving?" Tell children a specific number of crackers or snacks to eat: "Today you may have two square crackers."
3. At snack or meal times, what happens to the level of juice or milk as it is poured from a pitcher into individual cups? (See-through containers are best for this.) What can you say about all the plates, the cups, and the pitcher when the food or juice is gone? They are empty!"

4. At snack or meal times, serve sandwiches cut in half; fill juice or milk glasses half full; serve bananas or apples cut in half.
5. Use an alarm clock, a timer, or a clock radio to signal the end of rest time.
6. At the end of rest time, you could say, "I am going to slowly count to ten and then I want you to get up slowly and walk slowly over to _____."
7. As you walk or ride to and from the centre, call attention to the use of numbers on houses, stores, road signs, clocks, and thermometers: "Here we are at 215 Chestnut Street, Keiko's house."
8. Talk about tall and short buildings, things that are near and far, and big trucks and small cars while walking or busing.
9. Count familiar objects while in transit.
10. Call attention to basic concepts involved while dressing; for example, we need a pair of mittens, socks, or shoes (one for each hand or foot), or count how many children have blue coats, brown shoes, red mittens, etc.
11. At pickup time, ask for a specific number of objects: "Please give me two blocks to put on this shelf."
12. Comment on a child's ability at pickup time: "You put many books on the shelf."

Large Muscle Activities

1. Walking, running, or hopping can be done fast or slow. Call attention to how long it takes to go a certain distance by each method.
2. Throwing or rolling a ball can be done fast or slow. Did the ball go a long or a short way with each method?
3. Taking turns on the equipment requires that the children understand that there are not enough trikes, swings, or teeter-totters for everyone and they must wait. If a piece of equipment is in big demand, use a timer, a clock, or counting as a means of regulating length of turns.
4. Use of outdoor equipment offers opportunities to teach basic concepts. Swings can teach high or low, fast or slow. At the jungle gym, say, "Peter reached the top of the jungle gym first" (this is made as a statement of fact, not the result of a teacher-inspired race). At the sandbox: "I see Mary and Erika sitting beside each other in the sandbox." The teeter-totter teaches up and down, balancing each other's weight, and heavy and light.
5. Play *Two little blackbirds* (see the variation on p. 570).
6. When playing circle games, talk about who is in the middle, who is beside or next to someone else, and who is between, behind, or in front of, as appropriate.
7. Skill games:
   a. *Beanbag toss:* Use five beanbags. Talk about the results: "The first one got in; the second one didn't go far enough; the third one was close"; "You have two more to throw"; "Count how many you got in."
   b. *Johnny can you jump over the puddle?* Use a metre stick to see how far each child jumps.
   c. *Bowling:* Count how many pins are knocked down and how many are left standing.
   d. *Balls:* Use different-sized balls; talk about their shape and texture.

Extended Experiences

1. Take a ride on a bus and let each child deposit his or her own fare in the box. Look for uses of numbers as you ride around your community.

2. Take a trip to a store to buy something needed for the classroom or a special activity. Notice the use of numbers to mark prices of items and the use of scales, cash registers and money.
3. Take a trip to the post office to buy stamps or to mail letters or invitations.
4. Take a walk and look for uses of numbers on houses, stores, and street signs. Talk about things that are far and near, tall and short, high and low. Talk about directions: "Turn right," "Turn left." Count objects you see or find.

 # Teacher Resources

Pictures and Displays

☐ Clock display: Set out different kinds of clocks on a low table — wind-up alarm clock, electric alarm clock, clock radio, cuckoo clock, cooking timer, egg timer (hourglass), kitchen wall clock, and a clock that strikes on the quarter hour. Hang pictures of clocks that you are not able to obtain, such as a grandfather clock, a sunburst or other decorative clock, or a clock in a church or tower.

☐ Scales display: Set out metric scales, postal scales, bathroom scales, balance scales, kitchen scales, and baby scales. Hang pictures of those you cannot obtain, like doctor's and produce scales.

☐ Thermometer display: Set out different kinds of thermometers — indoor–outdoor, deep fat, candy, meat, and fever. Hang pictures of hot and cold objects.

☐ Display various kinds of measuring devices — metric ruler, metre stick, folding rule, metal tape measure, vinyl measuring tape.

☐ Display a stamp collection: Talk about the shapes, sizes, colours, and subjects. Find the numbers that tell how much the stamps are worth. Have different sizes of envelopes and different shapes — square, rectangular, large, medium, and small. Show postcards with and without pictures and postcards and envelopes with stamps printed on and with stamps glued on.

☐ Display coins and bills: Talk about shapes and sizes and identify by name.

☐ With older or experienced children, talk about the fact that there are pictures on the money.

☐ Make a calendar to mount on the wall near your group-time area. Use a sheet of construction paper for each month. Make squares at least 4 cm x 4 cm for each day. Use stickers to mark special days and birthdays. You can also paste on appropriate pictures or symbols to show trips or other special activities that were made or will be made.

☐ Rearrange your room so that a post office or grocery store can be set up between the home-living centre and the block-building centre to encourage interaction between these areas.

☐ Show pictures of subjects that can be counted or that will lead to discoveries about some of the basic concepts in this chapter, such as a bridge over water, an empty vase and one filled with flowers, or a picture that shows things close up and at a distance.

Books and Periodicals

Azzolino, Agnes. *Math Games for the Young Child.* Keyport, NJ: Mathematical Concepts, 1987.

Baroody, Arthur J. *Children's Mathematical Thinking: A Developmental Framework for Pre-School, Primary, and Special Education Teachers.* New York: Teachers College Press, 1987.

Blocksma, Mary. *Reading the Numbers: A Survival Guide to the Measurements, Numbers, and Sizes Encountered in Everyday Life.* New York: Penguin, 1989.

Charlesworth, Rosalind, and Karen K. Lind. *Math and Science for Young Children.* Toronto: Nelson, 1990.

Downing, Douglas. *Dictionary of Mathematics Terms.* Hauppauge, NY: Barron's, 1987.

Ginsberg, H., and S. Opper. *Piaget's Theory of Intellectual Development.* Englewood Cliffs, NJ: Prentice-Hall, 1979.

Lavatelli, Celia. *Piaget's Theory Applied to an Early Childhood Curriculum.* Boston: Boston American Science and Engineering, 1970.

Skemp, Richard. *The Psychology of Learning Mathematics.* Markham, ON: Penguin, 1971.

The following journals often have useful articles to support the teaching of mathematics:
The Canadian Journal of Early Childhood Education.
The Journal of the Canadian Association for Young Children.
The Journal of the National Association for the Education of Young Children.
The Ontario Journal of the Association for Early Childhood Education.

Films and Videos

NOTE: Check with your distributor about public performance rights.

Classifying: Juggling Shapes, Sizes, Colors, Textures. Manitoba Education and Training Instructional Resources Library, 1981.
One Was Johnny. Weston Woods.

Community Resources and Organizations

☐ Telephone teaching kit from phone company.
☐ Post office for stamps and posters of stamps.
☐ Stamp collectors.

Ten Red Apples

Anonymous

Key of F Major

Far - mer Brown had ten red ap - ples hang - ing on a tree.

Far - mer Brown had ten red ap - ples hang - ing on a tree. Then he

picked one ap - ple and he gave it all to me. Leav - ing

nine red ap - ples a - hang - ing on a tree.

1. Young children enjoy singing this counting song. Continue the verses with "nine red apples," "eight red apples," etc.
2. Have ten children stand, each holding a paper apple with a number (one to ten) on it. When each child's number is sung, that child sits down.
3. Another way to use the song is to draw an apple tree and "hang" ten applies on it. These are taken away one after the other as the song is sung.
4. Substitute other coloured objects, such as ten blueberries, ten green froggies, ten purple grapes, etc.

Appendix A

Canadian Publishers

Consult the *Canadian Publishers Directory*, published every December and June as a supplement to the magazine *Quill and Quire*, for up-to-date listings of Canadian publishers, book wholesalers, sales representatives, associations, and agencies concerned with publishing, audio-visual product sources, and foreign publishers and audio-visual producers represented in Canada.

You can reach *Quill and Quire* at 70 The Esplanade, 4th Floor, Toronto, Ontario M5E 1R2; telephone (416) 360-0044; fax (416) 360-8745.

Commercial Sources for Audio-Visual Producers and Suppliers

Atlantic Book
35 Cobequid Dr.
Truro, NS
B2N 5R1
(902) 468-3302
(902) 893-1464 (FAX)

B & B Publishing
4823 Sherbrooke St. W., Suite 115
Westmount, PQ
H3Z 1G7
(514) 932-9466
(514) 932-5929 (FAX)

BFA Educational Media (Canada)
47 Densley Ave.
Toronto, ON
M6M 5A8
(416) 241-3311
(416) 243-3287 (FAX)

CNIB National Library Division
1929 Bayview Ave.
Toronto, ON
M4G 3F8
(416) 480-7520
(416) 480-7700 (FAX)

Canadian Learning Company
63 Mack Ave.
Scarborough, ON
M1L 1M5
(416) 691-9094
(416) 691-8833 (FAX)

Canadian Museum of Nature/
Musée canadien de la nature
Box 3443, Station D
Ottawa, ON
K1P 6P4
(613) 990-6594
(613) 990-0318 (FAX)

Cannon Book Distribution
71 Orfus Rd.
Toronto, ON
M6A 1M4
(416) 781-3278
(416) 781-0350 (FAX)

Child's Play
120 Watline Ave., Unit 5
Mississauga, ON
L4Z 2C1
(416) 890-8111
(416) 890-3149 (FAX)

Children's Book Store
604 Markham St.
Toronto, ON
M6G 2L8
(416) 535-7011

(416) 535-7026 (FAX)
Copp Clark Pitman

2775 Matheson Blvd. E.
Mississauga, ON
L4W 4P7
(416) 238-6074
(416) 238-6075 (FAX)

Coronet Films & Video
1870 Birchmount Rd.
Scarborough, ON
M1P 2J7
(416) 293-3621
(416) 299-2539 (FAX)

Firefly Books
250 Sparks Ave.
Willowdale, ON
M2H 2S4
(416) 499-8412
(416) 499-8313 (FAX)

Fitzhenry & Whiteside
91 Granton Dr.
Richmond Hill, ON
L4B 2N5
(416) 764-0030
(416) 764-7156 (FAX)

Gage Educational Publishing
164 Commander Blvd.
Agincourt, ON
M1S 3C7
(416) 293-8141
(416) 293-9009 (FAX)

International Tele-Film Enterprises
47 Densley Ave.
Toronto, ON
M6M 5A8
(416) 241-4483
(416) 243-3287 (FAX)

Magic Lantern Communications
775 Pacific Rd., Unit 38
Oakville, ON
L6L 6M4
(416) 827-1155
(416) 827-1154 (FAX)

Magic Lantern Communications
201–6700 #3 Rd.
Richmond, BC
V6Y 2C3
(604) 273-8111
(604) 273-8171 (FAX)

Marlin Motion Pictures
211 Watline Ave.
Mississauga, ON
L4Z 1P3
(416) 262-4964
(416) 890-6550 (FAX)

Marvin Melnyk Associates
P.O. Box 220
Queenston, ON
L0S 1L0
(416) 262-4964
(416) 262-5303 (FAX)

McGraw-Hill Ryerson Limited
300 Water St.
Whitby, ON
L1N 9B6
(416) 428-2222
(416) 430-5020 (FAX)

McIntyre Media Limited
30 Kelfield St.
Rexdale, ON
M9W 5A2
(416) 245-7800
(416) 245-8660 (FAX)

National Film Board of Canada/
Office national du film du Canada
Customer Services
P.O. Box 6100, Station A
Montreal, PQ
H3C 3H5
(514) 283-9402
(514) 283-7564 (FAX)

Atlantic Canada: (800) 561-7104
Quebec (800) 363-0328
Ontario: (800) 267-7710
Northern and Western Canada:
(800) 661-9867

National Geographic Society
211 Watline Ave., Suite 210
Mississauga, ON
L4Z 1P3
(416) 890-1111
(416) 890-5080 (FAX)

Random House of Canada
1265 Aerowood Dr.
Mississauga, ON
L4W 1B9
(416) 624-0672
(416) 624-6217 (FAX)

The Resource Centre
P.O. Box 160
Waterloo, ON
N2J 3Z9
(519) 885-0826
(519) 747-5629 (FAX)

Scholar's Choice
Highway 100 and Trafalgar St.
P.O. Box 4214
London, ON
N5W 5W3
(519) 453-7470
(519) 455-2853 (FAX)

Scholastic Canada
123 Newkirk Rd.
Richmond Hill, ON
L4C 3G5
(416) 883-5300
(416) 883-4113 (FAX)

School Services of Canada
66 Portland St.
Toronto, ON
M5V 2M8
(416) 366-0903
(416) 366-0908 (FAX)

Tree House Press
610 Upper James St., Unit 4
Hamilton, ON
(416) 574-3399
(416) 574-0228 (FAX)

Visual Education Centre
75 Horner Ave., Unit 1
Toronto, ON
M8Z 4X5
(416) 252-5907
(416) 251-3720 (FAX)

Weston Woods Studios (Canada)
60 Briarwood Ave.
Port Credit, ON
L5G 3N6
(416) 278-0566
(416) 278-2801 (FAX)

Credits and Permissions

Birkenshaw, Lois. "Hot Potato," "The Ice Cream Cone," and "Ten Red Apples." From *Music for Fun, Music for Learning* (3rd ed.) by Lois Birkenshaw. Copyright © 1982 and reprinted by permission of Holt, Rinehart and Winston of Canada, Limited.

Cannon, Thea. "The Digger." Taken from *Finger Plays and Action Rhymes*, © 1952 by Standard Publishing, Cincinnati, Ohio, a division of Standex International Corporation. Used by permission.

Ebony Jr. For material from "Kwanza Feast" by Sharon Bell Mathis (December 1973); "Gifts of Love" by Norma R. Pointsett; "Candy Maker's Kitchen: Sweet Potato Candy" by Shirley A. Searey (December 1974); and "The Seven Lessons of Kwanza" by Karama Fufuka (December 1975). Permission to adapt granted by *Ebony Jr.*

Fowke, Edith. "The Little Skunk" and "Sally Go Round the Sun." From *Sally Go Round the Sun* by Edith Fowke. Used by permission of the Canadian Publishers, McClelland & Stewart, Toronto.

Heidbreder, Robert. "Little Robot," "Sticky Maple Syrup," and "Sun, Sun." From *Don't Eat Spiders*, poems © Robert Heidbreder 1985. Reprinted by permission of Oxford University Press, Canada.

Lutheran Church in America. "Guess What?" "Guess Who?" "Hide and Seek," "Hot Potato," "Skip Squat," "Together, Together," "Who Am I?" and "The Farmer Plants His Seed" from *The Bible for Three-Year-Olds* (1952); "Picture-Card Guess" from *Three-Year-Olds and Jesus* (1954); "Friend, Friend from over the Way" and "Look and See" from *Friends of Jesus* (1960); "Bobby Plants His Seed" from *Three-Year-Olds in Summer* (1951); "Match-Them," Name It," and "Scramble" from *My Storybook of Jesus* (1956); all by Darlene Hamilton, published by the Muhlenberg Press, Philadelphia.

Nash, Ogden. "The Guppy." From *Verses from 1929 On* by Ogden Nash. Copyright 1944 by Ogden Nash. First appeared in *The Saturday Evening Post*. By permission of Little, Brown and Company.

Author and Title Index

Books

Authors

Aardema, Verna, 430
Abolafia, Yossi, 403
Adams, Adrienne, 250, 271
Adler, D.A., 212, 243, 248, 249, 255, 256, 280, 281
Agell, Charlotte, 490
Alday, Gretchen P., 398
Alderson, Sue Ann, 182
Alexander, M., 553
Alexander, Martha, 171
Aliki, 110, 135, 147, 158, 172, 394
Allen, Jeffery, 553
Allen, Marjorie N., 309
Allen, Pamela, 567
Allington, Richard L., 135, 147, 355
Allix, Hereward, 403
Althea, 553
Amato, Sheila, 202
Ames, L.B., 101
Anastasiou, S., 379
Anderson, C.W., 379, 394
Anderson, Eugene, 101
Anderson, Karen, 73
Andrews, Jan, 135, 182
Anglund, Joan, 95
Anno, Mitsumasa, 309, 567
Arbuthnot, May Hill, 70
Ardizzone, Edward, 490
Ardley, Neil, 530
Armitage, Rhonda, 135
Arthur, Catherine, 124
Asch, Frank, 110, 124, 271, 394, 510
Aseltine, Lorraine, 171
Aska, Warabe, 310
Assanthiany, Sylvie, 458
Astrop, Caroline, 110, 124, 135, 158
Astrop, John, 110, 124, 135, 158
Atkinson-Keen, S., 332, 344
Atwood, M., 394

Aylesworth, Jim, 475
Azzolino, Agnes, 572

Bacon, 355
Baer, Edith, 445
Baggett, Nancy, 398, 409, 420
Bailes, Edith G., 434
Bains, Rae, 525
Baker, David, 514
Baker, Donald, 212
Balaban, Nancy, 68
Balian, Lorna, 271
Bancroft, Henrietta, 355
Bang, Molly, 525
Baratta-Lorton, Mary, 69
Barber, Mary, 212, 300
Barer-Stein, T., 212, 223, 300
Barkhouse, J., 394
Baroody, Arthur J., 573
Barrett, Judith, 567
Barrett, Norman, 322
Barry, Robert, 295
Bartlett, Nancy Lewis, 71
Bartoli, J., 403
Barton, B., 458, 475, 553
Batulla, Barbara, 430
Bauer, C., 445
Bauer, Judith, 198
Bauman, H., 403
Baumann, Kurt, 295
Baum, Arline, 310
Baylor, Byrd, 158
Bell, Bill, 183, 553
Bell, Caroline, 183
Bell, Cathie, 271, 318, 344, 394, 525
Bell, David, 271, 318, 344, 394, 525
Bemelmans, Ludwig, 172
Bennett, David, 510
Bennett, Jill, 124
Bentley, Roy, 458
Berne, Patricia, 101

Titles

Songs, Fingerplays, and Poems

Authors

Titles

Films and Videos

Subject Index

To the Owner of This Book:

We are interested in your reaction to the second edition of *Creative Teaching in Early Childhood Education*. With your comments, we can improve this book in future editions.

Please help us by completing this questionnaire.

1. What was your reason for using this book?
   _____university, college, or continuing education course
   _____program planning and development
   _____professional development
   _____other (please specify)

2. If you are a student, please identify your school and course. If you used this text for a program, what was the name of that program?

3. Which chapters or parts of this book did you use?

4. Did you omit any chapters or parts? If so, which ones?

5. What is the best aspect of this book?

6. Please identify any topics or information you would like to see added to future editions.

7. Please add any comments or suggestions.

(fold here and tape shut)

- -

Business
Reply Mail
No Postage Stamp
Necessary if Mailed
in Canada

POSTAGE WILL BE PAID BY

Heather McWhinney
Editorial Director
College Division
HARCOURT BRACE JOVANOVICH CANADA INC.
55 HORNER AVENUE
TORONTO, ONTARIO
M8Z 9Z9